ALSO BY MATTHEW J. BRUCCOLI

The Composition of *Tender Is the Night*

As Ever, Scott Fitz (editor, with Jennifer Atkinson)

F. Scott Fitzgerald in His Own Time
(editor, with Jackson Bryer)

F. Scott Fitzgerald: A Descriptive Bibliography

F. Scott Fitzgerald's Ledger (editor)

The Great Gatsby: A Facsimile of the Manuscript (editor)

Apparatus for a Definitive Edition of *The Great Gatsby*

Bits of Paradise: 21 Uncollected Stones by F. Scott and Zelda Fitzgerald (editor, with Scottie Fitzgerald Smith)

The Romantic Egoists (editor, with
Scottie Fitzgerald Smith and Joan P. Kerr)

"The Last of the Novelists": F. Scott Fitzgerald and
The Last Tycoon

The Notebooks of F. Scott Fitzgerald (editor)

The Price Was High: The Last Uncollected Stories
of F. Scott Fitzgerald (editor)

Ernest Hemingway, Cub Reporter (editor)

Ernest Hemingway's Apprenticeship (editor)

Hemingway at Auction (editor, with C. E. Frazer Clark, Jr.)

Kenneth Millar/Ross Macdonald: A Checklist

Raymond Chandler: A Descriptive Bibliography

Chandler Before Marlowe (editor)

Ring Lardner: A Descriptive Bibliography
(with Richard Layman)

Some Champions: Sketches & Fiction by Ring Lardner
(editor, with Richard Layman)

Lost American Fiction (series editor)

Screenplay Library (series editor)

Pittsburgh Series in Bibliography (series editor)

First Printings of American Authors (series editor)

The O'Hara Concern: A Biography of John O'Hara

"An Artist Is His Own Fault": John O'Hara on Writers
and Writing (editor)

John O'Hara: A Descriptive Bibliography

Selected Letters of John O'Hara (editor)

Scott and Ernest: The Authority of Failure and the
Authority of Success

Just Representations: A James Gould Cozzens Reader (editor)

Correspondence of
F. SCOTT FITZGERALD

Correspondence of F. SCOTT FITZGERALD

Edited by

MATTHEW J. BRUCCOLI

and

MARGARET M. DUGGAN

with the assistance of

Susan Walker

RANDOM HOUSE NEW YORK

 Published in the United States by Random House, Inc., New York, and simultaneously in Canada by Random House of Canada Limited, Toronto.

Library of Congress Cataloging in Publication Data
Fitzgerald, Francis Scott Key, 1896-1940.
Correspondence of F. Scott Fitzgerald.

1. Fitzgerald, Francis Scott Key, 1896-1940—Correspondence. 2. Authors, American—20th century—Correspondence. I. Bruccoli, Matthew Joseph, 1931- II. Duggan, Margaret M. III. Walker, Susan, 1954-

PS3511.I9Z53 1979 813'.5'2 79-4765
ISBN 0-394-41773-9

Manufactured in the United States of America
24689753
First Edition

Acknowledgments

This volume represents a vast collaboration. The editors could not have done their work without the help of many people who provided letters, information, permissions, and advice. We are gratefully indebted.

The following law firms, banks, and agencies generously granted permission to publish material: A. D. Peters & Co. Ltd., Writers' Agents; A. Watkins Literary Agency; American Play Company, Inc.; Brandt & Brandt Literary Agency; Halsey Lightly & Hemsley; Harold Ober Associates; London, Buttenweiser & Chalif; Mercantile–Safe Deposit and Trust Company, Baltimore, Maryland, Trustee under the Will of H. L. Mencken; Patterson, Belknap, Webb & Tyler; The Society of Authors; Union Trust Company.

The following publishers generously granted permission or provided information: Cassell & Collier Macmillan; Charles Scribner's Sons; Doubleday; E. P. Dutton; *Esquire*; Harcourt Brace Jovanovich; Harper and Row; Hill & Wang; Houghton Mifflin; John Murray; Macmillan; Random House; The Viking Press; William Collins Sons.

The following libraries and library collections generously provided letters: American Heritage Center, University of Wyoming; Archdiocese of Baltimore Archives; The Bancroft Library, University of California, Berkeley; Burlingame Family Papers, George Arents Research Library for Special Collections, Syracuse University; Carl Van Vechten Papers, V. F. Calverton Papers, H. L. Mencken Papers, and Crowell-Collier Publishing Co. Papers, Manuscripts and Archives Division, The New York Public Library, Astor, Lenox and Tilden Foundations; Charles Scribner's Sons Archives, Princeton University; The Charlotte Ashley Felton Memorial Library, Stanford University; Clifton Waller Barrett Library, University of Virginia; Collection of American Literature, The Beinecke Rare Book and Manuscript Library, Yale University; Columbia University Library; Cornell University Library; Department of Special Collections, Research Library, University of California, Los Angeles; Enoch Pratt Free Library; Ernest Hemingway Collection, John F. Kennedy Library; Goucher College Library; Guggenheim Foundation; Humanities Research Center, University of Texas, Austin; The Huntington Library, San Marino, California; James Boyd Papers, Southern Historical Collection, University of North

Carolina Library, Chapel Hill; The Lilly Library; Louisiana State University Library; Mary Colum Collection, State University of New York, Binghamton, Library; Metro-Goldwyn-Mayer Studios; Minnesota Historical Society, Division of Archives and Manuscripts; The Ohio State University Libraries; Pack Memorial Public Library, Asheville, North Carolina; Pennsylvania State University Library; Princeton University Library; Sherwood Anderson Papers, The Newberry Library, Chicago; Special Collections Department, University of Pittsburgh Libraries; University of Florida; Department, University of Pittsburgh Libraries; University of Florida Library; University of Northern Iowa Library; University of Pennsylvania Archives and Records Center; University of Pennsylvania Library; University of Tulsa Library; Wesley W. Stout Papers, Manuscript Division, Library of Congress; Western Reserve Historical Society.

The following librarians, scholars, literary executors, collectors, and patrons generously assisted by providing letters, permissions, and information: Sheldon Abend, Joan M. Allen, Duchess of Argyll, Virginia Ashley, Jo August, F. J. Avaloz, Julius P. Barclay, C. Waller Barrett, Scott Bartlett, Nava Bat-Avraham, Alice B. Beer, Doris Beer, Nathaniel Benchley, Jeanne Bennett, A. Scott Berg, Edmund Berkeley, Jr., Mrs. Livingston L. Biddle, II, Jonathan P. Bishop, Michael H. Blechner, Victor Bonham-Carter, John C. Broderick, Gladys Van Wyck Brooks, Mrs. James Branch Cabell, William Cagle, Morley Callaghan, Anne Cazeneuve, Dallas L. Chrislock, Providence Cicero, Alexander P. Clark, Alan Cohen, Malcolm Cowley, Joan St. C. Crane, F. J. Dallett, Margaret Dalrymple, Carolyn A. Davis, Frederick Dennis, Mrs. Charles W. Donahoe, Sr., Henry T. Donahoe, Honoria Murphy Donnelly, Mrs. John Dos Passos, John A. Daugherty, Ellen S. Dunlap, Peter Dzwonkoski, Donald D. Eddy, Mrs. T. S. Eliot, Don Erickson, Anne Freudenberg, Donald Gallup, Mrs. Arnold Gingrich, Paul Gitlin, Sylvia Goldman, Mary Ann Gray, Gene M. Gressley, David M. Hamilton, Marion Hanscom, Diana C. Haskell, Virginia R. Hawley, Mary Welsh Hemingway, J. P. Hennessey, Mrs. Thomas Hitchcock, Mrs. J. B. Holmes, Evelyn Saffold Holt, L. L. Hughes, Nancy Huntington, Norris D. Jackson, Neil R. Jandahl, Carol Johnston, Sarah D. Jones, Matthew Josephson, Mrs. Averil J. Kadis, William G. Kahlert, Ring W. Lardner, Jr., Betty Tenn Lawrence, Lady Iris Leslie, Richard Levinson, Eleanor M. Lewis, Kenneth Lohf, Ephraim London, Holger Lundbergh, Corona Machemer, Archibald MacLeish, Charles Mann, Kamy Mann, Floydette F. McCoy, Henry L. Meledin, Alan A. Meyer, Elizabeth C. Miller, Linda P. Miller, F. Lionel Monro, Irene Moran, Helen Morgan, Richard G. Moser, Anne Munro-Kerr, Elizabeth B. Nash, Julie Haydon Nathan, Dr. Frank Norris, Harriet B. Oglesbee, Dorothy Olding, S. J. Perelman, A. D. Peters, Gerald L. Peterson, Gerald Pollinger, Anthony Powell, Wanda Randall, Joan Redington, Victoria Reese, Lyman W. Riley, J. Albert Robbins, Ruth C. Rogin, Karen

Rood, Mrs. Edgar L. Rossin, R. L. Samsell, Budd Schulberg, Charles Scribner III, Timothy Seldes, Norma Shearer, Peter Shepherd, Robert Sherrod, Faye Simkin, Andrea Simon, Bernice Slote, Mrs. Curtis Smith, Mrs. C. A. F. Sprague, Eric Steele, Michael Stein, Robert Stocking, Albert Sturtevant, Phil Syracopaulos, Allen Tate, James D. Thueson, Robert S. Tibbetts, Rev. John J. Tierney, Barbara Trainer, Louis Trinkaus, Carolyn A. Wallace, Arthur W. Wang, Robert Penn Warren, Armitage Watkins, Mrs. Preston Watson, Joyce C. Werner, Glenway Wescott, Cara L. White, Brooke Whiting, Mrs. Edmund Wilson, Carl H. Winston, Daniel H. Woodward, Michele Yarus, Lois Moran Young, Carl E. Younger, V. J. William Zerbo.

The photographic work for this volume was efficiently performed by Richard Taylor and Willard Starks.

Albert Erskine of Random House improved this volume—as he improves everything he touches. Lynn Strong, the perfect copy editor, caught many blunders and made many useful suggestions.

A research grant from the National Endowment for the Humanities advanced work on this volume during the summer of 1977. The University of South Carolina Department of English provided many forms of help; we are grateful to the Chairmen of the Department during the time when this volume was edited, Professor William Nolte and Professor George Geckle.

The editors' greatest debt is to Scottie Fitzgerald Smith. Again.

This book is dedicated to the Keepers of the F. Scott Fitzgerald Papers at the Princeton University Library:

ALEXANDER CLARK, ANN VAN ARSDALE, MARGARETHE FITZELL, CHARLES E. GREENE, RICHARD M. LUDWIG, MARDEL PACHECO, JEAN F. PRESTON, WANDA RANDALL, AND AGNES SHERMAN.

Contents

Introduction

On 31 January 1941—six weeks after F. Scott Fitzgerald's death—Scottie Fitzgerald wrote to Maxwell Perkins of Scribners suggesting that a selection of her father's letters to her be included in *The Last Tycoon*: "these letters are so far beyond the average literary critic that they're incomparable."[1] Her idea was not acted on until Edmund Wilson published some of Fitzgerald's letters in *The Crack-Up* (New York: New Directions, 1945), which demonstrated that Scottie's assessment was correct.

One of the many ironies that inform the career of F. Scott Fitzgerald is that the writer who died "forgotten" in 1940 is the most fully documented American author of this century. We know more about Fitzgerald than about any of his contemporaries because he preserved the material; because Scottie Fitzgerald presented it to Princeton University; because the Princeton Library has been a superb custodian of the material; and because of thirty years of Fitzgerald scholarship. The best Fitzgerald scholar of us all was F. Scott Fitzgerald. He made everyone else's work possible by saving the evidence. Some of the best evidence is in his incomparable letters.

Fitzgerald was an active letter writer: some 3,000 of his letters have been located. This figure probably represents less than half the letters he wrote. After 1932 he worked with secretaries and kept carbons of most of his letters; but many of the pre-1932 letters are lost.

Correspondence of F. Scott Fitzgerald supplements the three published volumes of his letters. The principal collection is Andrew Turnbull's *The Letters of F. Scott Fitzgerald* (New York: Scribners, 1963). Jackson Bryer and John Kuehl edited a selection of the Fitzgerald/Perkins correspondence, *Dear Scott/Dear Max* (New York: Scribners, 1971). Bruccoli and Jennifer Atkinson published the Fitzgerald/Ober correspondence in *As Ever, Scott Fitz—* (New York and Philadelphia: Lippincott, 1972). None of the letters in those three volumes has been repeated here; however, when a letter in this volume bears on a previously collected letter, a footnote reference is provided. Some of the letters in this volume have appeared in books or scholarly journals, but none has been published in a

[1] Charles Scribner's Sons Archive, Princeton University Library.

collection of Fitzgerald's letters; they are included here to make them available in one place.

As indicated by its title, *Correspondence of F. Scott Fitzgerald,* this volume also includes letters written to Fitzgerald. These incoming letters are highly selective; they were chosen to provide an impression of Fitzgerald's literary correspondence and to fill in certain areas of his biography. For example, five letters from Monsignor Fay are included because this paternal friendship was so important in shaping—or confirming—the young Fitzgerald's ambitions. Since none of Fitzgerald's letters to Fay survives, Fay's letters constitute the total documentary evidence concerning his influence on Fitzgerald.

Inevitably, there are lacunae in Fitzgerald's extant correspondence, the most serious of which is the loss of nearly all the correspondence with his parents. This loss is particularly regrettable in view of Edward Fitzgerald's service as moral guide during his son's formative years.

The most significant relationship in F. Scott Fitzgerald's life was with his wife. After her 1930 breakdown, with its attendant separations, Fitzgerald wrote: "Do you remember, before keys turned in the locks,/When life was a close-up, and not an occasional letter. . . ."[2] Yet, for the reader, the force of their commitment to each other endures in their sometimes bitter and often heartbreaking letters. In the extraordinary forty-two-page letter published here Zelda Fitzgerald charts their mutual descent from a life of promise to one of disillusionment. This volume includes twenty-three Scott-to-Zelda letters and sixty-two Zelda-to-Scott letters. There are gaps in the Scott-to-Zelda letters because many of Zelda Fitzgerald's papers were destroyed after her death in 1948. Most of these survive as Fitzgerald's carbon copies.

Correspondence includes inscriptions by and to Fitzgerald. One of the ways writers communicate is by presenting books to each other. Moreover, Fitzgerald was a serious inscriber who usually tried to say something about the book—or, failing that, to make a personal comment. Wires have been included because Fitzgerald made frequent use of this form of communication, especially in cabling to America from Europe. Some of his most important messages were wired: see his last-minute attempt to change the title of *The Great Gatsby.* The record of Fitzgerald's correspondence would be incomplete without his inscriptions and wires.

Letters printed in dealer and auction catalogs have been included. These letters are now unlocatable, and some may disappear into private collections for a long time. There are certainly many Fitzgerald letters in private collections that are unknown to the editors because there is no effective way to search for them. It is anticipated that one of the benefits of this volume will be to turn up more letters. Research begets research.

[2] "Lamp in the Window," *The New Yorker* (23 March 1935), 18.

Near the end of his life Fitzgerald wrote: "Biography is the falsest of the arts. That is because there were no Keatzians before Keats, no Lincolnians before Lincoln."[3] His letters constitute the most authoritative biography of F. Scott Fitzgerald. Without conveying the impression that he was writing for posterity, they present the best portrait of the artist who was his own fault—as John O'Hara said of him. In addition to providing documentary evidence, these letters reveal the qualities of a finely sensitive literary mind. Fitzgerald spoke with the authority of a natural who had mastered his craft.

[3] *The Notebooks of F. Scott Fitzgerald* (New York and London: Harcourt Brace Jovanovich/Bruccoli Clark, 1978), p. 325.

Editorial Note

The format for the editorial headings of the letters is:

Recipient (or Writer)	Description. Location
Assigned date	Assigned place of writing

Dates specified in the original letters are treated as part of the letter text; if the year was omitted, it has been supplied in brackets. Since Zelda Fitzgerald did not date her letters, they have been placed in the chronology on the basis of internal evidence. Fitzgerald's return address is retained as part of the letter text, but the address of the recipient is omitted unless it has some significance. Some of Fitzgerald's letters from California in 1937–40 have been assigned to "Hollywood" although they may have been written in other parts of the Los Angeles area. With the exception of Zelda Fitzgerald's letters, no attempt has been made to assign the place of writing for letters sent to Fitzgerald.

ALS means autograph letter, signed by hand. TLS means typed letter, signed by hand. AL and TL indicate that the letter is not signed by hand. CC designates a carbon copy.

The most frequent location for letters is "Princeton"; but no attempt has been made to identify the several collections at the Princeton University Library (the F. Scott Fitzgerald Papers, the Charles Scribner's Sons Archive, or the John Peale Bishop Papers). However, letters that are in the Fitzgeralds' scrapbooks have been so identified.

This edition retains the spellings and punctuation in Fitzgerald's holograph letters. The position of quotation marks with punctuation has been regularized; and the length of dashes has been regularized to one em in most cases. Only meaningful deletions by Fitzgerald have been preserved. The placement of his insertions has not been duplicated: interlinear or marginal material is printed as part of the letter or at the end. The positioning of the headings and signatures in Fitzgerald's letters has been regularized.

It may be asked why it is necessary to retain Fitzgerald's misspellings in letters that were not written for publication. If he were overseeing the publication of his letters, he would insist they be copy-edited. The answer is that because these letters were private communications their character—

their personal quality—should be preserved. In editing letters the editor's chief duty is to refrain from textual editing. When letters are emended or improved, they are distorted.

The legend of Fitzgerald's bad spelling—like all the other Fitzgerald legends—is exaggerated. As these letters show, his spelling was bad but not illiterate. It seems worse than it was because he consistently misspelled certain common words: "yatch," "appartment," "ect."

Fitzgerald did not type; all of his typing was done by secretaries. Some obvious errors in his typed letters—strike-overs, transpositions, mis-strikes, space skips—have been silently emended. Similar errors in letters to Fitzgerald have also been corrected.

Editorial guesses for difficult readings are printed within brackets. Indecipherable words are indicated by empty brackets. Underlined words have been set in italic type; double underlines have been set as small capitals; triple underlines have been set as full capitals. When letters have been cut by the editor, the deletions are noted with a word count. Some of the telegraph companies' code material has been deleted from wires. The texts of letters reprinted from dealer and auction catalogs have not been verified since these letters are unlocatable.

Some of the references in the letters have not been footnoted. The policy on explanatory notes is to identify: (1) all of Fitzgerald's writings; (2) people or places important in his life; (3) references required for readers to understand the letters. Well-known figures are not identified, except to provide special information. Unidentifiable people are not so stipulated.

Chronology

24 September 1896

Birth of F. Scott Fitzgerald in St. Paul, Minnesota.

24 July 1900

Birth of Zelda Sayre in Montgomery, Alabama.

September 1908

Fitzgerald enters St. Paul Academy.

September 1911

Enters Newman School, Hackensack, New Jersey.

September 1913

Enters Princeton University with class of 1917. Meets Edmund Wilson, '16, and John Peale Bishop, '17.

December 1914

Production of *Fie! Fie! Fi-Fi!*, Fitzgerald's first Princeton Triangle Club show.

December 1914–December 1915

Writes for *Princeton Tiger* and *Nassau Literary Magazine.*

December 1915

Drops out of Princeton for rest of school year; though in academic difficulties, is allowed to leave for health reasons.

December 1915

Production of *The Evil Eye* by Triangle Club.

September 1916.

Returns to Princeton, dropping year behind.

December 1916

Production of *Safety First* by Triangle Club.

26 October 1917

Receives commission as second lieutenant in infantry.

20 November 1917

Reports to Fort Leavenworth, Kansas. Begins novel "The Romantic Egoist."

February 1918

Reports to Camp Taylor, Louisville, Kentucky.

March 1918

Completes first draft of "The Romantic Egoist" while on leave at Princeton and staying in Cottage Club; sends draft to Scribners.

April 1918

Reports to Camp Gordon, Georgia.

31 May 1918

Zelda Sayre graduates from Sidney Lanier High School.

June 1918

Fitzgerald reports to Camp Sheridan near Montgomery, Alabama.

July 1918

Meets Zelda Sayre at a country club dance in Montgomery.

August 1918

Scribners returns "The Romantic Egoist"; although Fitzgerald revises it, by the end of October the novel is finally rejected.

November 1918

Fitzgerald reports to Camp Mills, Long Island, to await embarkation; the war ends before his unit ships out.

December 1918

Returns to Camp Sheridan.

February 1919

Receives discharge from army and goes to work for Barron Collier advertising agency in New York City; lives in room at 200 Claremont Avenue. Informally engaged to Zelda Sayre.

Spring 1919

Visits Montgomery three times as Zelda remains reluctant to commit herself to marriage.

June 1919

Zelda breaks engagement.

July–August 1919

Fitzgerald quits New York job; returns to St. Paul and rewrites novel at 599 Summit Avenue.

16 September 1919

Maxwell Perkins of Scribners accepts *This Side of Paradise.*

November 1919

First sale to *The Saturday Evening Post*: "Head and Shoulders," published February 1920. Fitzgerald becomes client of Harold Ober at Reynolds agency.

November 1919

Visits Zelda in Montgomery; engagement resumed.

Mid-January 1920

Lives in boarding house at 2900 Prytania Street in New Orleans, where he stays less than a month.

26 March 1920

Publication of *This Side of Paradise.*

3 April 1920

Marriage at rectory of St. Patrick's Cathedral in New York; honeymoon at Biltmore and Commodore hotels.

May–September 1920

Fitzgeralds rent house in Westport, Connecticut.

10 September 1920

Publication of *Flappers and Philosophers,* Fitzgerald's first short-story collection.

October 1920–April 1921

Fitzgeralds rent apartment at 38 West 59th Street, New York City.

May–July 1921

First trip to Europe. Fitzgeralds sail to England on *Aquitania,* then travel to France and Italy; return home on *Celtic* and visit Montgomery.

August 1921–September 1922

Fitzgeralds move to St. Paul and rent house at Dellwood, White Bear Lake; after birth of Frances Scott (Scottie) Fitzgerald, 26 October 1921, take house at 646 Goodrich Avenue; in June 1922 move to White Bear Yacht Club for summer.

September 1921–March 1922

Serialization of *The Beautiful and Damned* in *Metropolitan Magazine.*

4 March 1922

Publication of *The Beautiful and Damned.*

22 September 1922

Publication of *Tales of the Jazz Age,* second collection of short stories.

Mid-October 1922–April 1924

Fitzgeralds rent house at 6 Gateway Drive in Great Neck, Long Island. Friendship with Ring Lardner.

27 April 1923

Publication of *The Vegetable.*

November 1923

The Vegetable fails at tryout in Atlantic City, New Jersey.

Mid-April 1924–Fall 1925

Fitzgeralds sail for France on *Minnewaska;* visit Paris, then Grimm's Park Hotel in Hyères, before settling in June at Villa Marie, Valescure,

St. Raphaël, on the Riviera. Fitzgerald writes *The Great Gatsby* during summer-fall 1924. Bitterness results from Zelda's involvement with French aviator Edouard Jozan.

Winter 1924–25

Fitzgeralds stay at Hotel des Princes, Rome, where Fitzgerald revises *The Great Gatsby*. Travel to Capri in February; stay at Hotel Tiberio.

10 April 1925

Publication of *The Great Gatsby*.

May–December 1925

Fitzgeralds rent apartment at 14 rue de Tilsitt, Paris, near Étoile. Fitzgerald meets Ernest Hemingway in May at Dingo bar.

August 1925

Fitzgeralds leave Paris for month at Antibes. Beginning of close friendship with Gerald and Sara Murphy.

January 1926

Zelda takes "cure" at Salies-de-Béarn.

January and February 1926

"The Rich Boy" appears in *Redbook Magazine*.

26 February 1926

Publication of *All the Sad Young Men*, third short-story collection.

Early March–December 1926

Fitzgeralds rent Villa Paquita at Juan-les-Pins on Riviera. Hemingways join Murphys and Fitzgeralds in May; accept offer to take over Villa Paquita. Fitzgeralds move to Villa St. Louis at Juan-les-Pins.

December 1926

Fitzgeralds return to America on *Conte Biancamano*.

January 1927

First trip to Hollywood, where Fitzgerald works on "Lipstick" (not produced) for United Artists.

March 1927–March 1928

Fitzgeralds take two-year lease on "Ellerslie," near Wilmington, Delaware. Zelda commences dancing lessons as student of Catherine Littlefield in Philadelphia.

April–August 1928

Fitzgeralds sail to Europe on *Paris;* rent apartment at 58 rue Vaugirard. Zelda studies ballet with Lubov Egorova.

September 1928–March 1929

Fitzgeralds return to America on *Carmania;* stay at "Ellerslie."

March 1929

Fitzgeralds sail to Genoa on *Conte Biancamano;* visit Riviera en route to Paris.

June 1929

Fitzgeralds rent Villa Fleur des Bois at Cannes, on Riviera.

October 1929

Fitzgeralds take apartment at 10 rue Pergolese, Paris.

February 1930

Trip to North Africa.

Spring–Fall 1930

Zelda Fitzgerald has breakdown in Paris: enters Malmaison clinic outside Paris, 23 April; Valmont clinic in Switzerland, 22 May; Prangins clinic near Nyon on Lake Geneva, Switzerland, 5 June. Fitzgerald stays in Geneva and Lausanne during summer and fall.

Late January 1931

Death of Fitzgerald's father. Fitzgerald returns alone to America on *New York* to attend funeral and for brief Montgomery visit to report to Sayres about Zelda.

July 1931

Fitzgeralds spend two weeks at Lake Annecy, France.

15 September 1931

Zelda Fitzgerald released from Prangins. Fitzgeralds sail to America on *Aquitania.*

September 1931–Spring 1932

Fitzgeralds rent house at 819 Felder Avenue in Montgomery. Fitzgerald travels alone to Hollywood to work on *Red-Headed Woman* for Metro-Goldwyn-Mayer in November-December.

17 November 1931

Death of Zelda's father.

February 1932

Zelda Fitzgerald has second breakdown: enters Phipps Psychiatric Clinic of Johns Hopkins University Hospital in Baltimore.

March 1932

Zelda Fitzgerald completes first draft of her novel *Save Me the Waltz* while at Phipps.

20 May 1932–November 1933

Fitzgerald rents "La Paix" outside Baltimore on Turnbull estate.

26 June 1932

Zelda Fitzgerald discharged from Phipps; joins family at "La Paix."

7 October 1932

Publication of *Save Me the Waltz.*

December 1933

Fitzgerald rents house at 1307 Park Avenue, Baltimore.

January–April 1934

Serialization of *Tender Is the Night* in *Scribner's Magazine.*

January 1934

Zelda Fitzgerald has third breakdown: enters Sheppard-Pratt Hospital outside Baltimore.

March 1934

Zelda Fitzgerald enters Craig House clinic in Beacon, New York.

29 March–30 April 1934

Zelda Fitzgerald's art exhibit in New York City.

12 April 1934

Publication of *Tender Is the Night.*

19 May 1934

Zelda Fitzgerald is transferred back to Sheppard-Pratt Hospital.

February 1935

Fitzgerald, convinced he has tuberculosis, stays at Oak Hall Hotel in Tryon, North Carolina.

20 March 1935

Publication of *Taps at Reveille.*

Summer 1935

Fitzgerald stays at Grove Park Inn, Asheville, North Carolina; visits Baltimore and New York.

September 1935

Takes apartment at Cambridge Arms, Baltimore.

November 1935

Stays at Skyland Hotel in Hendersonville, North Carolina; begins writing "The Crack-Up" essays.

8 April 1936

Zelda Fitzgerald enters Highland Hospital in Asheville.

July–December 1936

Fitzgerald stays at Grove Park Inn to be near Zelda.

September 1936

Death of Fitzgerald's mother in Washington, D.C.

January–June 1937

Fitzgerald stays at Oak Hall Hotel in Tryon.

July 1937

Travels to Hollywood for third and last time, with six-month MGM contract at $1,000 a week; works on script for *A Yank at Oxford.* Lives at Garden of Allah, where he meets Sheilah Graham.

September 1937–January 1938

Works on *Three Comrades* script, his only screen credit.

First week of September 1937

Visits Zelda in Asheville. Fitzgeralds spend four days in Charleston and Myrtle Beach, South Carolina.

December 1937

MGM contract is renewed for one year at $1,250 a week; Fitzgerald works on scripts (not used) for "Infidelity," *Marie Antoinette, The Women,* and *Madame Curie.*

March 1938

Fitzgeralds spend Easter at Cavalier Hotel, Virginia Beach, Virginia.

April 1938

Fitzgerald rents bungalow at Malibu Beach, California.

September 1938

Scottie enters Vassar.

October 1938

Fitzgerald moves to cottage on Edward Everett Horton estate, "Belly Acres," at Encino.

December 1938

MGM contract is not renewed.

February 1939

Fitzgerald travels to Dartmouth College with Budd Schulberg to work on *Winter Carnival;* fired for drinking.

April 1939

Fitzgeralds take trip to Cuba; Fitzgerald hospitalized on return to New York. Their final meeting.

Spring 1939–October 1940

Fitzgerald free-lances for Paramount, Universal, Fox, Goldwyn, and Columbia.

October 1939

Begins work on *The Last Tycoon.*

January 1940

Publication of the first Pat Hobby story, "Pat Hobby's Christmas Wish," in *Esquire;* seventeen-story series runs in *Esquire* from January 1940 to May 1941.

15 April 1940

Zelda Fitzgerald leaves Highland Hospital to live with mother at 322 Sayre Street in Montgomery.

May 1940

Fitzgerald moves to 1403 North Laurel Avenue, Hollywood.

May–August 1940

Works on "Cosmopolitan" ("Babylon Revisited") script.

21 December 1940

Dies of heart attack at Sheilah Graham's apartment, 1443 North Hayworth Avenue, Hollywood.

Correspondence of
F. SCOTT FITZGERALD

Letters

TO: Edward Fitzgerald

ALS, 1 p.[1] Scrapbook. Princeton University
Camp Chatham letterhead. Orillia, Ontario

July 15, 07

Dear Father,

I recieved the St Nickolas[2] today and I am ever so much obliged to you for it.

Your loving son.
Scott Fitzgerald

[1] The earliest known letter by Fitzgerald.
[2] *The St. Nicholas,* a popular children's magazine.

TO: Mrs. Edward Fitzgerald
Summer 1907

ALS, 1 p. Scrapbook. Princeton University
Camp Chatham, Orillia, Ontario

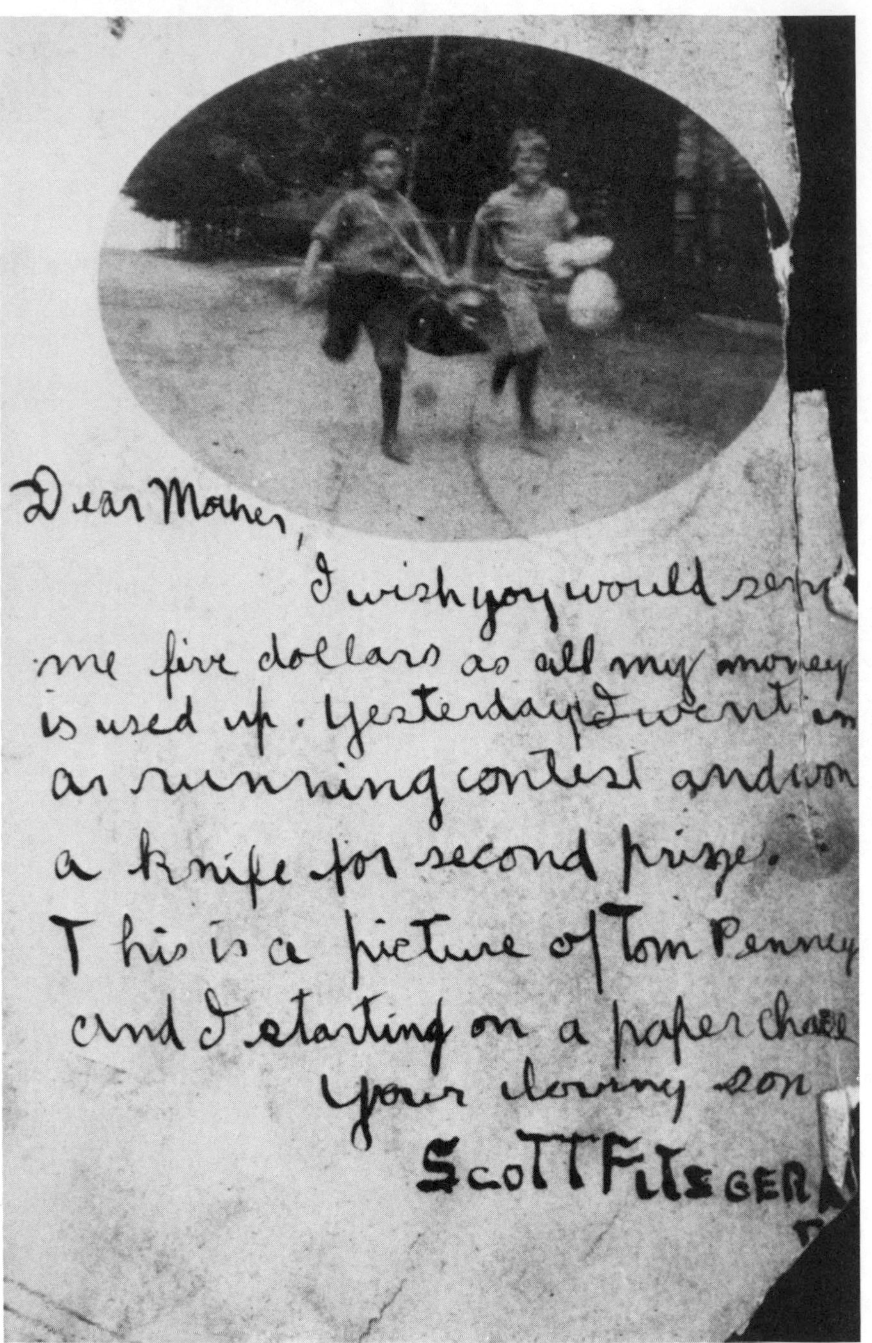

Dear Mother,
I wish you would send me five dollars as all my money is used up. Yesterday I went in a running contest and won a knife for second prize. This is a picture of Tom Penney and I starting on a paper chase
Your loving son
SCOTT FITZGER[ALD]

FROM: Edward Fitzgerald TL, 1 p. Scrapbook. Princeton University

July 30, 1909.

Master Scott Fitzgerald,
Frontenac, Minn.
My dear Scott:

Yours of July 29th received. Am glad you are having a good time. Mother and Annabelle[1] are very well and enjoying Duluth. I enclose $1.00. Spend it liberally, generously, carefully, judiciously, sensibly. Get from it pleasure, wisdom, health and experience.

[1] Fitzgerald's sister.

TO: Mrs. Richard Taylor[1] Postcard. Princeton University
Postmarked 14 February 1910 St. Paul, Minnesota

Dear Cousin Cece

Thank you ever so much for the picture of you house. I think it is aufully pretty. The one on the post card looks something like it. I think.

Your loving cousin
Scott Fitzgerald

[1] Cecilia Delihant Taylor, Fitzgerald's favorite cousin, of Norfolk, Va.; model for Clara in *This Side of Paradise*.

TO: Elizabeth Magoffin[1] ALS, 2 pp. Princeton University
Postmarked 12 January 1912 Newman School letterhead
Hackensack, New Jersey

Dear Miss Magoffin:

We arrived three hours late in New York. (Doggone it my pen spluttered tiny blots all over)

To begin again at a safe distance—Tell the girls that its disgracful they dont answer my letters. I wrote both MARIE! and ELENOR! and I intend to write all of them. Dont say anything but Marie promised me her picture and I havn't gotten it yet. Bob Clark is wild about Elenor Alair. Crazy about her. I hope she's not crazy about him To tell you the truth I am not crazy about anyone. Of course I fill my letters to my favorites with a lot of—well—nonsense but as far as telling them outright that you like them best i've come to the conclusion its foolish. A girl should always be kept guessing—always. I'm afraid I am boring you with my silly philosophy of human nature

So
~~Ta-Ta~~
~~So-Long~~
GOODBYE

Your Admirer
Francis Scott Fitzgerald
Playright

[1] Sponsor of Elizabethan Dramatic Club in St. Paul, for which Fitzgerald wrote four plays, 1911–14.

TO: Elizabeth Magoffin
Postmarked 17 February 1912

ALS, 2 pp. Princeton University
Newman School letterhead
Hackensack, New Jersey

My Dear Elizibeth:

Since you did not answer my other letter I suppose I will have to write you again. I addressed the other letter to Summit Avenue near Macubin but probably it is at the dead letter office and clerks with spectacles and red whiskers are vivesecting accounts of "Bear cats" and "Tongo Argentines." Tell Marie that I dont think she got my last letter as I didn't mail it. Tonight we have a dance followed by a minstrel show. I got two dollars for a poem.[1] Hurray for me. So you see if you can write verses about sparks and other combustibles I can dribble of Cavalier Ballads.[2]

Your friend
Scott
(Playright)

P.S. For Heavans sake send your adress

[1] Unidentified.
[2] Miss Magoffin had written a poem to Fitzgerald about his "spark."

TO: Marie Hersey[1]

ALS, 1 p. Scrapbook. Princeton University
Princeton, New Jersey

Thurs

My Very Very Dear Marie:
I got your little note
For reasons very queer Marie
You're mad at me I fear Marie
You made it very clear Marie
  You cared not what you wrote

The letter that you sent Marie
  Was niether swift nor fair
I hoped that you'd repent Marie
Before the start of Lent Marie
But Lent could not prevent Marie
  From being debonaire

So write me what you will Marie
  Altho' *I* will it not
My love you can not kill Marie
And tho' you treat me ill Marie
Believe me I am still Marie
  Your fond admirer

Scott

(Letter sent to Marie Jan 29, 1915)

[1] St. Paul friend with whom Fitzgerald corresponded when they were both away at school.

TO: Marie Hersey
Early 1915

ALS with collage, 8 pp. Unlocated[1]
Princeton, New Jersey

[1] *Modern First Editions . . . Sotheby Parke Bernet, Inc.*, Sale No. 3476 (20 February 1973), Item #207; pp. 2 and 3 were facsimiled in this catalog. The item was subsequently cataloged in *Autograph Letters Manuscripts Documents, Catalogue 102, Kenneth W. Rendell, Inc.* (1975), Item #37; pp. 7 and 8 were facsimiled in this catalog.

TO: Ruth Howard Sturtevant[1]
May 1915

ALS, 8 pp. University of Virginia
Princeton, New Jersey

May Something or other

Dear Howard

I have absolutly no excuse for writing you as you were careful to leave very few loopholes in your letter, but I want to write you and with most people thats reason enough. If you had begun that note "My Dear Mr. Fitzg—" I'd have never forgiven you and even "F. Scott Fitz" was a compromise. Its been very dull here since you left. Helen Walcott lightened our misery for a little while; Stu, Harold, and I took her to Cottage Club for tea.

As regards your Adjective—[2] let it wait. If I don't tell you what it is it'll always do for conversation—You see I'm very shy and sometimes have to fall back on that sort of subject. I tell you Ruth, I was a pretty enfuriated youth at your extreme partiality for Mr. O'brien-Moore at Campus. You told me what you thought of him and then when you prefered his conversation to mine—Well—Its pretty mean dope. It must be his "handsome face and daredevil manner." I like the way you say "Its too bad you can't come to our dance." How do you know we couldn't come—there are from three to five days between every exam.

Here I am writing to you, Ruth, when Ginevra's[3] letter lies unanswered on my desk. Pretty darn devoted I call it. Really Ruth I think you're fine. I like you a lot—I think

D—mit! ⟶ [ink blot]

especially we could have a wonderful quarrel if we ever got to know each other—because you see, we're both blondes + could find the other's weak points. It'd be a mean affair genererally and "more darn fun." I suppose you're having a dull time waiting for the Washington parlor snakes to float back from college + prep-school. I wish I was a Washington parlor Snake—I don't suppose it would be "all right" though—I was just thinking that if we both lived in St. Paul we could have a desperate affair—wouldn't it be interesting. (This savours 'un petit peu' of Mr. Obrien-Moore.)

As it is we'll probably never come across each other again. (Sob Stuff)

Ruth—(reading the letter)—"Why the *ridiculous* thing—Is *he* trying to slipover some second class stone-age sentiment when he's only *met* me *twice* in his life the fresh thing"

No Ruth—Far be it—I'm too suspicious of bloneds—however I think you're one of the cleverest ones I've ever met and I've another hunch we're going to be joyful, Ruth.

Ruth, just for fun answer this—will you Then I'll answer your answer and then we'll stop. How about it?

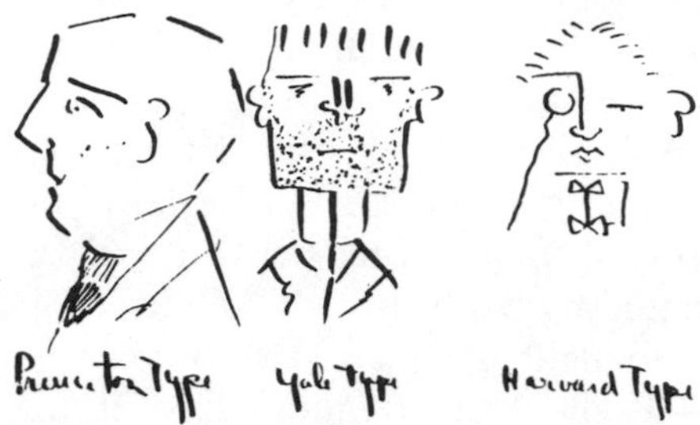

How is "dear Old Yale." By the time you get this we'll have beaten them in baseball. Remember in senior year your going to sit on the stage in the café scene of the △ show. Is that your debutante year. Au revoir. I am

[1] Fitzgerald met Ruth Sturtevant when she was a student at Farmington in Connecticut.

[2] One of Fitzgerald's lines with girls at this time was to say he had thought of an adjective for them—which he would reveal after he knew them better.

[3] Ginevra King, a Lake Forest, Ill., debutante who was Fitzgerald's first serious love. He met her at a party in St. Paul in January 1915 and maintained an elaborate correspondence with her while she was at Westover School. None of his letters to her survives.

TO: Ruth Howard Sturtevant
After 13 November 1915

ALS, 8 pp. University of Virginia
Princeton, New Jersey

Dear Ruth:

I'm feeling in a very blue and despondent mood so this is going to be a very blue and despondent letter

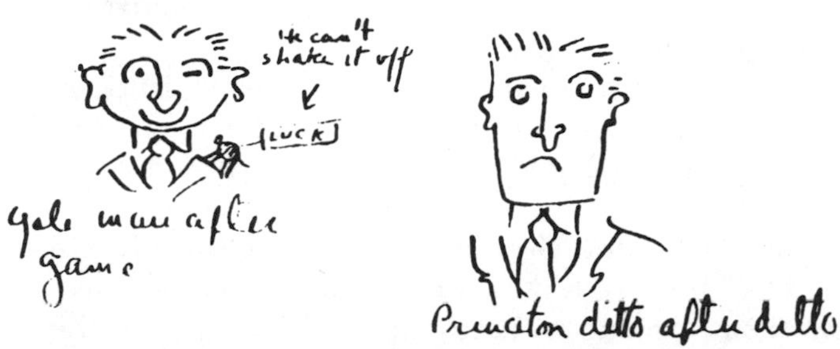

Saw Stu Walcott between halves and made a desperate effort to get over but the 2nd half started before I was out of the Princeton stand. It certainly was a heart-breaker wasn't it.[1] I gloomed all evening. While the rest of the college was drownding its sorrows in Busbys, Maximes, Jacks and other churches along Broadway I was sitting the Elton Hotel in Waterbury with Ginevra King, another Westover girl, and another Princetonian. All through dinner a Yale crowd kept singing "Bright College Beers"[2] their Univesity anthem and after dinner to heap insult apon injury we danced to "Boola-Boola" Its a wonder I didn't stand up and sing the undertaker's song; I had a corpse looking like the queen of the Folies Bergere. Then we rose at five-forty-five and sailed up to New York in the cold gray dawn.

Ruth Sturtevant I'd like to see you a lot right now. I imagine you'd be an awfully cheering person to talk to. I alway talk too D—— seriously with G.K. and end up with a pronounced case of melancholia but I think you'd be likely to leave a person in a good humor—I don't know why!

I suppose it must have been an awful relief to you to get out of the penententiary for a little carouse but now that you're again breaking stones with the other prisoners you're probably correspondingly lower. If you could only see me sitting alone in my room on a dismal unhappy tonight—Sunday night at that—with the rain pouring down outside and nothing to look forward to but weeks of grind and △ work

Why do you always begin your letters "My Dear Scott." Are we on such terribly formal terms. I should think that after our friendship of years and the weeks we have constantly spent together you might drop the my—or the my and the Scott.

No Ruth there is not a word not so compromising as either love or maledictions so until you make up your mind what to use you'd better just sign "Ruth Howard"

When I said you were like Aleda[3] I didn't mean at all that you looked like her because naturally you don't at all. Your resemblance to Aleda is purly in one thing which I won't put on paper as you'd surly show it to her and I don't think either of you would like it. Tell Aleda for me that she is very beautiful but extraordinarily stonyhearted. (Next time I see you I'll tell you why you're like her. Its a very essential and important point which you have, or lack, in common)

I suppose you trotted around at the St. Anthony dance, got rushed to death and by three oclock were the only girl in the room who had not lost her color and I suppose you met a perfectly wonderful Yale man who promised to "write you every day and send his picture.

Don't you think Ruth that for Sunday night this is a very brilliant letter. I'd illustrate it with those wonderful pen and ink sketches of mine but I havn't the pep but my next letter will be a regular "Life."[4] Best to Aleda and Curses to Margaret also remember me "very formally" to Helen James.—and in your next letter don't mention the football game. I'd been saving this letter so that I could gloat in it but doggone it I might as well have sent it a week ago. Committing Myself I am

With Love
Scott

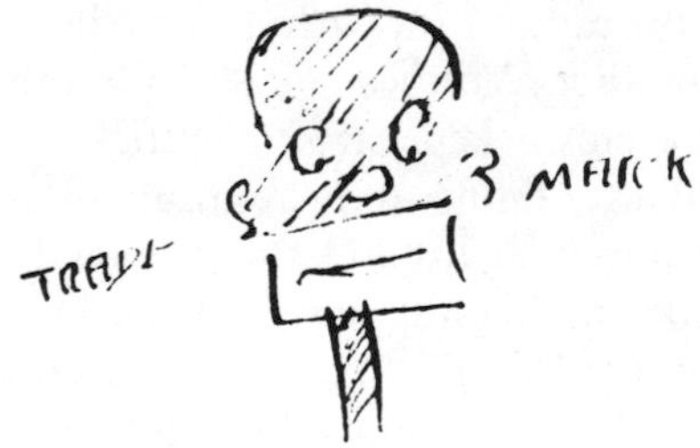

[1] Yale upset Princeton at New Haven, 13–7, on 13 November 1915.
[2] "Bright College Years," the Yale alma mater.
[3] Alida Bigelow, a St. Paul friend.
[4] *Life* was a humor magazine before Henry Luce bought the title for his picture magazine.

TO: Virginia Taylor[1]
1 November 1916

Signed postcard. Princeton University
Princeton, New Jersey

[1] Daughter of Fitzgerald's cousin Cecilia Taylor.

TO: Elizabeth Taylor[1] Signed postcard. Princeton University

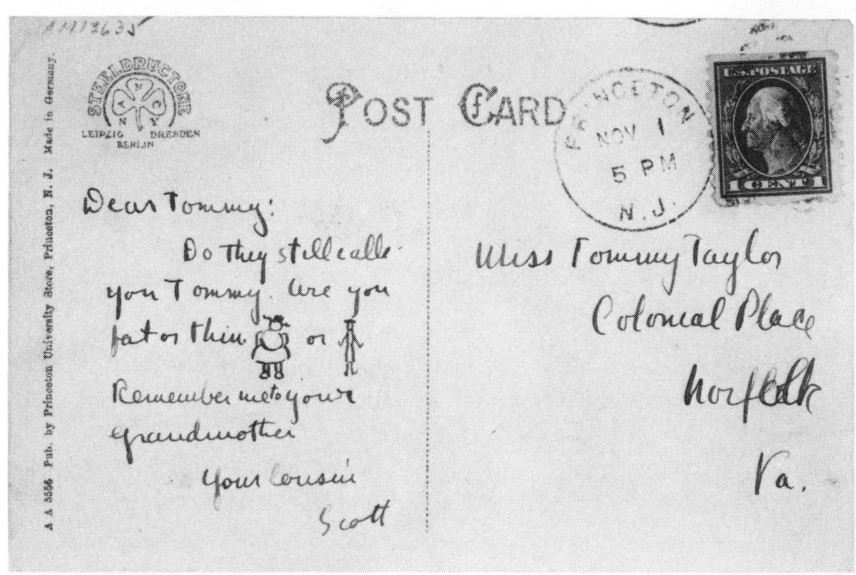

POST CARD

Dear Tommy:

Do they still call you Tommy. Are you fat or thin [drawing] or [drawing]

Remember me to your grandmother

Your cousin

Scott

Miss Tommy Taylor
Colonial Place
Norfolk
Va.

[1] Daughter of Fitzgerald's cousin Cecilia Taylor.

TO: Annabel Fitzgerald[1]
c. 1915

AL, 10 pp. Princeton University
Princeton, New Jersey

Written by me at 19 or so
Basis of Bernice[2]

The General Subject of Conversation

Conversation like grace is a cultivated art. Only to the very few does it come naturally. You are as you know, not a good conversationalist and you might very naturally ask, "What do boys like to talk about?'

(1) Boys like to talk about themselves—much more than girls. A girl once named Helen Walcott, told me (and she was the most popular debutante in Washington one winter) that as soon as she got a man talking about himself she had him cinched and harnessed—they give themself away. Here are some leading questions for a girl to use.

a) You dance so much better than you did last year.

b) How about giving me that sporty necktie when you're thru with it.

c) You've got the longest eyelashes! (This will embarrass him, but he likes it)

d) I hear you've got a "line"!

e) Well who's you're latest crush!

Avoid

a) When do you go back to school?

b) How long have you been home?

c) Its warm or the orchestras good or the floors good.

Also avoid any talk about relations or mutual friends. Its a sure sign you're hard up for talk if you ask Jack Allen about Harriette or Tuby about Martha. Dont be afraid of slang—use it, but be careful to use the most modern and sportiest like "line," camafluage etc. Never talk about a boy about about his school or college unless he's done something special or unless he starts the subject. In a conversation its always good to start by talking about nothing—just some fresh camafluage; but start it yourself—never let the boy start it: *Dont talk about your school—no matter where you* go. Never sing no matter how big the chorus.

2.

As you get a little old you'll find that boys like to talk about such things as smoking and drinking. Always be very liberal—boys hate a prig—tell them you dont object to a girl smoking but dont like cigarettes yourself. Tell them you smoke only cigars—kid them!—When you're old still you want always to have a line on the latest books plays and music. More men like that than you can imagine.

In your conversation always affect a complete frankness but really be only as frank as you wish to be. Never try to give a boy the affect that you're popular—Ginevra always starts by saying shes a poor unpopular woman without any beause. Always pay close attention to the man. Look at him in his eyes if possible. Never effect boredom. Its terribly hard to do it gracefully Learn to be worldly. Remember in all society nine girls out of ten marry for money and nine men out of ten are fools.

Poise: Carriage: Dancing: Expression

(1) Poise depends on carriage, expression and conversation and having discussed the last and most important I'll say a few words on the other two.

(2) A girl should hold herself straight. Margaret Armstrongs slouch has lost her more attention than her lack of beauty. Even Sandy is critiscized for stopping. When you cross a room before people nine out of ten look at you and if you're straight and self contained and have a graceful atheletic carriage most of them will remark on it. In dancing it is very important to hold yourself well and remember to dance hard. Dancers like Betty and Grace and Alice *work hard.* Alice is an entirely self made dancer. At sixteen she was no better than you, but she practised and tried. A dancer like Elizabeth Clarkson looses partners. *You can not be lazy.* You should try not to trow a bit of weight on the man and keep your mind on it enough to follow well. If you'd spent the time on dancing with me as I've often asked you instead of playing the piano youd be a good dancer. Louis Ordway taught Kit to dance the Castle walk one summer and as long as it lasted she was almost rushed at dances. And dancing counts as nothing else does.

(3) Expression that is facial expression, is one of your weakest points. A girl of your good looks and at your age ought to have almost perfect control of her face. It ought to be almost like a mask so that she'd have perfect control of any expression or impression she might wish to use.

a) A good smile and one that could be assumed at will, is an absolute necesity. You smile on one side which is *absolutely wrong.* Get before a mirror and practise a smile and get a good one, a radiant smile ought to be in the facial vocubulary of every girl. Practise it—on girls, on the family. Practise doing it when you dont feel happy and when you're bored. When youre embarrassed, when you're at a disadvantage. Thats when you'll have to use it in society and when you've practised a thing in calm, then only are you sure of it as a good weapon in tight places

(b) A laugh isn't as important but its well to have a good one on ice. You natural one is very good, but your artificial one is bum. Next time you laugh naturally remember it and practise so you can do it any time you want. *Practise anywhere.*

(c) A pathetic, appealing look is one every girl ought to have. Sandra and Ginevra are specialists at this: so is Ardita, Its best done by opening the eyes wide and drooping the mouth a little, looking upward (hanging

the head a little) directly into the eyes of the man you're talking to. Ginevra and Sandra use this when getting of their "I'm so unpopular speeches and indeed they use it about half the time. Practise this.
(d) Dont bit or twist your lips—its sure death for any expression
(e) The two expressions *you* have control over now are no good. One is the side smile and the other is the thoughtful look with the eyes half closed.

I'm telling you this because mother and I have absolutely no control over our facial expressions and we miss it. Mothers worse than I am—you know how people take advantage of what ever mood her face is in and kid the life out of her. Well you're young enough to get over it—tho' you're worse than I am now. The value of this practise is that whenever you're at a disadvantage you dont show it and boys hate to see a girl at a disadvantage.

Practise Now

Dress and Personality.

(A) No two people look alike in the same thing. but very few realize it. Shop keepers make money on the fact that the fat Mrs. Jones will buy the hat that looked well on the thin Mrs. Smith. You've got to find your type. To do so always look at girls about your *size* and *coloring* and notice what they look well in. Never buy so much as a sash without the most careful consideration   *Study your type.* That is get your good points and accentuate them. For instance you have very good features—you ought to be able to wear jaunty hats and so forth.

(B) Almost all neatness is gained in man or woman by the arrangement of the hair. You have beautiful hair—you ought to be able to do something with it. Go to the best groomed girl in school and ask her and then wear it that way—Dont get tired and changed unless you're sure the new way is better. Catherine Tie is dowdy about her hair lately   Dont I notice it? When Grace's hair looks well—She looks well   When its unkempt it looks like the devil. Sandy and Betty always look neat and its their hair that does it.

(2)

(C) I'll line up your good points against your bad physically.

Good	Bad
Hair	Teeth only fair
Good general size	Pale complexion
Good features	Only fair figure
	Large hands and feet.

Now you see of the bad points only the last cannot be remedied. Now while slimness is a fashion you can cultivate it by exercise—Find out now from some girl. Exercise would give you a healthier skin. You should never rub cold cream into your face because you have a slight tendency to grow hairs on it. I'd find out about this from some Dr. who'd tell you what you could use in place of a skin cream.

(D) A girl should always be careful about such things as underskirt showing, long drawers showing under stocking, bad breath, mussy eyebrows (with such splendid eyebrows as yours you should brush them or wet them and train them every morning and night as I advised you to do long ago. They oughtn't to have a hair out of place.

(E) Walk and general physical grace. The point about this is that you'll be up against situations when ever you go out which will call for you to be graceful—not to be physically clumsy. Now you can only attain this by practise because it no more comes naturally to you than it does to me. Take some stylish walk you like and imitate it. A girl should have a little class. Look what a stylish walk Eleanor and Grace and Betty have and what a homely walk Marie and Alice have. Just because the first three deliberately practised every where until now its so natural to them that they cant be ungraceful—This is true about every gesture. I noticed last Saturday that your gestures are awkward and so unnatural as to seem affected. Notice the way graceful girls hold their hands and feet. How they stoop, wave, run and then try because you cant practise those things when men are around. Its two late then. They ought to be incentive then

(F) General summing up.

- (1) dress scrupulously neatly and then forget your personal appearance. Every stocking should be pulled up to the last wrinkle.
- (2) Dont wear things like that fussy hat that aren't becoming to you—At least buy no more. Take someone who knows with you—some one who really knows.
- (3) Conform to your type no matter what looks well in the store
- (4) Cultivate deliberate physical grace. You'll never have it if you dont. I'll discuss dancing in a latter letter.

(G) You see if you get any where and feel you look alright then there's one worry over and one bolt shot for self-confidence—and the person you're with, man, boy, woman, whether its Aunt Millie or Jack Allen o myself likes to feel that the person they're sponsoring is at least externally a credit.

[1] Fitzgerald's sister was five years younger than he.
[2] "Bernice Bobs Her Hair," *The Saturday Evening Post* (1 May 1920).

TO: Stephen Leacock[1]
Before 16 March 1917

Not examined.[2]
Leacock Home, Orillia, Ontario

My Dear Mr. Leacock:

As imitation is the sincerest flattery I thought you might be interested in something you inspired. The Nassau Literary Magazine here at Princeton of which I'm an editor got out a "Chaopolitan number," as a burlesque of "America's greatest magazine."

The two stories I wrote "Jemina, a story of the Blue Ridge mountains, by John Phlox Jr" and "The Usual Thing" by "Robert W. Shamless [sic][3] are of the "Leacock school" of humour—in fact Jemina is rather a steal in places from "Hannah of the Highlands."

I'm taking the liberty of sending you a copy—needless to say it increased our circulation & standing in undergraduate eyes.

Hope you'll get one smile out of it for every dozen laughs I got from the Snoopopaths.[4]

Very appreciatively yours,
F. Scott Fitzgerald

1 Canadian humorist.

2 See Ralph L. Curry, *Stephen Leacock* (Garden City, N.Y.: Doubleday, 1959), pp. 119–20.

3 Brackets in printed text.

4 Leacock replied on 16 March 1917: "Your stories are fine. As Daniel Webster said, or didn't say, to the citizens of Rochester, 'Go on.' "

FROM: Father Sigourney Fay[1]

TLS, 2 pp. Princeton University

Deal Beach, New Jersey,
August 22nd, 1917.

Dear Fitz:—

I cannot tell you how delighted I am to have gotten your letter.

First of all as to money: Your $3600 will cover everything except your uniforms. There is no salary for any of us; they expect us to take it out in glory, and really there will be glory enough if we manage to do what I hope we will.

Now, in the eyes of the world, we are a Red Cross Commission sent out to report on the work of the Red Cross, and especially on the State of the civil population, and that is all I can say. But I will tell you this, the State Department is writing to our ambassador in Russia and Japan, the British Foreign Office is writing to their ambassador in Japan and Russia, and I have other letters to our ambassador in Japan and Russia, and to everybody else in fact who can be of the slightest assistance to us. Moreover I am taking letters from Eminence to the Catholic Bishops.

The conversion of Russia has already begun. Several millions of Russians have already come over to the Catholic Church from the schism in the last month. Whether you look at it from the spiritual or temporal point of view it is an immense opportunity and will be a help to you all the rest of your life.

You will be a Red Cross Lieutenant, and I will let you know as soon as I get your commission what your uniform will be.

Will you come on and join me in New York and get your uniforms there at the regular Red Cross place, where you can get them in 24 hours. You are measured at dawn, fitted at noon and fitted out at sunset. Or will you join me in Chicago and we can go thence to San Francisco and bid affectionate farewell to Peevie,[2] and get to Vancouver in time for the 27th. Or shall I come to St. Paul, and will we go by the C.P.R. But what will Peevie do then, poor fellow. It is hard enough on him in any case.

I think the best thing you and I can do is to write a book while we are away. I am going to take a Corona typewriter. I am so glad you know how to work one.

We shall have to work very hard going over on your French. Get a Rosenthal method at once and go right through it.

You will have to take plenty of warm clothes as we shall be in a very cold climate most of the time. You will be in Russia three months, not away only three months. Your money ought to be in this form: It costs $1600 for our traveling over and back, and $2000 in a letter of credit while we are living in Russia, as we shall have to keep at least some state.

Now, do be discreet about what you say to anybody. If anybody asks you say you are going as secretary to a Red Cross Commission. Do not say anything more than that, and if you show this letter to anybody, show it only in the strictest confidence. I would not show it to anybody but your mother, father and aunt.

To my mind the most extraordinary thing about it is that we may play a part in the restoration of Russia to Catholic unity. The schismatic church is crumbling to pieces; it has now no State to lean on.

I am tremendously glad you are going to have this experience. It really will change your whole life. Poor Peevie could not go. I was hoping that he might and I would have taken you both in that case.

Leslie[3] cannot go as he is not an American citizen, and the Red Cross is now the Government, so they cannot send anybody who is not an American. Besides he could not leave the Dublin; we cannot all be away.

I think the Dublin Review will be jolly glad to get anything we send them, signed with any initials we care to put to it. But I think we had better save our efforts for a book which we will write together, and to which we will put both our names.

Though we get no salary we all have to work hard, and you will have to help me with an enormous amount of correspondence. As you would elegantly express it, "the whole thing is a knock-out." I sincerely hope the war will be over long before you take to flying.

Now, last of all, whatever you surmise about the commission, keep your brilliant guesses to yourself. You guess far too well. Above all be careful what you say about religion. It is for that very reason that the attaches are Protestant. There will be no Catholice except yourself, myself and my servant. Whatever is done A.M.D.G.[4] will be done by you and me. For this reason I shall arrange for you to share my cabin, and we can take a room together when we get to Russia, as it will save some money at least and give us a chance to talk the things over which must be strictly confidential between us.

About your commission—give it up now, and say that as you have heard nothing you have decided to wait until you are of age and then go in for aviation. But I hope to goodness, as I said before that the war will be over before you take to that.

As soon as you have read this letter and shown it at home, burn it.

With best love,

S. W. Fay

[1] Cyril Sigourney Webster Fay became headmaster of the Newman School after Fitzgerald graduated. In 1917 he was planning to take Fitzgerald with him to Russia on a diplomatic mission for the Roman Catholic Church, using the cover that they were serving with the Red Cross. Fay provided the model for Father Darcy in *This Side of Paradise*, and the novel was dedicated to him. None of Fitzgerald's letters to Fay survives; they are believed to have been destroyed by Fay's mother after his death.

[2] Stephan Parrott, a Newman School protégé of Fay's. Fay had adopted Parrott and Fitzgerald as his spiritual sons.

[3] Sir Shane Leslie, Anglo-Irish author who became associated with Newman while Fay was headmaster. He encouraged Fitzgerald's literary ambitions.

[4] *Ad majorum dei gloria.*

FROM: Father Sigourney Fay — TLS, 1 p. Princeton University

Deal, N.J.
October 4, 1917.

Dear Fitz:

My note the other day was very short because I was frightfully rushed, and because I had not had time to read your story.[1] I have just finished it now and think it is first rate stuff. I should prefer it being called by your own name instead of that of Michael Fane, as that non de plume would give the impression that your story was an imitation of "Youth's Encounter" which it is not.[2] Your hero is curiously unlike Michael Fane, and very unlike you or me.

I was interested in your last letter—the way you tried to divide people up. I do not think there are as few classes as you think. There are many different types. I should take as the first type ourselves; the second class Leslie; third class Father Hemmick; fourth class Mr. Delbos;[3] fifth class Duc de Richelieu; sixth Aberdeen.

Then there are about four classes more. They dwindle down from the typical business men to the thug.

I think that is all the types there are, but I do not think you can get people under fewer heads than that. Of course in the type individuals vary, but the individual's variations are very slight. It's extraordinary how slight they are. Take ourselves, you and Pevy and I have many superficial differences. Each is due to age and environment. As for instance I am older than both of you. Pevy was educated almost entirely in Europe, you almost entirely here. My education is English, Pevy's French, yours American, but if you remember a long conversation we had in Washington at the University Club in June, you will also remember how we startled one another by our extraordinary likeness in essential things.

It is exactly the same way with Stephen. All my plans hang fire at present. I may go to Europe any day, but I will let you know in plenty of time, then we can make one last effort to go together. With best love.

Cyril S. W. Fay

[1] Unidentified.

[2] Michael Fane was the hero of Compton Mackenzie's *Youth's Encounter* (1913), which greatly impressed Fitzgerald and his friends.

[3] Hemmick and Delbos were on the Newman School staff.

FROM: Shane Leslie — ALS, 3 pp. Princeton University

2127 Leroy Place
Washington

Nov 26, 1917

My dear Fitz,

This letter of good cheer will follow you I hope to Kansas. All good wishes for a bright future literary as well as military. I shall be interested in your novel in verse—it sounds bold!

However there is no form of literature which should not be attempted or concocted before the farce of the Anglo-Celto-Latin civilisation is rung down.

I wish you would stick to your idea of a book of poems.[1] I was much interested in those you read to me at the Newman School. Thirty or forty would make a book or livret. Nobody has time to finish a book these days. They are served up scaffolding and design more than complete solid form. Do not let Kansas destroy your soul or rust your pen. We must meet again[2]

yours faithfully
Shane Leslie

[1] This project and the novel in verse were abandoned.
[2] See Fitzgerald's 22 December letter to Leslie in *The Letters of F. Scott Fitzgerald*, ed. Andrew Turnbull (New York: Scribners, 1963); hereafter referred to as *Letters*.

FROM: Father Sigourney Fay — TLS, 2 pp. Princeton University

Deal, N.J.
December 10th, 1917.

Dear Fitz:

As I told you when the lightning strikes one of us it strikes us all. You had hardly left when I got my walking papers, and I am waiting expecting every moment to be told where to take ship. First about your questions: Miss Grace will have your letters of introduction for you when you come East. Second: Your book should be called "The Romance of an Egoist."[1] Or, "A Child of the Last Days." I think the name you signed to your last letter is a very good name. Stephen is undoubtedly the right first name, and my own name is a very good last one. And the Fitz makes a good bridge, and might very well be there as the Fays were Normans originally. I want you to get a book called "The Three Black Pennies."[2] In fact I am going to send it you. It is something like us the same person being repeated, over and over. The explanation of our case is that we are all a repitition of some common ancestor. The only blood we have in common is the blood of the O'Donohue's. I am sure this man's name was Stephen O'Donohue. Before you get this I will probably be on the ocean. It seems only right and proper that I should be the first of us whose life would be put in danger. Then will come your turn and then Peevie's. I do hope you will write to me the night before we go into action. I hope to see you before that time, for I fancy you will go abroad sooner than you think. When you do, however, face the cannon, that you have two lives to take care of as well as your own, or rather that there is only one life amongst the three of us, and if anything happens to you Peevie and I will probably dry up and blow away. I suppose anybody but you would think this the most utter tosh, but the worst of it is, we all know it is perfectly true. How magnificent Streeter is.[3] It gave me a frightful shock when you wrote me he thought me splendid. How can he be so deceived? Splendid is exactly the one thing that one of three is.

We are many other things—we're extraordinary, we're clever, we could be said I suppose to be brilliant. We can attract people, we can make atmosphere, we can almost always have our own way, but splendid—rather not. Peevie writes me that he has given over his novel for the present. He thinks he is too young. I quite agree, but the real reason why he couldn't go on was that he wasn't writing about himself. I have had a rise since I saw you. Have been made Major and Deputy Commisioner for Italy. I am going to Rome with a wonderful dossier, and there will be "no small stir" when I get there. How I wish one of you were with me. This sounds like a rather cynical letter. Not at all the sort that a middle aged clergyman should write to a youth about to depart for the wars. The only excuse is that the middle aged clergyman is talking to himself. There are deep things in us and you know what they are as well as I do. We have great faith, and we have a terrible honesty at the bottom of us, that all of our sophistry cannot destroy, and a kind of childlike simplicity that is the only thing that saves us from being downright wicked. Oh, you will be delighted to know that Leslie thinks of you as the Rupert Brook of America. I was no end pleased at that. You assure me that it is not sentiment that makes you want to die in the last ditch. What is the use of telling me that, when I know well enough what it isnt and what it is, too. It is Romance, spelled with a large R, but do kindly remember about Peevie and me, and put off your rendezvous with death as long as possible. Send your next letter to Leslie, 2127 Leroy Place, Washington, D.C. with your picture enclosed, and write soon.

Best love.
Stephen Fitz Fay Sr.

P.S. You remember I told you when you were leaving that if you fell I would make a lovely "keen" for you, but I was so keen to keen that I couldn't wait so I made one for your going away, which I enclose.[4] I am sorry your cheeks are not up to the description I have written of them, but that is not my fault.

[1] The working title for the novel that became *This Side of Paradise* was "The Romantic Egoist."

[2] A 1917 novel by Joseph Hergesheimer.

[3] Henry Strater, Princeton '19, who provided the model for Burne Holiday in *This Side of Paradise.*

[4] Published in *This Side of Paradise* as "A Lament for a Foster Son, and He going to the War Against the King of Foreign."

FROM: John Peale Bishop[1] ALS, 5 pp. Princeton University
January 1918

O God! O God! How wonderful *Youth's Encounter* is! Perhaps it meant more to me now than it would have done at Princeton, but it has done more than all the sociology in the world to make me feel life is worth living. I rose from its reading with that "free" feeling you have when the first thaw of spring takes the courses of winter. What if the light is too golden, the half-light too blue? Who would have them otherwise in a story of youth is an ass and the father of asininity. This is undoubtedly the true, the undefiled aim of the novel—to present—but how shall I venture to speak to your ears, so fearful of banalities?—any how it's not sociology. That's the chief difference between the French and the English novel—the typical French and English novel. There's no preachment in the former.

Now to come to your own book.[2] Scott, I think if you will recollect the volume above, or the account of Wells' youthful heroes, or Anatole France's *Le Livre de Mon Ami,* the glaring defect of your book will be noted. I have a theory that novels as well as plays should be in scenes. The marvellous effect of *Crime and Punishment* is largely due to the cumulative effect of the successive climaxes. Each scene—chapter what you will should be significant in the development either of the story or the hero's character. And I don't feel that yours are. You see Stephen[3] does the things every boy does. Well and good. I suppose you want the universal appeal. But the way to get it is to have the usual thing done in an individual way. You don't get enough into the boy's reactions to what he does. Its the only way to awaken the memory which is the real source of pleasure in boy's stories for grown-olds. It's not in relating what a boy does that causes this awakening, but his own love in what he does. Think of Michael Fane's reaction to the iron bars of his crib. It's wonderful. Now your boy sleds, but I don't *feel* that he enjoys sledding. In matter of fact, I don't realize fully that he does sled. You see what I mean? Each incident must be carefully chosen—to bring out the typical: then ride it for all its worth.

You see I don't know what Stuart's[4] like. I don't feel the charm of Stephen's childish harem. While with Michael I successively fell just as deeply in love with Dora, Kathleen, and Lily as he did. You have got to be more leisurely. Fill out the setting. Make each incident a step. The successive chapters should be in *echelon,* each a step and yet all clear at once.

I have been pretty miserable lately, but today feel fairly like I'd prefer to keep living.

I'm thinking seriously of writing a novel myself. I have a room now—shared with one other man who is [not there] a great deal. I certainly can't write poetry.

Did I refer to the 45th Inf. again? Well, what I meant was that it was full of recruits and wouldn't be fit for foreign service for quite a while— That's nothing against it. It will probably give you better treatment than we get here. I am wild with rage over this last measure—All officers attend reveille—6oo A.M. O ye gods of the petit dejeuner! It takes an act of congress to make gentlemen out of us. No body would ever suspect it from the life you lead. Being an attached lieutenant is almost as bad as being a T.C. Candidate. Except for the social idea, I'd as soon be a sergeant. When do you come down? ANSWER THAT.

You certainly shat on my poem. Well, its not very good, but Bunny[5] liked it, so I chucked it in.[6] That last section has a good deal of drule. *Endymion, Sylvo* and *Nassau Street* are all right, but the rest are bum.

However, I don't think you have any right to compare it to R.B.[7] *Nassau Street* would be a fairer comparison. But you can't refer to his uplift, because our situation was so utterly different. Everybody felt it in England, but less because of the war than because of the frightful state England was in when war came. Decadent boredom and futile political wrangling. You damn well, nobody felt any lift at Princeton. And somehow, I've never reacted emotionally to the war. I am beginning to feel a fine hatred, if you will, but my chief emotion last spring was regret at seeing the fellows go and all that went into the last of *Nassau Street*. It was a banal emotion—we've discussed that before.

Adieu.
St James of Compostella.

[1] Fitzgerald's Princeton classmate who became the model for Thomas Parke D'Invilliers in *This Side of Paradise.*

[2] "The Romantic Egoist."

[3] The hero of Fitzgerald's novel in progress was named Stephen Palms.

[4] A character in "The Romantic Egoist."

[5] Edmund Wilson, Jr.

[6] Bishop had published *Green Fruit* (1917), a volume of verse.

[7] Rupert Brooke.

Note: In January 1918 John Peale Bishop was expecting to be sent to Italy and wrote Fitzgerald: "Even death there would be a compensation—Keats, Shelley, Browning, Wilde, Bishop various and gifted quintet, let us weep over all five." Fitzgerald responded with this drawing.

FROM: John Peale Bishop — ALS, 2 pp. Princeton University
January 1918

Now as to the book—The new chapters are much, much better. You didn't get the small boy's viewpoint very well. The schoolboy is far better done. I am beginning to know Stephen better, but I feel you are concealing a great deal of the young man's history that I ought to know. And it's just for this reason that I don't particularly like him. You see he isn't popular and on the whole one feels rather deservedly; you have been too hard on him and your reader is rather easily prejudiced against him. Why don't you give the other side. Show the boy's loneliness, his real suffering when alone, his mental and emotional states. *The history is not* SUBJECTIVE *enough.* I cant make that too strong. That's when the immense superiority of Youths Encounter comes in. You give us the *acts* of the boy. Mackenzie the *mind* and *soul* moving through the action. No body is particularly interested in what small boys do—except their individual parents—but we all love to recapture their attitude toward the world. In a way, it's the most mysterious thing in the world. To a grown man, woman is comparitively simple as against the adolescent youth. It apparently means nothing that we have been through it. It is exceedingly difficult to regain that curious mental life which is not rational, not clear, and uncolored by real emotion. It is the result of the beginning of clear reasoning and the uprising of the thousand obscure complexities of sex which permeate everything yet never identify themselves definitely with the sexual function That's my first criticism and the second is a further plea for simplification. Don't put in everything you remember. Retain only significant events and ride them hard. Pad them with Stephen's reactions. That's the great trouble with autobiographical material, it's so hard to arrange, so hard to distinguish as regards the incidental and the essential.

Send on more copy.

I haven't heard of the 45th going away.

> One face than autumn lilies tenderer
> And voice more soft than the far plaint of viols is
> Or the soft moan of any grey-eyed lute player
>
> —Heard the strange lutes on the green banks
> Ring loud with grief and delight
> Of the sun-silked, dark haired musicians
> In the brooding silence of night.
>
> O western winds when will ye blow
>   That the small rain down can rain.
> Christ! that my love were in my arms
>   And I in my bed again.

Till life us do part
Casabianca.

FROM: Shane Leslie ALS, 2 pp. Princeton University

Washington
May 11, 1918.

My dear Fitz

I read your book with real interest devoting thereto a whole Sunday. It will stand as it is very well and if there are to be operations I will see them through.[1] So you may depart in peace and possibly find yourself part of the Autumn reading banned by the Y.M.C.A. for use among troops! Let me know before you depart. Fay's last letter seemed to point to his return this month but he is far too useful in Rome where an American lever is needed to switch Austria on to President Wilson's policy.

By the way the Pope has made him Monsignore and clothed him in purple from thatch to toe. I hope we all meet again before the world is over—[2]

Yours ever
Shane Leslie

[1] Leslie sent Fitzgerald's novel to Charles Scribner with a covering letter that read in part: "I have read it through and in spite of its disguises it has given me a vivid picture of the American generation that is hastening to war. I marvel at it's crudity and its cleverness. It is naive in places, shocking in others, painful to the conventional and not without a touch of ironic sublimity especially toward the end. About a third of the book could be omitted without losing the impression that it is written by an American Rupert Brooke. I knew the poetic Rupert Brooke and this is a prose one, though some of the lyrics are good and aparently original. It interests me as a boy's book and I think gives expression to that real American youth that the sentimentalists and super patriots are so anxious to drape behind the canvas of the Y.M.C.A. tent. Though Scott Fitzgerald is still alive it has a literary value. Of course when he is killed it will also have a commercial value. Before leaving for France he has committed it to me and will you in any case house it in your safe for the time? If you feel like giving a judgment upon it, will you call upon me to make any alterations or perform whatever duties accrue to a literary sponsor?"

[2] See Fitzgerald's 8 May letter to Leslie in *Letters*.

FROM: Monsignor Sigourney Fay TLS, 2 pp. Princeton University

Deal Beach, New Jersey,
August 17th, 1918.

Dear Fitz:—

If I were accustomed to being affectionate with you this letter would sound like a letter of Mrs. Fay to Michael. I always think it such a shame that your very American training makes it impossible for me to pour out my paternal affection to you like I do to Peevie, for whom I notice you have the truly elder brotherly low opinion. I assure you he is not shallow, unless you and I are also, and he is becoming a very worthy member of society spending the summer in great discomfort at the Widow Nolan's at Cambridge tutoring diligently for the Tech. I have seen quite a good deal of him since he has been in the East, as he came here to Deal and also spent a Sunday with me at Southboro while I was there. We also had luncheon together, and tea at another time in Boston.

But the question which interests me at this moment is, when do I see you? You spoke of leave in August. I shall be here until the 30th. His Eminence and the Bishop of Richmond are staying here with me, and it is very hard to get a moment even to write, but I wish you could come if only for a week-end; or if you could come in September it would be even better. Or, again, if you could come as far as Washington in September I will go down and meet you. I have ten thousand things to say that I cannot write. There are intimacies that cannot be put upon paper.

The two chapters of your novel which I read gave me a queer feeling.

I seemed to go back twenty-five years. Of course you know that Eleanor's real name was Emily. I never realized that I told you so much about her. It was Swinburne, however, not Rupert Brooke, that we used to read together. How you got it in I do not know; her materialism and the preternatural circumstances—unless it is possible that you inherited my memory with the rest of my mental furniture. Really the whole thing is most startling; I am keen beyond words to read the rest of that book. I may be frightfully prejudiced but I have never read anything more interesting than that book. I think it beats Youth's Encounter hollow, if only in the brutal frankness in the use of the first person. There is always something far more arresting about a self revelation than there is about a story told about somebody else. If the rest of the book is up to the two chapters I have read it must be a corker. I suppose this is most ill-advised talk on my part, but really I cannot be bothered with the hypocracy of an elder damning with vain praise nor   my really great enthusiasm.[1]

Leslie told me himself that Scribner liked your book extremely and was reading it himself. I cannot understand their having told you that Scribner had not seen it. Do let me have the rest of the novel right away. I will read it quickly and send it back.

What a tremendous role the actual and cold fear of Satan does play in our make-up, and what a protection this sort of sixth sense by which we sense him, to use an American expression, is.

I am sorry you are in trouble again, but glad that at last you have time to remember my existence and to write to me.

Do write to Peevie. He is most anxious to correspond with you, and would really be a delightful correspondent, and you can speak quite as freely to him as you do to me. I should think you would find it rather fun to write to him as an older person to a younger, and to me as a younger person to an older. Youth and age both have their compensations.

What I shall do in the future is hanging rather in the balance, but I expect it will end in my going back. I wish the war were over and that I had a house in Washington, that you had digs in New York or somewhere near and could drop in for week-ends, and that Peevie were at a university. This war could very easily be the end of a most brilliant family.

Do try to get leave and come up to see me; and, above all, send me the rest of that book.

With best love,

Stephen Fitz Fay Sr

Lieut. F-Scott Fitzgerald,
Hq. Co. 67th Infantry,
Camp Sheridan, Alabama.

[1] The space in this line appears in the original.

FROM: Charles Scribner's Sons[1]

TLS, 1 p. Scrapbook. Princeton University
Charles Scribner's Sons letterhead
New York City

Aug. 19, 1918.

Lieutenant F. Scott Fitzgerald,
Hq. Co. 67th Infantry,
Camp Sheridan, Ala.

Dear Sir:

We have been reading "The Romantic Egoist" with a very unusual degree of interest;—in fact no ms. novel has come to us for a long time that seemed to display so much originality, and it is therefore hard for us to conclude that we cannot offer to publish it as it stands at present. Of course, in this we are considerably influenced by the prevailing conditions, including a governmental limitation on the number of publications and very severe manufacturing costs which make profitable publication far more difficult than ordinarily; but we are also influenced by certain characteristics of the novel itself. We generally avoid criticism as beyond our function and as likely to be for that reason not unjustly resented by an author but we should like to risk some very general comments this time because, if they seemed to you so far in point that you applied them to a revision of the ms., we should welcome a chance to reconsider its publication.

The chief of these is that the story does not seem to us to work up to a conclusion;—neither the hero's career nor his character are shown to be brought to any stage which justifies an ending. This may be intentional on your part for it is certainly not untrue to life; but it leaves the reader distinctly disappointed and dissatisfied since he has expected him to arrive somewhere either in an actual sense by his response to the war perhaps, or in a psychological one by "finding himself" as for instance Pendennis is brought to do. He does go to the war, but in almost the same spirit that he went to college and school,— because it is simply the thing to do. It seems to us in short that the story does not culminate in anything as it must to justify the reader's interest as he follows it; and that it might be made to do so quite consistently with the characters and with its earlier stages.

It seems to us too that not enough significance is given to some of those salient incidents and scenes, such as the affairs with girls. We do not suggest that you should resort to artificiality by giving a significance inconsistent with that of the life of boys of the age of the hero, but that it would be well if the high points were heightened so far as justifiable; and perhaps this effect could partly be gained by pruning away detail you might find could be spared elsewhere. Quite possibly all that we have said is covered by your own criticism of the ms, as at present a little "crude" and that the revision you contemplate will itself remove the basis of our criticism, and if when you make this you allow us a second reading we shall gladly give it. We do not want anything we have said to make you think we failed to get your idea in the book,—we certainly do not wish you to "conventionalize" it by any means in either form or manner, but only to do those things which it seems to us important to intensify its effect and so satisfy a reader that he will recommend it,—which is the great thing to accomplish toward a success.

We know how busy you are and how absorbed you must be in your present work, and it is rather difficult to think of you as being able to do this revising too; but as you have yourself spoken of it we have less hesitation in making suggestions toward it and in sending back the ms;—we hope we shall see it again and we shall then reread it immediately,—in fact our present delay was due to a misapprehension which led us to think you did not care about an early decision.

Very truly yours,
Charles Scribner's Sons

[1] This letter was probably written by Maxwell Perkins, who accepted *This Side of Paradise* in 1919.

TO: Zelda Sayre[1] | ALS, 1 p. Scrapbook. Princeton University
After July 1918 | Camp Sheridan, Alabama

Hq. 67th
Sheridan

Zelda:

Here is the mentioned chapter. . . . a document in youthful melancholy. . . .

However. . . . .the heroine does resemble you in more ways than four. . . . .

Needlessly I may add that the chapter and the sending of it are events for your knowledge alone. . .—Show it not to man woman or child.

I am frightfully bored today—

Desirously
F Scott Fit—

[1] At the time Fitzgerald met Zelda Sayre she was eighteen years old and a locally famous belle.

FROM: Monsignor Sigourney Fay TLS, 3 pp. Princeton University

Baltimore, Maryland.
October 19, 1918.

1st. Lieutenant Scott Key Fitzgerald,
67th Infantry,
Headquarters Company,
Camp Sheridan, Rifle Range,
Alabama.

Dear Fitz:

I hasten to send back the parts of your novel which you were good enough to let me read. The more I see of it the more amazingly good I think it is.

I wish you hadn't called me Taylor.[1] In fact I seem hardly to be like myself at all as a lay diplomat, and I do think a one syllable name is almost essential. Taylor gives a quite wrong impression,—Forbes, or something like that I think would be much better.

Besides I don't think my conversation sounds a bit like myself. The following bit of dialogue would explain what I mean:

"Have you got anything there I should like?"

"Do you like milk?"

"Rather."

"I have got crackers and jelly too, the jam is all out."

"Right. I think jelly is ripping, don't you?"

"Good Evening, Sir," I said uncertainly.

"Good Evening,—lets see the grub."

The rest is alright until you come to—

"Well" he said at length, "thats A-1."

The moon came out and we looked at each other unembarrassed.

"I say, you know" he said "you are a very unhappy boy aren't you?"

"Oh, well you look as if" etc.—"are there any more biscuits?"

"No, Sir."

"Well then, I'll cut along."

I do hope you can get to New York soon. There are about a million things that I cannot write about that I want to say to you, and when you come you must arrange to spend two or three days, as it is going to take forty eight hours to tell you all about last winter.

I think your book is way and beyond "His Family" or "The Harbor,"[2] or any of those self revolation sort of books. It is really very like "Youth's Encounter."

McKenzie has written a new book, "Sylvia Scarlet." You remember Sylvia in "Sinister Street." He has just simply taken Stella Fane gone wrong, and in order to excuse himself he has made her also a descendant of Lord Saxby. I think he has run out, Poor Michael is a proven ghost in this book, all the insides have gone out of him. As a matter of fact he cannot write the third volume of Michael's life. When I go to Europe I mean to get to know him and talk it out with him. In the meantime I am perfecting a sort of scheme which I will never publish without his permission of course.

The scheme is a collection of Michael's letters from Rome while he is studying and after he has been ordained, a diplomat in the service at the Vatican. I shall call them "The letters of Monsignor Fane." I felt a tremendous desire to do it lately.

With best love,
Stephen 1st

P.S. I have seen a lot of Peevie, who is at Harvard in the O.T.C. Peevie would have yelled at the idea of my writing anything for him. He says writing is your flare, architecture is his, and music is mine. But I tell him I could write if I chose, be an architect if I chose, and both of you could be musicians if you like,—so.

With best love, S 1st

N.B. Our letters are not at all what they ought to be, but I have been minus a secretary for a long time, and when on the rare occasions I can get one a lot of correspondence has piled up, and I never get a chance really to speak my mind. I think when we write one another, we ought always to think of the possibility of the other person some day publishing that letter.

S 1st

I have returned your letter as you said it was part of your novel

S.W. F S 1st
Stephen Fitz Fay Sr.

1 The name Taylor was changed to Darcy in the published novel.
2 Novels by Ernest Poole published in 1917 and 1915, respectively.

FROM: Charles W. Donahoe[1] ALS, 4 pp.[2] Princeton University

Trade Test Dept. (Alias Somewhere in France
Camp Lewis, Wash.
Sunday Oct 27, '18.

Dear Fitz:

Lost your address so am taking a chance on this reaching you. Received the three installments or chapters of your story and was very much interested in reading it. Recognized practically all the material of composition but as the well known WW[3] says "I would deem myself lacking in candor" did I not say that I was distinctly disappointed in your handling of the material "Nothing can be gained by leaving this essential thing unsaid." You remember in Stalky & Co the reference to St. Winifred's or the World of school and "Eric"[4] Well I have read Eric and realize, as you would, what spirit Kipling objected to in Eric. Think your book is very much an American "Eric." Of course I realize how damn hard it is to make the humorous scenes humorous, the serious ones serious and so on, but think you have failed entirely in getting it across as well as you could do had you taken more time. For instance the description of yourself hiding behind the rug when Dr —— came in the room. Also you have given a description of Princeton which while accurate enough overemphasizes the social climbing drinking etc. You have left all the fun out of it. Your description of the wrestling match with Izzy Hirsch fell rather flat. Your use of specific names of clubs etc is not going to be appreciated in the sense you have used them. Owen Johnson's[5] use of "Bones" was different. Everything seems have been skipt over the work is done too fast. There is none of the "je vous gloterai" spirit of "Stalky & Co." Think you could do ever so much better if you took more time and care. Noticed you placed JPB in the same position as Guy —— in Sinister Street (the one who was hero of Plasher's Mead[6])

[1] "Sap" Donahoe, Princeton classmate of Fitzgerald's. A visit to the Donahoe ranch in Montana in 1915 provided the setting for "The Diamond as Big as the Ritz."

[2] Only the first page and a half of this letter, discussing Fitzgerald's novel, are published here.

[3] President Woodrow Wilson.

[4] Rudyard Kipling's *Stalky & Company* (1899); Frederic W. Farrar's *Eric* (1858) and *St. Winifred's* (1862).

[5] Author of *Stover at Yale* (1911).

[6] A 1915 novel by Compton Mackenzie.

TO: Ruth Howard Sturtevant
Early 1919

ALS, 1 p.[1] University of Virginia
Montgomery, Alabama

The Sunny South

Ruth

I

am

in

love! Happy

New

Year!

You made a great impression on ma jeune soeur—Isn't she stoopid—

I am now aide-de-camp
to General Ryan—Sweet
is it not—

Ruth—I'm so glad we like each other again, or am I presuming?
I hope to Appollo
I'll be out in April—
I'll probably be out before
my book at that[2]

I beg to remain
Your obediant Servant
Geo Washington

[1] Written in slanted sections covering the paper.
[2] "The Romantic Egoist" was declined by Scribners; it was not accepted until September 1919, after Fitzgerald rewrote it as *This Side of Paradise.*

FROM: Shane Leslie ALS, 4 pp. Princeton University

128 West Fifty-Ninth Street
New York City
Jan 16 1919

My dear Fitz

I have been very anxious to see you and have a talk over Mgr Fay's death. I was ill my self and could not see him at the end but I crawled to the funeral, which he would have loved. It was magnificently Catholic and liturgical. Bishop Shahan sang solemn High Mass and Cardinal Gibbons gave the final absolutions. Bp Russell, Fr Sanderson, Delbos, Mrs Maloney, Fr Sargent, Fr Dolan were there and a host of friends and priests. I have been a week realising that his death was one of the sorrows of my life. His friendship was the choice find of my American years and I felt I had really settled down to a golden friendship such as only can be enjoyed by converts in the Church of their love and interest. But the inexorable shears have cut through all the threads which he had gathered into his hands. To me it was a haunting grief to see him lying in his coffin with closed hands upon his purple vestments. His face had not changed and as he never knew he was dying he shewed no pain or fear. It was just our dear old friend and the church was full of Newman people and all our friends with daft staring faces. The Cardinal looked the most stricken of all for as he said he was now left alone. It was a beautiful sight to see him like an Archangel in cope and mitre sprinkling the holy water while the choir sang the Requiem eternam.[1] I think of the dear Monsignor every night. I am sure his spirit must have come to you and Stephen Parrot. He was very fond of you both. Write or come to see me for I am very sad and lonely and feel a desire to become a Carthusian

Oh my grief and oh my sorrow ochone! ochone!

yrs ever
Shane Leslie

Heritage—feeling of safety with Burne[2]

[1] Monsignor Fay died in New York on 10 January 1919. Fitzgerald rewrote Leslie's description of Fay's funeral into the description of Monsignor Darcy's funeral in *This Side of Paradise*, pp. 286–87.

[2] Written at the bottom by Fitzgerald; Burne Holiday is a character in *This Side of Paradise*.

FROM: Shane Leslie — ALS, 4 pp. Princeton University

128 W 59 St
New York—

Jan 23 1919

My dear Fitz,

I have been just as miserable as you—desirous of death and sapped by the epidemic. There is nothing left except the Church and for that reason we must keep our lamps alive. Cheer up and come and see me when you are in N.Y. I hope to be here a few more weeks while Horace Plunkett is in the country. Take heart—I envy you your youth, your virginity, the tabula rasa of your mind, the sense of unknown literary adventure.

Mgr Fay's death removes the centre from your solar system. It twisted a planet out of mine. Cardinal Gibbons has lost his only satisfactory satellite—but you must set to work. Read wisely and well until Fr Hemmick returns. The country will be crammed with literary wanderers and men whose writing instincts have been touched by the war. I think you would be happier if you were anchored like Hugh Benson[1] to the priesthood. The American priests do not write but it is about time some of them began. Mgr Fay always wanted you and Stephen to be priests. Do not rush into Bohemia—Rome is the only permanent country the only patria to which we can all belong.

Write to me whenever you want a sympathetic hearer. Mgr Fay intended leaving you to me in his will. "Son, behold thy father—Father, receive thy son—"[2]

Yours ever
Shane Leslie

[1] English novelist; author of *None Other Gods* (1910).

[2] See Fitzgerald's late January letter to Leslie in *Letters*.

TO: Zelda Sayre — Wire. Scrapbook. Princeton University

CHARLOTTE NC 122AM FEBY 21ST 1919

MISS TELDA FAYRE

CARE FRANCES STUBBS[1]

AUBURN ALA

YOU KNOW I DO NOT YOU DARLING

SCOTT

1103AM

[1] Stubbs was Zelda's date at an Auburn party. Fitzgerald sent this wire from the train en route from Montgomery to New York following his army discharge.

TO: Zelda Sayre — Wire. Scrapbook. Princeton University
After 22 February 1919 — New York City

MISS SELDA SAYRE

DARLING HEART AMBITION ENTHUSIASM AND CONFIDENCE I DECLARE EVERYTHING GLORIOUS THIS WORLD IS A GAME AND WHITE I FEEL SURE OF YOU LOVE EVERYTHING IS POSSIBLE I AM IN THE LAND OF AMBITION AND SUCCESS AND MY ONLY HOPE AND FAITH IS THAT MY DARLING HEART WILL BE WITH ME SOON.[1]

[1] Fitzgerald was in New York trying to succeed in the advertising business in order to marry Zelda. When she became impatient, he began making quick trips to Montgomery.

TO: Zelda Sayre — Wire. Scrapbook. Princeton University

NEWYORK NY MAR 22 1919

MISS LILDA SAYRE

DARLING I SENT YOU A LITTLE PRESENT FRIDAY THE RING[1] ARRIVED TONIGHT AND I AM SENDING IT MONDAY I LOVE YOU AND I THOUGHT I WOULD TELL YOU HOW MUCH ON THIS SATURDAY NIGHT WHEN WE OUGHT TO BE TOGETHER DONT LET YOUR FAMILY BE SHOCKED AT MY PRESENT

SCOTT

[1] An engagement ring.

TO: Zelda Sayre
24 March 1919

AL.[1] Scrapbook. Princeton University
New York City

Darling: I am sending this just the way it came—I hope it fits and I wish I were there to put it on. I love you so much, much, much that it just hurts every minute I'm without you—Do write every day because I love your your letters so—Good bye, my own wife.

[1] Written on Fitzgerald's card.

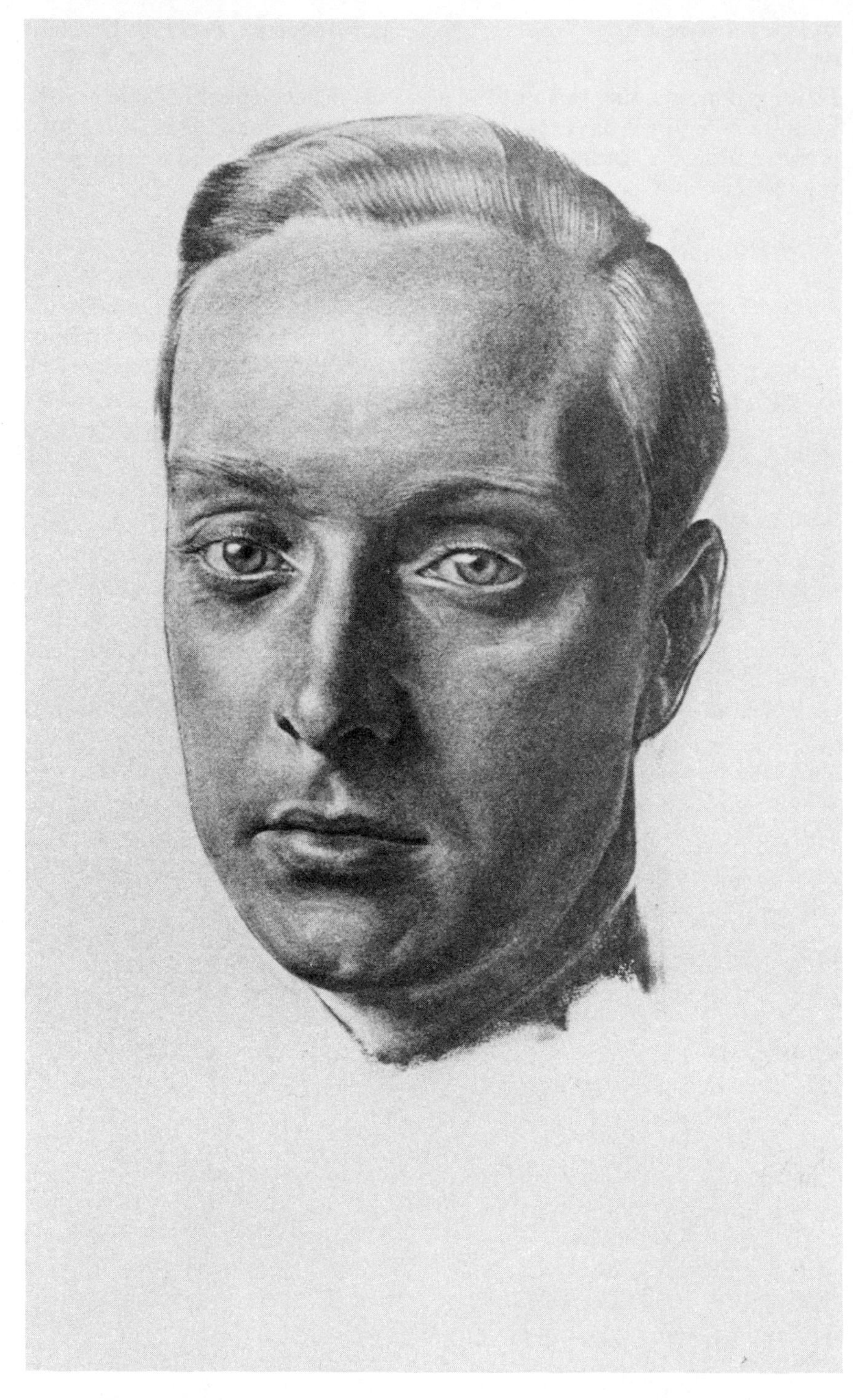

FROM: Stephan Parrott — ALS, 8 pp. Princeton University

5A Arlington Street

This letter sounds somewhat priggish but I don't mind what you say so [don't mind] what I say

Dear Fitz—It was quite unpardonable of me not to have written to you, but, damn it! I have'nt been able to write to a soul—Your conjecture in the letter is quite correct: I have been contemplating suicide since I left New York, and what's more never have I before imagined so many alluring methods of doing away with myself. Some were decadent—very much so—others dramatic—giving a large party, being as charming as possible and then going upstairs and—well, I have'nt quite decided whether it would be cutting a blood vessel or just taking an overdose of opium as I sliped into bed on a late summer night—The former has great possibilities, because I would naturally do it in a hot tub and my curious hair, long eyelashes, (which you very kindly noted), long ashen hands, and very white Renaissance figue would look charming as it was taken out of the tub all dripping blood, contrasting vividly with the afore mentioned whiteness of my skin—But however the contemplation of suicide must be carefully kept for times when I am very boared; to continue—Fitz—why are we so perverse? Just now when I feel like writing, the horrid clocks start ticking with unusual vehemence which reminds me painfully of the fact that I have some analytical jumble to do, and yet I know if I do'nt write to you now God knows when I ever will—I finished your book this afternoon. I won't discuss it at length in this letter: I will think more about it and then let you know specifically what I thought about it But just for a general criticism. I did'nt like the beginning it was too choped up and had too many rather animalistic females in it for *my* taste. The farther I got into it the more interested I became, but when I came to the place where you saw the man with the disgusting feet, I had to stop reading I know just what you felt. Your mood was exactly like some I have felt, of the worst kind; in fact it started a humour in me that was quite horrible—The chapter Eleanor was very vivid and convincing—The whole book seemed more to give an impression than an idea. It reminded me of a wonderful book: "Gösta Berling" by Selma Lagerloff. I wish I could see you and talk to you; about your book, and yourself, and myself. I have been thinking so much about you since I left New York. You could help me so much and I could help you so much, and I want to but I can't, perhaps it is because I am young, and I don't think that I have much hold on you, but while you were living faster than I was and developing more positive brilliancy, I was learning a great deal. At present, of course, I do feel useless and horribly weary, subconsciously I drag myself about, and it is lonely going up the hill all by myself everything seems so grey on either side and there does'nt seem much ahead, but then at least I know I am on the right road and have the right idea, whereas I know you have'nt. For instance I am aching to get drunk sometimes but then I don't. I would give anything to forget if only I could forget. At times I take the biretta[1] and stare at it until the eyes almost pop out of my head trying to conjure up his presence, but then I laugh and try to keep my mind from wandering like a nightmare. But I know I have a goal in view—oh well! "tout passe, tout lasse, tout casse!" so lets set our teeth and laugh at everything save intelect, for mind is our crowning glory—I am so glad that what I told you did not make any difference and as for your prigish conversation I did notice it but I did not mind it in the least it was all news to you and you had to have time to get adjusted, and then, I would stand almost anything from you, why, I can't explain but somehow I would—I felt exactly about Leslie as you do but unlike you the next time I go to New York for any length of time I will religiously call on him and, if all goes well, will be as pleasant as possible—I haven't written anything lately and if I did I don't think I could send it to you, it would be rather a waste of postage, you saw my feeble attempts about dear old Pan. I am afraid I am a hasish dreamer like Michael.

I wish I could meet a Zelda just now, I feel a horrible desire to fall in love with somebody, I feel so parched and wisely cold like a Babylonian scroll that has been buried for centuries, but the amusing part is that I can't or if I did I can picture myself at thirty with a red camelia in my hand + a laugh like Chris Hemmick, which is not a very pleasant thought: I think I would rather be an ascetic. Oh well! Spring is coming and all the exquisite fresh flowers have helped me tremendously. I passed by a man the other day who was selling daphne on the street: the odour was so fresh and perfect that I might have sung Pipa's song. Write soon!

Your brother Stephan

April whatnot 1919

[1] Monsignor Fay's biretta.

FROM: Zelda Sayre — ALS, 8 pp. Princeton University
April 1919 — Montgomery, Alabama

Dearest Scott—

T.G. that's over! The vaudeville, I mean, and I am a complete wreck—but everybody says the dance was a success—It nearly broke my heart to take off those lovely Oriental pants—Some actor with this week's Keiths tried to take me and Livye on the road with him—but I—can't ignore physical characteristics enough to elope with a positive APE. And now I've got just two weeks to train a Folly Ballet for Les Mysterieurs—

"Plasher's Mead" has been carefully perused—Thanks awfully for it—I haven't read in so long—but I don't really like it—People seldom interest me except in their relations to things, and I like men to be just incidents in books so I can imagine their characters—Nothing annoys me more than having the most trivial action analyzed and explained. Besides, Pauline is positively atrociously uninteresing—I'll save the book and re-read it in rainy weather in the Fall—I think I'll appreciate it more—

Scott, you've been so sweet about writing—but I'm so damned tired of being told that you "used to wonder why they kept princesses in towers"—you've written that verbatim, in your last SIX letters! It's dreadfully hard to write so very much—and so many of your letters sound forced—I know you love me, Darling, and I love you more than anything in the world, but if its going to be so much longer, we just *can't* keep up this frantic writing. It's like the last week we were to-gether—and I'd like to feel that you know I am thinking of you and loving you always—I hate writing when I haven't time, and I just have to scribble a few lines—I'm saying all this so you'll understand—Hectic affairs of any kind are rather trying, so please let's write calmly and whenever you feel like it.

I'd probably aggravate you to death to day—There's no skin on my lips, and I have relapsed into a nervous stupor—It feels like going crazy knowing everything you do and being utterly powerless not to do it—and thinking you'll surely scream next minute—You used to blame it all on poor Bill—and all the time, it was just my nastiness—

Mamma gave me this[1] to-day—I s'pose it's another of her subtle suggestions—

All my love

Zelda

[1] Missing; probably a clipping about a ruined writer.

TO: Zelda Sayre — Wire. Scrapbook. Princeton University
c. 14 April 1919 — New York City

MISS TELDA SAYRE

TELDA[1] FOUND KNOCKOUT LITTLE APARTMENT REASONABLE RATES I HAVE TAKEN IT FROM TWENTY SIXTH SHE MOVES INTO SAME BUILDING EARLY IN MAY BETTER GIVE LETTER TO YOUR FATHER[2] IM SORRY YOURE NERVOUS DONT WRITE UNLESS YOU WANT TO I LOVE YOU DEAR EVERYTHING WILL BE MIGHTY FINE ALL MY LOVE

[1] Zelda's sister Clothilde was called Tilde.
[2] Fitzgerald had written a formal letter to Judge Sayre requesting Zelda's hand in marriage.

FROM: Zelda Sayre
Spring 1919

AL, 4 pp. Princeton University
Montgomery, Alabama

Sunday—

Darling, darling I love you so—To-day seems like Easter, and I wish we were together walking slow thru the sunshine and the crowds from Church—Everything smells so good and warm, and your ring shines so white in the sun—like one of the church lillies with a little yellow dust on it—We ought to be together this Spring—It seems made for us to love in—

You can't imagine what havoc the ring wrought—A whole dance was completely upset last night—Everybody thinks its lovely—and I am so proud to be your girl—to have everybody know we are in love—It's so good to know youre always loving me—and that before long we'll be together for all our lives—

The Ohio troops have started a wild and heated correspondence with Montgomery damsels—From all I can gather, the whole 37th Div will be down in May—Then I guess the butterflies will flitter a trifle more—It seems dreadfully peculiar not to be worried over the prospects of the return of at least three or four fiancees—My brain is stagnating owing to the lack of scrapes—I havent had to exercise it in so long—

Sweetheart, I love you most of all the earth—and I want to be married soon—soon—Lover—Don't say I'm not enthusiastic—You ought to know—

FROM: Zelda Sayre
Spring 1919

AL, 8 pp. Princeton University
Montgomery, Alabama

Scott, my darling lover—everything seems so smooth and restful, like this yellow dusk. Knowing that I'll always be yours—that you really own me—that nothing can keep us apart—is such a relief after the strain and nervous excitement of the last month. I'm so glad you came—like Summer, just when I needed you most—and took me back with you. Waiting doesn't seem so hard now. The vague despondency has gone—I love you Sweetheart.

Why did you buy the "best at the Exchange"?[1]—I'd rather have had 10¢ a quart variety—I wanted it just to know you loved the sweetness—To breathe and know you loved the smell—I think I like breathing twilit gardens and moths more than beautiful pictures or good books—It seems the most sensual of all the sences— Something in me vibrates to a dusky, dreamy smell—a smell of dying moons and shadows—

I've spent to-day in the grave-yard—It really isn't a cemetery, you know—trying to unlock a rusty iron vault built in the side of the hill.

It's all washed and covered with weepy, watery blue flowers that might have grown from dead eyes—sticky to touch with a sickening odor—The boys wanted to get in to test my nerve—to-night—I wanted to *feel* "William Wreford, 1864." Why should graves make people feel in vain? I've heard that so much, and Grey is so convincing, but somehow I can't find anything hopeless in having lived—All the broken columnes and clasped hands and doves and angels mean romances and in an hundred years I think I shall like having young people speculate on whether my eyes were brown or blue—of cource, they are neither—I hope my grave has an air of many, many years ago about it—Isn't it funny how, out of a row of Confederate soldiers, two or three will make you think of dead lovers and dead loves—when they're exactly like the others, even to the yellowish moss?[2] Old death is so beautiful—so very beautiful—We will die together—I know—

Sweetheart—

[1] Fitzgerald had bought a bottle of liquor at the Exchange Hotel when he visited her.

[2] Fitzgerald used this graveyard description in *This Side of Paradise,* pp. 303–04.

TO: Ludlow Fowler[1]
October 1919

ALS, 2 pp. Princeton University

599 Summit Ave
St. Paul, Minn

Dear Lud:

Thot you might be int'rested to know that

SCRIBNER

has accepted my new novel

"This Side of Paradise"

Pretty swell? Eh!

Am coming East in November + will call you up and we'll have a supper or two together, wet or dry.

Hope you've guarded well the great secret.[2] God! Lud I'll never get over it as long as I live. There's still a faint chance. Thank fortune. Hope you've had better luck.

Yrs
Scott Fitz.

[1] Princeton classmate of Fitzgerald's; model for Anson Hunter in the 1926 story, "The Rich Boy."

[2] On the strength of the acceptance of his novel Fitzgerald was planning a trip to Montgomery in the hope of resuming his engagement, which Zelda had broken in June.

TO: Robert Bridges[1] ALS, 1 p. Princeton University

Oct 20th, 1919
St. Paul, Minn
599 Summit Ave.

Dear Mr. Bridges:

I was delighted to get your letter and find that you liked The *Four Fists*.[2] It has never been published elsewhere in any form. The price is quite satisfactory to me.

As you recommend I am sending *Barbara Bobs her Hair* to the *Women's Home Companion*.[3] *Benediction* sounds too much like Catholic propaganda so I guess I'll have to let it go by the boards. *Dalyrimple* goes to the *Smart Set* tho I think their stuff is rather punk as a rule and never send them anything until some better magazine has passed it up.[4]

Thanks especially for your letter. I am sending you a story next week that I think you'll like.

Sincerely
F. Scott Fitzgerald.

[1] Editor of *Scribner's Magazine*.
[2] *Scribner's Magazine* (June 1920).
[3] Published as "Bernice Bobs Her Hair" in *The Saturday Evening Post* (1 May 1920).
[4] "Benediction" and "Dalyrimple Goes Wrong" were both published in *The Smart Set* (February 1920).

TO: Robert Bridges ALS, 1 p. Princeton University
Before 1 November 1919

599 Summit Ave
St. Paul, Minn:

Dear Mr. Bridges:

I am sending you a new version of the *Cut Glass Bowl*[1] which I sent you on the 20th. The version you have is 9000 words and draggy in places. The new version is about seven thousand and makes a much more compact and readable thing. I also sent you a little story called A *Smile for Sylvo*.[2]

I am doing no more short stories at present but devoting a month to my "*Dairy of a Literary Failure*."

So please throw the long version of the *Cut Glass Bowl* away and if you can't use the short one I'm going to ask you to mail it to Mr. Reynolds[3] in the enclosed envelope—I am trying to get him to dispose of my stuff for me.

Sincerely
F Scott Fitzgerald

[1] *Scribner's Magazine* (May 1920).
[2] Published as "The Smilers," *The Smart Set* (June 1920).
[3] Literary agent Paul Revere Reynolds.

TO: Robert Bridges ALS, 2 pp. Princeton University

599 Summit Ave. St. Paul
November 1st, 1919.

Dear Mr. Bridges:

I was delighted that you liked the *Cut Glass Bowl*. Now between the two versions: undoubtedly when I cut the first version I sacrificed some wheat with the tares; still I think version II is more compact and continuous reading and on the whole I prefer it. Still I leave the descision entirely in your hands.

Do I understand from your letter that you pay on publication, on setting up or what? and that I am to correct my own proofs?

Your serial list seems pretty full all right but this *Dairy of a Literary Failure* is churning in my head and seems of itself to boil over occasionally in to ink so don't be surprised if it hops onto your desk some morning.

You might enclose that envelope adressed the Paul Revere Reynolds in your next.

Anyways Mr Bridges I certainly feel that I've gotten the best consideration from both the publishing and magazine side of Scribner's that I can possibly expect and be sure that whenever I write anything that seems to me first class I'll give you first whack at it.

Faithfully
Scott Fitzgerald

FROM: George Jean Nathan[1] TLS, 1 p. Scrapbook. Princeton University
Before 15 November 1919

F. Scott Fitzgerald, Esq.,
599 Summit Avenue,
St. Paul, Minn.

Dear Mr. Fitzgerald:

Both your short story and your one-act play please us—the play particularly.[2] We are accepting both manuscripts. The office sends you its cheques on Thursday morning.

I wish, in my office of dramatic critic, personally to congratulate you on the play. You have a decidedly uncommon gift for light dialogue. Keep at the dramatic form. You will do things. I believe that your talent is superior to Clare Kummer's.[3]

Our best thanks to you for the credos.[4] Three of them are excellent. We shall use them.

With best wishes,

George Jean Nathan

[1] Coeditor with H. L. Mencken of *The Smart Set*.

[2] "Dalyrimple Goes Wrong" and "Porcelain and Pink (A One-Act Play)," *The Smart Set* (January 1920).

[3] Prolific playwright, author of popular light comedies.

[4] Fitzgerald submitted items for "The American Credo" department of *The Smart Set*; he claimed twelve of the items in his copy of *The American Credo* (1920), edited by Nathan and Mencken.

TO: Robert Bridges
November 1919

ALS, 1 p. Princeton University

599 Summit Ave.
St. Paul, Minn.

Dear Mr. Bridges:

You ask me to send you everything first direct so I'm enclosing a story which is hands-down the best piece of light writing I've ever done.[1] However it just naturally *would* curl itself up into a little sneer at the end so I was going to send it to Reynolds, especially as I'm uncomfortably in need of ready money. In case its a little too vinegary I'm going to ask you to save me time by putting it in the enclosed envelope adressed to Reynolds.

The Dairy of a Literary Failure progresses haltingly and is becoming rather more poignant than I had at first intended. You shall certainly see it first.

Faithfully
F Scott Fitzgerald

[1] Possibly "Head and Shoulders," *The Saturday Evening Post* (21 February 1920).

TO: Ludlow Fowler
November 1919

ALS, 1 p. Princeton University

599 Summit Ave
St. Paul

Dear Ludow:

Im leaving here Saturday + going first to Montgomery then to New York. However not even the family know I'm going to Montgomery so keep it dark. I'll be in New York the 22nd to the 26th and I'll call you up so we can have dinner together or something.

Feeling pretty high. Selling short stories right and left. Novel wont be out until Feb.

God knows tho, Lud, I may be a wreck by the time I see you. I'm going to try to settle it definately one way or the other.

Scott Fitz.

FROM: John Peale Bishop — ALS, 1 p. Princeton University
18 December 1919

Dear Scott,

The most poetic thing in the novel is the Title—couldn't be better.
The most original character is Eleanor.
The best incident is the dramatic interlude at Alec's house.
The most realistic bit is the drunk.
The most amusing character is Tanaduke.
The best poem is "When Vanity kissed Vanity"
The cleverest poem is from *Boston Bards and Hearst Reviewers.*
The best-written part is the last.
The most unconvincing character is Amory's mother.
" " " incident is that with Ferrenby's father.

But it's damn good, brilliant in places, and sins chiefly through exuberance and lack of development.

I have been offered a job to go back to Europe for a year at $2800, but shan't take it if Scribner's comes through, and I think they will. I wish I could go up and just write but I am too poor. And I can't write here. Alec[1] and I are going to live together. I am throwing out several poems a day and have started a story. The idea is a knock-out, but I doubt my ability to handle it. I enclose two poems, for your criticism.

When are you to be married? When are you coming to New York?

John

[1] Alexander McKaig, Princeton '17.

TO: Robert Bridges — ALS, 1 p. Princeton University

Dear Mr. Bridges:

I'm in the most frightful literary slump—and I'm writing movies[1] to see if I can rest up my brain enough to start a new novel + also get the wherewithal to live until I finish it. "The Diary of a Literary Failure" was a literary failure. In the middle of its revision I gave out + consigned it to the drawer of unfinished manuscripts. As for short stories I've only done one since I left New York and its pitifully pathetic. So expect to see huge bill-boards announcing CHARLEY CHAPLIN in Scott Fitzgeralds new comedy "Slapstick Sam." As soon as I turn out anything repectable I'll send it on to you.

With Best Wishes
F. Scott Fitzgerald.

599 Summit Ave.
St. Paul, Minn
December 26th—
1919

[1] Fitzgerald was trying to write scenarios for silent movies but did not sell any.

TO: Zelda Sayre
Before 9 January 1920

Wire. Scrapbook. Princeton University
New York City

I FIND THAT I CANNOT GET A BERTH SOUTH UNTIL FRIDAY OR POSSIBLY SATURDAY NIGHT WHICH MEANS I WONT ARRIVE UNTIL THE ELEVENTH OR TWELFTH PERIOD AS SOON AS I KNOW I WILL WIRE YOU[1] THE SATURDAY EVENING POST HAS JUST TAKEN TWO MORE STORIES[2] PERIOD ALL MY LOVE

[1] Fitzgerald was going to New Orleans to write.
[2] Probably "Myra Meets His Family" (20 March 1920), "The Camel's Back" (24 April 1920), or "Bernice Bobs Her Hair" (1 May 1920).

FROM: Zelda Sayre
February 1920

ALS, 4 pp. Princeton University
Montgomery, Alabama

Dearest—

I wanted to for your sake, because I know what a mess I'm making and how inconvenient it's all going to be—but I simply *can't* and *won't* take those awful pills—so I've thrown them away I'd rather take carbolic acid. You see, as long as I feel that I had the right, I don't much mind what happens—and besides, I'd rather have a *whole family* than sacrifice my self-respect. They just seem to place everything on the wrong basis—and I'd feel like a damned whore if I took even one, so you'll try to understand, please Scott—and do what you think best—but don't do ANYTHING till we *know* because God—or something—has always made things right, and maybe this will be.[1]

I love you, Darling Scott, and you love me, and we can be thankful for that anyway—

Thanks for the book—I don't like it—

Zelda Sayre

[1] Zelda Sayre was not pregnant.

FROM: Zelda Sayre
February 1920

AL, 6 pp. Princeton University
Montgomery, Alabama

Darling Heart, our fairy tale is almost ended, and we're going to marry and live happily ever afterward just like the princess in her tower who worried you so much—and made me so very cross by her constant recurrence—[1] I'm so sorry for all the times I've been mean and hateful—for all the miserable minutes I've caused you when we could have been so happy. You deserve so much—so very much—

I think our life together will be like these last four days—[2] and I *do* want to marry you—even if you do think I "dread" it—I wish you hadn't said that—I'm not afraid of anything—To be afraid a person has either to be a coward or very great and big. I am neither. Besides, I know you can take much better care of me than I can, and I'll always be very, very happy with you—except sometimes when we engage in our weekly debates—and even then I rather enjoy myself. I like being very calm and masterful, while you become emotional and sulky. I don't care whether you think so or not—I do.

There are 3 more pictures I unearthed from a heap of débris under my bed—Our honored mother had disposed of 'em for reasons of her own, but personally I like the attitude of my emaciated limbs, so I solict your approval. Only I waxed artistic, and ruined one—

Sweetheart—I miss you so—I love you so—and next time I'm going back with you—I'm absolutely nothing without you—Just the doll that I should have been born—You're a necessity and a luxury and a darling, precious lover—and you're going to be a husband to your wife—

[1] During the early days of their engagement in 1919 Zelda Sayre continued to go out with other men, which elicited Fitzgerald's repeated comment that now he knew why princesses were locked in towers.

[2] They had renewed their engagement during Fitzgerald's recent visits to Montgomery.

TO: Zelda Sayre

Wire. Scrapbook. Princeton University

NEWYORK NY FEB 24 1920

MISS LIDA SAYRE

I HAVE SOLD THE MOVIE RIGHTS OF HEAD AND SHOULDERS TO THE METRO COMPANY FOR TWENTY FIVE HUNDRED DOLLARS[1] I LOVE YOU DEAREST GIRL

SCOTT

[1] Made as *The Chorus Girl's Romance* by Metro Pictures (1920).

FROM: Zelda Sayre
February 1920

AL, 8 pp. Princeton University
Montgomery, Alabama

O, Scott, its so be-au-ti-ful—and the back's just as pretty as the front.[1] I think maybe I like it a little better, and I've turned it over four hundred times to see "from Scott to Zelda." I try to feel so rich and fine but I'm so tickled I can't feel any way but happy—happy enough to bubble completely over and flow away into a sweet-smelling nothing. And I've decided, like I do every night before I go to sleep that you're the dearest, dearest man on earth and that I love you even more than this delicious little thing ticking on my wrist—

Mamma came in with the package, and I thought maybe it might interest her to know, so she sat on the edge of the bed while I told her we were going to marry each other pretty soon—She wants me to come to New York, because she says you'd like to do it in St. Patrick's. Now that she knows, everything seems mighty definite and nice, and I'm not a bit scared or shaky—What I dreaded most was telling her—Somehow I just didn't think I could—Both of us are very splashy vivid pictures, those kind with the details left out, but I know our colors will blend, and I think we'll look very well hanging beside each other in the gallery of life [This is *not* just another one of my "subterranean river" thoughts][2]

And I love you so terribly that I'm going to read "McTeague—[3] but you may have to marry a corpse when I finish. It certainly makes a miserable start—I don't see how any girl could be pretty with her front teeth lost in action, and besides, it outrages my sense of delicacy to have him violently proposing when she's got one of those nasty rubber things on her face—All authors who want to make things true to life make them *smell bad*—like McTeague's room—and that's my most sensitive sense. I do hope you'll never be a realist—one of those kind that thinks being ugly is being forceful—

When my wedding's going to be, write to me again—and if you'd rather have me come up there I will—I told Mamma I might just come and surprise you, but she said you mightn't like to be surprised about "your own wedding"—I rather think it's MY wedding—

"Till *Death do us part*"

[1] A platinum-and-diamond wristwatch Fitzgerald bought with the money from selling movie rights for "Head and Shoulders."

[2] Zelda Sayre's brackets.

[3] Frank Norris' 1899 novel that Fitzgerald greatly admired.

TO: Isabelle Amorous[1]
26 February 1920

ALS, 2 pp. Bruccoli

Cottage Club
Princeton, N.J.
Feb 26th

Dear Isabelle:

Excuse this wretched paper but being a hard working literary man its all I ever use. I hope you're a reader of the Saturday Evening Post, Smart Set, Scribners ect in which my immortal writings appear from time to time.

—And I read your letter with a mixture of impressions, the situation being some what complicated by the fact that Zelda and I have had a reconciliation. And Isabelle, much as I like being a "strong character," candor compells me to admit that it was she and not me who did the throwing over last June.

No personality as strong as Zelda's could go without getting critisisms and as you say she is not above reproach. I've always known that. Any girl who gets stewed in public, who frankly enjoys and tells shocking stories, who smokes constantly and makes the remark that she has "kissed thousands of men and intends to kiss thousands more," cannot be considered beyond reproach even if above it. But Isabelle I fell in love with her courage, her sincerity and her flaming self respect and its these things I'd believe in even if the whole world indulged in wild suspicions that she wasn't all that she should be.

But of course the real reason, Isabelle, is that I love her and that's the beginning and end of everything. You're still a catholic but Zelda's the only God I have left now.

But I want to thank you for your letter and the thought of it. You're a strange + rare combination, Isabelle: a woman who is at once very beautiful + very good and I hope your destiny won't lead you into the same devious paths that mine has. And don't reproach yourself for your letter. My friends are unanimous in frankly advising me not to marry a wild, pleasure loving girl like Zelda so I'm quite used to it. I wrote Martin but havn't heard from him. Tell him to write.

Faithfully
Scott Fitzgerald

[1] The sister of Fitzgerald's Newman School friend Martin.

TO: The Editor of *The Princeton Alumni Weekly* Before 10 March 1920

Unlocated.[1] Princeton, New Jersey

Dear Sir: I read with interest the letter of Mr. Edmund B. Wilson, Jr., '16, in The Alumni Weekly for Feb. 25, and I most heartily concur in his plea that the claims of the *Nassau Literary Magazine* to endowment should be prior to those of the Philadelphian Society. A scant fourth of every class, the more immature, impressionable, and timid fourth, are swept up yearly by the drag-net of the Philadelphian Society. By senior year most of them realize that the point of view therein camouflaged under the name of "social service" has little connection with modern life and modern thought—except with the present kill-joy spirit sweeping the Chautauquas—and the swarm of earnest youths diminishes to a mere scattering of mild and innocuous uplifters. But I believe that during the first three years inestimable harm is done to the impressionable fourth. Nothing could be less stimulating to that quickening of interest and intellectual curiosity which is the aim of all education than the depressing conviction of sin distilled by those prosperous apostles who go the rounds of the colleges frightening amiable freshmen. That a man such as the famous "bad example" should be permitted to sit smugly upon a Princeton lecture platform to be pointed at by the raucous lecturer as a reformed rake, and hence as an ideal, is a custom too ridiculous to be disgraceful but also too absurd to be endowed.

It seems inevitable that this herd of blue-nosed professional uplifters, at present at large in America appealing to the intellect of farmers' wives and pious drug-clerks, shall have a breeding place in Princeton, but that men to whom such ideas are distasteful and revolting should have to contribute to keep it alive and bawling when the *Lit.* goes unendowed is really too much.

It is an unnecessary truckling to the mediocre religious fanaticism of a dull and earnest minority. Princeton lives by its statesmen and artists and scientists—even by its football teams—but not by its percentage of puritans in every graduating class.

F. Scott Fitzgerald '17.

[1] *The Princeton Alumni Weekly*, 20 (10 March 1920), 514.

TO: H. L. Mencken

Inscription in *This Side of Paradise.*
Enoch Pratt Library
New York City

As a matter of fact, Mr Mencken, I stuck your name in on Page 224 in the last proof—partly, I suppose, as a vague bootlick and partly because I have since adopted a great many of your views. But the other literary opinions, especially the disparagement of Cobbs were written when you were little more than a name to me—

This is a bad book full of good things, a novel about flappers written for Philosophers, an exquisite burlesque of Compton McKenzie with a pastiche of Wells at the end—

F. Scott Fitzgerald
March 20th, 1920

Note: Irvin S. Cobb was a Kentucky humorist on whom Fitzgerald commented in *This Side of Paradise*: "This man Cobb—I don't think he's either clever or amusing—and what's more, I don't think very many people do, except the editors."

TO: Zelda Sayre Wire. Scrapbook. Princeton University

NEWYORK NY MAR 30 1920

MISS TILLA SAYRE

TALKED WITH JOHN PALMER AND ROSALIND[1] AND WE THINK BEST TO GET MARRIED SATURDAY NOON WE WILL BE AWFULLY NERVOUS UNTIL IT IS OVER AND WOULD GET NO REST BY WAITING UNTIL MONDAY FIRST EDITION OF THE BOOK IS SOLD OUT ADDRESS COTTAGE UNTIL THURSDAY AND SCRIBNERS AFTER THAT LOVE

SCOTT

[1] John Palmer was married to Zelda's sister Clothilde; Rosalind was another sister.

TO: Charles G. Norris[1]

Inscription in *This Side of Paradise.*
Stanford University
New York City

for Charles G. Norris
who in Salt wrote the
best American novel
since Vandover & the
Brute
with the sincere
admiration of
F Scott Fitzgerald
April 28th, 1920

[1] Novelist Charles G. Norris (1881–1945), whose realistic novel *Salt* (1917) impressed Fitzgerald; brother of author Frank Norris.

FROM: Charles G. Norris Wire. Scrapbook. Princeton University

5 MAY [1920]

SCOTT FITZGERALD

HOTEL COMMODORE NEWYORK NY

YOU WILL BE APPROACHED BY JAY PACKARD LITERARY AGENT FOR FILM RIGHTS TO THIS SIDE OF PARADISE[1] DONT TAKE A CENT LESS THAN FIVE THOUSAND REFUSE ANY ROYALTY ARRANGEMENT INSIST ON CASH PAYMENT ON SIGNING CONTRACT DONT LET REYNOLDS PERSUADE YOU TO ASK MORE OR TAKE LESS GOOD LUCK

CHARLES G NORRIS

[1] Movie rights to *This Side of Paradise* were not sold until 1923, when Famous Players–Lasky paid $10,000. The movie was never made.

FROM: John Grier Hibben[1] TLS, 2 pp. Scrapbook. Princeton University

May 27th, 1920.

My dear Mr. Fitzgerald:—

It has been in my mind for some time to write to you. Last evening I read your story in the current number of "Scribners" magazine, entitled "The Four Fists."[2] It is so admirably written and I finished it with a feeling of such deep satisfaction, that the long delayed purpose of writing you takes shape again today.

Let me first say that I feel that in this last story of yours you have shown not only your rare ability as an artist, but also your power to present a philosophy of life which I wish every young man of our country would feel and appreciate. Your description of "Samuel," attributing to him "some instinct stronger than will, deeper than training," presents a picture of human nature at its best. This philosophy of the instinctive nobility of man I hope may be further developed in your writings and prove a help and inspiration to many who may not be aware of the real power concealed within them.

Now I hope that you will allow me to add a word also in reference to your Princeton book, "This Side of Paradise." It is because I appreciate so much all that is in you of artistic skill and certain elemental power that I am taking the liberty of telling you very frankly that your characterization of Princeton has grieved me. I cannot bear to think that our young men are merely living for four years in a country club and spending their lives wholly in a spirit of calculation and snobbishness.

Your descriptions of the beauty and charm of Princeton are the most admirable that I have ever read and yet, I miss something in the book which I am sure you, yourself, could not wholly have missed in your college course.

You must not think that my point of view is merely that of an older man and that that accounts for my differing with you in reference to the Princeton life. From my undergraduate days I have always had a belief in Princeton and in what the place could do in the making of a strong vigorous manhood. It would be an overwhelming grief to me, in the midst of my work here and my love for Princeton's young men, should I feel that we have nothing to offer but the outgrown symbols and shells of a past whose reality has long since disappeared.

It would be a great satisfaction to me to have the opportunity of talking with you some time when you are in Princeton and I should appreciate your calling to see me.

I have written these words not in any spirit of carping criticism, but to let you know my full mind concerning you, and my pride in your power, already demonstrated in the world of letters and promise of a still richer fulfillment. I should like to learn from your own lips, in what you feel the Princeton of the present fails.[3]

With warm regards,

Faithfully yours,
John Grier Hibben

Mr. F. Scott Fitzgerald,
C/o Messrs Charles Scribner Sons,
48th and Fifth Avenue,
New York City.

[1] President of Princeton University.

[2] Fitzgerald was embarrassed by this story, which he regarded as obvious and didactic.

[3] See Fitzgerald's 3 June reply to Hibben in *Letters*, in which he characterizes *This Side of Paradise* as "a book written with the bitterness of my discovery that I had spent several years trying to fit in with a curriculum that is afterall made for the average student" but insists that he loves Princeton "now better than any place on earth."

TO: David Arnold Balch[1] — ALS, 2 pp. Unlocated[2]

Westport, Conn.
June 19th, 1920

Dear Mr. Balch:

I have unearthed so many esoteric facts about myself lately for magazines, etc., that I blush to continue to send out colorful sentences about a rather colorless life. However, here are some "human interest points."

(1) I was always interested in prodigies because I almost became one—that is in the technical sense of going to college young. I finally decided to enter at the conventional age of 17. I went in on my 17th birthday and, I

think, was one of the ten youngest in my class at Princeton. Prodigies always interested me and it seemed to me that the Harvard prodigy, Boris Siddis, offered grounds for a story. The original title of Head & Shoulders was "The prodigy" & I just brought in the chorus girl by way of a radical contrast. Before I'd finished she almost stole the story.

(2) I got four dozen letters from readers when it first appeared in the Post.

(3) It will be republished in my collection of short stories "Flappers & Philosophers" which the Scribners are publishing this fall.

(4) I'd rather watch a good shimmee dance than Ruth St. Dennis and Pavalowa combined. I see nothing at all disgusting in it.

(5) My story "The Camel's Back" in the S.E.P. (which you may be buying) was the fastest piece of writing I've ever heard of. It is twelve thousand words long and it was written in fourteen hours straight writing and sent to the S.E.P. in its original form.

I can't think of anything else just now that hasn't been used before. And I have no good picture. I expect to have some soon though and will send you one.

Sincerely
F. Scott Fitzgerald

[1] Editor of *Movie Weekly;* associated with Metro, which made *The Chorus Girl's Romance* from "Head and Shoulders."

[2] Text from "Two New Scott Fitzgerald Letters," *Modern Fiction Studies,* 11 (Summer 1965), 190–91. This letter was cataloged for sale by Sotheby Parke Bernet, Sale No. 3708, Item #577.

TO: David Arnold Balch — ALS, 2 pp. University of Virginia

Westport Conn, June 24th [1920]

Dear Mr. Balch:

Here are some "facts"

Born St. Paul, Minnesota, Sept 24th, 1896

Educated at The Saint Paul Academy in St. Paul, Minn
and at Newman School, Hackensack, NJ
and at Princeton.

Married on April 3d 1920 to Miss Zelda Sayre of Montgomery, Ala.

Served in war as 1st Lieut in the 45th + 67th Inf.
and as Aide-de-Camp to Gen. J. A. Ryan.

Am a decendent of Francis Scott Key + my whole name is Francis Scott Key Fitzgerald.

Stared writing when I was 10 yrs old + have been hard at it ever since

I wear brown soft hats in winter, panamas in summer, loathe dress suits and never wear one and prefer people with greenish-grey eyes.

I certainly would like to have lunch with you + will call you up soon. I don't think the new title is any good but you know best.

Sincerely
F Scott Fitzgerald.

TO: *The Editor* Unlocated[1]
June 1920 Westport, Connecticut

The idea of "The Ice Palace" (Saturday Evening Post, May 22d), grew out of a conversation with a girl out in St. Paul, Minnesota, my home. We were riding home from a moving picture show late one November night.

"Here comes winter," she said, as a scattering of confetti-like snow blew along the street.

I thought immediately of the winters I had known there, their bleakness and dreariness and seemingly infinite length, and then we began talking about life in Sweden.

"I wonder," I said casually, "if the Swedes aren't melancholy on account of the cold—if this climate doesn't make people rather hard and chill—" and then I stopped, for I had scented a story.

I played with the idea for two weeks without writing a line. I felt I could work out a tale about some person or group of persons of Anglo-Saxon birth living for generations in a very cold climate. I already had one atmosphere detail—the first wisps of snow weaving like advance-guard ghosts up the street.

At the end of two weeks I was in Montgomery, Alabama, and while out walking with a girl I wandered into a graveyard. She told me I could never understand how she felt about the Confederate graves, and I told her I understood so well that I could put it on paper. Next day on my way back to St. Paul it came to me that it was all one story—the contrast between Alabama and Minnesota. When I reached home I had

(1) The idea of this contrast.

(2) The natural sequence of the girl visiting in the north.

(3) The idea that some phase of the cold should prey on her mind.

(4) That this phase should be an ice palace—I had had the idea of using an ice palace in a story since several months before when my mother told me about one they had in St. Paul in the eighties.

(5) A detail about snow in the vestibule of a railway train.

When I reached St. Paul I intrigued my family into telling me all they remembered about the ice palace. At the public library I found a rough sketch of it that had appeared in a newspaper of the period. Then I went carefully through my notebook for any incident or character that might do—I always do this when I am ready to start a story—but I don't believe that in this case I found anything except a conversation I had once had with a girl as to whether people were feline or canine.

Then I began. I did an atmospheric sketch of the girl's life in Alabama. This was part one. I did the graveyard scene and also used it to begin the love interest and hint at her dislike of cold. This was part two. Then I began part three which was to be her arrival in the northern city, but in the middle I grew bored with it and skipped to the beginning of the ice palace scene, a part I was wild to do. I did the scene where the couple were approaching the palace in a sleigh, and of a sudden I began to get the picture of an ice labyrinth so I left the description of the palace and turned at once to the girl lost in the labyrinth. Parts one and two had taken two days. The ice palace and labyrinth part (part five) and the last scene (part six) which brought back the Alabama motif were finished the third day. So there I had my beginning and end which are the easiest and most enjoyable for me to write, and the climax, which is the most exciting and stimulating to work out. It took me three days to do parts three and four, the least satisfactory parts of the story, and while doing them I was bored and uncertain, constantly re-writing, adding and cutting and revising—and in the end didn't care particularly for them.

That's the whole story. It unintentionally illustrates my theory that, except in a certain sort of naturalistic realism, what you enjoy writing is liable to be much better reading than what you labor over.

[1] *The Editor*, 53 (Second July Number, 1920), 121–22.

TO: Maxwell Perkins

Postcard. Princeton University

Westport, Conn.
July 7th 1920

F.P.A.[1] is at it again. Here is his latest list

Old	*New Ones*
juvenalia	Christie Mathewson
born for borne	Confectionary
Cellini	Lyoff Tolstoi
Samuel Johnston	forborne
	inexplicably for inextricably
	Mont Martre
	tetotalling
	stimulous

Havn't my copy of the book so don't know where these occur

Sincerely
F Scott Fitzgerald

[1] Franklin P. Adams printed lists of errors in *This Side of Paradise* in his *New York Tribune* column, "The Conning Tower." Scribners made a total of forty-two alterations in the plates of the novel for the fourth and seventh printings.

TO: Maxwell Perkins ALS, 2 pp. Princeton University

Westport, Conn.
July 16th, 1920

Dear Mr. Perkins:

Last week in the Tribune F.P.A. balled out my book and gave a long list of mispellings—I find by looking at the *sixth* edition that many of those first list of corrections havn't been made—for instance *juvenalia* (twice) in the section called "Tom the Censor" in "Experiments in Convalescense." I really think it has been a mistake to let it go so long.

Met a friend of yours the other day named Amee Stone who said she had admired you ever since your Cambridge days.

The novel[1] progresses

Sincerely
F Scott Fitz—

F.P.A finds the following new misspellings
Frank on the Mississippi should be *Frank on the Lower Mississippi*
Chap I
Collar + Daniel's First-year Latin (mispelt)
Chap I
Cut a swathe (mispelt) Chap II
Poems + Ballades should be *Poems + Ballads*
(Chap II)
Fanny Hurst should be Fannie Hurst
Lorelie (mispelt)
Ghunga Dhin (mispelt)
Flambuoyant (mispelt
Come Into the Garden, Maude (mispelt?)

[1] Published as *The Beautiful and Damned* (1922).

TO: Stephan Parrott
August 1920

Inscribed photograph. Bruccoli
Westport, Connecticut

TO: Burton Rascoe[1] ALS, 1 p. University of Pennsylvania

Westport, Conneticut
Aug 6th 1920—

Mr. Burton Rascoe
The Chicago Tribune.

Dear Mr. Rascoe:

Just a line to ask you if you liked the story "*The Lees of Happiness*" which I wrote on order for your Sunday Magazine.[2] It's perhaps a little gloomy.

You were kind enough to praise my first novel—I am now in the midst of a second—and its very much harder sledding. Hope it won't dissapoint you and the other critics who were disposed to like "*This Side of Paradise.*"

Sincerely
F. Scott Fitzgerald.

[1] Book review editor of the *Chicago Tribune.*
[2] *Chicago Sunday Tribune* (12 December 1920).

TO: Carl Hovey[1] ALS, 2 pp. Huntington Library

Westport, Conn.
Aug 12th 1920

Dear Mr. Hovey:

I want to ask you a question. How long would it take to seriazize a 120,000 word novel? My plans have changed, I think. Here is new project.

(1) "Flappers + Philosophers" my 1st collection of short stories to appear in Oct.

(2) A second collection of short stories to appear next Spring + to include the Jellybean, three little plays and also four stories not yet written.[2]

(3) My new novel in which I am deeply absorbed "The Flight of the Rocket"[3] to appear next autumn.

Let us suppose you get the novel in Nov, like it + begin to serialze it in January or February. Then how about these three or four stories I intend to write when I finish the novel + which should be published before spring to be eligible for the collection. Could you publish them simultaeneously? Would you prefer only the novel? Would you prefer only the short stories?[4]

Of course the easiest way would be for me to do the short stories 1st but its utterly impossible as I'm plunged in the middle of the novel + wouldn't have it for $10,000.

The only solution it seems to me is for me to rewrite a fairly good novelette which appeared in the June Smart Set[5] instead of the new short stories + publish it in the Spring collection. Then I would devote the time between finishing my novel in Nov. and going abroad in Jan. to this revising and to writing a play which I've always wanted to do.

Let me hear from you. Went over to Miss Rita Willmans + I think she's a very striking personality + most attractive

Sincerely
F Scott Fitzgerald

[1] Editor of *Metropolitan* magazine, which serialized *The Beautiful and Damned* (September 1921–March 1922).

[2] *Tales of the Jazz Age* did not appear until September 1922.

[3] Original title for *The Beautiful and Damned.*

[4] The *Metropolitan* published two Fitzgerald stories in 1920–21: "The Jelly-Bean" and "His Russet Witch."

[5] Fitzgerald is referring to "May Day," which appeared in the July *Smart Set.*

FROM: Shane Leslie — ALS, 4 pp. Princeton University

London Eng
Sept 3 1920

My dear Fitz

I have been reading your book very carefully and I am suprised at the literary touch in places—the suprise that would be real pleasure if one had happed on a forgotten book of one's own. Your spelling is bad and you refer in your letter to "Austrailia"! The book was much improved on the MSS I persuaded Scribner to take and publish should you die like R. Brooke on the front. I should still like to have my autoautographed first edition if you can recover it from my New York address. Father Hemmick is here and we are both reviewing the book for the Dublin.[1] There will be more about Fay than you chiefly the mystical and devotional side. You only traced his political and international aspect. You did it very cleverly but I think the mystical note escaped you. You must not mind Catholic criticism for I think it is a Catholic minded book at heart and that you like Fay and myself can never be anything but Catholics however much we write and pose to make the bourgeois stare! I am glad you are married I hope liturgically or at least canonically—you know the subtle difference. My paternal love to Rosalind[2] for though my consent was not asked I feel I should have been consulted. The Mgr left you to me in his spiritual testament and I am responsible for seeing that your talent harms nobody including yourself. Why do you not bring Rosalind over here for a month say Nov. and we will go over to visit Fr Hemmick in Paris. I could give you enough literary material from my old Paris life to furnish you with a novel which you will kindly not dedicate to me! That is a literary give-away which is not generally practiced and if you published Fay's letters you ought not to have put his name in the frontispiece.[3] However you have a great deal like all clever men to learn. I am stupid-getting with learning. Men are only clever when they are on the pry for forbidden fruit of mind and body and better still for mystical or even non-existent fruitage. I shall be always glad to teach you a little literature or spelling though in the handling of the American language I shall always be your admiring inferior

Shane Leslie

You may write to me under the seal as a confessor and I shall respect the seal—on anything

[1] *Dublin Review* (October, November, December 1920).
[2] Rosalind Connage in *This Side of Paradise* was largely based on Zelda.
[3] Leslie is referring to the dedication of *This Side of Paradise* to Fay.

TO: H. L. Mencken
Before 4 September 1920

Inscription in *Flappers and Philosophers*.
Enoch Pratt Library
New York City

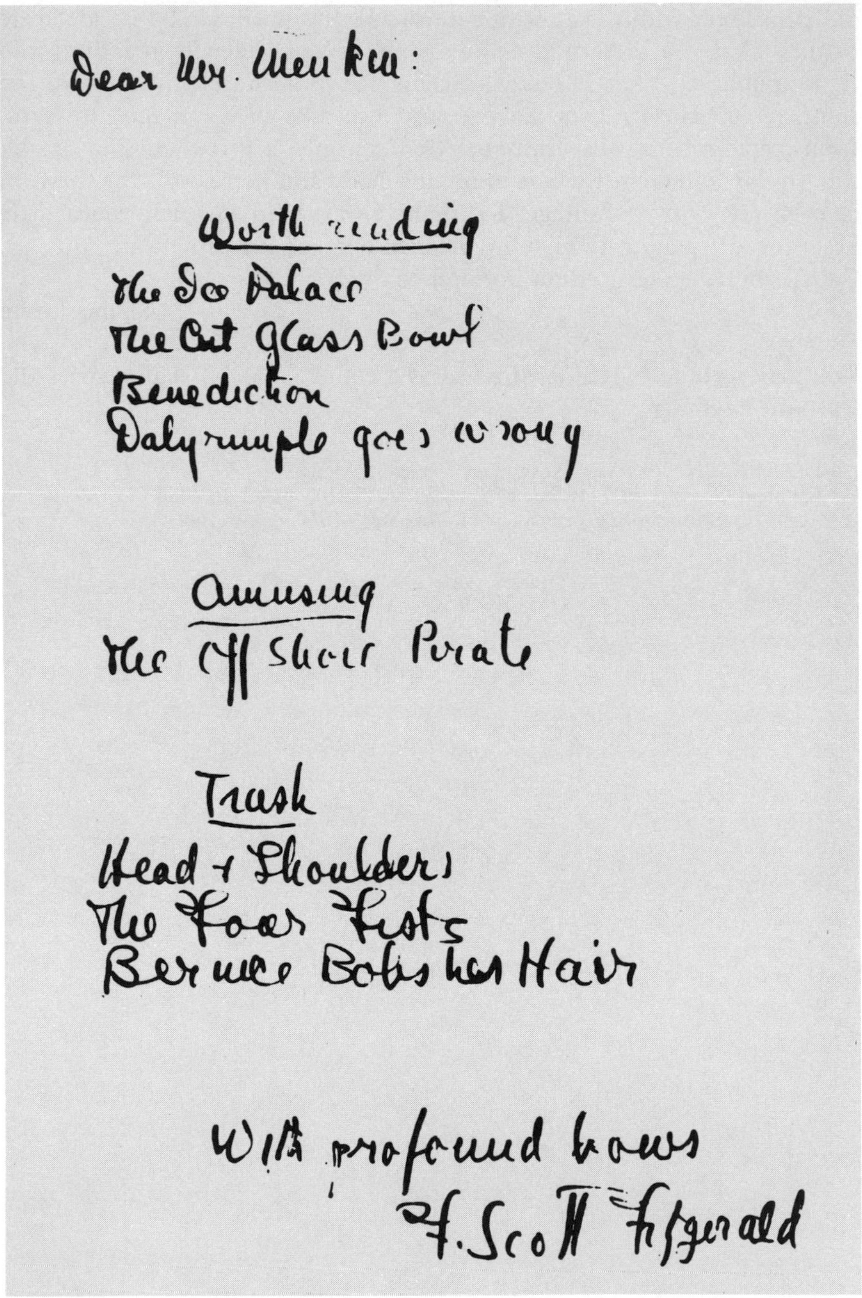

Dear Mr. Mencken:

Worth reading

The Ice Palace
The Cut Glass Bowl
Benediction
Dalyrimple goes wrong

Amusing

The Off Shore Pirate

Trash

Head + Shoulders
The Four Fists
Bernice Bobs her Hair

With profound bows
F. Scott Fitzgerald

TO: H. L. Mencken ALS, 1 p. New York Public Library

Westport, Conn
Sept 6th 1920

Dear Mr Menken:

Thank you for The "Symposium on H.L.M."[1] I read it with the greatest interest for I am a member of the rapidly increasing crew who consider you and Cabell at the head and front of American letters.

If you ever get tired of using the title "Prejudices" I discovered a good one for you out of your own manner—to wit: *Complexes.*

I am having the little red book bound up with *Pistols for Two*[2] as a permanency. ¶I am writing a brilliant novel called "Circumspecto, the Indian Chief." Nathan is a character in it.

Sincerely
F Scott Fitzgerald

P.S. Excuse pencil. No ink in house.

[1] *H. L. Mencken* (1920).
[2] A collaboration by Mencken and Nathan under the pseudonym Owen Arthur James Hatteras (1917).

TO: H. L. Mencken ALS, 2 pp. New York Public Library
Before 7 October 1920

38 W. 59th St.
New York City

Dear Mr. Mencken:

I'm going to take up a few minutes of your time to propound a sceme, which may bore you to death. Here it is. You know what Dutton did with those rather medeochre novels of Leanard Merrick—prefixed them with prefaces by W.K.[1] authors? and I believe they sold. Now I am a great admirer of Frank Norris's. I've had an awful time getting hold of Blix and Vandover + tho Mcteague is now accessible the others are buried full fathom fifty + about to be forgotten. Do you think it would be amusing for me to try and interest some publisher in this: Say a new edition, uniform—with short introductions by Americans after this fashion:

Vandover + the Brute with an introduction by H. L. Mencken
Mcteague " " " " Theodore Drieser
The Pit " " " " Joseph Hergeshimer
The Octupus " " " " Booth Tarkington
Moran of the Lady Letty " " " " Burton Rascoe
Blix " " " " Francis Hacket.
A Man's Woman (you say its no good! I've never read it)

If it'd do any good I'd do one that nobody else wanted + would be glad to do the organizing. I simply want to ask your advice. Do you think it would be worthwhile? If you do I'll write Charles Norris for data + commence planning it.[2]

I'm deep in a new novel at present. Edmund Wilson John Bishop + all my friends and I are eagerly awaiting Predjudices 2nd Series, even tho we've read most of the essays   Wilson, by the way, is doing an essay on you—not a mere blurb or puff but an analysis of your methods for the January or February Vanity Fair   We were both talking the other night about how hard it is not to imitate your style at times. Both of us are so saturated with Menckenia that we burst out with such phrases as "Baptist Bishop of Atlanta" ect. ect. when we want a simile for feeble mindedness. They, Bishop + Wilson, are finishing a really amazing book—32 ironic poems on death called "The Undertakers Garland."

John Williams[3] drove Zelda + I wild with laughter last night with the anecdote of how he + Nathan took you to remnants.[4]

Faithfully Yours
F. Scott Fitzgerald

[1] Well-known.

[2] Mencken responded on 7 October, offering to help, but Fitzgerald's plan for the Norris edition never developed further. A ten-volume edition was published by Doubleday in 1928.

[3] Editor at Appleton.

[4] Williams and Nathan had taken Mencken to a bad play, having assured him it was a masterpiece.

TO: Carl Hovey
October 1920

ALS, 1 p. Huntington Library

38 W. 59th St.
New York City

Dear Mr. Hovey:

Am about half thru my novel but went down to the bank last week + found my account so distressingly not to say so alarmingly low that I had to do a short story at once.

I hope you'll like it. I think its the best thing I've ever done.[1]

Sincerely
F Scott Fitzgerald

[1] "His Russet Witch," *Metropolitan* (February 1921).

TO: Phyllis Duganne Parker[1]
Fall 1920

ALS, 1 p. Princeton University

38 W. 59th St.
New York City

Dear Miss Parker:

I havn't read Prologue[2] yet but I've noticed that many reviewers have connected it with This Side Of Paradise and I've been intending to get it for weeks. I shall, within the day. "Rosalind" is really flesh and blood—I married her eventually and am now writing a very much better + more "honest" book about her.

I'm sorry to say that I like "Four Fists" less than any story I've written save one. It's so priggish + righteous. But many people think its the best.

I can tell much more if our ides of youth are in accord after reading your book.

Thanks for your note

Sincerely
F Scott Fitzgerald.

Miss Phyllis Duganne Parker
Scituate, Mass.
Second Cliff

[1] Novelist and playwright.
[2] Parker's 1920 novel about a New York girl during World War I.

TO: Carl Hovey

ALS, 1 p. Huntington Library

Oct 27th, 1920
38 W. 59th St.

Dear Mr. Hovey:

About the story. Glad you like it + I'll admit it'll be over the heads of a few people. I solemnly promise that the next one I send will be as jazzy + popular as The Offshore Pirate to make up for it.

As you can see the girl, of course, represents that inhibited attraction that all men show to a "wild + beautiful woman." The greyer a mans life is the more it comes out. *But* if I'd have explained the story in any way but a dream it would have been a regular Max Beerbohm extravaganza + hence furthur over people's heads that it is now. But I do think to come out + say "it was all a dream" in so many words would cheapen + rather spoil the story.

Sincerely
F Scott Fitzgerald

TO: Burton Rascoe ALS, 1 p. University of Pennsylvania

38 W. 59th St.
New York City
Nov 17th 1920

Dear Mr. Rascoe:

Thanks for the pamphlet.[1] I enjoyed your essay on Mencken—I think its a clever touch: his "being the only true American," just as Anatole France "is the only living Catholic." Also I agree with you that he is a greatman and bum critic of poetry. Why has no one mentioned to him or of him that he is in an intolerably muddled syllogism with several excluded middles on the question of Aristocracy. What on earth does he mean by it. Every Aristocrat of every race has come in for scathing comment yet he holds out the word as a universal panacea for art.

He + Nathan were up in the apartment drinking with us the other night + he was quite entheusiastic about Main Street.

This "Moon Calf"[2] is a wretched thing without a hint of glamor, utterly undistinguished, childhood impressions dumped into the reader's lap with a profound air of importance + the sort of thing that Walpole + Beresford[3] (whom I abominate) turn out twice a year with great bawlings about their Art. I'd rather be Tarkington or David Graham Phillips[4] and cast at least some color and radiance into my work! Wouldn't you?

Thanks again.

Yours
F Scott Fitzgerald

[1] *H. L. Mencken.*
[2] Novel by Floyd Dell that was favorably compared to *This Side of Paradise.*
[3] English novelists Hugh Walpole and John Davys Beresford.
[4] Prolific social novelist; author of *Susan Lenox: Her Rise and Fall* (1917).

TO: Burton Rascoe ALS, 1 p. University of Pennsylvania

38 W. 59th St.
New York
Dec 7th 1920

Dear Mr. Rascoe:

Mencken's code of honor springs from Nietche doesn't it?—the agreement among the powerful to exploit the less powerful + respect each other. To me it has no connection with Christian ethics because there is no provision for any justice to "the boobery."

Sorry I misquoted you. It was a slip of the pen. I still think Mooncalf is punk, Poor White[1] is fair, + Main Street is rotten. Everyone here is reading Well's History.[2] Most absorbing!

Faithfully
F. Scott Fitzgerald.

[1] A 1920 novel by Sherwood Anderson.
[2] *Outline of History* (1920) by H. G. Wells.

FROM: H. L. Mencken
Late 1920

Inscription in Mencken's *Prejudices: Second Series* (1920). Bruccoli

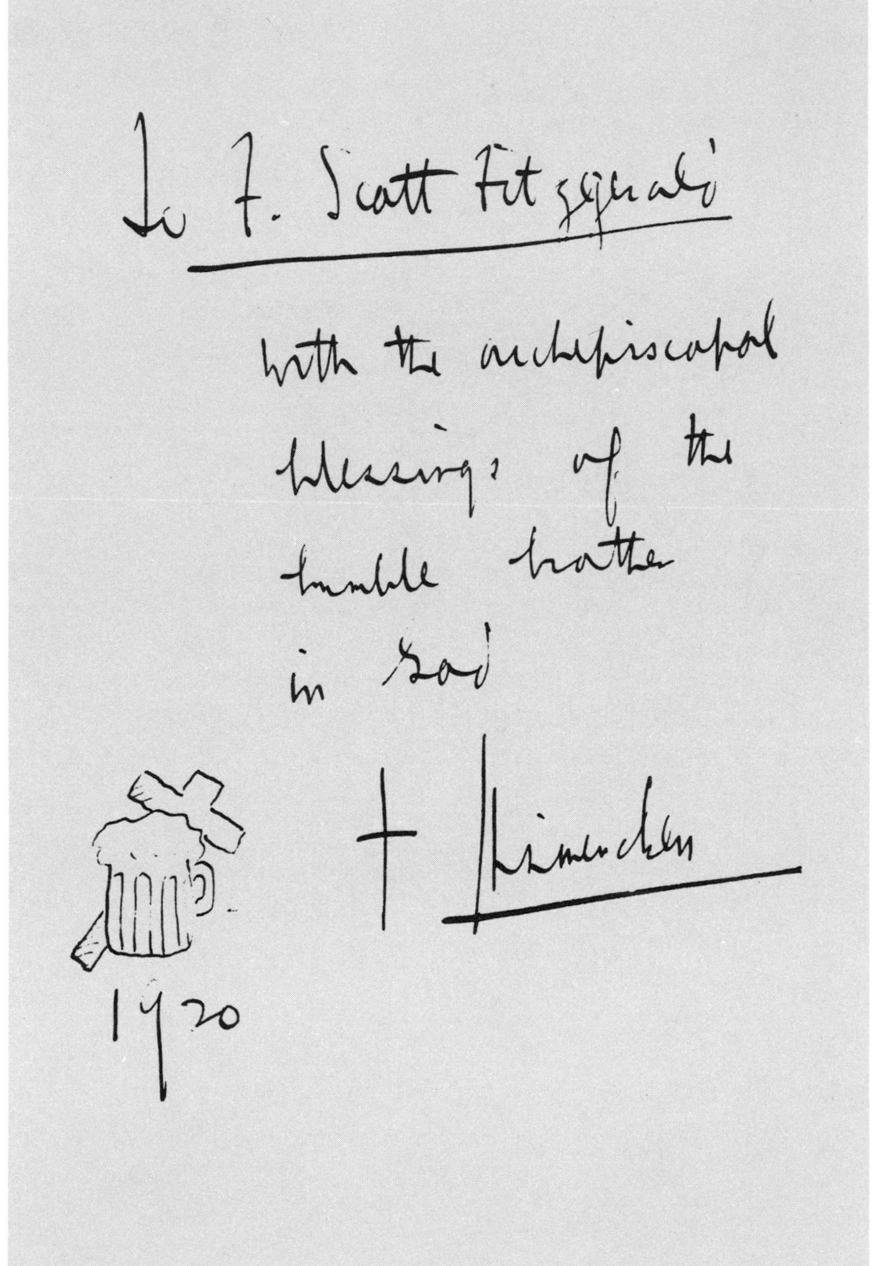

To F. Scott Fitzgerald

with the archiepiscopal
blessings of the
humble brother
in God

+ H L Mencken

1920

TO: H. L. Mencken — ALS, 1 p. New York Public Library

38 W 59th St.
New York.
Dec 30th 1920

To the Right Reverend H. L. Mencken
Good Sir: The Bookman asked me to review your latest blasphemy which I have done according to the council of Nicea.[1]

I am anxiously awaiting the next Smart Set. If you review the latest spud in the great potato tradition favorably, I refer to *Mooncalf* ("by Dostoieffski out of the Illinois corn crop") I shall be vilely dissapointed. I agree on Main Street; I hesitate at Poor White but at this wretched thing in the manner of "The Harbor" by a man who can't stand Cabell but does not hesitate to borrow freely from James Joyce + even F. Scott Fitzg (c.f. the last two pages of *Mooncalf*) I shall decide that the time to cavil at some of thy rulings has arrived.

You're going to like my new novel. If you object to the title of this review let me know and I'll have it changed.

Salve et Vale et Ora pro Nobis
F. Scott Fitzgerald

[1] "The Baltimore Anti-Christ," *The Bookman* (March 1921), a review of *Prejudices: Second Series*. Fitzgerald included a carbon copy of his review. The final paragraph in the typescript was not printed: "And to add—what a waste. Think of those dozens who would give everything for a chance to review a Mencken book. It seems cruel that the privilege could not have gone to Thorsten Veblen, to Paul Elmer More, to 'Dr. Wilson' or even to the great scapegoat, Harold B. Wright who would doubtless in his kindness have something to condone, something to cheer, something to joy in." It is not known who made this deletion.

TO: Edmund Wilson
Late 1920

ALS, 1 p. Yale University
New York City

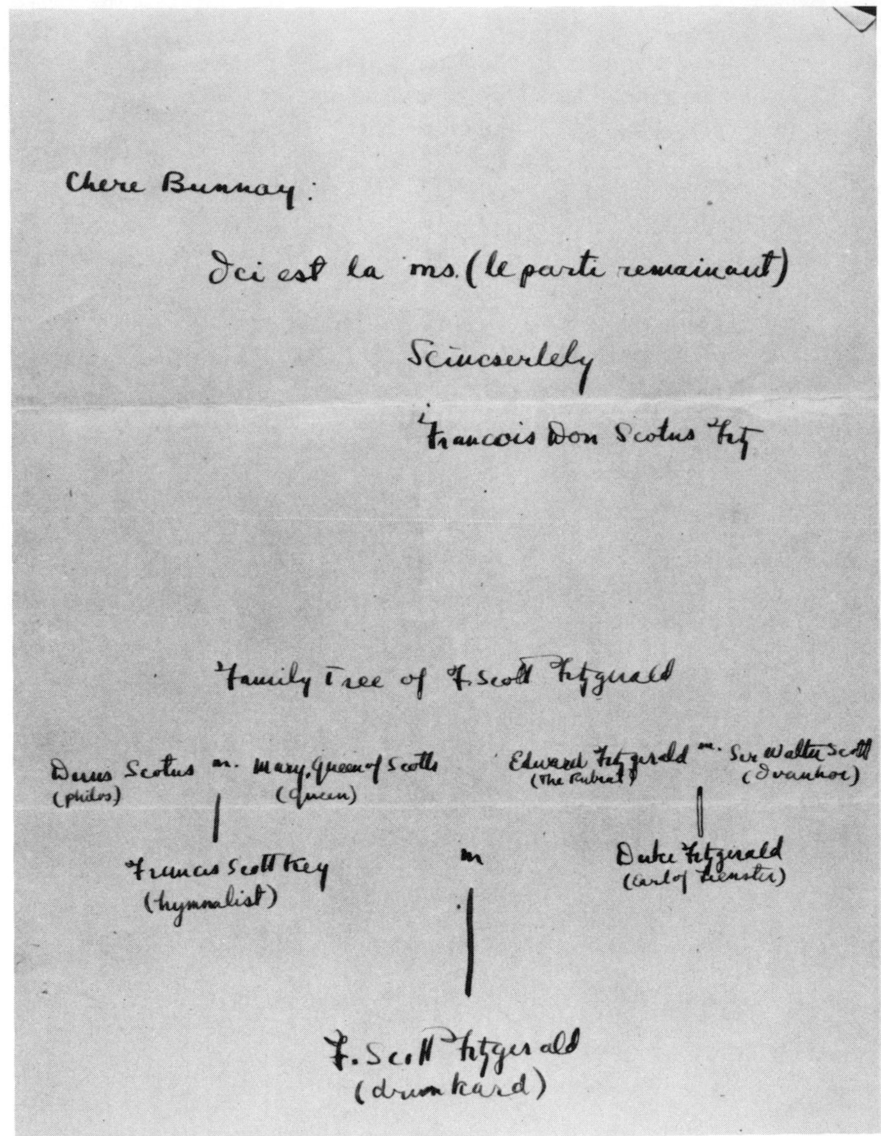

Chere Bunnay:

Ici est la ms. (le parti remainant)

Sciucserlely

Francois Don Scotus Fitz

Family Tree of F. Scott Fitzgerald

Duns Scotus (philos) m. Mary, Queen of Scotts (Queen)

Edward Fitzgerald (The Rubiat) m. Sir Walter Scott (Ivanhoe)

Francis Scott Key (hymnalist) m Duke Fitzgerald (earl of Leinster)

F. Scott Fitzgerald
(drunkard)

Note: The manuscript enclosed was either "This Is a Magazine," *Vanity Fair* (December 1920), or "Jemina, the Mountain Girl," *Vanity Fair* (January 1921).

TO: H. L. Mencken
January 1921

ALS, 1 p. New York Public Library

38 W. 59th St.
New York City
Jan 5th 1920

Dear Mencken:

I'm sorry you didn't care for the review + I'm also sorry I said that about Dell + my book. Lord knows I've borrowed freely in my time and again its only the people I detest like Frank Harris[1] + F. M. Hueffer[2] who quibble endlessly about "steals." It was probably my imagination anyhow.

I am anxious to consult you about something. Could you lunch with me Mon. or Tues. at Delmonicoes or are you all charted up this trip?

Yours
F Scott Fitzgerald

[1] Novelist and editor.
[2] Better known as Ford Maddox Ford.

TO: Henry Raleigh[1]
Before February 1921

ALS, 1 p. Princeton University

38 W. 59th St.
New York City

Dear Mr. Raliegh:

I want to thank you for the really stunning illustrations you did for my story.[2] I think the girl dancing is one of the best I've ever seen and the book-throwing scene is a wonder of its kind—you can just see the books flying! Honestly I think they're the best illustrations I've ever seen! and you must have put a lot of work on them.

They inspired me so that I rewrote the whole ending to get rid of the dream idea + I think now that its a really effective story.

Your girl on the table reminds me faintly of Zelda. My best regards to Mrs. Raliegh.

Yours
F. Scott Fitzgerald

[1] Magazine illustrator.
[2] "His Russet Witch," *Metropolitan Magazine* (February 1921).

TO: Helen Carson
1 February 1921

ALS, 1 p. Princeton University

38 W 59th St.
New York City
Feb 1st 1920

My Dear Miss Carson:

The Russet Witch is an awful muddle! I simply didn't consider time at all tho I suppose the "distant future" would do as well as anything. Its not a good story—too obscure.

Thanks for your note

Sincerely
F Scott Fitzgerald

TO: H. L. Mencken
2 February 1921

ALS, 1 p. New York Public Library

38 W 59th St
New York City
Feb 2nd 1920

Dear Mencken:

I am not waiting for an answer to this, but taking up your general offer to read exceptional but unfortunate novel mss. This is by a man my own age who is at present studying law at Cambridge.[1] To my mind it has the most beautiful writing—and I don't mean "fine" writing—that I've seen in a 'coon's age. I don't believe anyone in America can write like this—and the novel is also remarkable in the objectivity of its realism, that is, remarkable in so young a man. The man's in despair about it and wanted you to see it.

I took it to Scribners + Putnams who refused it on the grounds of obscurity. Can you give me some sort of opinion on it? The reverse side of the wrapper is readdressed and restamped.

As Ever
F. Scott Fitzgerald

Just finished "My Antonia"[2]—a great book! Mine is to be called "The Beautiful and Damned."

On second thought I'm enclosing stamps here as I don't know how many. Wrapper is readdressed

[1] John Biggs, Jr., Princeton classmate of Fitzgerald's.

[2] By Willa Cather (1918).

TO: Thomas Boyd[1] ALS, 4 pp.[2] Princeton University
9 February 1921

38 W 59th St
New York City
Feb 9th 1920

Dear Mr Boyd:

It seems to me that the overworked art-form at present in America is this "history of a young man." Frank Norris began it with *Vandover + the Brute*, then came Stephen French Whitman with *Predestined* and of late my own book and Floyd Dell's *Mooncalf*. In addition I understand that Stephen Benét has also delved into his past.[3] This writing of a young man's novel consists chiefly in dumping all your youthful adventures into the reader's lap with a profound air of importance, keeping carefully within the formulas of Wells and James Joyce. It seems to me that when accomplished by a man without distinction of style it reaches the depths of banality as in the case of *Mooncalf*. . . . . Up to this year the literary people of any pretensions—Mencken, Cabell, Wharton, Drieser, Hergeshiemer, Cather and Charles Norris have been more or less bonded together in the fight against intolerance and stupidity but I think that a split is due. On the romantic side Cabell, I suppose, would maintain that life has a certain glamor that detailed reporting—especially this reporting of the small mid-western town—can not convey to paper. On the realistic side Drieser would probably maintain that romantiscism tends immediatly to deteriorate to the Zane Grey–Rupert Hughes level, as it has in the case of Tarkington, fundamentally a brilliant writer. . . . . It is encouraging to notice that the number of pleasant sheep—i.e: people who think they're absorbing culture if they read Blasco Ibanez, H. G. Wells and Henry Van Dyke—are being rounded into shape. This class, which makes up the so called upper class in every American city, will read what they're told and now that at last we have a few brilliant men like Mencken at the head of American letters these aimable sheep will pretend to appreciate the appreciable of their own country instead of rushing to cold churches to hear noble but intelligable lords and meeting once a week to read papers on the afore-mentioned Blasco Ibanez. Even the stupidest people are reading *Main Street* and pretending they thought so all the time. I wonder how many people in St. Paul ever read *The Titan*[4] or *Salt* or even *Mcteague*. All this would seem to encourage insincerity of taste. But if it does it would at least have paid Drieser for his early stuggles at the time when such cheapjacks as Robert Chambers were being hailed as the "Balzacs of America."

F Scott Fitzgerald

[1] Literary editor of the *St. Paul Daily News*.

[2] Letter published as "The Credo of F. Scott Fitzgerald," *St. Paul Daily News* (20 February 1921), feature section, 8.

[3] *The Beginning of Wisdom* (1921).

[4] By Theodore Dreiser (1914).

TO: Robert D. Clark[1] ALS, 4 pp. Scottie Fitzgerald Smith
9 February 1921

38 W 59th St.
New York City
Feb 9th 1920

Dear Bob:

Your letter riled me to such an extent that I'm answering immediatly. Who are all these "real people" who "create business and politics"? and of whose approval I should be so covetous? Do you mean grafters who keep sugar in their ware houses so that people have to go without or the cheap-jacks who by bribery and high-school sentiment manage to controll elections. I can't pick up a paper here without finding that some of these "real people" who will not be satisfied only with "a brilliant mind" (I quote you) have just gone up to Sing Sing for a stay—Brindell and Hegerman, two pillars of society, went this morning.

Who in hell ever respected Shelley, Whitman, Poe, O. Henry, Verlaine, Swinburne, Villon, Shakespeare ect when they were alive. Shelley + Swinburne were fired from college; Verlaine + O Henry were in jail. The rest were drunkards or wasters and told generally by the merchants and petty politicians and jitney messiahs of their day that real people wouldn't stand it And the merchants and messiahs, the shrewd + the dull, are dust—and the others live on.

Just occasionally a man like Shaw who was called an immoralist 50 times worse than me back in the 90ties, lives on long enough so that the world grows up to him. What he believed in 1890 was heresy then—by by now its almost respectable. It seems to me I've let myself be dominated by "authorities" for too long—the headmaster of Newman, S.P.A, Princeton, my regiment, my business boss—who knew no more than me, in fact I should say these 5 were all distinctly my mental inferiors. *And that's all* that counts! The Rosseaus, Marxes, Tolstois—men of thought, mind you, "impractical" men, "idealist" have done more to decide the food *you* eat and the things *you* think + do than all the millions of Roosevelts and Rockerfellars that strut for 20 yrs. or so mouthing such phrases as 100% American (which means 99% village idiot), and die with a little pleasing flattery to the silly and cruel old God they've set up in their hearts.

A *letter*

Stratford-on-Avon
June 8th 1595

Dear Will:

Your family here are much ashamed that you could write such a bawdy play as Troilius and Cressida. All the real people here (Mr. Beef, the butcher and Mr. Skunk, the village undertaker) say they will not be satisfied with a brilliant mind and a pleasant manner. If you really want to ammount to something you've got be respected for yourself as well as your work

Affectionately
Your Mother, Mrs. Shakespeare

Concieted Ass! says Bob.

And I don't blame you for saying so, neither do I blame anybody much for anything. The only lesson to be learned from life is that there's no lesson to be learned from life.

Have you read Main Street? Its a great book. Had a letter from Sinclaire Lewis telling me we must not expect our books to sell in St. Paul. I expect my new one, just completed, "The Beautiful and Damned" to be barred from the St. Paul library—by the wives of Mr. Frost and Mr. Rietsky—and Mr. Severance.

Don Stuart[2] vowing he can stand business no longer has come to N.Y. to take up writing. He's a knock-out, I think.

But really Bob, fond as I am of you, I do think that was a silly letter to write me.

Come on east + look us up when you do.

Faithfully
F Scott Fitzg—

[1] Boyhood friend of Fitzgerald's in St. Paul.
[2] Donald Ogden Stewart became a successful humorist and screenwriter.

TO: Edmund Wilson
February 1921

ALS, 1 p. Yale University
New York City

Dear Bunny:

The kind of critisism[1] I'd like more than anything else—if you find you have the time, would be; *par example*

P. 10x I find this page rotten
P. 10y Dull! Cut!
P. 10z Good! enlarge!
P. 10a Invert sentence I have marked (in pencil!)
P. 10b unconvincing!
P. 10c Confused!

Ha-ha!

I'm glad you're going to the New Republic. It always seemed undignified for you to be on Vanity Fair.

F. Scott Fitz—

[1] Fitzgerald had probably given Wilson a working draft of *The Beautiful and Damned.*

TO: Carl Hovey ALS, 2 pp. Huntington Library

Fri, April 22nd 1921
38 W. 59th Street

Dear Mr. Hovey:

I'm sending you today, through Reynolds, the first of the three parts of *The Beautiful and Damned.* The second part should reach you Monday and the third part Tuesday.

After the ten months I have been working on it it has turned out as I expected—and rather dreaded—a bitter and insolent book that I fear will never be popular and that will undoubtedly offend a lot of people. Personally, I should advise you against serializing it—now that the damn thing is off my hand I can try a few cheerful stories. If you do not want it, I don't believe I shall offer it to anyone else but shall let Scribners bring it out in September—which is probably the psychological time anyhow.

On May 3d Zelda and I are going abroad for a few months (and I expect to write several movies and short stories while I'm over) so I'm sending you the thing in parts that I may get as early a decision as possible. Could you let me know; do you think, by Saturday the thirtieth? You see if you don't serialize it I shall have to depend on an advance from Scribner for our trip and of course I can't ask for that until I hear from you.

My best to Mrs Hovey

Sincerely
F. Scott Fitzgerald

TO: Ralph Block[1] ALS, 2 pp. Princeton University
2 May 1921

38 W. 59th St.
New York City

Dear Ralph:

You certainly were slick to remember about the letter. I probably never would meet Aldous Huxley. Very boiled at present but think you're a very good egg. Will get in touch with you when I return. My book appears in England (This Side ect.) the week I get there. Sail tomorrow. Have you heard about S. amuel G. oldwyn + G. eorge B. ernard S. haw:

Scene 1st + last

G.B.S: "The trouble is that you're thinking about art + I'm thinking about money. We never could get together."

This is vouched for. Is it *veritas?*

Yours in Christ
F. Scott Fitzgerald

% Goldwyn

[1] Associated with Goldwyn Studios; he apparently provided Fitzgerald with a letter of introduction to Huxley.

FROM: John Galsworthy — ALS, 2 pp. Scrapbook. Princeton University

May 13 [1921]

Dear Mr. Scott Fitzgerald,

Mr. Maxwell Perkins tells me you are just arrived over here. It would be a great pleasure to my wife + myself if Mrs. Fitzgerald and you could come and dine here with us at 8 o'clock.[1] The St. John Ervines[2] are coming, and possibly Lennox Robinson, the Irish playwright.

If you come by 'Tube,' take your train at 'Strand' station, to Hampstead station, and we are 4 minutes walk, up Holly Hill into The Grove, and turn to the left toward the tall white Admiral's House. Grove Lodge adjoins it.

Much hoping to see you. Sincerely yours

John Galsworthy

By taxi-cab its about twenty minutes from the Hotel Cecil.

J.G.

[1] The Fitzgeralds accepted the invitation.
[2] English playwright and novelist.

TO: Ruth Sturtevant Smith — ALS, 2 pp. Albert Sturtevant
Grande-Hôtel letterhead. Rome

The American Express Co.
Rome
Italy June 10th 1921

Dear Ruth:

In Venice we were bored one day and seeing an American destroyer in the harbor we took a gondola out to see it. A very polite officer showed us about + you can imagine my surprise when I saw in the mess room a large photograph of your brother, Al. It was destroyer 240, "The Sturtevant"

Below the picture was a bronze tablet—name, date of birth + death + rank.

I don't suppose you've ever seen the ship so I tried to make some snapshots—but the enclosed is the only one to come out. They were anxious to know all about your brother so I told them all I knew. They are sending you a painting of the ship.

We are having a rather punk time. Best to Curt.

As Ever
F. Scott Fitzg—

TO: Carl Hovey

ALS, 2 pp. Huntington Library
Claridge's Hotel letterhead. London

June 25th, 1921

Dear Mr Hovey:

What you say about the book fell sweetly on my ear. *This Side of Paradise* is having a checkered career in England. I'm not sure yet whether its going to be a sucess or not.

We spent a month in Italy + had a rotten time. We're coming to America early in July and I'm curious to see what you've done with the novel. Perhaps some of your cutting away may give excellent suggestion for further pruning of the book section.[1]

Zelda and I feel you've made a grave mistake about the illustrator. This Benson[2] did one of my stories in the Post + My God! you ought to see the grey blurs he made of my beautiful protagonists. But perhaps he'll rise to the occasion.

My best to Mrs. Hovey.

As Ever
F Scott Fitzgerald

[1] Fitzgerald's first version of *The Beautiful and Damned*—a 130,000-word typescript —was cut some 40,000 words by Hovey for serialization in *The Metropolitan;* Fitzgerald subsequently revised his original version for book publication.

[2] Leslie L. Benson illustrated *The Beautiful and Damned* serial.

TO: John Franklin Carter[1] ALS, 1 p. University of Wyoming

Montgomery, Alabama

Aug 3d 1921

Dear John:

The *Queen*[2] arrived here safely. She's excellent isn't she. Even such an old Tory as Viscount Bryce, with whom I had a talk on the boat coming back, thinks its a great book, tho he considered Eminent Victorians an outrage.

Yrs

F. Scott Fitz

[1] Writer and diplomat; Secretary to the American Ambassador in Rome in 1921.

[2] Lytton Strachey, *Queen Victoria* (1921).

TO: Maxwell Perkins ALS, 1 p. Princeton University

Dellwood, White Bear Lake

Minn, Sept 13th 1921

Dear Mr. Perkins:

Enjoyment of Poetry came today.[1] I have often heard of it as the best book of its sort ever written by an American—but I had no idea you published it. I'll read it with the greatest interest.

I wrote you yesterday asking for more alms—$650.00. I note it here so if my other letter went astray   Writing like a streak. Would it be imposing on your time to ask you to ask Wilcox downstairs to send me a 1st edition of Ben Hetch's *Eric Dorn*?

I'll read Eastman within the week—have just been reading a book you gave me last spring—Robert Lynde's essays.[2] They're slick

Faithfully

F Scott Fitzg—

[1] By Max Eastman, published in 1913.

[2] Robert Lynd, *The Art of Letters* (1921).

TO: Thomas Boyd ALS, 1 p. Elizabeth B. Nash

Dellwood, White Bear

Sept 19th 1921

Dear Boyd:

The enclosed is not typed—I have no typewriter![1] Also its written in Mencken's manner which I don't mind parodying for St. Paul consumption. I have a copy of the book—shall I return you the unbound one?

Please send me three copies of the issue containing it—will you? No excitement. The Metropolitan committed very little butchery on the 2nd installment—just enough to annoy me.

Yrs.
F Scott Fitzg—

P.S. Will Crafts sue me for libel?[2] If so cut out the word *sexual!*

[1] Fitzgerald's review of John Dos Passos' *Three Soldiers* in the *St. Paul Daily News* (25 September 1921).

[2] Dr. Wilbur F. Crafts, Superintendent of the International Reform Bureau and Prohibition leader, famous for his attacks on popular amusements. Fitzgerald referred to Crafts as giving "sexual thrills to the wives of prominent butchers and undertakers," which the paper printed as "bilogical thrills."

TO: Maxwell Perkins
Before 28 October 1921

ALS, 4 pp. Princeton University
St. Paul, Minnesota

599 Summit Ave

Dear Mr. Perkins:

One more thing I forgot to ask you about.

Which would be best. To have *Flappers* appear in England in the Spring or my new book.[1] The thing is I don't want to discourage them. Give me your advice.

As to this Reynold's business. It's grown complicated. How he ever got mixed up in it I don't quite understand. If Collins is sticking by me close enough to risk a book of short stories I'd rather keep on having him. In the first place why should I pay Reynolds 10% for changing publishers for me, maybe getting me $50 or so more advance royalty. I see no use of changing publishers anyhow—Collins are established and, moreover, they are darn good I think. And having books scattered around with different publishers, like James + Edith Wharton for instance, stands in the way of ever having collected editions if I ever get to that stage which I of course hope.

On the other hand he's been very good to me, advanced me nearly all that Metropolitan money even tho they havn't paid him very promptly. So if he wants to offer it in England I don't begrudge him the 10% and we can arrange it that the full 10% due to Scribners reaches you anyway. But I wouldn't want him to offer it to anyone but Collins, Why, suppose they brought out Flappers + someone else the new novel both this spring. It'd be silly!

Please advice me what to do. In any case send him the page proof + NOT the galley to offer to the movies as you see I've made many corrections.

I've written three short stories[2] since I've been here but havn't heard from any of them.

Sincerely
F Scott Fitzg—

[1] *Flappers and Philosophers* was published in London by Collins in March 1922; *The Beautiful and Damned* was published by Collins in November 1922.
[2] "Two for a Cent," "The Diamond as Big as the Ritz," and probably "The Popular Girl."

TO: Maxwell Perkins — AL, 1 p. Princeton University

Oct 28th, 1921
The Commodore Hotel
St. Paul, Minn

Dear Mr. Perkins:

Zelda had a girl day before yesterday. Both are doing excellently well.

I note what you say about the book + think you are entirely right about Collins. I'd appreciate it if you would, as you suggest, write Reynolds a letter explaining the contract (which, by the way, I had forgotten) to him when you send him the page proof.

I think the stenographer probably took the proof out to lunch because she couldn't decipher the corrections on an empty stomach. Maybe she didn't bring it back—you never can tell!

Faithfully

FROM: H. L. Mencken — ALS, 1 p. Scrapbook. Princeton University
After 26 October 1921

Dear Fitz:

Congratulations! A superb patriotic feat! I only hope young Ma is in her usual excellent health and spirits. The young one will be a prize beauty. Name her Charlotte after Charles Evans Hughes.

When are you coming east again?

Yours in Xt.
H. L. Mencken

TO: H. L. Mencken
After 26 October 1921

ALS, 1 p. New York Public Library

The Commodore Hotel
Western Ave
St. Paul, Minn

Dear Mencken—

Thank you for your note. Mother and infant are well and happy but I am feeling very old as I see the next forty years mapping themselves out for me. For God's sake tell me something to read—seriously I mean, don't send me a list of medical or spiritual titles. I am sick to my stomach with fiction and have been revelling in Paine's *Mark Twain*.[1]

Do you know where a fella could get the *Fireside Conversation in the time of Queen Elizebeth?*[2] Your fame is spreading apace into the religious homes of St. Paul

Yours in state of
extreme depression
F Scott Fitzgerald

[1] Probably Albert Bigelow Paine, *A Short Life of Mark Twain* (1920).

[2] *1601: Conversation, As It Was by the Social Fireside in the Time of the Tudors,* a privately printed scatological work by Mark Twain.

TO: Maxwell Perkins
Late 1921

ALS, 1 p. Princeton University
St. Paul, Minnesota

Dear Mr. Perkins—

I recieved your letter. Thank you for the information about *Who's Who*. Has Hill[1] done the cover—or are you waiting until he can see the galley proofs. I agree with you about *Eric Dorn* but at least Hetcht has vitality + can *write*. If *Mooncalf* is a good book then *Eric Dorn* is a masterpiece.

As to the adds—I think they should be dignified. I am apending a few suggestions on the next page.[3] I took out "soulecism" as you suggested. I do not like to italisze newspapers ect—I save italics *entirely* for emphasis, I hope you thinked I improved the midnight symposium.[2]

I don't know when I'll get east—next fall perhaps.

As Ever
Scott Fitz—

Am sending a picture you might use some time.

[1] The dust jacket for *The Beautiful and Damned* was illustrated by W. E. Hill.

[2] Perkins had asked Fitzgerald to revise the "Symposium" section of *The Beautiful and Damned,* which included satirical comments on religion and the Bible.

[3] Missing.

FROM: H. L. Mencken[1] TLS, 1 p. Princeton University
The Smart Set letterhead

December 22, 1921

Mr. and Mrs. F. Scott Fitzgerald,
599 Summit Avenue,
St. Paul, Minn.

Dear Mr. and Mrs. Fitzgerald:

As you have doubtless heard, both Mr. Nathan and Mr. Mencken are in Sing Sing Prison following a peculiarly dastardly assault upon a poor colored girl in the outskirts of Stanford, Conn. I am caring for their correspondence, and will forward your Christmas card to them. This crime was committed, unfortunately, while under the influence of strong drink. The colored lady's name was Miss Gladys Johnson of Nashville, Tenn., daughter of the late Rev. Hercules Johnson, D.D.

Sincerely
S. A. Golde
Secretary.

[1] Possibly also from George Jean Nathan.

TO: Maxwell Perkins Wire. Princeton University

STPAUL MINN 1111A DEC 23 1921
LILDA THINKS BOOK SHOULD END WITH ANTHONYS LAST SPEECH ON SHIP SHE THINKS NEW ENDING IS A PIECE OF MORALITY LET ME KNOW YOUR ADVICE IF YOU AGREE LAST WORD OF BOOK WOULD BE I HAVE COME THROUGH OR DO YOU PREFER PRESENT ENDING I AM UNDECIDED JACKET IS EXCELLENT[1]

F SCOTT FITHMERALD

[1] Perkins wrote on this wire: "I agree with Zelda." The original ending of the novel, as published in the serial, was a two-paragraph analysis of Anthony's and Gloria's idealism: "Their fault was not that they had doubted but that they had believed."

TO: Maxwell Perkins ALS, 2 pp. Princeton University
Before 27 December 1921

Dear Mr. Perkins—

Charlie Flandrau[1] has been reading my new book + either has an awful line of blarney or is tremendously impressed with it. Hope you liked the new ending. Also that you approved what I did to the sketch about the bible.

I have had my full advance of $3000 and the book won't be out for two months yet but I'm hoping enough has accumulated since September on the other two for you to let me have $500.00. Can you? And will you deposit it if you can. In the Chatham + Phenix as usual?

I am writing an awfully funny play[2] that's going to make me rich forever. It really is. I'm so damned tired of the feeling that I'm living up to my income.[3]

As Ever
F Scott Fitz—

626 Goodrich Ave.
St. Paul, Minn.

[1] St. Paul writer who was married to novelist Grace Flandrau; author of *The Diary of a Freshman* (1901) and *Harvard Episodes* (1897).

[2] Published as *The Vegetable* (1923).

[3] See Perkins' 27 December letter to Fitzgerald in *Dear Scott/Dear Max*, ed. John Kuehl and Jackson Bryer (New York: Scribners, 1971), hereafter referred to as *Scott/Max*.

FROM: Eugene O'Neill
1921

Inscription in O'Neill's *The Emperor Jones Diff'rent the Straw* (1921).
Princeton University

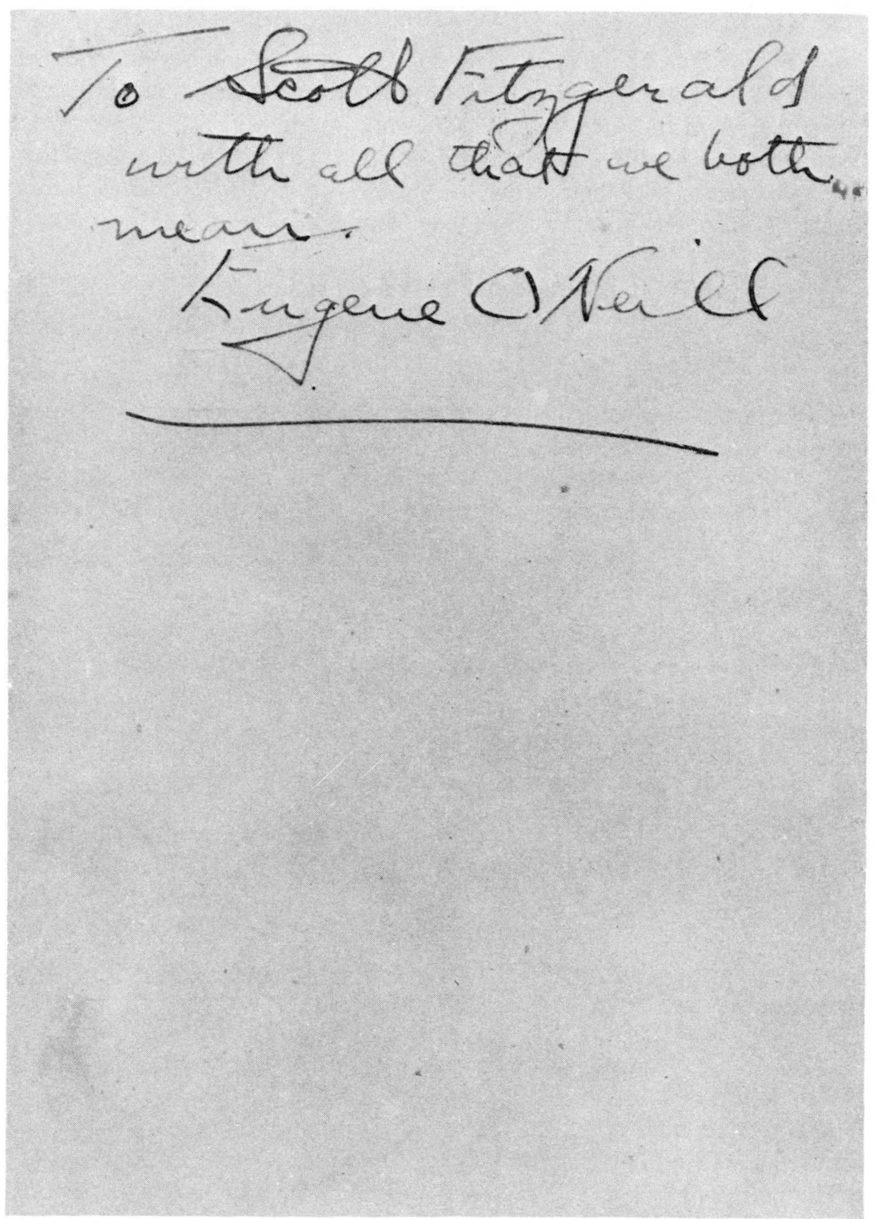
To Scott Fitzgerald
with all that we both
mean.
Eugene O'Neill

Note: This inscription is the only known communication between O'Neill and Fitzgerald.

TO: Maxwell Perkins
25 January 1922

ALS, 1 p. Princeton University

626 Goodrich Ave.
St. Paul, Minn

Dear Mr. Perkins:

Since *This Side of Paradise* came out I have given out about ½ dozen interviews + not one but has made me wince later when touched by the reportorial hand. If I give this Ward a good one it will use up material I can use myself shortly—if it is a bad one I will blush shamefully.[1] However once again I fall before the lure of the press. I will send tomorrow a picture of Zelda + one of me. I enclose two photos that he's got to return.

I expect to have this thing come out yellow as hell but I'll take the risk

Sincerely
F. Scott Fitzgerald.

P.S. For God's sake read this over. I give you my full permission to strike out or amend anything which Quirk[2] might twist to make an idiot out of me. I know what the newspaper men have done to Upton Sinclair + I dread them—not when they critisize me but when they twist my own words, with no ill intentions, but simply to make a sensational story. *Please* impress this on him. Am enclosing other pictures. Let him take his pick but I've got to have them all back.

I hope you give him a tremendous figure on the Paradise sales.
The Mind in the Making[3] has arrived + looks very interesting. Thanks immensely. I'm going to start it tonight

[1] The Ward interview has not been located.
[2] James Quirk, editor of *Photoplay*.
[3] James H. Robinson, *The Mind in the Making: The Relation of Intelligence to Social Reform* (1921).

TO: Maxwell Perkins
30 January 1922

ALS, 3 pp. Princeton University

626 Goodrich Ave.
St. Paul, Minn

Dear Mr. Perkins—

I wired you today because Edmund Wilson wrote me that he had recieved a copy of *The Beautiful + Dammed.* I was afraid it might go out to the newspapers + they'd review it too soon. There is a good sized article on me in March *Bookman.*[1]

I wish that the advertising man would be sure that review copies go to the following people[2]

The Review

√ " Freeman (VanWyck Brooks)

√ " Literary Review (N.Y. Evening Post)

√	F.P.A	World
×	Heywood Broun	World
×	Hanson	Chi. News
×	Benchley	Life
×	Sherwood	"
√	Boyd	St. Paul Daily News
×	Publishers Weekly	
√	Harry Dounce	
×	Carl Van Doren	% The Nation
√	Benjamin de Casseres—Judge	
√	Ludwig Lewisohn	% The Nation
×	Percy Hammond	N.Y. Tribune
√×	John Farrar	The Bookman
√	New Republic	
×	Max Eastman—	Liberator
√√	Gilbert Seldes	Dial
√	Yale Lit Magazine—	
×	Fanny Butcher	
√	Harvard [Lit]	
√	Nassau Lit.	
×	John A. V. Weaver	—Brooklyn Eagle
×	Edward Paramore	—Fashion Art
×	John Bishop	—Vanity Fair
√×	H. L. Mencken	—Smart Set.

√	Don Maquis—Sun	If you think advisable.
√	Christopher Morley—Post	If you think advisable.
×	Burton Rascoe	If you think advisable.
√	Dorothy Parker—	If you think advisable.

The ones checked should go as soon as possible

I will need 25 copies myself. I wish you'd send them as soon as possible—and charge me with nineteen of them. I'm allowed six, am I not?

No doubt the above list has already been attended to. Still I've followed closely the people who have kept my name in mind + think they should each recieve a copy. If I were in New York I'd autgraph all of them.

My twenty five are all for family, authors who have sent books + personal friends.

Am getting quite excited

F Scott Fitzg—

[1] "The Literary Spotlight," *The Bookman* (March 1922), an unsigned article by Edmund Wilson.

[2] Annotations on this letter in other hands have not been transcribed.

TO: Maxwell Perkins
22 February 1922

ALS, 2 pp. Princeton University

626 Goodrich Ave.
St. Paul, Minn

Dear Mr. Perkins:

By this time you'll have recieved *The Love Legend.*[1] It strikes me as a pretty fair first novel. Nothing wonderful but good stuff. Perhaps it needs more cutting tho I had her rip 10,000 words out of it.

You've never answered my question about an add in the St. Paul Daily News.

I found that thing by Anatole France very interesting. It's the same thing that Mencken says about Hardy + Conrad + Drieser the thing that lives them above the "cerberal" novelists like Wells—the profound gesture of pity.

Bishop's been asked to do 2500 words for the *Herald.*[2]

I have not heard anything from my book of importance—Nothing at all from [Cab]ell tho I sent him a copy   Will let you know when I do—though the blurb notices have become so frequent on covers that I doubt if they have the effect they used to. Still its worth doing.

I'm glad that was O.K. about the syndicate. I really think it will do me more good in the American + I don't trust these newspapers much. I was sorry though that you had gone to all that trouble about it. Needless to say I'm very much obliged to you. Will you return the photos? Saw the pictures Whitney[3] got out. They're excellent.

I am glad Biggs has sold you another story

We arrive east on March 9th for two weeks in New York.

As Ever
Scott Fitz.

[1] By Woodward Boyd, Thomas Boyd's wife. Scribners published the novel in 1922; Fitzgerald reviewed it in the *New York Post* (28 October 1922).

[2] John Peale Bishop, "Mr. Fitzgerald Sees the Flapper Through," *New York Herald* (5 March 1922).

[3] Whitney Darrow, advertising manager for Scribners.

Inscription in *The Beautiful and Damned*.
University of Virginia

For Mother —
This book which I feel sure you won't like but which I assure you is not about me.
with love from

F Scott Fitzgerald
St. Paul, Minn
Feb 6th, 1922

TO: Edmund Wilson
February/March 1922

ALS, 1 p. Yale University
St. Paul, Minnesota

Dear Bunny

The interpolated Harlequin episode is a *scream*—Zelda + I laughed ourselve's sick over it. I am charmed with the whole review.[1] I am in terror as to the book's success. We reach N.Y. on the 9th—will be probably at the Plaza.

Scott F

[1] "The Literary Spotlight."

TO: James Branch Cabell
c. March 1922

ALS, 1 p. Princeton University

626 Goodrich Ave.
St. Paul, Minn.

Dear Mr. Cabell:

I feel than by asking your permission to quote a private letter I have not acted in the best of taste. There have been, of course, innumerable precedents of late, but that does not excuse it. I appreciate your exceeding kindness and courtesy.

It seems that Perkins of Scribners had heard from some editor in Richmond that you liked the book. He had tried to get in touch with that editor to see if it was quotable—realizing how invaluable a word from you might be. For some reason he evidently failed, and he wired me Monday night—or Sunday—asking me if I had a letter from you which was quotable.[1] I wired you immediately.

Ive had the pleasure of a three day amour with an Exquisite Case of Spanish Influenza, and like all such illicit affairs it has left me weak + chastened. I hope you are *not* the same.

Faithfully
F Scott Fitzgerald

[1] Cabell wrote Fitzgerald on 24 February: "I have found it gratifyingly solid—moving, human, brilliant at times, and always nicely ironic." (*Between Friends*, ed. Padraic Colum and Margaret Freeman Cabell [New York: Harcourt Brace & World, 1962], p. 250)

TO: Maxwell Perkins
After 4 March 1922

ALS, 1 p. Princeton University
St. Paul, Minnesota

Dear Mr. Perkins—

By now you've seen Morley's little did in the Post[1] as well as the ambiguous review in the Book Review.[2] The last sentence in the latter might do to quote. I suppose it's too early to catch the wave of the book—my one hope is that the Metropolitan didn't hurt it violently.

Arrive Tuesday—Hope to God there'll be encouraging news by then. Two St. Paul stores + one Minneapolis have given big displays. One store sold 33 by three oclock the first day.

Scott Fitz—

Thank you for the thousand.

[1] Christopher Morley's review has not been found. *The Beautiful and Damned* was reviewed in the *New York Evening Post* by Henry Seidel Canby.

[2] R. S. Lynd wrote in the *Book Review:* "Mr. Fitzgerald continues to be one of the most original of our novelists, and reading him is an exhilerating experience, like zooming along in an airplane." This statement was used in Scribners promotional material.

TO: Maxwell Perkins

Wire. Princeton University

STPAUL MINN 1922 MAR 5 PM 11 48

PLEASE HOLD ALL MAIL THINK YOU COULD USE LAST SENTENCE IN BOOK REVIEW NOTICE ABOUT READING HIM IS AN EXHILIRATING EXPERIENCE ETC FANNY BUTCHER[1] DOES NOT LIKE BOOK AM WORRIED AS THE DEUCE WILL ARRIVE THURSDAY

F SCOTT FITZGERALD.

[1] Book reviewer for the *Chicago Tribune.*

TO: Shane Leslie
12 March 1922

ALS, 2 pp. Bruccoli

St Paul, Minn
626 Goodrich Ave.

Dear Leslie—

Don't tell me that having moved to the Riererra you're not going to get the copy of my new bitter book sent to 10 Talbot Square!

So you called the novel *The Oppidan.* As you know I have read some of it and was enormously interested. I do not understand what you mean when you say "Scribner is *taking* 1000 copies" but I shall certainly get one as soon as it can be got, and review it for either The Bookman or The Literary Review (N.Y. Post.)[1] I intended to review *Manning*[2] but by the time we were settled in one place and I took up writing again it was too late.

Your advertisments scattered about the page are hilarious—especially "Pawn *Main Street* and by *The Oppidan.*" I wish to heaven I was on the Riviera and perhaps I could think up something gay also. We often talk of you and of how meeting you in London was the best thing in our whole trip, not excepting Galesworthy and the Pope. We have been out in my home city, St Paul, for the winter but are going east for three weeks tommorrow. I doubt if we'll get abrood for a year. My compliments to Mrs. Leslie and your progeny.

Scribners have brought out my second novel in a 1st edition of 10,000—and the reviews—all except the puritan *Times* which damned it unmercifully—have been very favorable. I hope to heaven you havn't been reading the battered, shattered version of it which appeared in the Metropolitan.

Zelda and I both send entheusiastic greetings to you. She has never forgot that romantic walk through Wapping.[3] She would like to take it again—but me—give me a primrose path under the full sun

Yours
F Scott Fitzgerald

1 "Homage to the Victorians," *New York Tribune* (14 May 1922).
2 Leslie's biography of Cardinal Manning.
3 Leslie's notes with this letter read:
For Fitz' LIFE
if ever written
The romantic walk in the foggy East End refers to Zelda riding on my back when she tired. I wish we three cd have been photographed.

Letter Fitz wrote me in 1922
Shane Leslie
I took Zelda & Fitz through London Docks & Slums—ending at Wapping.

TO: George A. Kuyper — ALS, 1 p. Princeton University

You embarrass me, Mr Kuyper, beyond words. I did not suspect until your letter came that Gloria's birthday was a movable feast.[1] And then I looked it up—My God! And I can never straighten it out without re-writing the whole book.

It is really a most embarrasing predicament. God! This bugbear of in-accuracy. My first novel had 210 mispellings *when it issued from the press!*[2]

Thank you for your kindness in saying you liked the novel. It's a wretched novel, excellent in detail. I may do better later

Sincerely
F Scott Fitzgerald

626 Goodrich Ave.
St Paul, Minn
March 13th, 1922

[1] *The Beautiful and Damned* stipulated three different birth dates for Gloria.
[2] An exaggerated figure.

TO: Mr. Braddy

TLS, 1 p. Princeton University
Plaza Hotel letterhead. New York City

March 27, 1922.

Dear Mr. Braddy:—

I am amazed at the difference of opinion about the ending of my book. Mencken and Nathan insist that I botched the thing by having them get the money in the end, while Cabell and Benchley (of "Life") think that it is the best thing in the book. You seem to be one of the few people who even read those last two paragraphs in the Metropolitan, and I am still confused as to whether or not I made a mistake.

Again thank you for the praise which it pleases you to give me.

Sincerely,
F Scott Fitzgerald

TO: John Franklin Carter
Spring 1922

ALS, 1 p. University of Wyoming

626 Goodrich Ave.
St Paul, Minn.

Dear John:

Thanks for your letter. The *B. + D.* is a better book than *Paradise* tho I havn't the same affection for it.

Liking the people of Williamstown would cramp my style too. You'd better reread *My Antonia* before you revise.

Send me a copy of the Ladies Reading Club Article.

I remember Rome chiefly as the place where Zelda and I had an appalling squable. In fact that afternoon and noon with you was the only luminous spot in our stay.

Yours
F Scott Fitzgerald

We may go to Hollywood this summer.

TO: Maxwell Perkins
Spring 1922

ALS, 1 p. Princeton University

626 L'Avenue Goodrich
Sainte Paul, Minnesota

Dear Mr. Perkins—

Ici est l'article. Ne plus de la vin. Seulement de la travaille. Tout est bien. Notre mieux a Mme. Perkins et vous, a moi et Zelda.

Si vous ne comprenez pas cette lettre, le donnez a le departement Francais de Scribner pour la translation. Les petit histoires arriverez bientot

Tout A Vous
F. Scott Fitzgerald

auteur de "Cette coté de la paradis."

TO: Burton Rascoe
c. April 1922

ALS, 1 p. University of Pennsylvania

626 Goodrich Ave.
St Paul, Minn

Dear Burton:

I'm writing you at the behest of the famous author, my wife, to tell you that the great paper which you serve is with holding from her the first money she has ever earned[1] Whatever it be, from a rouble to a talent, prick your clerk into satisfying her avarice—for she has become as one mad.

You have certainly done wonders with the pages in the Tribune. Why not booklet form? Even the unspeakable *Herald* has an unspeakable literary booklet. Have you discovered that Vivian Shaw is *not* Bernard's daughter as was originally reported.[2] I wish we could have seen more of each other. My best regards to your wife

Clip for preservation on dotted line.

F Scott Fitzgerald

[1] Zelda reviewed *The Beautiful and Damned* for the *New York Tribune* (2 April 1922).

[2] Gilbert Seldes wrote reviews under the pseudonym Vivian Shaw.

TO: Chester B. Sikking[1]
Postmarked 7 April 1922

ALS, 2 pp. Princeton University

626 Goodrich Ave.
St Paul, Minn

Dear Chester:

Thanks both for the clipping,[2] which I had not seen and for (especially) your letter. I have thought about you frequently and thot of sending you a copy of my second book but I didn't know whether you'd even recognize my name on the cover.

One of the chapters in it is concerned with a southern camp and you'd doubtless recognize many of the incidents. In fact the hero's position in the army is, up to a certain point, very much like yours was. As you may know I married Zelda Sayre, the Montgomery girl I was so smitten with. We have one child and divide our time between St Paul and New York and Europe. Whenever I pass through Illinois I think of the motley crew with which you arrived—you especially, with a battered hat tipped rakishly over one ear and a beautiful pair of fallen arches.

I hope we will meet someday. Pay my respects to Mrs. Sicking + to young Chester (whose arrival gave you, as I recall, considerable worry). I remain

Most cordially yours
F Scott Fitzgerald

[1] An army acquaintance of Fitzgerald's at Camp Sheridan.
[2] An article about the 67th Infantry.

TO: Maxwell Perkins
After 17 April 1922

ALS, 2 pp. Princeton University
St. Paul, Minnesota

Dear Mr. Perkins

Your letter telling me that the B+D has not picked up is somewhat depressing but not very. I still think that it is going up to 50,000 and perhaps over within a year.[1]

I am returning the contract.[2] Of course for a novel I would not ask such high terms as for a book of short stories as there should be leeway for your advertising. I am enclosing a letter to Mr. Scribner.[3] Read it over and if it is bunk tear it up. If you think its worth doing, show it to him.

There is a heavy blizzard going on here + the world is dark and cold.[4]

As Ever
F Scott Fitzgerald

[1] *The Beautiful and Damned* probably reached 50,000 copies with the third printing in April 1922.

[2] The contract for *Tales of the Jazz Age* dated 12 April 1922 stipulated a 15 percent royalty on the list price on the first 20,000 copies, with an escalation to 20 percent after 40,000 copies.

[3] On 19 April Fitzgerald sent Scribner a plan for a reprint series to compete with The Modern Library. See *Letters,* pp. 155–57.

[4] See Perkins' 17 April letter to Fitzgerald in *Scott/Max.*

TO: Maxwell Perkins — ALS, 1 p. Princeton University
Postmarked 21 April 1922

626 Goodrich Ave.
St. Paul, Minn.

Dear Mr. Perkins:

I return the proofs herewith.[1] I have followed your suggestion about cutting the Henry James episode.[2] I have cut the dates of the stories except the recent ones and except in the case of *May Day,* for I want to show that it was published before *Three Soldiers.* When did I ever call you "astute"? And is it a slam? Also I have spared O'brien a bit.[3] Tell me if you think its all right. And I've inserted a dedication[4]

Did you see the review of the *B+D* in *Town and Country*?[5] Is there any new dope on the sale? I sold the movie rights to Warner Bros. for $2500.00 which seems a small price. But it was the best I could do. If you can think of some better typographical arrangement go ahead. And please strike out "Three Preposterous Plays" from the table of works. And please don't tell anyone what I got for the *B.+D* from the movies.

As Ever
F Scott Fitzgerald

[1] For the annotated table of contents for *Tales of the Jazz Age.*

[2] On 12 April Perkins commented on Fitzgerald's note for "The Lees of Happiness": ". . . I don't think Henry James had anything in the world to do with you at all, and so is not appropriate—but in all but details this material is admirable for our purposes." Fitzgerald probably revised the material, which appeared in *Tales of the Jazz Age* as "melodramas carefully disguised by early paragaphs in Jamesian manner which hint dark and subtle complexities to follow."

[3] Edward J. O'Brien, editor of the *Best Short Stories* series, which Fitzgerald frequently ridiculed.

[4] "Quite Inappropriately to My Mother."

[5] By William Curtis (15 April 1922).

TO: Burton Rascoe | ALS, 1 p. University of Pennsylvania
After 30 April 1922

626 Goodrich Ave. St Paul Minn

Dear Burton—

I have just seen that silly story printed in your book page in reference to Robert Bridges and myself.[1] Whether the lie is Mr. Stoke's or not I don't know—but it seems to me that it was rather bad taste to reprint anything which puts me in such an awkward and unpleasant position with people with whom I have to deal.

Yours
F Scott Fitzgerald

P.S. Zelda recieved the check. Thanks

F.S.F.

[1] Rascoe had printed publisher Frederick A. Stokes' report that Fitzgerald pulled the gray hairs from Bridges' beard: "A Bookman's Day Book," *New York Tribune* (30 April 1922). See Fitzgerald's May letter to Bridges in *Letters*.

TO: Maxwell Perkins | ALS, 2 pp. Princeton University
After 30 April 1922 | St. Paul, Minnesota

Dear Mr. Perkins:

Seven things:

(1) Write me when you've *got* to have the next copy on *The Jazz Age*

(2) Did you see that ghastly thing in the Tribune about Dr Bridges + me? I can't imagine who made up such a story out of thin air. If you ever see Mr. Stokes do ask him about it.

(3) The book business is dead out here. Nothing selling—but my book as well as any.

(4) Could you ask the retail dept. why they don't replace the defective copy of *The Revolt of the Angels*[1] that I sent them?

(5) I suppose you saw the good reviews in *Town + Country + The Freeman +* the bad one in the Bookman.[2] I suppose too that the books going as badly as ever

(6) Will you ask Darrow Whitney[3] if he has any pictures of me to send me one as I have to give it to somebody—almost any kind will do.

(7) I'm sure you skipped to the end to see if I wanted money— but for once I don't. Sold the movie rights of B+D for $2,500—did I tell you?—with the proviso of $1250 more if it did $250,000 gross busi-

ness.[4] Poor price. Keep it dark. Warner Bros bought it—they're the people who bought *Brass + Main Street*

As Ever
F Scott Fitzg—

626 Goodrich Ave.

We're going to White Bear for the summer again.

[1] By Anatole France.
[2] By Mary M. Colum in *The Freeman* (26 April 1922) and Burton Rascoe in *The Bookman* (May 1922).
[3] Whitney Darrow.
[4] Fitzgerald did not receive the bonus.

TO: Ernest Boyd[1] ALS, 1 p. Princeton University
Fall 1922(?)

Great Neck, Long Island

Dear Earnest—

I was in Vanity Fair office the other day (quite stewed) and Bunny was just dictating the letter to you. I had a dim idea it was one of those things like they ran before only the critics being rated by the novelists instead of vice-versa.[2]

I have a hunch that all the people in your letter will either take a crack at the obselete books or flog dead horses—all except Mencken, and frankly I'd rather not do it because I'd have ten men—half of whom have been kind to my stuff—after me with clubs and sling shots. And as far as pronouncing on the classics I have so little general culture that my opinions wouldn't be of the slightest value

When are you coming out? Any week-day or any week-end we'll always be glad to see you.

As Ever
F. Scott Fitzg—

[1] Editor and critic.
[2] In April 1922 *Vanity Fair* published a poll by critics in which Fitzgerald scored 1 on a scale of 25.

TO: Burton Rascoe TLS, 1 p. University of Pennsylvania

626 Goodrich Avenue,
St. Paul, Minn., May 5, 1922.

Dear Burton

This is a book just published by Scribners.[1] Leslie has rather a wide audience among people who have read his volume of Reminiscences, his Cardinal Manning, and his the Celt and the World.

Zelda is trying to think up something for McCall's, in fact, she has it about half written and will probably send it on soon.[2]

I hope you can use this in your book page.

As ever
F Scott Fitzgerald

P.S. You are all wrong about The Beautiful and Damned, but I don't care.

Thine.
Fitzg—

[1] *The Oppidan.*

[2] Zelda Fitzgerald wrote an article for *McCall's* called "Where Do Flappers Go?" that was not published. In addition to editing the book page of the *New York Tribune*, Rascoe was also at this time associated with *McCall's*.

FROM: John V. A. Weaver[1]
After 7 May 1922

TLS, 2 pp. Princeton University
Brooklyn Daily Eagle letterhead

Dear Scott,

I'm still sorta gaspin' with ecitement over the review![2] Gee, gosh, etc! It certainly was swell. I appreciate it all the more because, if there is one person who knows that stuff, you are it. You know, that dumbbell Broun and also, to my surprise, F.P.A. only wrote little squibs to the effect that they thought the slang was punk, being altogether exaggerated and overdone. They don't get it at all. I know the story itself, as I told you when you were here, is as light as the people in it. But the slang *is* correct, now isn't it?

You said in the review that you wanted more. Now I don't know whether that is merely a friendly gesture or what, but anyway, in the June Metropolitan, the same issue in which appears Zelda's Eulogy on the Flapper, is a story called "Enamel" by me. I enjoyed Zelda's article exceedingly. She can sure write. I'm doing an article called "The Younger Degeneration" for Metro, in which I tell what I think is the matter with these now young people. I'm a reactionary! 'ray!

I'm head over eardrums in work, trying to scrape enough dough together to depart around the first of June for Yurrup on a freight boat. Oh, God, if I can only get a little rest!

Thanks once more for the review which couldn't possibly have been more cheering. I am grateful to you from the cockle of my heart.[3]

Yours towjewers,
John

[1] Journalist and writer of vernacular verse.

[2] Fitzgerald reviewed Weaver's *Margey Wins the Game* in the *New York Tribune* (7 May 1922).

[3] See Fitzgerald's May letter to Weaver in *Letters*.

TO: Maxwell Perkins
13 May 1922

ALS, 1 p. Princeton University

626 Goodrich Ave.
St Paul, Minn

Dear Mr Perkins:

By this time you have got the letter defending my title.[1] The jacket is wonderful, the best yet and exactly what I wanted.[2] I wouldn't change the title for anything now.

Thanks.
F Scott Fitzgerald

[1] *Tales of the Jazz Age.*
[2] The dust jacket, by John Held, Jr., showed a dance scene.

TO: Edmund Wilson
Before 26 May 1922

ALS, 1 p. Yale University

Dear Bunny:

Havn't heard a word from the Theatre Guild. Did you ever give them the play[1]

Scott F.

626 Goodrich
St Paul.

For God's sake write me some dope on
(1) your play[2]
(2) undertaker[3]
(3) Literary Gossip ect ect ect ect
I think I dedicated my next book (Tales of the Jazz Age)[4] to you, but I have sent it off + I am not sure.[5]

[1] *The Vegetable* was produced in 1923 by Sam H. Harris.
[2] Possibly *The Crime in the Whistler Room* (1924).
[3] *The Undertaker's Garland* by Wilson and Bishop (1922).
[4] *Tales of the Jazz Age* was dedicated to Fitzgerald's mother. *The Vegetable* was dedicated: TO KATHERINE TIGHE AND EDMUND WILSON, JR. WHO DELETED MANY ABSURDITIES FROM MY FIRST TWO NOVELS I RECOMMEND THE ABSURDITIES SET DOWN HERE. Miss Tighe was a St. Paul friend of Fitzgerald's.
[5] Added vertically in the left-hand margin.

TO: Maxwell Perkins ALS, 3 pp. Princeton University
28 May 1922

F. SCOTT FITZGERALD
HACK WRITER AND PLAGIARIST
SAINT PAUL MINNESOTA[1]

Dear Mr. Perkins:

Your letter is at hand. I am glad you are taking the little man off the cover + all the jazz lettering and making it absolutely uniform with my other books (My God! There are almost four of them now!

I am thinking of starting a new novel this summer.

Use any typography you want for the Jazz Age. You can count on it running pretty close to a hundred thousand words.

As I am inserting two new things I will want another proof on the Table on Contents. Who did I dedicate it to? I've forgotten. It will reach you *sure* before the 15th.

Greatly to my distress I am compelled to ask you for money—for $1500.00 if it is convenient and O.K. If all right will you deposit it right away in The Chatham + Phenix Bank, 33d St.

How do you like my stationary?

What is the date on *Jazz Age*. First I was strong for Nov 15th but on thinking it over perhaps Oct 15th or even September would be better. What do you think?

As Ever
Scott Fitzg—

[1] Printed letterhead.

TO: Harry W. Winslow

ALS, 1 p. Unlocated[1]
St. Paul, Minnesota

For Harry W. Winslow A.B; M.D; PH.D
from
The Very Reverend F. Scott Fitzgerald
Archbishop of the Church of
St. Voltaire
Patterson, New Jersey.

"Now is the time for all good men to come to the aid of the party."

Ezekiel III V.2

May 31st, 1922

A self portrait of Mr. Fitzgerald just after the battle of Gettysburg

[1] *The Scriptorium* catalog (August 1972), #30.

TO: Edmund Wilson ALS, 1 p. Yale University
Summer 1922

White Bear Yatch Club, White Bear Lake, Minn.
new address

Dear Bunny:

Thanks for the funniest picture (of John + Margaret[1]) that I ever saw. Thanks ever so much for all the trouble you have taken with my play. I'd be delighted to have Mary Blair[2] show it to Craven + Bennet,[3] but I fear the former will write his own plays from now on + I doubt if the latter could see himself in the leading part. I wish you'd get *both* copies back from the theatre guild if you can. I don't think it would pay to have it published before production, unless I had other plays to put with it. My two one-act things are to be in my autumn collection (*Porcelain + Pink + Mr Icky* I mean). I am ordering Ullyses + will watch for your review—also New Jersey article.

You told me your novellette was not to be published in *The Smart Set*—it was for that I was commiserating you. What in God's name is the date on the *Undertaker*. I am thinking of starting a new novel or else writing another play. Wife + child both beautiful and healthy

Scott Fitzg—

I must stop. I have just seen a beautiful landscape and am unstrung.

[1] John Peale and Margaret Bishop.
[2] Actress who married Wilson in 1923.
[3] Broadway actors Frank Craven and Richard Bennett.

TO: Maxwell Perkins ALS, 1 p. Princeton University
14 June 1922

Dear Mr. Perkins:

I have the Jazz Age corrected all save one story + am sending it on Friday (day after tommorrow). Personally I think it's a million miles ahead of *Flappers* + a darn good book.

I have been lazy this month, trying to outline a new novel—consequently I am financially barren. Do you suppose ect? and Is it possible? ect. Am I good for another $1000.00. If I am I wish you'd deposit it for me in The Chatham + Phenix. If not, let me know by wire as I want to start to draw against it.

Is there any news on the B.+D.? If you see ~~Tom~~ Boyd tell him I've written Wilson about him + Wilson's ~~address~~ is 777 Lexington. As Ever

F Scott Fitzg—

Yatch Club, White Bear Lake, Minn.

TO: Maxwell Perkins
25 June 1922

ALS, 2 pp. Princeton University
White Bear Lake, Minnesota

Sunday,

Dear Mr Perkins:

The third section went to you Saturday + has no doubt reached you by this time. I neglected to put the section titles on separate pages and sending them.

The first title should, of course, come on a page before the first story. It is

My Last Flappers.

The second title should come on the page before The Diamond as Big as the Ritz. It is

Fantasies.

The third title which should come before the story The Lees of Happiness, has been changed from "And So Forth" to

Unclassified Masterpieces.

This arrangement may not seem seem to jibe with the table of contents but I have it all straight + will correct the Table of Contents as soon as you send me a proof of it.

I have numbered the 11 stories in order.

I hope you will be able to read the galley proofs and offer me any suggestions about cutting.

As Ever
F Scott Fitzgerald

TO: Maxwell Perkins
July 1922

ALS, 4 pp. Princeton University
White Bear Lake, Minnesota

Dear Mr Perkins:

I suspect you're on your vacation so I wrote the edit. dept. to deposit $1000.00 for me if possible.

The coupons were recieved but only two.[1] If its not two much trouble I wish your secretary would clip all that are due up to now. The proof of the Table of Contents came and I will correct it as you suggest. They did not send me the one which I had already partly corrected so I will put in both the new corrections and the old ones + return it tomorrow.

Thanks for the list of money remitted in 1921. As I feared I underestimated my earnings by $2,600. I will make the correction sometime this year

Were *Paradise* and *Flappers* published by the same people as the *B+D* in Canada + Austrailia respectively?[2] Also, another matter—you remember that Collins was to pay an advance on *This Side of Paradise.*

Do you remember how much it was? And will you let me know if you have it on record?

Whatever it was I recieved it in England, minus 10%. Now whether you got that 10% or whether it went to an English agent and you are still due 10% from the money I recieved I do not know.

Collins writes me that *Flappers* has not gone so well but that he hopes for the *B+D.*

Will the *Jazz Age* sell for $2.00? And what do you imagine will be its date?

I am asking you 1,000,000 questions, I know, but I am rather at sea about everything and they all bear on my problems. I have been working on a variety of things. Have written a remarkable play which just needs 2 wks. work to go on B'way next fall + have to get that started to write a novel. Also am bickering with 2 men who want to do *Paradise* as a movie with Zelda + I. in the leading rolls. Do not think it best to start a novel until I recieve a large amount either from play or movie or stories and have plenty of liesure. Especially as The *B.+D.* was not a big financial success and *Tales of the Jazz Age* probably will not be.

In fact I'm rather discouraged. Our expenses seem to grow bigger and my earning capacity smaller. I wish to God The B.+D. would pass the 40,000 mark + don't understand why it doesn't. I still get clippings showing it in demand all over the country.

Zelda sends her best. Don't forget to answer all questions

As Ever.
Scott Fitzg

[1] Fitzgerald had invested in a bond.

[2] *The Beautiful and Damned* was published in Canada by Copp, Clark, and sold in Australia by Collins. *This Side of Paradise* was sold in Canada by Copp, Clark, and in Australia by Whitcombe & Tombs. *Flappers and Philosophers* was sold in Canada by Copp, Clark, and in Australia by Whitcombe & Tombs.

TO: Maxwell Perkins — ALS, 1 p. Princeton University
July 1922 — White Bear Lake, Minnesota

Dear Mr. Perkins:

Enclosed are the revised proofs. If you have the other set I corrected please them so that there will be no confusion. I'm sorry I've had to do this. Please charge me with whatever it costs. I think that with the title, the jacket + the table of contents the *Jazz Age* will get a lot of publicity and may sell ten or fifteen thousand copies.[1] I don't suppose such an assorted bill-of-fare as these eleven stories, novellettes, plays + 1 burlesque has ever been served up in one book before in the history of publishing.

You mentioned in one letter that you did not like the type arrangement of The Table of Contents.[2] I think myself that there is something the matter with it—but I think the trouble proceeds from too many story titles + section titles. And I doubt if it could be repaired except by leaving out the section titles which of course I don't want to do.

As Ever.
F Scott Fitzgerald

[1] The first printing was 8,000 copies, followed by two printings in 1922; the total number of copies is not known.
[2] Fitzgerald wrote humorous annotations for the contents page.

TO: Maxwell Perkins
Mid-July 1922

ALS, 1 p. Princeton University

The Yatch Club,
White Bear Lake.

Dear Mr. Perkins:

Glad you liked the addenda to the Table of contents. I feel quite confident the book will go. How do you think *The Love Legend* will sell? You'll be glad to know that nothing has come of the movie idea + I'm rather glad myself. At present I'm working on my play—the same one. Trying to arrange for an Oct. production in New York. Bunny Wilson (Edmund Wilson Jr.) says that it's without *doubt* the best American comedy to date (that's just between you and me.)

Did you see that in that Literary Digest contest I stood 6th among the novelists? Not that it matters. I suspect you of having been one of the voters.

Will you see that the semi-yearly account is mailed to me by the 1st of the month—or before if it is ready? I want to see where I stand. I want to write something *new*—something extraordinary and beautiful and simple + intricately patterned.

As Usual
F Scott Fitzgerald

TO: A. L. Sugarman[1] — Inscription in *The Beautiful and Damned*. Bruccoli
2 August 1922

To a bookseller

Who declares himself
to be $\frac{3}{8}$ tight and promises
the other $\frac{5}{8}$ before night
and says he wouldn't
try to be too damn
clever if he was me —
after compromising with
you on this description,
A. L. Sugarman, I officially
declare myself to be —.

F. Scott Fitzgerald

and swear from this day
forward to take all books
to be autographed into the next room.

[1] Minneapolis bookseller.

TO: Arthur William Brown[1] ALS, 3 pp. Unlocated[2]
Fall 1922

To Mr. Brown—

Dear Mr. Arthur William Brown:

The story concerns a poor boy, his rise and his attempts to win a rich girl. He first sees her when he is a caddy about 14 years old and she is a little "*belle laide*" of 11. She comes on the golf course with her nurse carrying her clubs and tries to get a caddy. The sight of her stirs the poor boy to give up his job of caddying—He is too proud to caddy for a little girl as young as that—

He rises in the world. At 25 he is a guest at the golf club where he has been a caddy. He swims out to a raft one moonlit night. She comes by in a motor boat + they go surf-board riding under the moon (as you know in the inland lakes surfboard riding means being pulled behind a motor-boat on a board. They take turns.

My other scenes do not offer much pictorial possibility. I have just destroyed the second part of the story + am doing it over again—so I hope you can get two illustrations from the 1st page of this letter. Here are some suggestions.

(1) Little girl nervous at her 1st appearance. Nurse also out of depth + afraid to adress caddy. Caddy looking on intently.

(2) Little girl trying to hit nurse with golf club. Caddy looking on admiringly Caddy is a blond. Nurse is white linnen

(3) Caddy telling flabbergasted caddy-master that he won't caddy ever again. Little girl + nurse looking on—not sure enough of themselves to be angry. By the way the little girl is dark. And I have stressed in the story that she has big eyes + her lips turn down at the corners

(4) Man on raft. Girl hailing him from motorboat. Moonlight. Girl beautiful—lips turn down in corner.

(5) Man driving motorboat and girl on surfboard or vice-versa. Moonlight.

I'm sorry my suggestions are so few + so fragmentary but Mr. Hovey has asked me for them right away + it has been a most peculiar story—not nearly so obvious as it sounds here. I like all your work very much and was tremendously pleased at your illustrations for "The Camel's Back" and for "The Jellybean."

Most Sincerely
F Scott Fitzgerald

If you want a 3d picture there is a scene where the heroine—same age as in surf-board scene—drives a mashie-shot into the belly of a member of a foursome playing ahead of her. The foresome is composed of hero (25 yrs. old), one man of thirty—silly ass—and two old men—one of whom got hit in belly

[1] Illustrator of "Winter Dreams," *Metropolitan* (December 1922). In his unpublished memoirs, provided by Marcella Holmes, Brown wrote: "One day in 1920 the Saturday Evening Post sent me the galley proofs of a story to be illustrated, called 'The Camel's Back.' . . . In the next few years I did many of his stories for different magazines. 'The Camel's Back' was the first thing of his that the Post purchased. He was always late on deadlines and often I would have to make drawings from his vague descriptions."

[2] Cataloged in *Charles Hamilton Auction Number 111* (23 March 1978).

TO: H. L. Mencken
September 1922

Inscription in *Tales of the Jazz Age*.
Enoch Pratt Library
St. Paul, Minnesota

For the notorious
H. L. Mencken

under whose apostolic blessing five
of these things first saw the light.

from

F Scott Fitzgerald

Please read the Table of Contents

TO: Gelett Burgess[1] ALS, 1 p. University of California—Berkeley
c. October 1922

Great Neck, Long Island.

Dear Mr. Gellett Burgess:

My excuse for not answering your very kind letter is that I have been moving myself east, and family also. I have been enormously amused by the razzing of poor Liveright for his indescretion and also by the report that I arose and said

"Volstair—Volstair"!

and sat down.

As a matter of fact I wish I had but I couldn't think of anything so clever.[2]

Anyways you were an awfully good egg to console me with such a comforting note. I hope we'll meet soon + lunch together or something

Sincerely
F Scott Fitzgerald

[1] Humorist; author of "The Purple Cow" and "Are You a Bromide?"

[2] This occasion was reported in an unlocated clipping: "Horace B. Liveright, Gelett Burgess, F. Scott Fitzgerald and Others of Authors' League Fellowship Help Along 'Friendly Discourse.' "

TO: Mrs. Richard Taylor ALS, 2 pp. Princeton University
After October 1922

Great Neck, Long Island

Dear Cousin Cecie:

The pictures are wonderful—also you are a very sweet person (as always) to write me about Tales of the Jazz Age. We are established in the above town very comfortably and having a winter of hard work. I'm writing a play which I hope will go on about the 1st of Jan. I wish you could arrange to come up for the opening.

Great Neck is a great place for celebrities—it being the habitat of Mae Murray, Frank Craven, Herbert Swope, Arthur Hopkins, Jane Cowl, Joseph Santley, Samuel Goldwyn, Ring Lardner, Fontayne Fox, "Tad," Gene Buck, Donald Bryan, Tom Wise, Jack Hazard, General Pershing. It is most amusing after the dull healthy middle west. For instance at a party last night where we went were John McCormick, Hugh Walpole, F.P.A, Neysa Mcmien, Arthur William Brown, Rudolph Frimll + Deems Taylor. They have no mock-modesty + all perform their various stunts apon the faintest request so its like a sustained concert. I

don't know when we're going to have a chance to see you again. Zelda hasn't seen her mother now for almost two years and it doesn't look as tho we'll be able to get south till Spring.

Our Love to All of you
Yr. Devoted Cousin
Scott

FROM: Thomas Boyd
December 1922

ALS, 2 pp. Princeton University

Dear Scott:

To attempt to tell you of my honest gratitude would only show up my inability fully to express myself. When Scribner's turned down Through the Wheat I cried on reading the letter of rejection—as I also did when I wrote certain parts of the book. And besides, I felt that so long as it remained unpublished I could never write anything else: the best of which I am capable is in Through the Wheat, and to dam that would be to dam all subsequent transcriptions of thoughts and experiences. I feel quite aware that it is only through you and your inexhaustable exuberance that Scribner's took the book. I hope for all of your sakes that it exhausts one edition. Strange, but I doubted that you would like it; why, I don't know. And when I sent it I did not believe that you intended doing with it. I thought you wanted only to read it. Well, it was a surprise. The wire came early in the morning over the telephone and getting me angrily out of bed at seven—I had not planned to do anything with it for five or six more years. But while the ms. was sunk my ambition was sunk also. You know how much I appreciate what you have done, don't you.

The book shop is moved under the Womens City Club. It now has spacious and luxurious quarters. Alenèr Crosby has died which has had no effect upon *us*. Did you read Peggy's review of The Jazz Age?[1] Van[2] and I sent you a book today and it is a Christmas remembrance. It went early for fear, if it didn't, it would arrive late.

Perkins doesn't want to publish my book until Fall. What do you counsel?

If there ever is time in this Christmas *rush* I will write—

Love to Zelda
Tom

Peggy of couse inundates you both with pleasurable feeling toward you.

[1] *St. Paul Daily News* (10 December 1922).
[2] Cornelius Van Ness, Boyd's partner in the Kilmarnock Bookstore, St. Paul.

TO: C. O. Kalman[1] ALS, 3 pp. Princeton University
After 10 December 1922

Great Neck, L.I.

Dear Kaly:

I thought the enclosure might amuse you, as confirming a prophetic conversation we had in St. Paul. The conversation followed this scene:

Act I

The Kalman's house at Dellwood

Scott (to Lou Ordway[2])—"By the way, Lou, did you get that check I sent you?"

(He had lent me $5.00 the week before when a picnic caught me without my pocket-book)

Lou "No I didn't."

Scott (greatly surprised) "That's funny. I'm sure I addressed it right."

Lou "I never got it."

(Scott gives Lou $5.00 cash on the spot. Reports incident to C. O. Kalman next day. C. O. Kalman cynically advises Scott to look through his bank statement)

Act II

The enclosure

Curtain

First let me thank you for all your trouble about the Kahlert + Berg business.[3] I appreciate the time you devoted to it and especially your interest and advice in the matter.

What I'll do with the script I don't know. The B.+D. will not boost its chances. Kaly, Zelda and I saw it Sunday at the Strand and its by *far* the worst movie I've ever seen in my life—cheap, vulgar, ill-constructed and shoddy. We were utterly ashamed of it. I only hope you don't lose any money by it—and that's that.

Your letter of the 3d amused us both enormously. Ring is now on the wagon for a year at his wife's urgent request (as per your letter. We're going to try to go to Europe in the spring if we can afford it. The Metropolitan Magazine has, thank God, gone into the hands of a reciever and now I can write some stuff for the Post + perhaps collect on a few movie rights. Famous Players have been dickering for me to write a story for Bebe Daniels but its all in the air.[4]

Tales of the Jazz Age has sold beautifully. My poor play is still in abeyance. Blythe Daly, daughter to your friend Arnold, came over the other night. We didn't like her very much—affected, scrawny + not particularly amusing.

Scribner has now accepted Tom Boyd's book *Through the Wheat.* Its a wonder, I think. We expect you in February

Our best to both of you

Scott F—

Clip signature on dotted lines.

[1] St. Paul businessman. The Fitzgeralds and the Kalmans became close friends during the Fitzgeralds' 1921–22 residence in St. Paul.

[2] St. Paul boyhood friend of Fitzgerald.

[3] William G. Kahlert and Einar A. Berg were proprietors of Outlook Photoplays, Inc., of New York, which produced a movie version of Sinclair Lewis' *Free Air* in St. Paul. On 25 August 1922 Fitzgerald granted Kahlert and Berg movie rights to *This Side of Paradise* for $3,000 against a 15% share of the profits. The assignment was canceled on 12 December, when Kahlert and Berg failed to make the payment. The rights were sold to Famous Players–Lasky in 1923, but the movie was not made.

[4] Fitzgerald did not work on this movie.

TO: Thomas Boyd and Cornelius Van Ness — ALS, 1 p. Princeton University
After 10 December 1922

Great Neck, Long Island Dear Van + Tom—	Prelude
The book is mavellous, both in content and exterior, in close-ups and long shots. I have never heard of the gentleman with whom it is chiefly concerned but presume him to be one of our cleaner American humorists.	Gay Opening
Seriously I'm reading it now and enjoying it immensely—as I should the definative biography of my favorite poet. Thank you both immensely for the present and for the remembrance.	More Serious Stuff
Tom's namesake Earnest is coming out over New Years. Saw our own Mencken here in N.Y. today. If you want a good laugh see the screen version of the B.+D.	News Section
My love to both of you + to your wives and children with the august thanks and blessings of	Climax
Yours Ever F. Scott Fitzgerald	Fade Out

Released by Fitzgerald-Artcraft
to 4th + Cedar Sts.

TO: Thomas Boyd
December 1922

ALS, 4 pp. Princeton University
Great Neck, Long Island

Dear Tom:

While I'm in favor of Spring publication I wouldn't push it if I were you. One other thing—if Scribners object to a word or two—they don't mind "whore" + "goddamned" but they may chalk *merde* + *Oh christ* on the proof, maybe not—I wouldn't kick about it. I've sacrificed "Christ" several times.

In order to help along the idea of Spring publication I made those few minor changes myself—in brief they are

(1.) I'll, you'll, it's ect for I will, you will and it is in dialogue. I may have missed a few + you better pick them up in the proofs.

(2) About 4 sentences of Hick's philosophy—his occasional Mr. Britlingism.[1] Its not good, its stale + it doesn't fit Hicks. Hicks is a rather incoherent kid + his intelligence is *suggested* + not shown. On page one I put "Young Hicks" for the 1st "William Hicks" + I think it was a good move. If you give the impression that he's 25 or so you'd have to do as Perkins says and show more of his background. This is the best way to get around it by hinting that he's 19—as he actually was

(3) The satire was too heavy hitting in the Major Generals speech. I softened some of his coarsest inner refections.

(4) Just to hurry it along I supplied a few missing words where you left blanks. "The stars came out like ——" I put in "eyes" (which is cheap) just because of the printing. You can fix it in proof.

(5) I changed the "beast" to "the animal   Its not as good but you'd better keep it—"Beast" got a connotation of sentimal allegory in the more hysterical days of the war + people will think you're referring to "German Imperialism" or some such rot like Blasco Ibanez.[2] If you can think of a better word than animal put it in

(6) About a dozen little corrections—misprints, misspellings ect ect.

If you don't like any of these changes you can change them back in the proof. I'm pulling for Spring publication + I suggested a few blurbs to Scribner.

Have had some dealings with *Famous Players*. I suggested The Love Legend to them. I quote in part from the letter of the head of the scenario dept

> I looked up Woodward Boyd's "THE LOVE LEGEND" and find it makes wonderful reading, but the connected stories are so indeterminate in their results that it does not seem to me it would make a picture without such extensive re-writing as to destroy the original entirely. I certainly agree with you, however, that it is a very interesting story.
>
> Sincerely,
> Johnson[3]

Best to Peggy. Glad the acceptance made you happy. It needn't have. The more I see the book the more I'm convinced that its a perfectly superb piece of work. Quite as good as The Red Badge of Courage—which, by the way, you can now safely read. Be sure + send Peggy's review

Thine
FScottF

P.S. I suggested a marine green binding with a white tab or label on the front. Perkins agrees[4]

[1] Refers to *Mr. Britling Sees It Through* (1916) by H. G. Wells.
[2] Vincente Blasco-Ibáñez, author of *The Four Horsemen of the Apocalypse* (1916).
[3] Fitzgerald clipped and pasted on the paragraph from Johnson's letter.
[4] *Through the Wheat* was bound in a standard Scribners binding, without a label.

FROM: John Peale Bishop
and Edmund Wilson
1922

ALS, 1 p. Princeton University

To Zelda and Scott Fitzgerald, in the earnest belief that this book[1] deserves for to outsell This Side of Paradise—

Edmund Wilson, Jr.
John Peale Bishop

[1] *The Undertaker's Garland* (1922).

TO: Guy Holt[1]
c. 1922/1923

ALS, 1 p. University of Virginia

Great Neck, L.I.

Dear Holt:

You're asking me to read 50,000 words of the most terrific bunk.[2] If you're willing to let yours or Cabell's judgement serve for mine I'm perfectly willing for you to use my name. But I have no secretary and I know from experience that these things take up an awful lot of time. Movie publicity is not of the faintest value to book writers unless their sales go over two hundred thousand per vol.

I'd love to lunch with you. I will phone you when I'm next in

Sincerly
F Scott Fitzgerald

[1] Editor at Robert McBride & Co.
[2] Holt was editing *Jurgen and the Law* (1923), a protest against the suppression of James Branch Cabell's novel; he had solicited a statement from Fitzgerald.

TO: T. R. Smith[1]
1922–1924

ALS, 1 p. Unlocated

Great Neck, L.I.

Dear Tom:

The books arrived and I'm looking forward eagerly to reading the coon volume + the English book. The Waldo Frank novel[2] is I'm afraid just his usual canned rubbish. He seems to me to be an ambitious but totally uninspired person under the delusion that by filching the most advanced methods from the writers who originated them *to express the moods of their definate personalities,* he can supply a substitute for his own lack of feeling and cover up the bogus "arty-ness" of his work. He strains for a simile until his belly aches and brings up a mess of overworked words "lived and loved," "bronzed face" ect ect ect—three to a page. His horror of the cliche is entirely Freudian—and a man incapable of the disassociation of ideas can never think in any words except those that are immortally paired. His prose is of the relative importance of the bogus Ossian which colored theological writing in North Carolina from 1840–1847. I'm afraid Horace[3] has made a bad guess on him. I wish to God you'd republish Gertrude Stien's "Three Lives" and expose some of these fakers. Her book is utterly real. Its in her early manner before the attempt to transfer the technique of Mattisse + Picasso to prose made her coo-coo.

Thanks ever so much for sending the books. Come out again soon.

As Ever
F Scott Fitzgerald

[1] Editor at Boni & Liveright.

[2] Boni & Liveright published four of Frank's novels while Fitzgerald was living in Great Neck: *Rehab* (1922), *Holiday* (1923), *The Unwelcome Man* (1923), and *Chalk Face* (1924).

[3] Liveright.

TO: Maxwell Perkins
January 1923

ALS, 1 p. Princeton University
Great Neck, Long Island

Great Necking

Dear Mr. Perkins:

Thanks for "The hole in the sky"—its supreme.[1] Poor Andy. It opens up a vista—Jerry's[2] political enemies should *not* despise him—they should think of the poor ineffectual egg as a dangerous, vicious man—letting the audience themselves discover this is harmless.

Just finished my first Hearsts story[3] and am going to read *Magic Lanterns*[4] last of this week.

You evidently forgot to inclose the vitagraph letter[5]

Sincerely Thine
F Scott Fitz—

[1] Unidentified.

[2] Jerry Frost in *The Vegetable*.

[3] In December 1922 Fitzgerald contracted with the Hearst magazines for an option on his 1923 story output. The first story submitted was "Dice, Brass Knuckles & Guitar," *Hearst's International* (May 1923).

[4] A 1923 collection of plays by Louise Saunders, Perkins' wife, published by Scribners.

[5] Vitagraph was a movie company.

TO: Maxwell Perkins
Early 1923

ALS, 2 pp. Princeton University
Great Neck, Long Island

Dear Mr. Perkins:

I read Jackolanterns[1] and enjoyed it enormously—while I don't think [Jackolanterns] is a very good selling title I've wracked my brains to think of a better one which would convey the spirit of the plays, and without success.

It really is an excellent book—quite Dunsanyesque: I liked them in the following order

(1) King + Commoner
(all except the "jester" part which seemed a little obvious
(2) Poor Maddalena
(3) Our kind
(which I had read before in the S.S.)
It strikes me as being enormously witty
(4) Figureheads
(5) See-saw (which I didn't like nearly so well as the others.

If the plays had been on the order of *Our Kind* as I thought they were, I would certainly have reccomended a Shavian title—but as the proportions of fantasies are three to two the name has got to be in keeping with them.

It seems to me they ought to sell, but of course they'll be in competition with these three anthologies of one-acters which I see are on the market. As in the case of the Dunsany things an attempt to sell them by Babbitry would merely vulgarize them.

"Saunders hits bull's eye with red-blooded fantasy."

—So I am out of my province. I've enjoyed reading them immensely + want to talk to you about them when I come in this week.

Sincerely
F Scott Fitzgerald

[1] *Magic Lanterns.*

TO: Holger Lundbergh[1] — ALS, 1 p. Princeton University
Early 1923(?) — Great Neck, Long Island

Dear Mr Lundberg:

In the long sad tale of an author's correspondence it seldom he recieves such a pleasant, appreciative and intelligent letters as yours. Of course the Scandanavians as the present heroes of the Nordic theory can stand anything in the way of a slight—but I will say that the *Ice Palace* was written in the middle of a Minnesota winter when I felt that I could have been blood-brother to a warm-blooded ethiope. Its utterly unfair of course to judge a race by its lowest class.

It might interest you to know that I'm writing or rather have written a play which I hope will appear soon. I'm not starting my new novel until Spring.

With many thanks for your kind letter + hopes that we may some day meet I am

Sincerely
F Scott Fitzgerald

[1] Swedish-born poet and magazine writer.

TO: Edmund Wilson — ALS, 1 p. Yale University
Before March 1923

Great Neck, L.I.

Dear Bunny:

Nominating Ring Lardner as America's most popular humorist,[1]

Because he is really inimitable, as is shown by the lamentable failure of his many imitators,

Because he does not subscribe to a press-clipping bureau and is quite unaware of the critical approval he is recieving in recondite circles,

Because he is frequently covered with bruises from being the Yale football team against his four Harvard-bound boys.

And finally because with a rare, true ear he has set down for the enlightenment of posterity the American language as it is talked today

---

Dear Bunny: Chop this up if you want. See you soon.

F. S. Fitzgerald

[1] "We Nominate for the Hall of Fame," *Vanity Fair*, 20 (March 1923), 71. The published caption reads: "Because he is quite unaware of the approval he is receiving in erudite circles; because he is covered with bruises from representing the Yale football team against his Harvard-bound boys; and finally, because with a rare true ear he has set down for posterity the accents of the American language."

TO: Thomas Boyd
March 1923

ALS, 5 pp. Princeton University

Great Neck—(Force of habit)
c/o A. D. Sayre
6 Pleasant Ave, Montgomery, Ala.

Dear Tom:

Sorry I've been so long in writing:

(1.) Enclosed find check for book. There is a rumor that it is the first of Abelards letters + has been published in English before. Is there any Truth in this?

② The Hearst price was $1750.00 per story. It totals $10,500.00

③ Glenn Hunter is going to do *This Side of Paradise* for Paramount.[1] They paid me fifteen thousand dollars cash for it. So you see I'm now a purse proud millionaire + as good a business man as Hergeshiemer.

④ "The Vegetable" (my same play) comes out on April 15th or 20th. In a previous version Hopkins[2] turned it down. No one has seen this version—it is the 6th +, like all the others, *absolutely perfect*. It will sell 20,000 in book form + be eagerly bid for by 20 managérs—and run one solid year in New York.[3]

⑤ Perkins is a wonder—the brains of Scribners since the old man has moved into another generation. I'd be glad to review Thru the Wheat. I wrote one blurb for it + will try another. I'll see that Wilson reviews it.

⑥ I shall never write another document-novel. I have decided to be a pure artist + experiment in form and emotion. I'm sure I can do it much better than Anderson.

⑦ The butler would let you in with pleasure. We get home around April 1st + you'll have to spend at least a night with us.

⑧ I am offended that Peggy thinks my productive days are so nearly over that I should go to Scribners as a sort of Grant Overton.[4] I assure her I'm not dead yet. Does she imagine that such jobs are well paid?

⑨ I reviewed Grace's book.[5] Thought it was magnificent of its type. Liked it better than *Babbit* as I never could sufficiently tolerate the middle-class booster Babbit to get near him.

⑩ Thanks for the Doran book. I am enjoying it immensely. I feel I should return it to you as obtained under false pretenses but I have no attention of doing so.

⑪ All these "marvellous" places like Majorca turn out to have some one enormous disadvantage—bugs, lepers, Jews, consumptives or philistines.

⑫ I wrote Glenn Hunter's next picture "Braver + Braver."[6] Also he's to play in "This Side of Paradise." A pleasant affiliation as he's a nice kid. Paramount are now paying him $156,000 a year and two years ago he was starving in Central Park

③ You're wise to stick with one publisher. Nobody's ever gained a damned thing by switching around unless they've actually been treated like a son of a bitch

④ St Paul with three weeks more of winter must be hell. Down here it's heaven. Commend me to Peggy.

Yours Prosperously
F Scott Fitzgerald

(No figures in this letter are for publication)

F.S.F

[1] Not produced.
[2] Broadway producer Arthur Hopkins.
[3] *The Vegetable* closed after its Atlantic City tryout. The book sold fewer than 8,000 copies.
[4] Editor and anthologist.
[5] Fitzgerald reviewed Grace Flandrau's *Being Respectable* for *The Literary Digest International Book Review* (March 1923).
[6] Possibly *Grit*, produced by Film Guild (1924).

FROM: Sherwood Anderson — ALS, 2 pp. Princeton University
After 4 March 1923

Dear Fitz—One of my brothers sent me your review of my novel and I read it with delight.[1] It's a kind of satisfaction to get broken away from the ["realist"] notion.

It is pretty evident I did not handle with entire success the notion of the little stone given the daughter by Webster or the fellow in Poor White sitting in the train and playing with the handful of bright stones.[2]

You see it may well be that the idea I have isn't well digested in me. Maybe I'm a [serious] ass. Vulgarity and ugliness often hurt me physically like sitting on a board full of nails.

And at such times some little thing—a well made chair, a bit of jewelry, a touch of color remembered from some painting seems to cheer me up and make me [ ] again.

Wish I had had some chance to talk with you—with neither of us tanked.

Did Boyd—Minneapolis tell you the charming ironic story—how I went about saying you could write but your style bothered me and your people seemed to me insignificant and not worth while, while you were, at the same moment, taking the same shots at me, in the same words.

I grinned with joy when I heard it.

Am in the west—having chucked our well known centers of civilization for the time. Some day I hope really to become acquainted with you and Mrs Fitz.

Sincerely
Sherwood Anderson

[1] Fitzgerald reviewed *Many Marriages* in the *New York Herald* (4 March 1923).

[2] Fitzgerald commented in his review: "Again the significance of the little stone eludes me. I believe it to have no significance at all."

TO: Edmund Wilson
After 18 March 1923

ALS, 1 p. Yale University

6 Pleasant Ave.
Montgomery, Ala

Dear Bunny:

The servants are not permanently gone. They were simply on a vacation and I can get in touch with them if you want. And there's probably plenty of coal in Great Neck by now. In any event why won't you + Mary spend the week-end of April 7th with us?

I'd seen Rascoe's customary botch—He seems to be devoid of any sense of humor. I hope Ring never sees the Fox story.[1]

For a moment you scared me about "The Adding Machine"—I thot someone had my President scene.[2] No news. I'm bored to death.

As Ever
Scott—

[1] Rascoe's "A Bookman's Day Book" column in the *New York Tribune* (18 March 1923) included an anecdote about Fitzgerald and Wilson, and disparagingly repeated a Ring Lardner joke about foxes.

[2] Elmer Rice's surrealistic play *The Adding Machine;* Fitzgerald was concerned that Rice had anticipated the second act of *The Vegetable.*

TO: Thomas Boyd
April 1923

ALS, 2 pp. Elizabeth B. Nash

Great Neck

Dear Tom—

Thanks for the book, the pre-review and the scrumptious inscription[1] and also for liking the Vegetable. Your book is quite a sensation here and you certainly have to thank Perkins for the best press of the spring. As to the sale it depends on that incalculable element—the public mood, the psychological state they're in. There's been so much exploitation lately that its almost impossible for a press to create a mood. However its certainly made you among the literati. I got Wilson to read it. He liked it enormously + is reviewing it. Also I sent a copy to Mencken with sections of the jacket marked off (deleted) lest he get a false impression. He said of Peggy's book[2] in his reply that it was a good substantial canny piece of work marred by some high school crudities. When she gets her royalty report in August please let me know just how many it sold. I gave your name to Charlie Towne of the American Play Co. He is a first class literary agent in case either of you have any commercial short stories. Also he's a damn good man for a young writer to know—I mean he goes everywhere, is entheusiastic and *talks*.

Best to Cornelius   I'm busy as hell. Hope you'll like my review.

As Ever
Scott

P.S. Is *the Vegetable* selling at all there?

[1] Boyd's inscription in *Through the Wheat*: "for F. Scott Fitzgerald the most generous and engaging individual I've ever known—and without whom Saint Paul is a pretty sallow spot Thomas Boyd." (Princeton)

[2] *The Love Legend.*

TO: Elinor Wylie[1]
May 1923(?)

Inscription in *The Vegetable.*
Yale University

Eleanor Wylie
poet
Hers admiringly

F Scott Fitzgerald
in memory of
"Liar and Braggard, he had no friend"
which we both agree is the
best American poem to date.

[1] Poet and novelist; Fitzgerald's inscription refers to the first two lines of her poem "Peregrine."

TO: Samuel Hopkins Adams[1]
c. 14 May 1923

ALS, 1 p. Princeton University

Great Neck, L.I.

Dear Mr. X:

Thanks ever so much for the copy of "Flaming Youth." I had of course been reading it as it appeared in the Metropolitan and enjoying it immensely. It will be a great pleasure to start from the beginning and read it thru as I had missed several installments.

Who in the devil are you? Do you know at least a dozen people have asked me if I wrote it. I wish I had but I'm sure I didn't—so who did. Tell me immediately and oblige

Yours Admiringly + Gratefully

F Scott Fitzgerald

[1] Author of *Flaming Youth* (1923), under the pseudonym Warner Fabian.

TO: H. L. Mencken
Before 18 May 1923

Inscription in Thomas Boyd's *Through the Wheat* (1923). Enoch Pratt Library
Great Neck, Long Island

Dear Menck——

This strikes me as something extraordinary good. I got an enormous kick out of it. It's by Boyd of St Paul, who is keeping literature alive west of the Mississippi— Yrs.

F Scott Fitzgerald

TO: A. Philip Randolph[1] Unlocated[2]

Great Neck, L.I.,
May 25, 1923.

DEAR MR. RANDOLPH:

I read THE MESSENGER from cover to cover and thoroughly enjoyed its intelligent editing and its liberal point of view. Many congratulations to you, and many thanks for sending it to me. . . .

Sincerely,
F. SCOTT FITZGERALD.

[1] Leader of the Brotherhood of Sleeping Car Porters and editor of *The Messenger*. The May special book review number of *The Messenger* included a review of *Tales of the Jazz Age*. Fitzgerald was sent a copy of the magazine and was probably asked to respond.

[2] *The Messenger*, 5 (June 1923), 749.

TO: Holger Lundbergh ALS, 1 p. Princeton University
Summer(?) 1923

Great Neck, Long Island

Dear Mr. Lundberg—

Sam Harris has taken *The Vegetable* for fall production and of course I'm very much excited. Earnest Truax (sp) is going to play Jerry. I've just finished reading what I consider is the most wonderful novel of the 19th century—*Le Rouge et Le Noir* by Henri Beyle-Stendahl. Your countryman George Brandes was the first to appreciate—wait tho! He was a Dane on second thought. My new novel is started and progressing—but too slowly. Tonight I'm going to chart out a schedule of work for the rest of the year.

I hope we will meet some day soon. I seldom come to N.Y. now but some of these days I will give you a ring + we must have lunch together

Sincerely
F Scott Fitzgerald

FROM: Max Gerlach[1] ALS, 1 p. Scrapbook. Princeton University
20 July 1923

"THE BEAUTIFUL AND DAMNED"
DOES NOT LOOK ALL OF THAT

F. Scott Fitzgerald, his wife and their 2-year-old daughter, "Scotty," at their summer home on Long Island. Mrs. Fitzgerald is the heroine of her husband's successful novel, "The Beautiful and Damned." —Fotograma

[1] One of the models for Jay Gatsby. Gerlach sent Fitzgerald this clipping with the note: "Enroute from the coast—Here for a few days on business—How are you and the family old Sport?" See Bruccoli, " 'How Are You and the Family Old Sport?'—Gerlach and Gatsby," *Fitzgerald/Hemingway Annual* 1975.

TO: Mary M. Colum[1] ALS, 1 p. State University of New York—Binghamton
c. September 1923

Great Neck, L.I.

Dear Mrs. Colum:

I have turned over your letter to my attorneys and they inform me that your case against me for the stamps is very strong. Perhaps some compromise could be reached. Thanks enormously for writing me. The unanimity with which most of the critics decided that *The Vegetable* would flop on the boards has made me violently anxious for a big success. I have hopes that it'll be in rehearsal within the fortnight.

Bunny Wilson has promised to take me to see you sometime soon. Anticipating the pleasure of the encounter for me, I will now close. Please convey my respects to your husband.

Sincerely
F. Scott Fitzgerald

[1] Critic; wife of writer Padraic Colum.

TO: C. O. Kalman
After 17 November 1923

ALS, 2 pp. Princeton University

Great Neck Long Island
5.30 A.M.
(not so much up already
as up still)

Dear Kaly;—

I hear that you have given two seats to this nonsensical game between the Yale blues vs. the Princeton Elis, to F. Scott Fitzgerald. For what reason, is what I want to know.

Ring W. Lardner

Dear Kaly:

This is a letter from your two favorite authors. Ring + I got stewed together the other night + sat up till the next night without what he would laughingly refer to as a wink of sleep. About 5.30 I told him he should write you a letter. The above is his maudlin extacy.

The tickets arrived and I am enclosing check for same. I'm sorry as the devil you didn't come. We could have had a wonderful time even tho the game was punk.

We took Mr + Mrs Gene Buck (the man who writes the Follies + Frolics.)[1] This is a very drunken town full of intoxicated people and retired debauchés + actresses so I know that you and she to who you laughingly refer to as the missus would enjoy it.

I hope St Paul is cold + raw

I discover this tell tale evidence on the paper[2]

so that you'll be driven east before Xmas.

Everything is in its usual muddle. Zelda says ect, asks, ect, sends ect.

Your Happy but Lazy friend
F Scott Fitzgerald

[1] Buck was a Great Neck resident who was associated with Ziegfeld.
[2] A ring from a wet glass.

TO: Ernest Truex[1] — Inscription in *The Vegetable*. Bruccoli

Ernest Truex
"The best post man in the world"
Atlantic City
Nov 19th, 1923
F Scott Fitzgerald

[1] The leading man in the theatrical production of *The Vegetable*. This copy was inscribed during the tryout of the play; two other copies with the same inscription are known.

TO: Gelett Burgess
c. 1923

ALS, 2 pp. University of California—Berkeley

Great Neck, L.I.

Dear Gelett Burgess:

I located Eleanor the Second Hand[1] at last + read it with much interest. It is written, I see, in much the same sort of staccato prose Hutchinson[2] uses in "If Winter Comes." It seems to me well-constructed, frequently witty and occasionally brilliant as in the cocktail description. It is, however, rather more sentimental than I like a story to be and for this reason seems to me fundamentally unreal. I don't mean that I mind the sentimentalism in the characters but I do mind it being condoned by the author.

However I enjoyed it immensely and I thank you for calling it to my attention. I shall certainly watch for her work in future. I critisize its sentimentality chiefly because I'm so often guilty of the same myself when trying to make a magazine story poignant + moving.

Most Sincerely
F Scott Fitzgerald

[1] Unidentified.
[2] A. S. M. Hutchinson.

TO: Bernard Vaughan[1]
December 1923

Unlocated[2]

Great Neck, L.I.

Dear Bernard: You ask me for the news from literary New York. Outside of the fact that Rebecca West and Frank Swinnerton[3] are in town, there isn't any. Tom Boyd, after being feted on all sides by admirers of his books, got off for France and is sending back short stories for Scribner's Magazine by every boat.

The books of the fall seem to have determined themselves as "A Lost Lady,"[4] Thomas Beer's life of Stephen Crane and Eleanor Wylie's "Jennifer Lorn," a remarkable period romance which just misses—but misses—being a classic. Floyd Dell's new book ("Janet March") is a drab, dull statistic throughout. How such an intelligent, sophisticated man can go on year after year turing out such appalling novels is a question for the psychoanalysts, to whom, I understand, he resorts.

Aldous Huxley's "Antic Hay," while a delightful book, is inferior on all counts to Van Vechten's "The Blind Bow-Boy."

But the real event of the year will, of course, be the appearance in January of the American Mercury. The Smart Set without Mencken and Nathan is already on the stands, and a dreary sight it is. In their nine years' association with it those two men had a most stupendous and far-reaching influence on the whole course of American writing. Their influence was not so much on the very first-rate writers, though even there it was considerable, in many cases as on the cultural background. Their new venture is even more interesting. We shall see what we shall see.

You ask for news of me. There is little and that bad. My play ("The Vegetable") opened in Atlantic City and foundered on the opening night. It did better in subsequent performances, but at present is laid up for repairs.

—Scott Fitzgerald

[1] St. Paul newspaperman who collaborated with Fitzgerald on *The St. Paul Daily Dirge*, a parody newspaper Fitzgerald distributed at a dance in 1922.

[2] *St. Paul Daily News* (23 December 1923), II, 5.

[3] English novelists.

[4] A 1923 novel by Willa Cather.

TO: Thomas Boyd
Early 1924

ALS, 1 p. Princeton University

Great Neck, L.I.

Dear Tom:

I was talking to Perkins on the phone today and he says *The Dark Cloud*[1] is a rather remarkable piece of work. He's going to send me the proof of it. No news here—I've been sweating out trash since the failure of my play but I hope to get back to my novel by March 1st. We're coming abroad either to write it or when its done. I'm not sure which. Zelda got Peggy's letter + sends her best—I enjoyed your letter a lot; you sound just faintly bored but as tho you were getting a lot of work done. Rebecca West + a rather (not *too*) literary crowd are coming out Sunday for a rather formal party + Zelda's scared.

Best to Peggy—Tell her I thot *Lazy Laughter*[2] was fine and I think she ought to have sent me an autographed copy for my library.

Yours in Terrific Haste
Scott

[1] Boyd's second novel (Scribners, 1924).

[2] Scribners (1923).

TO: Moran Tudury[1] ALS, 1 p. Unlocated[2]
Postmarked 11 April 1924 Great Neck, Long Island

I am so anxious for people to see my new novel which is a new thinking out of the idea of illusion (an idea which I suppose will dominate my more serious stuff) much more mature and much more romantic than This Side of Paradise. The B & D was a better book than the first but it was a false lead . . . a concession to Mencken . . . The business of creating illusion is much more to my taste and my talent.

[1] *Adventure* editor.
[2] Samuel T. Freeman catalog (29 June 1979), #41.

For Carl Van Vechten
with all the
proper deference which
authors always
inscribe in their
books on presenting
them to other authors
— but with
real admiration and
envy besides
F Scott Fitzgerald
New York.
Feb 9th 1924.

[1] Music critic and novelist; author of *Peter Whiffle* (1922), *The Blind Bow-Boy* (1923), *The Tattooed Countess* (1924), *Firecrackers* (1925), *Nigger Heaven* (1926), *Spider Boy* (1928), *Parties* (1930).

TO: Thomas Boyd — ALS, 6 pp. Princeton University
May 1924 — Grimm's Park Hotel letterhead. Hyères, France

Dear Tom:

Your letter was the first to reach me after I arrived here. This is the lovliest piece of earth I've ever seen without excepting Oxford or Venice or Princeton or anywhere. Zelda and I are sitting in the café l'Universe writing letters (it is 10.30. P.M.) and the moon is an absolutely *au fait* Mediteraenean moon with a blurred silver linnen cap + we're both a a little tight and very happily drunk if you can use that term for the less nervous, less violent reactions of this side.

We found a wonderful English nurse in Paris for *$26.00 a month* (My God! We paid $90.00 in New York) and tomorrow we're going to look at a villa that has a butler + cook with it for the summer + fall. I have 100 feet of copper screen against the mosquitoes (we brought 17 pieces of baggage) + on the whole it looks like a gorgeous working summer.

We missed Edith Wharton by one day—she left yesterday for Paris + won't return until next season. Not that I care, except that I met her in New York + she's a very distinguished grande dame who fought the good fight with bronze age weapons when there were very few people in the line at all.

I'm going to read nothing but Homer + Homeric literature—and history 540–1200 A.D. until I finish my novel + I hope to God I don't see a soul for six months. My novel grows more + more extraordinary; I feel absolutely self-sufficient + I have a perfect hollow craving for lonliness, that has increased for three years in some arithmetical progression + I'm going to satisfy it at last.

I agree with you about Bunny + Mencken—though with qualifications as to both. Bunny appreciates feeling after its been filtered through a temperment but his soul is a bit *sec*—and in beginning the Joyce cult on such an exalted scale he has probably debauched the taste of a lot of people—(who of course don't matter anyhow)—but these unqualified admirations! Poor Waldo Frank!

My God! Do you know you once (its been a year) thought that *Middleton Murray*[1] was an important man!

Paul Rosenfeld[2] is quite a person—(he admires Sandburg though!)— + the "Port of New York" is quite an adventure in our nervous critical entheusiasm; its nicer tho to be sitting here, to watch slow dogs inspect old posts. (I don't kid myself Ive got away from anything except *people* in the most corporeal sense.)

Well, I shall write a novel better than any novel ever written in America and become par excellence the best second-rater in the world.

Good night old kid
F Scott Fitz—

P.S. Brentano's (Paris) seems to have had some *Thru the Wheat* but are sold out—Max is entheusiastic about The Dark Cloud + promised to send it to me. I made a suggestion about brighter color in the jacket. Between you + me the background of the first proof suggested a story of the steel mills. It should be rather rich, I think, like Melvilles Moby Dick jacket. This is *entre nous*

For Christs sake don't blame Scribners because of that ass Bridges. Perkins + Old Charles would make 20 Bridges bearable. What do you mean you lost $1200.00.

The Jellybean[3] is junk! I've written a fine story called The Baby Party[4] (a bit soft but good stuff) that will appear in Hearsts for July or August.

F.S.F

Message from Zelda ⟶ (Hello *Tom* + *Peggy*)

[1] English critic.
[2] Literary and music critic.
[3] *Metropolitan Magazine*, LII (October 1920).
[4] *Hearst's International*, XLVII (February 1925).

TO: Thomas Boyd — ALS, 2 pp. Elizabeth B. Nash

Villa Marie, Valescure
St. Raphael, Var, France
June 23d, 1924

Dear Tom:

Hyerès proved too hot for summer. I loved it but the bathing was bad + we couldn't find a new clean villa. So we're up the coast between St. Maxime + Cannes in a charming villa we've got untill November 1st.

I saw a lot of Hyeres during the week we were there—the castle on the hill I liked especially—then one day I met a twelve year old girl on the street whose faces had been eaten off with congenital syphillis. She had the back of her head and in front of that nothing but a scab slit three times for her mouth and eyes. It rather spoiled the streets for me.

Anyways after seeing Cannes, Hyeres, Nice, St. Maximes + Antibles I think St. Raphael (where we are) is the lovliest spot I've ever seen. Its simply saturated with Shelley—tho he never lived here. I mean its like the "Eugenean Hills" + "Lines written in Dejection"—cooler than Hyeres, less tropical, less somnolent, perhaps less Romanesque—still Frejus which has aqueducts + is both Roman + Romanesque is in sight of my window.

We have bought a little Reynault car + Zelda + the Baby + the Governess swim every day on a sandy beach—in fact everything's idyllic and for the first time since I went to St. Paul in 1921 (the worst move I ever made in my life) I'm perfectly happy.

Lewis'[1] prosperity makes me boil with envy. I am only asking $25,000 or $20,000 for my novel.[2] Its almost done. The man who sent the remembrance was the manager of your hotel at La Plage d'Hyeres. I spoke to Paul R. Reynolds about your work (he's my agent + the best in New York—The Post people come to see him every week. Liverite[3] isn't any good) and he said he'd like to try your stuff. Explain to him in your letter if you write him (70 5th Ave.) that you wrote *Through the Wheat* + are the man I spoke off. And if you send him anything that Liverite's had be sure + tell him everywhere its been. Send me *The Dark Cloud* please when it appears.

We expect to be in Europe three or four years—maybe longer.

Yours Ever
F. Scott Fitzg—

[1] Sinclair Lewis.

[2] Serial rights to *The Great Gatsby* were not sold. Fitzgerald declined $10,000 from *College Humor*.

[3] Horace Liveright.

TO: Robert Kerr[1] — ALS, 1 p. Doris K. Brown
June 1924

Great Neck—I mean
St. Raphael, France
Villa Marie.

Dear Bob:

Thanks for your letter + for selling the membership many thanks indeed.[2] One hundred and fifty is more than I expected. I hope some time that I may be able to return the favor.

The part of what you told me which I am including in my novel is the ship, yatch I mean, + the mysterious yatchsman whose mistress was Nellie Bly I have my hero occupy the same position you did + obtain it in the same way.[3] I am calling him Robert B. Kerr instead of Robert C. Kerr to conceal his identity (this is a joke—I wanted to give you a scare. His name is Gatsby).

Best to you all from all of us and again thanks enormously for your courtesy + your trouble

Sincerely
Scott Fitzg—

[1] Great Neck friend of the Fitzgeralds.

[2] Fitzgerald's membership in a Great Neck golf club.

[3] As a boy Kerr had been befriended by yachtsman Edward Gilman, and Fitzgerald drew upon Kerr's experiences for Gatsby's association with Dan Cody. See Joseph Corso, "One Not-Forgotten Summer Night," *Fitzgerald/Hemingway Annual* 1976.

TO: Carl Van Vechten
Summer 1924

ALS, 1 p. New York Public Library

Villa Marie, Valescure
St Raphael, France

Dear Carl:

The book[1] is great and you were a mighty good egg to send it to me. I have only finished three chapters as Zelda has snatched it away but the resumé of her past + the 1st "sketches" of Iowa as you call them (the Parcae, the Reception) ect. are unbeatable. I couldn't resist writing you this premature line to thank you.

As Ever
Your Friend
Scott Fitzg—

[1] *The Tattooed Countess* (1924).

TO: Ludlow Fowler
August 1924

ALS, 2 pp. Princeton University

Villa Marie, Valescure
St Raphael, France

Dear Lud: I knew there wasn't a chance of seeing you when your trip was so short but I wrote a note to Sap[1] asking him to drop in on us if he stayed over and got down this far. I sent it care of Eleanor Maurice, American Express. I wonder if he ever got it.

My novel is finished and I'm doing the last revision of it. We've had a quiet summer and are moving on in the fall either to Paris or Italy. I'm going to write another play and I hope it'll be less disastrous than the last.

The real purpose of this letter is sordid + material is this. The field glasses you gave me were out of whack—they showed two ships instead of one and made the Olympic look as if it had 8 smokestacks which can't be true according to the papers.

So I'm going to ask you to send mine to Ring Lardner, Steamship *Paris*, sailing Sept. 10th + he'll bring them to me. And will you wrap a newspaper around them so the Captain won't appropriate them for himself. About yours I'll do just as you say—send them home by somebody or have them fixed in Paris and leave them at some definate place there so you can call for them on your annual jaunt last summer.

I remember our last conversation and it makes me sad. I feel old too, this summer—I have ever since the failure of my play a year ago. Thats the whole burden of this novel—the loss of those illusions that give such color to the world so that you don't care whether things are true or false as long as they partake of the magical glory.

We both send our best love to you, Lud.

Scott

PS. Don't forget the glasses—I'm awfully anxious to get them. I'm sorry I've been such a bother about it.

[1] Sap Donahoe.

TO: Maxwell Perkins
After 8 August 1924

ALS, 1 p. Princeton University

Villa Marie
Valescure, St Raphael
France.

Dear Max:

Thanks for your long + most interesting letter. I wrote you yesterday so this is just a note. I feel like saying "I told you so" about the Bobbs-Merril + Doran books of Rings but I know that it is mostly Bobbs-Merrils fault and a good deal Ring's.[1] The ad was great—especially the Barrie. I imagine that Mr. Scribner was pleased—and a little surprised. Poor Ring—its discouraging that he keeps on drinking—how bored with life the man must be. I certainly think his collection for 1925 should include all *fantasies*. Certain marvellous syndicate articles such as the "fur coat + the worlds series" + the "celebrities day-book" should be saved for the "My Life and Loves" volume.[2] Do read Seldes on Ring in "The Seven Lively Arts." Be sure to. I'll really pay you to do it before making the selections.[3]

As Ever
Scott

[1] Scribners had recently published Ring Lardner's *How to Write Short Stories* at Fitzgerald's urging, and was negotiating for the Lardner volumes previously published by Bobbs-Merrill and Doran.

[2] *What of It?* (Scribners, 1925).

[3] See Perkins' 8 August 1924 letter to Fitzgerald in *Scott/Max*.

TO: Maxwell Perkins — ALS, 2 pp. Princeton University

Villa Marie, Valescure
St Raphael, France
Sept 10th 1924

Dear Max:

I am in rather a predicament. Mr. + Mrs. Gordan Sarre (Ruth Shepley) have my house, as you know, until the 1st day of October—that is for twenty days after the date heading this letter. Now we left in the house for purposes of subletting.

1 Blue figured dinning room rug
1 Stair carpet

and since I want the former I think its advisable to get it out by Oct 1st—otherwise Mrs. Miller may claim its hers, a way landladys have.

As Ring has gone and my others friends there are drunk and unreliable I'm going to ask you to send the enclosed to some reliable New York warehouse and ask them to call for the rugs and store them on Oct 1st.

I have left the name of the warehouse blank as I don't know one—thats why I'm asking you to pick one out + send it to them. I'm sure they do that sort of thing. This is a hell of a thing to ask anybody but I don't know what else to do as everybody in Great Neck is either incapable or crooked. I'm writing the tenants to deliver the property in question. God almighty! If I only knew a warehouse I could do it myself, but I don't.

Tom's book arrived.[1] I've only read 40 pages but so far its remarkably interesting. The writing is curiously crude, almost Drieserian but I suppose that's deliberate.

Now for a promise—the novel will absolutely + definately be mailed to you before the 1st of October. I've had to rewrite practically half of it—at present its stored away for a week so I can take a last look at it + see what I've left out—there's some intangible sequence lacking somewhere in the middle + a break in interest there invariably means the failure of a book. It is like nothing I've ever read before.

As Ever
Scott

[1] Thomas Boyd's *The Dark Cloud.*

TO: Sidney Howard[1] ALS, 1 p. University of California—Berkeley
Winter 1924

Hotel Quirinal, Rome

Dear Sid:

Perkins sent us your book and I can't tell you how extraordinarily good I think the two middle stories are.[2] Especially Transatlantique. I loved Mrs. Vietch too (the grandmothers attitude—with its absolute lack of any appeal to sentimentality) and so did Zelda. She was in fact the first who read the book. Transatlantic however was my favorite. It seems quite as good to me as Katherine Mansfield + Ruth Suckow—the only touch I objected to was when the good sport broke down and wept. But the pool auction, and the engineers story, and all about Harry were wonderful. I felt horribly like Harry all through.

Many congratulations and I hope it sells. Its nice to be able to write you with real entheusiasm because you've liked my books too. Please believe me I look forward to your doing some gorgeous things—if Mrs. Vietch had been only 10,000 words longer it might have been wise to publish it as a short novel + get the rather larger intention that that insures. However several short story books have made enormous hits lately + I hope this gets the attention it diserves. Zelda joins me in congratulations + best wishes

Sincerely
F Scott Fitzgerald

1 Playwright and short-story writer.
2 *Three Flights Up* (1924) included "Mrs. Vietch: A Segment of Biography" and "Transatlantic."

TO: John Myers O'Hara[1] ALS, 1 p. University of Northern Iowa
Postmarked 13 December 1924

Hotel des Princes
Rome, Italy

Dear Mr. O'Hara

The Sapho[2] followed me around Europe + reached me here. We had some people to dinner the night it came + we took turns reading it and almost finished the book. Its gorgeous—I'd always wanted to read

Sapho but I never realized it would be such a pleasure as you've made it.

Thank you, + for your courtesy in sending me a copy thanks again

Sincerely
F. Scott Fitzgerald.

[1] Translator of Greek poetry. Fitzgerald later sent him a copy of *This Side of Paradise* inscribed: "For John Myers O'Hara who first introduced me to Sapho in his translations, with a thousand thanks. 'Much have I travelled in the Realms of gold'? his most cordially, F Scott Fitzgerald, Washington D.C." (*Antiquarian Bookman* [7 July 1975], 99)

[2] *The Poems of Sappho* (1924).

TO: Thomas Boyd
Late 1924(?)

ALS, 1 p. Elizabeth B. Nash

Guaranty Trust Co. Paris.

Dear Tom:

I like the book enormously.[1] First I'll say that. Not quite as well as the first because the style bothered me. Its not as simple as the first—"shore line like a womans neck!" for example.

On the other hand its far bigger feat of imagination—something quite new + more in line with a big development. You might have been a one book man + written the other, but in this you show you have the novelists temperment of sticking within within your own concieved sceme—instead of my talent which is merely to interest people, in the accidental form of writing novels. I want to write you more but Im in the middle of my own last revision[2] + I'm about crazy with nervousness. I'll write again next week. Anyways the book interested me from beginning to end—the fights, the beautifully done idea of the slaves caught in Detroit—all of it. Many congratulations.

As Ever
Scott

[1] *The Dark Cloud.*

[2] *The Great Gatsby* was published before Fitzgerald settled in Paris in May 1925. This letter was probably written from Rome in late 1924, using the Paris forwarding address.

TO: Mrs. A. D. Sayre
1924(?)

Inscription in *The Diary of Otto Braun* (1924). Bruccoli

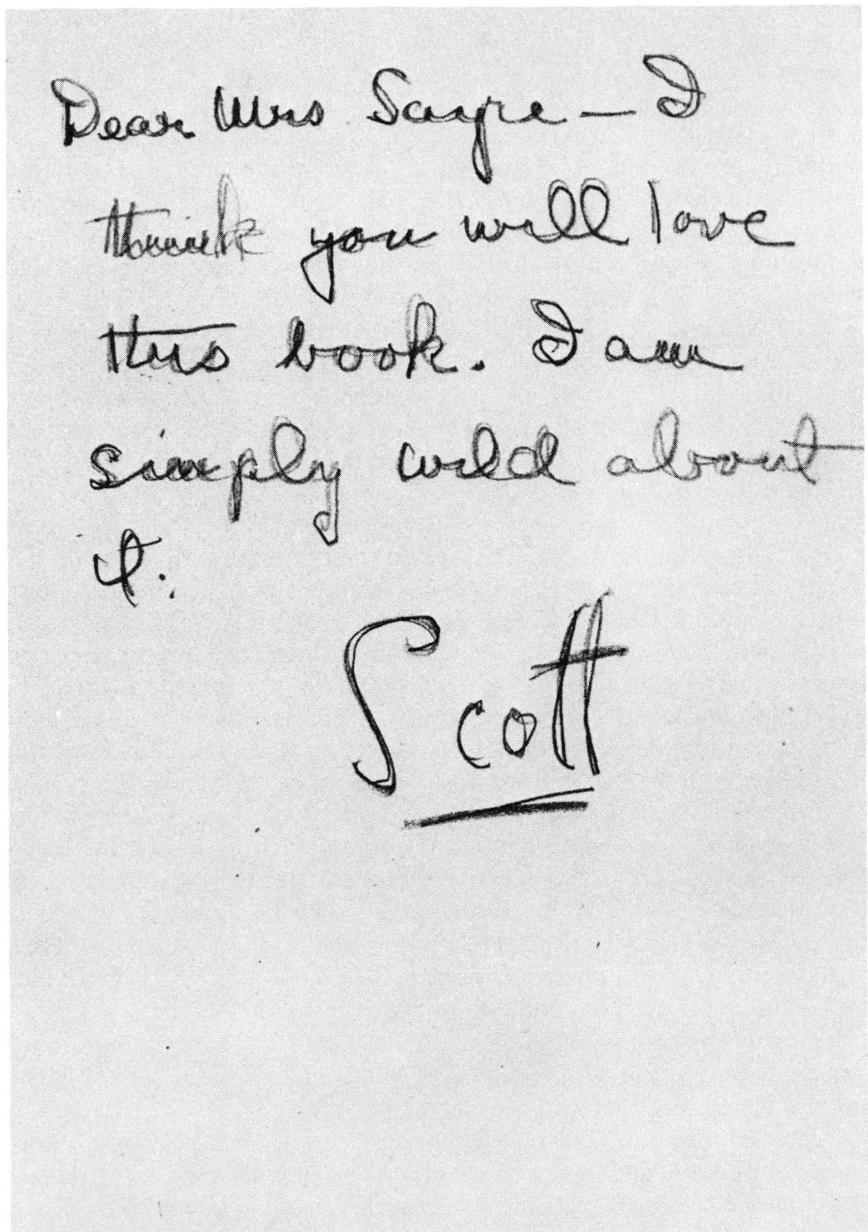
Dear Mrs Sayre—I think you will love this book. I am simply wild about it.

Scott

Note: The inscription was traced over by an unknown hand. Braun was a young German intellectual killed in the war.

FROM: Ring Lardner TL, 3 pp. Princeton University

Friday, January 9, 1925.

Dear Wops:—

You would get a lot more mail from me if you had a decent and permanent address. I hate to write letters and think all the time that they'll never get anywhere.

I have talked with Max Perkins several times since he received Scott's novel. He is very enthusiastic about it, saying it's much the best thing Scott has done since "Paradise," that parts of it are inspired, and etc. He wasn't crazy to have anybody use it serially on account of the delay it meant in getting out the book, but he told me today that "College Humor" had made a good offer which he thought you might accept. "College Humor" seems to be l—y with money and careless of how it spends it—not knocking Mr. Fitzgerald. My brother was strong for the book and wanted "Liberty" to run it, but some of the other readers thought it was better as a book than it would be as a serial, meaning that it couldn't be arranged so that the reader would be left in suspense at the end of each installment.

I've been on the wagon since Armistice Day and Ellis[1] and I have seen a lot of shows. Laurence Stallings' play is a bear, even with a few of the words left out.[2] I see no reason why it shouldn't beat a record or come near it. Dorothy Parker's "Close Harmony" got great notices and was, we thought, a dandy play, but it flopped in three weeks. Dorothy, Beatrice Kaufman and Peggy Leech gave a party at the Algonquin six or seven weeks ago. I was enjoying an intellectual conversation with Mary Hay when Peggy tore me away to talk to a lady who seemed kind of lonely. The lady was Mrs. Ernest Boyd and I'd have been with her yet if June Walker hadn't come in with a bun and rescued me.

We got back from the other side (Europe) in time to see the Yale-Princeton game. Art Samuels was host to a huge party of us—Swopes, Brouns, etc.—at lunch at the Cottage club. The Princeton team, which had made a sucker of Harvard the Saturday before, acted on this occasion as if football was a complete surprise and novelty. We stood up all the way home and I swore it would be my last trip to old Nassau.

Instead of working on the ship coming home, as I intended, I did nothing but lap them up. But as soon as I was home and on the wagon, I wrote the five European articles in nine days.

I have quit the strip[3] and Dick Dorgan is doing it, with help from Tad.[4]

The Society of Composers and Authors, of which Gene[5] is president, gave him a clock for Christmas that must have cost $1000 at least.

Gene and Helen were over the other night and in the midst of one of Gene's stories, Helen said, "Stop picking your nose, sweetheart." That's all the dirt I know.

Speaking of noses, Rube and Irma[6] gave a New Year's Eve party to which 150 people were invited and 300 came. Rube said he never saw so many strangers in his life. Billy Seeman had a lot of the Follies people there to help entertain, but the affair was such a riot that little attention was paid to the entertainment. Ellis and I missed this party. Speaking of noses again, I was in the hospital having my antrum cut open. I'm nearly all right again now, I think, though if I get up suddenly or stoop over, a regular Niagara of blood pours forth from my shapely nostrils.

I took "Vanity Fair" (Thackeray's, not Crowninshield's) to the hospital with me and one day the nurse asked me what I was reading and I told her and she said, "I haven't read it yet. I've been busy making Christmas presents."

Ellis is at present in Danville, Illinois, where her last brother is being married tomorrow to a gal named Bredehoft. I was kept at home by my nose. We are leaving next Tuesday, with the Grant Rices,[7] for Miami and then Nassau, to be gone till nearly the first of March. Our address at Nassau will be New Colonial Hotel. I think I'll take up golf again, but won't stick to it if I don't like it.

And I think you've staid away long enough.

Mrs. Nell.

1 Mrs. Lardner.
2 *What Price Glory?*
3 Lardner provided continuity for a syndicated comic strip, "You Know Me Al."
4 Cartoonist Tad Dorgan.
5 Gene Buck.
6 Cartoonist Rube Goldberg and his wife.
7 Sportswriter Grantland Rice.

TO: Maxwell Perkins
Late January 1925

ALS, 1 p. Princeton University

Rome

American Express Co.

Most important of all, I've thought it over + decided the Tom + Myrtle episode in Chap III isn't half as rough as lots of things in the B.+D. and should stand. Havn't heard from you on the subject but sure you agree

Dear Max:

Three things

(1.) The Plaza Hotel scene (Chap VII) is now wonderful and that makes the book wonderful. It should reach you in 3 days

(2) I hope you're sending Irene de Moirier[1] the page proof and not the galley. Sure!

(3) Didn't you think I was heroic to turn down $10,000.[2] God! I wish I'd been a month earlier with it.

No news. Proof should all reach you within 10 days after this letter

Scott.

Starved for news!!!

[1] Miss de Moirier was planning to translate *The Great Gatsby* into French, but dropped the project.

[2] *College Humor* had offered $10,000 for serial rights to *The Great Gatsby*, which would have delayed publication.

TO: Ludlow Fowler
March 1925

ALS, 2 pp. Princeton University
Capri, Italy

Guaranty Trust Co.
1 Rue des Italiens
Paris

Dear Lud:

This is a last desperate appeal. Twice I've written you in vain—have you or havn't you got my field glasses. If they are permanently mislaid do let me know—I shall accept the fact with equanimity as I had no business to make you responsible for them for six years. But I want to *know* because I need field glasses all the time over here and the ones you lent me are cross-eyed and myoptic and always have been. I don't mind buying a new pair because they add so to every excursion but I'd rather not if there's any chance of getting my own back in June. Are you coming over? What on God's earth has become of you?

Now, having bawled you out I'll give you the news. We've been over a year during which I've done a lot of work, saved money and had a facinating and most instructive time. We have spent the spring here in Capri but next month (April) we go to Paris for 8 mos. so adress me there.

I have written a fifteen thousand word story about you called *The Rich Boy*—it is so disguised that no one except you and me and maybe two of the girls concerned would recognize, unless you give it away, but it is in a large measure the story of your life, toned down here and there and symplified. Also many gaps had to come out of my imagination. It is frank, unsparing but sympathetic and I think you will like it—it is one of the best things I have ever one. Where it will appear and when, I don't as yet know.[1]

Question? How did Connie Bennet take Phil Plants engagement.[2] Had they split up before? Is Judy Smith that 30 year-old prom trotter or another Judy Smith.

How of Virgina, Dot Mc[ ], Ada? The law business? Eleanor and Al? Your Mother? Powell? John Bishop and Ring Lardner send me my only news and I have none at all from you.

With all good wishes and hopes of seeing you in June.

Ever your Friend
Scott

[1] *Redbook* (January and February 1926).
[2] Plant, a millionaire playboy, married actress Constance Bennett in November 1925.

TO: Charles Scribner's Sons — Wire.[1] Princeton University

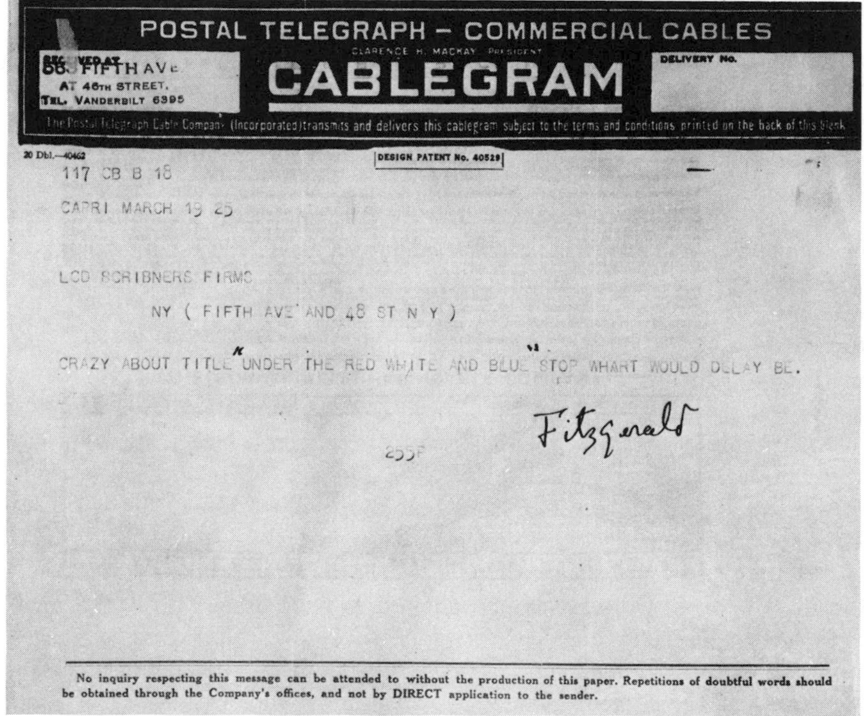

POSTAL TELEGRAPH – COMMERCIAL CABLES
CLARENCE H. MACKAY, PRESIDENT
CABLEGRAM

RECEIVED AT 55 FIFTH AVE AT 46TH STREET. TEL. VANDERBILT 6395

DELIVERY No.

The Postal Telegraph Cable Company (Incorporated) transmits and delivers this cablegram subject to the terms and conditions printed on the back of this blank

20 Dbl.—40462

DESIGN PATENT No. 40529

117 CB B 18

CAPRI MARCH 19 25

LCD SCRIBNERS FIRMS

NY (FIFTH AVE AND 48 ST N Y)

CRAZY ABOUT TITLE UNDER THE RED WHITE AND BLUE STOP WHART WOULD DELAY BE.

Fitzgerald

255P

No inquiry respecting this message can be attended to without the production of this paper. Repetitions of doubtful words should be obtained through the Company's offices, and not by DIRECT application to the sender.

[1] Fitzgerald never felt confident about "The Great Gatsby" as a title and tried to change it shortly before publication. Fitzgerald's name and the quotation marks were written on the wire by Perkins.

Perkins wired that changing the title would delay publication and that he preferred "The Great Gatsby." On 22 March Fitzgerald wired: YOURE RIGHT.

FROM: Ring Lardner TL, 3 pp. Princeton University

March 24th. [1925]

Dears Mr. and Mrs. F.—

Max Perkins reports that Mrs. F. is or has been sick, which we hope isn't true, but would like to know for sure.

I read Mr. F's book (in page proofs) at one sitting and liked it enormously, particularly the description of Gatsby's home and his party, and the party in the apartment in New York. It sounds as if Mr. F. must have attended a party or two during his metropolitan career. The plot held my interest, too, and I found no tedious moments. Altogether I think it's the best thing you've done since Paradise.

On the other hand, I acted as volunteer proof reader and gave Max a brief list of what I thought were errata. On Pages 31 and 46 you spoke of the news-stand on the *lower level,* and the cold waiting room on the *lower level* of the Pennsylvania Station. There ain't any lower level at that station and I suggested substitute terms for same.[1] On Page 82, you had the guy driving his car under the elevated at Astoria, which isn't Astoria, but Long Island City.[2] On Page 118 you had a tide in Lake Superior[3] and on Page 209 you had the Chicago, Milwaukee & St. Paul running out of the La Salle Street Station.[4] These things are trivial, but some of the critics pick on trivial errors for lack of anything else to pick on.

Michael Arlen, who is here to watch the staging of The Green Hat, said he thought How To Write Short Stories was a great title for my book and when I told him it was your title, he said he had heard a great deal about you and was sorry to miss you. He also said he had heard that Mrs. Fitzgerald was very attractive, but I told him he must be thinking of somebody else. Mike is being entertained high and low. He was guest of honor at a luncheon given by Ray Long.[5] Irv Cobb[6] and George Doran[7] sat on either side of him and told one dirty story after another. Last Sunday night he was at a party at Condé Nast's, but who wasn't? I was looking forward to a miserable evening, but had the luck to draw Ina Claire[8] for a dinner and evening companion and was perfectly happy, though I regretted being on the wagon. The last previous time I saw her was at the Press Club in Chicago about eight years ago and she says I was much more companionable on that occasion. George Nathan said he heard you were coming home soon. George, they say, is quitting the associate editorship of the Mercury, but will continue to write theaters for it.

So far as I know, Zelda, Mary Hay[9] and Richard are still together; they were when I met them.

Beatrice Kaufman and Peggy Leech have gone abroad.

We had a dinner party at our little nest about two weeks ago; the guests were the Ray Longs, the Grantland Rices, June Walker[10] and

Frank Crowninshield. As place cards for Ray, Crownie and Grant, we had, respectively, covers of Cosmopolitan, Vanity Fair and The American Golfer, but this didn't seem to make any impression on June and right after the soup she began knocking Condé Nast in general and his alleged snobbishness in particular. Finally Crownie butted in to defend him and June said, "What do you know about him?" "I live with him," said Crownie. "What for?" said June. "Well," said Crownie, "I happen to be editor of one of his magazines, Vanity Fair." "Oh!" said June. "That's my favorite magazine! And I hate most magazines! For instance, I wouldn't be seen with a Cosmopolitan." After the loud laughter had subsided, I explained to her that Ray was editor of Cosmopolitan. "I'm always making breaks," she said, "and I guess this is one of my unlucky evenings. I suppose that if I said what I think of William R. Hearst, I'd find that even he has a friend here or something."

The annual Dutch Treat show[11] comes off this week. I have a sketch in it which is a born flop.

I met Gene on the train the other day and he said, "Come over and play bridge with us tonight," and I said I couldn't because Arthur Jacks was coming to our house. When I got home, I called up Arthur to inform him of this and he said it was tough luck, but it just happened that he had been invited, several days before, to dine at Gene's that very night.

Write.

Bob Esselstyn.

[1] These changes were not made.
[2] This change was not made.
[3] Fitzgerald changed "ebb-tide" to "wind."
[4] The La Salle Street Station was changed to Union Station.
[5] Hearst magazine editor.
[6] Irvin S. Cobb.
[7] Partner in Doubleday, Doran.
[8] Actress.
[9] Actress married to movie actor Richard Barthelmess.
[10] Actress.
[11] New York club for writers and artists.

TO: Willa Cather — ALS, 1 p. Princeton University
Late March/early April 1925

Hotel Tiberio, Capri, Italy

My Dear Miss Cather:

As one of your greatest admirers—an admirer particularly of *My Antonia, A Lost Lady, Paul's Case* and *Scandal* I want to write to explain an instance of apparent plagiarism which some suspicious person may presently bring to your attention.

To begin with, my new book *The Great Gatsby* will appear about the time you recieve this letter (I am sending you the book besides). When I was in the middle of the first draft *A Lost Lady* was published and I read it with the greatest delight. One of the finest passages is the often-quoted one toward the end which includes the phrases "she seemed to promise a wild delight that he has not found in life . . . "I could show you" . . . ect (all misquoted here as I have no copy by me).[1]

Well, a month or two before I had written into my own book a parallel and almost similar idea in the description of a woman's charm—an idea that I'd had for several years. Now my expression of this was neither so clear, nor so beautiful, nor so moving as yours but the essential similarity was undoubtedly there. I was worried because I hated the devil to cut mine out so I went to Ring Lardner and several other people and showed them mine and yours and finally decided to retain it. Also Ive kept the pages from my first draft to show you and am enclosing them here. The passage as finally worked out is in my Chapter One. Hoping you will understand my motive in communicating this to you I am[2]

With Best Wishes and Most Sincere Admiration
F. Scott Fitzgerald

[1] See *A Lost Lady* (New York: Knopf, 1923), pp. 171–72.

[2] Cather's 28 April reply is in Fitzgerald's scrapbook but cannot be quoted. She wrote him that she had enjoyed reading *The Great Gatsby* before receiving Fitzgerald's letter and had detected no duplication of *A Lost Lady*. See Bruccoli, " 'An Instance of Apparent Plagiarism': F. Scott Fitzgerald, Willa Cather, and the First *Gatsby* Manuscript," *Princeton University Library Chronicle*, XXXX (Spring 1978), 171–78.

TO: Robert Kerr
April 1925

Inscription pasted in *The Great Gatsby*.[1]
Doris Kerr Brown
Capri, Italy

Dear Bob:
Keep reading and you'll finally come to your own adventures which you told to me one not-forgotten summer night. Your Friend
F. Scott Fitzgerald

[1] Fitzgerald sent Scribners a number of inscriptions on slips of paper to be pasted in presentation copies.

TO: Van Wyck Brooks[1] — Inscription pasted in *The Great Gatsby*.
April 1925 — Bruccoli
Capri, Italy

Dear Brooks: I'm taking the liberty of sending you this, after having run across a copy of *America's Coming of Age* in a book store here and bought and read it with enormous pleasure.

Capri, Italy.

F Scott Fitzgerald

[1] Literary historian and critic.

TO: Carl Van Doren[1] — Inscription pasted in *The Great Gatsby*.
April 1925 — Unlocated
Capri, Italy

Dear Mr. Van Doren:

This is really not a moral book. I swear before God that if it seems to be I'm going to a psychoanalist

F Scott Fitzgerald

[1] Critic and historian.

TO: Sinclair Lewis — Inscription pasted in *The Great Gatsby*.
April 1925 — University of Tulsa
Capri, Italy

Dear Sinclair Lewis: I've just sent for Arrowsmith. My hope is that this The Great Gatsby will be the second best American book of the Spring.

F Scott Fitzgerald

TO: H. L. Mencken
April 1925

Inscription pasted in *The Great Gatsby*.
Enoch Pratt Library
Capri, Italy

Dear Menck: This is a grand book. I see you don't review fiction any more. If you like this will you write me a line about it? If not— just say you received it and will read it presently. Always Sincerely
F Scott Fitzgerald

FROM: H. L. Mencken

TLS, 1 p. Scrapbook. Princeton University

April 16th [1925]

Dear Fitz:—

"The Great Gatsby" fills me with pleasant sentiments. I think it is incomparably the best piece of work you have done. Evidences of careful workmanship are on every page. The thing is well managed, and has a fine surface. My one complaint is that the basic story is somewhat trivial—that it reduces itself, in the end, to a sort of anecdote. But God will forgive you for that.

I'll probably do a review of it for the Chicago *Tribune*, which supplies 25 or 30 papers, with a total circulation of 3,000,000.[1] I assume that one reader in every 30,000 will read the review.

You are missing many spiritual immensities by staying away from the Republic. Future generations will look back to the Coolidge era as upon a Golden Age. I wake up every morning with a glow of anticipation, and am roaring with mirth by the time my senile tea and Zwieback come on.

Yours in Xt.,
H L Mencken

1 Mencken's review appeared in the *Baltimore Evening Sun* (2 May 1925) and was syndicated in other papers.

FROM: Roger Burlingame[1] ALS, 2 pp. Scrapbook. Princeton University
Before 19 April 1925

Dear Scott:

I can't help writing you how grand I think the Gatsby is; I've read it twice now and I'm going to read it again and I've got to like a book something terrible to read it 3 times.

Of course I liked The Beautiful + D. + I suppose, in a way, that is a more substantial novel, but nowhere have you ever touched the warmth and living quality of this Gatsby; or its beauty or its strange nostalgia or its amazing color.

In the ¶ "For Daisy was young and her artificial world was redolent . . . etc.," you have done something that I think no one will ever do better. That's so damn beautiful it hurts + makes you cry out with pain. The one after too, is good but nothing in the book or any where that I know is so adequate for that particular thing. It does so much. It gives in 11 lines that whole phase of her life, of anyone's, of everyone's life. It's tremendous.

I could go on for a long time quoting things that delight me. The beginning of Ch. II, for instance, + that gorgeous place where she cried into the shirts, + the night "when we hunted through the great rooms for cigarettes."

Someone said once that the thing that was common to all real works of art was a nostalgic quality, often indefinable, not specific. If that is so then The Great Gatsby is surely one because it makes me want to be back somewhere as much, I think as anything I've ever read.

Congratulations!

As ever
Roger Burlingame

[1] An editor at Scribners who was also a novelist.

TO: Roger Burlingame ALS, 2 pp. Syracuse University
19 April 1925 Dollar Steamship Line/
S.S. *President Garfield* letterhead

(Bound from Naples to Marsielle
en route to Paris
April 19th, 1924

Dear Roger:

I think that's about the nicest letter I ever recieved about my work. I was tremendously pleased that it moved you in that way "made you want to be back somewhere so much" because that describes, better than I could have put it myself, whatever unifying emotion the book has, either in regard to the temperment of Gatsby himself or in my own mood while writing it. Thank you so much for taking the trouble to write.

As yet I know nothing. Zelda has been too sick for the long overland trip to Paris in our French Ford so we had to catch a boat on a days notice to get the car back to France within the 6 mos. period of the International touring arrangement. (She's better now—Italy depressed us both beyond measure—a dead land where everything that could be done or said was done long ago [for whoever is decieved by the pseudo activity under Mussolini is decieved by the spasmotic last jerk of a corpse. In these days of critisism it takes a weak bunch of desperates to submit for 3 years to a tyrant, even a mildly benificent one]—).[1]

—but leaving suddenly I have heard nothing about Gatsby—nothing except you and Ring since Perkins letters three months ago. I don't know how many were printed or what advance orders or what notices or advertising not to mention reviews tho by this time all that information is probably waiting for me in Paris, having been forwarded from Capri. (By the way will you ask Max to pass on any movie nibbles to Reynolds)

Thank you again and again for your letter. I shall always keep it.

Scott Fitz—

Guaranty Trust Co.
1-3 Rue des Italiennes
Paris. France

[1] Fitzgerald's brackets.

FROM: Van Wyck Brooks — ALS, 3 pp. Scrapbook. Princeton University

Westport, Connecticut
April 22d 1925

Dear Fitzgerald:

It was ever so kind of you to send me "The Great Gatsby." I have just read it, with the greatest delights, and it seems to me by far the best thing you've done—certainly a real creation and one that leaves in the mind a most haunting impression. Your values are so true, although that isn't what makes the book so appealing: it is merely the thing full of glamour, and so it is—your own kind—this time for me more glamorous than ever.

I am sending you my book on Henry James[1] because you spoke in such a friendly way of the opening chapters. I hope it will not strike you as too bleak. It is the last thing of the kind I mean to do. Next time I hope to give you something more "constructive," as they say.

Capri must be wonderful now. I knew every inch of the island once. Have you been up to the little church on the top of Monte Solaro. And do they still have there those pictures at the stations of the cross that were lithographed in Bleeker street, New York?

Won't you remember me most kindly to your wife and believe me, with thanks and warm regards, Yours sincerely,

Van Wyck Brooks

[1] *The Pilgrimage of Henry James* (1925) which he inscribed: "For Scott Fitzgerald. With friendly greetings Van Wyck Brooks April 22nd. 1925." (Princeton)

FROM: James Branch Cabell TLS, 1 p. Scrapbook. Princeton University

My dear Scott Fitzgerald:

It was good of you to send me The Great Gatsby. But it is upon another count that I am most grateful to you,—upon the count that you have here written a solidly and sharply excellent book.

It is, I think, coherent and individual and clean-cut, in a fashion—if you don't mind,—wholly unpredicted by your earlier work. And it is full, too, of good bits. That last glimpse of Daisy and Tom, in particular,—I mean, upon page 174 5,—surprises and, in a half-instant, delights.

Altogether, I tender you my most cordial congratulations upon this book,—and am

Yours faithfully,
James Branch Cabell

2 *May* 1925

TO: James Branch Cabell ALS, 1 p. Princeton University
After 2 May 1925

14 Rue de Tillsit (sp.)
Paris,

Dear Mr. Cabell:

Thank you for writing me such a nice letter about my novel. I know it (the letter) by heart and carry it around constantly to show people. I'm afraid the book isn't a popular success but two or three letters, of which yours is one, have made it a success for to me.

Sincerely
F Scott Fitzgerald

FROM: Alexander Woollcott ALS, 1 p. Scrapbook. Princeton University

May 15 [1925]

Dear Scott,

This is a line to report that I read "The Great Gatsby" with the deepest interest. It is, I think, your best job by a long jump. I have the profoundest respect for the man who could write it/A. Woollcott

TO: Gertrude Stein[1]
Before 22 May 1925

Inscription in *The Great Gatsby*. Yale University
Paris

For Gertrude Stein
with best wishes from
F. Scott Fitzgerald

Note: Hemingway took the Fitzgeralds to meet Gertrude Stein shortly after their arrival in Paris.

FROM: Gertrude Stein ALS, 4 pp. Scrapbook. Princeton University

22 May [1925]

My dear Fitzgerald

Here we are and have read your book and it is a good book. I like the melody of your dedication[1] it shows that you have a background of beauty and tenderness and that is a comfort. The next good thing is that you write naturally in sentences and that too is a comfort. You write naturally in sentences and one can read all of them and that among other things is a comfort. You are creating the contemporary world much as Thackery did his in Pendennis and Vanity Fair and this isn't a bad compliment. You make a modern world and a modern orgy strangely enough it never was done until you did it in This Side of Paradise. My belief in This Side of Paradise was alright. This is as good a book and different and older and that is what one does, one does not get better but different and older and that is always a pleasure. Best of good luck to you always, and thanks so much for the very genuine pleasure you have given me. We are looking forward to seeing you and Mrs. Fitzgerald when we get back in the Fall. Do please remember me to her and to you always

Gtde Stein.

I find that at the last moment of departure I did not copy your address into my address book, and so am sending this care of Hemingway. do give it to me again.[2]

G.S.

[1] *The Great Gatsby* was dedicated: ONCE AGAIN TO ZELDA.
[2] See Fitzgerald's June 1925 letter to Stein in *Letters*.

FROM: Gilbert Seldes TLS, 1 p.[1] Scrapbook. Princeton University

26th of May [1925]

My dear Scott:

Of course you know that you have written a fine book; but it may be news to you that we know it too. Amanda and I are madly enthusiastic about it, and some of that has gone into a very severely analytical boost of the truly great Gatsby for The Dial.[2] (It probably won't be out for months, but I am doing a little propaganda elsewhere.) It's so good, Scott; so satisfying, and so rich in stuff. And written; and by the Lord, composed; it has structure and direction and an internal activity.

I'm told it's going well, but the reviews, apart from Mencken and Bill Benet[3] have made me sour. Van Wyck Brooks and Paul Rosenfeld told me they admire it; from Bunny you've no doubt heard; and your admirer, and the best critic hereabouts (Mrs Mary Colum) is doing it for the New Republic so you'll have some sort of a press. For God's sake Scott, if it doesn't go well, don't be persuaded not to go on with this, your real line of genius. I hope you're writing another already, and that it is as good.

I trust I suggest, in a way, my enthusiasm.[4]

Gilbert

[1] Cut by Fitzgerald from a longer letter.
[2] Seldes' review appeared in the August 1925 issue of *The Dial.*
[3] William Rose Benét.
[4] See Fitzgerald's June letter to Seldes in *Letters.*

TO: Sidney Howard — ALS, 1 p. University of California—Berkeley
Spring 1925

14 Rue de Tilsitt
Paris

Dear Sid:

Many thanks for *They Knew What They Wanted*[1] which after an adventurous buffeting here and there was finally forwarded to me here from Capri. I read it immediately and with greatest pleasure, moved throughout and easily understanding how it has achieved its great success. I think in life she would have kept on staying with Joe but of course that would have made the idea of her being taken back profoundly unsympathetic. A thousand congratulations—I only hope the reception of the play won't keep you from writing more *Transatlantic's* and Mrs. *Veach's.*

As Always, Your friend
F. Scott Fitzg—

[1] Howard's play, produced in 1924.

FROM: George Jean Nathan — ALS, 1 p. Scrapbook. Princeton University
Spring 1925

Dear Scott: A thousand congratulations! "The Great Gatsby" is an excellent job. It is leagues in advance of anything you have ever done.

As ever,
George Jean Nathan.

TO: Thomas Boyd — ALS, 1 p. Princeton University
Spring/Summer 1925

14 Rue de Tilsitt
Paris, France

Dear Tom:

You malign me. I am a faithful and punctillious correspondent. I wrote you that I was crazy about *Points of Honor*.[1] Since then I have read them both over (I must have given away 2 doz. copies of *Through the Wheat*.) and I think they are about my favorite modern books. Feeling the war, as one still does over here, they grow in stature.

I am anxiously awaiting *Samuel Drummund*—[2] of course in choosing a field that so many men + women from Zola + Hardy to Shiela Kaye-Smith have tilled you set yourself a problem—that is you must bring twice as much freshness, data and communicable emotion to it to make it absorbing, as those who like Geo. Elliot first saw something in the subject, were required to do. No doubt you have—I hope so and I'm looking forward with enormous interest. Did you agree with me that *The Apple of the Eye*[4] was a big fake?

Was your description of Mrs. Sinclair Lewis sincere or ironic? I've always heard she was a pretentious fright.[5]

Sorry you didn't like *Gatsby*—and thank you for being so nice about concealing the fact (I mean this); I think you're wrong but time will tell.

Ever your Friend Scott

Watch for a book by young Ernest Hemminway.

[1] Boyd's collection of war stories published by Scribners in March 1925.
[2] Boyd's novel (Scribners, 1925).
[3] Sheila Kaye-Smith, English regional novelist.
[4] A 1924 novel by Glenway Wescott.
[5] Grace Hegger Lewis.

TO: Joseph Hergesheimer — ALS, 1 p. University of Texas—Austin
May/June 1925

14 Rue de Tilsitt
Paris, France

Dear Hergeshiemer:

Scribners forwarded me a copy of the letter you were kind enough to write about *The Great Gatsby*. Thank you for what you said about it as well as for the permission you so courteously gave to use your opinion. I'm afraid its a financial failure and I enclose you one of comments which may interest you. I don't do Rascoe's[1] intelligence to think he really believes I am like Chambers—*La Cousine Bette* or *Linda Condon* could be "critisized" on the same grounds, if one wanted to make out such a preposterous case—the trouble is that we snubbed his wife. None the less I find the enclosure rather saddening.

Looking forward to *From an Old House* of which I've read with delight the three parts I came across in Italy.

Again thank you, and most cordial good wishes

Scott Fitzg—

Excuse the blots!
I'm awfully anxious to see the Döwer House.[2] You promised to invite us but never did.

[1] Burton Rascoe's comment on *The Great Gatsby* has not been identified.
[2] Hergesheimer's Pennsylvania home.

FROM: John Galsworthy ALS, 1 p. Princeton University

June 2. 1925

My Dear Scott FitzGerald

I have only just had the chance to read your novel The Great Gatsby' which you were good enough to send me with some very charming words.

Find it very interesting indeed, and prefer it to 'This Side Paradise.' Thank you so much for sending it; and forgive this thready line of acknowledgment. I write to you after a fortnight of fever. Our best wishes,

very sincerely
John Galsworthy

FROM: John Peale Bishop TLS, 4 pp. Scrapbook. Princeton University

108 East 86th Street, New York City
June 9th, 1925

Dear Scott, I have delayed unpardonably in acknowledging your letter and the book, having waited to get some inkling of your spring and summer address. All I know is that you can't be in Rome at this season, and yet it is to Rome that I suppose this will have to go.

I might begin as regards the Great Gatsby by telling you that I had dinner with Seldes and Van Wyck Brooks last night, and that Seldes is reviewing the GG in the Dial saying that you have written a grand book which leaves all your contemporaries behind (contemporaries specifically including Lewis and Cather, not to mention the Stevie-dear Benéts etc and in the hogswill) Brooks admitted modestly and with characteristic quietness that he had read the book and liked it.

On all sides, in fact, I gather that you have rather bowled them all over, intelligentsia and the more or less intelligent public. Johnson, the famous players gent who occasionally gives me some money for doing captions, thinks it one of the greatest books of all time etc.

As for myself, I think that you have definitely in this book, as you never did in its predecessors, crossed the line which distinguishes the artist from whatever you like, but not-artist. It has all the old fire, the instinctive gift of the novelist, which Godknows you've always had but it has also, what you never before showed, a fine and rigorous control, a clear sense of planning and an execution quite up to the plan. In brief you have got rid of your worst enemy, your ungodly facility. But—I could go on showering compliments on you quite as ferevently as those you have already received and are about to receive. But as you'll undoubtedly get more of those than you can possible have need for, I am going to put down, very briefly what I've got against the book. If I do, please don't think that I don't admire it with the most ardent; I do, but I also think that having come over the aforementioned line into the artist class you have got to be taken seriously and scrupulously to task for shortcomings which before were pardonable enough.

In the first place, I object to the inaccuracy of a great deal of the writing. For instance, in the paragraph in which you introduce the two girls buoyed up by the sofa, the first impression is a stroke of genius, but as you go on, you in one phrase add and in the next detract from that impression. I am not here talking about the strict Dictionary, Edmund Wilson, use of words, I am talking about a quality of clear visualization. You admit things into that paragraph which could not, the first conditions being granted, have been seen. There are details which could not have been as you describe them. This may seem a picayune point, but it is, to my mind, the final distinction of good writing, accuracy at once to the emotion of the scene and its sensible facts. My own feeling is that you would profit by doing what Joyce, James etc, have done, taking notes on the spot, working them up as practice descriptions, and then carefully analyzing the result. This may seem like an amateur advising a professional, and it is. For there are a number of things which you can do already which no amount of note-taking will teach you or another. But I still think that you would gain by a very strict consideration of the elements which go into a description, whether of things only seen or of things felt. Different as they are, both Joyce and James are superbly accurate writers. The one is true to a visual, the other a nervous experience. Your own experience of things outside your self still seems to me a bit blurred, whether considered as a thing felt or a thing seen. This may seem to you splitting hairs that had better be left in the horse's tail, or surrounding the horse's ass. But I assure you that though a great many people will pass over such inaccuracies as I have noted, practically all of them will feel the gain in intensity of a complete realization of the thing—person, object, scene, situation—which in the GG now seems to me not quite there.

I feel this lack of complete realization also in the broader aspects of the book—in the character of Gatsby and in his relation to the girl. What you have got is all right as far as it goes, but it does not, to my mind, go far enough. I grant of course that Gatsby should remain a vague mysterious person to the end, but though he is seen through a mist, always, one should feel his solidity behind that mist. And it's because you don't entirely "get" him, that the violent end seems abrupt. Emotionally it is beautifully prepared for, but it does to me seem in action just a little "willed." Everything of Gatsby is specified, but it as though you saw him in patches instead of getting casual glimpses of what is after all a complete man. Great characters—Falstaff or Bloom or the Baron de Charlus—continually offer new and surprising aspects of themselves (somehow James characters don't, and I am inclined to think that this is one of the reasons why one resents James' overelaboration); so does Gatsby, but the transition, not in the scene but in the character, is not quite managed. The only way out of this is I suppose, a more lengthy preparation before writing another novel—after it is conceived and the characters placed in your mind.

I think too that the book is too short. I remember what you said to me in Paris about the excessive length of modern novels, and guess that you deliberately imposed the present length on your book. I grant the virtues you have gained by this; the impression of complete control, of nothing that is not strictly necessary, of the ultimate concision possible to your tale. Still I think the book would have gained by a greater elaboration and a slower tempo in the early portions. Your end is so violent that it seems to me you should have done, what Dickens and Conrad both do when they are working toward a bloody and extravagant end, so set the characters in a commonplace attitude, in everyday situations, that the reader completely accepts them, and hence, ultimately anything they may do or suffer.

But you have done wonders both as a writer and as a social critic. And you have, a thing after all, very few novelists succeed in doing, broken new ground. Gatsby is a new character in fiction, and, as everybody is now saying, a most familiar one in life. You have everything ahead of you; Gatsby definitely admits you to importance. For god's sake take your new place seriously. Scrutinize your own impressions, distrusting your facility which will continue to work anyhow as far as it is needful, and cultivate the acquaintance of writers who are both subtle and accurate, especially those who are different in temper from yourself. A little more subtlety, a little more accuracy, and you'll have every living American novelist, and most of the dead ones, wiped off the critic's slate.

Are you going to stay in Europe? We may come over in the fall to stay a couple of years. Though it's all very uncertain.[1]

John.

[1] See Fitzgerald's 9 August letter to Bishop in *Letters*.

TO: Van Wyck Brooks
Postmarked 13 June 1925

ALS, 1 p. Bruccoli

Paris, France

Dear Brooks:

I read the James book, so did Zelda + Ernest Hemminway + everyone I've been able to lend it to and I think it rises high above either Bunny's carping or Seldes tag on it. I like it even better than the Mark Twain.[1] It is exquisitely done + entirely facinating

One reason it is of particular interest to us over here is obvious. In my own case I have no such delicate doubts—nor does anyone need to have them now since the American scene has become so complicated + ramified but the question of freshening material always exists. I shall come back after one more novel.

Why didn't you touch more on James impotence (physical) and its influence? I think if hadn't had at least one poignant emotional love affair with an American girl on American soil he might have lived there twice as long, tried twice as hard, had the picaresque past of Huck Finn + yet never struck roots. Novelists like he (him) + in a sense (to descend a good bit) me, have to have love as a main concern since our interest lies outside the economic struggle or the life of violence, as conditioned to some extent by our lives from 16–21.

However this is just shooting in the dark at a target on which you have expended your fine talent in full daylight. It was a really thrilling pleasure for a writer to read. Thanking you for writing me about my book so kindly + for sending me yours.

Scott Fitzgerald

[1] *The Ordeal of Mark Twain* (1920).

FROM: Paul Rosenfeld
Spring/Summer 1925

TL, 1 p. (fragment). Scrapbook.
Princeton University

The Great Gatsby would have given me a diving rock better than any I had, May Day included.[1] It's beautifully done, breezy throughout like Daisy's sitting-room. And extraordinarily American, like ice cream soda with arsenic flavoring, or jazzmusic in a fever-dream. I could have wished to have known a little more of the quality of Gatsby's passion for Daisy: what made him so naive, and what made him with his bootleg and wandering bonds love a girl who was as weak as she. Not that I doubt the reality of his passion; but there was not quite enough of it to make me feel at home in it. Also, I could have wished the narrator more positively dramatized. Don't you find him, at present, a trifle too passive; and the cause of his narration within himself not sufficiently developed? There were hints, to be sure, but he too was a Great Gatsby who learned vicariously, I imagine. But really, Mr.F.Scott, the story is unfolded with all the suavity of the late H. James. And the writing! The garden before the first supper party, and "It was already midsummer on the rooves of garages," and the Rabelaisian chronicle of the people who came to Gatsby's house! Really virtuosic, and a delight to read. The book felt like a dawn, for all the time I had to say to myself "This is the last time he asks life to do something for him! This is the last time he tries to play with life itself! This is the moment when he realizes that the flowing something he has been looking for outside is really within himself!" Isn't that so, or am I too projecting?

Paul Rosenfeld

[1] Rosenfeld had written about Fitzgerald in *Men Seen* (1925).

FROM: Edith Wharton

ALS, 1 p. Princeton University
Stationery of Pavillon Colombe

Thursday, July 2 [1925]

Dear Mr Fitzgerald,

Will you + Mrs Fitzgerald come to tea next Sunday? I shall be in at 4—. Perhaps you wd be kind enough, if Sunday suits you, to let Mr Parrett know, as I know he is a friend of yours, + to suggest his coming also, with Teddy Chanler?—I am helpless as I stupidly forgot to ask Mr Parrett his number in the rue du Bac—

I hope in any case to see you + Mrs Fitzgerald.[1]

Yrs sincerely
E. Wharton

[1] Fitzgerald went without Zelda. This encounter with Edith Wharton generated a widely recounted anecdote of how Fitzgerald was humiliated by her. The American composer Theodore Chanler, who was present, has reported his version of the day: "On the way back to Paris he showed no sign of feeling squelched, or that the failure of the occasion was due to him rather than to Mrs. Wharton." See "What Really Happened at the Pavillon Colombe," *Fitzgerald Newsletter*, #7.

TO: Ellingham Brooks

Inscription in Norman Douglas' *South Wind* (1917). Bruccoli

For T. Ellingham Brooks
this book of the first edition
(vice one copy signed
Faith Compton Mackenzie
strayed or stolen)
from his friend
F Scott Fitzgerald
(responsible and
violently apologetic
for above incident)
His other book may have
been the first copy of the first
edition available in London
This, I do swear before God,
is the last.
Paris, July 1925

Note: Brooks, a long-time resident of Capri and a friend of Norman Douglas', provided the model for Mr. Eames in *South Wind*. Douglas counter-inscribed this book on the title page: "My Dear Brooks, I like the fellow's impudence! He pretends to forget that I gave you this book—almost the first copy that reached me. To Hell with him Yours ever Norman Douglas."

FROM: Shane Leslie

Holograph document signed, 1 p.
Scrapbook. Princeton University

STATEMENT OF SHANE LESLIE

I think this is a marvelous picture book. It brings back to me the world of Long Island like an Arabian Night mixed with a subway swound. I can see the exact big mansion and the flow of guests and the riotous hospitality and the greenlight blinking on the pier and I can hear the foghorn bleating like a ghost suffering vivisection all night. Long Island cannot have an Epic because it's inhabitants are not Sagalike or heroic—only locusts and fireflies that float in an ephemeral radiancy. But this is a wonderful idyll of Long Island—How well I remember the Ash heap off Flushing.

The writer has brought back dead months and dead people to me and nailed down sights and scents and days and atmospheres with nice brass tacks of phrases. Three or four dwell with me—perhaps I shall remember the book long after I have forgotten the background. Yet the background is real and the book is art—artificial art but really wonderful.

Shane Leslie
Paris, July 1925

TO: Shane Leslie
July 1925

ALS, 1 p. Princeton University

14 Rue de Tilsitt
Paris, France

Dear Leslie:

Thank you many times for what you wrote on the back of *Gatsby*. Needless to say I'm having it bound into the novel—its curious that my first sight of Long Island was when I went with you to Port Washington Great Neck, where we later lived, is, you'll remember two stations on the New York Side.

The purpose of this letter is chiefly to say that we're coming to England in mid-November for three or four days and we want to see you. We'll be at the Savoy or Cecil probably, and I want your adress which you forgot to give me. Will you drop me a line, telling it to me.

Also, what is Mrs. Leslie's Paris adress? We want her to dine with us one night if she will and I've forgotten where she is (we've been swimming for two months in the south of France—where we met, among various people, your Washington friends, the Willards* [the Times Correspondent].[1] I liked them very much.) If Mrs. Leslie is in London please thank her for the complimentary note she enclosed on returning the *Great Gatsby*. In the more serious literary reviews the press on it has really reached a crecendo of entheusiasm but the sale has not been large, a little over 25,000. Still I am thoroughly satisfied, and not least because you liked it

Your friend
Scott Fitzg—

**Willarts*

[1] Fitzgerald's brackets.

FROM: John Peale Bishop
August 1925

TL, 1 p. (fragment). Scrapbook.
Princeton University

I was delighted to get your letter—with the Paris address. I wrote, belatedly it is true, thanking you for the Great Gatsby, to Rome, but with no very lively hopes that my strictures on the book would ever reach you.

Curiously enough I have seen almost no reviews of it, beyond the not very interesting, even though decidedly laudatory account which Stallings gave of it in the World, and the, also published in the World Menckenian drool. The man has become a sausage machine, grinding out the same old highly spiced weenies and hot dogs we've been consuming for years.

As for myself, I liked the book, liked it enormously, though, as I told you in the Italian letter, I thought it too short—a thing I haven't said of a novel ever before in my life—and the character of Gatsby insufficiently elaborated. I can't understand your resentment of the critic's failure to perceive your countenance behind Gatby's mask. To me it was evident enough. I haven't watched you living up to the Fitzgerald legend since 1917 for nothing. But it seems to me interesting, if at all, privately only. The point is that you have created a distinct and separate character, perhaps the first male you have ever created on the scale [ ] a novel, whom you have filled, as is inevitable, with your own emotional life. But to ask people to see you in Gatsby seems to me an arrant piece of personal vanity; as an artist it should flatter you that they did not see it.

Since sending it to you I have read the Apple of the Eye. I think you underrate it. But then I didn't regard it as a picture of American peasants; on the contrary it seems to me a rather fine projection of personal emotion on the part of Westcott. He is by instinct an artist, as yet not especially original, and, for a prosateur, too much under the influence of the imagist poets; but the consciousness is there, both of the material and the effects he means to produce. And on the whole it seems to me a very creditable performance. At least I am interested in what he will do next, and for most of my compatriots I have an indifference to their future which to say the least gives me a good deal of time for reading the works of dead men and foreigners. Nothing, I think, will ever persuade me to do more than glance through a Lewis novel, a Hecht novel, even I am afraid to say a Dos Passos novel.

The great thing about you is, aside from the fact that your material is always new and interesting in itself, is that you are quite likely at any time to do something radically different from anything you have ever done before. And the ordinary American's incapacity to do more than endlessly repeat himself, or rather his first success, is what makes contemporary American letters a desert of inanity. Besides, practically none of them no how to write.[1]

[1] See Fitzgerald's 9 August letter to Bishop in *Letters.*

FROM: Ring W. Lardner TL, 2 pp. Princeton University

Signing this letter "Bucky" reminded me that Bucky[1] bought himself a Chevrolet or something and nobody would ride with him but Isabelle, so he took her riding and drove her into a tree and raised hell with the bridge work.

Great Neck, August 8, 1925.

Dear Sir:—

I enclose a fragment from one of your former letters. Zelda isn't here, but when I see her I certainly will give her your best love.

I might consider visiting Paris if you will guarantee me an introduction to Miss La Gallienne who is my favorite actress and with whom I have been secretly in love ever since Liliom.

Thanks to the Great Neck Playhouse we hardly ever have to go to New York any more. Nearly all the shows play a night or two here before going to Broadway. Twenty-two try-outs are booked for this season and you can buy season tickets if you want to.

Gene didn't make any comment on "The Love Nest," but evidently had no suspicion.[2] Anyway, we are still pals. He told Dorothy Parker in my presence one night that the new house had been bought as a memorial to the kiddies.

Dorothy visited the Lardners for a week at my invitation. She had been having an unfortunate affair and for some reason or other, I thought a visit to us would cheer her up. I got into this sympathetic mood on the seventh of May and it lasted till the tenth of July; during the two months I was constantly cock-eyed, drinking all night and sleeping all day and never working. Fortunately I was eight weeks ahead in syndicates before the spree started.

One night during Dorothy's visit, Herman Mankiewicz[3] called up from

Petrova's and said he would come and see us if we'd come after him. We did and I took them, Mank and Dorothy, to Durand's, Ellis (very sensibly) refusing to go. The place was full of Durand's big, husky Irish clients. After a few drinks, Mank remembered that he had been in the Marines and ought to prove it by licking all the inmates of the joint. I (as usual) acted as pacifist and felt next day as if I'd been in a football game against Notre Dame. We finally got Mank home (our house) and put him to bed and he arose next day at ten and said he had to go right to town and do some work for the Sunday Times. Ellis gave him a few highballs to brace him up and he finally left at five in the afternoon.

George Nathan and Lillian[4] are still very thick so far as I know.

Harry Frazee, who is making millions out of "No, No, Nanette" (with four companies in America, three in England and two in Australia), promises to stage a small revue, written by Jerry Kern and me, late this fall. But you know how those things go.[5]

Dick Barthelmess is living in Great Neck and we see him occasionally. The papers announced that Mary was through with him, though she didn't intend to get a divorce.

Mrs. Lardner and I will be highly honored by the dedication of your book to us.[6] I hope "The Great Gatsby" is going better. It certainly deserves a big sale. I think it probable that the reason it got no notice from Frank Adams was that he was on a vacation and getting married about the time it came out. Max Perkins said he thought the size of the book was against it (in the eyes of the buyers). That is a great commentary on American life and letters. What is your new novel going to be about?

Gene called up the other day and said he had sold the play "we" wrote to Ziegfeld, but that it would have to be rewritten into musical comedy form. Ziegfeld had given him contracts for us to sign. There were clauses in them which I wouldn't sign even with a manager I could trust. I told Gene so and he cabled Ziegfeld, who is now in France, and said we objected to certain clauses. Ziegfeld cabled back that he wouldn't make any changes. Gene then wanted me to sign the contracts as they stood and I wouldn't. So that's that. I've got a story coming out in "Liberty" for October 3, of which Flo is the hero.[7] When, and if, he reads it, he won't offer me any more contracts, even lousy ones.

On the Fourth of July, Ed Wynn gave a fireworks party at his new estate in the Grenwolde division. After the children had been sent home, everybody got pie-eyed and I never enjoyed a night so much. All the Great Neck professionals did their stuff, the former chorus girls danced, Blanche Ring kissed me and sang, etc. The party lasted through the next day and wound up next evening at Tom Meighan's, where the principal entertainment was provided by Lila Lee and another dame, who did some very funny imitations (really funny) in the moonlight on the tennis court. We would ask them to imitate Houdini, or Leon Errol, or Will Rogers, or

Elsie Janis; the imitations were all the same, consisting of an aesthetic dance which ended with an unaesthetic fall onto the tennis court.

Charley Chaplin's new picture, "The Gold Rush," opens here next week and we are going to a party in his honor at Nast's.

I seem to have written a good many words, most of them about myself, and not many of them of much interest.

We do miss you and Zelda a great deal. Write again and tell her to write, too. And I might add that I have a little money to lend at the proverbial six per cent, if worst comes to worst.

Bucky.

[1] Gene Buck.
[2] Lardner's story was loosely based on Buck.
[3] Drama critic who later became a prominent screenwriter.
[4] Lillian Gish.
[5] The Jerome Kern–Lardner collaboration did not materialize.
[6] *All the Sad Young Men* (1926) was dedicated: "To Ring and Ellis Lardner."
[7] "A Day with Conrad Green."

FROM: Gerald Murphy[1] TLS, 1 p. (with holograph postscript). Princeton University

19 September '25.

Dear Scott and Zelda:—

There *really* was a great sound of tearing heard in the land as your train pulled out that day. Sara and I rode back together saying things about you both to each other which only partly expressed what we felt separately. Ultimately, I suppose, one must judge the degree of one's love for a person by the hush and the emptiness that descends upon the day,—after the departure. We heard the tearing because it was there,—and because we were'nt able to talk much about how much we do love you two. We agreed that it made us very sad, and sort of hurt a little—for a "summer holiday."

Most people are dull, without distinction and without value, even *humanly,*—I believe (even in the depths of my expansive Irish heart). For Sara most people are guilty of the above until they are proved innocent. All this one can believe without presumption or personal vanity,—and the proof that it's true is found for me in the fact that you two belong so irrevocably to that rare race of people who are *valuable.* As yet in this world we have found four. One only *really* loves what is rare and valuable to one, in spite of the fact that one loves first.

We four communicate by our presence rather than any means: so that where we meet and when will never count. Currents race between us regardless: Scott will uncover for me values in Sara, just as Sara has known them in Zelda through her affection for Scott.

Suffice it to say that whenever we knew that we were to see you that evening or that you were coming to dinner in the garden we were happy, and showed it to each other. We were happy whenever we were with you. My God** How *rare* it is. How rare.

The matter of the bath-house, umbrella, etc. is fixed and I owe you 50 francs. Albert is very leisurely putting the Renault in order. You can stop the engine now without running up the steps of the Hotel de Ville to stall it. The painting comes next, replacing of mudguards, etc., and then I think we'll be able to enter it in the Flower Parade at Pasadena,—as it stands.

We are coming to Paris toward the end of the month for a week of hilarity at the Exposition. We'll wire you in advance. My heart leaps up, etc. at the idea of seeing you both.

One thing I regret: that we did'nt all go out on a short cruise on the "Picaflor." But if you come to Nice there'll be plenty of chances: she'll be in commission all the time and we'll seize a good spell and make for the open seas. We might all four take that Compagnie Generale trip to Tunisia. Just three weeks, very cheap. High-powered cars with Arab chauffeurs meet you at the boat and you course thro' the country staying as long as you want in each town. More like being a guest than a tourist, they say. Wonderful hotels even in the desert. Beaumont told us about it.

Honoria's teacher is Madame Egórova (Princess Troubetzkoy),[2] top floor over the Olympia Music Hall on the Boulevard. The stage entrance is on the side street, 8 or 10 Rue Caumartin. You walk up thro' the wings while the performance is going on, and her studio!! A big, bare room just for learning to dance in.

Sara's yelling that she misses you. Good-bye until the end of the month. It gives me an awful thrill to think of the imminence of the novel. For me such things are the most important in the world. I suppose for the same reason that you two are important. Take care of yourselves, please.

Thank God for you both,

Devotedly,
dow dow

What lovely letters you both wrote. It did our hearts good. The children are *still* at the hotel. Fevers running. It was the grippe they had.

1 Gerald and Sara Murphy were American expatriates who became the Fitzgeralds' intimate friends in France. The Murphys provided partial models for the Divers in *Tender Is the Night*, and the novel is dedicated to them. See Linda Patterson Miller, "'As a Friend You Have Never Failed Me': The Fitzgerald-Murphy Correspondence," *Journal of Modern Literature*, 5 (September 1976), 357–82.

2 Lubov Egorova became Zelda Fitzgerald's ballet teacher; she was married to Prince Troubetskoy.

For T. S. Elliot

Greatest of Living Poets

from his enthusiastic

worshipper

F Scott Fitzgerald.

Paris,
Oct,
1925,

TO: Ludlow Fowler — ALS, 2 pp. Princeton University

[2 enclosures]
as we used to
say in the army

14 Rue de Tilsitt
Paris, France:
Nov. 6th, 1925

Dear Lud:

Promptly (within two hours) after recieving your letter I wired *Reynolds* to make what changes you wished about *The Rich Boy*.[1] The letter from him (enclosed explains why they have not been made in *The Red Book*. You told me explicitly to *wire him, not you.*

The changes have been made in the book *All the Sad Young Men*[2] where it appears as the first story + unless you've talked about it that is (the book) all anybody will ever see and remember It appears Jan + Feb in *The Red Book* + I got $5000.00 for it so see you are a most profitable aquaintance. I wish I had $1,000,000,000 worth of law business to swing your way.

Anyhow everybody agrees that it, with *Gatsby*, is the best thing I've ever written: I mean everybody that's read it. It should be amusing for you to hear yourself critisized by the critics!

Enclosed is a sheet that evidently got left out of the ms.[3] I sent you—which must have been incoherent without it.

Did those glasses ever turn up, Lud? Wish you would have one more search made for them.

Our plans are vague. We are here till Jan: then three or six months on the Rivierra, followed by sixth months in England (in the former case) or three more months in Paris (in the latter). Next fall we're coming back for awhile, for how long I can't say—that will make 2 yrs. and six months. We intended to stay three.

Sorry we didn't get together last Spring. I wanted so much to see you + talk to you. Sap was great but he + I have grown apart in some things.

Saw Paul Nelson[4] the other day; a purely comic experience—(by the way he didn't seem so obnoxious to me as you'd led me to expect). Buzz Law,[5] an old hero of mine, passed me on the street the other day looking by no means distinguished.

Write me, answering questions + telling me about what you thought of *The Rich Boy*—different parts, ect. *Please!* Ernest Hemminway, a fine young writer here, says its a swell story *but* Anson *would* have raped Dolly—I hadn't the priviledge of telling him that, in life, he *did!*

As Ever, Your Devoted Friend
Scott.

Are you going to marry Isabelle MacMillan?

[1] There are more than 500 substantive changes between publication of the story in *Redbook* and in *All the Sad Young Men*. In general, the effect of the alterations was to render Anson more self-centered and Paula more appealing.

[2] Published February 1926.

[3] "The Rich Boy."

[4] Princeton classmate of Fitzgerald and Fowler.

[5] Princeton football star.

TO: Maxwell Perkins — ALS, 1 p. Princeton University

14 Rue de Tilsitt
Paris, France
December 1st [1925]

Dear Max:

I have taken the liberty of arranging for a French translation of *Gatsby*. It is being done by Victor Llona who translated Ambrose Bierce + Willa Cather into French, and will be published by Kra, Grassi or The *Nouvelle Revue Français* who all stand very high here.[1]

I am paying the translator

2000 francs ($80) on delivery of ms. to me.
1500 " ($60) " contract being signed by French publisher (he acts as agent)

And I am also agreeing to pay $80 toward the advertising, a total outlay of $220. Also I give him 20% after I have my outlay back on all copies sold up to 50,000 after which he gets 10%.

Please write me telling me what arrangement I should make with you to obtain French copyright + how much I shall owe you of the proceeds—if any. I have no idea of the usual proceedure—but as I am awfully anxious to have it done I have gone ahead, counting on your consent. The money, of course, I will pay myself.

The novel progresses slowly but brilliantly.[2]

Scott Fitzgerald's new book
All the Sad Young Men
(containing THE RICH BOY)
CHAS. SCRIBNERS

← I suggest somthing *very* simple like this for the announcement of the short stories. In my opinion the blurb has had its day.

Would Bridges be interested in Hemminways new short pieces

As Ever
Scott

The *Post* have raised my regular price to $2500. a story. This is confidential.

[1] *Gatsby le magnifique* (Paris: Kra, 1926).
[2] Fitzgerald was working on an early version of the novel that became *Tender Is the Night*.

TO: Horace Liveright and T. R. Smith
Before 30 December 1925

ALS, 2 pp. Princeton University

14 Rue de Tilsitt
Paris

Dear Horace and Tom:

Ernest Hemminway showed me his new book the other day (the satiric book: *The Torrents of Spring*) and seemed a bit in doubt as to how you were going to recieve it.[1] I don't know how much value, if any, you attach to my opinion but it might interest you to know that to one rather snooty reader, at least, it seems about the best comic book ever written by an American. It is simply devastating to about seven-eighths of the work of imitation Andersons, to facile and "correct" culture and to this eternal looking beyond appearances for the "real," on the part of people who have never even been conscious of appearances. The thing is like a nightmare of literary pretensions behind which a certain hilarious order establishes itself before the end—so it hasn't that quality of leaving a painful passionate *funnyness* as the last taste in your mouth. Like Alice in Wonderland it sends you back to the sane world above cant and fashion in which most of us flatter ourselves that we live—sometimes.

Beyond that it is absorbingly interesting—the failure to be that is the one unforgivable sin. Frankly I hope you won't like it—because I am something of a ballyhoo man for Scribners and I'd some day like to see all my generation (3) that I admire rounded up in the same coop—but knowing my entheusiasm and his own trepidation Ernest agreed with me that such a statement of the former might break the ice for what is an extraordinary and unusual production.

With Best Wishes to you Both

Your Friend
F. Scott Fitzg—

[1] Boni & Liveright had published Hemingway's *In Our Time* (1925) and held an option on his next three books.

FROM: Horace Liveright TL(CC), 2 pp. Princeton University

December 30th, 1925.

Dear Scott:

I'm enclosing a copy of a letter which I have just sent to Hemingway in Austria. Frankly, I am less violently opposed to Torrents of Spring than is anyone else who has read it. I thought it was pretty funny and in spots extremely well done. But I do know that unless it gets a tremendous lot of publicity from some of the third-rate ultra-conservative reviewers who hate Sherwood Anderson and all of his school, the book won't have a chance in the world of selling more than several hundred copies. I do see, though, the possibility of a much larger sale if some publisher like Doran first runs it in The Bookman, gets a lot of advance publicity for it, and then brings it out with a great fanfaronade of trumpets. I know how to handle a book like this and if my office believed in it and we were willing to pander to the very elements of American life that we have all been fighting against for eight years, we might be able to put the book over. T.R. and Julian[1] and Donald Friede, my new partner whom you don't know, and everyone else around here thinks the book is just bad, and that it hasn't a chance. As I've just said, I can't quite agree with them. I'd like to see Hemingway make a lot of money on the book, and although you may want to give it to Scribner's, I think Doran could do a good deal more with it.

You know we have a contract with Hemingway for three more books and you know too that we all, and I, especially, believe in Hemingway. I think he has a big future. And I'd hate you to get so hilariously enthusiastic about our rejection of Torrents of Spring that you would make yourself believe that we were in any way giving up Hemingway. We're not, and we expect to absolutely go through on our contract with him.[2]

Did I write you how absolutely swept off my feet I was by The Great Gatsby? As I dictate this, Miss Goldman tells me I did. I'm eager to see just what sort of play it's going to make.[3] She tells me, too, that when I wrote you about The Great Gatsby, I told you to do a play for me. My Hamlet in modern dress has been a tremendous succes d'estime. It has actually run 8 weeks and it looks as though it might run 4 more. This doesn't mean that it has made any money, but it has done a great deal for me in many ways. I have a new play now almost ready for rehearsal that I hope to do in February. Our publishing season which is just closing has been the best we've ever had. The book-trade says that our entire list has gone better than that of any other publisher, although only one of our books has been among the six best-sellers. Tom expects to leave for the other side the latter part of January. I suppose he'll see you in Paris when he gets there. My best wishes to you always.

Faithfully,

Mr. Scott Fitzgerald
14 Rue de Tilsitt,
Paris, France.

[1] Thomas R. Smith and Julian Messner.

[2] The Boni & Liveright contract with Hemingway became invalid when *The Torrents of Spring* was declined.

[3] *The Great Gatsby* ran on Broadway for 112 performances in 1926.

FROM: Ernest Hemingway
Late 1925(?)

Inscription in typescript (CC)
of *The Torrents of Spring* (1926).
Princeton University

THE TORRENTS OF SPRING

A Romantic Novel In Honor of The Passing Of

A Great Race.

By ERNEST HEMINGWAY.

To Scott and Zelda
with love from Ernest.

And perhaps there is one reason why a comic writer should of all others be the least excused for deviating from nature, since it may not be always so easy for a serious poet to meet with the great and the admirable; but life everywhere furnishes an accurate observer with the ridiculous.

Henry Fielding.

TO: Maxwell Perkins — Wire. Princeton University

JAN 8 1926

PARIS 1906

YOU CAN GET HEMINGWAYS FINISHED NOVEL PROVIDED YOU PUBLISH UNPROMISING SATIRE HARCOURT HAS MADE DEFINITE OFFER WIRE IMMEDIATELY WITHOUT QUALIFICATIONS[1]

FITZGERALD

[1] Perkins wired back the same day: PUBLISH NOVEL AT FIFTEEN PERCENT AND ADVANCE IF DESIRED ALSO SATIRE UNLESS OBJECTIONABLE OTHER THAN FINANCIALLY. On the 11th Perkins cabled Fitzgerald: CONFIDENCE ABSOLUTE KEEN TO PUBLISH HIM. Scribners published *The Torrents of Spring* and *The Sun Also Rises* in 1926. See Bruccoli, *Scott and Ernest* (New York: Random House, 1978).

TO: Carl Van Vechten — ALS, 1 p. New York Public Library

January 1926

In the Pyrenes
Adress c/o Guaranty Trust
1 Rue des Italiens
Paris

Dear Carl:

I can't tell you how I enjoyed the essays.[1] The one on "*Out of Season*" gave me the most persistent nostalgia for the Rivierra—I wanted to be in Nice immediately—you know we *have* spent two summers out of season there. Also I loved the ones on *Fuller* + *Saltus*. The former I knew only by name. *Dedications* was fine. *Machen* I'd read before. The musical ones I liked without altogether understanding—that is one of my many blind eyes.

Thank you, Carl, for the pleasure it gave me. Zelda sends her best

As Ever, your friend
Scott Fitzg—

[1] *Excavations* (1926).

TO: Carl Winston[1] ALS, 1 p. Winston
c. January 1926

14 Rue de Tilsitt
Paris, Frane

Dear Carl:

Thanks for your letter (and for your gloves and your cane—the latter together with Jack's[2] cane and Zelda's opera cloak was returned next day by an honest taxidriver. The gloves lie reproachfully, neatly folded waiting for you on our mantlepiece. I will send them some day soon. The cane I claim by right of salvage and in return will hand over any cane I may be carrying when we next meet in New York) God! what a parenthesis that was:

The Grand Duke[3] still functions.

McAlmon[4] is still a bitch—I suppose so, anyhow.

If you read my last book *The Great Gatsby* you will understand how I happened to be so interested in Jack's Oxford gag.[5]

Good luck to you always

Sincerely
F Scott Fitzgerald

P.S. I stayed up till two oclock next day!

[1] Newspaper reporter who met Fitzgerald during an altercation at Bricktop's, a Paris nightclub. See Winston's "My Night with the Scott Fitzgeralds," *Saturday Review* (16 November 1963).

[2] Jack Thorne.

[3] A Paris nightclub.

[4] Robert McAlmon, expatriate American author and publisher of the Contact editions in Paris, which included his own work and that of other writers. Winston recalls that Fitzgerald and McAlmon quarreled at Bricktop's.

[5] Thorne, who was with Winston that night, told Fitzgerald that he had gone to Oxford after the war under an international student exchange program.

FROM: Ring W. Lardner TL, 3 pp. Princeton University

Feb. 23, 1926.

Heap Big Zelda and Scott:—

I am in the Indian and Mexican country and am learning the language rapidly.[1]

The elegant picture, "The Fitzgeralds' Christmas," was forwarded to us here and we really did and do like it.[2] We agree that Scotty is the second best looking one in the outfit, or shebang, to use the colloquial.

We and the Rices, including their daughter, went to Belleair, Florida, the first week in January and staid there three weeks. Then I had to go home for a few days and view a Tommie Meighan picture, to which I was engaged to write the titles. The picture, I believe, will be the worst ever seen on land or sea, and the titles are excrutiatingly terrible. They will look as if Jack Hazzard had written them.

On the tenth of February, if you are still interested, we set out for New Orleans, stopping fifteen minutes in Montgomery, where we shed a tear. (But I almost forgot to say that while in New York, Ellis and I saw "The Great Gatsby." It was a matine on a day of the worst weather ever seen in the city or anywhere else; yet the house was over three-quarters full. The blizzard was so bad that all the schools were closed and the commuters had a terrible time getting to New York at all. The man who plays Buchanan lives on Long Island and arrived during Act 2. But we thought the show was great and that Rennie[3] was just about perfect. I regretted that they left out the drunken apartment scene, but I presume Davis[4] figured that one party scene was enough. Every now and then one of Scott's lines would pop out and hit you in the face and make you wish he had done the dramatization himself.

Well, anyway, we got to New Orleans for the Mardi Gras and were rushed by a bunch of morons and I couldn't stand it and fell off the wagon and we all got the flu and had a very sick trip from New Orleans to this place, where we are resting. From here we go to Los Angeles (including Hollywood), Monterey and San Francisco; then home, arriving there the first week in April. The Rices have been with us right along and we are still all speaking.

Write soon, both of you. You, Zelda, come home and show up the Charleston dancers. You, Scott, also come home and write a play.

And Oh, yes, we had two long and entertaining sessions with Sherwood Anderson and wife in New Orleans. We took them along with us to one of the dinners given, for no reason, in our honor and Sherwood was very frank in stating his opinion of the host and local guests.

Tallulah.

[1] Lardner wrote from the Hotel Del Coronado in Coronado Beach, Calif.

[2] The frequently reproduced photograph of Scott, Scottie, and Zelda in a chorus line in front of the Christmas tree in their Paris apartment.

[3] James Rennie had the title role.

[4] The play version of *The Great Gatsby* was written by Owen Davis.

FROM: Carl Van Vechten — TLS, 1 p. Scrapbook. Princeton University

Dear Scott,

Thanks for ALL THE SAD YOUNG MEN, which I read with mixed emotions. Of course, Absolution is one of your very best, and I liked The Rich Boy, and Winter Dreams, but I don't think you should have published the rest of the book, that is as a book; it is so far inferior to my grand Gatsby. However, you probably won't agree with me and anyway it is silly to talk of not publishing something that is already published and it is easier to read Absolution again in this form than to take down a heavy volume of the Mercury. By the way your titles are all superb. My next one—I have just finished a novel—is Nigger Heaven.

sweet-peas and mimosa to you and Zelda!
Carl Van Vechten

March 4, 1926

TO: H. L. Mencken
March 1926

ALS, 1 p. New York Public Library

Villa Paquita
Juan-les-Pins
Alpes Maritime
France

Dear Menck—

for the man who wanted a school for his backward boy I suggest Dummer Academy, South Byfield, Massachusettes

F. Scott Fitzgerald.

Tear on dotted line

Dear Menck:

The article on the writing of novels never materialized. I scarcely dared hope you'd like the other one, since it discussed you and since it was a blurb for Hemmingway whom you don't like.[1] But I thought I'd make the gesture of offering it to you so that if there was anything you thought unfair you could arrange public punishment.

After we come back will you sometime give me a chance to talk with you—I mean socially and with liesure? I've never met you without being either shy or drunk.

Yours
F Scott Fitzgerald

[1] "How to Waste Material: A Note on My Generation," *The Bookman* (May 1926), which had been declined by *The American Mercury.*

FROM: Ring W. Lardner TL, 2 pp. Princeton University

Monday, May 10, 1926.

Dear Scott and Darling Zelda:—

I just got through reading the current Bookman and it certainly gave me the impression that you, Scott (or Fitz), are having a violent affair with Johnnie Farrar.[1] I was touched particularly by his assertion that he was glad you were coming back this fall, though you and he quarreled a great deal.

Ellis and I are exceedingly grateful to you, Scott, not you, Zelda, for dedicating "All The Sad Young Men" to us. I had read all of it except the first story, which, I think, is the best story.[2] I think also that you were a sap not to have made a novel of it.

"Gatsby," I see by the papers, closed Saturday night owing to Rennie's impending trip to England. It's too bad it couldn't have run on, but it would have been a mistake to continue it with somebody else in the lead. If there was ever a man that fitted a part and vice versa, etc.

In case you haven't heard of the Pulitzer awards—George Kelly got first prize for his play "Craig's Wife." Aleck Woollcott said he would have given it to Marc Connelly's "The Wisdom Tooth," which is a damn good play, and Percy said he would have placed both "Gatsby" and "The Wisdom Tooth" ahead of the winner. The fact that Owen Davis was on the committee may have ruined "Gatsby's" chance. It's too bad you couldn't have seen "Gatsby." I think you'd have been pleased. Red Lewis got the book prize with "Arrowsmith" and turned it down. I can see his point. I am against all that kind of stuff, meaning the Pulitzer awards and the All America football team and "The Best Short Stories of so-and-so," even when Mr. O'Brien honors me with a place or three or four stars in the last named.

Reviews of "The Love Nest" have been perfectly elegant. I don't know whether you've seen the book, but I had an introduction to it written as if I were dead. The Sunday Times ran a long review and played up the introduction strong, saying it was too bad I had died so young, etc. and the result was that Ellis was kept busy on the telephone all that Sunday evening assuring friends and reporters that I was alive and well. It just happened that I was at home and cold sober; if I'd been out, she might have worried a little. Or maybe not.

Max Perkins tells me you have sold "Gatsby" to the movies. It ought to make a great picture and it would be a knock-out if they got Rennie to play in it.[3]

Speaking of pictures, I rewrote a lousy baseball-Florida real estate story for Tom Meighan,[4] some one else having written it first, and I also wrote the titles after seeing the uncut film. When the picture came out, it was a complete surprise to me and one of the worst pictures I ever saw. But it seems to be going all right and I am told that it compares very favorably with most of Tom's recent releases.

I can't remember when I wrote to you last, so I may be telling you old stuff. (Stop me if you have heard this one). Ellis and I toured California with the Grantland Rices and their daughter. I'd have had a much better time in Hollywood if I'd been drinking. Anyway, Charlie Chaplin had us out to dinner and was more or less amusing and we met all the nuts.

Gene and Helen[5] spent six weeks in Palm Beach while Gene was working on Ziegfeld's "Palm Beach Nights," a girl show which Flo put on down there with somebody else's money and which proved a dismal flop. However, Gene and Jimmy Hanley had a good song in it—"No Foolin' "—and I think he (Gene) will make some money out of the song. He has bought a Lincoln "town car," but the old homestead is still on the market. I suggest that you two take it off his hands when you come back. Anyway, I insist on your living somewhere in Great Neck. You have no idea how I miss you, Zelda, not you, Scott.

Tom and Peggy Boyd are expected in New York soon and will be invited out here to dinner.

Burton and Hazel[6] are also threatening to visit us. I think Burton is doing pretty well, writing a daily syndicate letter for Johnson Features and also acting as editor for the concern's other features.

Harry Hansen has quit the Chicago News and taken Laurence Stallings' place on the World.

Max Perkins gave me your address over the telephone and I hope I got it approximately right.

Write and tell me your plans. If you want me to be looking up a house in Great Neck, let me know and I'll be glad to serve.

I went on the wagon April 18, theoretically for a year, but I might get a week off when you come back.

Gil Boag.

[1] The review of *All the Sad Young Men* was headed: "The Best of His Time." John Farrar was editor of *The Bookman*.

[2] "The Rich Boy."

[3] A silent version (now lost) of *The Great Gatsby* was made by Famous Players in 1926 with Warner Baxter in the title role.

[4] *The New Klondike*.

[5] The Bucks.

[6] The Rascoes.

TO: Ernest Hemingway[1]
June 1926

AL, 10 pp. Kennedy Library
Juan-les-Pins, France

Dear Ernest: Nowdays when almost everyone is a genius, at least for awhile, the temptation for the bogus to profit is no greater than the temptation for the good man to relax (in one mysterious way or another)—not realizing the transitory quality of his glory because he forgets that it rests on the frail shoulders of professional entheusiasts. This should frighten all of us into a lust for anything honest that people have to say about our work. I've taken what proved to be excellent advice (On The B. + Damned) from Bunny Wilson who never wrote a novel, (on Gatsby—change of many thousand wds) from Max Perkins who never considered writing one, and on T. S. of Paradise from Katherine Tighe (you don't know her) who had probably never read a novel before.

[This is beginning to sound like my own current work which resolves itself into laborious + sententious preliminaries].[2]

Anyhow I think parts of *Sun Also* are careless + ineffectual. As I said yestiday (and, as I recollect, in trying to get you to cut the 1st part of 50 Grand)[3] I find in you the same tendency to envelope or (and as it usually turns out) to *embalm* in mere wordiness an anecdote or joke thats casually appealed to you, that I find in myself in trying to preserve a piece of "fine writing." Your first chapter contains about 10 such things and it gives a feeling of condescending *casuallness*[4]

P. 1. "highly moral story"
"Brett said" (O. Henry stuff)
"much too expensive
"something or other" (if you don't want to tell, why waste 3 wds. saying it. See P. 23—"*9 or 14*" and "or how many years it was since 19XX" when it would take two words to say That's what youd kid in anyone else as mere "style"—mere horse-shit I can't find this latter but anyhow you've not only got to write well yourself but you've also got to scorn NOT-DO what anyone can do and I think that there are about 24 sneers, superiorities, and nose-thumbings-at-nothing that mar the whole narrative up to p. 29 where (after a false start on the introduction of Cohn) it really gets going. And to preserve these perverse and willfull non-essentials you've done a lot of writing that *honestly* reminded me of Michael Arlen.[5]

[You know the very fact that people have committed themselves to you will make them watch you like a cat. + if they don't like it creap away like one][6]

For example.

Pps. 1 + 2. Snobbish (not in itself but because the history of English Aristocrats in the war, set down so verbosely so uncritically, so exteriorly and yet so obviously inspired from within, is *shopworn.*) You had the same problem that I had with my Rich Boy, previously debauched by Chambers ect. Either bring more thot to it with the realization that that ground has already raised its wheat + weeds or cut it down to seven sentences. It hasn't even your rythym and the fact that may be "true" is utterly immaterial.

That biography from you, who allways believed in the superiority (the preferability) of the *imagined* to the *seen* *not to say to the merely recounted.*

P. 3. "Beautifully engraved shares" (Beautifully engraved 1886 irony) All this is O.K. but so glib *when* its glib + *so* profuse.

P. 5 Painters are no longer *real* in prose. They must be minimized. [This is not done by making them schlptors, backhouse wall-experts or miniature painters][7]

P. 8. "highly moral urges" "because I believe its a good story" If this paragraph isn't maladroit then I'm a rewrite man for Dr. Cadman.[8]

P. 9. Somehow its not good. I can't quite put my hand on it—it has a ring of "This is a true story ect."

P. 10. "Quarter being a state of mind ect." This is in all guide books. I havn't read Basil Swoon's[9] but I have fifty francs to lose.

[10][About this time I can hear you say "Jesus this guy thinks I'm lousy, + he can stick it up his ass for all I give a Gd Dm for his 'critisism.'" But remember this is a new departure for you, and that I think your stuff is great. You were the first American I wanted to meet in Europe—and the last. (This latter clause is simply to balance the sentence. It doesn't seem to make sense tho I have pawed at it for several minutes. Its like the age of the French women.[11]

P. 14. (+ therabout) as I said yesterday I think this anecdote is flat as hell without naming Ford[12] which would be cheap.

It's flat because you end with mention of Allister Crowly.[13] If he's nobody its nothing. If he's somebody its cheap. This is a novel. Also I'd cut out actual mention of H. Stearns[14] earlier.

Why not cut the inessentials in Cohens biography?[15] His first marriage is of no importance. When so many people can write well + the competition is so heavy I can't imagine how you could have done these first

20 pps. so casually. You can't *play* with peoples attention—a good man who has the power of arresting attention at will must be especially careful.

From here Or rather from p. 30 I began to like the novel but Ernest I can't tell you the sense of disappointment that beginning with its elephantine facetiousness gave me. Please do what you can about it in proof. Its 7500 words—you could reduce it to 5000. And my advice is not to do it by mere pareing but to take out the worst of the *scenes.*

I've decided not to pick at anything else, because I wasn't at all inspired to pick when reading it. I was much too excited. Besides this is probably a heavy dose. The novel's damn good. The central theme is marred somewhere but hell! unless you're writing your life history where you have an inevitable pendulum to swing you true (Harding[16] metaphor), who can bring it entirely off? And what critic can trace whether the fault lies in a possible insufficient thinking out, in the biteing off of more than you eventually cared to chew in the impotent theme or in the elusiveness of the lady character herself.[17] My theory always was that she dramatized herself in terms of Arlens dramatatization of somebody's dramatizatatg of Stephen McKenna's[18] dramatization of Diana Manner's[19] dramatization of the last girl in Well's *Tono Bungay*—who's original probably liked more things about Beatrix Esmond than about Jane Austin's Elizibeth (to whom we owe the manners of so many of our wives.)

Appropos of your foreward about the Latin quarter—suppose you had begun your stories with phrases like: "Spain is a peculiar place—ect" or "Michigan is interesting to two classes—the fisherman + the drummer."

Pps 64 + 65[20] with a bit of work should tell all that need be known about *Brett's* past.

(Small point) "Dysemtry" instead of "killed" is a clichês to avoid a clichê. It stands out. I suppose it can't be helped. I suppose all the 75,000000 Europeans who died between 1914–1918 will always be among the 10,000,000 who were killed in the war.

God! The bottom of p. 77 Jusque the top p. 78 are wonderful,[21] I go crazy when people aren't always at their best. This isn't picked out—I just happened on it.

The heart of my critisim beats somewhere apon p. 87.[22] I think you can't change it, though. I felt the lack of some crazy torturing tentativeness or insecurity—horror, all at once, that she'd feel—and he'd feel—maybe I'm crazy. He isn't *like an impotent man. He's like a man in a sort of moral chastity belt.*

Oh, well. It's fine, from Chap V on, anyhow, in spite of that—which fact is merely a proof of its brilliance.

Station Z.W.X. square says good night. Good night all.

[1] Hemingway and Fitzgerald were both on the Riviera, where Fitzgerald read the typescript of *The Sun Also Rises* for the first time. See Philip Young and Charles W. Mann, "Fitzgerald's *Sun Also Rises*," *Fitzgerald/Hemingway Annual* 1970.
[2] Fitzgerald's brackets.
[3] Fitzgerald had persuaded Hemingway to cut an anecdote about Jack Brennan and Benny Leonard from "Fifty Grand."
[4] The first chapter included a series of comments and anecdotes about the Paris Latin Quarter; Hemingway cut these in proof.
[5] Armenian-born English society novelist, best known for *The Green Hat*.
[6] Fitzgerald's brackets.
[7] Fitzgerald's brackets.
[8] Samuel Parkes Cadman, inspirational preacher.
[9] Basil Woon, author of *The Paris That's Not in the Guidebooks*.
[10] Fitzgerald's bracket.
[11] A reference to the epigraph for Hemingway's *in our time* (1924).
[12] An anecdote about Ford Madox Ford, which Hemingway later used in *A Moveable Feast*.
[13] Aleister Crowley, English diabolist; Hemingway later salvaged the anecdote about him in *A Moveable Feast*.
[14] Harold Stearns, alcoholic American journalist in Paris; model for Harvey Stone in *The Sun Also Rises*.
[15] Hemingway made this cut.
[16] President Warren G. Harding, who often had trouble with his rhetoric.
[17] Duff Twysden, an alcoholic and promiscuous English woman; model for Brett Ashley.
[18] English society novelist.
[19] English actress.
[20] Ch. 5 scene in which Jake tells Cohn about Brett.
[21] Ch. 6 scene in which Frances Clyne, Cohn's mistress, berates him for abandoning her.
[22] Ch. 7 scene in which Brett comes to Jake's flat.

FROM: Sara Murphy — ALS, 3 pp. Princeton University
June 1926

Tues.

Dear Scott,—I've generally said to you what I've thought. And it seems another of those moments.

We consider ourselves your friends—

(of course if you don't want us as such but as objects for observation or something—you have only to say so,— + if I were you I shouldn't even bother to read this—)

However we do.—But you can't expect anyone to like or stand a *Continual* feeling of analysis + sub-analysis, + criticism—on the whole unfriendly—Such as we have felt for quite awhile. It is definitely in the air,— + quite unpleasant.—It certainly detracts from any gathering,— + Gerald, for one, simply curls up at the edges + becomes someone else in that sort of atmosphere. And last night you even said "that you had never seen

Gerald so silly + rude"—It's hardly likely that I should Explain Gerald,—or Gerald me—to you. If you don't know what people are like it's *your* loss—And if Gerald was "rude" in getting up + leaving a party that had gotten *quite bad,*—then he was rude to the Hemingways + MacLeishes too—[1] No, it is hardly likely that you would stick at a thing like *Manners*—it is more probably some theory you have,—(it *may* be something to do with the book),—But *you ought to know at your age* that you *Can't have Theories about friends*—If you Can't take friends largely, + without suspicion—then they are not friends at all—. We *Cannot*—Gerald + I—at our age— + stage in life—*be bothered* with Sophomoric situations—like last night—We are very simple people—(unless we feel ourselves in a collegiate quagmire)—and we are *literally* + *actually* fond of you both—(There is no reason for saying this that I know of—unless we meant it.)

And so—*for God's sake* take it or leave it,—as it is meant,—a straight gesture, *without* subtitles—

Yr old + rather irritated friend

Sara

[1] Fitzgerald had spoiled a party given by the Murphys to welcome Hemingway to the Riviera.

TO: James Rennie
c. 17 July 1926

ALS, 1 p. M. J. Smith

Villa St. Louis
Juan-les-Pins
Alpes Maritime
France

Dear Jimmy:

Your wire came just as I was about to wire you. I sobered up in Paris and spent three days trying to get Brigham[1] into shape. Then down here I worked on it some more and made a tentative working outline. But I don't believe that I could make the grade and the more I struggle with it the more I'm convinced that I'd simply ruin your idea by making a sort of half-ass compromise between my amateur idea of "good theatre" and Werner's book. I think your instinct has led you to a great idea but that my unsollicited offer was based more on entheusiasm than on common sense. So I bequeath you the notion of the girl which I think in other hands could be made quite solid and rather ungracefully retire hoping that Connolly or Craig[2] will make you the sort of vehicle of it that's in your imagination.

It was great seeing you You're a man after my own heart and I feel that we have by no means seen the last of each other, even in a theatrical way. My love to Dorothy—it was so nice of you both to come and see Zelda.[3] Take care of yourselves.

Always Your Friend
F Scott Fitzgerald

[1] A play based on M. R. Werner's *Brigham Young.*
[2] Marc Connelly; possibly actor-manager John Craig.
[3] Rennie and his wife, Dorothy Gish, had visited Zelda in the hospital after her appendectomy.

TO: Holger Lundbergh
Summer 1926

ALS, 1 p. Princeton University

Villa St. Louis
Juan-les-Pins
A—M—

Dear Mr. Lundberg

I read every word of the article and enjoyed it immensely.[1] I believe now that all critisism should be read in a language one doesn't understand. It adds poignancy, mystery, glamour.

But I could figure out a lot and God will forgive you for your enconiums. I too. Thank you. King Gustave has sent me orchids.

I hope my next book won't disappoint you. I don't think it will.

Most Gratefully Yours
F. Scott Fitzgerald

[1] A Swedish article by Lundbergh in *Våra Nöjen.*

TO: Thomas Beer[1]
Summer 1926

ALS, 1 p. A. Beer

Villa St. Louis
Juan-les-Pins
France

Dear Tom:

The Mauve Decade never arrived but I bought a copy as I was too impatient to wait and wallowed in every paragraph of it. Its wonderful, and, with *Stephen Crane,* a great achievment. Thanks for your thought of sending it.

Is it professional jealousy that makes me say that to me *Sandoval* was a brilliant failure? I started to include it in my lousy article in the *Bookman*[2] because I sympathize with and admire your intenions in it, and got a lot of place feeling and time feeling all through. But Sandoval himself was concieved, I thought, with too much of the Conrad-Hergeshiemer quality which is also my bête noir. I thought it was miles ahead of *The Fair Rewards* and your next ought to be a wonder.

Always with best wishes
Scott Fitzg—

[1] Novelist and biographer.
[2] "How to Waste Material: A Note on My Generation."

TO: Willerd D. Firestone
Summer 1926

ALS, 1 p. University of Tulsa

Villa St. Louis
Juan-les-Pins
France

Dear Mr. Firestone.

Gatsby took about a year and a half all told.

I should go to college—that is unless you've got something more interesting such as a war, or travel, or crime, to do instead.

Sincerely
F Scott Fitzgerald

TO: Ludlow Fowler
Summer 1926

ALS, 4 pp. Princeton University

Villa St. Louis
Juan-les-Pins
A—M—
France

Dear Ludlow—

More congratulations than I can express and so many good hopes for you that if laid end to end they would reach from here to Winnetka.[1] Someone sent us a picture of Elsie, and I congratulate you again. What's more you sound as if you were really in love again—a thing which you didn't think would ever happen.

And now for the terribly bad news that we won't be back in time for the wedding. If we were free I wouldn't hesitate to come back a few months early, for your wedding Ludlow, but I can't *possibly* finish my novel before Christmas and our plans—we talked it over carefully when your swell letter came—can't possibly be beaten into shape. God! What we would give to come you can imagine. It sounds marvellous. Your bachelor dinner ought to be the best since Trimalchios feast, but please, *please* Ludlow don't end up in Charleton, Carolina next morning

II (I'm following your numerology)

Everyone seems to have recognized you in *The Rich Boy*. Even an unknown autograph hunter from Mercersberg School wrote complimenting me on my "picture of Ludlow Fowler." I discussed it at length with Virginia DeHaven in Paris last June. She didn't seem to mind it a bit—probably didn't know what it was about.

I thought all the critics, at least all the good ones, gave the *Rich Boy* the most space. Almost everyone thinks its the best short story I've ever done

III.

There's no news from us. Zelda had her appendix out in June at the American hospital in Paris and for the first time in a year and a half is really well. We sold the movie of *Gatsby* for $50,000. of which I got a third. We have rather a nice place here on the Rivierra between Antibes + Cannes and half the Americans I know have been or are hereabouts this summer—Gerald Murphys, Archie Mclieshes, Marice Hamilton,[2] Deering Davis, the Wymans, Grace Moore, Ruth Goldbeck, Anita Loos, John Emerson, Hemmingway, Picasso, Mistinguet, Ben Finney, Don Stuart, the Debt Commission + so many others I can't enumerate. I've been slowed up in my work with parties but I'm getting along at last. *Gatsby* reopens in Chicago this winter. I hope Al and Eleanor find more happiness than they have lately. I wouldn't think of taking the glasses—*it was absolutely my fault* for asking you to keep them for me for nearly five years. I simply pressed you because I wanted to be sure you'd made a thorough search. Keep them + use them on your honeymoon if you pass any girls' schools. If you sent them they'd never reach me anyhow as the posts are awful.

Ludlow, that was a wonderful letter and we are so happy to know that you are happy. If you come abroad on your honeymoon you must surely visit us in November. Our best love to you both

Always Your Devoted Friend
Scott

[1] Fowler married Elsie Blatchford of Winnetka, Ill., on 21 October.

[2] Mrs. Pierpont Morgan Hamilton, a Riviera resident and acquaintance of the Fitzgeralds'.

TO: Roger Burlingame ALS, 1 p. Syracuse University
Summer 1926

Villa St. Louis
Juan-les-Pins

Dear Roger:

Thanks enormously for *Susan Shane*. I think it's immensely well done, so much better and more original both in conception and in the writing than *You Too*. There is something about the end that doesn't satisfy me but its rather too difficult to explain in a letter. Susan herself, though, has three dimensions throughout. A really novel and accomplished portrait.

Altogether my most cordial congratulations

As Ever Your Friend
Scott Fitzg—

FROM: Ring Lardner TL, 2 pp. Princeton University

October 13, 1926

Fitzgeralds one and all:—

I have said to myself a hundred times, "Ring, you just must write to those sweet Fitzgeralds," and then I have added (to myself, mind you), "Better wait, perhaps, until there is something to write about." But the days come and the days go and nothing happens—nothing may ever happen. Best not delay any longer.

Very, very glad to hear you are returning soon to God's Country and the Woman. Don't you dare live anywhere but Great Neck, but if I were you, I'd rent awhile before I thought of buying. If you want me to, I will be on the look-out for a suitable furnished house.

Ellis had two babies this summer. They are both girls, giving us two girls and four boys, an ideal combination, we think.[1]

On a party with the Rices, at the Sidney Fishes' in East Hampton, we ran into Esther Murphy[2] and her father and mother. I had an interesting talk with Miss Murphy (Interesting to me, mind you).

The Ziegfeld show (Gene's) didn't do well in New York, but is going better (they say) on the road.

I was in deadly earnest when I said I liked "The Peasants."[3] I knew damn well it would be over your head (Not yours, Zelda).

May Preston[4] reports that she saw you (not you, Zelda) on your way to the hospital, in Paris, and that you were carrying a bouquet of corsets to give your wife.

I enclose a copy (nearly complete) of the story I wrote about the "fight" in Philadelphia. Heywood Broun refused, at the last moment, to cover it and as a favor to Herbert,[5] and to my syndicate, I said I would do it. We had terrible wire trouble on account of the rain and only about half my story got into the World. It broke off (the story) in such a manner that people must have said to themselves that I was very drunk. It made me so mad that I am going to quit newspapers as soon as the last of my present contracts expires, which will be in six months. After that I am going to try to work half as hard and make the same amount of money, a feat which I believe can be done. I bet $500 on Dempsey, giving 2 to 1. The odds ought to have been 7 to 1. Tunney couldn't lick David[6] if David was trying. . . .[7]

You ought to meet this guy Tunney. We had lunch with him a few weeks before the fight and among a great many other things, he said he thought the New York State boxing commission was "imbecilic" and that he hoped Dempsey would not think his (Tunney's) experience in pictures had "cosmeticized" him.

. . . .[8]

We have just had a world's series that neither club had any right to be in, let alone win, and that is all I will say about sports, excepting that Heywood, who has become quite a Negrophile, wrote column after column on the fistic prowess of Harry Wills and the dread that he was held in by Dempsey et al., and how unfair it was not to give Harry a chance, and—Well, last night Wills deliberately fouled Jack Sharkey in the 13th. round after Sharkey (who isn't even as good as Tunney) had beaten the life out of him from the very beginning.

I have been on the wagon since early in July, when Ellis' mother died. Before that I had a spree that broke a few records for longevity and dullness.

A couple of months ago, the Metro-Goldwyn people asked me to write a baseball picture for Karl Dane, the man who made such a hit as "Slim," one of the doughboys in "The Big Parade." We talked matters over several times and finally the man asked me how much I would want. I told him I didn't know what authors were getting. He said, "Well, we are giving Johnnie Weaver $7,500 and Marc Connelly the same," so he asked me again what I wanted and I said $40,000 and he threw up his hands and exclaimed, "Excuse me, Mr. Lardner, for wasting your *valuable* time!" Maybe I told you that before; I have no idea how long ago it was I wrote to you.

It might not be very lively for you, but why not come and stay with us awhile before or after you go to Montgomery.

Keep me posted on your plans and accept the undying love of the madam and

I.

[1] Mrs. Lardner did not give birth to any children that summer.
[2] Sister of Gerald Murphy.
[3] Possibly a novelette by Chekov.
[4] Magazine illustrator.
[5] Broun was a columnist on the *New York World;* Herbert Bayard Swope was editor of the *World.*
[6] Lardner's son. The reference is to the first Dempsey-Tunney fight, which Tunney won.
[7] One hundred six words omitted by the editor.
[8] Fifty-six words omitted by the editor.

TO: Ludlow Fowler
Fall 1926

ALS, 2 pp. Princeton University

Villa St. Louis
Juan-les-Pins
A—M—

Dear Ludlow:

Of *course* you must stop off and see us. You seem to think we're in a wilderness ("some sort of Inn in the vicinity"). You'll stay with us in the house but if it interests you in these exciting days, there are two de Luxe Hotels here, the gayest and third largest Casino on the Rivierra and three wild night clubs.

Now some dope. The trip from Biaritz to Marseille by train is *terrible.* Three changes + no sleepers unless you go way back to Bordeaux
But by auto its wonderful. (Through Pau, Carcassonne, Nimes ect)
Why not go to Biarritz by *train* from Paris? Everyone agrees that the Chateau country by auto is a dud anyhow. From Marseille to us is all right—is about five hours by train. But from Biaritz to Marseille by train is two terrible days and a sit-up all night (or else stop-offs) + by auto is three beautiful days in the Pyrenees-Pau, Lourdes ect ect.

From Juan-les-Pins you can take in Monte Carlo, Nice, Cannes ect. Cannes is ten minutes, just across the bay.

We're *mad* to see you. We'll be here till Dec 8th. Come for four or five days anyhow—a week if you can. We'll go off the wagon—while you're here.

We will present you with your wedding gift when you arrive here. Hurry!

Always Your Devoted Friend
Scott

Villa St. Louis
Juan-les-Pins
A-M-

Dear Ludlow:

Of course you must stop off and see us. You seem to think we're in a wilderness ("some sort of Inn in the vicinity"). You'll stay with us, in the house, but if it interests you in these exciting days, there are two de Luxe Hotels here, the gayest and third largest Casino on the Riveria and three wild night clubs.

Now some dope. The trip from Biarritz to Marseille by train is terrible. Three changes + no sleepers unless you go way back to Bordeaux

Paris
Bordeaux
Biarritz
Spanish Border
Marseille
Cannes
Juan-les-Pins
Antibes
Nice
Monte Carlo

But by auto its wonderful. (Through Pau, Carcassonne, Nimes ect)

Why not go to Biarritz by train from Paris? Everyone agrees that the Chateau country by auto is a dud

(2)

anyhow. From Marseille to us is all right — about five hours by train but from Biarritz to Marseille by train is two terrible days and a sit up all night (or else stop-offs) + by auto is three beautiful days in the Pyrenees - Pau, Lourdes ect ect.

From Juan-les-Pins you can take in Monte Carlo, Nice, Cannes ect. Cannes is ten minutes, just across the bay.

We're mad to see you. We'll be here till Dec 8th. Come for four or five days anyhow — a week if you can. We'll go off the wagon while you're here.

We will present you with your wedding gift when you arrive here. Hurry!

Always Your Devoted Friend
Scott

TO: Lois Moran
Early 1927

Inscription in *This Side of Paradise*.
Bruccoli
Hollywood, California

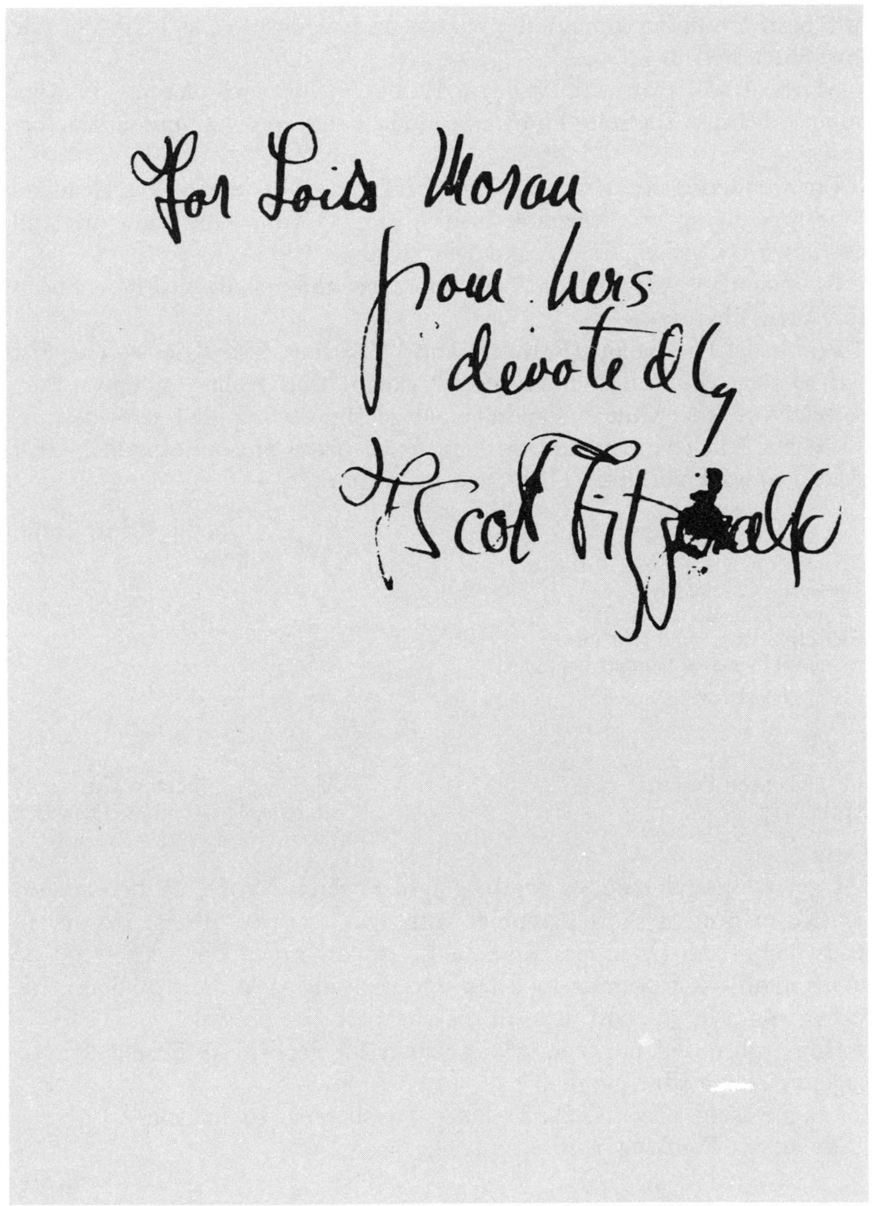
For Lois Moran
from hers
devotedly
F Scott Fitzgerald

Note: Probably inscribed at the time Fitzgerald met Miss Moran, an actress who became the model for Rosemary Hoyt in *Tender Is the Night*.

FROM: Lois Moran
Spring 1927

ALS, 3 pp. Princeton University

Darling Scott—

I miss you enormously—Life is exceedingly dull out here now—Have just been bumming around the studios and seeing people I am not the least interested in—

Maybe I will play with William Haines in his next picture—I rather hope so because I admire him tremendously and he gives very satisfactory kisses—

I'm wondering what sort of a trip you had—You must have spent all your time filling out telegraph blanks, judging from the numerous and hectic wires Carmel,[1] John,[2] and I received—

Rosamond[3] leaves for New York tomorrow and I shall miss her—She is absolutely charming—

Finished "The Sailor's Return"[4] and "The Sun Also Rises"—The first was so tragically real and the second caught that feeling of unrest very perfectly—For a while I couldn't analyze the feeling that pervades the book, but I believe it is that, isn't it? Both books are quite perfect, each in its own way, methinks. Thank you again for them—

Good-by, dear child,
Lois

[1] Actress Carmel Myers.
[2] Actor John Barrymore.
[3] Actress Rosamond Pinchot.
[4] Novel by David Garnett (1925).

TO: Maxwell Perkins
April 1927

ALS, 1 p. Princeton University
"Ellerslie," Edgemoor, Delaware

Dear Max:

I get continual requests for biographical data. Would it be very expensive to print a short pamphlet with two or three articles on me already published (Wilsons, Rosenfelds, Boyds—say about 12,000–15,000 words in all)—a picture or so, a few appreciations + a short bibliography. What would be the cost done in the cheapest way possible?

Hope you found the cane. Many thanks for deposit. Will send title + pages at 1st possible moment.[2]

Let me know about O'Hara's book. It was great to see you

No news. Working hard

Scott.

[1] A pamphlet was not published.
[2] Perkins had requested the title and a sample of the text of Fitzgerald's novel in order to start designing the book. Fitzgerald submitted "The Boy Who Killed His Mother" as a working title.

TO: Richard Halliburton[1]
c. 30 June 1927

ALS, 1 p. Princeton University

"Ellerslie"
Edgemoor, Delaware

Dear Dick:

I hope this will reach you before you disappear into Brooklyn to imagine and write another travel book—because don't think I really believe you've been in all these places and done all these things like you say. That bathtub was pretty well faked up to look like the Helespont, but what is the cake of soap and the patent back-washer doing on the so-called "shores of Asia Minor"? The family chimney does well enough for the "throne of Zeus" but when you call Ellis Island "Corfu City" and fake up an old photo of Coney as "Gozo" or "Gazabo," I feel that, like all missionaries to foriegn parts you are taking away money from those who can use it and spend it on those who can't.

It is a good book, better planned and better written than the first. I'd hope it sells better too but I want "the dear public" to have some cash left for mine.

Your Friend
Scott Fitzg—

That must have been a good cigar you were smoking (facing P. 217) and I'm glad to repairs on Nassau Hall are getting along (facing p 69)[2]

[1] Princeton-educated adventurer and author.

[2] Halliburton had sent Fitzgerald a copy of his book *The Glorious Adventure* (1927) inscribed: "For F. Scott Fitzgerald The world's swellest fiction writer from Richard Halliburton America's noblest travel writer June 1 1927." (Princeton) The postscript references are to illustrations of Stromboli and the Acropolis.

TO: Maxwell Perkins
September 1927

ALS, 1 p. Princeton University
"Ellerslie," Edgemoor, Delaware

Dear Max:

One million matters

(1) Terribly sorry you can't come down. How about the first wk. end in October. Will that suit you both—I do hope so. The last fortnight of Sept is bad for us.

(2.) Thanks for the royalty report. You were nice to say what you said—too nice, alas, for I'm going to ask you, if you possibly can, to deposit for me $200.00. That still keeps it under 5000. Can you?

(3.) What do you know of Hemmingway, save his marriage?

(4.) I'm hoping now to finish the novel by the middle of November.

(5.) This enclosed letter is self explanatory. The entire European vogue of *Gatsby* (except the Scandanavian rights) rests on the French translation which I paid Llona to make. Evidently what he feared has happened and it seems a shame I wasn't informed about it before money was accepted from the Knauer Verlag. I don't know what arrangement you made with them but I hope it wasn't an outright sale—in any case if it is possible I wish you'd cancel the matter + take up the enclosed contract instead as neither Victor Llona or I who inaugurated the whole European business with your authorization were consulted by Knauer and I'd much rather come out there under Joyces publisher and translated by a known good man. Do let me know at once what you can do. It is of vital importance to me as I feel I am going to have more + more a European public. Also please return Llona's letter.

No more now. Always Your Affectionate Friend

Scott

P.S. I love my cane. I carry nothing else.

FROM: Ring W. Lardner — TL, 1 p. (fragment). Bruccoli

Sunday, Sept. 25. [1927]

Dear Sir and Madam:—

Our son Jimmie has joined our son John at Andover, and Jimmie is pretty homesick, so Ellis is going up there to spend next week-end with him. If she broke that engagement, he would die. So, you see, we can't visit you and we are both sorry. I hope you are, too.

If you care to know anything about my affairs, I had quite a wet summer, but have now been on the wagon since the 22nd. of August. During the dry intermissions, I wrote a baseball play which George Cohan accepted.[1] He says he is going to put it on this fall, but you know these d------------------------d producers. If he does, and if he should happen to try it out at Atlantic City, I'd expect the Fitzgeralds to be in attendance as a belated reward for the Lardners' sacrifice of time and money in 1924 or whatever year "The Vegetable" was staged.

I have written three short stories this month in an effort to ease the financial situation brought about by weeks of idleness and weeks of work on the play. To make that situation a little more desperate, the Pittsburgh ball club seems ready to lose the National League pennant and finish behind the Giants. Last spring I bet $800 to $2400 that Pittsburgh would win the pennant and $800 to $800 that it would beat out New York. A week ago, it looked as if I could begin spending my $3200 winnings, but now, with New York having all the best of the remaining schedule, I appear to be sunk.[2] To offset that, I am thinking of covering the world's series for Jack Wheeler.[3] Two years ago I swore I would never work on another one, but when poverty

[1] *Elmer the Great.*
[2] The Pittsburgh Pirates won the National League pennant in 1927.
[3] Proprietor of the Bell Syndicate.

TO: H. L. Mencken
c. October 1927

Inscription in Ernest Hemingway's *Men Without Women* (1927). Enoch Pratt Library

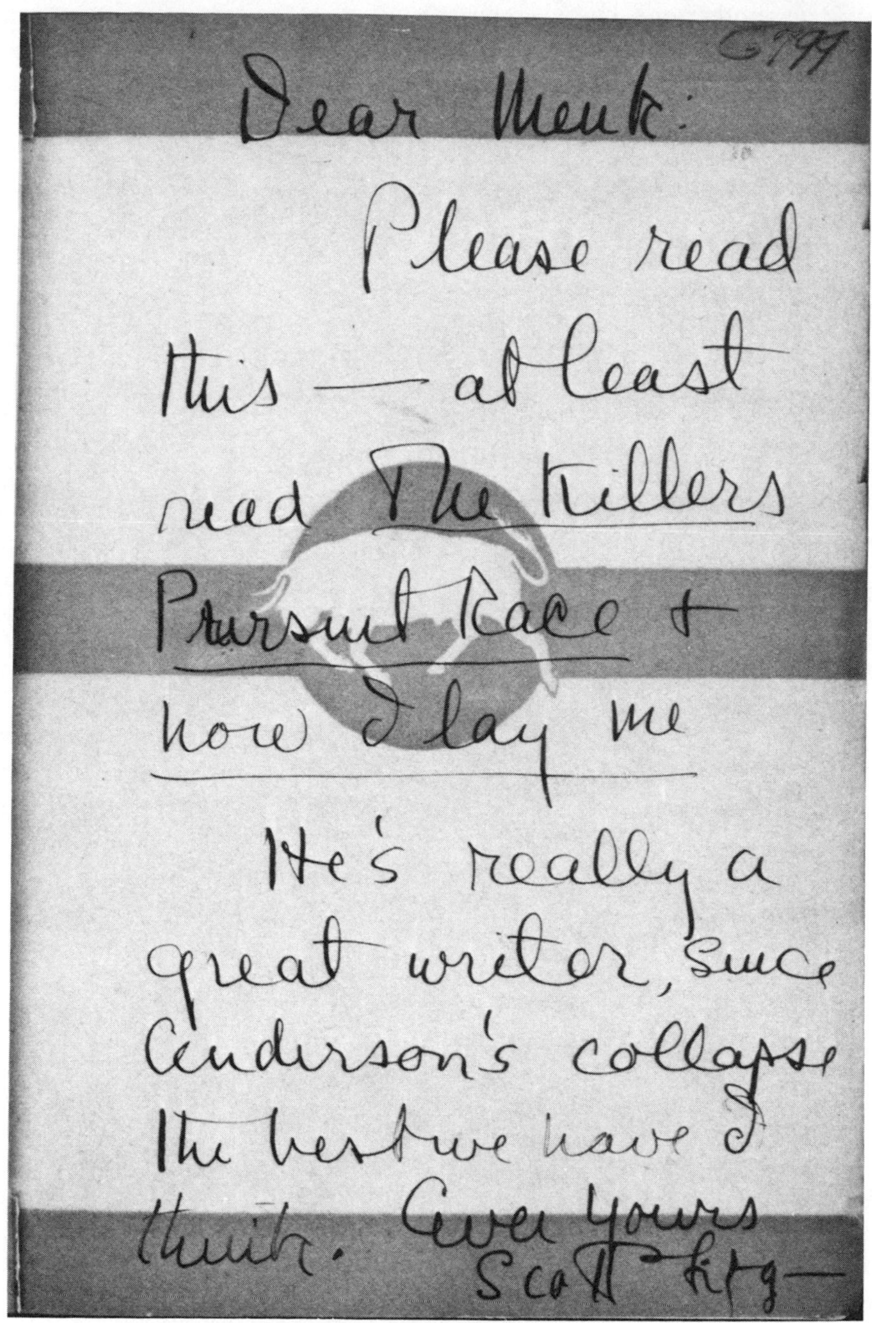

Dear Menk:
Please read
this — at least
read *The Killers*
Pursuit Race &
Now I lay me

He's really a
great writer, since
Anderson's collapse
the best we have I
think. Ever yours
Scott Fitzg—

TO: Ring and Ellis Lardner
December 1927(?)

TL, 1 p. Scrapbook. Princeton University
"Ellerslie," Edgemoor, Delaware

To the Ring Lardners[1]

You combed Third Avenue last year
  For some small gift that was not too dear
—Like a candy cane or a worn out truss—
  To give to a loving friend like us
You'd found gold eggs for such wealthy hicks
  As the Edsell Fords and the Pittsburgh Fricks
The Andy Mellons, the Teddy Shonts
  The Coleman T. and Pierre duPonts
But not one gift to brighten our hoem
—So I'm sending you back your God damn poem.

1 Written in response to the Lardners' printed poem about their inability to find suitable Christmas gifts.

FROM: Maxwell Perkins

TL(CC), 2 pp. Princeton University

Dec. 8, 1927

Dear Scott:

I am sorry you were troubled about that check for one hundred and fifty. When busy at other things, I thought a number of times of wiring you. I had it on my mind, but I thought, "He will know we did it anyhow." Now I am enclosing a check in behalf of Ernest Hemingway on orders just received from him. We sent him a check for a thousand dollars the other day, although he had not asked for it, and he does not seem to want it much. He says he may not ever cash it, and that he finds he lives according to the amount he has, however little it may be. "Men without" has gone to 13,000. I shall see John Biggs tomorrow, and hear about how you get on.

By the way, if you want an easy and amusing exercise, do as I have done, and get a set of quoit—tennis. It is practically the same game as deck tennis, and can be put up even on a piazza,—although I do not think yours is wide enough. *I* have it on a piazza and play it almost every night. Half an hour a day would keep you pretty fit, I believe, and Zelda would like it.

Ever yours,

TO: Mr. Barret
1927–1929

ALS, 1 p. University of Virginia

Edgemoor, Delaware

Dear Mr. Barret:

The priest gives the boy a form of Absolution[1] (not of course sacramental), by showing him that he (the priest) is in an even worse state of horror + dispair.

Thanks for your letter. I've been working on a novel for several years—hence so few stories

Sincerely
F. Scott Fitzgerald

[1] "Absolution" appeared in *The American Mercury* (June 1924) and was collected by Fitzgerald in *All the Sad Young Men* (1926).

FROM: Thornton Wilder

ALS, 2 pp. Princeton University

Jan 12 1928

Dear Scott Fitzgerald:

I have been an admirer, not to say a student, of The Great Gatsby too long not to have got a great kick out of your letter. It gives me the grounds to hope that we may sometime have some long talks on what writing's all about. As you see I am a provincial schoolmaster[1] and have always worked alone. And yet nothing interests me more than thinking of our generation as a league and as a protest to the whole cardboard generation that precedes us from Wharton through Cabell and Anderson and Sinclair Lewis. I know Ernest Hemingway. Glenway Westcott, I think, is coming down here for a few days soon. I'd like to think that you'd be around Princeton before long and ready for some long talks. I like teaching a lot and shall probably remain here for ages; a daily routine is necessary to me: I have no writing habits, am terribly lazy and write seldom. I'd be awfully proud if you arrived in my guestroom some time.

I spent last Xmas with a pack of Rhodes Scholars (I'm not one) at Juan-les-Pins. The dentist-doctor-ex-sailor-adventurer on the plage told me you were working on a novel based upon a pathological situation seen in the hotel crowd. You'd do it wonderfully and to hell with Scribners. The new firm of Coward-McCann would do their share wonderfully well. I'm sending you my Second—[2]

We're looking for some more tremendous pages from you. Thanks a lot for writing me

Sincerely yours
Thornton Wilder

Jan. 12. 1928

Later: God, I write a bad letter. I hoped this was going to carry more conviction. Fill in with the energy I'd have had if I hadn't just taught four classes in French. T.W.

[1] At the Lawrenceville School in New Jersey.
[2] *The Angel That Troubled the Waters and Other Plays* (1928).

TO: Maxwell Perkins
After 24 January 1928

ALS, 1 p. Princeton University
"Ellerslie," Edgemoor, Delaware

Dear Max:

Novel not finished. Christ I wish it were! Thanks for Hemmingway's letter. Was Dudly Lunt's law book any good?[1]

That's fine about Morly Callagan.[2] I'll come up but give me plenty of warning. I think he really has it—personality, or whatever it is. One can't be sure yet and I doubt if he's as distinctive a figure as Ernest (Gosh! hasn't he gone over big?)

Will you ask the bk. keeping dept. not to spare my shame but to send me my bi-ennial report, for the income tax?

As Ever
Scott.

[1] Possibly Dudley Lunt's *The Road to the Law,* published in 1932.
[2] Morley Callaghan, Canadian novelist whose short-story collection, *Native Argosy,* had just been accepted by Scribners. See Perkins' 24 January letter to Fitzgerald in *Scott/Max.*

TO: Scottie Fitzgerald
24–25 January 1928

Three holograph postcards signed.
Scottie Fitzgerald Smith
Montreal, Quebec

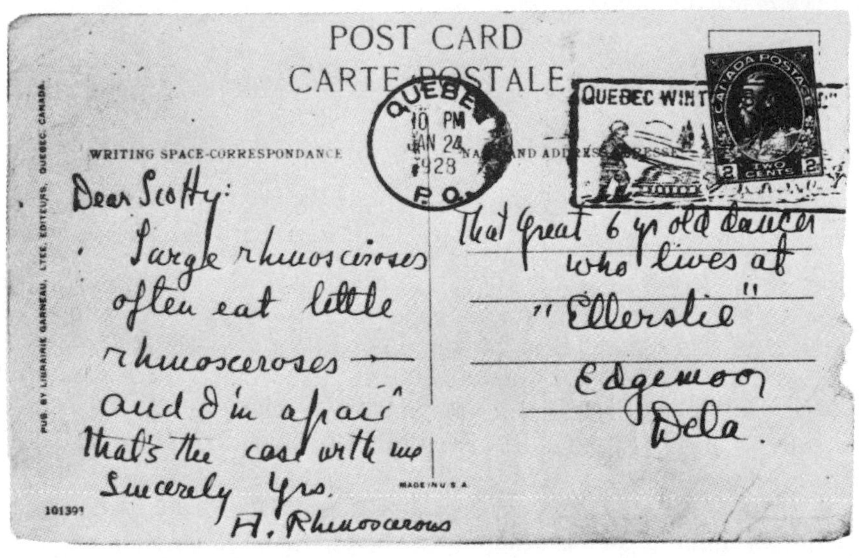

POST CARD
CARTE POSTALE

PUB. BY LIBRAIRIE GARNEAU, LTEE. EDITEURS, QUEBEC CANADA.

QUEBEC
10 PM
JAN 24
1928
P.Q.

QUEBEC WINT

WRITING SPACE-CORRESPONDANCE

Dear Scotty:
Large rhinoscerosses
often eat little
rhinosceroses —
and I'm afraid
that's the case with me
Sincerely Yrs.
A. Rhinoscerous

That Great 6 yr old dancer
who lives at
"Ellerslie"
Edgemoor
Dela.

MADE IN U.S.A.

101391

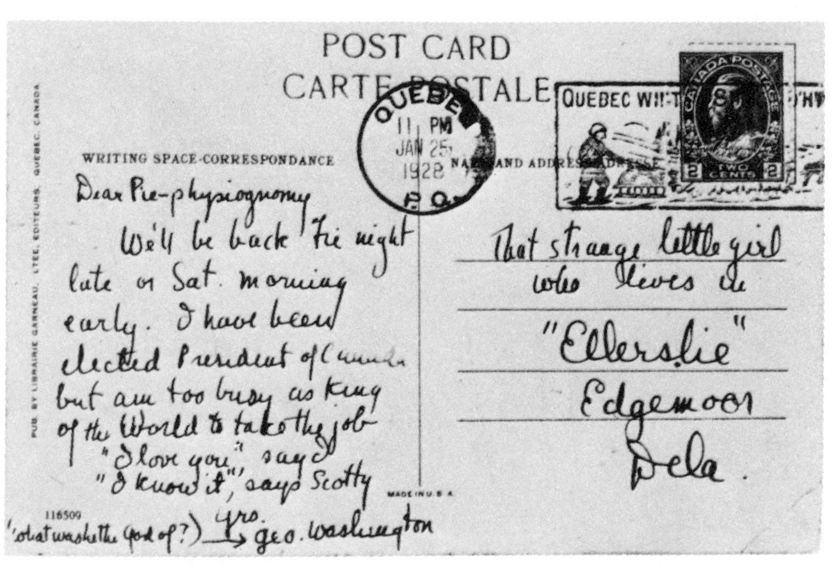

POST CARD
CARTE POSTALE

QUEBEC 11 PM JAN 25 1928 P.Q.

WRITING SPACE-CORRESPONDANCE

NAME AND ADDRESS—ADRESSE

Dear Pie-physiognomy

We'll be back Fri night late or Sat. morning early. I have been elected President of Canada but am too busy as King of the World to take the job

"I love you," says

"I know it", says Scotty

Yrs. Geo. Washington

(what was he the God of?)

That strange little girl who lives in "Ellerslie" Edgemoor Dela.

PUB. BY LIBRAIRIE GARNEAU, LTEE, EDITEURS, QUEBEC, CANADA.

116509

MADE IN U.S.A.

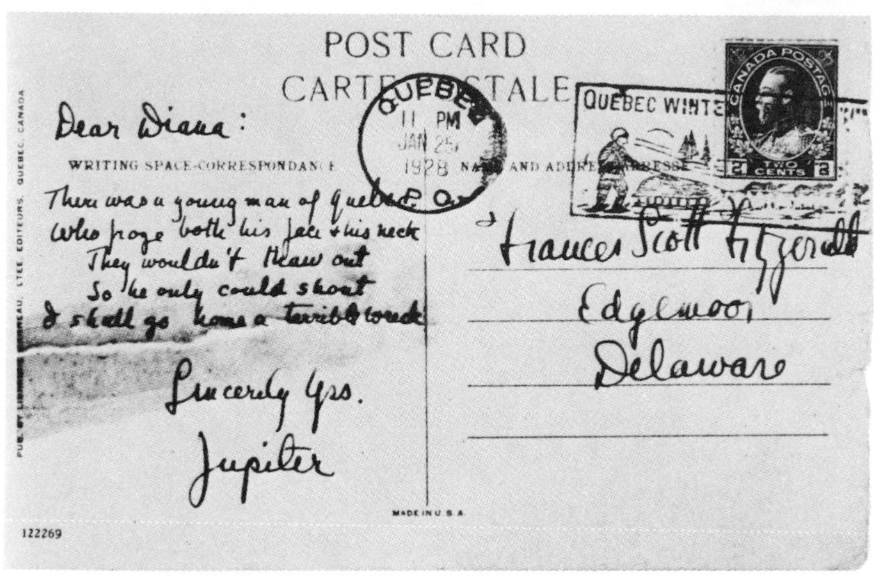

POST CARD
CARTE POSTALE

QUEBEC
11 PM
JAN 25
1928
P.Q.

QUEBEC WINTE

CANADA POSTAGE
TWO CENTS

Dear Diana:

WRITING SPACE-CORRESPONDANCE

NAME AND ADDRESS-ADRESSE

There was a young man of Quebec
Who froze both his feet & his neck
They wouldn't thaw out
So he only could shout
I shall go home a terrible wreck

Sincerely Yrs.
Jupiter

To Frances Scott Fitzgerald
Edgemoor,
Delaware

MADE IN U.S.A.

122269

MONTMORENCY FALLS, QUEBEC, CANADA.

Went swimming here today. It was very exciting—but they turned on the cold instead of the hot.

CHUTES MONTMORENCY, QUEBEC, CANADA.

FROM: Thornton Wilder
February 1928

ALS, 2 pp. Princeton University

Dear Scotty:

Dont brood about your speech in the evening; your speech in the afternoon was a raring wow and the audience wants more.[1] Can you have me on Sat the 25th: I can leave Trenton at any time after 10:30 and as always when I'm going towards any place I will be thinking with strange concentration about you for the length of the whole train-ride. It is wonderful to have been liked by you and to have been told so, for the self-confidence I have exhibited toward my work I have never been able to extend to my person.

Up here I'm dog-tired just now: the House is always restless during the Winter-term and espec. just before the 3-day Prom.

Heaven bless you and your book. And the two ladies whom I shall straight off call by their first names.

All for you
Thornt.

[1] Fitzgerald spoke at the Princeton Cottage Club in February.

TO: Norris D. Jackson[1]
Postmarked 23 March 1928

ALS, 1 p. Princeton University
"Ellerslie" letterhead. Edgemoor, Delaware

Dear Nor

This letter is inspired by a desire to tell Betty that in a story of mine called The Scandal Detectives which will be in the Post in April[2] I've tried to pay some tribute to that celebrated children's meeting place, the Ames' backyard. Please clip it and save it for your children, for sooner or later time will wipe out that pleasant spot.

How are you? And Betty? and all your illegitimate children who I suppose are even now clogging up the juvenile courts with their delinquencies. We have taken an old place on the Delaware River where we live in splendor surrounded by a nubian guard of sling throwers, eunuchs, back-slappers and concubines.

I miss you enormously. If you + Betty come East this Spring would you please come and spend a few years with

Your Old and Always Devoted Friend
Scott—

[1] Boyhood friend of Fitzgerald in St. Paul, married to the former Betty Ames.
[2] *The Saturday Evening Post*, CC (28 April 1928).

FROM: Sylvia Beach[1] — ALS, 1 p. Princeton University

June 23 1928

Dear Scott Fitzgerald,

Don't forget that you and Mrs Fitzgerald are coming to dine with us next Wednesday at 8, (to meet Mr and Mrs Joyce)[2] and we are counting on you. Adrienne[3] and I live at 18 rue de l'Odéon on the 4th floor no lift.

Yours very sincerely
Sylvia Beach

[1] Owner of the Paris bookstore Shakespeare and Company, and publisher of *Ulysses*.

[2] This occasion was the "Festival of St. James."

[3] Adrienne Monnier, owner of the Paris bookshop La Maison des Amis des Livres.

TO: Sylvia Beach — ALS, 1 p. and inscription in *The Great Gatsby*.[1] Princeton University

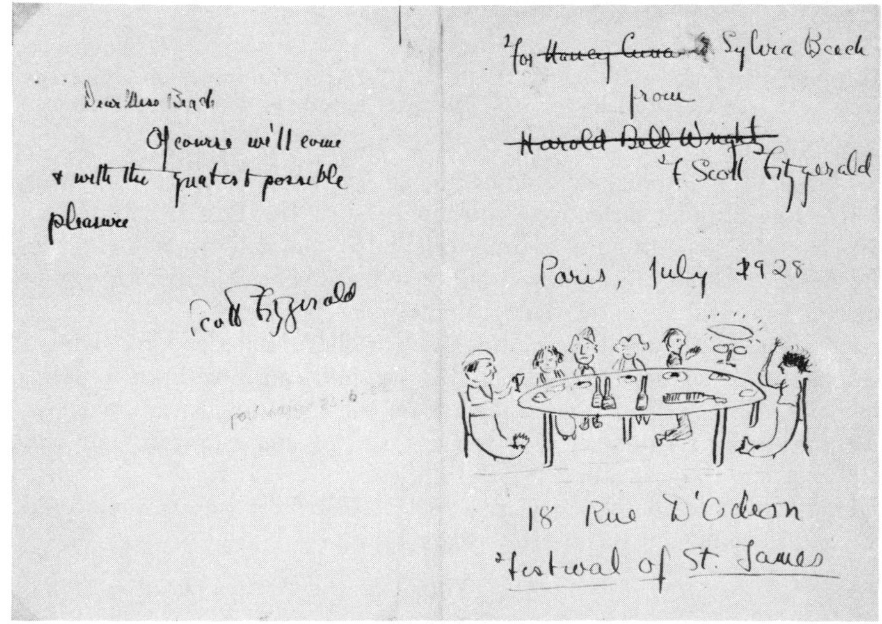

Dear Miss Beach

Of course we'll come & with the greatest possible pleasure

Scott Fitzgerald

for ~~[illegible]~~ Sylvia Beach
from
~~Harold Bell Wright~~
F Scott Fitzgerald

Paris, July 1928

18 Rue D'Odeon
Festival of St. James

[1] Fitzgerald's note to Beach is mounted on the front pastedown endpaper and is dated "25–6–28" in another hand. The inscription is on the free front endpaper.

FROM: James Joyce
11 July 1928

ALS, 1 p.[1] Bruccoli

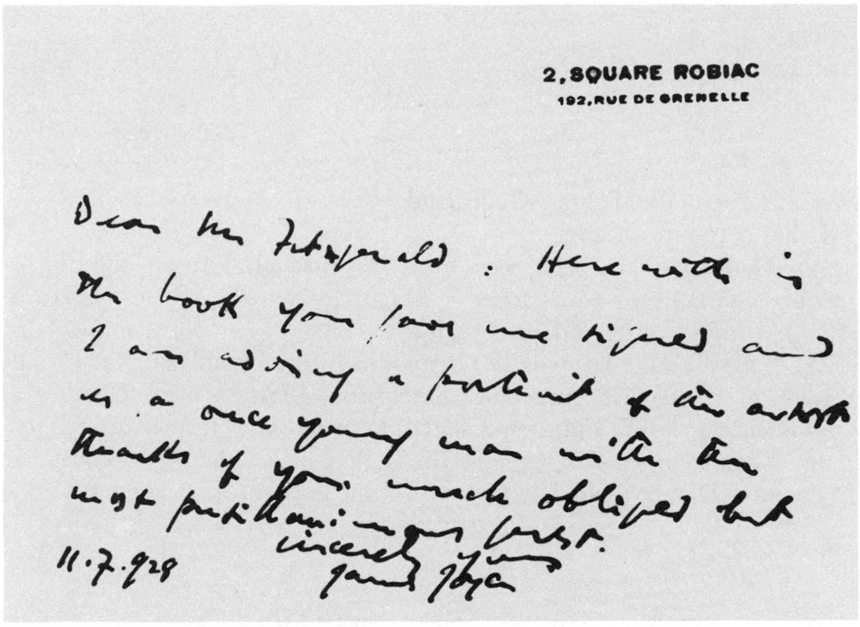

2, SQUARE ROBIAC
192, RUE DE GRENELLE

Dear Mr Fitzgerald: Here with is the book you gave me signed and I am adding a portrait of the artist as a once young man with the thanks of your much obliged but most pusillanimous guest.

Sincerely yours.
James Joyce

11.7.928

Dear Mr Fitzgerald: Here with is the book you gave me signed and I am adding a portrait of the artist as a once young man with the thanks of your much obliged but most pusillanimous guest.

Sincerely yours.
James Joyce

11.7.928

[1] Letter pasted in Fitzgerald's copy of *Ulysses*, which is not signed by Joyce. The copy of A *Portrait of the Artist as a Young Man* is inscribed: "To/Scott Fitzgerald/ James Joyce/Paris/11•7•928." (Bruccoli)

Joyce's description of himself as "pusillanimous" probably refers to the occasion when Fitzgerald worried him by offering to jump out the window to express his admiration.

TO: Ernest Hemingway
c. July 1928

ALS, 2 pp. Kennedy Library
Paris

Teenie-weenie Corner
Sunshineville.

Precious Papa, Bull-fighter, Gourmand ect.

It has come to my ears

ⓐ That you have been seen bycycling through Kansas, chewing + spitting a mixture of goat's meat + chicory which the natives collect + sell for artery-softener and market-glut

ⓑ That Bumby[1] has won the Benjamin Altman scholarship at Cundle School + taken first prizes in *Comparitive Epistemology, Diseases of Cormorants + Small Vultures, Amateur Gyncology + Intestinal Hysterics*

ⓒ That you are going to fight Jim Tully[2] in Washdog Wisconsin on Decoration Day in a chastity belt with your hair cut á la garconne.

Is it all true?

We are friends with the Murphys again. Talked about you a great deal + while we *tried* to say only kind things we managed to get in a few good cracks that would amuse you—about anybody else—which is what you get for being so far away. Incidently called twice on Hadley[3]—she was both times out but saw Bumby once + think he's the best kid I ever saw by 1000 miles.

Well, old Mackerel Snatcher,[4] wolf a Wafer + + a Beaker of blood for me,—and when you come Shadowboxing into my life again with your new similes for "swewa" and "wousy" (which, as you doubtless notice, you've given to the world) no one will be glader than your

Devoted Friend
Scott Fitzg—

While in America don't cast any doubt on my statement that you held a bridgehead (or was it a hophead) at Caporetto for three days + utterly baffled the 2nd Austrian Army Corps. In 50 yrs all the people that could have denied it will be dead or busy holding their own bridgeheads—like Lawrence Stallings, who is slowly taking to himself the communal exploits of the 5th + 6th Marines. "Hebuterne—of course I know it—I took that village."

Do send Lorimer[5] a story. I Read Mencken's public apology.[6] Not bad for an old man who has had his troubles. God help us all! Have seen a good deal of Joyce. Please come back—will be here till Aug 20th 58 Rue de Vaugirard. Then back to America for a few months.

Best to Pauline!

[1] Hemingway's first son, John Hadley Nicanor.
[2] Hobo writer.
[3] Hemingway's first wife, whom he had divorced in 1927.
[4] Hemingway had converted to Catholicism at the time of his marriage to Pauline Pfeiffer.
[5] George Horace Lorimer, editor of *The Saturday Evening Post.*
[6] Possibly a reference to Mencken's review of *Men Without Women* in *The American Mercury* (May 1928).

TO: Maxwell Perkins
After 6 August 1928

ALS, 1 p. Princeton University
Paris

Dear Max:

Terribly sorry about Bishop.[1] Delighted about Chamson.[2] But this is *very important!—The Road Menders* is not accurate—they are *not* mending a road but pushing a new road thru + this becomes a great part of their lives; they are creaters + belong to their creation. Of course the difficulty of the literal "Men of the Road" is that it suggests Highwaymen to us. I suggest (without thinking any of these titles are good)

The Road Builders
The Road Makers
Creation
Toilers of the Road
Makers of the Road
Work on the Road[3]

In Haste
Scott

[1] Perkins had declined to publish a novel by John Peale Bishop.
[2] Andre Chamson, author of *Les hommes de la route,* whom Fitzgerald had recommended to Perkins. The novel was published by Scribners in 1929 as *The Road.*
[3] See Perkins' 6 August letter to Fitzgerald in *Scott/Max.*

TO: Maxwell Perkins
October/November 1928

ALS, 1 p. Princeton University
"Ellerslie," Edgemoor, Delaware

Dear Max:

Am going to send you two chapters a month of the final version of book beginning next week + ending in Feb.[1] Strictly confidential. Don't tell

Reynolds! I think this will help me get it straight in my own mind—I've been alone with it too long.

I think Stearns will be delighted + hereby accept for him.[2] Send me a check made out *to him*—he hasn't had that much money since I gave him $50 in '25—the poor bastard. If you leave out his name leave out mine too—or as you like.

Ever Yrs
Scott

Sending chapters Tues or Wed or Thurs.

[1] Fitzgerald sent only one installment of the novel.
[2] Harold Stearns, "Apology of an Expatriate," *Scribner's Magazine* (March 1929)—written in the form of a letter to Fitzgerald.

FROM: Victor Llona — TLS, 1 p. Ernest Kroll

"Les Glycines," Marlotte (S.&M.)
Dec. 9, 1928.

Dear Scotty,

Look who's here! I have received the following letter:

> "Mon cher Llona,
>
> Voulez-vous faire savoir à F. Scott Fitzgerald que son livre m'a permis de passer des heures très dures (je suis dans une clinique). C'est un livre *céleste;* chose la plus rare du monde.
>
> Vous lui demanderez qu'il vous félicite d'en être le traducteur—*car il faut une plume mystérieuse pour ne pas tuer l'oiseau bleu,* pour ne pas le changer en langue morte.
>
> Je vous embrasse,
> Jean Cocteau.

Too bad he did not write this in the papers when the book came out—the sales would have gone up 2 or 300 per cent. Apparently he read the book quite recently.

When will you bless us with another heavenly book? I am most anxious to read you.

Our best wishes to you all.

Yours for ever,
Victor Llona

P.S. The itilization is J.C's.

FROM: Maxwell Perkins TL(CC), 2 pp. Princeton University

Jan. 23, 1929

Dear Scott:

I enclose a check for one hundred dollars which is from Ernest Hemingway in payment of that loan. He has also written, "Unless you come and get the book you can't have it," so I expect to go and get it next week.[1] Why don't you come too, and swear to stick with me and I will have you back inside of nine days. I would feel much safer with you too. Without you I may leave a leg with a shark, or do worse,—because alone I would lack the courage of my cowardice which would otherwise prompt me not to have anything to do with sharks. It seems Hemingway and Waldo[2] have a theory that the sharks are more afraid of them than they are of the sharks,—but they are much more likely to be afraid of them than they are of me.

I am going to post an office boy sentry to watch the elevators to see when you come into this building and go out of it unless you break the habit of skipping the fifth floor.

Ever your friend,

[1] *A Farewell to Arms* (1929). Hemingway was in Key West, Fla.
[2] Artist Waldo Peirce.

TO: Maxwell Perkins ALS, 2 pp. Princeton University
February 1929

Edgemoor, Dela

Dear Max

This is about four things

1st Can you have my "royalty" report sent me this week as I need it for my income tax. The last one Aug 1st 1928 with chivalrous delicacy does not mention the monies I had from you during 1928 and the government is insistant.

2nd Will you look out for a war book by one Wm. A. Brennan, a friend of a cousin of mine. It just might amount to something

3d Ditto in the case of a novel by Katherine Tighe Fessenden (Mrs. T. Hart Fessenden) who read proof on T. S. of P. + to whom I dedicated *The Vegetable*. Its her 1st novel + might be excellent. Will you let me know privately what you think of it?

4th Reynolds says Mr. Chas. Scribner was opposed to Cerf[1] using one of my stories in a modern library collection to be called *The Best Modern*

Short Stories; a 20th Century Anthology and to include Conrad, E. M Forster, D. H. Lawrence, Kath. Mansfield, Anderson + Maugham. In the cases of Hemmingway + Lardner who are chiefly known as short story writers I can see the objection, especially as they are still selling. But as my three collections sold about 150 books last year I don't see it makes much difference in a financial way.

Personally I should like very much to be in the collection—but there are only three or four short stories, Absolution, The *Rich Boy, Benjamin Button, The Diamond as Big as the Ritz + May Day* that I'd put in a book with the people I've mentioned—everything recently has a certain popular twist, even when its pretty good. So without your permission I'll have to forgo the matter. Please advise me.[2]

I'll be up next week

As Ever

Scott

[1] Bennett Cerf, a founding partner of Random House.

[2] *Great Modern Short Stories,* ed. Grant Overton (1930), included Fitzgerald's "At Your Age" and Hemingway's "Three-Day Blow" but nothing by Ring Lardner.

TO: Sinclair Lewis
After March 1929

ALS, 1 p. Syracuse University

% Guaranty Trust Co.
1 Rue des Italiennes
Paris

Dear Sinclair Lewis:

Since I read "*Dodsworth*" I've been full of it—I like it better than any book of yours and can't resist telling you how big a success I think you've made of a difficult theme. At least a dozen of the scenes are among your most vivid, which is saying a lot—and those are the ones which you most wanted to bring off + which give it its character—tho you could always do that. Anyhow most hearty congratulations—since "*Le Temps Retrouvé*"[1] no book has given me so much real personal pleasure—Mencken's review seemed curiously inadequate—Dorothy Parker's seemed ill-humored. If it wasn't so late + I so far away I'd try to disagree with them publicly—I can only say that beside such neat, suave tinsel as "*The Plutocrat*"[2] it shouts its verity—dozens of people have become "Dodsworth" for me within the last fortnight. (Oscar Kalman among others) Always best wishes—thanks for your courteous word to my father at some reception(?) in Washington, D.C.

Always Yr. Admirer
F. Scott Fitzgerald

[1] The final volume of Proust's *A la recherche du temps perdu*.
[2] By Booth Tarkington (1927).

TO: Louis Adamic[1] ALS, 1 p. Princeton University

℅ Guaranty Trust Co.
1 Rue des Italiennes
Paris

Dear Mr. Adamic:

I've been meaning to offer my congratulations for months on *Superman*.[2] I think it's one of the best American short stories in some years—very vivid and facinating. Seeing you in the Mercury again this month reminded me of it.

Most Appreciatively Yrs.
F. Scott Fitzgerald

April 2nd, 1929

[1] Yugoslav-born fiction writer and political commentator.
[2] *American Mercury* (December 1928).

TO: Ernest Hemingway[1] AL, 9 pp. Kennedy Library
June 1929 Paris

114–121 is slow + needs cutting—[2] it hasn't the incisiveness of other short portraits in this book or in yr. other books. The characters too numerous + too much nailed down by gags. *Please* cut! There's absolutely no psycholical justification in introducing those singers—its not even bizarre—if he got stewed with them + in consequence thrown from hospital it would be O.K. At least reduce it to a sharp + self sufficient vignette. It's just rather gassy as it is, I think.

For example—your Englishman on the fishing trip in T.S.A.R. contributes to the tautness of waiting for Brett. You seem to have written this to try to "round out the picture of Milan during the war" during a less inspired moment.

(Arn't the Croats Orthodox Greeks?[3] or some Byzantine Christian Sect—Surely they're not predominantly Mohamedens + you can't say their not Christans

122ect[4]

In "Cat in the rain" + in the story about "That's all we do isn't it, go + try new drinks ect,"[5] you were really listening to women—here you re only listening to yourself, to your own mind beating out facily a sort of sense that isn't really interesting, Ernest, nor really much except a sort of literary exercise—it seems to me that this ought to be *thoroughly* cut, even re-written.

(Our poor old friendship probably won't survive this but there you are—better me than some nobody in the Literary Review that doesn't care about you + your future.)

P. 124 *et sequitur*[6]

This is definately *dull*—it's all right to say it was meant all the time + that a novel can't have the finesse of a short story but this has got to. This scene as it is seems to me a shame.

Later I was astonished to find it was only about 750 wds. which only goes to show the pace you set yourself up to that point. Its dull because the war goes further + further out of sight every minute. "That's the way it was" is no answer—this triumphant proof that races were fixed!

—I should put it as 400 word beginning to Chap XXI

Still later Read by itself it has points, but coming on it in the novel I still believe its dull + slow

---

Seems to me a last echo of the war very faint when Catherine is dying and he's drinking beer in the Café.

Look over Switzerland stuff for cutting

(ie. 2nd page numbered 129)[7]

129 (NW) Now here's a great scene—your comedy used as part of you + not as mere roll-up-my-sleeves-+ pull-off a-tour-de-force as on pages 114–121

P. 130—[8]

This is a comedy scene that really becomes offensive for you've trained everyone to read every word—now you make them read the word cooked (+ fucked would be as bad) *one dozen times*. It has ceased to become amusing by the 5th, for they're too packed, + yet the scene has possibilities. Reduced to five or six *cooked* it might have rythm like the word "wops" in one of your early sketches. You're a little hypnotized by yourself here.

133–138[9]
This could stand a good cutting. Sometimes these conversations with her take on a naive quality that wouldn't please you in anyone else's work. Have you read Noel Coward?
Some of its wonderful—about brave man 1000 deaths ect. Couldn't you cut a little?

134[10]
Remember the brave expectant illegitimmate mother is an OLD SITUATION + has been exploited by all sorts of people you won't lower yourself to read—so be sure every line rings *new* + has some claim to being incarnated + inspired truth or you'll have the boys apon you with scorn.

By the way—that buying the pistol is a *wonderful* scene.[11]

Catherine is too glib, talks too much physically. In cutting their conversations cut some of her speeches rather than his. She is too glib—
I mean—you're seeing him in a sophisticated way as now you see yourself then—but you're still seeing her as you did in 1917 thru nineteen yr. old eyes. In consequence unless you make her a bit fatuous occasionally the contrast jars—either the writer is a simple fellow or she's Eleanora Duse disguised as a Red Cross nurse. In one moment you expect her to prophecy the 2nd battle of the Marne—as you probably did then. Where's that desperate, half-childish dont-make-me-think V.A.D. feeling you spoke to me about? It's there—here—but cut *to* it! Don't try to make her make sense—she probably didn't!

The book, by the way is between 80,000 + 100,000 wds—not 160,000 as you thought

P. 241[12] is one of the best pages you've ever written, I think

P 209— + 219[13] I think if you use the word cocksuckers here the book will be suppressed + confiscated within two days of publication.

All this retreat is marvellous the confusion ect.
The scene from 218[14] on is the best in recent fiction

I think 293–294[15] need cutting but perhaps not to be cut altogether.

Why not end the book with that wonderful paragraph on P. 241.[16] It is the most eloquent in the book + could end it rather gently + well.

A beautiful book it is!

Kiss my ass
EH[17]

[1] In June 1929 Fitzgerald and Hemingway were in Paris when Fitzgerald read a typescript of *A Farewell to Arms* while the novel was being serialized in *Scribner's Magazine*. The nine unnumbered pages of this memo are printed here as units in the order of the references to Hemingway's typescript—except for the pages on which Fitzgerald departed from numerical order. See Charles W. Mann, "F. Scott Fitzgerald's Critique of *A Farewell to Arms*," *Fitzgerald/Hemingway Annual* 1976.

[2] Ch. 19, pp. 126–29, of *A Farewell to Arms* (New York: Scribners, 1929): the meeting with Meyers and his wife through the conversation with the opera singers and Ettore Moretti. This material is crossed out on Hemingway's typescript, perhaps indicating that he considered cutting it.

[3] Ch. 26, p. 189: possibly a reference to the priest's statement "The Austrians are Christians—except for the Bosnians."

[4] Ch. 19, pp. 134–35: Frederic and Catherine's conversation about the rain: "I'm afraid of the rain because sometimes I see me dead in it."

[5] "Hills like White Elephants."

[6] Ch. 20, pp. 136ff.: the account of Frederic and Catherine's day at the races.

[7] Ch. 22, pp. 152–55: Miss Van Campen's discovery of the empty bottles in Frederic Henry's hospital room.

[8] Ch. 21, pp. 142–43: Henry's report of the British major's analysis of the war. "Wops" refers to the Ch. VIII vignette of *In Our Time* or Ch. 9 of *in our time*.

[9] Ch. 21, pp. 146–51: the scene in which Catherine announces she is pregnant.

[10] Ch. 21, p. 147: "I'm going to have a baby, darling."

[11] Ch. 23, pp. 158–59.

[12] Ch. 34, pp. 266–67: Frederic Henry's night soliloquy after his reunion with Catherine at Stresa: "If people bring so much courage to this world the world has to kill them to break them, so of course it kills them." Fitzgerald wrote in the margin of the typescript: "This is one of the most beautiful pages in all English literature." The note was erased but is still readable.

[13] Ch. 30, pp. 228, 238. The word was replaced with dashes in print.

[14] Ch. 30, pp. 237–41: Frederic Henry's arrest by the *carabinieri* and his escape.

[15] Opening of Ch. 40. This passage was cut by Hemingway.

[16] Ch. 34. See note 12.

[17] Added by Hemingway.

FROM: Morley Callaghan
June(?) 1929

TLS, 1 p. Princeton University

2 Square du Port Royal,
15 Rue de la Sante.

Dear Scott,

Please forgive me using the typewriter but there is no ink at hand, and I want to tell you at once that we can not accept your invitation to have lunch with you on Wednesday. It was very kind of you to ask us, but, if I remember correctly, I made it almost impossible for you to do otherwise.

I do hope that both you and Zelda will pardon my rather abrupt visit last night. I had intended simply to leave a note for you. The first time I called on you was equally unfortunate because you were both tired after the theatre. I ought to have explained then that Max Perkins, asking me to call on you, had said to me, when I pointed out that I did not know you, that any formality would be unnecessary and I ought simply to call on you. And I asked you to read the novel[1] because in the first place, you, as you said, made the gesture, and then I felt that I simply had to have someone's opinion of it.

Your frank opinion of the book is honestly appreciated. It was what I wanted. If I had caught you at any other time I would have been the poorer for it. Please don't think that I resent the way you told me the novel was rotten. It would have been much easier for you, I am sure, to have said that it was a nice piece of work, and so I am grateful to you.

Perhaps we'll be able to see each other sometime at one of the cafes. And I am sure you'll understand why we can not have lunch together on Wednesday.

With best wishes,
Morley Callaghan

[1] *It's Never Over* (1930).

TO: Holger Lundbergh — ALS, 1 p. Princeton University

12 Blvd. Eugene Gazagnaire
Cannes
July 14th [1929]

Dear Holger:

Your letter just reached on a bright French day with the tri-colors raising hell and the bistrots full of cannon fodder. We miss you too and your ever kind memories of us. Did Edward Coffee[1] tell you of the time he was center + I quarterback on the Newman seconds + when he with his drawing (then) + me with poetry were the schools professional dunces?

Voices without
In haste
Always Afftly Yrs.
Scott Fitzg—

[1] Arthur Herbert Coffey, who wrote under the pseudonym Edward Hope.

TO: Maxwell Perkins ALS, 1 p. Princeton University

Villa Fleur des Bois
Cannes
Sept 1st [1929]

Dear Max:

Working hard at the novel + have sworn not to come back this fall without completing it. Prospects bright. Two things.

① My clipping Bureau (The Author's) has gone out of business. Will you send me the adress of another.

(2) *Most important*—can you get me copies of *The Great Gatsby* in German, Swedish, Norwregan Danish ect. I should like very much to have them + if they go out of print never will even see them.' Can you take care of this for me?

Ever Yours
Scott

TO: Ernest Hemingway ALS, 1 p.[1] Kennedy Library
After 8 October 1929 Paris

As you'll see from this, while Ober was simply wondering if you wanted to use him Reynolds went ahead + constituted himself your agent, though as his only approach to you was through me, he was stepping forth. Of course this letter is nothing but Ober being sore and your work is financially safe with Reynolds so long as he doesn't go senile. I simply pass this on to show how the battle over your work increases in speed now that you don't need any help. In any case I shall step out here, not even answering this letter except in the vaguest terms I liked Cowly's review in Sun. Tribune.[2] First intelligent one I've seen

Scott

[1] Written in the margin of Harold Ober's 8 October letter to Fitzgerald, which Fitzgerald sent to Hemingway. Ober's letter is printed in *As Ever, Scott Fitz—*, eds. Bruccoli and Jennifer Atkinson (Philadelphia and New York: Lippincott, 1972). Fitzgerald made two other marginal notes: On the second paragraph, "This was sixth months back it seems to me—maybe not"; on the third paragraph, "(This is the offer of $300 or 600 you told me about months ago) F.SF."

[2] Malcolm Cowley's review of *A Farewell to Arms*.

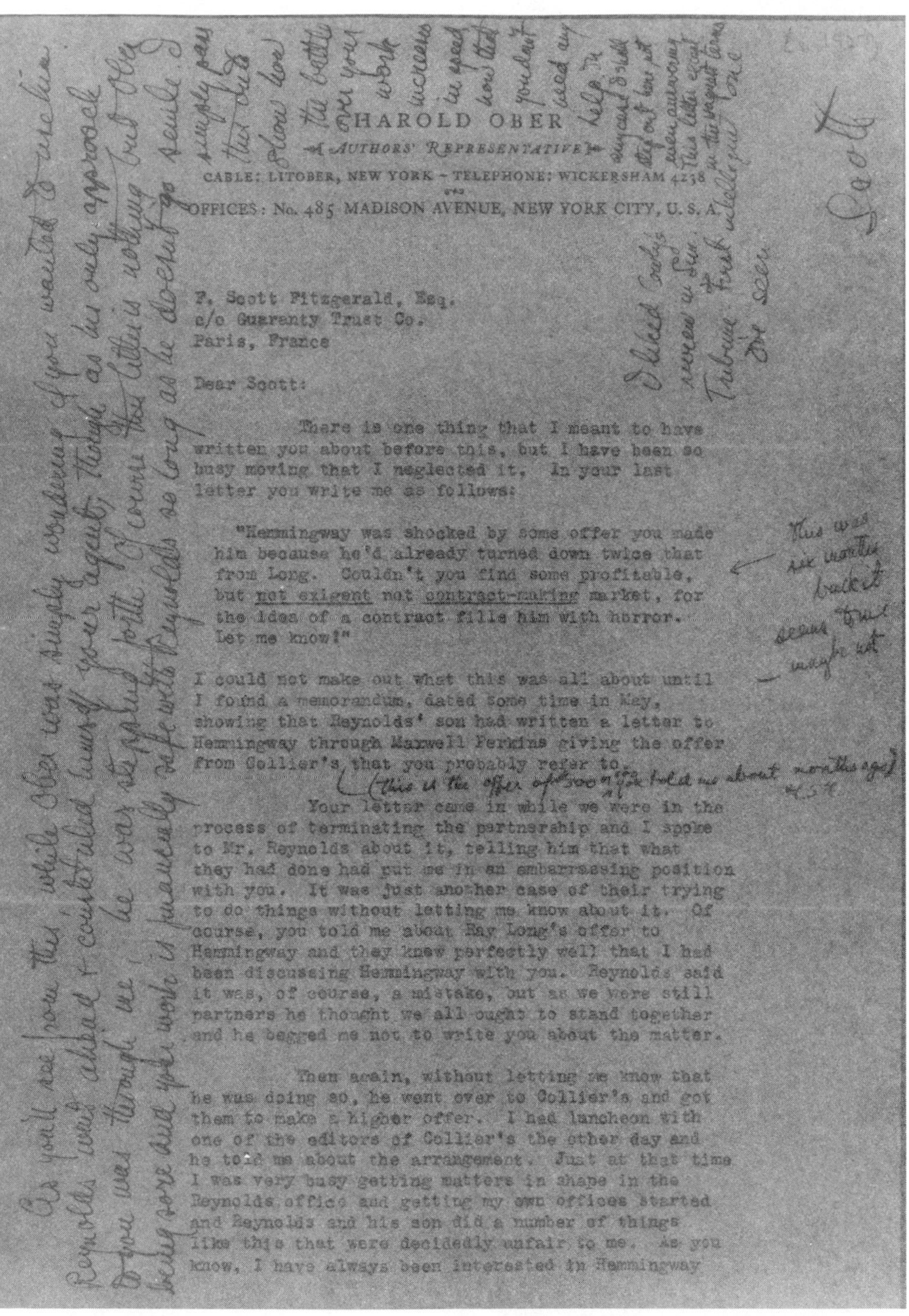

HAROLD OBER

AUTHORS' REPRESENTATIVE

CABLE: LITOBER, NEW YORK – TELEPHONE: WICKERSHAM 4238

OFFICES: No. 485 MADISON AVENUE, NEW YORK CITY, U. S. A.

F. Scott Fitzgerald, Esq.
c/o Guaranty Trust Co.
Paris, France

Dear Scott:

There is one thing that I meant to have written you about before this, but I have been so busy moving that I neglected it. In your last letter you write me as follows:

> "Hemmingway was shocked by some offer you made him because he'd already turned down twice that from Long. Couldn't you find some profitable, but <u>not exigent</u> not <u>contract-making</u> market, for the idea of a contract fills him with horror. Let me know!"

This was six months back it seems true — maybe not

I could not make out what this was all about until I found a memorandum, dated some time in May, showing that Reynolds' son had written a letter to Hemmingway through Maxwell Perkins giving the offer from Collier's that you probably refer to.

Your letter came in while we were in the process of terminating the partnership and I spoke to Mr. Reynolds about it, telling him that what they had done had put me in an embarrassing position with you. It was just another case of their trying to do things without letting me know about it. Of course, you told me about Ray Long's offer to Hemmingway and they knew perfectly well that I had been discussing Hemmingway with you. Reynolds said it was, of course, a mistake, but as we were still partners he thought we all ought to stand together and he begged me not to write you about the matter.

Then again, without letting me know that he was doing so, he went over to Collier's and got them to make a higher offer. I had luncheon with one of the editors of Collier's the other day and he told me about the arrangement. Just at that time I was very busy getting matters in shape in the Reynolds office and getting my own offices started and Reynolds and his son did a number of things like this that were decidedly unfair to me. As you know, I have always been interested in Hemmingway

Scott

FROM: Edmund Wilson

Inscription in Wilson's *Poets, Farewell!* (1929). Bruccoli

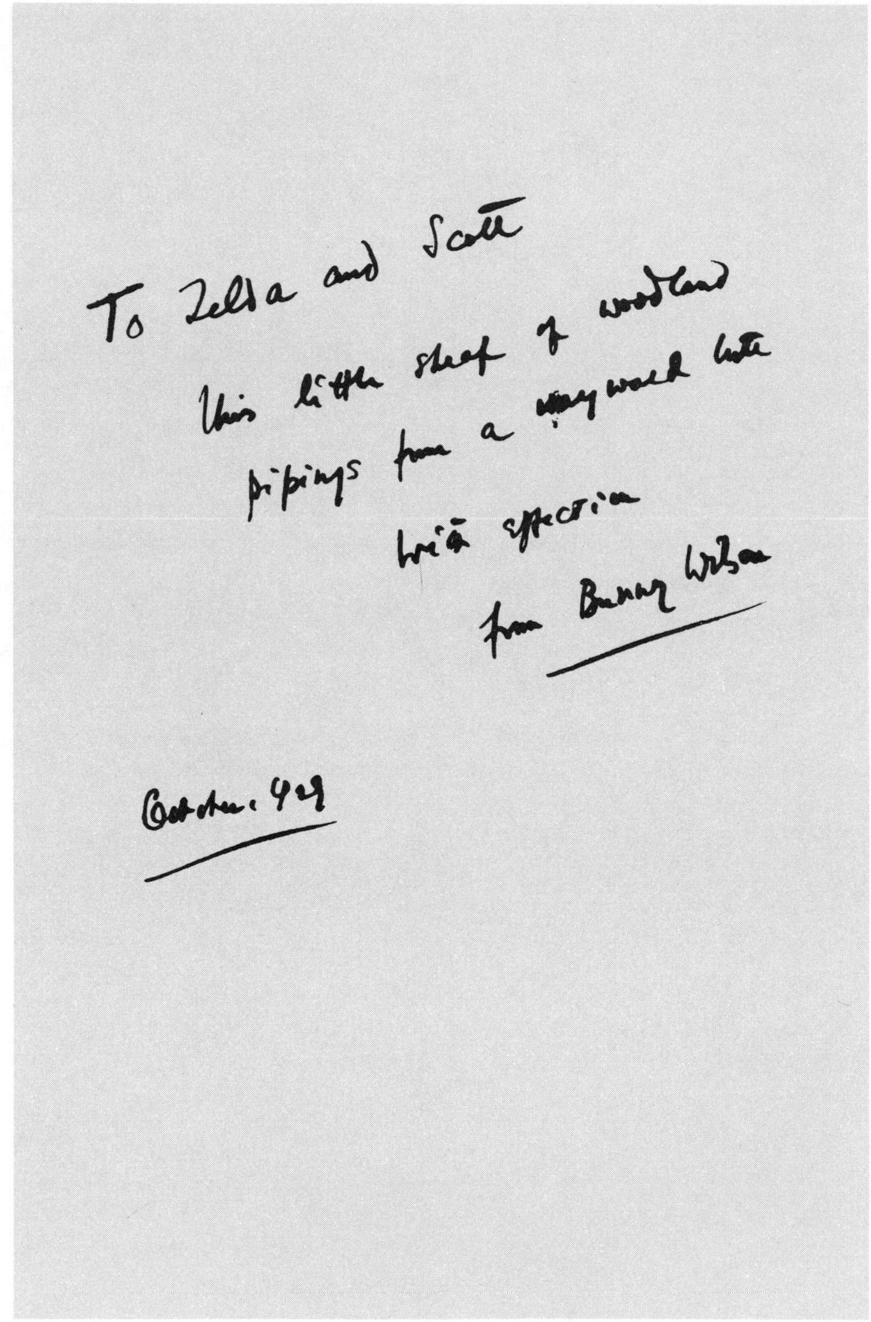

To Zelda and Scott
this little sheaf of woodland
pipings from a wayward lute
with affection
from Bunny Wilson

October 1929

FROM: Maxwell Perkins TL(CC), 3 pp. Princeton University

November 20, 1929

Dear Scott:

Harold Ober was telling me today of a letter he had from you which said you would not come back until mid-February. Well, do come then anyhow. He told me the novel seemed to be going on, but I suppose we can hardly expect to publish until fall,—unless perhaps you will be sending it over before you yourself leave France.

I was terribly sorry to have to decline John Biggs'[1] last book. It did not seem to have the life and power of his others;—and besides he had been Hemingway'd. Many young writers have, but one would not expect it of so marked an individual as John. He picked up the superficial traits of Ernest's method without anything else. It is possible, though, that this book represents a transition with John. He has probably outgrown his old fantastic phaze with its almost insane imaginative quality, and the next thing he writes may be much more natural, and if he gets into a new mood he may do better and also more successful things. I think he felt greatly disappointed, but I could not do anything else in his interests, even more than in ours.

Everything goes well to date with "A Farewell to Arms." Ernest has cabled me several times to report on the sale, but it is hard to do it because there are always complications like those which come from dealers and jobbers splitting their orders so that part go into one month, and others into another, so that sometimes the sale is several thousand larger than the card actually shows. And yet I am always careful not to give an over-statement. In reality, between ourselves, the sale must now be 50,000, and perhaps more, but only about 47,000 show on the card. Somehow rumors very damaging to us have got about that Ernest is dissatisfied with his publisher. He knew about this before we did, and wrote me there was nothing in it whatever, but there is nothing that can be done to stop it, and every other house is perfectly willing to pass it on, and to take the excuse for going to Ernest with an offer. Here is one publisher rushing to him who, when "The Sun Also" appeared said of Scribners:—"A great publisher sunk to the gutter," and another publisher sends over a delegation whose younger men read aloud passages from "The Sun Also" in derision, at a director's meeting. You would think they would be too ashamed of their original position to do this. I enclose herewith a paragraph from the Eagle which I suppose was written by a man who came in to see me to tell me that there was nothing in these reports of Ernest's dissatisfaction; and then he turns right around and puts into the paper something which will spread them everywhere. It is just an annoyance that can't be avoided, I suppose, but it is hurtful with writers in general who hear of it, as they all must.

I was impressed with McAlmon's "Village,"[2] a copy of which he gave me. Some of the passages in it are very fine, but he does not seem to have any attractiveness of style, but rather the reverse. I think though, that if he will be patient, we shall be able to publish a book made up of some of the better things in "Village" and some other things which he has that he thinks will combine with these. I would certainly like to do this even on his own account because he is entitled to publication.—And I understand that he has had much to do with bringing other writers forward, although I never knew exactly what it was. Was he the originator and publisher of "Transition"?[3]

I hope you will send me a line some day, but don't do it if you are too busy. Remembrances to Zelda.[4]

Ever yours,

[1] Scribners had published two of Biggs' novels: *Demigods* (1926) and *Seven Days Whipping* (1928).

[2] *Village: As It Happened Through a Fifteen Year Period* (1924).

[3] McAlmon had slandered both Fitzgerald and Hemingway during his meeting with Perkins.

[4] See Fitzgerald's c. 15 November letter to Perkins in *Scott/Max*.

TO: Mrs. Edward Fitzgerald
Late 1929

ALS, 1 p. Princeton University

10 Rue Pergolèse
Paris

Dear Mother

No—we are here + won't be home before February + can't imagine where you heard I was home. Max Perkins had heard the same thing.

Glad Annabel is having a good time in Annapolis. We are dining with the John Peale Bishops tonight + tomorrow going to the annual dance of the Princeton Club of Paris, but on the whole no news—all well. Scotty has a fine governess but goes to a sort of recitation and examination school twice a week. Also she skates at the Palais du Glace.

Never could trace the Herald interview you speak of—[1] have you read Hemmingway's "Farewell to Arms"?

Much Love to you both
Scott

[1] Possibly "Turns with a Bookworm," *New York Herald Tribune Books* (24 November 1929), which included a distorted account of the Hemingway-Callaghan boxing match at which Fitzgerald was the timekeeper.

TO: Maxwell Perkins
After 11 February 1930

ALS, 1 p. Princeton University
Paris

Dear Max:

Just a last word about the Bishop story. He (and I too) is in doubt about the episode of the Union boy murdered + mutilated by the nigger. It is too melodramatic + not too clear, as the whole thing is already harrowing enough.

Will you consider the question of cutting it from the story. It is a short episode + not *really* important[1]

Ever
Scott

[1] "Many Thousands Gone" (*Scribner's Magazine* [September 1930]), which Fitzgerald had recommended to Perkins. The murder and castration of the soldier were retained in the story. See Perkins' 11 February letter to Fitzgerald in *Scott/Max*.

TO: Ruth A. Conley[1]
Spring 1930

ALS, 1 p. University of Virginia
Grand Hôtel de la Paix letterhead
Lausanne, Switzerland

Dear Madame:

You are a darling to have written me. I will be at the corner of Boston Common on Monday Evening, April 22nd, 1930 wearing a red rose as you suggest, a quiet suit of royal purple and red white and blue suspenders.

As to my photograph—simply write to Sears Roebuck, c/o Mrs. Potter Palmer, Chicago. I am even better in my later films.

I am enclosing carfare

Your Chattel
F Scott Fitzgerald

P.S. Seriously thanks for your letter. I was
pleased + touched

F.S.F.

[1] Miss Conley had sent Fitzgerald a fan letter.

FROM: Maxwell Perkins

TL(CC), 2 pp. Princeton University

May 14, 1930

Dear Scott:

I hope Zelda is O.K. now. I am mighty sorry she was ill.[1] You ought to spend next winter in Key West,—the healthiest, sunniest, restfullest place in the world (so far as I know it) and enough good company.

I have never found any flaw in your judgment about your work, yet. I think you are dead right in holding back the Basil Lee story until you get out the novel. The only thing that has ever worried me about you was the question of health. I know you have everything else, but I have often been afraid on that account, perhaps because I myself can stand so little in the way of late hours, and all that goes with them.

But don't blame me for being impatient once in a while. It is only the impatience to see something one expects greatly to enjoy and admire, and wishes to see triumph. That's the truth.

Ever yours,

[1] In April 1930 Zelda Fitzgerald suffered a nervous breakdown in Paris. While she was being treated at a Swiss clinic Fitzgerald shuttled between Switzerland and Paris, where Scottie was living with a governess.

TO: Rosalind Sayre Smith
After 8 June 1930

AL (draft), 2 pp. Princeton University
Paris or Lausanne

Dear Rosalind

After three agonizing months in which I've given all my waking + most of my sleeping time to pull Zelda out of this mess, which itself arrived like a thunderclap. I feel that your letter which arrived today was scarcely nessessary. The matter is terrible enough without your writing me that you wish she would die now rather than go back to the mad world you and she have created for yourselves." I know you dislike me, I know your ineradicable impression of the life that Zelda and I led, and evident your dismissal of any of the effort, and struggle success or happiness in it and I understand also your real feeling for her—but I have got Zelda + Scotty to take care of now as ever and I simply cannot be upset and harrowed still further. Also that since the Sayres can't come over and that Zelda can't for the moment go to America, I beg you to think twice before you say more to them than I have said. That is your business of course but our interests in this matter should be the same. Zelda at this moment is in no immediate danger—and I have promised to let you know as I already have if anything crucial is in the air.

I had collapsed in that fashion and Zelda were here taking every care of me   imagine the effect on Zelda of recieving such a letter from my sister in America

FROM: Zelda Fitzgerald
June 1930

ALS, 2 pp. Princeton University
Prangins Clinic, Nyon, Switzerland

Dear Scott:

Just at the point in my life when there is no time left me for losing, I am here to incapacitate myself for using what I have learned in such a desperate school—through my own fault and from a complete lack of medical knowledge on a rather esoteric subject. If you could write to Egorowa a friendly impersonal note to find out exactly where I stand as a dancer it would be of the greatest help to me—Remember, this is in no way at all her fault. I would have liked to dance in New York this fall, but where am I going to find again these months that dribble into the beets of the clinic garden? Is it worth it? And once a proper horror for the accidents of life has been instilled into me, I have no intention of joing the group about a corpse. My legs are already flabby and I will soon be like Ada ——, huntress of coralled game, I suppose, instead of a human being recompensed for everything by the surety of a comprehension of one manifestation of beauty—Why can't you write me what you think and want instead of vague attempts at reassurance? If I had work or something it would be so much decenter to try to help each other and make at least a stirrup cup out of this bloody mess.

You have always had so much sympathy for people forced to start over late in life that I should think you could find the generosity to help me amongst your many others—not as you would a child but as an equal.

I want you to let me leave here—You're wasting time and effort and money to take away the little we both have left. If you think you are preparing me for a return to Alabama you are mistaken, and also if you think that I am going to spend the rest of my life roaming about without happiness or rest or work from one sanatorium to another like Kit you are wrong. Two sick horses might conceivably pull a heavier load than a well one alone. Of cource, if you prefer that I should spend six months of my life under prevailing conditions—my eyes are open and I will get something from that, too, I suppose, but they are tired and unhappy and my head aches always. Won't you write me a comprehensible letter such as you might write to one of your friends? Every day it gets harder to think or live and I do not understand the object of wasting the dregs of me here, alone in a devasting bitterness.

Zelda

Please write immediately to Paris about the dancing. I would do it but I think the report will be more accurate if it goes to you—just an opinion as to what value my work is and to what point I could, develop it before it is too late. Of cource, I would go to another school as I know Egorowa would not want to be bothered with me. Thanks.

FROM: Zelda Fitzgerald — AL, 8 pp. Princeton University
After June 1930 — Prangins Clinic, Nyon, Switzerland

Dear Scott:

You said in your letter that I might write when I needed you. For the first time since I went to Malmaison I seem to be about half human-being, capable of focusing my attention and not walking in black horror like I have been for so long. Though I am physically sick and covered with eczema I would like to see you. I'm lonely and do not seem to be able to exist in the world on any terms at all. If you do not want to come maybe Newman[1] would come.

Please don't write to me about blame. I am tired of rummaging my head to understand a situation that would be difficult enough if I were completely lucid. I cannot arbitrarily accept blame now when I know that in the past I felt none. Anyway, blame doesn't matter. The thing that counts is to apply the few resources available to turning life into a tenable orderly affair that resembles neither the black hole of Calcutta or Cardinal Ballou's cage.[2] Of cource, you are quite free to proceed as you think best. If I can ever find the dignity and peace to apply myself, I am sure there must be something to fill the next twenty years of a person who is willing to work for it, so do not feel that you have any obligations toward me, sentimental or otherwise, unless you accept them as freely as you did when I was young and happy and quite different from how I am now—

I am infinitely sorry that I have been ungrateful for your attempts to help me. Try to understand that people are not always reasonable when the world is as unstable and vacillating as a sick head can render it—That for months I have been living in vaporous places peopled with one-dimensional figures and tremulous buildings until I can no longer tell an optical illusion from a reality—that head and ears incessantly throb and roads disappear, until finally I lost all control and powers of judgement and was semi-imbecilic when I arrived here. At least now I can read, and as soon as possible I am going on with some stories I have half done. Won't you send me "Technique of the Drama" please? I have an enormous desire to try to write a play that I have begun a little.

Scottie has not written but I know she is happy with Madamoiselle. I'm glad you are better. It seems odd that we were once a warm little family—secure in a home—

Thank you for the books—

Was it fun in Paris? Who did you see there and was the Madeleine pink at five o'clock and did the fountains fall with hollow delicacy into the framing of space in the Place de la Concorde, and did the blue creep out from behind the Colonades of the rue de Rivoli through the grill of the Tuileries and was the Louvre gray and metallic in the sun and did the trees hang brooding over the cafés and were there lights at night and the click of saucers and the auto horns that play de Bussey—

I *love* Paris. How was it?

[1] Newman Smith, husband of Zelda's sister Rosalind.
[2] Cardinal Balue was imprisoned in a cage for six years by Louis XI.

TO: Zelda Fitzgerald
Summer(?) 1930

AL, 7 pp.[1] Princeton University
Paris or Lausanne

Written with Zelda gone to the Clinique

I know this then—that those days when we came up from the south, from Capri, were among my happiest—but you were sick and the happiness was not in the home.

I had been unhappy for a long time then—When my play failed a year and a half before, when I worked so hard for a year, twelve stories and novel and four articles in that time with no one believing in me and no one to see except you + before the end your heart betraying me and then I was really alone with no one I liked In Rome we were dismal and was still working proof and three more stories and in Capri you were sick and there seemed to be nothing left of happiness in the world anywhere I looked.

Then we came to Paris and suddenly I realized that it hadn't all been in vain. I was a success—the biggest man in my profession everybody admired me and I was proud I'd done such a good thing. I met Gerald and Sara who took us for friends now and Ernest who was an equeal and my kind of an idealist. I got drunk with him on the Left Bank in careless cafés and drank with Sara and Gerald in their garden in St Cloud but you were endlessly sick and at home everything was unhappy. We went to Antibes and I was happy but you were sick still and all that fall and that winter and spring at the cure and I was alone all the time and I had to get drunk before I could leave you so sick and not care and I was only happy a little while before I got too drunk. Afterwards there were all the usuall penalties for being drunk.

Finally you got well in Juan-les-Pins and a lot of money came in and I made of those mistakes literary men make—I thought I was "a man of the world—that everybody liked me and admired me for myself but I only liked a few people like Ernest and Charlie McArthur[2] and Gerald and Sara who were my peers. Time goes bye fast in those moods and nothing is ever done. I thought then that things came easily—I forgot how I'd dragged the great Gatsby out of the pit of my stomach in a time of misery. I woke up in Hollywood no longer my egotistic, certain self but a mixture of Ernest in fine clothes and Gerald with a career—and Charlie McArthur with a past. Anybody that could make me believe that, like Lois Moran did, was precious to me.

Ellerslie, the polo people, Mrs. Chanler[3] the party for Cecelia[4] were all attempts to make up from without for being undernourished now from within. Anything to be liked, to be reassured not that I was a man of a little genius but that I was a great man of the world. At the same time I knew it was nonsense—the part of me that knew it was nonsense brought us to the Rue Vaugirard.

But now you had gone into yourself just as I had four years before in St. Raphael—And there were all the consequences of bad appartments through your lack of patience ("Well, if you were [ ] why don't you make some money") bad servants, through your indifference ("Well, if you don't like her why don't you send Scotty away to school") Your dislike for Vidor, your indifference to Joyce I understood—share your incessant entheusisam and absorbtion in the ballet I could not. Somewhere in there I had a sense of being exploited, not by you but by something I resented terribly no happiness. Certainly less than there had ever been at home—you were a phantom washing clothes, talking French bromides with Lucien or Del Plangue[6]—I remember desolate trips to Versaille to Rhiems, to La Baule undertaken in sheer weariness of home. I remember wondering why I kept working to pay the bills of this desolate menage. I had evolved. In despair I went from the extreme of isolation, which is to say isolation with Mlle Delplangue, or the Ritz Bar where I got back my self esteem for half an hour, often with someone I had hardly ever seen before. In the evenings sometimes you and I rode to the Bois in a cab—after awhile I preferred to go to Cafe de Lilas and sit there alone remembering what a happy time I had had there with Ernest, Hadley, Dorothy Parker + Benchley two years before. During all this time, remember I didn't blame anyone but myself. I complained when the house got unbearable but after all I was not John Peale Bishop—I was paying for it with work, that I passionately hated and found more and more difficult to do. The novel was like a dream, daily farther and farther away.

Ellerslie was better and worse. Unhappiness is less accute when one lives with a certain sober dignity but the financial strain was too much. Between Sept when we left Paris and March when we reached Nice we were living at the rate of forty thousand a year.

But somehow I felt happier. Another spring—I would see Ernest whom I had launched, Gerald + Sarah who through my agency had been able to try the movies.[7] At least life would less drab; there would be parties with people who offered something, conversations with people with something to say. Later swimming and getting tanned and young and being near the sea.

It worked out beautifully didn't it. Gerald and Sara didn't see us.

Ernest and I met but it was a more irritable Ernest, apprehensively telling me his whereabouts lest I come in on them tight and endanger his lease. The discovery that half a dozen people were familiars there didn't help my self esteem. By the time we reached the beautiful Rivierra I had developed such an inferiority complex that I couldn't fase anyone unless I was tight. I worked there too, though, and the unusual combination exploded my lungs.

You were gone now—I scarcely remember you that summer. You were simply one of all the people who disliked me or were indifferent to me. I didn't like to think of you—You didn't need me and it was easier to talk to or rather at Madame Bellois and keep full of wine. I was grateful when you came with me to the Doctors one afternoon but after we'd been a week in Paris and I didn't try any more about living or dieing. Things were always the same. The appartments that were rotten, the maids that stank—the ballet before my eyes, spoiling a story to take the Troubetskoys to dinner, poisening a trip to Africa. You were going crazy and calling it genius—I was going to ruin and calling it anything that came to hand. And I think everyone far enough away to see us outside of our glib presentation of ourselves guessed at your almost meglomaniacal selfishness and my insane indulgence in drink. Toward the end nothing much mattered. The nearest I ever came to leaving you was when you told me you thot I was a fairy in the Rue Palatine but now whatever you said aroused a sort of detached pity for you. For all your superior observation and your harder intelligence I have a faculty of guessing right, without evidence even with a certain wonder as to why and whence that mental short cut came. I wish the Beautiful and Damned had been a maturely written book because it was all true. We ruined ourselves—I have never honestly thought that we ruined each other.

1 Draft for a letter which may not have been sent.
2 Charles MacArthur, playwright and screenwriter; married to actress Helen Hayes.
3 Probably Mrs. Winthrop Chanler, a wealthy friend of Father Fay's.
4 Daughter of Fitzgerald's cousin Cecilia Taylor.
5 Movie director King Vidor.
6 Scottie's governess.
7 Gerald Murphy had worked with King Vidor on *Hallelujah*.

TO: Dr. Oscar Forel[1] AL (draft), 6 pp.[2] Princeton University
Summer(?) 1930 Lausanne, Switzerland(?)

For translation with carbon. But
not on hotel stationary.

This letter is about a matter that had best be considered frankly now than six months or a year from now. When I last saw you I was almost as broken as my wife by months of horror. The only important thing in my life was that she should be saved from madness or death. *Now that, due to your tireless intelligence and interest, there is a time in sight where Zelda and I may renew our life together on a decent basis, a thing which I desire with all my heart, there are other* considerations due to my nessessities as a *worker and to my very existence that I must put before you.*

During my young manhood for seven years I worked extremely hard, in six years bringing myself by tireless literary self-discipline to a position of unquestioned preeminence among younger American writers, also by additional "hack-work" for the cinema ect. I gave my wife a comfortable and luxurious life such as few European writers ever achieve. My *work is done on coffee, coffee and more coffee, never on alcohol. At the end of five or six hours I get up from my desk white and trembling and with a steady burn in my stomach, to go to dinner.* Doubtless a certain irritability developed in those years, an inability to be gay which my wife—who had never tried to use her talents and intelligence—was not inclined to condone. It was on our coming to Europe in 1924 and apon *her* urging that I began to look forward to wine at dinner—she took it at lunch, I did not. We went on hard drinking parties together sometimes but the regular use of wine and apperatives was something that I dreaded but she encouraged because she found I was more cheerful then and allowed her to drink more. *The ballet idea was something I inaugurated in 1927 to stop her idle drinking after she had already so lost herself in it as to make suicidal attempts.* Since then I have drunk more, from unhappiness, and she less, because of her physical work—that is another story.

Two years ago in America I noticed that when we stopped all drinking for three weeks or so, which happened many times, I immediately had dark circles under my eyes, was listless and disinclined to work.

I gave up strong cigarettes and, in a panic that perhaps I was just giving out, applied for a large insurance policy. The one trouble was low blood-pressure, a matter which they finally condoned, and they issued me the policy. I found that a moderate amount of wine, a pint at each meal made all the difference in how I felt. When that was available the dark circles disappeared, the coffee didn't give me excema or beat in my head all night, I looked forward to my dinner instead of staring at it, and life didn't seem a hopeless grind to support a woman whose tastes were daily diverging from mine. She no longer read or thought or knew anything or liked anyone except dancers and their cheap satellites People respected her because I concealed her weaknesses, and because of a certain complete fearlessness and honesty that she has never lost, but she was becoming more and more an egotist and a bore. Wine was almost a nessessity for me to be able to stand her long monalogues about ballet steps, alternating with a glazed eye toward any civilized conversation whatsoever

Now when that old question comes up again as to which of two people is worth preserving, I, thinking of my ambitions once so nearly achieved of being part of English literature, of my child, even of Zelda in the matter of providing for her—must perforce consider myself first. I say that without defiance but simply knowing the limits of what I can do. To stop drinking entirely for six months and see what happens, even to continue the experiment thereafter if successful—only a pig would refuse to do that. Give up strong drink permanently I will. Bind myself to forswear wine forever I cannot. My vision of the world at its brightest is such that life without the use of its amentities is impossible. I have lived hard and ruined the essential innocense in myself that could make it that possible, *and the fact that I have abused liquor* is something *to be paid for with suffering and death perhaps but not with renunciation.* For me *it would be as illogical as permanently giving up sex because I caught a disease* (which I hasten to assure you I never have) I cannot consider one pint of wine at the days end as anything but one of the rights of man.

Does this sound like a long polemic composed of childish stubborness and ingratitude? If it were that it would be so much easier to make promises. What I gave up for Zelda was women and it wasn't easy in the position my success gave me—what pleasure I got from comradeship she has pretty well ruined by dragging me of all people into her homosexual obsession. Is there not a certain disingenuousness in her wanting me to give up all alcohol? Would not that *justify her* conduct completely to herself and prove to *her relatives, and our friends that it was my drinking that had caused this calamity, and that I thereby admitted it? Wouldn't she finally get to believe herself that she had consented to "take me back" only if I stopped drinking? I could only be silent.* And any human value I might have would disappear *if I condemned myself to a life long ascetisim to which I am not adapted either by habit, temperment* or the circumstances of my metier.

That is my case about the future, a case which I have never stated to you before when her problem needed your entire consideration. I want very much to see you before I see her. And please disassociate this letter from what I shall always feel in signing myself

Yours with Eternal Gratitude and Admiration

FIN

[1] Head psychiatrist at Prangins.
[2] Italics in this draft represent passages underlined by Fitzgerald for emphasis.

TO: Zelda Fitzgerald — AL (draft), 4 pp. Princeton University
Summer(?) 1930 — Lausanne(?)

When I saw the sadness of your face in that passport picture I felt as you can imagine. But after going through what you can imagine I did then and looking at it and looking at it, I saw that it was the face I knew and loved and not the mettalic superimposition of our last two years in France. . . .[1]

The photograph is all I have: it is with me from the morning when I wake up with a frantic half dream about you to the last moment when I think of you and of death at night. The rotten letters you write me I simply put away under Z in my file. My instinct is to write a public letter to the Paris Herald to see if any human being except yourself and Robert McAlmon has ever thought I was a homosexual. The three weeks after the horror of Valmont when I could not lift my eyes to meet the eyes of other men in the street after your stinking allegations and insinuations will not be repeated. If you choose to keep up your wrestling match with a pillar of air I would prefer to be not even in the audience.

I am hardened to write you so brutally by thinking of the ceaseless wave of love that surrounds you and envelopes you always, that you have the power to evoke at a whim—when I know that for the mere counterfiet of it I would perjure the best of my heart and mind. Do you think the solitude in which I live has a more amusing decor than any other solitude? Do you think it is any nicer for remembering that there were times very late at night when you and I shared our aloneness?

I will take my full share of responsibility for all this tragedy but I cannot spread beyond the limits of my reach and grasp. I can only bring you the little bit of hope I have and I don't know any other hope except my own. I have the terrible misfortune to be a gentleman in the sort of struggle with incalculable elements to which people should bring centuries of inexperience; if I have failed you is it just barely possible that you have failed me (I can't even write you any more because I see you poring over every line like Mr. Sumner[2] trying to wring some slant or suggestion of homosexuality out of it)

I love you with all my heart because you are my own girl and that is all I know.

[1] Sixty-two words omitted by the editor.
[2] John S. Sumner, secretary of the New York Society for the Suppression of Vice.

FROM: Zelda Fitzgerald
Late summer/early fall 1930

AL, 42 pp. Princeton University
Prangins Clinic, Nyon, Switzerland

Dear Scott:

I have just written to Newman[1] to come here to me. You say that you have been thinking of the past. The weeks since I haven't slept more than three or four hours, swathed in bandages sick and unable to read so have I.

There was:

The strangeness and excitement of New York, of reporters and furry smothered hotel lobbies, the brightness of the sun on the window panes and the prickly dust of late spring: the impressiveness of the Fowlers and much tea-dancing and my eccentric behavior at Princeton. There were Townsend's[2] blue eyes and Ludlow's rubbers and a trunk that exhuded sachet and the marshmallow odor of the Biltmore. There were always Ludow and Townsend and Alex and Bill Mackey[3] and you and me. We did not like women and we were happy. There was Georges[4] appartment and his absinth cock-tails and Ruth Findleys gold hair in his comb, and visits to the "Smart Set" and "Vanity Fair"—a collegiate literary world puffed into wide proportions by the New York papers. There were flowers and night clubs and Ludlow's advice that moved us to the country. At West Port, we quarrelled over morals once, walking beside a colonial wall under the freshness of lilacs. We sat up all night over "Brass Knuckles and Guitar."[5] There was the road house where we bought gin, and Kate Hicks and the Maurices and the bright harness of the Rye Beach Club. We swam in the depth of the night with George before we quarrelled with him and went to John Williams parties where there were actresses who spoke French when they were drunk. George played "Cuddle up a Little Closer" on the piano. There were my white knickers that startled the Connecticut hills, and the swim in the sandaled lady's bird-pool. The beach, and dozens of men, mad rides along the Post Road and trips to New York. We never could have a room at a hotel at night we looked so young, so once we filled an empty suit case with the telephone directory and spoons and a pin-cushion at The Manhattan—I was romanticly attached to Townsend and he went away to Tahatii—and there were your episodes of Gene Bankhead and Miriam. We bought the Marmon with Harvey Firestone and went south through the haunted swamps of Virginiia, the red clay hills of Georgia, the sweet rutted creek-bottoms of Alabama. We drank corn on the wings of an aeroplane in the moon-light and danced at the country-club and came back. I had a pink dress that floated and a very theatrical silver one that I bought with Don Stewart.

We moved to 59th Street. We quarrelled and you broke the bathroom door and hurt my eye. We went so much to the theatre that you took it off the income tax. We trailed through Central Park in the snow after a ball at the Plaza, I quarrelled with Zoë about Bottecelli[7] at the Brevoort and went with her to buy a coat for David Belasco.[8] We had Bourbon and Deviled Ham and Christmas at the Overmans[9] and ate lots at the Lafayette. There was Tom Smith and his wall-paper and Mencken and our Valentine party and the time I danced all night with Alex and meals at Mollats with John[10] and I skated, and was pregnant and you wrote the "Beautiful and Damned." We came to Europe and I was sick and complained always. There was London, and Wopping with Shane Leslie and strawberries as big as tomatoes at Lady Randolph Churchills. There was St. Johns Ervines wooden leg and Bob Handley in the gloom of the Cecil—There was Paris and the heat and the ice-cream that did not melt and buying clothes—and Rome and your friends from the British Embassy and your drinking, drinking. We came home. There was "Dog"[11] and lunch at the St. Regis with Townsend and Alex and John: Alabama and the unbearable heat and our almost buying a house. Then we went to St. Paul and hundreds of people came to call. There were the Indian forests and the moon on the sleeping porch and I was heavy and afraid of the storms. Then Scottie was born and we went to all the Christmas parties and a man asked Sandy[12] "who is your fat friend?" Snow covered everything. We had the Flu and went lots to the Kalmans and Scottie grew strong. Joseph Hergesheimer came and Saturdays we went to the university Club. We went to the Yacht Club and we both had minor flirtatons. Joe began to dislike me, and I played so much golf that I had Tetena.[13] Kollie[14] almost died. We both adored him. We came to New York and rented a house when we were tight. There was Val Engelicheff and Ted Paramour[15] and dinner with Bunny in Washington Square and pills and Doctor Lackin And we had a violent quarrell on the train going back, I don't remember why. Then I brought Scottie to New York. She was round and funny in a pink coat and bonnet and you met us at the station. In Great Neck there was always disorder and quarrels: about the Golf Club, about the Foxes, about Peggy Weber, about Helen Buck, about everything. We went to the Rumseys,[16] and that awful night at the Mackeys[17] when Ring sat in the cloak-room. We saw Esther and Glen Hunter[18] and Gilbert Seldes. We gave lots of parties: the biggest one for Rebecca West. We drank Bass Pale Ale and went always to the Bucks or the Lardners or the Swopes when they weren't at our house. We saw lots of Sydney Howard and fought the week-end that Bill Motter was with us. We drank always and finally came to France because there were always too many people in the house. On the boat there was almost a scandal about Bunny Burgess. We found Nanny and went to Hyeres—Scottie and I were both sick there in the dusty garden full of Spanish Bayonet and Bourgainvilla. We went to St. Raphael. You wrote, and we went sometimes to Nice or Monte Carlo. We were alone, and gave big parties for the French aviators. Then there was Josen[19] and you were justifiably angry. We went to Rome. We ate at the Castelli dei Cesari.

The sheets were always damp. There was Christmas in the echoes, and eternal walks. We cried when we saw the Pope. There were the luminous shadows of the Pinco and the officer's shining boots. We went to Frascati and Tivoli. There was the jail,[20] and Hal Rhodes at the Hotel de Russie and my not wanting to go to the moving-picture ball[21] at the Excelsior and asking Hungary Cox[22] to take me home. Then I was horribly sick, from trying to have a baby and you didn't care much and when I was well we came back to Paris. We sat to-gether in Marseilles and thought how good France was. We lived in the rue Tilsitt, in red plush and Teddy[23] came for tea and we went to the markets with the Murphies. There were the Wimans[24] and Mary Hay and Eva La Galliene and rides in the Bois at dawn and the night we all played puss-in-the-corner at the Ritz. There was Tunti and nights in Mont Matre. We went to Antibes, and I was sick always and took too much Dial.[25] The Murphy's were at the Hotel du Cap and we saw them constantly. Back in Paris I began dancing lessons because I had nothing to do. I was sick again at Christmas when the Mac Leishes came and Doctor Gros said there was no use trying to save my ovaries. I was always sick and having picqures[26] and things and you were naturally more and more away. You found Ernest and the Cafe des Lilas and you were unhappy when Dr. Gros sent me to Salies-de Bearn.[27] At the Villa Paquita I was always sick. Sara brought me things and we gave a lunch for Geralds father. We went to Cannes and and listned to Raquel Miller[28] and dined under the rain of fire-works. You couldn't work because your room was damp and you quarrelled with the Murphys. We moved to a bigger villa and I went to Paris and had my appendix out. You drank all the time and some man called up the hospital about a row you had had. We went home, and I wanted you to swim with me at Juan-les-Pins but you liked it better where it was gayer: at the Garoupe[29] with Marice Hamilton and the Murphys and the Mac Leishes. Then you found Grace Moore[30] and Ruth and Charlie[31] and the summer passed, one party after another. We quarrelled about Dwight Wiman and you left me lots alone. There were too many people and too many things to do: every-day there was something and our house was always full. There was Gerald and Ernest and you often did not come home. There were the English sleepers that I found downstairs one morning and Bob and Muriel and Walker[32] and Anita Loos, always somebody—Alice Delamar and Ted Rousseau and our trips to St. Paul[33] and the note from Isadora Duncan and the countryside slipping by through the haze of Chamberry-fraises and Graves—That was your summer. I swam with Scottie except when I followed you, mostly unwillingly. Then I had asthma and almost died in Genoa. And we were back in America—further apart than ever before. In California, though you would not allow me to go anywhere without you, you yourself engaged in flagrantly sentimental relations with a child.[34] You said you wanted nothing more from me in all your life, though you made a scene when Carl[35] suggested that I go to dinner with him and Betty Compson. We came east: I worked over Ellerslie incessantly and made it function. There was our first house-party and you and Lois—and when there was nothing more to do on the house I began dancing lessons. You did not like it when you saw it made me happy. You were angry about rehearsals and insistent about trains. You went to New York to see Lois and I met Dick Knight[36] the night of that party for Paul Morand.[37] Again, though you were by then thoroughly entangled sentimentally, you forbade my seeing Dick and were furious about a letter he wrote me. On the boat coming over you paid absolutely no attention of any kind to me except to refuse me the permission to stay to a concert with whatever-his-name-was. I think the most humiliating and bestial thing that ever happenned to me in my life is a scene that you probably don't remember even in Genoa. We lived in the rue Vaugirard. You were constantly drunk. You didn't work and were dragged home at night by taxi-drivers when you came home at all. You said it was my fault for dancing all day. What was I to do? You got up for lunch. You made no advances toward me and complained that I was un-responsive. You were literally eternally drunk the whole summer. I got so I couldn't sleep and I had asthma again. You were angry when I wouldn't go with you to Mont Matre. You brought drunken under-graduates in to meals when you came home for them, and it made you angry that I didn't care any more. I began to like Egorowa—On the boat going back I told you I was afraid that there was something abnormal in the relationship and you laughed. There was more or less of a scandal about Philipson, but you did not even try to help me. You brought Philippe[38] back and I couldnt manage the house any more; he was insubordinate and disrespectful to me and you wouldn't let him go. I began to work harder at dancing—I thought of nothing else but that. You were far away by then and I was alone. We came back to rue Palantine and you, in a drunken stupor told me a lot of things that I only half understood:[39] but I understood the dinner we had at Ernests'. Only I didn't understand that it matterred. You left me more and more alone, and though you complained that it was the appartment or the servants or me, you know the real reason you couldn't work was because you were always out half the night and you were sick and you drank constantly. We went to Cannes. I kept up my lessons and we quarrelled You wouldn't let me fire the nurse that both Scottie and I hated. You disgraced yourself at the Barry's[40] party, on the yacht at Monte Carlo, at the casino with Gerald and Dotty.[41] Many nights you didn't come home. You came into my room once the whole summer, but I didn't care because I went to the beach in the morning, I had my lesson in the afternoon and I walked at night. I was nervous and half-sick but I didn't know what was the matter. I only knew that I had difficulty standing lots of people, like the party at Wm J. Locke's and that I wanted to get back to Paris. We had lunch at the Murphy's and Gerald said to me very pointedly several times that Nemchinova[42] was at Antibes. Still I didn't understand. We came back to Paris. You were miserable about your lung,[43] and because you had wasted the summer, but you didn't stop drinking I worked all the time and I became dependent on Egorowa. I couldn't walk in the street unless I had been to my lesson. I couldn't manage the appartment because I couldn't speak to the servants. I couldn't go into stores to buy clothes and my emotions became blindly involved. In February, when I was so sick with bronchitis that I had ventouses[44] every day and fever for two weeks, I had to work because I couldn't exist in the world without it, and still I didn't understand what I was doing. I didn't even know what I wanted. Then we went to Africa and when we came back I began to realize because I could feel what was happenning in others. You did not want me. Twice you left my bed saying "I can't. Don't you understand"—I didn't. Then there was the Harvard man who lost his direction, and when I wanted you to come home with me you told me to sleep with the coal man. At Nancy Hoyt's[45] dinner she offerred her services but there was nothing the matter with my head then, though I was half dead, so I turned back to the studio. Lucienne[46] was sent away but since I knew nothing about the situation, I didn't know why there was something wrong. I just kept on going. Lucienne came back and later went away again and then the end happenned I went to Malmaison. You wouldn't help me—I don't blame you by now, but if you had explained I would have understood because all I wanted was to go on working. You had other things: drink and tennis, and we did not care about each other. You hated me for asking you not to drink. A girl came to work with me but I didn't want her to. I still believed in love and I thought suddenly of Scottie and that you supported me. So at Valmont I was in tortue, and my head closed to-gether. You gave me a flower and said it was "plus petite et moins etendue"—[47] We were friends—Then you took it away and I grew sicker, and there was nobody to teach me, so here I am, after five months of misery and agony and desperation. I'm glad you have found that the material for a Josepine story[48] and I'm glad that you take such an interest in sports. Now that I can't sleep any more I have lots to think about, and since I have gone so far alone I suppose I can go the rest of the way—but if it were Scottie I would not ask that she go through the same hell and if I were God I could not justify or find a reason for imposing it—except that it was wrong, of cource, to love my teacher when I should have loved you. But I didn't have you to love—not since long before I loved her.

I have just begun to realize that sex and sentiment have little to do with each other. When I came to you twice last winter and asked you to start over it was because I thought I was becoming seriously involved sentimentally and preparing situations for which I was morally and practicly unfitted. You had a song about Gigolos: if that had ever entered my head there was, besides the whole studio, 3 other solutions in Paris.

I came to you half-sick after a difficult lunch at Armonville and you kept me waiting until it was too late in front of the Guaranty Trust.

Sandy's[49] tiny candle was not much of a strain, but it required something better than your week of drunkenness to put it out. You didn't care: so I went on and on—dancing alone, and, no matter what happens, I still know in my heart that it is a Godless, dirty game; that love is bitter and all there is, and that the rest is for the emotional beggars of the earth and is about the equivalent of people who stimulate themselves with dirty post-cards—

[1] Newman Smith.

[2] Townsend Martin, Princeton classmate of Fitzgerald's.

[3] Alexander McKaig and possibly William Mackie.

[4] George Jean Nathan.

[5] "Dice, Brass Knuckles & Guitar" was written in January 1923—not in Westport in 1920.

[6] Summer 1920; this trip provided material for "The Cruise of the Rolling Junk," *Motor* (February, March, April 1924).

[7] Playwright Zoë Akins; Botticelli is a parlor game.

[8] Theatrical producer.

[9] Lynne Overman, stage and screen actor.

[10] John Peale Bishop.

[11] A comic song Fitzgerald had written.

[12] Xandra Kalman.

[13] Possibly tetany, a condition resembling tetanus.

[14] Oscar Kalman.

[15] Prince Vladimir N. Engalitcheff, son of the former Russian Vice Consul in Chicago and a wealthy American mother; the Fitzgeralds met Engalitcheff aboard the *Aquitania* in 1921 while he was an undergraduate at Brown University. E. E. Paramore, writer best known for "The Ballad of Yukon Jake"; later a Hollywood collaborator with Fitzgerald.

[16] Charles Cary Rumsey, sculptor and polo player who had an estate at Westbury, Long Island.

[17] Probably financier Clarence MacKay.

[18] Actor Glenn Hunter appeared in *Grit* (1924), a silent movie for which Fitzgerald wrote the scenario.

[19] Edouard Jozan, French naval aviator with whom Zelda Fitzgerald was romantically involved in the summer of 1924.

[20] In the fall of 1924 Fitzgerald was jailed in Rome after a drunken brawl.

[21] A Christmas party for the cast of *Ben-Hur*.

[22] Howard Coxe, journalist and novelist.

[23] Possibly composer Theodore Chanler.

[24] Producer Dwight Wiman.

[25] Preparation containing alcohol; used as a sedative.

[26] Probably *piqûres*, ("injections").

[27] Spa in the Pyrenees where Zelda Fitzgerald took a "cure" in January 1926.

[28] Raquel Meller, internationally known Spanish singer.

[29] A beach at Cap d'Antibes.

[30] Opera singer and actress whom the Fitzgeralds knew on the Riviera.

[31] Ruth Ober-Goldbeck–de Vallombrosa, an American married to the Count de Vallombrosa; Charles MacArthur.

[32] Walker Ellis, Princetonian with whom Fitzgerald had worked on *Fie! Fie! Fi-Fi!*

[33] St.-Paul-de-Vence, a town in the mountains above the Riviera where Zelda was angered one night by Fitzgerald's attentions to Isadora Duncan.

[34] Zelda resented Fitzgerald's friendship with Lois Moran.

[35] Carl Van Vechten.

[36] New York lawyer Richard Knight.

[37] French diplomat and author; best known for *Open All Night* (1923) and *Closed All Night* (1924).

[38] Paris taxi driver whom Fitzgerald brought to "Ellerslie" in 1928 to serve as chauffeur.

[39] Fitzgerald had come home after a drinking session with Hemingway and passed out. In his sleep he said "No more baby," which Zelda interpreted as evidence that Fitzgerald and Hemingway were engaged in a homosexual affair.

[40] Playwright Philip Barry.

[41] Dorothy Parker.

[42] Prima ballerina Nemtchinova.

[43] Fitzgerald believed he had tuberculosis.

[44] French medical term for cupping.

[45] Novelist; sister of Elinor Wylie.

[46] Ballerina in Madame Egorova's studio.

[47] Fitzgerald used this phrase in one of Nicole's letters from the sanitarium in *Tender Is the Night*.

[48] In 1930 Fitzgerald began a series of five stories for *The Saturday Evening Post* about Josephine Perry, a teenaged girl who undergoes a process of "emotional bankruptcy."

[49] The Kalmans were in Paris at the time of Zelda Fitzgerald's breakdown in the spring of 1930.

TO: H. L. and Sara Mencken — ALS, 1 p. Enoch Pratt Library

% Guaranty Trust
4 Place de la Concorde
Paris, France

Dear Menk and Sarah:

Excuse these belated congratulations,[1] which is simply due to illness. Zelda and I were delighted to know you were being married + devoured every clipping sent from home. Please be happy

Ever your Friend
Scott (and Zelda)
Fitzgerald

Oct 18th, 1930

[1] Mencken had married Sara Haardt, who grew up in Montgomery with Zelda Fitzgerald.

FROM: Zelda Fitzgerald | AL, 3 pp. Princeton University
Fall 1930 | Prangins Clinic, Nyon, Switzerland

Goofy, my darling, hasn't it been a lovely day? I woke up this morning and the sun was lying like a birth-day parcel on my table so I opened it up and so many happy things went fluttering into the air: love to Doo-do and the remembered feel of our skins cool against each other in other mornings like a school-mistress. And you 'phoned and said I had written something that pleased you and so I don't believe I've ever been so heavy with happiness. The moon slips into the mountains like a lost penny and the fields are black and punguent and I want you near so that I could touch you in the autumn stillness even a little bit like the last echo of summer. The horizon lies over the road to Lausanne and the succulent fields like a guillotine and the moon bleeds over the water and you are not so far away that I can't smell your hair in the drying breeze. Darling—I love these velvet nights. I've never been able to decide whether the night was a bitter [   ] or a grand patron—or whether I love you most in the eternal classic half-lights where it blends with day or in the full religious fan-fare of mid-night or perhaps in the lux of noon—Anyway, I love you most and you 'phoned me just because you 'phoned me to-night—I walked on those telephone wires for two hours after holding your love like a parasol to balance me. My dear—

I'm so glad you finished your story—Please let me read it Friday. And I will be very sad if we have to have two rooms. Please.

Dear. Are you sort of feeling aimless, surprised, and looking rather reproachful that no melo-drama comes to pass when your work is over—as if you ridden very hard with a message to save your army and found the enemy had decided not to attack—the way you sometimes feel—or are you just a darling little boy with a holiday on his hands in the middle of the week—the way you sometimes are—or are you organizing and dynamic and mending things—the way you always are.

I love you—the way you always are.

Dear—

Good-night—

Dear-dear dear dear dear dear dear
Dear dear dear dear dear dear dear
Dear dear dear dear dear dear
Dear dear dear dear dear dear
Dear dear dear dear dear dear
Dear dear dear dear dear dear
dear dear dear dear dear dcar
dear dear dear dear dear dear
dear dear dear dear dear dear
dear dear dear dear dear dear

TO: Judge and Mrs. A. D. Sayre TL(CC), 3 pp. (fragment)
Princeton University

Paris, the 1st December 1930.

My dear Judge Sayre and Mrs. Sayre,

Herewith a summary of the current situation shortly after I wrote you: at length I became dissatisfied with the progress of the treatment—not from any actual reason but from a sort of American hunch that something could be done, and maybe wasn't being done to expedite the cure.

The situation was briefly that Zelda was acting badly and had to be transferred again to the house at Praugras reserved for people under restraint—the form in her case being that if she could go to Geneva alone she would "see people that would get her out of her difficulties."

When Forel told me this I was terribly perturbed and had the wires humming to see where we stood. I wrote Gros who is the head of the American hospital in Paris and the dean of American medecine here. Through the agency of friends I got opinions from medical specialists of all sorts and the sum and substance of the matter was as follows:

1°—That Forel's clinique is as I thought *the best* in Europe, his father having had an extraordinary reputation as a pioneer in the field of psychiatry, and the son being universally regarded as a man of intelligence and character.

2°—That the final rescourse in such cases are two men of Zürich—Dr. Jung and Dr. Blenler,[1] the first dealing primarily with neurosis and the second with psychosis, which is to say, that one is a psychoanalist and the other a specialist in insanity, with no essential difference in their approach.

With this data in hand and after careful consideration I approached Dr. Forel on the grounds, that I was not satisfied with Zelda's progress and that I had always at the back of my mind the idea of taking her home, and asked for a consultation. I think he had guessed at my anxiety and he greeted the suggestion with a certain relief and thereupon suggested the *same two men* I had already decided to call in—so that it made a complete unit. I mean to say there was nothing left undone to prove that I was dealing with final authorities.

After much, much talk I decided on Blenler rather than Jung—this was important because these consultations cost about five hundred dollars and one can't be complicated by questions of medical etiquette. He came down a fortnight ago, spent the afternoon with Zelda and then the evening with Forel and me. Here is the total result.

1°—He agreed *absolutely* in principle with the current treatment.

2°—He recognized the case (in complete agreement with Forel) as a case of what is known as *skideophranie*, a sort of borderline insanity, that takes the form of double personality. It presented to him *no feature that was unfamiliar* and no characteristic that puzzled him.

3°—He said in answer to my questions that over a field of many thousands of such cases three out of four were discharged, perhaps one of those three to resume perfect functioning in the world, and the other two to be delicate and slightly eccentric through life—and the fourth case to go right down hill into total insanity.

4°—He said it would take a whole year before the case could be judged as to its direction in this regard but he gave me hope.

5°—He discussed at length the possibility of an eventual discovery of a brain tumor for the moment unlikely and the question of any glandular change being responsible. Also the state of American medical thought on such matters. (Forel incidently was at the Congress of Psychiatrists at Johns Hopkins last spring). But he insisted on seeing the case as a case and to my questioning answered that he did not know and no one knew what were the causes and what was the cure. The principles that he believes in from his experience are those that he and the older Forel, the father, (and followed by Myers[2] of John Hopkins) evolved are rest and "re-education," which seems to me a vague phrase when applied to a mind as highly organized as Zelda's. I mean to say that it is somewhat difficult to teach a person who is capable now of understanding the Einstein theory of space, that 2 and 2 actually make four. But he was hardboiled, regarded Zelda as an invalid person and that was the burden of his remarks in this direction.

6°—The question of going home. He said it wasn't even a question. That even with a day and night nurse and the best suite on the Bremen, I would be taking a chance not justified by the situation,— that a crisis, a strain at this moment might make the difference between recovery and insanity, and this question I put to him in various forms i.e. the "man to man" way and "if it were your own wife"—and he firmly and resolutely said "NO"—not for the moment. "I realize all the possible benefits but no, not for the moment."

7°—He changed in certain details her regime. In particular he felt that Forel was perhaps pushing her too much in contact with the world, expediting a little her connection with me and Scotty, her shopping expeditions to Geneva, her going to the opera and the theatre, her seeing the other people in the sanitarium (which is somewhat like a hotel).

8°—He not only confirmed my faith in Forel but I think confirmed Forel's own faith in himself on this matter. I mean an affair of this kind needs to be dealt with every subtle element of character. Humpty Dumpty fell off a wall and we are hoping that all the king's horses will be able to put the delicate eggshell together.

9°—This is of minor importance and I put it in only because I know you despise certain weaknesses in my character and I do not want during this tragedy that fact to blur or confuse your belief in me as a man of integrity. Without any leading questions and somewhat to my embarrassment Blenler said "This is something that began about five years ago. Let us hope it is only a process of re-adjustment. Stop blaming yourself. You might have retarded it but you couldn't have prevented it.

My plans are as follows. I'm staying here on Lake Geneva indefinately because even if I can only see Zelda once a fortnight, I think the fact of my being near is important to her. Scotty I see once a month for four or five days,—it's all unsatisfactory but she is a real person with a life of her own which for the moment consists of leading a school of twenty two French children which is a problem she set herself and was not arbitarily

[1] Dr. Paul Eugen Bleuler.

[2] Dr. Adolf Meyer, psychiatrist at the Phipps Clinic of Johns Hopkins Hospital, who later treated Zelda Fitzgerald.

TO: Mrs. Edward Fitzgerald — ALS, 1 p. Princeton University
1930 — Lausanne, Switzerland

Dear Mother

No news. I'm still here waiting. Zelda is better but very slowly. She can't cross the ocean for some time yet + it'll be a year before she can resume her normal life unless there's a change for the better. Adress me Paris, care of Guaranty. Actually I'm in Lausanne + migrate to Paris once a fortnight to see Scotty who has a small apartment. So we're all split up.

Got the Swiss book. Its no good.

Love to you both
Scott

TO: Scottie Fitzgerald
c. 1930

Holograph postcard signed.
Scottie Fitzgerald Smith
Lausanne, Switzerland

Sweet darling — this makes various sized doll's chairs + tables

The secret of putting it together again is to put all the curved surfaces next to the curved surfaces + the straight surfaces next to the straight surfaces. Do not force it.

I love you so, my child

Daddy

Lithographie Simplon, Lausanne

FROM: Zelda Fitzgerald
1930/1931

AL, 4 pp. Princeton University
Prangins Clinic, Nyon, Switzerland

Dear Scott:

Will you mail this to Sara please? I seem to have lost her address amongst other things. I wrote you a long rig-a-marole yesterday, I don't know why, which you can believe or not as you choose—since I do not know whether it was true

I keep thinking of Provence and thin brown people slowly absorbing the deep shade of Aix—the white glare on the baking dust of a country pounded into colorless oblivion by an incessantly rotating summer—I'd like awfully to be there—Avignon must be perfect now, to feel the wide quiet of the Rhone, and Arles obliterating its traces with the hum of cafés under the great trees— I'd like to be eating the lunch we had at Chateau Neuf du Pap, where the air was not vibrant and full of the whole spectrum—looking over a deep valley full of grape-vines and heat and far away the palace of the Popes like a mirage—

I would like to be walking alone in a Sirocco at Cannes at night passing under the dim lamps and imagining myself mysterious and unafraid like last summer—

I would like to be working—What would you like? Not work, I know, and not lone places. Would you like to be in New York with a play in rehearsal like you always said? and to have decorative people about you—to be reading Spengler, or what?

It is not possible that you should really want to be in the hurry and disorder of the Ritz Bar and Mont Matre and the high excitability of scenes like the party we went to with McGowan where you passed so much of your time recently—

FROM: Zelda Fitzgerald
1930/1931

AL, 3 pp. Princeton University
Prangins Clinic, Nyon, Switzerland

My dearest and most precious Monsieur,

We have here a kind of a maniac who seems to have been inspired with erotic aberrations on your behalf. Apart from that she is a person of excellent character, willing to work, would accept a nominal salary while learning, fair complexion, green eyes would like correspondance with refined young man of your description with intent to marry. Previous experience unnecessary. Very fond of family life and a wonderful pet to have in the home. Marked behind the left ear with a slight tendency to schitzoprenie.

We thought it best to warn you that said patient is one of the best we have at present in the irresponsible class, and we would not like any harm to come to her. She seems to be suffering largely from a grand passion, and is easily identifiable as she will be wearing the pink of condition and babbling about the 6.54 being cupid's arrow. We hope this specimen will give entire satisfaction, that you will entrust us with all future orders and we love you with all all all our hearts and souls and body.

Wasn't it fun to laugh together over the 'phone? You are so infinitely sweet and dear—O my dear—my love, my infinitely inexpressible sweet darling dear, I love you so much.

Our picnic was a success and I am cooked raw from the sun. A lady came with us who behaved about the row-boat like I used to about the Paris taxis so it was a lively expedition. What fun, God help us—

Goofy! I'm going to see you to-morrow to-morrow! You said you wouldn't 'phone, so what time will I expect your call?

If all the kisses and love I'm sending you arrive at their destination you will be as worn away as St. Peter's toe and by the time I arrive have practically no features left at all—but I shall know you always by the lilt in your darling person

Dearest!

FROM: Zelda Fitzgerald
January 1931

ALS, 2 pp. Princeton University
Prangins Clinic, Nyon, Switzerland

Dear Scott:

Knowing that our meeting was inadequate and that the sympathy and tenderness that I would liked to have expressed more clearly were lost in the disorder of your sudden leaving I hope this note will reach you before you are on the sea. Once in America the loss of your father will seem closer home than it does from Europe. Reconstructing the scenes of your youth is going to be a painful affair and [ ] I would like to offer you the little comfort there is in the knowledge that someone who is close to you appreciates the fullness of your heart in thinking of a definately finished part of your world. Your father was a happy man at the end. He liked Washington and his hotel friends and had grown to imagine himself a part of government machinery. You must not be too sorry for his lot. By the time the failures of his middle years had grown far enough away to be fitted retrospectively into his career he was already old and tired with life less pressing on his heels. Luckily they have always had money and he did not feel the necessity to struggle and keep alert his intelligence in the great scramble for a place in the world. He was at any rate spared that in his old age and spent his time in a vague dream.

Don't be anxious about us. Madamoiselle is exceedingly capable and can communicate with me when necessary.

I would have been so happy to help you. A neurose is not much good in times of distress to others. And its hard to extract solace from the past. I can only send my profoundest sympathy—

Zelda

TO: Bert Barr[1]
29 January–6 February 1931

ALS, 2 pp. Princeton University
Hamburg-Amerika Line letterhead

Bremen
Feb 3d 1881

Madame—I hope to God you got some kind of sleep. No human being could possibly have all the stuff that I think you have, but you could divide that by two and still have enough left over to make a whole row of mixed debutantes and Tiller girls[2] or what have you.

This letter is a sort of tender homage or would you like that big lilac tree in front of the dining room or a cargo mast (the latter covered with the facial hair of any man on board including the captain)?

Your Chattel
Scott Fitzgerald

[1] When Fitzgerald sailed for America on 29 January to attend his father's funeral, he met Bert Barr (Mrs. Louis Goldstein) on the *New York*, which docked 6 February. She was a member of the party with Texas oilman Herman Cornell and convinced Fitzgerald that she was a professional card sharp. The story "On Your Own" was inspired by this shipboard meeting. See *Esquire* (30 January 1979), 67, for a note on Bert Barr.

[2] Troupes of dancers for musical comedies.

TO: Bert Barr
29 January–6 February 1931

ALS, 3 pp. Princeton University
Hamburg-Amerika Line letterhead

Somewhat later

Canal Boat "Staten Island"
"Spend-a-dollar day" 1901

Pearl of the Adriatic: Another note because I am in terror you will wake up with an open trunk in front of you + confuse it with the trunk you last saw early this [ ] morning tottering, I might say weaving from your palatial suite—what I mean is I am sober, de-alcoholized, de-nicotinized de-onionized and I still adore you. Jay Obrien himself could say no more.

Is every member of you entourage so inflamed with jealousy at my wakefulness that it will be difficult to see you?—Douglass Fairbanksova Dostoieffski for example? I arrived on the last day but we parvenus have to be pushing or My God the rush of modern life would just—just well, devour us—that doesn't sound right, but whatever the rush of modern life does.

Be generous; don't be a lower bert' but an upper 'bert—even forgive that. I miss you. Will you meet me in the boiler room just inside the first canary cage at 12:15? I miss you. If you have breath in your body answer this.

Jay
(Doctor of Medicine)

TO: Bert Barr
29 January–6 February 1931

ALS, 2 pp. Princeton University
Hamburg-Amerika Line letterhead

Even Later

Graf Zeppelin
Stowaways Quarters

Are you just going to sleep and sleep? And sleep and sleep? Havn't you any feeling of public responsibility. Havn't you any invitations to fine country houses. Mrs. Jay Obrien would blush for you. I woke up thinking of you—I have tried to get my mind a decent break by feeding books to it but you are too much alive to let them have any reality.

Wake up. The sun is shining, the clocks are ticking, the nose is running. Life is tearing along, and you an old sleepy-head.

Dudley Field Malone
Bishop of Bordeaux

I enclose my photograph

TO: Bert Barr
29 January–6 February 1931

ALS, 3 pp. Princeton University
Hamburg-Amerika Line letterhead

The "Alps," 6th Ave at 58th
Near Nightfall

I put in a new razor blade for you + the texture of my skin is like duveteen or *Gloria Morgan* "Pond's Extract" Vanderbilt—it would not shame the greatest fairy that ever knitted a boudoir cap—and still no word. Are you recieving? Do you ever recieve? Did you ever think who killed Rothstien + Dorothy King?[1] I did. After the fourth note + no answer I said if they like sleeping I'll help go on with it. Thats *my* story and no transfer connieseur from Brooklyn can shake it. What if your father is President? What if Scott Fitzgerald did try to make you? Every girl's got to get off on her own initiative and any paddles broken or bloomers-ripped should be reported to Miss Rorer at the small cottage. Have I got to have the whole Hapag S.S. Line installed with room telephones to know you're still alive?

Fitzg—

[1] Gambler Arnold Rothstein and Dorothy King were victims of unsolved murders; Rothstein was the model for Wolfshiem in *The Great Gatsby*.

TO: Bert Barr
ALS, 3 pp. Princeton University
New Yorker Hotel letterhead. New York City

feb 7th [1931]

So then you were gone + I couldn't whisper any more into the wooly top-knot of your hat. Everything was unreal again with all the women sitting naked on the tables + the men snarling among themselves + so I went behind my convenient bush—which is to say I got quite a lot drunk. I talked a lot to thisman thatman + that girl who was in ballet school with my wife but when I heard myself from the calm detached listening post that part of me was sitting in, telling her that she was mosh beautiful woom in a worl and asking Douglas f'ee had any ajections—I decided to get out which took twenty minutes of slow motion—I left the three of them in front of some cafe + came back to this lousy hotel with my briefcase in my arms, wondering about you + what you had gone home to + how long hours and days are.

So Mrs. Goldstien (Neé Mr. and Mrs Jay O'brien) so—there's some hours gone and to that extent you're nearer

Scott

TO: Bert Barr
ALS, 3 pp. Princeton University
After 7 February 1931
Hotel Napoleon letterhead. Paris

Micky Mouse: This is Virginia with names like Manassas and Culpepper full of the Civil War + I've been thinking about my father again + it makes me sad like the past always does. So I'll think of you because that's happy, *Dear* Bert.

The management of *Grand Hotel* had two of their men scurrying about New York all afternoon trying to get seats for Charley + me. Finally they had to buy in two singles from different agencies + change around two parties to get a pair of seats together. Charley arrived at the theatre at eight o'clock, took his seat + went sound asleep for three hours. He remembers the curtain going up + a man coming on the stage but nothing after that except that at one point a woman asked him to take his head off her shoulder. I reached the theatre at the moment when the last curtain was going down and saw the knees + feet of what appeared to be a lot of bellboys. So no one can say that Scott Fitzgerald + Charles MacArthur havn't been to "Grand Hotel"—at least in spirit. I left him in a speakeasy with the indignant manager, Charley looking very wild + helpless as if a whole series of tournedos had xploded in his mouth

I sent the books to 50 Plaza St. If they havn't come please call Scribners retail dept. I'm particularly anxious for you to have them.

I miss you so Goddamn much

Scott

TO: H. L. Mencken | Wire. New York Public Library

MONTGOMERY ALA[1] 1931 FEB 15 PM 6 35

H L MENCKEN

WILL YOU KINDLY WIRE ME THE NAME OF THE BIGGEST PSYCHIATRIST AT JOHNS HOPKINS FOR NONORGANIC NERVOUS TROUBLES ADDRESS 2400 16TH ST WASHINGTON DC REGARDS

SCOTT FITZGERALD.

[1] After his father's funeral Fitzgerald went to Montgomery to report to the Sayres on Zelda's condition.

TO: Bert Barr | ALS, 2 pp. Princeton University
March 1931 | Grand Hôtel de la Paix letterhead
Lausanne, Switzerland

Darling Micky Mouse: Arrived here in bum condition + took to bed—immediately a pile of the most depressing American mail arrived so I got up + organized myself + my affairs + now things look brighter (by the way if you have any lingering jealously of that lady you'll be glad to know that I found a week-old note here saying she was leaving for America because of the serious illness *of her ex-husband!*)

It was too bad about us this time—we met like two crazyy people, both cross + worried + exhausted + as we're both somewhat spoiled we took to rows + solved nothing. It was rough too about the hotel—at the time I was angry at that woman but later the scene of her in the hall returns to me as something terribly sordid, a scene in a cheap boarding house, and both of us too dazed to face it + her properly.

It certainly indicates that we're not too good for each other at this precise moment—as you suggested we'd each better try to straighten out our affairs first, because we're so different that we *have* to have a certain patience toward each other + that's impossible in a condition of agitation. All of which doesn't mean that my tenderness toward you is diminished in the slightest *but only that I want it to go on,* + one more siege like those three days would finish us both + spoil everything for ever.

In any case I find I'm in debt again which means two weeks hard work and a life of complete ascetisism. As I told you the first two weeks in July belong to my family. Meanwhile if your own plans get clearer—and believe me dear child I appreceate what of a hell of a time you've had—the Guaranty Trust always reaches me quickest, because I may be here or in Nyon with my invalid.

I hope things are better + that you'll try to remember the best + not the worst of that bad time

Your
Krazy Cat

TO: Alice Lee Myers[1]
c. March 1931

ALS, 2 pp. Mrs. Richard Myers
Grand Hôtel de la Paix letterhead
Lausanne, Switzerland

Sweet Alice (Ben Bolt or no Ben Bolt):

What a hell of time all my friends have been having this year! Even the Bishops have twins. But when I think of poor Dick with part of his flesh cloven to another part I have the horrors thinking what it must feel like. But those things leave no mental scars. I had my nosebones sawed without anaesthetics at his age and it only taught that all misery is over eventually.

All right about Scotty if you'll trade Fanny for her. But tell Dick not to tell her she's pretty because she gets ugly for a week afterwards grimacing at herself in mirrors. You've been so damn nice to her and there's nobody I'd rather have her with than your children This must be an exception to the fact that children of friends invariably loathe each other. Scotty + the little Murphys begin to glare as soon as they're in a radius of a hundred yards from each other.

Christ knows about this summer. I'd certainly love to have Scotty visit you for a time—she'll be some, maybe a lot with her mother + I plan taking her for a months swimming. It's all vague.

I hope you have a great time in America. In spite of the heavy gloom of up-to-my-neck-in-crêpe, I enjoyed the way people are getting down to work.

Zelda is much, much better. Only a few months from being well. I've skiied with her yesterday.

Much Much love from us both to all of you
Scott

[1] Mr. and Mrs. Richard Myers were close friends of the Murphys.

TO: Bert Barr

ALS, 1 p. Princeton University
Guaranty Trust, Paris
March 1931

Darling Micky Mouse:

When are you coming over?—about when? approximately when? I know you buyers don't get here usually until about Août while we contact men just go hither + thither at will—but I have mothers to take to Carlsbad, daughters to arrange vacations for, and I want to know when you're coming + how much of you I can see. Are you coming in Apr.;? May?; June? Your telegram made me think sooner. I'll meet you anywhere (like Mr. Cornell) and just so long as you go in for white evening purses I know it'll be worth my while.

Oh Bert! I remember:

"No jam tomorrow"—and

"I've got my *gloves* on" (preceded by a shriek of laughter) and

"I g't a paarler", and

The exploding tournedos, and best of all

"Not *one* of the nicest episodes, *the* nicest episode."

And I miss you so Goddamn much

So, as we agreed, let's not have such a long time interval between these Honalulu Beaches. Bert, dear.

Scott

TO: C. O. Kalman

ALS, 1 p. Princeton University
Grand Hôtel de la Paix letterhead
Lausanne, Switzerland

Guaranty Trust
4 Concorde
March 11th 1931

Dear Kaly:

I can't thank you enough for your kindness to mother. I love your "There is no charge for this as we are doing it every day." Such a wonderful reason. I'm going to write Lorimer that I make no charge for my writing as I'm doing it every day. Can't you hear the barber's: "No, *please* sir—I won't take a penny—I'm doing it every day." However there's probably some catch to it—you've found that *caché* of old prayer books I left in your mother's cellar or something like that + your conscience is troubling you. Far be it from me not to look for the motive behind—I suppose you think I'm going to write another story about you—well, I'm not—unless you get in some more interesting trouble.

I hear you're the only prominent Minnesotan that didn't get a Nobel Prize last year + that's why you're afraid to show your face in Europe.

Zelda is *almost well—really* well. I hope we'll be home in the fall. She's still in the *clinique* but I went ski-ing with her this afternoon.

All love, sacred + profane to Sandy + yourself

Scott F

TO: Alfred Dashiell[1]
June 1931

ALS, 1 p. University of Virginia
Grand Hôtel de la Paix letterhead
Lausanne, Switzerland

Dear Mr. Dashiell:

As I wired—I'd like to do the article[2] (It's already paid for!) It'll be ten days before I can send it, tho It'll reach you about early in July. Thanks for the idea

Yrs.
Scott Fitzgerald

[1] Editor of *Scribner's Magazine.*

[2] "Echoes of the Jazz Age," *Scribner's Magazine* (November 1931).

FROM: Zelda Fitzgerald
Spring/Summer 1931

AL, 3 pp. Princeton University
Prangins Clinic, Nyon, Switzerland

Darling, Berne is such a funny town: we bumped into Hansel and Gretel and the Babes in the Wood were just under the big clock. It must be a haven for all lost things, painted on itself that way. Germanic legends slide over those red, peeling roofs like a fantastic shower and the ends of all stories probably lie in the crevasses. We climbed the cathedral tower in whispers, and there it was hidden in the valley, paved with sugar blocks, the home of good witches, and I asked of all they painted statues three wishes

That you should love me
That you love me
You love me!

O can you? I love you so.

The train rode home through a beautiful word: "alpin-glun."[1] The mountains had covered their necks in pink tulle like coquettish old ladies covering scars and wrinkles and gold ran down the hill-sides into the lake.

When we got home they said you had 'phoned, so I phoned back as indiscreetly as possible since I couldn't bear not having heard your voice, that lovely warm feeling like an emotional massage.

O my love—how can you love a silly girl who buys cheese and plaited bread from enchanted princes in the public market and eats them on the streets of a city that pops into life like a cucoo-clock when you press the right note of appreciation

I *love* you, dear.

[1] *Alpenglühen,* the glow of the Alps at sunset.

TO: Maxwell Perkins | ALS, 1 p. Princeton University
Summer 1931 | Lausanne, Switzerland

Dear Max: Here's the article—I found that I had pretty well exhausted my ideas on the subject but I think this is all right. Charge off my account what you think right, for it is shorter than you wanted.

Did you get me the Scandanavian copies of *Gatsby*?

Zelda is well, thank God, and is writing some amazing stuff We sail for America on the Aquitania Sept 19th, so I'll see you about the twenty fifth. So will you tell your secretary to hold mail.

We are going to Alabama for the winter + there I hope to God I'll finish the novel

What are these wine cubes? Will you get me a couple and keep them in your desk till I come—I'm curious, + afraid they'll disappear before I come.

I'm so anxious to see you

Always Yours Devotedly
Scott F

FROM: Gerald Murphy | TLS, 1 p. (with holograph postscripts). Princeton University
Summer 1931

Sunday.

Dear Scott:—

How great that everything seems to be going so well and that you can all really come here. We had begun to worry a little and expect an ugly letter from you. You've doubtless got my telegram saying that the fourth August will be fine. We return from Salzburg on the afternoon of the *third* after Patrick's next injection which takes place *that* morning. We stay at the Grand Hotel de l'Europe when there. It's not a bad idea that we see each other there that day, unless you're coming by another way (Zurich—Munich) to Bad Aussee.

Bring bathing suits.

The name of the property is RAMGUT, Bad Aussee, Steyrmark, Austria. Telephone number I. We are about 85 kilometres or two hours and one half easy going from Salzburg. I should suggest that you come by Zurich, Buchs, Innsbruck, Salzburg,—or if you want to go to Germany from the Swiss border and then South to Salzburg, go by Munich,—but by Innsbruck and the Austrian Tyrol is lovely.

Our schedule may be too tight a one to allow of our going to Vienna with you, as it will be just the moment that we are without a trained nurse for Patrick, the present one leaves August 3rd and Miss Stewart does not land until the 10th. But you and Zelda must go, Scottie can stay with us so easily until you come back to get her. It will give you and Zelda kind of a fling alone;—and we are on your way back.

The termination of your letter with it's patter of baby feet had what you would consider the desired effect upon Sara: sharp local pains followed by excessive retching.

Our love to you all. We *are* looking forward to seeing you,

Gerald.

[Across the top] Vienna is 5 hrs. (at most) due East of us by motor. We are on the direct road between Salzburg + Wien.

[Along left margin] Bring Express or A.B.A. checks for Austria + Germany,—otherwise it's difficult,—and if possible put USA somewhere on your car,—otherwise you're apt to be eaten for a Frog. With USA they strew roses.

FROM: Zelda Fitzgerald — AL, 6 pp. Princeton University
After August 1931 — Prangins Clinic, Nyon, Switzerland

Dearest, my Love—

Your dear face shining in the station, your dear radiant face and all along the way shimmering above the lake—

It's so peaceful to be with you—when we are to-gether we are apart in a high indominatable place, sweet like your room at Caux swinging over the blue. I love you more always and always—

Please don't be depressed: nothing is sad about you except your sadness and the frayed places on your pink kimona and that you care so much about everything—You are the only person who's ever done all they had to do, damn well, and had enough left over to be dissatisfied. You are the best—the best—the best and genius is so much a part of you that when you find a person you like you think they have it too because it's your only conception—O my love, I love you so—and I want you to be happy. Can't you possibly be just a little bit glad that we are alive and that all the year that's coming we can be to-gether and work and love and get some peace for all the things we've paid so much for learning? Stop looking for solace: there isn't any and if there were life would be a baby affair. Johnny takes his medicine and Johnny get well and a quarter besides. Think! Johnny might get some mysterious malady if left to develop and have it named for him and live forever, and if Johnny died from not having his syrup the parable would have been a moralistic one about his mother.

Dear, I'm tired and in an awful muddle myself and I don't know what to tell you—but love is important and we can make life do and you are greater than any of them when you're well and rested enough not to know they exist.

Stop thinking about our marriage and your work and human relations—you are not a showman arranging an exhibit—You are a Sun-god with a wife who loves him and an artist—to take in, assimilate and all alterations to be strictly on paper—

Darling, forgive me, I love you so. I can't find anything to say beyond that and I'd like a wonderful philosophy to comfort you.

Dear, my love.

Think of me some—

It's so happy to touch you.

FROM: Ernest Hemingway
October 1931

Inscribed photograph. Bruccoli

FROM: Zelda Fitzgerald — ALS, 3 pp. Princeton University
11 November 1931 — Montgomery, Alabama

Darling—

Four days have gone so now we have only thirty-eight 'till you'll be home again.[1] We are like a lot of minor characters at table waiting for the entrance of the star. It's very lonely in the morning and afternoon and at night. I had the rubbeuse last night but it was only half a massage—since you weren't there to have the other half. I kept the light burning on your desk so I'll think you're there when I wake up, but then it's awful to have to turn it out when it's day. Your room is warm and fuzzy with you and I sit and look where you left things.

There was a parade to-day but I didn't go. I love the still desertion of the back streets when men are marching. The weather here is a continual circus day—Smoky with the sun like a red balloon and soft and romantic and sensual. I hope it's as nice in California

I found the old blind buglar from the Civil War that used to sell me candy when I was a child. I said "Uncle Bob I used to buy your candy twenty-five years ago" and he said "That's nothing new"—So I felt very part of the generations, struggling and pathetic. I bought Scottie a cream bar. It tasted of buried treasure so we gave it to the cat who has reappeared.

I am send off the murder story again.[2] There is no word from "Nurts"[3] and I'm afraid I am just "writing for myself"

Va. Browder phoned me about Sanctuary.[4] Said she couldn't sleep for three nights it gave her the horrors so terribly. Do you think we should give it to all these people? Two came last night for Mathilde (her aunts) of the clever type: when the word "year" comes up they say "a year has twelve months, you know—" or a person has only to say "Sat." to bring forth "*that's* after Sunday"—God! You know the kind: women of fifty still known as "Baby." Darling; I am escapeless in an awful world when you are not here.

If I could only *some*way make you feel how much I love you—

Zelda.

I read "The Off Shore Pirate" to-day. You were younger than anybody in the world once—what fun you must have had in that curious place that's younger than life—It's a good story   Can they make clocks out of cellos in Hollywood?[5]

[1] In November/December 1931 Fitzgerald was in Hollywood working on the screenplay for *Red-Headed Woman* at MGM; his script was not used.

[2] Unidentified.

[3] Probably "A Couple of Nuts," *Scribner's Magazine* (August 1932).

[4] Novel by William Faulkner (1931).

[5] Line from a song in "The Offshore Pirate," *The Saturday Evening Post* (29 May 1920).

FROM: Zelda Fitzgerald
November 1931

AL, 4 pp. Princeton University
Montgomery, Alabama

Dearest, my love:

I had the most horrible dream about you last night. You came home with a great shock of white hair and you said it had turned suddenly from worrying about being unfaithful. You had the big leather carry-all trunk you have always talked about buying and in it were two huge canvasses, landscapes, with the trees stuffed and made of cloth and hanging off like doll's arms, O Goofo! I love you so and I've been mad all day because of that dream.

The people came in hoards, (each one) for lunch, *ten*, and it was very successful. Mrs McKinney, Eva Mae Clark (useful for golf) Marjorie Allen, Virginia Julia, Francis Stevenson and the director of the Little Theatre. He said he'd give Private Lives if I'd play it. I thought he would fly out the window, but he's very pleasant.

Did you see this in the New Yorker?

Dear, I miss you more every day—These sultry days when everything feels like an interlude after a big event and the woods are introspective and the heavens old and sober I want you near so much. But one week has gone to-night—one week more to realize how much I love you. De-e-o.[1]

Its wonderful that we have never had a cross word or done bad things to each other. Wouldn't it be awful if we had? Dear—I can't seem to get started writing. I havent got that inner happiness or desperation that leaves a person free in the external world of imagination, but just a sort of a plugging along feeling—When you come home we can be happy

If we seem dim and far away sometimes, dear please think of us anyway even if it should seem like a useless emotional disciplining. You are all I care about on earth: the past discredited and disowned, the future has doubled up on the present; give me the peace of my one certitude—that I love you. It's the only instance in my life of my intelligence backing up my emotions—That was an awful dream—awful dear. I didn't want to live and you were only formally sorry—

Oddly enough, I always think of Dolf Patterson when I think of Hollywood—His illusions seem realer to me than my own sporadic despair of the time—

I don't mean any of this: I want you to have a good time and take what you can from everywhere and love me if you want to and be kind—

But I Love you

Zelda

[1] One of Zelda's pet names for Fitzgerald was "Deo," which she variously wrote as "De-e-o," "D.O.," or "Do-Do."

FROM: Zelda Fitzgerald
Before 17 November 1931

ALS, 4 pp. Princeton University
Montgomery, Alabama

Darling O my Own Love!

I wrote you such a silly egocentric non-sensical letter yesterday—I was haunted by the night-mare. To-day I played tennis from ten to twelve-thirty with Noonie[1] and we swam about ten minutes and I am all cheerful and not a bit depressed anymore except by thinking that there might have been something in that absurd letter to worry you.

Dear, I've finished "All The Sad Young Men"—except "The Rich Boy that I saved for to-night. They are all so good—fine stories. I wanted to cry over the Sensible Thing. Reading your stories makes me curious more than ever about you. I don't suppose I really know you very well—but I know you smell like the delicious damp grass that grows near old walls and that your hands are beautiful opening out of you sleeves and that the back of your head is a mossy sheltered cave when there is trouble in the wind and that my cheek just fits the depression in your shoulder.

Scottie and Mlle went on horse-back to-day. They are very enthusiastic—and Mlle has started lessons in ball-room dancing. I am so glad she has found some distraction. The house goes along listening for you and we are terribly lonely.

Daddy is sinking rapidly the Doctors say. I only go once a day and take Mamma for a long drive, since he is completely unconscious and does not know us or seem to want anybody about.

To-day I went to sleep on your bed. It was like dozing in a lullaby swung on the ends of time and space. Your cane is still always where you left it. Do you want it sent?

I had planned to spend Thanksgiving with the three of us and Noonie at a place near Dothan, Panama City, that they say is the equal of the Bay of Biscay. If Daddy's condition permits we will go for the week-end and if its nice we can go when you're back. Its only 150 miles, and perfect beach and bathing. Noonie plays fine tennis: she give me 30 but I won so she made me take 15. We are going to play every day so I can play with you—

Goofo, my dear, I think of you always and at night I build myself a warm nest of things I remember and float in your sweetness till morning—

All my love and heart and everything, everything

Zelda

[1] Zelda's niece, the daughter of her sister Marjorie Brinson.

FROM: Zelda Fitzgerald
18 November 1931

ALS, 2 pp. Princeton University
Montgomery, Alabama

Dearest:

This is all very sad: The struggle is over and this is the end of another brave, uncompromising effort to preserve conceptions—

Daddy died last night but I was not called till morning.

Anthony is here and Tilde arrives to-morrow—[1]

Mamma is very brave and cheerful but it's very sad.

I wonder what ironic sequence, what stamina of spirit Daddy has carried over that made him think so little of the world and so much of justice and integrity? I have not seen his body. But I am glad that he is released at last from a consciousness that knew only pain at the end. The last time I saw him he seemed glad to see Scottie and very gentle and glad of his flowers—and apart from that oblivious—

I am glad he is in peace—

All my love, my dear—dear—dear

Zelda.

[1] Zelda's brother and sister.

FROM: Zelda Fitzgerald
After 18 November 1931

ALS, 2 pp. Princeton University
Montgomery, Alabama

Darling:

The fire burns contentedly like many ladies swishing their silk petticoats and Chopin[1] passes invisible delicacies judiciously about in his mouth. I have sore throat, asthma, grippe and indigestion and I am making Mamma a picture of myself for Christmas that looks like a Florentine fish-monger. The rain keeps up and the ground is heavy as a sponge and receeds from everything. The country clay-banks are washed to deep folds of a heavy fabric and the trees are limp and gummy. I am delighted your Mother is coming after all. It will be pleasanter for her than a lone Christmas. Please *wire*: shall I put her down-stairs? The house is fresh as a candy-store. The curtains are washed and starched to paper and the rugs are cleaned and bright, owing to hap-hazard animal excretions. We have had a zoo here since you left and its only Mamma who kept me from buying a monkey from the circus.

I love climbing out on the tin roof and brandishing my empty pistol and yelling "Who's there?" as if I had a mob at bay. But I am, secretely, always the escaping criminal. My bravado instincts do not function on the side of law and order, as do not also a great many other interesting facets of myself: ie, to me, interesting, of cource.

Minor tried to teach Scottie a break-down. It's terribly hard since it consists of dangling yourself by your shoulder while your feet bounce like drum-sticks. It's the real nigger tap dancing and I'm crazy to have her learn it. It has nothing in common with musical comedy and is very distinguished and would be nice to know when calling on the President.

I miss my Daddy horribly. I am losing my identity here without men. I would not live two weeks again where there are none, since the first thing that goes is concision, and they give you something to butt your vitality against so it isn't litterred over the air like spray of dynamite. D.O. darling, I love you—

Zelda, the dowager duchess of detriment.

[1] A cat.

FROM: Zelda Fitzgerald
After 18 November 1931

ALS, 2 pp. Princeton University
Montgomery, Alabama

Dearest:

I fell down to-day and sprained my ankle: I won't be able to walk for a week but luckily it isn't very swollen so perhaps it will be well quicker: Scottie stumbled and burnt her arm very slightly on the stove and has a bandage—and this is accident prevention week. The Boy-Scouts are tormenting innocent pedestrians with ropes and flags and the police look very stylish in their badges for afternoon wear. Perhaps I will be able to write while my foot subsides.

That's a fine article:[1] I hope it cured you of some of your loss of confidence. Deo, my Darling—You are the best of all.

I'm sorry your work isn't interesting. I had hoped it might present new dramatic facets that would make up for the tediousness of it. If it seems too much drudgery and you are faced with "get to-gether and talk-it-over" technique—come home, Sweet. You will at least have eliminated Hollywood forever. I wouldn't stay and waste time on what seems an inevitable mediocrity and too hard going.

Scottie and I are hideously lonesome for you: I have sunk into a conservative apathy and can't seem to produce anything at all. I worked on the automobile story, changed the name to "Sweet Chariot"[2] and sent it off. Also Elsa Maxwell, which, in spite of your criticism, still seems good to me. Thought of calling it "Foie Gras"—[3] What do you think? The plot is banal, but the writing is the best I ever did—

I don't know what to think about with you away—My mind stumbles about the shadows of your room and thinks of nothing at all except that you were there a week ago—

Darling my own love—*Don't* stay if you're miserable. There's warmth and content and happiness waiting here and you don't *have* to struggle through experimental mazes with all you've got behind you—

I love you so—I wish I could do all the badness for you—

A very nice man I don't remember said he was in the army with you and asked very cordially after you—as do all our friends—

Mr. Indespensable Dudo, I love you.

Zelda

1 "Echoes of the Jazz Age."
2 Unpublished.
3 Unpublished.

FROM: Zelda Fitzgerald
After 18 November 1931

ALS, 2 pp. Princeton University
Montgomery, Alabama

Dearest, my Own Love:

This has been such a discouraging day: if there weren't the thought of you at the end to make everything have a compensation existence would be too dispiriting. I have been able to walk for the first time. The body is given us, I presume, as a counter-irritant to the soul. And my story at last is started. We closed up Daddy's office. It was very musty and masculine and cerebral and the great bulk of all those old men impressive. Daddy had a big butterfly pinned over the map of the L+N. lines and some shirt samples and a copy of Josephus. We hope the state will buy his library. It's just the little personal things we care about in people, we being what we are—only his historians bother about what a man has contained of time and race. Who cares what good or evil dies? And all of us care that we will never hear a certain chuckle again or see the fingers meet a certain way. The things we can do ourselves are all that really move us: Which is why our intellects and our emotions subsist in different spheres and ceaselessly destroy us with their battles. It is a beautiful warm night like steam from a savory cauldron and I want to be happy and glad of the rutted moon and the birds in the bare baked trees. Life is horrible without you because there's not another living soul with whom I have the slightest communion.

Scottie is a fiend on horse-back. We love you and miss you—

O *Dee-o* I love you so. It is very good to have something to love

Zelda

FROM: Zelda Fitzgerald
23 November 1931

ALS, 3 pp. Princeton University
Montgomery, Alabama

Dearest, My Own Darling

I went to get my hair washed th[is] afternoon and shades of Hollywood Boulev[ard] in walked her the hairdressers sister straight from Los Angeles, and fried to the eyes It reminded me of the Helen Buck era "Bessie Love?"[1] she'd say "well she's *out*," with the finality of Ring. And "I haven't had a bite yet" by which I inferred that she was on her way to supper and "Say *listen*!" every other word and then at the end opening her big 35 year old eyes very innocently "I'm tight" Then a long wait for laudatory exclamations. Hearing her talk was like being two people at once, one of them dim and far away in the past. Equivalent spectres floated thru so many of our early years. "The Talmadge girls are absolute *rag-pickers*—say friend, have you got a match?"

O dear, this beneficent weather—and a pink rose in the garden and the cat rolling a sun-beam over the grass and the nights like a child's prayer. I wish we were sharing the expansiveness of this benevolent country. I have never never missed you so much as I do. Do you think of me out there amongst the vibrations where everything quivers and waits to fall like swelling drops from a dropper?

And Daddy's grave so sad on the side of an old and sinking hill. To-[day] was Mamma's birthday—I had [ ] all to lunch—Anthony's wife is [aw]fully nice and Tilde is pretty and Marjorie is good and kind and there we were: All Daddy had to leave behind. Mamma sat in that more aristocratic world where she and Daddy have always lived. She is so sweet and foolish and infinitely courageous—I have been feeling very proud and simple lately. How have you been feeling? I do not examine myself very closely or my reactions since you are away and there is no one to talk to—Life is just the essence of zero without you and it somehow seems a very distant affair—as it were taking place in California perhaps—I love you so—Please write Scottie that she must learn her American history. Her information on the Revolution is lamentable and she has discovered that she can get by without work. They have long finished it at the school, and she is completely ignorant of both details and conception. Her French is fine—the work, I mean—very thorough + lively—The school thing is *important*!

Dearest—I love you so dearly

Zelda

[1] Movie actress.

FROM: Zelda Fitzgerald
November 1931

ALS, 2 pp. Princeton University
Montgomery, Alabama

Darling, My Love:

The second check has arrived I will keep it until I need it, however it is dated Nov 27—

The kitten caught, tortured and ate his first mouse. Shall I give him a coming out party?

Mamma and I drove to a pottery in the hills to get some vases for the cemetery and I bought a lump of clay to mould. It is very fascinating. You feel like a plastic surgeon and the things are very rubbery and alive. It is really fine to cup my hands about a head, and stick my thumbs into the eyes and mash the neck as if it were my own I were rectifying.

My foot is still too bad to either dance or exercise. Va. likes my story very very well.[1] I would like to mail it to you but I know you are absorbed in your own so I'll do the best I can and send it on to Ober. Darling I miss you so not having anyone to trust and talk to intellectually. There's no use asking anybody else's opinion because I don't care what it is.

I love a Sunday in Montgomery with all the people on their porches and the cars all full of children and those augmented Sunday families and I love walking home when the lights get tangled in the dusk and the houses seem to be awaiting some gay reception, posing expectantly as the very stately home or the giddy young bungalow, the house just out of college or the house that made its way in the world. This is a pleasant place. I am sorry I find difficulty in simplicity, but I would be happy if you were here.

$75,000! Goofo—I would do anything for that! We could build us a house with the surplus. A great denuded square I want with frank windows that frame the world in cold impersonal rigidity. And it is to be all over yellow. We will have all the children we can and call them Dementia Praecox Fitzgerald—Dear, how gruesome!

Our car seems to be passing into senility—It goes to the garage tomorrow for monkey-glands. I suppose they will use a local anesthetic—perhaps on the passengers. Maybe you'd better bring yours home.

Darling, my own I love you so—and I'm so sleepy and thinking about the back of your head

Zelda

[1] Unidentified.

FROM: Zelda Fitzgerald
December 1931

ALS, 2 pp. Princeton University
Montgomery, Alabama

Dearest My D.O—

Sunday in a trance and sleeping all afternoon like a deserted cat on your bed and now its night and the house seems to be nothing but overtones with you away—Tho you hat is in the hall and your stick still on the bed and you could not tell that it's all just a bluff and a make-shift without you. I feel like going to Florida for the week-end. It's only six hours in the car, and I imagine at this time of year it would be very reedy with lone fowls strung on the horizon and the seaflinging loose gray cowls on the sand and long yellow beaches that look like womens' poetry and belong to the Swinburne apostles.

The cat is the most beautiful fellow. He broods over ancient Egypt on the hearth and looks at us all contemptuously. Julia and Freeman[1] are very good and considerate and Mlle and I get along very well and have not yet come to blows. She is a nice girl. Scottie is engrossed in protecting herself against being disillusioned about Santa Claus and is as pretty as a moon-beam. She dresses herself by my fire and it's a joy to watch her long sweet delicate body and the cool of her pale hair quenching the light from the flames. However, my disposition is very bad and asthmatic and it is just as well that you are out of this homely lyric. I am going to dig myself a bear-pit and sit inside thumbing my nose at the people who bring me carrots and then I will be perfectly happy. My mother and father are civilized people: it is strange the rest of us should be so inadequate. There are some lovely bears in Berne who live in a mythical world of Sunday afternoon and little boys and itenerant soldiers and the one in Petrouschka is very pleasant and sometimes they live on honey and wild-flowers when they are off duty from the fairy-tales. But I will be a very dirty bear with burrs in my coat and my nice silky hair all matted with mud and I will growl and move my head about disconsolately.

There are no grands évènements to report. I am sending my story to Ober as it now seems satisfactory to me, but nobody will buy it since it is mostly about champagne. They wouldn't buy it anyway even if it was about hydrochloric-acid or mystic anti-kink so what ho!

Darling I miss you so terribly—You can never go off again. It's absolutely impossible to be very interested in anything without you or even to get along very well—at all.

Love and Love and Love

Zelda

[1] The Fitzgeralds' servants.

FROM: Zelda Fitzgerald
December 1931

ALS, 4 pp. Princeton University
Montgomery, Alabama

Dearest my love:

I am positively tormented by all sorts of self-reproaches at leaving. Scottie is so sweet and darling and the house is so pleasant and I have everything in the world except you. And yet I am nervous and too introspective and stale—probably because since you left I haven't felt like amusement and recently I have not been able to exercise at all. So I am leaving for the week-end only, in the hopes that just long riding rolling along will give me back the calm and contentment that has temporarily disappeared with my physical well-being. Please understand and do not think that I leave in search of any fictitious pleasure. After the utter solitude of Prangin there have been many people lately and people that I love with whom my relations are more than superficial and I really think I need a day or two by myself. I will leave Sun. and be back Wed. night—While we are away, Julia is thorough cleaning. She is a peach.

D.O. I realize more completely than ever how much I live in you and how sweet and good and kind you are to such a dependent appendage.

Chopin has his nest in our bath-room. He is so lovely with a face like a judicial melancholic bear, the Polly scornfully eats peanuts, and Uncle rakes the leaves like father Time sorting over the years of the past.

Scottie and I have had a long bed-time talk about the Soviets and the Russian idea. I lent her "The Russian Primer"[1] to read and will be curious to hear her reactions when I get back. She is so responsive and alert. You will be absolutely ravished by her riding trousers and yellow shirt and Scottie rearing back in her saddle like a messenger of victory. Each time she goes she conquers herself and the pony, the sky, the fields and the little black boy who follows on a fast shaven mule. I wish I were a fine sweet person like you two and not somebody who has to go 200 miles because they have a touch of asthma.

The house is full of surprises—but as usual I did everything at once and there's nothing left for the end, except finish my story which is too good to do uninspirationally and out of sorts.

God! I hope you haven't worked yourself to death. We *must* reduce our scale of living since we will always be equally extravagant as now. It would be easier to start from a lower base. This is sound economics and what Ernest and most of our friends do—

Darling—How much I love you.

Zelda

[1] M. Ilin, *New Russia's Primer* (1931).

FROM: Zelda Fitzgerald
December 1931

ALS, 2 pp. Princeton University
Montgomery, Alabama

Dearest Sweetheart and Darling:

My nice quiet time when I look in the fire and think you are working in the next room went in visitors: Mary Ceil who talked about the times when people wanted her to take a drink and Tillis about the times she got people to take them "You know that boy—Aw *you* know. I know you know who I mean—The one that was so drunk that night."

"I never saw him in my life. I never even laid eyes on him."

"You know. I know you know. Don't you remember who I mean?" From eight until eleven! Tillis is, au fond, a cigar-wrapper and Mary Ceil is a Louis Bromfield heroine. This place is like one of those cracked phonograph records that plays always in the same place where you have to push the needle over but each revolution it sticks till you push it again and you never can come to the tune. Save me, Deo, from the darkness and the blight. God! I will be glad when you get home. Two weeks from to-day.

I'm sorry about your mother. Old people are very tragic. gestures left from the days when they expressed desires and unconscious responses to tones in the voice when they know no more authority or submission and all those placative phrases with which they've managed to piece the rents and tears of the current of life and patch away the meaning of things. I suppose she does not want to be bothered with the effort of a new place. I would love to have her.

I am drugged with atmosphere. It's a shock moving about as we do—or is it growing old—suddenly finding yourself on unremembered corners surrounded by a flood of forgotten association. When places and experience have contributed their tuning and stretching of the emotional range their contribution should be equally applicable anywhere and at your service for a voluntary projection into remembered qualities, not situations. An experience of unabsorbed detail is a recurrent repetitive storehouse and almost useless and means living in the past (see Eddington: direction of time)[1] waiting with a subconscious hope of finding the same yellow jasmine on the same June wall. It's hurt lots of writers: Hergesheimer, for one, and Wells for another.

D.O., Monsieur—I love you very dearly and you never write which is OK because I know you are busy but I must complain since this is a very ill-tempered day and Darling my Own Darling I love you.

Your Very Insignifigant
Zelda

[1] Arthur Stanley Eddington, English astrophysicist who developed theories concerning physical reality and relativity.

FROM: Gertrude Stein[1]
December 1931

Inscription in Stein's *How to Write* (1931).
Bruccoli

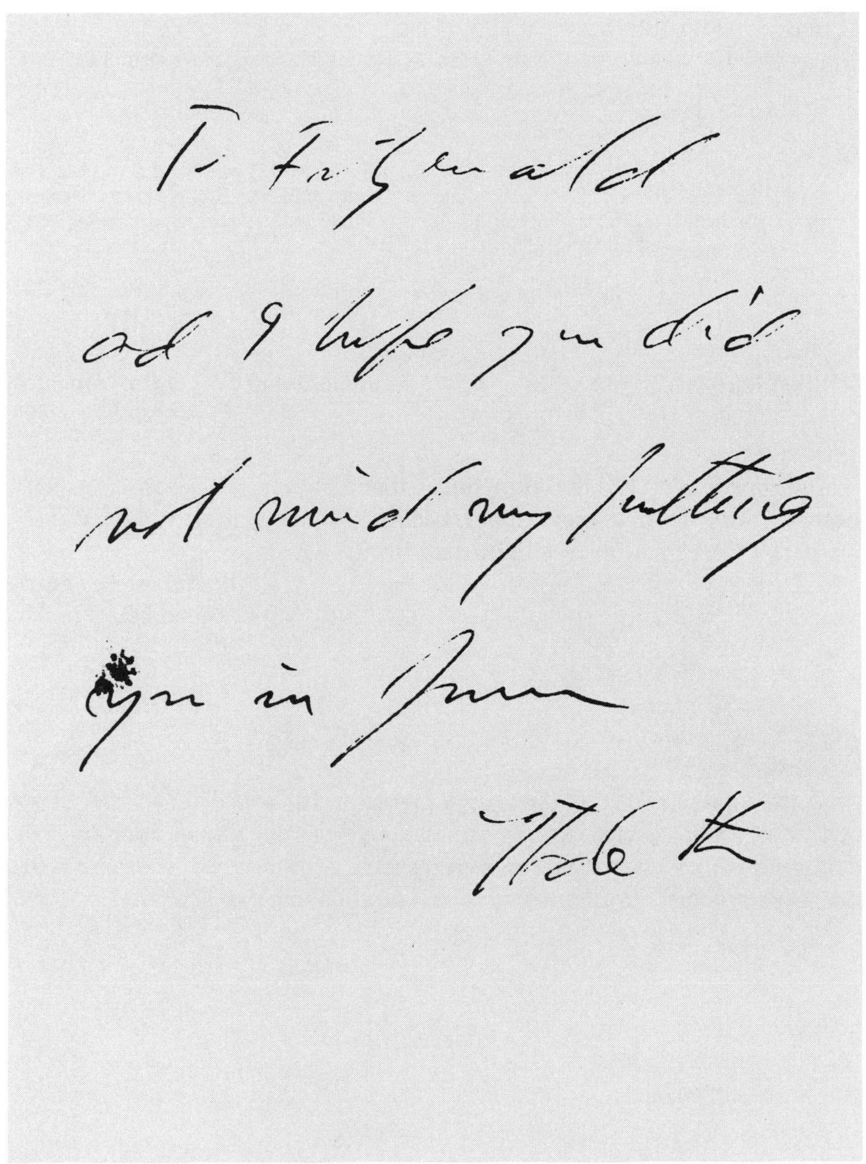

To Fitzgerald
and I hope you did
not mind my putting
you in
Gtde Stein

Note: On p. 30 of *How to Write* (Paris: Plain Edition) Fitzgerald marked the sentence "That is the cruelest thing I ever heard is the favorite phrase of Gilbert." In *The Autobiography of Alice B. Toklas* (1933) Stein later wrote: "Fitzgerald always says . . . her doing it is the cruelest thing I ever heard of." See Fitzgerald's 28 April 1932 letter to Stein in *Letters*.

FROM: Norma Shearer Thalberg[1] Wire. Scrapbook. Princeton University
c. December 1931

SCOTT FITZGERALD

CHRISTIE HOTEL HOLLYWOOD CALIF

I THOUGHT YOU WERE ONE OF THE MOST AGREEABLE PERSONS AT OUR TEA

NORMA THALBERG.

[1] Actress; wife of Irving Thalberg, production head of MGM and model for Monroe Stahr in *The Last Tycoon.* While working in Hollywood on *Red-Headed Woman,* Fitzgerald got drunk at a party in the Thalbergs' home and performed for the guests. "Crazy Sunday" is based on this incident.

TO: Bert Barr Inscription in *This Side of Paradise*. Princeton University
1931

Dear Bert:

This book is silly + dated now but it made me a name when I was very young. It was the first book about necking + the younger generation—way back before Flaming Youth or such things

Affectionately Yours
F Scott Fitzgerald

TO: Maxwell Perkins Wire. Princeton University

MONTGOMERY ALA 1228P 1932 JAN 5 PM 1 58

HAVE YOU SEEN KAUFFMANS OF THE I SING JUDGING FROM REVIEWS THE INFLUENCE OF THE VEGETABLE OVERSTEPS THE BOUNDARY OF DECENCY WILL YOU MAKE DISCREET INQUIRIES AND WIRE ME YOUR OPINION REGARDS

SCOTT FITZGERALD

TO: Maxwell Perkins Wire. Princeton University

MONTGOMERY ALA 1102A JAN 29 1932

HAVE BEEN TRYING UNSUCCESSFULLY TO DO HOLLYWOOD ARTICLE AT NIGHT AND WORKING FURIOUSLY ON NOVEL SIMPLY DONT DARE STOP WILL DO ARTICLE AT FIRST BREAK IN ENTHUSIASM TERRIBLY SORRY

SCOTT FITZGERALD.

1244P

FROM: Zelda Fitzgerald
February 1932

AL, 3 pp. Princeton University
Phipps Clinic, Baltimore, Maryland

Dearest—

It seemed very sad to see you going off in your new shoes alone.[1] Little human vanities are somehow the most moving poignant things in people you love—Struggles and deep emotions when you are closely identified with are apt to assume the unconscious epic quality but the little things about people are always so touching—

I didn't finish your socks. It seems awful that you should be doing them again. You could easily teach Julia I'm sure she'd be conscientious about it.

I have been trying to make myself a picture of you—It's just one of those usual black faces that look doughy and embryonic I'd give anything to have my beautiful picture that looks as if you were inventing special heavens to go to on June Sundays.

I brought the little chess set and the manual—so when you miss them don't think the social revolutionists have looted the house—

If Freeman goes to jail it will save you the humanitarian reproaches of having to fire him.

The row of brick houses from the window at night present a friendly conspiracy to convince us of the warmth and pleasantness of life—but its cold here and there is no communication yet between the swept chilly pavements and the sky—

Sunday we went to a museum and I saw some directoire wall lights with stars that would be perfect for the house that we'll never have—

You are my darling, darling, darling one and I love you so, D.O.

Think of me—If my room is as empty to you as yours was when you were away you will find yourself living in an ether dream—as if there was a veil between you and reality—

D.O—I love you—

[1] After Zelda Fitzgerald suffered a relapse during a trip to Florida in January, Fitzgerald placed her in the Phipps Clinic and returned to Montgomery.

FROM: Zelda Fitzgerald
After February 1932

AL, 4 pp. Princeton University
Phipps Clinic, Baltimore, Maryland

Dearest:

Life has become practicly intolerable. Everyday I devellop a new neurosis until I can think of nothing to do but place myself in the Confederate Museum at Richmond. Now it's money: We must have more money. To-morrow it will something else again: that I ran when Mamma needed me to help her move, that my hips are fat and shaking with the vulgarities of middle-age, that you had to leave your novel, that there are unemployed, or millionaires, people better than I am and people worse, a horrible sickening fear that I shall never be able to free myself from the mediocrity of my conceptions. For many years I have lived under the disastrous pressure of a conviction of power and necessity to accomplish without the slightest ray of illumination. The only message I ever thought I had was four pirouettes and finité. It turned out to be about as cryptic a one as Chinese laundry ticket, but the will to speak remains.

O Darling! My poor dear—watching everything in your life destroyed one by one except your name. Your entire life will soon be accounted for by the toils we have so assiduously woven—your leisure is eaten up by habits of leisure, your money by habitual extravagance, your hope by cynicism and mine by frustration, your ambition by too much compromise. D.O. it is very sad and utterly meaningless and the only real emotion I have which will bear inspection is an overwhelming desire to expose the charlatanism and ignominious harlotrys of what we so eruditely refer to as our civilizations. Freud is the only living human outside the Baptist church who continues to take man seriously.

Bunny's[1] mind is too speculative—Nothing but futures, of the race, of an idea, of politics, of birth-control. Just constant planning and querulous projecting and no execution. And he drinks so much that he cares more than he would.

Darling:

I want to go to fabulous places where there is absolutely no conception of the ultimate convergence of everything—

I *Love You*

[1] Edmund Wilson.

FROM: Zelda Fitzgerald — ALS, 4 pp. Princeton University
March 1932 — Phipps Clinic, Baltimore, Maryland

Darling, Sweet D.O.—

Your dear letter made me feel very self-condamnatory. I have often told you that I am that little fish who swims about under a shark and, I believe, lives indelicately on its offal. Anyway, that is the way I am. Life moves over me in a vast black shadow and I swallow whatever it drops with relish, having learned in a very hard school that one cannot be both a parasite and enjoy self-nourishment without moving in worlds too fantastic for even my disordered imagination to people with meaning. So: it is easy to make yourself loved when one lives off love. Goofo—I adore you and worship you and I am very miserable that you be made even temporarily unhappy by those divergencies of direction in myself which I cannot satisfactorily explain and which leave me eternally alone except for you and baffled. You are absolutely all in the world that I have ever been able to think of as having any vital bearing on my relations with the evolution of the species.

"Freaks" gave me the horrors.[1] God! the point of view of sanity, normality, beauty, even the necessity to survive is so utterly arbitrary. Nobody has ever been able to experience what they have thoroughly understood—or understand what they have experienced until they have achieved a detachment that renders them incapable of repeating the experience. And we are all seeking the absolution of chastity in sex and the stimulation of sex in the church until sometimes I think I would loose my mind if I were not insane.

Darling, darling. The Zola is wonderful. Had he ever fallen into the hands of the authorities, we should have missed his contribution to neurasthentic symptology sadly. It is a long time since I have had any new symptoms and I am bored with all the old tricks of my shatterred organism

I love you and I would like us to be covered with the flake of dried sea water and sleeping to-gether on a hot afternoon. That would be very free and fine. Dear Heart!

I have got so fetid and constantly smell of the rubbery things about here—It's ghastly, really. I do not know to what depths the human soul can sink in bondage, but after a certain point everything luckily dissolves in humor. I want to fly a kite and eat green apples and have a stomach-ache that I know the cause of and feel the mud between my toes in a reedy creek and tickle the lobe of your ear with the tip of my tongue.

If Trouble[2] still bites give him a good kick in the ass for me.

Darling, I love you so.

Zelda.

P.S. I do not see how Dr. Squires[3] can remain a sprig of old English lilac in this seething witches cauldron. Did you know the Furies turned out to be respectable old women who went about the countryside doing good and laying eggs in their night shirts? So much for Eschyllus. The old moralist!

[1] A 1932 movie.

[2] Scottie's dog.

[3] Dr. Mildred Squires of the Phipps clinic, to whom Zelda Fitzgerald dedicated *Save Me the Waltz.*

FROM: Zelda Fitzgerald
March 1932

ALS, 4 pp. Princeton University
Phipps Clinic, Baltimore, Maryland

Dearest D.O—

I'm sorry to be so nagging house-wife about the money. I did not realize that things like laundry and stuff were hard cash and no refund and, as usual, I am penniless and about to spend three chapters of Dickens in a mental debtors'-prison. Since you did not understand either, I suppose you think that I have been sloshing my insides at Marconis, or tearing up to the Atlantic City Baby Parade.

When are you coming to Baltimore? There is a night-club and some good shows. I have had a terrible proclivity towards the baubles and tawdry doo-dads of life recently—feeling like the ex-wife of Diamond Jim Brady, mentally. I am secretly awfully suppressed in the fancy-goods line—was just coming to in Montgomery.

Darling—I miss you so—It's very interesting here, however. Every now and then somebody opens the door and I say

"And what do you see my sister". and they answer "Nothing but the dust up on the hills," and I go back to wishing I had never stolen the golden-key and awaiting the return of Blue-Beard.

I am proud of my novel,[1] but I can hardly restrain myself enough to get it written. You will like it—It is distinctly École Fitzgerald, though more ecstatic than yours—Perhaps to much so. Being unable to invent a device to avoid the reiterant "said" I have emphasized it à la Ernest much to my sorrow. He is a very determined writer, but I shall also die with my boots on.

I mailed Zola—Found he was helping me to nourish my psychological disorders too much for my own good. Eschyllus is infallible and and to read him is to wallow in a lush and golden roll of prose that would force you to write if you knew nothing but the Syrian alphabet.

The days wheeze in on these creaky March days like the last moments of a dying novelist. Sometimes I feel like a titan and sometimes like a three-months abortion—But always I love you in spite of the fact that you are infinitely superior to me and I forgive you your many superlative merits—

Dear—I do not want to keep Mlle. It is very irritating to have a person in such close contact whom you feel is not co-operating except by giving in to avoid trouble. Scottie is not fond of her, so I have no regrets. It's too bad, but I have done my best and I am sure she will not feel that her trip has yielded her nothing. It's so annoying to have a person in your own house who is distasteful to you. There must be plenty of French women out of work in the east. Mlle is, au fond, very dogmatic and intolerant and both Scottie and I hate making the constant effort of pulling our punches to get along at all.

Damn Serez[2] for forsaking us! More + more I realize her perfections. I cannot live any more with people under thirty—harmoniously. They have too much to learn from experiences which I have already achieved—and do not care to be reminded of or have to explain to others—Chaque-un a son gout! Love and Love and Love—Zelda.

[1] *Save Me the Waltz* (Scribners, 1932).
[2] Scottie's governess in France.

FROM: Zelda Fitzgerald | ALS, 2 pp. Princeton University
March 1932 | Phipps Clinic, Baltimore, Maryland

Dearest

My letters sound dry and composed, I suppose, because there isn't much external data with which to embellish them. I assure you they are not the gleanings of my meagre note-book. My writing went so successfully that I didn't have time to make my usual observations on our social state. It's an amusing book which I will mail to you Monday. I sent a copy direct to Max, but I know Scribner's will refuse it. Knopf is the place I suppose since it has no more weight than Nigger Heaven and many things on his list I have some slick psychological stuff which will have to be written in future under more tranquil circumstances when I feel more egotistical since I mean to lambaste our whole mass of concepts. Now, I can hardly afford to whip myself to the necessary frenzies to attack the primal deep-seated hypocracies of our kind. But I shall have some words to say of the baseness and beauties of man.

Dear, I'm sorry about the money's going so fast. This week it was a permanent wave—next week I hope God in his plush heavens with toss me out some old moth-eaten repose that none of his customers could use and I can stop castigating myself long enough to buy nothing, wish for nothing and achieve the infinite: nothing. I have finished a rhapsodic fizzle of a story about the Auerbacks which I shall send to Ober with instructions to try Physical Culture on account of the gymnastics in the prose.[1]

I'm sorry Montgomery is so dull: It always was, but Daddy presence seemed to bolster it up to a semblance of being the end of more noble times. Now we see it as very tentative and unsophisticated snatching at the turmoils brewed in bigger kettles. I'm all for savagery and its discard always moves [meet] to lament. However all my social sorrows are of the École Burne-Jones[2] just at present: rather voluptuous and symbolical; vague fleshly figures floating in a ghostly nebulum playing the harp. Or else they are cartoons bearing such legends as "Bologny," otherwise known as what the hell—

Dearest, I love you—which is not a dead Narcissus but just one of those things: perhaps a boutonnière from the trick shop on the Boulevard des Italiens which squirts water in your eyes when you try to smell it—

Anyway, the Baby is very intent on Establishing herself in the unquestionable benefits of our dubious policies of organization, and at considerable loss to know how to proceed since Ober will not dispose of my gems, some of which are as good as Mr Faulkners—the murder story for instance. I'm going to put them in the want ads—pretty soon—

Your wife, otherwise known as the mendacious, mendiant, maniacal

Mme. X—

Please let me ask somebody for a job on the paper somewhere—

[1] Unpublished.

[2] Sir Edward Burne-Jones, English painter of the Pre-Raphaelite school.

FROM: Zelda Fitzgerald
March 1932

ALS, 2 pp. (with Fitzgerald's annotations).[1]
Princeton University
Phipps Clinic, Baltimore, Maryland

Dearest, my own Darling D.O—

I hadn't realized how much I wanted to see you till night came and you had telegraphed your delay—Here, living so that every action is a ritual and every smallest bit of energy expended is of interest to *somebody*, there's not much time left for projecting yourself into distant places and speres of an ordinary existence. One day goes and then another and the cradle rocks on in the continuous lullaby of recapitulations. My heart fell with a thump that you didn't come—So I have been very cross and rude and blaming the Sicilian Vespers[A] and St. Bartholemew's on Dr. Myers.

Dearest:

Dr. Squires tells me you are hurt that I did not send
1 √ my book to you before I mailed it to Max. Purposely I
didn't—knowing that you were working on your own
and honestly feeling that I had no right to interrupt you
? to ask for a perious opinion. Also, I know Max will not
(perilous) want it and I prefer to do the corrections after having
FSF his opinion. Naturally, I was in my usual rush to get it
2 √ off my hands—You know how I hate brooding over
This things once they are finished: so I mailed it poste haste,
is hoping to have yours + Scribner's criticisms to use for
an revising. (all this reasoning is specious or else there is
evasion no evidence of a tornado in the state of
Alabama[B]

Scott, I love you more than anything on earth and if
you were offended I am miserable. We have always
shared everything but it seems to me I no longer have the
right to inflict every desire and necessity of mine on you.
I was also afraid we might have touched the same
material.[C] Also, feeling it to be a dubious production due
3 √ to my own instability I did not want a scathing criticism
such as you have mercilessly—if for my own good given
4 √ my last stories, poor things. I have had enough discour-
5 √ agement, generally, and could scream with that sense of
inertia that hovers over my life and everything I do. So,
Dear, my own, please realize that it was not from any
sense of not turning first to you—but just time and other
6 ill-regulated elements that made me so bombastic about
Max.

I have two stories that I save to show you, and a fantastic sketch.

I am going to begin a play as soon as I can find out about length etc—for which I ordered Baker's[D] book—

(7.) √ Goofo, please love me—life is very confusing—but I
love you. Try, dear—and then I'll remember when you
need me to sometime, and help.

I love you—
Zelda

[1] The numbers and check marks in the margin are Fitzgerald's. Editorial footnotes are identified by letters A–D.

[A] September 1931 Mafia murders.

[B] Fitzgerald's note; there had recently been a tornado in Alabama. The words "of Alabama" are smeared.

[C] Probably underlined by Fitzgerald.

[D] George Pierce Baker, professor of playwriting.

TO: Maxwell Perkins — Wire. Princeton University

MONTGOMERY ALA 1932 MAR 16 PM 10 21

PLEASE DO NOT JUDGE OR IF NOT ALREADY DONE EVEN CONSIDER ZELDAS BOOK UNTIL YOU GET REVISED VERSION LETTER FOLLOWS[1]

SCOTT FITZGERALD.

[1] Zelda had written the first version of *Save Me the Waltz* at Phipps and sent it directly to Perkins. When Fitzgerald learned about it, he was bitterly angry because he felt she had used material that belonged to him. The first draft of *Save Me the Waltz* does not survive.

TO: Maxwell Perkins — Wire. Princeton University

MONTGOMERY ALA 1932 MAR 25 PM 11 52

THINK NOVEL CAN SAFELY BE PLACED ON YOUR LIST FOR SPRING IT IS ONLY A QUESTION OF CERTAIN SMALL BUT NONE THE LESS NECESSARY REVISIONS MY DISCOURAGEMENT WAS CAUSED BY THE FACT THAT MYSELF AND DAUGHTER WERE SICK WHEN ZELDA SAW FIT TO SEND MANUSCRIPT TO YOU YOU CAN HELP ME BY RETURNING MANUSCRIPT TO HER UPON HER REQUEST GIVING SOME PRETEXT FOR NOT HAVING AS YET TIME READ IT AM NOW BETTER AND WILL WRITE LETTER TOMORROW IN MY OPINION IT IS A FINE NOVEL STOP WILL TAKE UP ARTICLE AS SOON AS I HAVE FINISHED CURRENT POST STORY WHICH WILL BE ON ARRIVAL BALTIMORE WEDNESDAY BEST REGARDS FAITHFULLY

SCOTT FITZGERALD.

TO: Maxwell Perkins — Wire. Princeton University

MONTGOMERY ALA 1150A 1932 MAR 28 PM 1 41

READ MANUSCRIPT BUT IF YOU HAVE ALREADY RETURNED IT WIRE AND ILL SEND COPY STOP IF YOU LIKE IT AND WANT TO USE IMMEDIATELY REMEMBER ALL MIDDLE SECTION MUST BE RADICALLY REWRITTEN STOP TITLE AND NAME OF AMORY BLAINE CHANGED[1] STOP ARRIVING BALTIMORE THURSDAY TO CONFER WITH ZELDA WILL IMMEDIATELY DECIDE ON NEW TITLE AND NAME CHANGES REVISING SHOULD TAKE FORTNIGHT

SCOTT FITZGERALD.

[1] The original title of *Save Me the Waltz* is not known. David Knight, the hero, was named Amory Blaine after the hero of *This Side of Paradise*.

FROM: Zelda Fitzgerald — ALS, 2 pp. Princeton University
April 1932 — Phipps Clinic, Baltimore, Maryland

Dearest:

Of cource, I glad submit to anything you want about the book or anything else. I felt myself the thing was too crammed with material upon which I had not the time to dwell and consequently lost any story continuity. Shall I wire Max to send it back? The real story was the old prodigal son, of cource. I regret that it offended you. The Pershing incident[1] which you accuse me of stealing occupies just one line and will not be missed. I willingly relinquish it. *However, I would like you to thor-*

oughly understand that my revision will be made on an aesthetic basis: that the other material which I will elect is nevertheless legitimate stuff which has cost me a pretty emotional penny[2] to amass and which I intend to use when I can get the tranquility of spirit necessary to write the story of myself versus myself. That is the book I really want to write. As you know my contacts with my family have always been in the nature of the raids of a friendly brigand. I quite realize that the quality of this book does not warrant so many excursions into the bizarre—As for my friends: first, I have none; by that I mean that all our associates have always taken me for granted, sought your stimulus and fame, eaten my dinners and invited "the Fitzgeralds" place. You have always been and always will be the only person with whom I have felt the necessity to communicate and our intimacies have, to me, been so satisfactory mentally that no other companion has ever seemed necessary. Despised by my supiors, which are few, held in suspicion by my equal, even fewer, I have got all external feeding for my insignifgant flames from people either so vastly different from myself that our relations were like living a play or I have cherished my inferiors with color; to wit; Still [ ] etc. and the friends of my youth. However, I did not intend to write you a treatise on friendship in which I do not believe. There is enough difficulty reconciling the different facets in one single person to bear the context of all human communication, it seems to me. When that is accomplished, the resultant sense of harmony is what is meant by benevolent friendship.

D.O. I am so miserable at not being able to help you. *I know how upset you get about stories. Don't worry.*[3] If we have less money—well, we can always live. I promise to be very conciliatory and want nothing on earth so much as for you to feel that you can write what you want.

About my fish-nets: they were beautiful gossamer pearl things to catch the glints of the sea and the slow breeze of the weaving sea-weed and bubbles at dawn. If a crab filtered in and gnawed the threads and an octpus stagnated and slimed up their fine knots and many squids shot ink across their sheen and shad laid comfortable row on their lovely film, they are almost repaired once more and the things I meant to fish still bloom in the sea. Here's hope for the irridiscent haul that some day I shall have. What do you fish with, by the way? that so puts to shame my equipment which I seriously doubt that you have ever seen, Superior Being—

With dearest love, I am your irritated
Zelda

[1] In Book I, Ch. 18, of *Tender Is the Night* Abe North pretends to be General Pershing at the Paris Ritz.

[2] Possibly underlined by Fitzgerald.

[3] Possibly underlined by Fitzgerald.

TO: Dr. Oscar Forel TL(CC), 3 pp. Princeton University

Hotel Rennert
Baltimore, Md.
April 18, 1932

Dear Dr. Forel:

Forgive me for not having written before, but things have been in a turmoil. Now for the news.

A week after I last wrote you (about February 1st), Lelda[1] had another period (about two hours) of psychotic delusions, with attendant hysteria, and suggested herself that we go to a clinic. I took her (without any trouble—this was not anything like as serious as 1930, save for these short periods), and I left her with Dr. Myers in Baltimore, and returned to Montgomery. My haste was lest she begin to turn against me again (*which she did not at any time*).

It appears that, as you fondly hoped, this may indeed be the "classical case" though nothing is yet entirely certain. She has behaved almost perfectly at Johns Hopkins. They do not take "committed" patients there and they told me that during the whole time she had not done or said anything that would warrant committing her. She wrote, or finished, a novel in the clinic that is excellent—in it she told, in veiled terms, of her dancing life of 1928-29 and our quarrels and I think it raked up a lot of the past and for awhile the doctors reported her tense and driven by nervous energy, (she refused to talk to the doctors about herself or her case). She is not yet absolutely stable (the unmotivated smile returned and is now disappearing). In most ways she seems externally better than she was at Prangins at Easter, 1931, and a little less well than she was in mid-summer, 1931. There was too much tragic strain on her this fall, and then the awful sleep-killing asthma from October to February when she came here. (We think we have traced it, by the way, to *moose hair*. Isn't that extraordinary? In every house where she has had asthma there has been a moose head).

My only immediate worry is that, with her writing, a little of the old tendency to "take the bit in her teeth" has come back. In the American atmosphere some of the "reeducation" has worn off, yet even that may have been part of the relapse (it showed itself in much talk about how she was going to drink all she wanted to, etc.); in this regard, she is better in this last month, during which I've been in Baltimore. My plans are to take a house here and, if things continue to improve, to let her slip gradually into it and resume domestic life again—this, with the clinic within reach and with Lelda insulated against such strains as lingering death in the family and asthmatic attacks. There were no circumstances or rift in our personal life which could have contributed to this relapse—we were very happy.

During the crisis, I longed for you, but a trip to Europe is at present financially impossible. I read Dr. Myer some excerps from your recent letter, leaving out *of course,* your advice to return to Prangins, and your recommendation of another psychiatrist (which arrived too late). Until recently Myer has seen much less of Lelda than you did; she has been more directly under the care of his chief assistant, a woman doctor (more intelligent than Mlle. Byasni) whom Lelda likes, but to whom, I think, she has given a more romantic and self-justifying presentment of herself than she should, as a person who really wants to be understood and integrated. Recently, on my urging, she has opened up to Dr. Myers as to the reasons for her coming here, and is doing her best to help. One factor in this is her realization that these are hard times and we're feeling it like everyone else. One week, through an oversight, I didn't send her allowance. One can't charge at Johns Hopkins and she couldn't pay her hairdresser—the doctors say the change in her was extraordinary. She was tractable, serious and it was the beginning of her improvement—the liberal stream of money which I have been providing for a dozen years, was temporarily cut off—perhaps in that way I have done my share in unhealthily shielding her for so long from the realities of life—perhaps after all she's been a victim of our decade of prosperity.

Ever your devoted friend,

P.S. Please do write Dr. Myers anything you think would be useful and I will be enormously grateful. He has your last report, consultation with Bleuler, etc.

P.S.–2 No excema.

1 "Zelda" was typed thus throughout the surviving carbon copy of the letter.

FROM: Zelda Fitzgerald
Spring 1932

ALS, 2 pp. Princeton University
Phipps Clinic, Baltimore, Maryland

D.O, dearest:

I am utterly miserable that we should have parted so un-happily.

You have been working to hard. While I do not know what could possibly relieve the strain on you, I wish I could be of some help. Love and affection is not of much practical use but it may be of a little comfort to you to know it is there.

Dear—You know that if I could sell any of my stories I would not have written this book. Ober is swamped with my things, and it seems worthless to plague him with more. The fact that I have had time to write it while you have had to put aside your own is due to circumstances over which I had no control and cannot bring myself to feel a sense of guilt. You, of all people, certainly would not have preferred my folding my hands during my long unoccupied hours. You must not forget that that the Toxologic (?) part of my illness is cured and I can no long sit for endless blank periods in a trance as I did with Eczema at Prangins.

It was impossible to fulfill my obligations as a normal sane person at home with three hours sleep a night. It seems to me that, in spite of your obligations, I had no alternative but to come here.

It is dreadful that I am not un-happy, but I would not be away any sooner if I sat and cried.

Believe me, dear. I quite appreciate the strain and depression under which you are existing. If there is any way on earth in which I can speed matters up you have only to indicate it to me.

In the meantime, please try to be calmer. At present I realize that there is little that your life has to offer as a substitute, but I wish you could drink less—do not fly into a rage, I know you stay *sober*—but you need some rest and I can't think how you can get it except by using those miserable moments that gin helps to dispel and turn into activity by resting.

I love you D.O—I would have collapsed years ago if I'd had me on my hands—but there's Scottie and we can be happy—and about money: when there isn't any will be time to be desperate. We never have more than we have now, really, only we usually have just finished spending so much that we feel God-awful rich and as if it were not actual, our constant and present poverty. Financially, we have trod our precarious path until it has become almost a high-way by this time—garnished by municipal bridges and garlanded by county lights and other public loot till you'd think the thing led somewhere—

When you're worried about one thing, think of how far ahead on worry you were from the last time you felt as strongly—

Love, dear
Zelda

TO: H. L. Mencken
April/May 1932

ALS, 1 p. New York Public Library
Hotel Rennert letterhead
Baltimore, Maryland

Dear Menk:

The above proves that I am now a resident of your city. Zelda is taking a precautionary rest cure at Hopkins (nothing serious—she's just finishing a fine novel) + I am standing by.

The immediate purpose is to ask you if you can put me in touch with a reliable and unextorionate bootlegger, I have been depending on the whimsical brews of bell-boys.

I want to see you—at present we are nessessarily in retirement but wouldn't want to leave without a glimpse of you.

Best to Sarah + yourself
F Scott Fitzgerald

TO: H. L. Mencken
July 1932

ALS, 1 p. New York Public Library

La Paix
Roger's Forge, Md

Dear Menck

The enclosed story has a history.[1] It was written specifically for Cosmopolitan, and the editors liked it but as it was about to be set up the Hearst policy man forbade it on the ground that it discussed well-known figures in Metro which Hearst controlls.[2] The Post was afraid of it as being risque and I have concluded that its a little too good for the popular magazines. Perhaps it will interest you

Ever Yours
F Scott Fitzgerald

[1] "Crazy Sunday," *American Mercury* (October 1932).

[2] William Randolph Hearst did not control MGM, but he financed the Marion Davies movies made there.

TO: H. L. Mencken
Before 29 July 1932

ALS, 1 p. New York Public Library

Dear Menck:

Appropos of your idea that you'd like to see a few communists seated in congress may I make a suggestion. I'm afraid it hasn't much reality in our attempt to govern a *continent* but it might be amusing + exciting + clarify some things. Why not appoint one of your yes-men to draw up an exact list of senators + *representatives ranging from right to left as in the French* SENATE + CHAMBRE. At least our departure from "Parlimentary" proceedure has become more pronounced than has the French (and German) sceme from our still functioning method.

It would be parallel to your series about states + I have an idea that it's one of my best hunches. Naturally, in order to send the boys protesting or scurrying to cover, it ought to come out before elections. I havn't the political knowledge to do it myself but if it doesn't interest you please let *me know so I can pass it on immediately to Max Perkins*

I'm sure you'll see amusing slants, such as finding strange bed-fellows, if the comparative radicalism or conservatism of delegates are grouped in fours or eights. But it ought to be done by a "heavy," not a reporter.[1]

It is nice to be living near you

Faithfully
F. Scott Fitzgerald

"La Paix"
Roger's Forge, Towson, Md.

If you take the idea it will cost you a first edition of one of your books chosen by me from among *five* submitted titles.

[2]Dear Menck

Could they strike an extra galley for me? + send it *with* the proof galley?

Faithfully
Scott Fitz

[1] On 29 July Mencken replied: "I think your idea for the coöperative lists of Senators and Representatives is an excellent one. Unfortunately, it would take a great deal of special knowledge to complete it and the only man really competent to do the job is probably Paul Y. Anderson, of the St. Louis Post Dispatch. However, Frank Kent could certainly make a good stab at it. Inasmuch as he is already working for Scribner, I suggest that you propose the whole scheme to Perkins. It would fall a bit outside the present plans of The American Mercury." (Princeton)

[2] Holograph note attached to first page of letter.

TO: Bennett Cerf[1] TLS, 1 p. Columbia University

"La Paix," Rodgers Forge,
Towson, Maryland.
August 29, 1932.

Dear Mr. Cerf:

Of course I think Ulysses should be published legally in America. In the first place time has crept up on Ulysses and many people are under the daisies who were horrified ten years ago. In the second place compared to pornography on the news stands Ulysses is an Elsie book. And in the third place people who have the patience to read Ulysses are not the kind who will slobber over a few little Rabelaisian passages.

Very truly yours,
F Scott Fitzgerald

[1] The founding partner of Random House who was trying to reverse the ban on Joyce's *Ulysses* and had solicited statements from leading writers.

TO: Cary Ross[1] TL(CC), 4 pp. Princeton University

"La Paix," Rodgers Forge,
Towson, Maryland,
September 3, 1932.

Dear Cary:

Your formidable letter, is at hand. Since *The American Tragedy,* nay! since *A la Richerche de temps Perdus* no one has attempted such a task as answering it would be. Even the heading makes it necessary to drag out *The Last of the Mohicans* and look up the history and geography of Lake George—then one must gape at the date August 26th 1932 and the eclipse that ensued (with all the astronomical ramifications) prefiguring, paralleling and indirectly precipitating the fall of capitalism and here one must read *Das Capital* at last. The handwriting alone is a lifetime study for a triumverate of calligraphist, psychiatrist and specialist in Nagari, Devanagari and Brahmi.

So instead of answering the letter I will write one. First as to your car—little you'd reck (not "wreck") how rash you were. It's now our car—we seem to have taken it over for its board. How it runs, the little green darling, and such care we take of it! Not a night that it isn't washed, that is, not a *rainy* night. And if it isn't simonized once a week then the word simony doesn't mean that the Popes waxed their mustaches. Does it pant, does it pull—oh God, hold me back, I want to go back to the garbage can, open the lid and kiss that car.

Now, you refer to some pictures—Zelda doesn't remember any pictures but she does remember that she missed a few paper cloths that she used to take off make-up, and Aquilla, the small black energy, says that some of his shoe rags are gone while—but enough. So for "pictures" we read "fixtures," and now, Cary, we would never accuse you of taking off the fixtures. There *was* the unfortunate matter of Zelda's diamond ring that, as you explained, got stuck to a wad of your gum, as well as Dr. Gluccks curious loss of the watch marked "love from Dicky Loeb," but we have missed nothing—except you, Cary, we have missed you.

About the poems, *please* do some weeding, *please* offer a selection, *please* after you have worked over the best ones add one or two in the highly critical mood that the working over will induce, a few written in that utter boredom and despair that I have seen sometimes as a mood in you but never expressed. Go on the cross as the last Jesus of decadent Capitalism, but let's see all five wounds—it is only from the fifth, the unrememberable one, that the holy grail is collected; it is only the last bored glance that finds the purse which we could least afford to lose.

I'm writing Max Perkins. Unfortunately, he doesn't know any poetry and hands it all to the poetry editor whose name I can never remember though he is a poet himself and has been there for years. If you will find out his name from any clerk in Scribner's book store I'll write him too. I'll recognize the name if I see it.

All goes well here. I went to the Hopkins with a temperature of 104 degrees diagnosed as typhoid, but incorrectly. I came back in a week to find Zelda overstrained with worry but she has recovered the lost ground, driven in the Japanese outposts, and can be reached c/o the American Consulate, Shanghai. Meanwhile, we shall be here indefinitely—which is to say I am extending our lease for six months more. You are welcome here at any time with or without warning although the latter is preferable because when my mother is here I get in a nervous humor and growl at all forms of animal life as well as at a few bright minerals.

Have been reading *Sanctuary* and *Little Lord Fauntleroy* together—chapter by chapter (this is serious) and am simply overwhelmed by the resemblance. The books are simply two faces of the same world spirit and only by putting them together do you get anything as integral as, say, "*Smoke*"[2] or "*Moll Flanders.*"

Young doctors come here in the long afternoons. Mr. Crossly is old and brown on the verandah. There is an ungodly lot of animal life trying to end the fair weather with a non-stop concert. Scotty comes home from picnics with her hair wet and one last unexpended laugh.

My warm regards to the Paul Rosenfeld and to the Stieglitzs[3] who probably don't remember me. Naturally Zelda and I are intensely grateful to Stieglitz and Rosenfeld for the interest they show in Zelda's pictures. We will talk about an exhibition when you arrive.

We both send five gallon jars of good feeling and gratitude to stand on the shelves of your apartment while you dismantle it.

Till soon,

[1] An aspiring writer who later became the proprietor of the gallery where Zelda Fitzgerald's paintings were exhibited in 1934.

[2] An 1867 novel by Turgenev.

[3] Photographer Alfred Stieglitz.

TO: Alice Lee Myers

TL(CC), 1 p. (fragment)
Princeton University

"La Paix," Rodgers' Forge,
Towson, Maryland,
September 29, 1932.

Dear Alice Lee,

Your letter destresses me, in spite of the really fine tone you take. These sudden reverses seem to be part of our time but when they happen to people like you and Dick, who used your resources so wisely and generously it seems terrible, and drives me more and more toward the red flag about which I have been may-poling at a distance all through the decade. I don't any more feel that the money I make belongs to me and while pretending to dispense it grudgingly in the current manner I feel it is all a farce and that an adjustment must come soon.

However I know you don't feel that way and will take this as a burden on your own strong shoulders—and of course with your talents and the double wits of two people with a common cause you will survive and flourish long after the Fitzgeralds collapse.

TO: Alfred Dashiell — ALS, 1 p. Princeton University
October 1932

"La Paix"
Roger's Forge, Md.

Dear Mr. Dashiell:

I seem to have put all the stuff I had on Hollywood into "*Crazy Sunday*" which you couldn't use, + which is in the current *Mercury*. I have about twenty pages on *Hollywood Revisted*, and if I wasn't on my novel again I could workup something, but nothing extraordinary that would matter to you, I'm afraid. So for the present I'll simply have to "put the matter to our account." The article, as happens sometimes, died in mid-air when several editors (including Lorimer) didn't like the story version of my material* + chilled my own entheusiasm, which was probably ill-founded[1]

Sincerely
F. Scott Fitzgerald

*Think Mencken only bought it for fancied value of name.

[1] Fitzgerald did not complete this article.

TO: Gregg Dougherty[1] — TL(CC), 2 pp. Princeton University

"La Paix," Rodgers' Forge,
Towson, Maryland,
December 6, 1932.

Dear Gregg:

I should have written you before but on the eve of receiving your data went to bed with grippe—when I called you I already had one foot in the grave. A thousand thanks for the whole thing which I believe will be of great aid. I am inclosing check for thirty dollars for you to dispose of as you see fit as a small payment for the work involved in doping out the two experiments. If the story sells (as I believe it will) I feel that I will owe a further contribution to science.[2] I have figured such things at various prices. Once I gave a man ten per cent of the net for giving me his entire life story with full permission to use it, and on the other hand I presented two young Hopkins internes with free trips to the Yale game for checking inaccuracies in a medical story. When I see whether or not this sells I will figure out what should be a proper reimbursement for the amount of help of yours that I have been able to use.

It is fun being in touch with an old friend if only in brief correspondence. You told me something once years ago that has been of help to me several times in my life. You said it in a moment of extreme impatience. It happened on an evening in the dark spring of 1918. Do you remember it? With best wishes

Faithfully,

[1] Princeton classmate of Fitzgerald's who joined the Princeton chemistry department.
[2] Probably "On Schedule," *The Saturday Evening Post* (18 March 1933).

TO: Zelda Fitzgerald
1932(?)

AL, 2 pp. (fragment). Princeton University
"La Paix," Towson, Maryland

Honey, when you come out into the world again I wish you would try to realize what I can only describe as the:

Nub (NUB) of Experience.

The fact that in your efforts you have come up *twice* against insuperable facts 1st against Lucienne 2nd against me—both times against long desperate heart-destroying proffesional training beginning when we (ie Lucienne + I) were seven, probably;

There has never been any question as to your value as a personality—there is however a question as to your ability to use your values to any practical purpose. To repeat the phrase that became anathema in my ears during the last months of our trying to make a go of it "*expressing oneself.*" I can only say there isn't any such thing. It simply doesn't exist. What one expresses in a work of art is the dark tragic destiny of being an instrument of something uncomprehended, incomprehensible, unknown—you came to the threshold of that discovery + then decided that in the face of all logic you would crash the gate. You succeeded merely in crashing yourself, almost me, + Scotty, if I hadn't interposed.

TO: Zelda Fitzgerald — AL (draft), 11 pp. Princeton University
After 1932 — "La Paix," Towson, Maryland

Do you feel that you are now able to be your own doctor—to judge what is good for you?

If no—do you know what should be done?

Should you be in a clinic do you think?

Would a trained nurse help?

An experienced one?

An inexperienced one?

If you were really not yourself and in a fit of temper or depression would you ask the judgement of such of woman or would you come to me?

Are these bursts of temper part of the derangement you mentioned?

Or are they something that is in your surroundings?

If they are in your sickness how can you accept another's opinion when the nature of your attack has taken away your power of reasoning?

If they are in your home surroundings in what practical ways would you like your home surroundings changed?

Must there big changes which seriously affect the life of husband and children?

If you feel that you are now able to be your own doctor—to judge what is good for you.

Of what use would a nurse be?

Would she be a sort of clock to remind you it was time for this and that?

If that function in your husband is annoying would it not be more annoying in the case of a stranger in your own house?

Is there not an idea in your head sometimes that you must live close to the borders of mental trouble in order to create at your best?

Which comes first your health or your work?

Are you in delicate health?

If a person sacrificed some of their health to their work is that within their human rights?

If a sick person sacrificed some of their health to their work is that within their human rights?

If a sick person sacrificed some of their health to their work and sacrificed others also would that be within their rights

If the other people felt that they would not willingly be sacrificed could they refuse?

What recourse would the determined worker have *if well*?

What recourse if sick?

Must he not wait until he is well bringing such matters to a decision, because being sick he will be inevitably worsted in trying to infringe on the rights of others?

Is there any enlightened opinion which considers that you are liable to be strong for another year?

Can you make yourself strong by any means except the usual ones?

Are you an exceptional person who will be cured differently from anyone else

---

Will you make the usual return to society for its protection of you during your sickness and convalesence

Is the return usually the virtues of patience and submissiveness in certain important regards?

In case the ill person (suppose a man with small pox) runs around hurting and infecting others will society tend to take stern measures to protect itself?

Are you ill?

Are your husband and child, in their larger aspects, society?

If one of them were contagiously sick and wanted to return to the home during convalescence would you let him infect the other and yourself?

Who would be your natural guides in determining what was the end of convalescence?

Did "good" behavior in the clinic preceed your previous recovery?

Was it better behavior than any other?

Did not furious activity and bad behavior preceed the previous denoument at Valmont and Prangins?

Are you or have you been ill?

Does furious activity lead often to consequent irritability even in well persons?

Would not this be terribly accentuated by an ill person?

Does a person recovering from heart trouble start by moving boulders

---

Is "I have no time" an answer to the previous questions?"

What is the order of importance of everything in your mind—

Is your health first?

Is it always first?

Is it first in the midst of artistic creation when the two are in conflict?

If it is not, and you should be well, should society coerce you into putting health first?

If you should be ill should society so act apon you?

Does your child have the same priviledges when ill as when well?

Are not lessons stopped?

Is this logical?

What does logic mean?

Is it important to be logical?

If not, is it important to be dramatic?

Is it important to have been dramatic?

If an illness becomes a nuisance to society does society act sternly?

Is it important to be dramatic or logical in the future?

Is an ill person or a well person more capable of being logical or dramatic?

Can a very ill person try to be only a little ill?

Why does madness not enlarge the artistic range?

What is disaccociation of ideas?

How does it differ in an artistic person and in a mentally ill person?

Who pays for illness?

Who pays in suffering?

Does only the ill person suffer?

When you left Prangins would you have taken any patient there into your home if they came in a refractory way

Would you constitute yourself a doctor for them?

Suppose the choice was between two patients and one patient would accept your judgement while the other one said he would not   Which would you choose

---

When doctors recommend a normal sexual life do you agree with them?

Are you normal sexually?

Are you retiscent about sex?

Are you satisfied sexually with your husband?

TO: Edmund Wilson   Wire. Yale University

ROGERSFORGE MD 1933 JAN 30 PM 10 05

HAVE BEEN WORRIED BY THE UNFORTUNATE CONDITIONS OF OUR MEETING THAT I HAD LOOKED FORWARD TO FOR SO LONG[1] STOP STILL COUNTING ON YOU TO COME DOWN HERE AND WE ALL HOPE YOU CAN BRING ROSALIND[2] WHAT ABOUT THIS WEEKEND STOP HAVE ASKED NONE OF THE QUESTIONS NOR SAID ANY OF THE THINGS THAT I WANTED TO ASK AND SAY

SCOTT.

[1] Fitzgerald was on a bender when he met Wilson and Hemingway in New York, and he quarreled with both of them.

[2] Wilson's daughter.

FROM: T. S. Eliot

Inscription in Eliot's *Ash-Wednesday* (1930).
Bruccoli

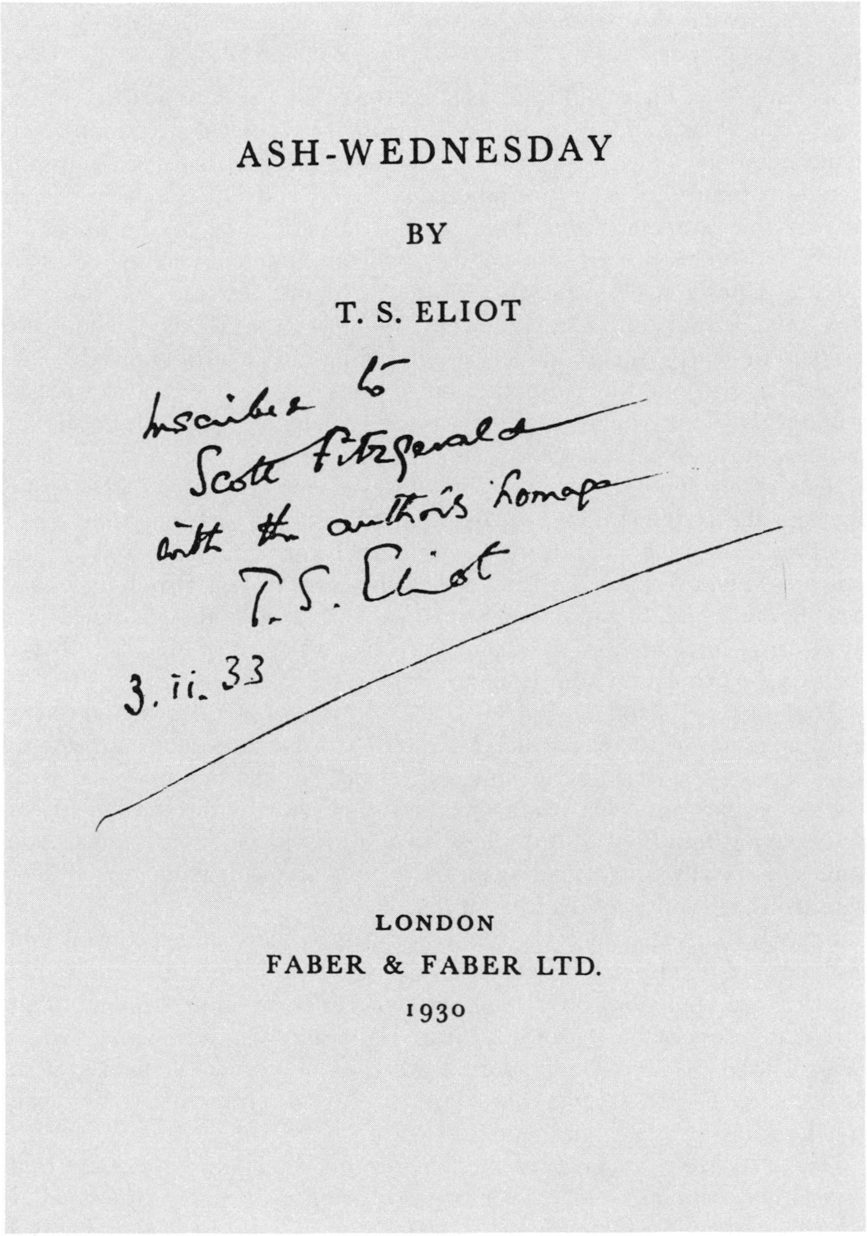

ASH-WEDNESDAY

BY

T. S. ELIOT

Inscribed to
Scott Fitzgerald
with the author's homage
T. S. Eliot

3. ii. 33

LONDON
FABER & FABER LTD.
1930

Note: Eliot met Fitzgerald when he lectured in Baltimore in 1933.

TO: Dr. Adolf Meyer TL(CC), 7 pp. Princeton University

"La Paix"
Roger's Forge, Md.
April 10th, 1933

Dear Dr. Myer:

Taking Zelda Fitzgerald's case as it existed in a purer form—last October, say, when I was standing up under the thing—I would like to submit you some questions which might clarify things for me. I've had the feeling of a certain futility in our conversations with you and Dr. Rennie,[1] though at first they did much good because she was still close to the threat of force and more acutely under the spell of your personality. Certain questions never really came to a head—no doubt you saw the thing in flux. And I know also that you were trying to consider as a whole the *millieu* in which she is immersed, including my contributions to it—nevertheless in one way or another our discussions have gotten so wide in scope that they would properly have to include the whole fields of philosophy, sociology and art to lead anywhere.

This is my fault. In my own broodings about the case, I have gone through the same experience—arriving at the gate of such questions as to whether Zelda isn't more worth saving than I am. I compromised on the purely utilitarian standpoint that I was the wage-earner, that I took care of wife and child, financially and practically, and beyond that that I was integrated—integrated in spite of everything, in spite of the fact that I might have two counts against me to her one.

That fact has stood up for the last three years (save for her mother's little *diversion* to the effect that I wanted to spirit away her daughter to a madhouse.) It began to collapse, bit by bit, six months ago—that is to say the picture of Zelda painting things that show a distinct talent, of Zelda trying faithfully to learn how to write is much more sympathetic and, superficially, more solid than the vision of me making myself iller with drink as I finish up the work of four years.

But when I began to compromise my case by loss of self-control and outbreaks of temper, my own compensation was to believe in it more and more. I will probably be carried off eventually by four strong guards shrieking manicly that after all I was right and she was wrong, while Zelda is followed home by an adoring crowd in an automobile banked with flowers, and offered a vaudeville contract. But to return to last October, may I ask my first categorical question.

Does Dr. Meyer suspect, or did Dr. Squires lead him to suspect that there were elements in the case that were being deliberately concealed? I ask this because for a month Zelda had Dr. Forel convinced that I was a notorious Parisien homo-sexual.

The second question also requires a certain introduction. It goes back to something we've talked about before and if I restate it in detail it is chiefly to clarify it in my own mind.

All I ever meant by asking authority over her was the power of an ordinary nurse in any continental country over a child; to be able to say "If you don't do this I shall punish you." All I have had has been the power of the nurse-girl in America who can only say, "I'll tell your Mama."

It seems to me that one must either have

(1) A mutual bond between equals

(2) Direct authority

(3) Delegated authority

To give responsibility without authority seems to me impossible. If a nurse can and does punish, or instead of "punish" let me say "enforce"—there is a certain healthy action and reaction set up between nurse and child, perhaps from the nurse's remorse at her strictness or the child's sense that the punishment was just—at the very worst, in the case of real injustice or over-punishment, the child has recourse to the parents. We once had a nurse of that sort—we were aware of it before the child was.

Naturally I can't rush in and turn out Zelda's lights when its her bedtime. I can't snatch strong cigarettes away from her, or countermand orders for a third cup of strong coffee given to a servant. Through moral suasion I might but more of that later.

Here is my second question:

Will Doctor Meyer give me the authority to ask Zelda when she is persistently refactory to pack her bag and spend a week under people who can take care of her, such as in the clinic?

If Doctor Meyer is in doubt about my ability to decide when such force is necessary, then hasn't the case reached such a point of confusion psychologically that I had better resort to legal means to save myself, my child and the three of us in toto.

My third question:

I have noted throughout our conversations a reluctance on your part to impose any ideas of morality upon her, save ideas of moderation in various directions. It has seemed to me that she has taken advantage of this difference of attitude from that of the continental physicians with whom she was most in contact to draw a false inference. Because Dr. Forel believes in the strictly teutonic idea of marriage and Dr. Meyer does not she imagines that the latter's attitude is nihilistic and that it somehow negates all mutual duty between husband and wife except the most casual profession of it.

Now this idea of mutual duty was, from Zelda's youth, the thing most lacking in her personality, much more lacking than in the average spoiled American girl. So that it shocked other women, even gay society women and theatrical women, again and again. At the same time she is the type who most clearly needs a guiding hand. There is the predisposition of her family to mental troubles, and in addition her mother tried hard to make everlasting babies of her children. Zelda played the baby with me always except when an important thing came up, when she was like a fire-horse in her determination and on the principal occasion she ended in Switzerland. In that moral atmosphere—which I admit can't be transported entire to the U.S.A.—she changed very much, became less dependent and more mature in smaller things and more dependent on my advise on a few main issues.

The nine months before her second breakdown were the happiest of my life and I think, save for the agonies of her father's death, the happiest of hers. Now all that is disappearing week by week and we are going back to the agonizing cat and dog fight of four or five years ago.

To recapitulate—since her personality began to split about 1928, the two main tendencies have been:

(1) Self-expression, extreme neglect of home, child and husband, exageration of physical and mental powers . . .[2] bullheadedness (Beautiful psychiatric term!).

(2) Conservatism, almost Victorianism, dread of any extremes or excess, real domesticity, absorbtion in child, husband, family and close friends, quick amenity to moral suasion.

One of her reasons for gravitating toward the first state is that her work is perhaps at its best in the passage from the conservative to the self-expressive phase, just before and just after it crosses the line—which, of course, could be the equivalent of the period of creative excitement in an integrated person. Just before crossing it is better—over the line she brings that demonaic intensity to it that achieves much in bulk with more consequent waste. I could make you a list in parallel lines but refrain out of respect for your patience.

Creatively she does not seem able to keep herself around that line. A healthful approach with all that implies, and a limited work time never to be exceeded, gives the best results but seems to be impossible outside of the dicipline of a clinic. We came nearest to this last August and September. With much pushing and prodding she lived well, wrote well and painted well.

But the question of her work I must perforce regard from a wider attitude. I make these efforts possible and do my own work besides. Possibly she would have been a genius if we had never met. In actuality she is now hurting me and through me hurting all of us.

First, by the ill-will with which she regards any control of her hours.

Second, by the unbalanced egotism which contributes to the above, and which takes the form of an abnormal illusion cherished from her ballet days: that her work's success will give her some sort of divine irresponsibility backed by unlimited gold. It is still the idea of an Iowa high-school girl who would like to be an author with an author's beautiful care-free life. It drives her to a terrible pressing hurry.

Third, by her inferiority complex caused by a lack of adaptation to the fact that she is working under a greenhouse which is my money and my name and my love. This is my fault—years ago I reproached her for doing nothing and she never got over it. So she is mixed up—she is willing to use the greenhouse to protect her in every way, to nourish every sprout of talent and to exhibit it—and at the same time she feels no responsibility about the greenhouse and feels that she can reach up and knock a piece of glass out of the roof at any moment, yet she is shrewd to cringe when I open the door of the greenhouse and tell her to behave or go.

Fourth, by her idea that because some of us in our generation with the effort and courage of youth battered a nitch in an old wall, she can make the same kind of crashing approach to the literary life with the frail equipment of a sick mind and a berserk determination.

With one more apology for this—my God, it amounts to a booklet!—I arrive at my last question.

Doesn't Dr. Meyer think it might be wise to let Zelda have the feeling for a minute of being alone, of having exhausted everyone's patience—to let her know that he is not essentially behind her in any way for she interprets his scientific impersonality as a benevolent neutrality?

Otherwise the Fitzgerald's seem to be going out in the storm, each one for himself, and I'm afraid Scotty and I will weather it better than she.

Yours gratefully always, and in extremis

[1] Psychiatrist at Phipps Clinic.
[2] Two words omitted by the editor.

TO: Dr. Adolf Meyer
Spring 1933

AL (draft), 6 pp. Princeton University
"La Paix," Towson, Maryland

Dear Dr. Myer:

Thanks for your answer to my letter—it was kind of you to take time to reply to such an unscientific discussion of the case. I felt that from the difference between my instinctive-emotional knowledge of Zelda, extending over 15 years, and your objective-clinical knowledge of her, and also from the difference between the Zelda that everyone who lives a hundred consecutive hours in this house sees and the Zelda who, as a consumate actress, shows herself to you—from these differences we might see where the true center of her should lie, around what point its rallying ground should be. When you qualify or disqualify my judgement on the case, or put it on a level very little above hers on the grounds that I have frequently abused liquor I can only think of Lincoln's remark about a greater man and heavier drinker than I have ever been—that he wished he knew what sort of liquor Grant drank so he could send a barrel to all his other generals.

This is not said in any childish or churlish spirit of defying you on your opinions on alcohol—during the last six days I have drunk *altogether* slightly less than a quart and a half of weak gin, at wide intervals. But if there is no essential difference between an overextended, imaginative, functioning man using alcohol as a stimulus or a temporary *aisment* and a schitzophrene I am naturally alarmed about my ability to collaborate in this cure at all.

Again I must admit that you are compelled to make your judgements apon the basis of observed behavior but my claim is that a true synthesis of the totality of the behavior elements in this case has not yet been presented to you.

If you should for example be in a position to interview an indefinate number of observers—let me say at random my family as opposed to hers, my particular friends as opposed to hers, or even my instinctive protection of Zelda as opposed to her instinctive protection of me—you could formulate simply nothing—you would have to guess, rather like a jury sitting on the case of a pretty girl and a plausible man. Or if as you say (and I must disagree) that this is a dual "case" in any sense further than that it involves the marriage of two artistic temperments, you should interview Dr. Squires or any of Zelda's nurses while she was in Phipps—there would be the fault of Zelda being the subject and me becoming the abstraction so that there would be real play of subjective forces between us to be observed.

But if, to follow out my (fable) there should be another series of people to be examined to whom our life bares a nearer relation in its more basic and more complex terms, I mean terms that are outside "acting" and personal charm because they are in each case qualified by a hard an objective reality—you might be confronted with my child and what she thinks; by any professional writer of the first rank (say Dos Passos, Lewis, Mencken, Hemmingway, any real professional) on being told that their amateur wives were trying to cash in secretly on their lust for "self expression" by publishing a book about your private life with a casual survey of the material apon which you were currently engaged; by my business associates a publisher each of fourteen years standing; by every employee, secretaries, nurses, tennis-instructors, governesses; and by every servant almost without exception—if you could meet an indefinate series of these people extending back long before Zelda broke down I think there would be less doubt in your mind as to whence this family derives what mental and moral stamina it possesses. There would be a good percentage who liked her better than me and probably a majority who found her more attractive (as it should be); but on the question of integrity, responsibility, conscience, sense of duty, judgment, will-power, whatever you want to call it—well, I think that 95% of this group of ghosts; their judgment would be as decided as Solomon pronouncing apon the two mothers.

This beautiful essay (I find that manic-depressives go in for such lengthy expositions and I suspect myself + all authors of being incipient manic-depressives) is another form of my old plea to let me sit apon the bench with you instead of being kept down with the potential accomplices —largely on the charge of criminal associations.

The witness is weary of strong drink and until very recently He had had the matter well in hand for four years and has it in hand at the moment, and needs no help on the matter being normally frightened by the purely physical consequences of it. He does work and is not to be confused with the local Hunt-Club-Alcoholic and asks that his testimony be considered as of prior validity to any other.

Sincerely

P.S. Please don't bother to answer the above—its simply a restatement anyhow. In answer to your points—I can concieve of giving up all liquor but only under conditions that seem improbable—Zelda suddenly a helpmate or even divorced and insane. Or, if one can think of some way of doing it, Zelda marrying some man of some caliber who would take care of her, *really* take care of her This is a possibility Her will to power must be broken without that—the only alternative would be to break me and I am forwarned + forearmed against that

P.S. ② All I meant by the difference between the Teutonic + American ideas of marriage is expressed in the differences between the terms Herr + Frau and the terms Mr + Mrs

TO: Lawrence Lee[1] TLS, 2 pp. University of Pittsburgh

La Paix, Rodgers' Forge,
Towson, Maryland,
June 12, 1933.

Dear Lawrence:

I waited to write you until I could read *Summer Goes On.*[2] It seems to me excellent—the advance over the rather Alfred Noisy Highwayman poem is astounding. If I chose the piece that pleased me most I should simply have to mention them all but I particularly liked *Headstone for a Quarrel, When Summer's In Full Bloom, Noon in Barbour County, Lines to a Dead Lady* (in spite of the touch of Eliott) and all the sonnets. I must warn you that *Bequest to my Daughters* is an idea that was pretty well enshrined in the will of Citizen George Francis Train, or am I thinking of the wrong man? Maybe, though, it is one of those recurrent ideas that pop up every decade or so. In all my hearty congratulations.

And thank you for your hospitality and for a most pleasant afternoon which gave me a haunting impression of one of the most beautiful places this side of the Atlantic.[3]

With very best wishes,
F Scott Fitzgerald

[1] A member of the University of Virginia staff.

[2] Scribners, 1933.

[3] Fitzgerald had visited Charlottesville in May. See Lee's "Tender Was the Man: Memories of F. Scott Fitzgerald," *The Pittsburgh Press Family Magazine* (14 July 1974).

TO: Mrs. H. H. Prouse — TLS, 1 p. Unlocated[1]
18 July 1933 — "La Paix," Towson, Maryland

The Keys settled in Maryland with a tremendous grant about 1698 in St. Marys County. They were rich with no special record of service to the state until after the Revolution. You and I are both descended from Philip Key, who died about 1800, you through his grandson Francis Scott Key, and I through Francis Scott Key's uncle Philip Barton Key[2] . . . In my branch of the Key family (descendants of Philip Barton Key) there has been no money or achievement of note for four or five generations though some of the descendents have married well. . . . I am told here in Baltimore that two men bearing the Key name, descendents of the aforementioned Philip Key, died poverty stricken in the Confederate Home at the beginning of the century. So I am afraid we must forget past glories, if there were any, and look forward to the future.

[1] *The Collector*, No. 854 (1977), #K-746.

[2] Fitzgerald was an enthusiastic but inaccurate amateur genealogist. Francis Scott Key was the great-grandson of the original Philip Key; his father was John Ross Key, brother of Philip Barton Key, from whom Fitzgerald was not descended. Philip Barton Key's father, Francis Key, was the brother of Dr. John Key, from whom Fitzgerald was descended. Francis Scott Key was F. Scott Fitzgerald's second cousin, three times removed.

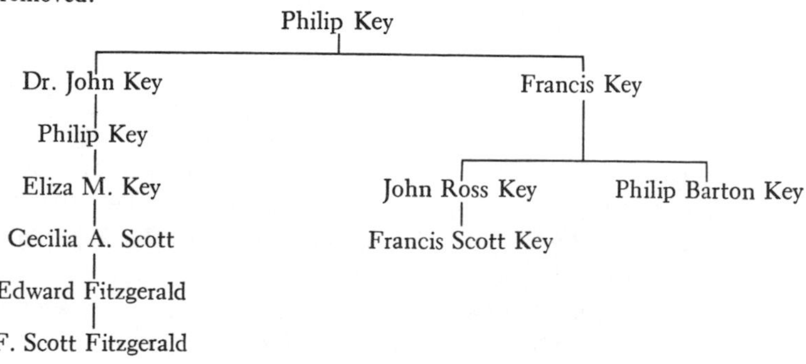

TO: Zelda Fitzgerald
Summer 1933

ALS, 2 pp. Princeton University
"La Paix," Towson, Maryland

Dearest: Im writing because I don't want to start the day with an arguement—though I had thought that what has become controversial was settled before you left the clinic.

Darling, when you shut yourself away for twenty four hours it is not only very bad for you but it casts a pall of gloom and disquiet over the people who love you. To spend any reasonable time in your room has been agreed apon as all right, but this shouldn't be so exagerated that you can't manage the social side any further than sitting at table It would help everything if you could enter a little into Scotty's life here on the place, and your reluctance to play tennis and swim is a rather reckless withdrawal; for whatever of the normal you subtract from your life will be filled up with brooding and fantasy. If I know that there is excercise scheduled for morning and afternoon and a medical bath in the afternoon + that you have half an hour for us after supper and you stop work at ten, my not very exigent list, *insisted apon by Dr. Myers,* is complete. When you throw it out of joint I can only sit and wait for the explosion that will follow—a situation not conducive to work or happiness. If this week has been too much it is easy to return to the clinic for three days and it needn't be done in a spirit of dispair any more than your many returns to Prangins.

I believe however you are not giving it, giving us, a fair trial here. If I didn't love you so much your moods wouldn't affect me so deeply and excitedly. We can't afford scenes—the best protection is the schedule and then the schedule and again the schedule, and you'll get strong without knowing it.

S.

TO: Francis Swann[1]

TLS, 1 p. (with three-page annotated TS).
Bruccoli

La Paix, Rodgers' Forge,
Towson, Maryland,
July 19, 1933.

Dear Francis:

Enclosed is the plan. I won't be starting my part of it for another three or four weeks but I send you this so that if you have any brain waves you can note them down. In any case stick it away someplace and don't let it get lost around the Vagabonds.[2] See you soon.

Ever yours,
F Scott Fitzgerald

Francis

It is agreed that for eleven weeks we produce one skit a piece each week trying to fit it into the general plan outlined so that at the end of three months we will have thirty-three skits from which to choose. Skits must fit in with general line of plot. Rough assignment to Francis Swann:

All plot scenes in Act II

1, *8 in Act II*

4, 6, 13 in Act I

Plot numbers to be dramatized and jazzed if possible. Try to have one of your four numbers a tap number; one number should have to do with percussion value of firearms used in a muffled way.

Avoid the morbid and bloodthirsty, on the other hand don't lean over backward as attempt to make gangsters feminine would be equally bad effect. Skits should expose trivial and cheap motives in back of gangsters without moralizing.

When a theme line for song occurs to you simply write it down, don't write lyric till we get music line-up.

Don't write anything that disagrees with main theme or will confuse it. Use main characters when possible but use them *in character*. In addition each of us is to invent a series of two or three characters *not too important*, to run through our own skits. Those characters must be definitely subordinated to the simple lines of the plot and nothing that occurs in plot scenes can be permitted to turn on these characters. In other words we can each write a little comedy of our own running through the play or else do four or five stunt numbers with or without music. Remember: the minor characters are not to be tied directly to the main plot.

Act I (The Civic Building)

Background city of Chicago in pandemonium state of civil war. Gangsters under handsome executive taking over control and finally win control only to find pretty young girl alone at helm, everybody having walked out on her.

1—Chorus and skit
2—*Plot Scene*—Establish character of girl and gangster executive. Song if it seems convenient.
3—Song or skit (Comic)
4—Song or skit (Sentimental)
5—Song or skit (Dramatic or Pictorial)
6—Song or skit (Comic)
7—*Plot Scene*—Establish girl's relation with Idealist. Song if convenient.
8—Song or skit (Sentimental)
9—Song or skit (Dramatic or Pictorial)
10—Song or skit (Comic)

11—*Plot Scene*—Prepare finale of act. Establish interrelation of three main characters. Hint Master Mind. Song if convenient.
12—Song or skit (Sentimental)
13—Song or skit (Dramatic or Pictorial)
14—*Plot Scene*—Lead into finale
15—*Plot Scene*—Finale. Song—Closing Chorus

Act II (The Streets)

It develops that mystery man who is backing gangsters is also backing reformers. Girl threatens exposure thereby winning back city to the side of good, but is attracted by gangster's nephew and elopes with him at the end.

1—Chorus and skit
2—*Plot Scene*—Girl's predicament—bring out that Idealist is controlled by Master Mind. Song if convenient.
3—Song or skit (Comic)
4—Song or skit (Sentimental)
5 (Long)—*Plot Scene*—Audience guesses Master Mind. In same scene disclose that Executive depends on Master Mind. Song if convenient.
6—Song or skit (Comic)
7—Song or skit (Sentimental)
8—Song or skit (Comic)
9—*Plot Scene*—Girl's ultimatum. Song if convenient.
10—*Plot Scene*—Girl elopes with ex-Executive'

[1] A member of the Vagabond Players, a Baltimore amateur theatrical group.

[2] The proposed collaboration between Fitzgerald and Swann on a musical comedy was abandoned.

TO: George Jean Nathan — TLS, 1 p. Cornell University

La Paix, Rodgers' Forge,
Towson, Maryland,
July 27, 1933.

Dear George:

My interest in finding the *Spectator* in six pages this issue reminded me that you asked me to contribute. My phantom novel which is now really in its last stages absorbes every second of time that I don't have to devote to making a living so that for months even all correspondence has gone by the boards. As a matter of fact I have several pieces which I would like to work up for you but that eventuality seems some months off.

Please give my affectionate souvenirs to Ernest[1] whose letter I also omitted to answer. We often think of you and read everything you write, but we seem to see each other only at intervals of three years.

With cordial best wishes always,

F Scott Fitzgerald

[1] Ernest Boyd, an editor of *The American Spectator*.

Appointment of Literary Executor — Typed document signed, 1 p. Princeton University

"La Paix," Towson, Maryland

I would like my novel in its unfinished form to be sent to John Peale Bishop, c/o Guarantee Trust Company, Paris, who I appoint as my literary executor in case of misfortune. What necessary work Mr. Bishop conceives should be done on it before publication he should award himself as seems just on a percentage basis, the rest going to my heirs and assigns.

Signed F. Scott Fitzgerald
Witness Essie Jackson[1]
Witness Isabel W Owens[2]

August 9, 1933.

[1] Servant at "La Paix."
[2] Fitzgerald's secretary.

TO: Sara Haardt Mencken — TLS, 1 p. New York Public Library

La Paix, Rodgers' Forge,
Towson, Maryland
August 23, 1933.

Dear Sara:

Please don't think me a Doubting Thomas if I remind you once more that what I said last night about Schribner's was indiscreet. Max saw only a few chapters of the book and we discussed vaguely the possibility of serialization.[1] That is the only practical basis on which the matter rests but if that were even mentioned in any literary circles you know it would immediately appear in the gossip columns as an affair all clinched and set; which might in itself prejudice the whole matter beyond redemption. —It will be several months before I am sure what's going to happen.

Such a pleasant evening we had with you both! It was absolutely necessary for me to see someone who had some nourishment to offer because I have the sense of giving it out and taking none in for the past six months.

Ever yours,
Scott

[1] *Tender Is the Night* was serialized in *Scribner's Magazine* (January–April 1934).

TO: W. F. Clarkson[1] TL(CC), 2 pp. Princeton University

La Paix, Rodgers' Forge,
Towson, Maryland,
September 19, 1933.

Dear Floyd:

I haven't lost interest at all, only like everybody else, I have been absorbed in personal affairs, and also the exhibit that I was to and will send to you seemed to me to have a somewhat overwhelmingly exhibitionistic cast to it, and I lost enthusiasm in that particular. However, I shall send it off the end of this week. It seems to me that a piece of writing done in the club, which has subsequently obtained national attention, should be an interesting exhibit, and that an excerpt from it dealing with an actual scene at Princeton should be of interest—but whether Monsieur Palmer or Monsieur McGrath or Monsieur Orrick would agree with me is another matter. In other words: I am not a lamb going to the sacrifice. So for Christ's sake use your judgment and do not present this as the first fruit of our efforts unless it is surrounded by at least a dozen photographs of the boys making touchdowns and other successes, which in the republic are considered really worthy of mention.

Also, in what way can I serve on your committee? Though I have begun to do some research in Baltimore, the first thing shoved into your lap is a beautiful memoribilium of Fitzgerald; so I send it to you as something to keep out of sight for the present. You needn't be ashamed of it, because it has only bitten three people so far; but don't put it forward with the first batch of offerings.

P.S. Also please instruct your secretary about the spelling of my name or warn her that she will shortly be bombed from her love nest.

[1] Member of a committee assembling memorabilia for the Cottage Club. Fitzgerald donated two pages from the manuscript of *This Side of Paradise*, corresponding to pp. 117–19 of the book, with the poem "Good Morning, Fool."

TO: Sherwood Anderson TLS, 1 p. Newberry Library

La Paix, Rodgers' Forge,
Towson, Maryland,
October 11, 1933.

Dear Sherwood:

It was damn kind of you to write me about the article.[1] I'm sure we feel the same way about Ring.

Ever yours,
Scott Fitzgerald

[1] "Ring," *The New Republic* (11 October 1933), Fitzgerald's tribute to Ring Lardner.

FROM: Dorothy Parker ALS, 1 p. Princeton University
After 11 October 1933

I think your piece about Ring is the finest + most moving thing I have ever read

Dorothy Parker
N.Y. City

TO: Alfred Dashiell TL, 2 pp. Princeton University

Rodgers' Forge,
Towson, Maryland,
October 29, 1933.

Dear Dashiell:

I cannot come to a decision about the title before Monday or Tuesday. It is, naturally, to me a tremendously important question. My reasons against the lyrical title I've already told you, my reasons against the title which used the word "Doctor" I've already told you, I can also see reasons against "Dick and Nicole Diver"; so I think that I will simply have to dope over the whole thing again; but remember, if I come to no conclusion (no new conclusion) that "Richard Diver" will be the title.

The second section will reach you about the 12th of November. If there is any special reason for wanting it sooner I could probably manage it but I would prefer to have that much time at it.

About the other two installments: I had already talked to Max—after finishing the second installment, I am practically compelled to do a *Post* story. So the third installment may be delayed five weeks beyond the second, then the fourth will follow in three weeks more.

If this arrangement is unsatisfactory let me know but I gathered from Max that it would be all right.

Ever yours,

Mr. Fitzgerald had to leave immediately after dictating this letter so could not sign it.

I. W. Owens

TO: Alfred Dashiell — Wire. Princeton University

TOWSON MD 109P 1933 OCT 31 PM 1 24

HAVENT YET BEEN ABLE TO THINK UP A THING THAT I CONSIDER SATISFACTORY FOR A TITLE WHY DOES A TITLE HAVE TO BE PUBLISHED IN A PREVIEW ANYHOW IVE ALWAYS BEEN AGAINST IT THE IMPORTANT THING IS THAT A NOVEL BY ME IS APPEARING NO ONE WOULD REMEMBER THE TITLE OVER A WHOLE MONTH AND THIS IS NOT THE ANNOUNCEMENT OF A SPECIAL VOLUME BUT SIMPLY THAT A BOOK WILL APPEAR IN SCRIBNERS IN ANY CASE THIS IS BETTER THAN HAVING AN UNSATISFACTORY TITLE PLEASE ANSWER

F SCOTT FITZGERALD.

FROM: Edward Shenton[1] — ALS, 1 p. (fragment). Scrapbook.
Fall 1933 — Princeton University

I just finished reading the final installment and will start the drawings this week. I wish I could tell you precisely how your novel affected me. Nothing comes readily to hand, except the kind of glib phrases, reviewers use. The pattern of disintegration you've created, is so subtle, adroit, so techinically proficient—and so completely moving—that the book seems to have a new form; something entirely it's own.—That's not what I mean, at least only partially. It's a swell job! Any writer would give his right arm and both legs to have done it. It's the best thing that's been written since "The Great Gatsby"—(This is going to become a "fan-letter" if I don't curb it)

Anyway—by these few incoherent sentences—you may see why I am delighted to have my drawings a permanent part of the book.[2] I hope to have the pleasure of meeting you sometime. Our paths have crossed often in the offices of Scribners.

Cordially
Edward Shenton

[1] Illustrator for the *Scribner's Magazine* serialization of *Tender Is the Night.*
[2] Some of Shenton's drawings were included in the book form of the novel at Fitzgerald's request.

TO: Edmund Wilson — TLS, 1 p. Yale University

La Paix, Rodgers' Forge,
Towson, Maryland,
November 2, 1933.

Dear Bunny:

Why wasn't Ring a great and good American? Who is? I meant the mixed metaphor about tearing a medallion which I thought afterwards would be rather a Herculean feat.[1]

Ever yours,
F Scott Fitzgerald

[1] On 21 October Wilson complimented Fitzgerald on "Ring" but criticized its closing lines: "A great and good American is dead. Let us not obscure him by the flowers, but walk up and look at that fine medallion, all abraded by sorrows that perhaps we are not equipped to understand." Wilson explained on 4 November that "great and good American" sounded to him "like a political speech."

TO: Maxwell Perkins — Wire. Princeton University

TOWSON MD 417A 1933 NOV 3 AM 8 59

SEXTONS NOTE DISTURBED ME[1] STOP PLEASE REQUEST THEY LAY OFF ALL PUBLICITY STOP YOUR PLAIN STATEMENT WAS ENOUGH STOP IF FURTHER STUFF GOES OUT NOW IT WILL KILL DEAD THE STRATEGIC POSITION IN WHICH WE FIND OURSELVES STOP FAR BETTER IT APPEAR AS MYSTERY SERIAL BY A MASKED UNKNOWN STOP NOT DESIRABLE ALIENATE BIG PEOPLE TO PLEASE LIBRARIANS WHO ARE JUST SHEEP STOP HAVE NO PRIVATE LIFE EXCEPT OF INTEREST TO FRIENDS STOP WRITING FULLY MONDAY

F SCOTT FITZGERALD.

[1] Fitzgerald was reacting to the advance publicity for the *Scribner's* serialization of *Tender Is the Night.*

TO: Maxwell Perkins Wire. Princeton University

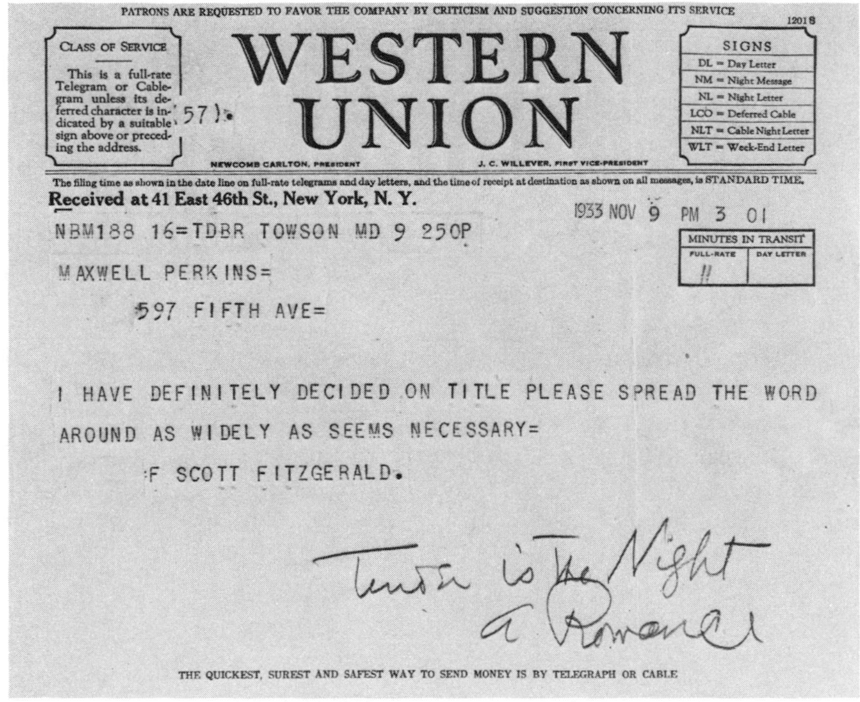

PATRONS ARE REQUESTED TO FAVOR THE COMPANY BY CRITICISM AND SUGGESTION CONCERNING ITS SERVICE

1201 S

CLASS OF SERVICE

This is a full-rate Telegram or Cablegram unless its deferred character is indicated by a suitable sign above or preceding the address.

57)

WESTERN UNION

NEWCOMB CARLTON, PRESIDENT J. C. WILLEVER, FIRST VICE-PRESIDENT

SIGNS
DL = Day Letter
NM = Night Message
NL = Night Letter
LCO = Deferred Cable
NLT = Cable Night Letter
WLT = Week-End Letter

The filing time as shown in the date line on full-rate telegrams and day letters, and the time of receipt at destination as shown on all messages, is STANDARD TIME.

Received at 41 East 46th St., New York, N. Y. 1933 NOV 9 PM 3 01

NBM188 16=TDBR TOWSON MD 9 250P

MINUTES IN TRANSIT	
FULL-RATE	DAY LETTER
11	

MAXWELL PERKINS=

597 FIFTH AVE=

I HAVE DEFINITELY DECIDED ON TITLE PLEASE SPREAD THE WORD AROUND AS WIDELY AS SEEMS NECESSARY=

F SCOTT FITZGERALD.

Tender is the Night
a Romance

THE QUICKEST, SUREST AND SAFEST WAY TO SEND MONEY IS BY TELEGRAPH OR CABLE

Note: The title was written on the Western Union form by Perkins.

FROM: John Peale Bishop AL, 2 pp. (fragment). [2] Scrapbook.
December 1933/January 1934 Princeton University

Dear Scott,

The first installment of the novel confirms what I have long thought, that your gifts as a novelist surpass those of any of us. It is so skilful, so subtle, so right that I have only praise for it. You get the whole romance of that period, which is now like history.

The only thing I question in the whole installment are some of the names. Your list of queer names is right. But I don't like Hengist and Horsa. They are too funny for the text. And your French man's name[1] is confusing, particularly so early in the novel. It's hard to grasp the duel accordingly. Giving him an English prénom is excellent, but he needs a new surname. And have somebody beside the Scribner staff watch the [ ][2] They are no good, and [ ] pass over

[1] On p. 102 of the book Abe North addresses two Englishmen as "Major Hengest and Mr. Horsa." Tommy Barban was named Tommy Costello in the serial version.

[2] The bottom left corner of this letter was cut off when Fitzgerald pasted it in his scrapbook, deleting those words indicated by brackets.

TO: E. S. Oliver — TLS, 2 pp. Unlocated[1]
January 1934 — Baltimore, Maryland

The first help I ever had in writing in my life was from my father who read an utterly imitative Sherlock Holmes story of mine and pretended to like it.[2] But after that I received the most invaluable aid from . . . headmaster of the St. Paul Academy[3] . . . from Courtland Van Winkle in freshman year at Princeton . . . he gave us the book of *Job* to read and I don't think any of our preceptorial group ever quite recovered from it . . . Most of the professors seemed to me old and uninspired, or perhaps it was just that I was getting under way in my own field. I think this answers your question. This is also my permission to make full use of it with or without my name. . . .

[1] *Charles Hamilton Auction Number 61* (14 September 1972), Item #160. On 1 February Fitzgerald wrote to Oliver: "I don't want to be quoted . . . anything you may want to use from my letter is to be summarized." (#161)

[2] Probably "The Mystery of the Raymond Mortgage," *The St. Paul Academy Now and Then* (February 1910).

[3] C. N. B. Wheeler.

TO: Cameron Rogers[1] — TLS, 2 pp. University of California—Los Angeles

1307 Park Avenue,
Baltimore, Maryland,
January 24, 1934.

Dear Cameron Rogers:

I hasten to thank you for your kind letter. It is really the nicest thing I have heard yet. It arrived simultaneously with one from Archie McLeish[2] so altogether I have had a good morning.

It is sometimes surprising to have a novel give an effect which was not exactly intended in the plan. Obviously Nicole is going to steal the book when it was intended as Dick Diver's story, and Nicole was to be scarely more important than Rosemary.

Again thank you for the whole-hearted cordiality of your congratulations. Let me warn you though that sections three and four have been cut for serial publication and some of their best scenes unfortunately omitted as being too racy by the Post Office department. They will be reinstalled in the book.

Sincerely,
F Scott Fitzgerald

P.S. Would it seem too much like scratching your back in return for your kind words if I mentioned in this letter how much I enjoyed your book on Walt Whitman[3] which I read on the way to Bermuda? Also, did you notice that in the second issue of Scribner's that really great story by Tom Wolfe[4] and the quality of all those wood cuts of Shenton running through the magazine?

[1] Biographer who had written Fitzgerald after reading the first two installments of *Tender Is the Night:* "I can think of no more moving character in contemporary fiction than Nicole nor do I readily recollect finding elsewhere writing so sensitive, so admirable in its restraint and yet so very rich in the capacity to arrest and touch the reader. . . . Nothing in these bleak latter years has cheered me so much as this evidence that you are still so conclusively to be reckoned with as one of the four or five best American writers now alive." (Scrapbook. Princeton)

[2] Archibald MacLeish had written: "Great God Scott you can write. You can write better than ever. You are a fine writer. Believe it. Believe It—not me." (Scrapbook. Princeton)

[3] *The Magnificent Idler* (1926).

[4] "Four Lost Men," *Scribner's* (February 1934).

TO: Chatto & Windus — TL(CC), 2 pp. Princeton University

1307 Park Avenue,
Baltimore, Maryland,
January 24, 1934.

Dear Sirs:—

In particular, Mr. Frank Swinerton,[1] if he is still with you, my novel "Tender is the Night," the very dilatory successor to "The Great Gatsby," will be issued by Scribner's late in March. It is a long book, which is to say about 110,000 words, and you might have better luck with it than with "Gatsby." Mr. T. S. Eliot of Faber and Faber is interested[2] and for that reason could I ask you to make your approximate decision from the first half which appears in the January and February numbers of Scribner's magazine. They are indicative of the tone and scope of the book. This is in order to obtain, if possible, simultaneous publications in England and here. Another question to be considered is that the book contains certain episodes which Scribner's have found not advisable to print in the magazine, in general would you say that what will get by the censors in book form here will get by the censors in England? Such things are very much liberalized here, for instance, the unexpurgated "Ulysses" is permitted. Do you know whether Hemingway's "Farewell to Arms" was published in England exactly as it was here? So consider in making your decision whether you would be using Scribner's plates or setting up the whole thing from a faintly expurgated text in London.[3] I may tell you that the book is getting an extraordinary response here.

Yours very truly,
F. Scott Fitzgerald

[1] English novelist Frank Swinnerton was an editor with Chatto & Windus.

[2] On 15 January Eliot wrote Fitzgerald: "Chatto and Windus is a good firm, and it would in any case be contrary to publishing ethics to attempt to seduce you away from them, but of course if you are quite free in this matter, it is up to you to send the manuscript first to whatever firm you elect." (Princeton)

[3] Chatto & Windus reset the type for *Tender Is the Night,* but the text was not bowdlerized.

TO: Victor Llona — TL(CC), 2 pp. Princeton University

1307 Park Avenue,
Baltimore, Maryland,
January 25, 1934.

Dear Victor:

The novel is finished and will be published here in March, it is running in Scribner's magazine now. The name is "Tender is the Night" taken from Keats' "Nightingale." As to translation into French, which you have several times mentioned to me there are two points to consider: first, the remark of Simon Kra to me some years ago to the effect that Europeans would not be interested in a novel written by an American with scenes laid in Europe. I think, however, this can be qualified by the statement that all the leading characters are American, or partly American, and even such minor characters who are not American are German Swiss. The second point to be considered is that the novel is more than twice as long as "The Great Gatsby." So far as royalty arrangements are concerned, both translator's share and my own I would be more than willing to allocate that more liberally than before as I have never expected to make any money out of French rights anyhow, but this time we should manage to get it some time in advance to someone like Jean Cocteau. From this end the novel looks like a hit already, having increased the circulation of Scribner's magazine etc. etc.

If, on the other hand, you have other designs for the immediate future which would preclude your attempting this please let me know as someone else might be interested in the task.[1] If you can get hold of a copy of Scribner's magazine for January, which contains the first quarter of the book, you may be able to form some opinion from that. As soon as I hear from you I can ship you off complete proofs.

With very best wishes to you both.

[1] *Tender Is the Night* was first published in French in 1951, translated by Marguerite Chevalley.

TO: Maxwell Perkins — Wire. Princeton University

BALTIMORE MD 1934 JAN 28 PM 8 29

DECIDED REGRETFULLY DONT LIKE JACKET MUCH TOO ITALIANATE TOO RED AND YELLOW SKY DOES NOT GIVE WHITE AND BLUE SPARKLE OF FRENCH RIVIERA AM SENDING REAL RIVIERA POSTER SHOWING MAXFIELD PARRISH COLORS IF IMPRACTICAL WOULD PREFER SHENTON WOODCUT OR PLAIN JACKET WAIT FOR LETTER[1]

FITZGERALD.

[1] The dust jacket on the published book has a Riviera scene in red, yellow, blue, white, and green.

TO: Louis Bromfield[1] — TLS, 2 pp. Ohio State University

1307 Park Avenue,
Baltimore, Maryland,
January 29, 1934.

Dear Louis:

It was certainly damn nice of you to write me that telegram.[2] I have been alone with this book so long that I eagerly gobble up any morsel of praise, walk around my study for half an hour going over the book in the mind of one who so far happened to like it.

I was living in the country when I heard that you were considering Baltimore as a residence and was disappointed when a few hours later I learned that you had moved to Princeton. I wonder where you finally settled. Am out of touch with most of our mutual friends though I occasionally correspond with Ernest, Marice and Archie.[2] (By the way, the latter also seems to like the book so far, so maybe I am going to have some sort of *succès d'estime* out of it.) A writer's praise is worth that of a hundred critics, don't you think? And wasn't Gertrude Stein pretty sweet to us?[3] Or was she pretty sweet to us? (as my daughter says)[4]

Again thank you for your gracious and generous telegram. With cordial best wishes to you and your family.

As ever,
F. Scott Fitzg—

P.S. By the way I must warn you, if you continue to read the story in the magazine, that the fourth + last section is cut from what it will be in book form.

FSF.

[1] Novelist Bromfield, who knew Fitzgerald in Paris, had wired him: JUST READ SECOND INSTALMENT NOVEL WONDERFUL REGARDS LOUIS BROMFIELD. (Princeton)
[2] Marice Hamilton and Archibald MacLeish.
[3] *The Autobiography of Alice B. Toklas* mentions Fitzgerald and Bromfield favorably.
[4] This sentence was added in holograph.

TO: Maxwell Perkins — TLS, 3 pp. Princeton University

1307 Park Avenue,
Baltimore, Maryland,
February 1, 1934.

Dear Max:

Confirming my telegram I wish to God I had thought of this a week ago, but having put the proof aside to do my story it didn't occur to me. Now you know what my galleys look like. To transfer twenty-eight pages of those corrections from one kind of galley proof to another kind of galley proof will be a matter, to me, of many days work and it will obscure all the advantage of doing my final revision on clean galleys. My idea was originally to use the benefit of the magazine galley as an extra chance at corrections. As I said in my wire the reinsertion of the cut scenes is the work of only an afternoon.[1]

Of course if you have gone ahead with Section IV from the manuscript I suppose there is nothing to be done except strike off another galley for me when I have done all that spade work over again, altogether, probably a more expensive process, if Section IV is not already completely set up for the book. This is an awful mess. The ideal way would be, if you haven't already set up a whole block of Section IV, to wait for corrected magazine proof of IV and have some editor roughly dub in the two big cuts, the scene of the fairies and the scene of the Lesbians, and send that to me with my own typescript containing the minor blue underlined magazine cuts. In that way I can work swiftly and efficiently. Meanwhile you could show the Book of the Month Club magazine galley of IV supplemented, just to be honest, with my typescript of the Lesbian scene *if* The Book of Mo. can get it back to you in time to insert it in my book galley for Section IV. From what you said to me on the phone last night about Wallace Myers' accuracy, perhaps he could handle it.

This is all the result of haste and nobody's fault except mine, but I worried about it all last night and it is essential that it be straightened up. I wish you would wire me immediately. Accept your decision about the jacket but be sure and do your best about that yellow as well as the red. I think every bit of yellow could be changed to white. Maybe somebody who knows about color printing could think of some way of introducing a little of that crimson-purple, as in the last poster I sent you, into the mountains. Oh God, it's hell to bother you about all this but of course the book is my whole life now and I can't help this perfectionist attitude.

You'll see Section I will come out all right.

Ever yours,
Scott

[1] Fitzgerald was working on proofs of the serial and book texts of *Tender Is the Night* at the same time.

TO: Gilbert Seldes — TLS, 2 pp. Princeton University

1307 Park Avenue,
Baltimore, Maryland,
February 2, 1934.

Dear Gilbert:

On second thoughts I am not very sold on "First and Last" as a Lardner title.[1] I keep thinking of Lears' "Book of Nonsense" and of "Alice in Wonderland." While I know Ring's book will not be for children it is aimed at a somewhat childish side of us all and the title "First and Last" has a faint knell of his funeral bells in it. It is just a bit literary, and even sentimental. Please think this over. Constructively I have nothing to offer, but God damn it, that Thurber title "My Life and Hard Times" would have been wonderful. I have been fooling with the idea "On All Fours, or Compendium of the Jocose Adventures of Ring Lardner," etc. or "Life as Viewed by a Natural" or "May I Arise and Protest." Maybe that note will suggest something to you.

I have just thought of another item which may have been overlooked. It is the preface of "How to Write Short Stories" and explanatory notes. The preface would have to be cut; the notes containing such gems as:

"This story was written on top of a Fifth Avenue bus, and some of the sheets blew away, which may account for the apparent scarcity of interesting situations." Also another one: "This story is an example of what can be done with a stub pen." And: "This story is an example of a story written from a title, the title being a line from Tennyson's immortal 'Hot Cross Buns.' A country-bred youth left a fortune, journeys to London 'to become a gentleman.' Adventures beset him, not the least of them being that he falls out of a toy balloon." Could any of these wisecracks or the ones in the preface be fitted into your scheme, which I gather has been planned to be quite elastic? (I didn't see "Round Up" but I don't think that they used any of that material.)

Love to you both.

As ever,
F. Scott Fitzg—

[1] Seldes was editing a posthumous collection of Ring Lardner's writings. *First and Last* was the final title.

TO: Alfred Dashiell TLS, 2 pp. Princeton University

1307 Park Avenue,
Baltimore, Maryland,
February 2, 1934.

Dear Fritz:

A woman named Pauline Reinsch, 1904 Kendall Avenue, Madison, Wisconsin, has read the book and been interested enough to send me a rather thorough list of errors in French and German for Sections I and II. In spite of everything there were a hell of a lot of them. I wish you would make a special note to send her page proofs of Sections III and IV the minute they are available, otherwise I am going to get one of those terrible bawlings out like Zelda did.[1] There is a certain sort of critic, who, when he is over his head, takes refuge in school marm quibbling, and another type of reader who is legitimately annoyed by inaccuracy.

By the way, where is the page proof of Sect. III you promised; also I could use another copy of your January issue, which is unprocurable around here. Have you got any report yet as to the February sales of the magazine? And have you any other reports that would be of interest to an anxious author? I am doing three galleys an evening of Section IV.

Ever yours,
Scott Fitzgerald

[1] *Save Me the Waltz* was ridiculed by critics for its many errors.

TO: Maxwell Perkins Wire. Princeton University

BALTIMORE MD 1934 FEB 5 AM 1 28

FEEL CANNES JAIL SCENE SHOULD GO INTO SERIAL OPINIONS INDICATE SAME OTHERWISE DICKS CHARACTER WEAKENS AND NOVEL FORSHOTENS TOWARD END IT IS NEEDED AND WAS WRITTEN TO BOLSTER HIM UP IN INEVITABLY UNDIGNIFIED CUCKOLD SITUATION STOP PLEASE PERMIT WILL TREAT TACTFULLY WIRE

FITZGERALD.

1 Ch. 10 of Book 3. This scene was included in the serial version, but is set in Antibes.

TO: Maxwell Perkins Wire. Princeton University

BALTIMORE MD 1248P 1934 FEB 5 PM 1 29

FEEL DOWNRIGHT ESSENTIAL FOR READER TO GET GLIMPSE OF DICK THROUGH IMPERSONAL EYES NOT TOMMYS AND NICOLES TO SUSTAIN HIM AT THE END OTHERWISE FINAL TRIAL OFF INSPIRES SCORN INSTEAD OF PATHOS CANT REPEAT MISTAKE OF BEAUTIFUL DAMNED STOP SCENE IS FOURTEEN HUNDRED WORDS BUT CANT YOU ARRANGE IT SOMEHOW[1]

SCOTT.

1 Two drafts for Perkins' wires to Fitzgerald on 5 February are in the Scribners Papers. In the first of these Perkins asks Fitzgerald to condense the jail scene to 800 words; but the second Perkins wire draft reads: "Will work it out somehow but cut anywhere you rightly can." See Fitzgerald's 5 February letter to Perkins in *Scott/Max.*

TO: John Palmer TL(CC), 2 pp. Princeton University

1307 Park Avenue,
Baltimore, Maryland,
February 12, 1934.

Dear John:

I am sending you this letter merely as a matter of record and not with any idea of alarming any member of Zelda's family, as there is absolutely no cause for alarm. Frankly, though I know you have troubles of your own, I am doing it as a measure of self-protection, and if Newman were not so far away I would write this letter to him instead as he has been more in touch with Zelda's case. After a tremendous improvement she has had a slight relapse which makes it necessary for her to enter a clinic once more for a rest period which may be no longer than two weeks and may stretch into a month or so. To tell Mrs. Sayre a fact like this or to tell it to Marjorie, which would be the same thing, would be taking five years off her life because she would immediately link it up with Anthony's troubles.[1] Zelda and I consider it would be *absolutely disastrous to do* such a thing. I may even add (that I would rather you did not communicate this to Tild) as it may, in some round-robin way, reach Montgomery. I simply want to put it as a matter of record with some member of Zelda's family that she is vountarily hospitalizing herself under the advice of the same Dr. Myers who has been in charge of the case for the past two years and that it is with my entire agreement. Her own letters to her mother during this time will be headed as if she were still here with Scottie and me.

With best wishes to you all and hopes that both Tild and young John have fully recovered from their indispositions of last year and that all goes well with you, I am

Faithfully,

[1] Zelda's brother suffered a breakdown and committed suicide in 1933.

FROM: Glenway Wescott TLS, 2 pp. Princeton University

228 Madison Avenue, New York.
February 20, 1934

Dear Scott Fitzgerald,

My past and present publishers seem to be dreamy fellows, and your letter did not reach me until today. Thank you for the friendliness with which you refer to our overlapping inspiration.[1] I am glad that you have read my sailor story, liking to think that I write for such as you, and not merely for those who keep me going in our profession; I am glad that Hemingway remembered it; I am glad that you did not read it too soon, since my accidental precedence might have embarassed you somehow—it shouldn't have. I shall defend you spiritedly, if anyone is so foolish as to mention it. If need be, we can pretend that you told me of your intention to make use of the festivities of my Villefranche, years ago when we first met in your Antibes—when, in fact, I think, we talked only of Hemingway. You may wish to defend me before long on the same score: I haven't read any of TENDER IS THE NIGHT; I hear that your hero is a doctor; the sad hero of my new novel is a doctor; and God knows what similarities may result from that fact.

Miss Stein and I have never been either friends or the reverse; but if she hears some of the offensive things I've been saying about her since she worked up for herself such general celebrity, I'm afraid I can't expect her to feel friendly. We met one day last spring at Mme Pecci-Blunt's, and she asked if I had heard any news of you; presently I expressed my admiration of you, with some casual, perhaps hair-splitting reservations, saying that I did think you had a much more natural novelist's talent, a more vigorous narrative gift, than either Hemingway or myself, wondering if you felt that yourself, and felt responsible, and cared . . . Oh, she replied, of course he is infinitely better than you and Hemingway; if you two had talent enough you wouldn't have to work so hard; all this fuss and constipation and *cuisine* and rewriting . . . etc. Of course I thought that the amiable old bluffer had considerably missed the point, all the points. I was sure of it when she began bracketting you with Charles Henri Ford[2] *and* Bromfield *and* Defoe *and* Sir Rose, Bart., as he used to be called in Villefranche.[3] She herself, I think, hasn't done an honest day's work between THREE LIVES and the AUTOBIOGRAPHY, and this last job was done just to make money; like most autobiographers, taking a rebate on the money she has spent on herself all these years. I think that her remarks on Hemingway, so sly and hard to rebut, are odious; and that her effort, aided and abetted by my old friend Fay, to set herself up as a model of normality and a judge of wholesomeness in literature, is odious and ridiculous. You see, my troubles have only begun; what if Miss Toklas should now write an autobiography of Miss Stein. . . ? I didn't really mind her epigram about my "syrup not flowing." It doesn't, indeed. When people began condoling with me and baiting me, I said as much, and said that since I had been complaining about it for years and living around the corner from Miss S. for years, I wasn't surprised at her having heard it; finally the local talkers began to say that the epigram had been my own, and that she had swiped it; which of course I corrected, but still felt revenged and cheered . . .

Please excuse my loquacity. We're all Stein-conscious in New York just now.

With warm greetings, and my respectful compliments to Mrs Fitzgerald, if she remembers me.[4]

Yours,
G Wescott

[1] *Tender Is the Night* and Wescott's story "The Sailor" in *Good-Bye Wisconsin* (1928) both treat American sailors at Villefranche.

[2] Editor, writer, and artist.

[3] Sir Francis Rose, English artist; Riviera acquaintance of Fitzgerald's.

[4] See Fitzgerald's 6 February letter to Wescott in *Letters*.

FROM: Thomas Wolfe TLS, 1 p. Scrapbook. Princeton University
March 1934

Dear Scott:

Thanks for your note. It's good to hear from you again. I'll be delighted to visit Zelda's exhibition when I'm in town. I live in Brooklyn now and it's sometimes hard to get over to Manhattan in daytime, but I should like to see her painting before the exhibition is over.

Scott, I want to tell you how glad I am that your book is being published next month, and also what a fine book it is. I read it as it came out in *Scribner's Magazine* and even read the proofs of the last two installments. I tell you this because I got the jump on most readers in this way. I thought you'd be interested to know that the people in the book are even more real and living now than they were at the time I read it. It seems to me you've gone deeper in this book than in anything you ever wrote. I don't pretend to know anything about the book business and have no idea whether it will have a big sale or not, but I do know that other people are going to feel about it as I do. I think it's the best work you've done so far, and I know you'll understand what I mean and won't mind if I get a kind of selfish hope and joy out of your own success. I have sweated blood these last four years on an enormous manuscript of my own, and the knowledge that you have now come through with this fine book makes me want to cheer. I felt a personal interest in parts of the book where you described places we had been together, particularly Glion and Caux and that funicular that goes up the mountain. I don't think anyone will know just how good that piece of writing is unless he has been there.

This is all for the present. I am still working like hell but I'd like to see you if you come up here. Meanwhile, I am wishing for the best kind of success in every way for your book when it is published.[1]

Yours,
Tom Wolfe

[1] See Fitzgerald's 2 April letter to Wolfe in *Letters*.

TO: Maxwell Perkins Wire. Princeton University

BALTIMORE MD 920A 1934 MAR 15 AM 9 31

PLEASANT NICE THOUGHTS IT WOULD BREAK MY HEART IF THE PROOF READERS ARE STICKING BACK ALL THOSE ITALICS I TWICE ELIMINATED STOP IN THE FIRST PROOF THEY HAD ALL THE FRENCHMEN TALKING IN ITALICS

SCOTT.

TO: Houghton Mifflin | Wire. Princeton University

BALTIMORE MD 440A 1934 MAR 17 AM 5 02
HATE QUIBBLING IN NARROW TIMES BUT YOUR NEWS CARRIES IMPLICATION THAT BOTTOME GIVES FULL LOAF TO MY HALF LOAF ABOUT PSYCHIATRY[1] STOP ITS FAIR TO CAPITALIZE RESEMBLANCE BUT SINCE YOU MADE MISSTATEMENT IN USING WORDS QUOTE CONCLUDING CHAPTERS UNQUOTE FEEL YOU SHOULD AMEND IN NEXT ISSUE

F SCOTT FITZGERALD.

[1] In the promotional material for Phyllis Bottome's *Private Worlds*, a novel that dealt with psychiatry, Houghton Mifflin compared it with *Tender Is the Night*.

TO: Samuel Marx[1] | TLS, 2 pp. Princeton University

1307 Park Avenue,
Baltimore, Maryland,
March 22, 1934.

Dear Sam:

You were wrong! The letter to Cukor[2] dealt with the idea of Gable playing "*Gatsby*." "*Tender is the Night*" is still an unknown quanity.[3] Would rather like to come out there now that the main chore is finished. It seems to be that or the *Saturday Evening Post* and I long for variety—but at any price (and I am cherishing none of the illusions of 1931 about money) I wouldn't come out there with any such lineup as I had to face last time. Who is this Joan Crawford? Is she the one who preaches in the Los Angeles temple, or is that Greta McArthur?

With best wishes to Madame and to you,

Ever yours,
Scott Fitzgerald

[1] MGM story editor.
[2] Director George Cukor.
[3] Neither of these movies was made.

TO: Dale Warren[1] | TLS, 1 p. Princeton University

1307 Park Avenue,
Baltimore, Maryland,
March 28, 1934.

Dear Dale:

My God! My God! I didn't think when I made all that fuss about nothing that I was digging at an old Princetonian. Forget it and forgive *me*. I enjoyed Phyllis Bottome's book but my own instinct is for things more dynamic and more closely knit and I've never been able to get deeply absorbed about these long chatty English novels.

With best wishes and hoping to see you soon.

Yours
Scott Fitzgerald

[1] Warren had answered Fitzgerald's 17 March wire to Houghton Mifflin. See Warren's "(Signed) F.S.F.," *Princeton University Library Chronicle* (Winter 1964).

FROM: Zelda Fitzgerald
March 1934

ALS, 6 pp. Princeton University
Craig House, Beacon, New York

Dear Scott:

I quite realize the terrible financial pressure of the last year for you, and I am miserable that this added burden should have fallen on your shoulders. All the beauty of this place must cost an awful lot of money and maybe it would be advisable to go somewhere more compatible with our present means.[1] Please do not think that I don't appreciate the strain you are under. I would make the best possible effort to rehabilitate myself under any less luxurious conditions that might be more expedient.

Please don't give up Scottie's music. Though she is at an age when she resents the practice, I feel sure that later she will get an immense satisfaction out of the piano. About the French, do as you think best. She will never forget it at her age and could pick it up again quickly as soon as she heard it around her

It's too bad about Willie She was the best cook we've ever had in years and I've always held Essie in suspect: there've been such a long succession of rows over missing things since she became part of the household.

The trunk arrived. I am very much oblidged. However, I would also like my blue bathing-suit which may be in the box with moth balls in the back room on the third floor, and also the rest of my clothes: a blue suit, a green checked skirt and the evening clothes. ALSO PLEASE ask Mrs Owens to send me a $2 pointed camel's hair brush from Webers and the two unfinished canvases from Phipps, and a pound can of Weber's permalba.

Dear: I am not trying to make myself into a great artist or a great anything. Though you persist in thinking that an exaggerated ambition is the fundamental cause of my collapse, knowing the motivating elements that now make me wa[nt] to work I cannot agree with you and Dr Forel— though of cource, the will-to-power may have played a part in the very beginning. However, five years have passed since then, and one matures. I do the things I can do and that interest me and if you'd like me to give up everything I like to do I will do so willingly if it will advance matters any. I am not headstrong and do not like existing entirely at other peoples expense and being a constant care to others any better than you like my being in such a situation.

If you feel that it is an imposition on Cary to have the exhibition, the pictures can wait.[2] I believe in them and in Emerson's theory about good-workman-ship. If they are good, they will come to light some day.

About my book: you and the doctors agreed that I might work on it.[3] If you now prefer that I put it aside for the present I wish you would be clear about saying so. The short story is a form demanding too concentrated an effort for me at present and I might try a play, if you are willing and don't approve of the novel or something where the emotional purpose can be accomplished by accurate execution of an original cerebral conception. *Please say what you want done,* as I really do not know. As you know, my work is mostly a pleasure for me, but if it is better for me to take up something quite foreign to my temperament, I will—Though I can't see what good it does to knit bags when you want to paint pansies, maybe it is necessary at times to do what you don't like.

Tilde 'phoned that she and John would drive over to see me. I will be very glad to see them.

Love
Zelda

[1] Zelda Fitzgerald failed to show improvement at Phipps, and Fitzgerald moved her to Craig House in Beacon, N.Y., where the minimum rate was $175 a week.

[2] Zelda Fitzgerald's paintings and drawings were shown at Cary Ross's gallery in Manhattan 29 March–30 April, with a smaller exhibit at the Algonquin Hotel.

[3] A second novel that was never finished; possibly "Caesar's Things."

FROM: Zelda Fitzgerald
March 1934

ALS, 1 p. Princeton University
Craig House, Beacon, New York

Dearest Do-Do.

Please ask Mrs. Owens to hurry with my paints. There are so many winter trees exhibiting irresistible intricacies, and there are many neo-classic columns, and there are gracious expanses of snow and the brooding quality of a gray and heavy sky, all of which make me want terribly to paint

I have been working on the hotels,[1] and will mail them as soon as they're finished. Also what of my book I get done for you to have typed. Be sure to write me what you think of the chapters you read.

Do-Do:

It was so sad to see your train pull out through the gold sheen of the winter afternoon. It is sad that you should have so many things to worry you and make you unhappy when your book is so good and ought to bring you so much satisfaction. I hope the house won't seem desolate and purposeless; if you want to, you could board Scottie at Bryn Mawr,[2] or maybe even the Turnbulls[3] and stay in New York with the people you're fond of.

This is a beautiful place; there is everything on earth available and I have a little room to paint in with a window higher than my head the way I like windows to be. When they are that way, you can look out on the sky and feel like Faust in his den, or an alchemist or anybody you like who must have looked out of windows like that. And my own room is the nicest room I've ever had, any place—which is very unjust, considerring the burden you are already struggling under.

Dear—I will see you soon. Why not bring Scottie up for Easter? She'd love it here with the pool and the beautiful walks—And I *promise* you absolutely that by then I will be much better—and as well as I can.

Dear:

PLEASE remember that you owe it to the fine things inside you to get the most out of them.

Work, and don't drink, and the accomplished effort will perhaps open unexpected sources of happiness, or contentment, or whatever it is you are looking for—certainly a sense of security—If I were you'd, I'd dramatize your book—yourself—I feel sure it contains a good subtle drama suitable to the purposes of the theatre Guild: a character play hinging on the two elements within the man: his worldly proclivities and his desire to be a distinguished person—I wish I could do it.

Love, dear—
Zelda

[1] " 'Show Mr. and Mrs. F. to Number—,' " *Esquire* (May and June 1934). This autobiographical article was by-lined "F. Scott and Zelda Fitzgerald," but Fitzgerald credited it to Zelda in his Ledger.

[2] Scottie was a day student at Bryn Mawr School in Baltimore.

[3] The Turnbull family owned the estate on which "La Paix" was situated.

FROM: Zelda Fitzgerald — AL, 3 pp. Princeton University
March 1934 — Craig House, Beacon, New York

Dear, Monsieur, D.O;

The third installment is fine. I like immensely that retrospective part through Nicole's eyes—which I didn't like at first because of your distrust of polyphonic prose. It's a swell book.

. . . .[1]

I am sorry Charlie[2] is still so charming. I have never felt Charlie to be a legitimate attraction somehow and suspect him of not really being from Borneo at all, though no amount of research yields up the slightest false whiskers. However, he has a parasitical flavor—

I am glad you are a lion Dr Rennie says you are a lion so I am glad. You deserve to be. I hope there will be enough Christians left to make it worth while; though there is some talk amongst the lions of eeking out the winter with Barnum Bailey—just for the experience—

Borrow $1000 from your mother and write a play. It will make her feel very virtuous and will become what she has been waiting for all these years. The play will be a big success; if it isnt you can stick in some propaganda —Then you can support Mr. Lorimer in his old age without the stories.

I wish I could write stories. I wish I could write something sort of like the book of revelations: you know, about how everything would have come out if we'd only been able to supply the 3-letter word for the Egyptian god of dithryambics. Something all full of threats preferably and then a very gentle confession at the end admitting that I have enfeebled myself too much by my own vehemence to ever become very frightened again.

If Scottie sneezes you will find the proper method of proceedure in Louis Carrol; the Katzenjammers also are full of constructive ideas about bringing up children Only you have to have children who explode when banged with a stick to use the latter as a text book—

If we had $500 we could all go to Greece—The Vale of Shalimar still settles to earth somewhere in the east; capitals with short bombastic names drown in the tides of the Black sea; metro polese of many syllables are being mispronounced by travellers like missionaries in Cook's most inefficient out-posts In Indo-Chine in the newsreels the clouds are full as treasure-sacks. Natives all over those foreign places treaddle, and migrate, and think of the world as a very big place. If only the signifigance of roads had not left the western hemisphere!

Please ask Cary to come to see me if he wants to. And tell him that I am sorry I was rude and that if he will lend me the Satie[3] I will make him a pink and dreamy picture filled with the deepest appreciation of the most superficial emotions—

D.O:

You *don't* love me—But I am counting on Pavloff's dogs to make that kind of thing all right—and, in the mean-time, under the added emotional stress of the break-up of our state, perhaps the old conventions will assume an added poignancy—Besides, personal love should be incidental music, maybe—Besides, *anything* personal was never the objective of our generation—we were to have thought of ourselves heroicly; we agreed in the Plaza Grill the pact was confirmed by the shaking of Connie Bennets head and the sonority of Ludlow's premature gastritis—

1 Fifty-seven words omitted by the editor.
2 Possibly Charles MacArthur.
3 Composer Erik Satie (1866–1925).

FROM: Zelda Fitzgerald
April 1934

ALS, 4 pp. Princeton University
Craig House, Beacon, New York

Dearest Do-Do:

I have now got to the Rosemary-Rome episode. It makes me very sad—largely because of the beautiful, beautiful writing. Recapitulation of casual youth in the tenderer terms one learns to cling to later is always moving. You know I love your prose style: it is so fine and balanced and you know how to achieve the emphasis you want so poignantly and economicly. It's a fine book, suggestive to me of these black tree formations, aspiring or despairing, scatterring their white petals to make another valley spring.

Please don't be alarmed if I don't write; there is much outside to look at and my room inside reflects the softness of new greens and harbors the squares of mountain sun

I am so happy that it is hot again.

Mrs Kellam and I hammered at golf-balls yesterday, taking enough swings to have built the Roxy Center—at least I did. She plays very well. You know my psychological attitude toward golf: it was just the sort of thing they would have brought into England during the reign of Chas. II. The French probably played it in high-heels with stomachs full of wine and cheated a little.

I hope all goes well at home. All you *really* have to do for Scottie is see that she does not go to Bryn Mawr in dirty blouses. Also, she will not voluntarily wash her ears: I noticed when she was here and hope Louise Perkins didn't. I can't say that I blame her but some people might, so am afraid you will have to go through a thorough inspection every now and then—

Love
Zelda

TO: Maxwell Perkins

TLS, 1 p. Princeton University

1307 Park Avenue,
Baltimore, Maryland,
April 2, 1934.

Dear Max:

In the usual confusion of leaving your city I don't know whether I paid my bill at the Algonquin, whether you paid it or whether it was paid at all. Have you got any dope on the subject?

All in all, I am deeply satisfied with the get-up of the book. My only regret is that the dedication isn't to You, as it should be, because Christ knows you've stuck with me on the thing through thick and thin, and it was pretty thin going for a while.

Got a fine letter from Tom Wolfe. Thank you for your hospitality and courtesy to Scottie and me, more than I can say.

Ever yours,
Scott

P.S. I could use a dozen copies of the book if you could send them here.

FROM: John Peale Bishop — ALS, 2 pp. Scrapbook. Princeton University

April 3, 1934.

Dear Scott,

I come fresh from reading *Tender Is the Night* and am overcome with the magnificence of it. It surpasses *The Great Gatsby*. You have shown us, what we have wanted so long and impatiently to see, that you are a true, a beautiful and a tragic novelist. I have only praise for its understanding, its characterization, and its deep tenderness. I write you much enthusiasm. Like a good wine, you mature and gain in richness. There is no loss of strength. Nor, to drop the figure, of invention. And I may tell you that I am very happy that you have carried it off. I think I can say honestly that I am always gratified when an American does a good book. But that you should do this book pleases me beyond measure. I can guess what it means to you. And with all of old affection, I congratulate you.

I'm glad you changed Costello's name. The one point in the book which stuck for me was the incest. I couldn't quite believe it. Nor do I think it was necessary. But it's done, and is being forgotten—if I should need to forget it—in the midst of so many Triumphs.

I'm sorry I couldn't dine with you at Alec's. We are now mud-bound as a month ago snow-bound. M was stuck for nearly an hour this morning in the Valley Forge Road. But I'll see Zelda's show if I can possibly get into New York.[1]

As ever,
JB

[1] See Fitzgerald's 7 April letter to Bishop in *Letters*.

FROM: John Peale Bishop — ALS, 2 pp. Princeton University

April 4, 1934

Dear Scott:

I wrote you last night just after finishing *Tender Is the Night*. But this morning I received your letter, which demands a reply.

I don't remember talking to anyone in New York about the novel except Esther[1] and she did all the talking. Certainly the quoted remark means nothing to me. I haven't been in New York for three weeks at least, and at that time I had read only the first installment in Scribner's. I hate reading novels in magazines and decided to put yours off until I had the complete copy.

It is true that the tone of the first section bothered me when I read it in Scribner's. But I know now that it was right—To see the Divers through Rosemary's romantic and naïve eyes. And as for the end of your novel, I don't see how it could be bettered. It moved me profoundly.

You can understand my worrying over your beginning, because technically my novel[2] does the same thing—That is, there is a long stretch, seen through a young boy's eyes, in which no ironic view of the other characters is possible. That can only come as the plot unfolds. If I can succeed in sustaining the reader over this half as well as you do, I shall be immensely gratified. I exaggerated none of my enthusiasm when I wrote you last night. I admire Tender is the Night tremendously. One sentence in my letter may convey a false meaning—I wanted to say that we had waited a long time for this novel—not for you to prove yourself a novelist.

I want to see you very much. I have been terribly slowed up in my work lately. I suspect a profound boredom with Connecticut as being at the bottom of it. The winter here has about annihilated all vitality.

affectionately,
JB

[1] Probably Esther Murphy.
[2] *Act of Darkness* (Scribners, 1935).

TO: Louis Bromfield — TLS, 2 pp. Ohio State University

1307 Park Avenue,
Baltimore, Maryland,
April 7, 1934.

Dear Louis:

Again it was good to hear from you. My book comes out the twelfth and meanwhile, I sent you an advanced copy in care of your publishers.

Indeed, we are not only growing middle-aged, we *are* middle-aged, and being treaded down by that very young generation, that I agree with you, hasn't as much talent as ours. But remember, we flowered, or failed to flower, in days of Florentine splendor, while most of these kids have been up against it for half a decade. However, I must frankly admit that all their work does essentially bore me (haven't read this Farrell[1]) and seems very thin and doctrinaire and unworked at and giving the final effect of all having been derived from some Work I never saw by some Great Craftsman I never saw and am not sure ever existed. All in all, I feel patient with them though for they didn't know what now seems the Golden Age.

With very best wishes to you and yours, I am

Faithfully,
F Scott Fitzgerald

[1] James T. Farrell, author of *Young Lonigan* (1932).

FROM: Zelda Fitzgerald
April 1934

ALS, 1 p. Princeton University
Craig House, Beacon, New York

Mr. Scott Fitzgerald
1307 Park Avenue
Baltimore Md

Dear—The book is grand. The emotional lift sustained by the force of a fine poetic prose and the characters *subserviated* to forces stronger than their interpretations of life is very moving. It is tear-evoking to witness individidual belief in individual volition succumbing to the purpose of a changing world. That is the purpose of a good book and you have written it—Those people are helpless before themselves and the prose is beautiful and there is manifest an integrity in the belief of both those expressions. It is a reverential and very fine book and the first literary contribution to what writers will be concerning themselves with some years from now.

Love
Zelda

FROM: Louis Bromfield
April 1934

ALS, 2 pp. Princeton University

Dear Scott—

Two copies of the book—one signed—arrived and I was delighted to have them. Needless to say they are in great demand among the neighbors. All of us—and that means 3 hard-boiled readers—Mary myself and George Hawkins who keeps me at work and squeezes the pennies from wretched movie magnates editors etc—found it full of the real stuff. There are certain pages which are unforgettable and there is a beautiful *quality* about the whole performance. It is I should think permanent. That we should see deeper into it than the older or younger reader is inevitable. They dont know what its about. Ive just embarked on a ponderous novel on the same theme—save that the whole setting is as different as possible. I've gone the whole hog. My "hero," surrounded by all the blessings in the world, simply goes out to the garage and shoots himself—fifteen years after the war.[1] Anyway its all a fascinating business, this writing. As to the "Younger generation" most of them seem pretty "arty" and self-conscious and the hard-boiled school is the most tiresome of all. Perhaps when they become middle-aged like ourselves they'll outgrow it. We did know the golden age. Hot or cold, we were very lucky. I never knew it more profoundly than during the past winter when a lot of Princeton undergraduates crossed my path.

Life here is extremely quiet. I fiddle around the garden all day and work at night. I never liked Paris and now it is a morgue. I haven't spent a night there since my return a month ago. But I'm saving up for London where I have fun.

Drop me a line with news of yourself. I'm planted here until October save for a month in Cornwall. Then back to Broadway and Mr. Jed Harris[2] for a play, which will be [my new] experience. Thank you for the book and for having written it.

As always—
Louis Bromfield

[1] *The Man Who Had Everything* (1935).
[2] Theatrical producer.

FROM: James Branch Cabell TLS, 1 p. Scrapbook. Princeton University

Dear Scott Fitzgerald:

Completely, admiringly, and a bit enviously, have I relished each page of Tender Is the Night. I think it a superb piece of writing—solid (in the word's best sense), urbane, true, and unfailingly picturesque. To call it your best book were mere idle understatement: it is immeasurably your best book.

All luck to it and you. And all my thanks for remembering me thus handsomely, in a fashion so pleasure giving.

Yours faithfully,
James Branch Cabell

11 April 1934

TO: Malcolm Cowley[1]
Early April 1934

Inscription in *Tender Is the Night*. Unlocated[2]
Baltimore, Maryland(?)

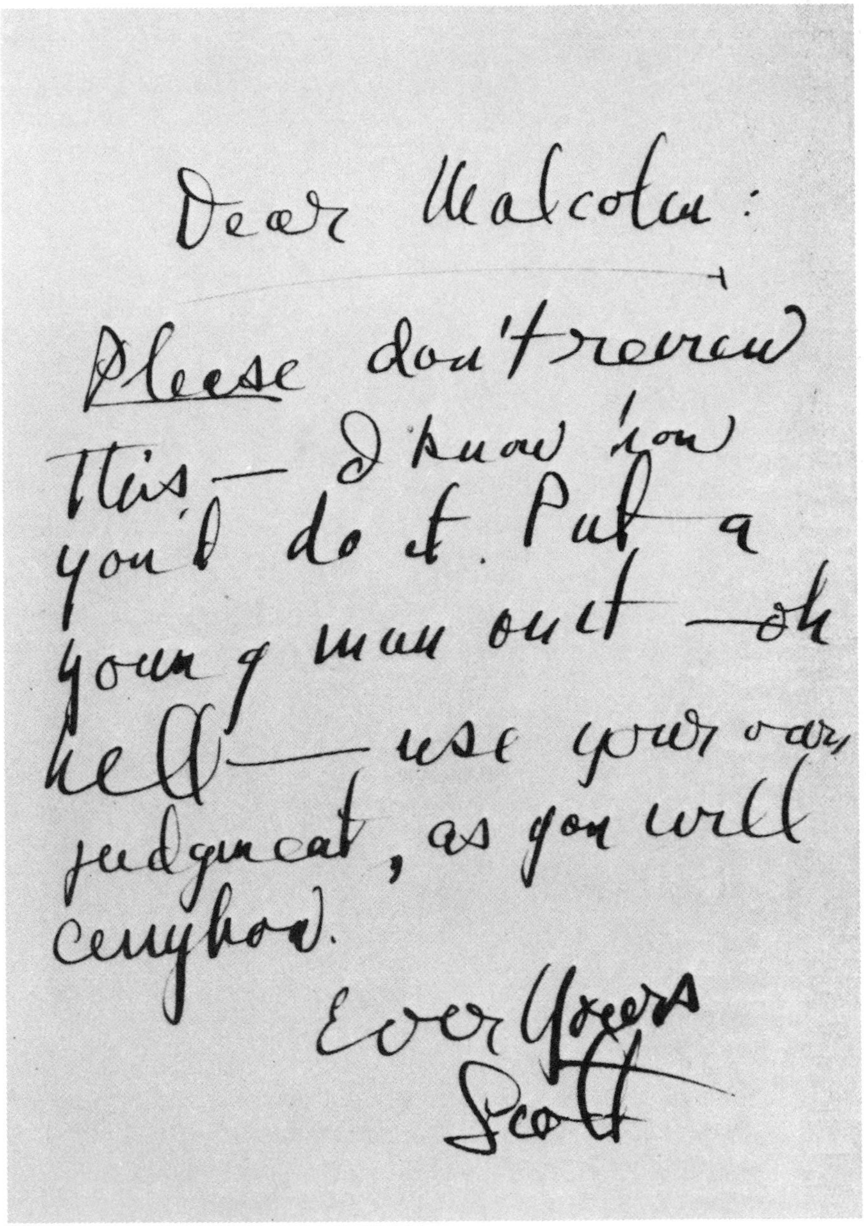
Dear Malcolm:

Please don't review this—I know you'll do it. Put a young man out—oh hell—use your own judgement, as you will anyhow.

Ever Yours
Scott

[1] Book review editor of *The New Republic*.
[2] Sotheby Parke Bernet catalog #3966 (1977), #114.

TO: Dorothy Parker
April 1934

Inscription in *Tender Is the Night*. Bruccoli
Baltimore, Maryland(?)

Splendid presentation

Dear Dotty

This is better
than the magazine

Love Always
Scott

Dorothy Parker
c/o The New Yorker

TO: Carl Van Vechten
April 1934

Inscription in *Tender Is the Night*.
Yale University
Baltimore, Maryland (?)

Dear Carl:

Glad you liked This is
the thing
better than the
serialyzed version

Scott Fitzgerald

FROM: Carl Van Vechten TLS, 1 p. Scrapbook. Princeton University
April 1934

Dear Scott, Thanks for sending me Tender is the Night. I read it at once and it seems to me to be a very poignant book. I was swept almost at once into the undertow of meanings and feelings. It is by no means as clear as Gatsby, but very possibly it is even a greater performance. There are passages which are almost unbearable in their deflected intensity. But I didnt believe the end. Anyway, congratulations.

Love to Zelda!

Someday when you are in town, please give me a ring and come in to be photographed. The number is Circle 7-3399.

best silver dolphins to you!

Wednesday. Carlo V. V.

Perhaps best of all I like the way your gallant creatures carry on against time, against space, almost against history.

TO: John O'Hara
April 1934

Inscription in *Tender Is the Night*.
Pennsylvania State University
Baltimore, Maryland (?)

Dear John:

May we meet
soon in equally
celebre but more
communicable
condition

Scott Fitz

FROM: John O'Hara TLS, 1 p. Scrapbook. Princeton University
April 1934

Dear Scott:

Thank you, for myself and my bibliophile grandchildren, for the inscribed copy of Tender Is the Night. The little bastards will have to be satisfied with cut leaves, because I am reading the novel once again, having read it in the magazine, in galley proof, and now. I will say now that Tender Is the Night is in the early stages of being my favorite book, even more than This Side of Paradise. As I told you once before, I don't read many books, but the same ones over again. Right now I can't think of any other book clearly enough to make a comparison between it and Tender Is the Night, and I guess in its way that is the most important thing I've ever said about any book.

You helped me finish my novel.[1] I finished it yesterday. The little we talked when you were in New York did it. I reasoned that the best parts of my novel will be said to derive from Fitzgerald, and I think I have muffed my story, but I became reconciled to having done that after talking to you and reading Tender Is the Night in proof. No one else can write like that, and I haven't tried, but the best parts of my novel are facile pupils of The Beautiful and Damned and The Great Gatsby. I was bushed, as Dottie[2] says, and the fact that I need money terribly was enough to make me say the hell with my book until you talked to me and seemed to accept me. So then I went ahead and finished my second-rate novel in peace. My message to the world is Fuck[3] it! I know this is not the right, the classical (as Hergesheimer would punctuate it), attitude, but I can write better than Louis Bromfield, Tiffany Thayer, Kathleen Norris, Erskine Caldwell or Mike Gold, so I am not the worst writer there is. I never won anything, except a German helmet for writing an essay on Our Flag, and a couple of Father Lasance's My Prayer Book's for spelling bees.

Please look me up when you come to New York, and thank you for the book.

John O'Hara

[1] *Appointment in Samarra* (1934).
[2] Dorothy Parker.
[3] Fitzgerald crossed out this word.

TO: Howard Coxe[1] TLS, 1 p. Princeton University

1307 Park Avenue,
Baltimore, Maryland,
April 15, 1934.

Dear Hungry:

There wasn't the faintest intention of using you as a character in my novel. There was only an intention of reproducing what was just about the rottenest thing that ever happened to me in my life.[2] I don't think that anyone would possibly associate the character of Collis Clay[3] with you; nor do I think that it recapitulates in any way what happened during that eventful night. I must say, however, that having gone through hell on that occasion, I am often groggy about recalling it, and I do remember, through the dim midst of blood, that it was you as well as Zelda who helped me out of jail.

The fact that I happened to remember a breach of tact on your part at the time springs probably from a quarrel we had a month and a half later, which I resented very deeply, perhaps unjustly, perhaps because I was still a little cuckoo on account of the shock of the beating.

But I hope that when we met years afterwards in the Ritz bar (I believe you were with George Piper) that the thing was written off as far as I was concerned, because I don't believe in carrying on old quarrels, and have gotten beyond the age when it gives me any satisfaction.

So, let me reassure you—my use of *Collis Clay* was purely a part of my artistic purpose in the book (remember, for instance, I started him in Paris, and this was *before* I had any intention of associating him with the character in Rome). And so, there is no question of renewing old grudges on my part, and you can show this letter to anybody.

Also, if this does not seem a satisfactory account for what I have written, I will be glad to meet you at any place at any time and make what proper physical amends you might deem necessary.

What you did that night, as I say, I am perhaps not prepared to properly estimate.

In any case, I read your Florentine novel with the greatest delight, and have only failed to see the new book because of tremendous pressure of work.

So you see from the foregoing that the character was not intended to be any possible portrait of my impression of you, but simply was part of the (so called) artistic intention of the book.

With best wishes,

Scott

[1] Author of *Passage to the Sky* (1929), a novel set in Florence. Coxe graduated from Princeton in 1920 and had met Fitzgerald in Rome in 1924.

[2] Fitzgerald was beaten by the Roman police in 1924.

[3] In Book II, Ch. 21, of *Tender Is the Night* Dick Diver is beaten by the police in Rome after getting drunk with Collis Clay.

FROM: Malcolm Cowley TLS, 1 p. Scrapbook. Princeton University

April 13, 1934

Dear Scott:

I am reading snatches of "Tender is the Night"—one chapter here, one chapter there, as I usually do with novels before I can bring myself to sit down ambitiously and read them straight through. All I can say so far is that there are some swell side-shows in it. The one very near the end, of the English Countess and Mary North and the kick in the sailor pants, is absolutely immense. In spite of what you say, I think I ought to review the book myself[1] rather than pass it along to one of the young guys who would ask why you weren't a proletarian novelist. I am sure to be late with it, because I am just finishing up the last six pages of my own book.[2] The hungry linotype machines are now eating the rest of it.

Thanks a lot for your list of neglected novels.[3] The next time you jump into New York, U.S.A., let me know you are in town instead of sitting mournfully at Tony's.

As ever,
Malcolm

[1] In his review in *The New Republic* (6 June 1934) Cowley said that some of the characters in *Tender Is the Night* are "self-contradictory" because Fitzgerald had changed his attitudes during the long period of working on the novel.

[2] *Exile's Return* (1934).

[3] "Good Books That Almost Nobody Has Read," *The New Republic* (18 April 1934), 283. Fitzgerald's list included *Miss Lonelyhearts, Sing Before Breakfast, I Thought of Daisy, Through the Wheat.*

TO: Maxwell Perkins | TLS, 1 p. Princeton University

1307 Park Avenue,
Baltimore, Maryland,
April 15, 1934.

Dear Max:

I got swell personal letters from James Branch Cabel, Carl Vanvechten, Shane Leslie, John O'Hara, and various members of the New Yorker crowd, but don't think I would care to quote them—especially as the press has been so profuse in using big names. After all, a letter is written in a few minutes and a man may change his opinion the next minute on such a detail as his opinion of, or reaction from, a work of fiction. And while I believe that this praise has been sincere, I do not think that they (any more than myself) would want to be quoted until they have had time for mature reflection.

So I think that all the personal stuff that has come in had better be buried.

As ever,
Scott

FROM: Zelda Fitzgerald | ALS, 3 pp. Princeton University
After 12 April 1934 | Craig House, Beacon, New York

Dearest D.O.:

I was afraid you might worry about some of the silly reviews[1] which I have not seen until to-day *Please don't* All the opinion which you respect has said everything you would like to have said about the book. It is not a novel about the simple and the inarticulate, nor are such a fitting subject for literature one of whose primary functions is to enrich the human mind. Anybody granted a certain talent can express direct action, or even emotion segregated from the activities of the world of their day but to present the growth of a human tragedy resultant from social conditions is a big feat. To me, you have done it well and at the same time preserved the more simple beauties of penetrating poignancy to be found in the use of exquisite prose.

Don't worry about critics—what sorrows have they to measure by or what lilting happiness with which to compare those ecstatic passages?

The atomists who followed Democritus said that quantity was what differentiated one thing from another—not quality—so critics will have to rise one day to the high points of good books. They cannot always live on reproductions of their own emotions in simple enough settings not to distract them: the poor boy having a hard time which is all very beautiful because of the poverty, etc.

It's a swell heart-breaking book, because the prose compels you to respond to the active situations—which is as it should be.

I am very worried about the finances. PLEASE don't hesitate to do *anything* that would relieve the strain on you.

Love
Zelda

[1] The reviews of *Tender Is the Night* were mixed, with several critics expressing confusion at the structure of the novel.

FROM: Zelda Fitzgerald
After 12 April 1934

ALS, 4 pp. Princeton University
Craig House, Beacon, New York

Dearest Do-Do:

I was so worried that you would be upset about some of those reviews—What critics know about the psycholocgy of a psychiatrist, I don't know, but the ones I saw seemed absurd, taking little account of the fact that a novel not in 18 volumes *can't* cover everything but must rely on the indicative You know yourself that as people yours are moving and heart-rending creations; as instruments of your artistic purpose they arrive at an importance which they would otherwise not have had, and that is the function of characters in a novel, which is, after all, a way of looking at life Do you suppose you could get Menken to write an intelligent review? The rest do not seem to know what they think beyond the fact that they have never thought of such problems before. And *don't* let them discourage you. It is a swell evokation of an epoch and a very masterly presentation of tragedies sprung from the beliefs (or lack of them) of those times which bloomed from the seeds of despair planted by the war and of the circumstance dependent on the adjustment of philosophies—Woolcot might be good to review it, since he had some appreciation of the spectacle which it presents, but I have seen some very silly and absurd commentaries of his lately, and he may have succumbed to the pseudo-radical formulas of Kaufman and Gershwin by now.[1]

Let Bromfield feed their chaotic minds on the poppy-seed of farm-youth tragedies and let them write isolated epics lacking any epic quality save reverence Yours is a story taking place behind the scenes, and I only hope that you will not forget that most of the audience has never been there—

Anyway, they all seem to realize that much thought and a fine equipment has gone into its making and maybe—if they only could understand—

D.O.—darling—having reached the people you wanted to reach, what more can you ask? Show man ship is an incidental consideration, after all—they have its glitterring sequins in the circus and the Hippodrome and critics yelling for more in literature seems a little like babies crying for things they can't have between meals—put card-board cuffs on their elbows—Those antiquated methods are the only ones I know.

XXXX

Since writing your letter has come. Of cource, I missed all but a few reviews. Bill Warren has a swell sense of the dramatic and I hope he'll separate out the points that will appeal to Mr. Mayer.[2] My advice is to revert to the money-triangle as you can't possibly use the incest. Or make the man a weak and charming figure from the first, always gravitating towards the center of things: which would lead him, when he was in the clinic, to Nicole and later to Rosemary. Regret could be the motif of the last section—Naturally, it's only advice, and I don't know if a male star would like to play something so far removed from Tarzan and those things about the desert where people are so brave, and only minor figures make mistakes

Love
Zelda

[1] Alexander Woollcott did not review *Tender Is the Night*. George S. Kaufman collaborated with George Gershwin on *Of Thee I Sing*.

[2] Charles Marquis Warren was working on a screenplay of *Tender Is the Night* that Fitzgerald hoped to sell to MGM.

FROM: Zelda Fitzgerald
April 1934

ALS, 4 pp. Princeton University
Craig House, Beacon, New York

Dearest Scott:

I am glad you did not let those undiscerning reviews upset you—You have the satisfaction of having written a tragic and poetic personal drama against the background of an excellent presentation of the times we matured in. You know that I have always felt that the chief function of the artist was to inspire *feeling* and certainly "Tender" did that. What people will live on for the next ten years I do not know: because, with the synchronization of light and sound and color (still embryonicly on display at the world's Fair) there may be a tremendous revision of aesthetic judgments and responses. Some of the later movies have cinematic effects unachievable with a brush—all of which tends to a communistic conception of art, I suppose. In this case, I writing might become the most individualistic of all expressions, or a sociological organ.

Anyway, your book is a sustained and exalted piece of prose—

Bill Warren, in my opinion, is a silly man to get to transcribe its subtleties to a metier that is now commanding the highest talents: because people will be *looking* thus expecting to be carried along by visual emotional developments as well as story and you will be robbed of the inestimable value of your prose to raise and cut and break the tension. But you know better than I. In the movies, one symbolic device is worth a thousand feet of explanation (granted you haven't at your disposal those expert technicians who have turned out some of the late stuff) Go to see Ruth Chatterton and Adolph Menjou in the last thing about murder.[1] It's a swell straight psychological story—I simply thought that with all the stuff in your book so much could have been done: the funicular, the beach umbrellas, the garden high above the world, and in the end the two people swimming in darkness.

When Mrs O. sends

1) Dramatic Technique

2) Golden Treasury

3) Pavlowa's Life

4) The Book on Modern Art, I will return Scottie's Treasury. Until then, I have nothing to read as I can't stand the Inferno or the pseudo-noble-simplicity of that book Dorothy P. gave me.

Won't you ask her to? Also the paint from Webers. She said she would—They would mail it.

Love
Zelda—

[1] *Journal of a Crime.*

FROM: Zelda Fitzgerald
After 12 April 1934

ALS, 4 pp. Princeton University
Craig House, Beacon, New York

Dearest Do-Do:

I'm so glad all the good people liked your book. It's swell about Mary Column and Seldes[1] and I can't understand your not using Elliot's[2] opinion of your works in the adds. That man J.A.D.[3] in the Times is the one I told you dismissed a novel completely on moral grounds not long ago. He is an imbecile and it would be a good thing if somebody attacked him. He knows nothing of art, aestheticly or sociologicly or of anything that's going on in the world to-day. However, you had already had a good review in the Times[4] so what ho! Only it does make me sore to give people books to review who have no idea of the purpose behind them or of their artistic intent. I Hope you didn't mind; it is such a fine book, as everybody else seems unanimously agreed.

Cary wrote that Ernest was back in N.Y.; that he had been to see my pictures. Why don't you ask him down? You've got more room than people in the house and Mrs. Owens would get you a maid. He also said the Murphys bought the acrobats. I am going to paint a picture for the Murphy's and they can choose as those acrobats seem, somehow, singularly inappropriate to them and I would like them to have one they liked. Maybe they aren't like I think they are but I don't see why they would like that Buddhistic suspension of mass and form and I will try to paint some mood that their garden has conveyed.

I wish I could see the review in the New Republic, Forum, etc. Won't you send them? I'll mail them back immediately.

And don't pay any attention to that initialled moth-hole in the Times.

Apparently the Tribune man[5] still believes that movie stars got there via the gutters of Les Miserables—But we can't buy him a ticket to Hollywood, and, on the whole, it was an intelligent and favorable review—and he liked the book even if he didn't know what it was about psychologicly. He will like it better when he reads it again.

I hope Ernest liked it; I guess Morley Callaghan is sore at having his adds reduced.[6] Please send me a copy—

Love
Zelda

[1] Mary Colum reviewed *Tender Is the Night* in *Forum and Century*; Gilbert Seldes' review appeared in the *New York Evening Journal*.

[2] T. S. Eliot.

[3] J. Donald Adams in the *New York Times Book Review*.

[4] By John Chamberlain.

[5] Lewis Gannett.

[6] Callaghan's novel *Such Is My Beloved* was published by Scribners in the same season as *Tender Is the Night*.

TO: Zelda Fitzgerald — TL(CC), 3 pp. Princeton University

1307 Park Avenue,
Baltimore, Maryland,
April 26, 1934.

Forgive me for dictating this letter instead of writing it directly, but if you could see my desk at the moment and the amount of stuff that has come in you would understand.

The thing that you have to fight against is defeatism of any kind. You have no reason for it. You have never had really a melancholy temperament, but, as your mother said: you have always been known for a bright, cheerful, extraverting attitude upon life. I mean *especially* that you share none of the melancholy point of view which seems to have been the lot of Anthony and Marjorie. You and I have had wonderful times in the past, and the future is still brilliant with possibilities if you will keep up your morale, and try to think that way. The outside world, the political situation, etc., is still gloomy and it *does* effect everybody directly, and will inevitably reach you indirectly, but try to separate yourself from it by some fotm of mental hygiene—if necessary, a self-invented one.

Let me reiterate that I don't want you to have too much traffic with my book, which is a melancholy work and seems to have haunted most of the reviewers. *I feel very strongly about your re-reading it.* It represents certain phases of life that are now over. We are certainly on some upsurging wave, even if we don't yet know exactly where it's heading.

There is no feeling of gloom on your part that has the *slightest* legitimacy. Your pictures have been a success, your heath has been very much better, according to the doctors—and the only sadness is the living without you, without hearing the notes of your voice with its particular intimacies of inflection.

You and I have been happy; we haven't been happy just once, we've been happy a thousand times. The chances that the spring, that's for everyone, like in the popular songs, may belong to us too—the chances are pretty bright at this time because as usual, I can carry most of contemporary literary opinion, liquidated, in the hollow of my hand—and when I do, I see the swan floating on it and—I find it to be you and you only. But, Swan, float lightly because you are a swan, because by the exquisite curve of your neck the gods gave you some special favor, and even though you fractured it running against some man-made bridge, it healed and you sailed onward. Forget the past—what you can of it, and turn about and swim back home to me, to your haven for ever and ever—even though it may seem a dark cave at times and lit with torches of fury; it is the best refuge for you—turn gently in the waters through which you move and sail back.

This sounds allegorical but is *very* real. I want you here. The sadness of the past is with me always. The things that we have done together and the awful splits that have broken us into war survivals in the past stay like a sort of atmosphere around any house that I inhabit. The good things and the first years together, and the good months that we had two years ago in Montgomery will stay with me forever, and you should feel like I do that they can be renewed, if not in a new spring, then in a new summer. I love you my darling, darling.

P.S. Did I tell you that, among others, Adele Lovett came in and bought a picture and so did Louise Perkins and the Tommy Daniels from St. Paul? Will see that the Dick Myers get one free.

FROM: Zelda Fitzgerald
April 1934

ALS, 4 pp. Princeton University
Craig House, Beacon, New York

Dearest Do-Do:

Thanks for your long sweet letter: I have just finished part I of your book again. It is the most beautiful prose, without a wasted or irrelevant word. It is also very moving and a fine presentation of those sun lit places, which its bright glare finally faded and streaked—perhaps to dimmer nuances. In fact, Do Do, it's a swell book and well imbued with that sense of impersonal tragedy, as good books should be: of individual happiness drained to fill out the schemas for momentary pleasure-theories. Also, you have kept beautifully intact the personalities against so vivid a mise en-scene that any lesser creations would have been submerged in the glitter. It is a beautiful book.

You seem afraid that it will make me recapitulate the past: remember, that at that time, I was immersed in something else—and I guess most of life is a re-hashing of the tragedies and happinesses of which it consisted in days before we started to promulgate reasons for their being so Of cource, it is a haunting book—everything good is haunting because it calls to light something new in our consciousness

Scott: this place is most probably hidiously expensive I *do not want you to struggle* through another burden like the one in Switzerland for my sake. You write too well. Also, you know that I live much within myself and would feel less strongly now than under normal circumstances about whatever you wanted to do. You have not got the right, for Scottie's sake, and for the sake of letters to make a drudge of yourself for me.

I'm awfully glad the pictures go well: you know the ones that are yours and I gave those white anenomies to Dr Rennie. Also I do not want that portrait of Egorowa sold. Cary has been so nice—Ask what he would like and I will try to paint it for him. I have just finished one of the Plage at Antibes. Maybe you'd like to swop it for your foot-ball players—though it is not so good—

Love
Zelda.

FROM: Robert Benchley

TLS, 1 p. Scrapbook. Princeton University
April 29th, 1934

Dear Scott:

It was damned nice of you to write in your book for me. I don't remember ever having said anything that appears on page 25,[1] or on any other page, but I would have given my two expensivly-filled eye-teeth to have written just one page of the book.

Honestly, Scott, I think that it is a beautiful piece of work, not only technically, but emotionally. I haven't had a book get hold of me like that for years. As a journeyman writer, I can not even conceive of anyone's being able to do that scene in the Guaranty Trust, just from the point of view of sheer manipulation of words, to say nothing of the observation contained in it. And the feeling of the whole book is so strong upon me, even now, that I am oppressed by a not-quite-vague-enough fear that several people I am fond of are very unhappy.

I hope that you, yourself, are not any unhappier than is called for in the general blueprint specifications for Living. Please don't be. Anyone who gets down on his stomach and crawls all afternoon around a yard playing tin-soldiers with a lot of kids, shouldn't be made too unhappy. I cry a little every time I think of you that afternoon in Antibes.

Thanks again for thinking of me, and look me up the next time you come to town. My number is Vanderbilt 3-6498.

Gratefully,
Bob.

[1] Book I, Ch. 4, of *Tender Is the Night:* the conversation on the beach among Abe, Mary, and Nicole. The copy sent to Benchley is unlocated.

FROM: John Dos Passos
April 1934

ALS, 3 pp. Scrapbook. Princeton University

Dear Scott—

Reading Tender Is the Night—the book—I got entirely a different impression from reading the couple of [ ] in Scribners. It's so tightly knit together that it cant be read in pieces. The layout and construction of the damn thing is enormously impressive, all building up to a final paragraph that'll certainly be quoted in all the future textbooks. The only thing of that sort that disappointed me was the end of book II—where Rosemary first catches on that there's something wierd about Nicole. Something about the phrasing 'verbal inhumanity' threw me off the track. The whole conception of the book is enormous—and so carefully understated that—so far as I know—not a single reviewer discovered it. I think probably the less the reviewers can find out about a book the better it is. The part I liked best was the stuff about the clinic in Zurich & Diver's clinic later—the chapter where Nicole goes off her head at the little carnival is a knockout. I like Baby Warren & the English bitch best among the characters. For some reason I couldn't believe very thoroughly in the main people—how much that is due to knowing some of the models from which the various phases were sketched I dont know. For some reason all American books about us in Europe make me feel as if I were reading

The Marble Faun[1]—I got that feeling from The Sun Also Rises & I get the feeling from Tender is the Night—I don't know if that's entirely a knock, but I think it is. Still even Turgeniev's people aren't so hot when they're in foreign parts. Maybe characters are like the President of the United States & go to pieces when they leave home. But as the picture of the collapse of one of the great after the war imperial illusions, it's great. The way you first lay in the pretty picture and then start digging under the surface is immense—and gives you a kind of junction of your two types of writing that ought to be damned useful in the future: the Sat. Eve. Post wish fulfilment stuff as a top layer and the real investigation of living organisms underneath. I think you pulled it off in every detail except the main characters—& after all most main characters are a lot of dummies (if it had pulled off the main characters it would have been in the War & Peace class) I certainly felt impressed when I finished it, and I must admit that I was enormously thrown off by the beginning (that later turns out to have been very good). By the time I was half way through I was entirely under the book's thumb, in spite of it being written in a style I'm a little leary of, and in spite of continuous doubts about the people. It's a damned impressive piece of work—Hope to see you in Baltimore Friday or Saturday—we are going down to assist Horsley Gantt in a matrimonial venture—

Yrs
Dos

[1] By Nathaniel Hawthorne (1860).

FROM: Cary Ross ALS, 4 pp. Princeton University

525 East 86th Street
N.Y.C.
May 4 '34

Dear Scott

I figure my expenses on the exhibition to be around $\$150^{\underline{00}}$. I sold four of Marian Hines' photographs for $\$15^{\underline{00}}$ a piece + she insisted that I deduct her share of expenses from the amount I had taken in, so I kept $\$45^{\underline{00}}$ and sent her a check for $\$15^{\underline{00}}$.

I have so far collected $\$250^{\underline{00}}$ for Zelda's pictures as follows:

The Gerald Murphys—oil "Chinese Theater"	—$\$200^{\underline{00}}$
Dorothy Parker—two water color drawings	$35^{\underline{00}}$
Mrs. Thomas Daniel—water color drawing	$15^{\underline{00}}$
Total	$\$250^{\underline{00}}$

I am enclosing check for $\$150^{\underline{00}}$ representing this amount less $\$100^{\underline{00}}$ which I have kept for my expenses. I am still owed $78.75, as follows:

Thomas Hitchcock Jr.	$\$15^{\underline{00}}$
Mrs. Robert Lovett	$16^{\underline{25}}$
Muriel Draper	$15^{\underline{00}}$
Mrs. Maxwell Perkins	$32^{\underline{50}}$
Total	$78.75

And will of course turn this amount over to you when collected. Mrs. Perkins took two water-color drawings. "The Plaid Shirt" and "Spring in the Country" preferring these two to the "Russian Stable," oil, on second thought, she told me on the telephone early this week.

I am delivering all pictures sold to-day or to-morrow with careful labels giving name of artist, title, when + where exhibited on the back, but am holding "Au Claire de la Lune" purchased by Hitchcock until we can arrange about Zelda's signature which he requested.

It is quite possible that I may be able to take it to her to Beacon to sign sometime between May 14 and May 26 if that turns out eventually to be the best way to have it done. I would like to see the place in any case—Zelda writes me that it is so pretty there.

If I don't hear from you in the mean time I will try to reach you by telephone in Baltimore some time the week-end of March 12—+ I wonder if *High Quist* will win the Preakness? I hope I can get a tip from Mrs. Owens before the race.

Ever yours
Cary

Oh I forget to say that Mabel Luhan[1] wrote from the west that she would like to buy Zelda's oil "Portrait in Thorns" if it weren't too expensive. I wrote her that I had it priced at $\$200^{\underline{00}}$ but that I remembered Zelda saying once she did not want to sell it + would have to inquire of you + Zelda + let her know later—which I will.

C.R.

[1] Mabel Dodge Luhan, friend of writers and painters. "Portrait in Thorns" was a painting of Fitzgerald with a crown of thorns. Mrs. Luhan apparently did not buy this portrait, and it remains unlocated. See James Thurber, "Scott in Thorns," *The Reporter* (17 April 1951).

TO: Maxwell Perkins Wire. Princeton University

BALTIMORE MD 215P MAY 11 1934

FINISHING POST STORY STOP CANT EXPECT PAY UNTIL NEXT WEEK END STOP MUST GET ZELDA OUT OF HOCK AT THAT EXORBITANT CLINIC AND ENTER HER HERE IN REASONABLE PLACE STOP CAN I RAISE SIX HUNDRED FROM YOU ON MOVIE BASIS OR ANY OTHER EVEN MORTGAGE ON THIS STORY

F SCOTT FITZGERALD

249P

FROM: Matthew Josephson[1] TLS, 1 p. Scrapbook. Princeton University

Gaylordsville, Conn.
May 15, 1934

Dear Mr. Fitzgerald,

I was delighted to find your book waiting for me when I returned about two weeks ago from a long stay in the very geography it evokes. I waited until I could read it before writing you about your kindness in thinking of me and saying all those nice things about one of my things.[2]

I found my mind going back to the novel repeatedly, several days after I had put it aside. It certainly looks like the best thing you've done since This Side of Paradise—and of course utterly different. (I have always hoped for the opportunity to tell you that this young novel is a landmark in the history of morals as well as literature, not to mention its general riotousness.) In Tender Is the Night, it is significant that the author changes and grows. I felt that the first half represented the best work in it, its best writing. Both selection of materials and style seemed a little less well in the second half, roughly speaking, (almost too roughly), though there were pages I liked a good deal there too. But throughout the book the ambitious form or structure lent importance and unity, in a degree not found in your other novels. The apotheosis of Nicole accompanied by the steady decline and fall of Diver made a contrapuntal music; a very strange "situation" (such as old Henry James would have loved, and certainly would have concealed, restrained and developed in the same way). Light fell backward over the whole book, from the very end.

Rosemary was for me the best characterization, because I have always felt so much mystification about the type. Diver, who was achieved as a tragic figure, after all, was also full of a special interest for me. And a piece of experimental writing in a middle, transitional passage—the retrospective airplaine–honeymoon flight across resort Europe struck me as an awfully good, poetic performance; by itself, as good a thing of its kind as I have seen anywhere in recent years.

Thanks very much again for a novel that is not easily classified nor easily forgotten.

Matthew Josephson

[1] Critic, editor, and biographer.

[2] Fitzgerald had sent Josephson an inscribed copy of *Tender Is the Night*: "Dear Mathew Josephson Save for the swell organization of 'Zola' + your reproduction of it, this would never have reached the stalls—I'll skip the obvious remarks with best wishes + high hopes for you Scott Fitzgerald." (University of Rochester Library) Josephson's *Zola and His Time* (1928) included the plans for *Les Rougon-Macquarts*.

FROM: Richard L. Simon TLS, 1 p. Princeton University

May 16th, 1934.

Dear Mr. Fitzgerald:

My horrible signature embarrasses me. I wrote to you as a reader of your book. Now you forge my signature on an envelope and ask me, dear sir, who are you? That's the embarrassing part. I am Richard L. Simon, known to the trade as Simon of Simon and Schuster. In emerging from the anonymity of an undecipherable signature, I can only that I wrote you the other day, as I do now, not as a publisher, but as if I were a lady of the lady's club of Grand Rapids who thinks you are a grand writer and has the impulse to tell you so.

Cordially yours,
Richard L. Simon

Mr. F. Scott Fitzgerald,
1307 Park Avenue,
Baltimore, Maryland.

TO: T. S. Eliot TL(CC), 1 p. Princeton University

1307 Park Avenue,
Baltimore, Maryland,
May 21, 1934.

Dear Eliot:

I want to thank you for your generous remark about my work which you permitted Scribner's to use and also to apologize and regret terribly that they used a line from a personal letter of yours on the jacket.[1] They promised me that they wanted to use some material like that only to show to their salesmen and I was shocked when I saw what they had done. If Chatto & Windus would be inclined to use the American edition blurbs I think you could head it off by phoning them to cut out the one about Henry James. I know how I would feel if anyone used as publicity what I had written in a personal letter. With very best wishes always and a great desire to see you again.

Faithfully,

[1] The dust jacket of *Tender Is the Night* quoted Eliot: "I have been waiting impatiently for another book by Mr. Scott Fitzgerald, with more eagerness and curiosity than I should feel towards the work of any of his contemporaries, except that of Mr. Ernest Hemingway." At the time of *The Great Gatsby* Eliot wrote Fitzgerald that the novel "seems to me to be the first step that American fiction has taken since Henry James."

TO: Dr. William Elgin[1] TL(CC), 3 pp. Princeton University

1307 Park Avenue,
Baltimore, Maryland,
May 21, 1934.

Dear Dr. Elgin:

While I covered most of the old ground on Saturday there are a couple of immediate things that I'd like to go into. I don't think I stressed how much such a matter as swimming means to my wife and her morale. It will be convenient for my secretary, Mrs. Owens, to pick her up there any morning, take her for a swim and deliver her back in two hours. I stress this because I think the swimming really saved her for two summers here and I know that the skiing had a tremendous effect on her in Switzerland while certain elements of ergo-therapy[2] are not very effective with her because of her poor eye sight and consequent occasional headaches.

I will of course abide by any decision of yours not to see her for a couple of weeks, but in regard to this remember that I have only seen her twice in two months and neither time long enough to have had the faintest nervous friction with her—and sometimes I have a very strong power of raising her morale when she inclines toward apathy.

I inclose a note to her on practical matters which you would be kind to have delivered.

I must tell you that while I have been very convinced and even dogmatic about the idea that she should not write serious fiction at present still I am not unamenable to change in that regard. For it there is to be said that she grew better in the three months at Hopkins where it was allowed and she grew apathetic in the two months at Craig House where she was continually disuaded. Also, it provides a direction and might lessen the sense that I am frustrating her.

The things against it, such as reawakening betes noires, my inability to keep her writing within reasonable bounds at home, her inability to take disappointments healthily, etc. I went over with you Friday but would appreciate it if you would weigh these factors, one set against the other, because there you can control automatically the time she works at it and because even in the broader aspect of the matter my initial position may be absolutely wrong.

[1] Psychiatrist on the staff of Sheppard and Enoch Pratt Hospital in Towson, Md.
[2] Work therapy.

TO: Samuel Marx — TLS, 2 pp. Princeton University

1307 Park Avenue,
Baltimore, Maryland,
May 21, 1934.

Dear Sam:

Apropos of a proposed treatment of my book which went to you (by the way *Publishers Weekly* lists it as national third best seller this week) you will remember that I collaborated on that first treatment with a kid named Charles Warren who has shown a remarkable talent for the theatre in writing, composing and directing two shows which have packed them in and had repeat weeks here in Baltimore and in Princeton. My intention, if *Tender is the Night* was sold immediately, was to back him in going out there and seeing if he could help round it into shape. So far the offers have been unsatisfactory, considering the work put on it—nevertheless, Warren has planned to brave Hollywood even without the permit to enter which a definite connection would be to him. He will be without acquaintance there save for such letters as I can give him. I would be much in your debt if you will see him, give him what advice you can about finding an opening. His talents are amazingly varied—he writes, composes, draws and has this aforesaid general gift for the theatre—and I have a feeling that he should fit in there somewhere within a short time and should go close to the top, in fact I haven't believed in anybody so strongly since Ernest Hemingway. Incidentally, he is not a highbrow, his instincts are toward practical showmanship, which is why I engaged him, as a sort of complement to me.

Perhaps you could arrange to let him look around the lot for a few hours, lend him a few sample treatments that he could take back to his hotel and study and also some story that he could work on without salary.[1]

With best regards to the madam and to yourself.
Ever your friend,
Scott Fitzgerald

[1] Warren did not succeed in finding employment as a screenwriter at this time, but later became a writer-producer for television.

TO: Zelda Fitzgerald TL(CC), 4 pp. Princeton University

1307 Park Avenue,
Baltimore, Maryland,
May 31, 1934.

Talked with Dr. Murdoch[1] on the phone and he thought that you were worrying about my worrying about you—if you can get that complicated point. I am always worrying about you and Scottie when you are not near me but that is simply a temperamental peculiarity that I have gotten used to. It is just worrying for worrying's sake and is not founded on any reality. Actually I am very cheered by the thought that you are within hearing distance again and am looking forward to the time when you will be closer that that. Life here has been very tranquil. Have made one of my usual mistakes in judgment in embarking on about five mutually exclusive enterprises: 1. a *Post story*,[2] 2. a second story for the *Red Book*,[3] 3. a funny offer from United Artists to jazz up some episode from Cellini's biography to help the sale of the picture release which is imminent,[4] 4. an idea of staging Ring's short plays—which has just come out with Gilbert Seldes doing the editing.[5] I am thinking of lopping off the two last and getting down to business.

The trip to Virginia Beach was a complete flop as far as weather was concerned—we ran into what amounted to a very dismal mistral—and while, as you know, I always love to see the Taylor clan, things were all indoors. Perhaps it was just as well because Scottie, being inflicted with poison ivy on her bottom, didn't have to see other people using the surf for a good time. However, I sat around and smoked too much and got no special profit out of the trip.

While I think of it I am enclosing a letter from Tommy Hitchcock[6] which came with his check for the drawing he bought. I opened it by mistake.

To go back to domestic matters, Scottie is in good health generally and my plan is, roughly, to send her for a week that will elapse between her examinations and the beginning of a camp down to Norfolk with Cousin Ceci who would devote good attention to her and to board them at some reasonable hotel at Virginia Beach. That is to avoid a whole week here where I would have to spend much of my time playing nurse maid for her because I do not entirely like the way the children of this neighborhood behave when they run loose and the business of transportation out to the suburban districts is a little onerous especially on Saturday afternoons and Sundays when Mrs. Owens is not here. By the way she has just been invited to spend the week-end after examinations with the Ridgelys. About the camps, she seems to want to go to one of the bigger ones so I suppose she will go to either Aloha or Wyonegonic, both of which I started to investigate last year. I am still hoping that we can go to Europe toward the latter half of the summer, even if only for six weeks, whether we decide to go alone or leave Scottie in camp.

We went to tea at the Woodwards yesterday. I got into a heavy political argument with a Hitlerite. Then our incessant friend, Madam Swann,[7] telephoned for Scottie and me to come there for dinner, which we did and which reinforced my feeling that she is a beheaded poullet trying to do her best but without any consistent method.

Honey, may I ask you seriously to control your reading, not going in so much for heavy books or books that refer you back to those dark hours in Paris? I know what ill effects on my ease, sleep, appetite, etc. can be caused by getting disturbed by something I've read and I should guess that would be doubly true in a case like yours where you are trying to get a real rest cure. However, the doctors will probably keep an eye on that.

[1] Dr. Harry M. Murdock, psychiatrist on the staff of the University of Maryland School of Medicine and College of Physicians and Surgeons, Baltimore.

[2] Possibly "No Flowers" (July 1934).

[3] The second Philippe story, "The Count of Darkness" (June 1935).

[4] Fitzgerald did not act on this offer.

[5] This project did not develop.

[6] War hero and polo player whom Fitzgerald greatly admired.

[7] Baltimore journalist Rita Swann; wife of artist Don Swann.

FROM: Malcolm Cowley — TLS, 1 p. Scrapbook. Princeton University
May 1934

Dear Scott:

Here is the review. I'm not especially proud of it. After waiting all this time, and writing it against your wishes, I should have given you something better. I wanted to write you a long letter about the book, which I liked more and was more deeply impressed by than the review seems to say.—Outside of all I said here, I think the double introduction interfered with the novel more than anything else—I mean the presenting of all the characters through Rosemary's eyes and then the going back to tell the story from 1919 to 1924; there is confusion of time here that bothers most of the readers with whom I have talked. Wouldn't it have been better to have the story develop directly from Rosemary's meeting with the Divers?[1] As soon as Dick fell in love with Rosemary his first instinct would be to tell her all about himself, even at the risk of a spiritual infidelity to his wife—that would have obviated the second introduction. You were certainly right in saying that the sideshows were fine—some of them are unforgettable.

My own book is out today, and I'm getting a swell run-around from the critics. I wish some of them had read it.

If I pass through Baltimore around the first of July, is there any chance of my seeing you?

As ever,
Malcolm

[1] Fitzgerald subsequently attempted to reorganize a copy of *Tender Is the Night* into straight chronological order. This edition was edited by Cowley in 1951 as "The Author's Final Version."

FROM: Zelda Fitzgerald — ALS, 2 pp. Princeton University
After 9 June 1934 — Sheppard and Enoch Pratt Hospital, Towson, Md.

Dearest Do-Do—

I was amused to read in the New Yorker the praise of Gilbert for his recognition of Ring.[1] Never mind: your biography will be written. Dr. Ellgin said you wanted me to read more so I am reading: The Alchemist and Edward II——also I am absorbed in the travel adds. For $600 (2) dollars we could go to Oberamagrau, tourist class via Berlin + Munich—including all expenses for a 3 wks trip. *We could!* I look nostalgicly on all the sun-burned people in the advertizements lolling on boats and beaches and think of the good times we only half appreciated. They are so young and soignées in the pictures.

It seems rather Proustian to be rambling these deep shades again so close to La Paix. It makes me sad, but it is a lovely landscape—the trees, and clouds like cotton-candy, very still and festive about the clover. And I think of your book and it haunts me. So beautiful a book.

I wish we could spend July by the sea, browning ourselves and feeling water-weighted hair flow behind us from a dive. I wish our gravest troubles were the summer gnats. I wish we were hungry for hot-dogs and dopes[2] and it would be nice to smell the starch of summer linens and the faint odor of talc in blistering bath-houses. Or we could go to the japanese gardens with Kay Laurel and waste a hundred dollars staging conceptions of gaiety. We could lie in long citroneuse beams of the five-o'clock sun on the plage at Juan-les-Pins and hear the sound of the drum and piano being scooped out to sea by the waves. Dust and alfalfa in Alabama, pines and salt at Antibes, the lethal smells of city streets in summer, buttered pop-corn and axel grease at Coney Island and Virginia beaches—and the sick-sweet smells of old gardens at night, verbena or phlox or night-blooming stock—we could see if all those are still there.

It is rather disquieting to read of the importance of bangs and linen hankerchiefs, new brands of perfume and new lines to bathing-suits in the papers. *I wish I had something*—D.O!

When are you coming to see me?

Love, darling and love to my sweet little Scottie
Zelda

[1] Clifton Fadiman had reviewed *First and Last* in the 9 June issue of *The New Yorker*.
[2] Coca-Cola spiked with aromatic spirits.

TO: Zelda Fitzgerald

TL, 4 pp. (incomplete; possibly not sent).
Princeton University

1307 Park Avenue,
Baltimore, Maryland,
June 13, 1934.

Dear Zelda:

I am dictating this letter because there is so much that it's got to cover and I want you to have it there for reference because each point is important.

First and foremost I called Perkins this morning on an idea that I have had for a long time which is the publication of a representative group of your short pieces.[1] I want to do this if only for the salutary effect on you of keeping your hand in during this period of inaction. I did not call Max with the idea of getting him to publish such a collection which, since he is committed to an amalgamation of mine for the same season, he naturally would shy away from it but with the idea that he could suggest a publisher who would take a chance on the idea. I break off here to include a suggestion for the general line up of the book:

Table of Contents

Introduction by F. Scott Fitzgerald (about 500 words)

I. Eight Women (These character sketches and stories appeared in *College Humor, Scribner's* and *Saturday Evening Post* between 1927 and 1931, one of them appeared under my name but actually I had nothing to do with it except for suggesting a theme and working on the proof of the completed manuscript. This same cooperation extends to other material gathered herein under our joint names, though often when published in that fashion I had nothing to do with the thing from start to finish except supplying my name.)

The Original Follies Girl	(about 2000 words)
The Girl the Prince Liked	" 2500 "
The Southern Girl	" 2250 "
The Girl with Talent	" 3500 "
The Millionaire's Girl	" 8000 "
Miss Bessie[2]	" 4000 "
A Couple of Nuts	" 4000 "

(There will also be joined to this two hitherto unpublished stories which are also character studies of modern females.)[3]

II. Three Fables[4] (estimated about 5000 words)

The Drought and the Flood
A Workman
The House

III. Recapitulation

Show Mr. and Mrs. F. to Number—
Auction Model 1934

All in all about 50,000 words. This will give you plenty of work for the next three or four weeks if you can find time for it, especially that item of the two possible stories which I am afraid will have to go through some more revision to measure up to the rest. I am having Mrs. Owens send you (a) All living copies of your Mary McCall story.

(b) All living copies of your Katherine Littlefield story.[5]

In the first case I think you have got to cut out the mystical element about the dogs because the story itself is so haunted by suggestion of more or less natural vice that the introduction of the supernatural seems excessive and breaks the pattern. In the second case my feeling is that it is largely a question of cutting "down to its bare bones." I am seldom wrong about the value of a narrative and feel that my continued faith in this one is not misplaced. It may take two workings over, but the first one is undoubtedly stripping it to its girders and then seeing what, if any, plaster you want to slap on it. These two stories would seem to be necessary to make up the bulk of a volume, the aim of which is to compete with such personal collections of miscellany as Dorothy Parker's, etc. The very fact that the material is deeply personal rather than detached and professional make it expedient that it be presented in some such way as this.

This letter has been interrupted by having a phone conversation with the small publisher (respectable, but with[6]

[1] The projected collection was not published.
[2] Published as "Miss Ella."
[3] Unpublished and unidentified.
[4] Unpublished.
[5] These two stories were not published.
[6] The rest of the page has been torn off.

FROM: Zelda Fitzgerald
After 13 June 1934

ALS, 3 pp. Princeton University
Sheppard and Enoch Pratt Hospital
Towson, Maryland

Dearest Do-Do:

Do-Do you are so sweet to do those stories for me. Knowing the energy and interest you have put into other people's work, I know how much trouble you make appear so easy. Darling—

I will correct the stories as soon as I can—though you know this is a very regimented system we live under with every hour accounted for and not much time for outside interests. There was a better, later version of the dance story—but maybe I can shift this one since I remember it.

You talk of the function of art. I wonder if anybody has ever got nearer the truth than Aristotle: he said that all emotions and all experience were common property—that the transposition of these into form was individual and art. But, God, it's so involved by whether you aim at direct or indirect appeals and whether the emotional or the cerebral is the most compelling approach, and whether the shape of the edifice or the purpose for which it is designated is paramount that my conceptions are in a sad state of flux. At any rate, it seems to me the artists business is to take a willing mind and guide it to hope or despair contributing *not* his interpretations but a glimpse of his honestly earned scars of battle and his rewards. I am still adamant against the interpretive school. Nobody but educators can show people how to think—but to open some new facet of the stark emotions or to preserve some old one in the grace of a phrase seem nearer the artistic end. You know how a heart will rise or fall to the lilt of an a-laden troche or the sonorous dell of an o—and where you will use these business secrets certainly depends on the author's special evaluations. That was what I was trying to accomplish with the book I began: I wanted to say "This is a love story—maybe not your love story—maybe not even mine, but this is what happened to one isolated person in love. There is no judgment."—I don't know—abstract emotion is difficult of transcription, and one has to find so many devices to carry a point that the point is too often lost in transit—

I wrote you a note which I lost containing the following facts

1) The Myers have gone to Antibes with the Murphys—

2) Malcom Cowley arrested for rioting in N.Y.

3) I drink milk, one glass of which I consider equal to six bananas under water or two sword-swallowings—

There didn't seem to be anything else to write you except that I love you. We have a great many activities of the kind one remembers pleasantly afterwards but which seem rather vague at the time like pea-shelling and singing. For some reason, I am very attached to this country-side. I love the clover fields and the click of base-ball bats in the deep green cup of the field and the sky as blue and idyllic as parts of your prose. I keep hoping that you will be in some of the cars that ruffle the shade of the sycamores. Dr. Ellgin said you would come soon.

It will be grand to see Mrs. Owens—I wish it were you and Scottie. Darling.

Don't you think "Eight Women" is too big a steal from Dreiser[1]—I like, ironicly, "My Friends" or "Girl Friends" better. Do you suppose I could design the jacket. It's very exciting.

My reading seems to have collapsed at "The Alchemist." I really don't care much for characters named for the cardinal sins or cosmic situations. However I will get on with it—

Thanks again about the book—and *everything*—In my file there are two other fantasies and the story about the judge to which I am partial—and I would be most grateful if you would read "Theatre Ticket"[2] to see if it could be sold to a magazine maybe—

Love
Zelda.

Why didn't you go to reunion?

Do you think the material is too dissimilar for a [co]llection? It worries me.

[1] Theodore Dreiser's *Twelve Men* (1919).
[2] Unidentified.

FROM: Zelda Fitzgerald
After 13 June 1934

ALS, 2 pp. Princeton University
Sheppard and Enoch Pratt Hospital
Towson, Maryland

Mon chère Monsieur:

Here are some titles—Maybe you can paste them on the unidentifiable bottles in the medicine cabinet if they don't seem to apply

1) Even Tenor
2) Rainy Sunday
3) How It Was.
4) Ways It Was.

I admit frankly that they are not much good, but then neither am I at quick inventions. I will let you know if the next brain storm should bring to light something more pertinent—

"Authors Wife" sounds as if it's an intimate revelation of the blacker side of how we writers live. Again I admit frankly it makes me sick. For your book,[1] would it be a good idea to add up how much those stories brought in and call the book "Eighty Thousand Dollars"—ho! Or "Words"—(sounds to experimental)—and I don't know what to call *anything*. Had I a pet canary, he should be nameless—Call it a day—There are some fine ideas for titles in the Victor record catalogue—which is where I found "Save Me the Waltz—"

Couldn't Scottie come swimming next time with Mrs Owens—if she's back? I keep hoping you'll show up but you don't—and neither does Christmas or other holidays before their time, I suppose.

I am become an expert seamstress and laundress and am, in fact, thoroughly equipped to make you exactly the kind of wife you most detest. However, I am going to read Karl Marx so we can give a parade if the day of exodus ever arrives—bombs on the house, and a cigar for every Lord Mayor you hit.

Well—

Recevez, Monsieur, mes felicitations les plus distinguées—

And many thanks for the perfectly useless check to Mrs Owens. Now that the blind tiger is no more, I couldn't think of any place to cash it so I tore it up as emotionally and dramaticly as $34.50 seemed to warrant—Of cource, a hundred would have made a better scene—

With deepest devotion—

Love
Zelda.

[1] Published as *Taps at Reveille* (1935).

FROM: Dr. O. L. Forel   TLS, 1 p.[1] Scrapbook. Princeton University

13 July 1934
Mr. F. Scott Fitzgerald
c/o Charles Scribner's Sons
New-York City

Dear Sir,

I am truly ashamed at having waited so long to thank you for the book that you sent me. I read it with great interest, particularly because of the observations that were made at Prangins and that you used. I congratulate you however for having been able to treat your subject freely by transposing reality into a world of fiction. I admit that I am always a little on the defense when I see laymen approach subjects as complicated as those that regard psychiatry. And I am relieved when I discover that the amateur point of view has been maintained. The development of the personality of your characters is described in a very suggestive manner and I greatly appreciated your picture of American life in the United States and in Europe.

I hope that you have every reason to be satisfied with Mrs. Fitzgerald's state of health. Here all is well, although we regret, it goes without saying, that we hardly see any Americans anymore.

Once again thank you and I remain yours sincerely,

O. L. Forel

[1] Forel wrote in French; the letter has been translated by Mary Borelli, Professor of Romance Languages, University of South Carolina.

TO: Rosalind Sayre Smith — TL(CC), 4 pp.[1] Princeton University

1307 Park Avenue,
Baltimore, Maryland,
July 19, 1934.

Dear Rosalind:

It was good to have our second conversation but your letter has snapped me back to our first which is the essential trouble between us. I am not going to call your mother into consultation nor have I ever called anybody into consultation on this problem except the trained technicians who are dealing with it. In any given case there has got to be one doctor, one man who must stand for a final solution. When I called on you and Newman in Switzerland in 1930 it was only to have one member of your family know what I was doing and why I was doing it. (I did not fail to appreciate his interest and yours on that occasion, but after all he has other commitments and could only give me what help he could spare.) The final reservations in this case must remain with me. To disparage all the sweat that has gone off me and out of me since it began is simply absurd, and every time it is done it causes more harm than good because it upsets me and makes things hard for Zelda. Whenever I handle the case by myself it goes well; whenever I have an impulse that I haven't been keeping you posted and tell you about it I run into that same old Puritanism that makes drinking unmoral, that makes all thinking done with the help of drink invalidated and I am put down to a level of a person whose opinion can't be trusted and that reaches the doctors in the case and they get confused and it all has to start over again.

To summarize: somebody in your family, preferably Newman, must get it straight in his mind that Mrs. Sayre is an old woman, that you are irreparably prejudiced against me, that Newman himself naturally hasn't the time to go into this thing very deeply and that it must all be left to me. If it were practical for you to investigate this case like Sherlock Holmes you would find in the first corridor the proper clues. They are: that somebody is trying to reconstruct a broken egg shell, which is a terrible problem, and that there is the money and effort that must contribute to this solution, the definite things that are near it and bearing on it, such as Scottie to be explicit.

But, Rosalind, every time that I tried to face what I consider facts I've run up against obsolete family prides, against such situations as that of the real facts of Anthony's death were concealed from me.

So I have come to think that outside of formal letters which I will try to do once a month I had best conceal what facts emerge and what decisions are to be made from all of you until they are *faits accomplis*.

I agree with you absolutely that none of us have either spare time or spare energy at this moment to devote to recriminations but I must cling to my point of view that despite what wisdom you may show in helping me with the problem of Scottie, on the problem of Zelda you are completely blinded, even I accuse you of being purposely blinded.

Faithfully,

P.S. To say that my conclusions have ever been influenced by drink is as absurd as to think that Grant's '64 and '65 campaigns were influenced by the fact that he needed stimulant and used it. There is the tangible fact of a very successful novel and many highly-paid-for short stories in my case and in holding to any such point of view and allow yourself to be placed with those who put over prohibition and almost ruined the nation with it.

P.S.S. The question of Scottie's future is not decided but I like Mrs. Robinson-Duff[2] and that bats highest with me at the moment. Will keep you informed.

[1] "*Not to be mailed* File only" appears at the top of the letter.

[2] Frances Robinson-Duff, director of an acting studio in New York. Scottie was not sent there.

TO: Don Swann

TLS, 1 p. Unlocated

1307 Park Avenue,
Baltimore, Maryland,
July 26, 1934.

Dear Don:

This is the best I can do. Only thing I want to ask you is first, that after your book is published all rights to use this in any way, such as in a collection of stray pieces, etc. reverts to me.

Secondly, that you do not make any changes, that is, if you want to change the word "mansion" to the word "manor" that is O.K. with me, but if you want to change "beautiful mansion" to "magnificent manor" that would utterly defeat the rhythm and so the purpose of the introduction. It would be exactly as if I took one of your etchings of Holder Hall at Princeton and drew a black oblong around one of the windows to indicate to my mother where I lived.[1]

Ever yours,
Scott

[1] Swann was working on *Colonial and Historic Homes of Maryland* (Baltimore: Etchcrafters Art Guild, 1939), for which Fitzgerald wrote the foreword.

TO: Rosalind Sayre Smith — TL(CC), 8 pp. Princeton University

1307 Park Avenue,
Baltimore, Maryland,
August 8, 1934.

Dear Rosalind:

Your letter unsettled my intentions, or rather my idea of the means by which to put them into effect. I was trying to do so many things in New York that I must have been confused in leaving with the idea that you approved of the governess business. I had foreseen the difficulties attendant upon such a radical step as this but had determined to overcome them somehow. The problem of Scottie was so adequately solved during Zelda's sickness in Switzerland by the combination of the *Cours Dieterlen* and Mlle. Sereze that I hoped to repeat it on a larger scale this winter.

Let me list first what is impractical about the present regime and about alternatives:

1. There is no probability (let alone certainty) that Zelda and I will be able to make a place for her in the east beyond that of bearing a well known name.

2. I would not want to deliberately make of her a middle-westerner, or a southerner.

3. So the purely social education that she is now getting is essentially directionless.

4. All indications point to the fact that in the next generation there ain't going to be any young millionaires to snatch off.

5. Scottie has an essentially artistic temperament; though at present she is at the most conventional of all ages; I can't see her settling down at eighteen into a conventional marriage.

6. The actual objections to her going to day-school here are that either she would be living alone with me—with unending work ahead of me and not too much good time to give to a child—or else with Zelda and me in case it is recommended that Zelda spend the fall and winter in a new attempt to brave the world. In either case the atmosphere will not be conducive to the even tenor advisable for a child at that important age.

7. Such social alternatives as a straight country boarding school, or semi-boarding school in New York (such as you suggest) or else Spence or Brierly—all these lead into the same blank alley. Scottie has no talent such as a musical one that could be developed locally at the Peabody here or the Boston Conservatory.

To isolate Scottie with a governess wasn't my idea. The governess would serve as chaperone, teacher, and general guide, to a planned regime which I would constantly oversee; Scottie would go to a "social" dancing class in New York, and also to some sort of gymnastic association or club where she could have swimming and basket-ball. She would pass the week-ends either here or with friends in New York—I have friends there who have children exactly her age and if she managed to find so many friends in Paris among foreign people the question of her being lonely in New York is absolutely non-existent.

Now let me list what is in favor of my plan as conceived:

1. Scottie seems to have a varied talent which may express itself in any one of a number of ways. The theatre is the great universal of *all* talents. In the modern theatre every single bent is represented and by starting in early she would be learning the fundamentals not of one career but of half a dozen.

2. One of the reasons that the world shows little practical achievement by sons and daughters of talented people—with notable exceptions, of course—is that the son or daughter of a man who has sung an opera, written a book, or painted a picture, is inclined to think that that achievement will stand in place of any effort of his own. It is much easier for Scottie to play being the daughter of a writer than to get down and write something herself, and I have noticed increasing tendencies toward that under present conditions. She used to write, with real pleasure and pride, little poems or stories for our Christmases and anniversaries. Now she's inclined to say, "What's the use? Daddy will do my writing for me" —Beyond that, Rosalind, she accepts the idea of most American children that Constance Bennett will do her acting for her and Bing Crosby her crooning. If I didn't see Scottie grimacing, posing, practising in front of mirrors and dressing herself up to the gills on all possible occasions, I would conclude that she had no desire for a public existence, but the contrary is true. She wants a lime-light and the question is whether it will be a healthy one of effort, or else one of these half-botched careers like Zelda's—of running yourself ragged for purely social ends and then trying to give the broken remnants to people and getting melancholia because people won't snap at it.

My point here is, that, as far as I can judge, Scottie is by nature and destiny a potential artist.

3. Broke off here for a moment to discuss the question with Mrs. Owens and was reminded of the fact that Scottie can always change from an

artistic to a social career but the reverse is very difficult. (My God, Rosalind! if you would see the manuscripts that come my way from idle lawyers and bored housewives, who decided that they would take up literature in their "spare time"! It's as if I rushed into Johns Hopkins this afternoon, asking for a scalpel and an appendicitis patient, on the basis that I had an uncle who was a doctor, and people told me in my youth that I would make a good surgeon.) The pith of this is that only professionals function—capably within a profession—just as the time to begin ballet is about eleven years old, so the age to get used to the stage is at about thirteen or fourteen.

4. New York is the only possible center for Show Business (the boys and girls of Broadway persist in leaving the definite article out of that phrase.) The position of amateur teachers in society schools is less than nothing. To put Scottie with some defeated actress teaching for Miss This-Or-Thats would be to devitalize the whole idea. The moment Zelda entered Eglarova's ballet school she saw the difference between amateur and professional training. The fact that the shift from play to work led to disaster in Zelda's case has no bearing on this situation; if at any moment I find that Scottie has not the physical or nervous vitality to stand the rigors of real work, I shall snatch her out as quick as a blink.

But in the case of Miss Duff-Robinson I think of how the Renaissance artists trained men in their studios and trained them well because the pupils did a great portion of their work for them—the system of apprenticing in the middle ages derives its value from that fact. Her whole livelyhood depends not on any fake "diplomas" but on the actual accomplishments of her pupils. As for the amateur teachers—well, I could teach Scottie as much about the stage here in our own parlor.

5. Having gone this far with the French I want to keep it up, and with a few more years of this part-time tutoring she will inevitably lose her bilinguality that I spent thousands of dollars sustaining by importing governess, etc. Even the private tutoring here has started to slip, insofar as her accent and vocabulary are concerned, though her constructions are still holding up well enough.

And now to discuss such factors as might militate against this plan:

1. Child snatched from healthy home influences, neighborhood activities, etc. thrown immature into the great world. But where are these healthy home influences, neighborhood activities, etc? Though I forbid a radio in the house she can go around the corner at any moment and sit in with other innocents on "Oh You Nasty Man" and other bucolic classics.

2. As to friends: with every move we make Scottie has kicked about leaving tried and true friends behind her. In the upshot, however, it is a struggle to get her to so much as answer the letters of her late pals. She makes friends so easily and has so much curiosity about people that she is

not essentially a loyal child or one who is ever liable to be very lonely. She has been to two camps from here without any untoward sense of pining away. Only once in her life have I seen her actively miss anyone for more than a few days and that was in the case of Mlle. Sereze.

3. She will be less outdoors but she will have compensatory indoor exercise. One can't have everything.

I wish you would read this letter a couple of times, because I have written it partly to help me make up my own mind about Scottie's year, and I've spent a conscientious morning at it. If you see any loop-holes in my reasoning, please let me know. I am always ready to reconsider and there is a whole month before I will get to the actual engaging of a governess. (By the way she will have to be an actual native born Frenchwoman.) Miss Duff-Robinson, in tentatively agreeing to take her, made a point of her advantage in having that language. Zelda, in a clear-thinking moment was enthusiastic about the idea (though of course she would rather have had ballet for which Scottie is totally unfitted both physically and rhythmically.)

Best wishes to you both and hopes that your annoying uncertainty of domicile will be shortly liquidated.

TO: Mrs. Richard Taylor

TLS, 1 p. Princeton University
Baltimore, Maryland

1307 Park Avenue
August 17, 1934.

Sweet Cecie,

My reactions always about leaving your vicinity are a curse at its uncertain weather and a feeling that I have come to see you in an exhausted condition. This trip was no exception to the rule. Perhaps my very need for you and your descendants to keep my life going along is the explanation—however, when my visits happen, these situations repeat themselves.

In my most systematic manner:—

1. Do I owe any money, do you think?, on the last day that I haven't accounted for? I am pretty dim about leaving the Monticello, and told Mrs. Owens only a resumé of what I might have spent there.
2. Do you and your children love me as much as I love you?
3. *Did I forget a safety pin in the middle of your parlor rug?—this is probably the most important point of all.*

Every moment with you all has a quality immediately of something so far remembered that it calls up half-forgotten things: like something somebody said to you when you were ten; or else something so far in the future that it makes one think of an inspiration and a hope.

I suppose that is always true of experiences that one has undergone at an emotional age. I am so afraid of spoiling anything in my relation to you and the daughters, and having been rather a bull in china shops lately, have been conscious of heading in that direction.

I am now reading Baron Marlot's "Reminiscences of the Napoleonic Campaigns" and going in for tactics on a big scale. Also awaiting the arrival of Scotty in about ten days and may ship her off to you for two or three days if plans coincide.

My respect and love to Aunt Elise[1] and warnings to all four progeny and for yourself my dearest love always.

Scott

P.S. Any advice that you can give Mrs. Owens I will appreciate. She seems to be a little bit undecided what she will do or where she will stay; but if she does end up in your region and calls you, advise her to the best of your capacities. Could you realize that this is the first vacation she has had in almost three years?

[1] Eliza Key Delihant.

TO: Bennett Cerf

TLS, 1 p. Columbia University
Baltimore, Maryland

1307 Park Avenue
August 17, 1934.

Dear Bennett,

Called up about the preface, with which I am not satisfied;[1] talked with Don Klopfer,[2] telling him that I would like proof as quickly as possible on the piece.

Thanks for your generous offer. I could not take advantage of it without asking for so many books that it would confuse me to have them around. I am going to ask you this, however. I would like one copy of Tom Wolfe's "Look Homeward, Angel" sent to Mr. and Mrs. Thomas Hitchcock, at Old Westbury, Long Island, with my compliments. (Incidentally, I congratulate you on bringing it out, because it is certainly one of the finest books of the last ten years)—and I would like a copy for myself.

Also I would like ten or fifteen copies of "The Great Gatsby" when it is issued.

With congratulations for having profited, as I gather you did, from your foreign explorations,

Yours ever,
Scott Fitzg—

[1] In 1934 *The Great Gatsby* was reprinted in The Modern Library, and Fitzgerald received $50 for writing an introduction. Another letter to Cerf dated 17 August returns the corrected proof for the introduction. For an account of Fitzgerald's correspondence with Random House in 1934 see Andrew B. Myers, "'I Am Used to Being Dunned,'" *Columbia Library Columns*, XXV (February 1976), 28–39.

[2] Co-founder of Random House.

TO: Dr. Harry M. Murdock — TL(CC), 4 pp. Princeton University

1307 Park Avenue
Baltimore, Maryland
August 28, 1934.

Dear Dr. Murdock,

As you probably know, I saw my wife yesterday and spent an hour and a half with her. It was much better than any of the nine or ten times that I have seen her since she broke down again last January. She seemed in every way exactly like the girl I used to know. But, perhaps for that reason, it seemed to both of us very sad and she cried in my arms and we felt that the summer slipping by was typical of the way life is slipping by for both of us. Which brings me to the point of this letter.

As I tried to indicate to you:

Dr. Forel's treatment of this problem was very different from Dr. Meyer's and all my sympathies were with the former. During the entire time with Dr. Meyer, I could never get from him, save in one letter, an idea of his point of view. He seemed to believe:

(1) that Zelda should not get too hospital-minded;

(2) that I drank too much, which complicated the whole matter; and

(3) that I was a work horse with the nervous system of a Swiss peasant.

He was very generous with his time, but that time (save that he always had rather a temporary moral effect on Zelda) seemed largely unprofitable. Great sheaves of notes on our interviews were taken by Dr. Rennie but the notes disappeared into the archives with no upshot. He would not permit her to return to his clinic for short stays, which was my favorite point.

Just suppose that the fear of her growing hospitalized is valid. I would many times rather have Zelda live with me part of the time and go to rest cures and hospitals for part of the time than have her remain for long years of our lives in hospitals on the faint chance that when she came out she would suddenly become completely social. And from *my* point of view, the feeling that I could call on a hospital for a month or two—have her come back to me provisionally and then return for a few weeks—would have been a tremendous relief.

Now for the second point: I realize that the following theory is qualified by the fact that perhaps a first cure of the malady is easier than a second or a third. Yet I believe that if Dr. Meyer had seen the situation in a less Puritan light he had more chance to help her to a permanent cure than either Dr. Forel at the time of her terrible eczema and total disorientation, or you at the time of her katatonic state. But he made less use of his advantage, because he could never seem to appreciate that my writing was more important than hers by a large margin because of the years of preparation for it, and the professional experience, and because my writing kept the mare going, while Zelda's belongs to the luxury trade. In other words, he encouraged the damn woman's desire to express herself as if she hadn't broken down on that point twice before.

He never bothered to compare our books nor, living in his own generation and in his own cerebral world, would he have got the counter-implications or the nuances of either of them. There are, of course, universals both medical and moral behind this case but in a changing world he failed to get any of the contemporary sidelights which change their values. He never really *believed* that I worked very hard, had a serious reputation or made money.

Once he had done what he could with Zelda, he simply shoved her on to me during two and a half years of the most tremendous work of my life, refused to take her back, and offered instead the singularly barren three-cornered conversations. At the end of a year I was half crazy myself and then the heavy drinking began. He laid down a schedule for Zelda but gave me no power to enforce it. And what threat could I hold over Zelda—save some kind of brute force—unless I had the right to say that if she did not do this or that, she must go back to the clinic. Zelda, for the most part, puts up a much more sympathetic face than I do. She is generally, paradoxical as it may seem, in much better control of her nerves and she sold Dr. Meyer the idea that her life was as socially useful as mine. But she never could sell it to our daughter or to our immediate household. She walked out on too many things.

This letter is drawing on but it is so hard to make a series of points over a telephone. I am getting at last to the main thesis about which I was circling. When Zelda became better after the year and a half of her first illness, Dr. Forel encouraged us to take short trips of ten miles or so, at first with a nurse, to dinner in Geneva for instance; then a few long day-time trips; then to visit me for a night at the hotel where I was living, always with the understanding that her permanent headquarters was the clinic and holding her room for her there. After a half-dozen of these, we went on a ten-day holiday, after which she again returned to the clinic for two or three weeks. In other words, his method was to wean her away, while Dr. Meyer's was God knows what.

I am not trying to discuss the comparative merits of the two, except from the pragmatic attitude: in Zelda's case the first one worked because it gave her hope and refuge at the same time, while Dr. Meyer's theoretical plan was, in her case, a failure. He gave back to me both times a woman not one whit better than when she went in. She seemed to have more self-control, less tension, and he assumed that if these conditions did not persist at home, the guilty element must be myself. If that is reasoning, then San Francisco Bay is full of grape juice.

Of course, the *immediate* putting into effect any such plan if you should approve of it, may be affected by her collapse up at Dr. Slocum's,[1] but I wish you would think this over and discuss it with whatever doctors are in touch with the case out there—if any of them have the time to read this letter. It would give both Zelda and me some practical hope for the future and something upon which I could found my plans.

Could you give me an appointment for some time during the next week, so I might hear your opinions?

With many thanks for your interest and best wishes,

[1] Director of Craig House.

TO: Bennett Cerf

TLS, 2 pp. (with 1 p. typed list).
Columbia University

1307 Park Avenue,
Baltimore, Maryland,
August 30, 1934.

Dear Bennet

It was nice to take a look at you through sober eyes, + in spite of the fact that the afternoon was largely devoted to Fitzgeraldiana the impression remains with me. The reason I didn't head the subject into more impersonal channels was because you all seemed to be interested—and intimate details of another's past are always interesting.

Hey! do you think that I am so illiterate as to have only the few Modern Library books that are in the British-American section of fiction of my library? It is scattered all over the house at the moment, but in the different shelves of history, philosophy, etc. I counted twenty-five after you left. For your stupidity I am going to take you up on your offer, pick ten titles and ask you for them. They are appended to this letter.

Anyhow I had a most pleasant afternoon seeing you and shall certainly call on you when I come to New York.

Ever yours,
Scott Fitzg—

Golden Ass	88
Beaudelaire	70
Jungle Peace	30
Don Quixote	174
Borgias	192
Tom Jones	185
W.S.Gilbert	113
Suetonius	188
Gibbon	G6 G7
Restoration Plays	G10

TO: Elizabeth Lemmon[1]

TLS, 2 pp. (with holograph postscript). Princeton University

1307 Park Avenue,
Baltimore, Maryland,
September 6, 1934.

Dearest Beth

This is the story that I got out of "Welbourne," with my novelist instinct to make copy out of social experience.[2] I don't think for a moment that this does any justice to "Welbourne" but it might amuse you as conveying the sharp impression that the place made on me during a few week-ends. Am sorry that this is not a transcription of the final draft as the *Post* will publish it, but in its general outlines it is the story as written.

Of course the detail about the initials of the "Gallant Pelham" will identify the place to such neighbors of yours who read the *Saturday Evening Post*. As the story is so detached from any reality I am sure it won't cause you or family any annoyance.

With Love
Scott Fitzg—

Just wired you the weather killed my Mannassus trip. Hope to hell you're all right now.

[1] Maxwell Perkins' cousin.

[2] Miss Lemmon lived at a house called "Welbourne" in the Virginia hunt country. The story was "Her Last Case," *Saturday Evening Post* (3 November 1934).

FROM: Nathanael West TLS, 1 p. Princeton University

September 11, '34

My dear Mr. Fitzgerald,

You have been kind enough to say that you liked my novel, Miss Lonelyhearts.

I am applying for a Guggenheim Fellowship[1] and I need references for it. I wonder if you would be willing to let me use your name as a reference? It would be enormously valuable to me. I am writing to you, a stranger, because I know very few people, almost none whose names would mean anything to the committee, and apparently the references are the most important part of the application.

As you know, the committee will probably submit my plan for future work to you if you give me permission to use your name as reference. This will be a nuisance, of course, but the plan is a very brief one and you are only obliged to say whether you think it is good or not.

If you can see your way to do this, it will make me very happy.

Sincerely,
Nathanael West

[1] West was planning "A novel about the moral ideas of the generation which graduated from college in 1924." He did not receive the grant. See Jay Martin, "Fitzgerald Recommends Nathanael West for a Guggenheim," *Fitzgerald/Hemingway Annual* 1971.

TO: Bennett Cerf TLS, 1 p. Columbia University

September 15th, 1934
1307 Park Ave.
Baltimore, Md.

Dear Bennett:—

I want to: thank you first for the generous present of books;

Second, to acknowledge the check for the preface;

And, third, to make a grumble, not against you but against myself. I do not like the preface. Reading it over it seems to have both flipness and incoherance, two qualities which the story that succeeds it manages to avoid. Please answer for me the following questions: Can it be changed in subsequent editions?[1] I should naturally be willing to pay for it myself, out of respective royalties or even in cash. If this is practical—the whole thing being naturally in foundry,—Wouldn't it be simpler for me to rewrite the whole preface, in spite of the fact that my revisins will comprise merely the excision of a paragraph and the change of a couple of key sentences?

Planning to be in New York toward the end of the week (meaning week of 16th), and will deliver copy—*if you answer me these questions upon receipt of this letter.*

It was fine seeing you. Sorry This complication mars my satisfaction in the handsome re-issue.

Ever Yours,
Scott

F. Scott Fitzgerald
Per Scottie Fitzgerald, typing

Note This

[1] Cerf replied on 17 September: "If you want to write a new preface to appear in second and all subsequent editions in the Modern Library, go to it." (Columbia) Fitzgerald did not have an opportunity to revise his introduction because the Modern Library reprinting of *The Great Gatsby* was discontinued.

TO: Guggenheim Foundation — TLS, 1 p. Guggenheim

Dear Sirs:

Today Nathanael West asked me for a letter of reference on behalf of his application for a Guggenheim fellowship.

—and, in the same post, came a consignment of a reprint by the Modern Library of a novel of mine, THE GREAT GATSBY, which had a new preface that included the statement that I thought young writers in America were being harmed now for the lack of a public, and I had mentioned specifically Nathanael West.

I don't know on what basis the Guggenheim fellowships are given but I know some of the people who have profited by them, and, while many of the men have been chosen worthily and well, such as Thomas Wolfe and Allen Tate, there have been others who have been sent to Europe who have not been worth their salt, and who—in the eventuality—have proved nothing.

I have sometimes felt that you have put especial emphasis on poetry while I think that the most living literary form in America at the moment is prose fiction. In my opinion Nathanael West is a potential leader in the field of prose fiction. He seems to me entirely equipped to go over on the fellowship.

With best wishes to the custodians of the great idea.

Sincerely yours,
F. Scott Fitzgerald

1307 Park Avenue
Baltimore, Maryland
September 25, 1934

TO: Marvin Chauncey Ross[1] TLS, 1 p. Yale University

1307 Park Avenue,
Baltimore, Maryland,
September 26, 1934.

Dear Mr. Ross:

I will do everything in my power to add to the pleasure of Miss Gertrude Stein's triumphal return visit to Baltimore but she has older friends than me here, such as Miss Etta Cohn, who also are in a position to do more for her as I am a most recent resident. My suggestion is that you assign me any particular service I can render in that connection and I will be glad to do it, but outside of entertaining here in my house, if she has the time to spare, I cannot see exactly how I can be of much assistance.

Please let me hear further on this because I am under much obligation to Miss Stein and am very fond of her.

Sincerely,
F. Scott Fitzgerald

[1] Manager of Stein's American lecture tour.

TO: V. F. Calverton[1] TLS, 1 p. New York Public Library

1307 Park Avenue,
Baltimore, Maryland,
September 26, 1934.

Dear Calverton:

Your letter reached me on my return from an arduous and unsuccessful foray to New York during which I left my hotel room only once and that once to have my story curtly turned down. Am here in slews of work but am still looking forward to our next meeting if you give me plenty of notice.

I did see Grattan's review in the *Modern Monthly*[2] and I believe it pleased me more than any that I got. Sometime I want to meet him and thank him personally for his interest—and I thank you for yours which probably called the book to his attention.

Am waiting for "Passing of the Gods" and will report on it either by letter or in person.

Yours ever,
Scott Fitzg—

[1] Nom de plume of George Goetz, editor of *The Modern Monthly* and author or editor of some twenty books on political and sociological topics.

[2] Hartley Grattan's review of *Tender Is the Night* (July 1934).

TO: Bennett Cerf TLS, 1 p. Columbia University

1307 Park Avenue,
Baltimore, Maryland,
October 10, 1934.

Dear Bennett:

I meant it about rewriting that preface. Please give me a couple of weeks warning when and if you are going to print up another batch. The preface *is* incoherent. I am not even going to revise it, but simply do it over again.

Ever yours,
Scott Fitzg

TO: V. F. Calverton TLS, 2 pp.[1] New York Public Library

1307 Park Avenue,
Baltimore, Maryland,
October 17, 1934.

Dear George:

Someone called here today representing herself as your secretary, though why in God's name you should have a secretary in Maryland I don't know, and asked if I had got a copy of "The Passing of the Gods." I have been absorbed with it for the last four days and never suspected anybody of such erudition. It is inevitable that in destroying a moral system you should, in the same breath, create one—and I did not adhere in all points to the creation. *You are a modern Lecky and I congratulate you on the achievement.* My one objection is the high overtone of economics, which eventually defeats its own purpose, or so it seems to me. *For the rest, the synthesis of anthropology, sociology and philosophy, salted with good eighteenth century rationalism, seem like a triumph.*

Please give me jiggers on this date with Grattan.

Best always,
Scott

[1] The italicized sentences in this letter may not have been underlined by Fitzgerald.

FROM: Zelda Fitzgerald
October 1934

ALS, 4 pp.[1] Princeton University
Sheppard and Enoch Pratt Hospital
Towson, Maryland

Dearest Do-Do-

Thanks for your letter. Since you are slowly dissolving into a mythical figure over the long period of years that have elapsed since two weeks ago, I will tell you about myself:

1) I am lonesome

2)I have no relatives or friends and would like to make acquaintance with a Malayean warrior

3) I do not cook or sew or commit nuisances about the house

The Sheppard Pratt hospital is located somewhere in the hinterlands of the human consciousness and I can be located there any time between the dawn of consciousness and the beginning of old age.

Darling: Life is difficult. There are so many problems. 1) The problem of how to stay here and 2) The problem of how to get out. And I want so desperately to go to Guatemala still and ride a bicycle to the end of a long white road. The road is lined with lebanon cedars and poplars and ancient splendors crumble down the parched bleached hills and natives sleep in the shade beside a high grey wall. Whereas here Grace Moore sings very prettily over the radio and obscure kings get themselves killed by what I am convinced are Mussolinis henchmen so that Lowell Thomas will not disappoint the old ladies—It is all very depressing

We had a swell ride through the woods very proudly aflame with a last desperate flamboyance. The paths are like tunnels through the secrets of a precious stone, all green and gold and red and under the maples the world is amber.

Can we go to the Russian ballet? or can I go with Mrs Owens? or will you ask Father Christmas to bring me a Russian ballet—or have the cook put some in the next pudding—or something.

I liked New Types.[2] The girl was nice with breezes in her bangs. Like all your stories there was something haunting to remember: about the lonliness of keeping Faiths—I love your credos—and your stories. I meant to write you about The Darkest Hour.[3] It was sort of stark and swell and full of the pressure of history in the making—but I would have liked more description and less of the battle. Mrs. Ridgely took me to see the hunt start. There is a story in that atmosphere—There is a grandfather little and guarded like the Pope and Miss Ludy of the love letters here in the hospital and none of them fought in the Civil War. Of cource, it might not be Family history but its an awfully good story.

[1] The sketch of Fitzgerald appears to be the fourth page of this letter.
[2] *The Saturday Evening Post* (22 September 1934).
[3] "In the Darkest Hour," *Redbook* (October 1934).

FROM: Zelda Fitzgerald
Fall 1934

ALS, 3 pp. Princeton University
Sheppard and Enoch Pratt Hospital
Towson, Maryland

Dearest *Dearest* Do-Do—

Please pay no attention to any Splenglarian collapses or other portentious disasters should any take place between now and the time for your visit, and I will slit my tongue and stop up my ears to prevent further communication until you come. It seems as if we have not seen each other in years and I live in terror of some cataclysmic event's preventing—Darling!

Don't mind about the book sale. Few people in these times concern themselves with the honest serving of a human heart—especially when the yield is poetry, and ecstatic and a singing of other happinesses not yet in retrospect. It's so good. Only, of cource, it makes me quite sick to think of the hard work you are having to do. It was awfully nice of you to send Scottie to camp. She is so charming now—

I am busy with a Promethesus complex—largely due to the washing and ironing and the lack of drawing materials. He really had a horrid time; Io, now, was more like it—just wanderring

Monsieur, it is hot—and at Antibes people on beaches finish the Chablis and think of their stomachs and think themselves uncomfortable because of the sand down their backs. Pleasure of life are, indeed, relative. The earth is hotter than the air and insistent and the breeze moves spasmodicly through resentful siasmic trees—There are so many nice places, even if we leave out Guatemala. Did you see in the Sunday paper about all the things they've found in Greece? And the statues were still painted, red and blue. The plains in the picture were flat and vast and as unbrokenly harmonious as the Greeks conception of the cosmos; the views all ended at a paling of poplars—

I am very offended by the girl with the dog—I consider that I have a very interesting face due to so much experience with life and so little with Elizabeth Arden. But maybe it was the terrier which bore the resemblance—

Anyway, I love you—pie-face or not—

Zelda—

I'm awfully sorry about Annabel and hope it isnt serious—

Please come to see me.

Please come to see me

Please come to see me—

TO: Bennett Cerf TLS, 1 p. Columbia University

1307 Park Avenue,
Baltimore, Maryland,
November 20, 1934.

Dear Bennett:

Goldwin is considering "Tender is the Night" with Miriam Hopkins in the role of Nicole.[1] If you can honestly see her in that light for God's sake drop her a line telling her so, though I don't know whether she will have any say in the final choice. When I thought that the thing would be sold immediately she was one of the three (the others were Hepburn and Harding) that I could see in the role, which requires intelligent handling, but of all of them she was my favorite.

People still marvel at your giant editions which I keep on display but the daughter can't understand why a modern library publishes Apuleuis and Suitonieus.

Ever yours
Scott Fitzg—

[1] The movie was not made.

TO: Carmel Myers[1] TL(CC), 3 pp. Princeton University

1307 Park Avenue,
Baltimore, Maryland,
November 21, 1934.

Dear Carmel:

This will seem the voice of a ghost out of the past, but you are equally a ghost to me since I was unable to reach you through Metro with a copy of my last spring's book which I was trying to force upon you. The point is this: there is a personal favor that I want done out there and I have been at sea about whom to call on because I am so out of touch with the coast. Asking King Vidor to do something is about as impractical as asking Franklin Roosevelt to run out in the pantry and bring me a box of matches, I hardly know Dick Barthelmess any more and by an irony of fate the younger generation seems a little bit younger and farther away than any other, so it's to a poor frail defenseless female that I turn in my predicament.

There is a kid (male) out there of whom I am very fond. He went out working on a treatment of "Tender is the Night" with some money that I had paid him for his collaboration on the job and Sam Marks at Metro finally gave him a job writing script on the lot; whereupon young Bill proceeded to come in for hard luck developing four weeks of sickness in a hospital and then, after a fortnight on his feet, a relapse which shot him back into boarding house hospitalization for another three weeks. Metro believed in him and saw him through his first illness but of course in the second one began to lose faith. I haven't, however, because if there's a finer universal talent in his generation than he has (he's only twenty-two) I will be astonished. My intention is to back him insofar as my means will allow. The immediate occasion is that his family here are half crazy with worry about him because he has that Spartan quality of depriving himself of food when he has an objective in mind. I want some responsible person to call on him at his headquarters, 6434 Yucca Street, Hollywood, and look over his physical condition and if it looks as if he is in bad shape get in touch with his doctor—and if, God forbid, the situation seems in any way menacing, *to wire me here immediately.*

Carmel, if I weren't so fond of this boy and if my affection for you had suffered with the years, I would not dare call on you for this. My only other idea was to ask Bart Cormack or Dwight Taylor[2] to do it for me but young Warren (for some reason, although his name is Charles Warren, he is universally known here as Bill Warren) is very proud and would be much more likely to put on a crust before a man and conceal his real condition, where with a woman he would be more inclined to let the truth emerge. Please do this for me, Carmel. I am sure in any case that you will like Warren who is a gifted free-hand composer among his many talents. Any courtesy that you could show him would be tremendously appreciated because he is in one of those sloughs of despond when he needs help and if the help gets there a little late it might get too late indeed.

Ever yours devotedly,

P.S. Could not for the hell of it think of how Ralph spelled his last name and had to wire Madam Selznick to be sure of this reaching you.

[1] Fitzgerald had met Miss Myers in 1924 when she was making *Ben-Hur* in Rome.
[2] Screenwriters.

TO: Mrs. Richard Taylor

TLS, 2 pp. (with holograph postscript). Princeton University

1307 Park Avenue,
Baltimore, Maryland,
November 22, 1934.

Dearest Ceci:

In these parts it has been only a round of unending work. When you see Hume thank him for his legal advice but tell him that, alas! the story came to no proper fruition. I have been concentrating on this medieval series which started in the *Red Book* in the early autumn and will be continued all winter; and also I am correcting proofs on my collection "*Taps at Reveille*" which will come out in the spring. All my movie plans seem to be cursed, though there is now a very promising nibble on "Tender is the Night." (for Miriam Hopkins, one of you rebel gals from "Joja") Zelda does well, though she still doesn't want to make the leap back into life. Scottie is a dear and is doing her work better than last year, and the process of growing up with its accompanying struggles and disillusions absorbs more of her energy than I like. I don't quite see her making a trip at Thanksgiving but be sure that when the proper occasion arises there is no one I would rather she had a holiday with than you.

Love
Scott—

"Tender" hasn't come thru financially in England but it got fine reviews from the important press, *London Times*, *Manchester Guardian* Spectator, G. B. Stern in *the Telegraph* ect its being translated into Hungarian + some Syrian dialect! My God!

FROM: Gertrude Stein — ALS, 4 pp. Scrapbook. Princeton University
November 1934

My dear friend,

I do so much want to see you to be with you and to have a long talk with you, here we are and it has been a most lively time, and very very often during that time I have been thinking of you. We will be in Baltimore between Christmas and New Year, and I do hope you will be there too,[1] I want so much to see you and talk to you and listen to you, I liked a lot of Tender is the Night, and I am sure that you will do some more, and I will very carefully order another one. Will you let me know care of Mrs. Julian Stein, Rose Hill, Pikesville Md. whether you will be there when I am there, I do most awfully want to see you, I am liking being here immensely it means a lot to me in every way but all that and everything else we will tell about when we meet[2]

Always
Gtde St—

[1] Gertrude Stein and Alice B. Toklas visited the Fitzgeralds in Baltimore during the Christmas holidays.

[2] See Fitzgerald's 23 November letter to Stein in *Letters*.

TO: Ernest Hemingway | Wire. Kennedy Library

BALTIMORE MD 1934 DEC 3 PM 1 03

DEAR ERNEST SEEMS IMPOSSIBLE TO GET DOWN THIS WEEK AND I CERTAINLY REGRET IT AND I APPRECIATE YOUR INVITATION[1] HAD SO MANY THINGS TO TALK TO YOU ABOUT WITH BEST ALWAYS TO YOU AND YOURS

SCOTT.

[1] Fitzgerald had been invited to go fishing with Hemingway at Key West.

TO: Maxwell Perkins | TLS, 2 pp. Princeton University

1307 Park Avenue,
Baltimore, Maryland,
December 3, 1934.

Dear Max:

Do you realize that they are sending me a whole series of new galleys which repeat from the beginning of my old galleys? I don't know whether this was accidental or intentional, in any case, I am very glad—but I must remind you that it will inevitably slow up the completion of the book—as well as defeat your purpose of being able to free the type. A proof is to me as a covey of partridges to Ernest Hemingway. I can't let it alone.

Will you give me a straight story about when you actually want this in, because I am still feeling my way around in a wilderness of work and want to aligne what must be done. The complications are:

I have your first proofs to do
Your second proofs to do
Proofs from Balmer on the Medieval novel[1]
Originals for Balmer
Extra work for "Esquire" to keep alive
And a "Saturday Evening Post" story in the offing (which looks so remote as to be practically hypothetical.)

I want to keep all these things straight and I'd be terribly obliged for any final decision as to a favorable date of publication for *Taps at Reveille* this spring, and the corresponding zero hour for the final version—and please tell me the truth, Max. I am no longer in diapers in this game and hurrying me *honestly* does no good.

Just had to turn down a wonderful invitation to fly south with Gingrich of "Esquire" to see Ernest at Key West, the whole trip free including champagne. However, I still have a faint hope of accompanying you when you go.

Ever yours,
Scott

[1] Fitzgerald was attempting to write an historical novel in the form of a serial for *Redbook Magazine*. He completed four segments of this work, usually referred to as the "Count of Darkness," or "Philippe," stories; the first was "In the Darkest Hour."

TO: Maxwell Perkins — TLS, 3 pp.[1] Princeton University

1307 Park Avenue,
Baltimore, Maryland,
December 17, 1934.

Dear Max:

Enclosed are two galleys and also a short short story called "The Night Before Chancellorsville" which I wish could be included into the book. This story and "The Fiend" together are not as long as "Her Last Case" so I think they would fit in your space originally allowed for that.

2. On original galley 84 six lines from the bottom (in story "First Blood") there occurs the phrase "their eyes were blazing windows across the court of the same house." This phrase I find occurs in *Tender is the Night* and I am VERY ANXIOUS to cut it if I haven't already done it on the galley I returned you. This is awfully important to me and I wish you would have it checked up before you put it into page proof.[2] Certain people I know read my books over and over again and I can't think of anything that would more annoy or disillusion a reader than to find an author using a phrase over and over as if his imagination were starving. *Please let me know if you find it!*

3. You have not told me whether you wanted me to correct the typescript of "The Fiend" or whether you are going to send me galleys.

You will notice that "Crazy Sunday" is scarcely corrected at all in contrast to previous stories so I think that it will all even out. I hope that whoever is going over my proofs knows that my reason for cutting or changing some of the best passages is that they were used in *Tender is the Night*.

This makes about half the stories but you can be sure the other half will not take as long as these first ones; six of these latter I will hardly have to touch at all, the proof was largely a matter of getting started. It looked so formidable and there's been so much to do. I can do two a week without fail.

Please answer those first three questions, Max.

Ever yours,
Scott

P.S. If you do not like "The Night Before Chancellorsville" please tell me frankly. My idea is that this and "The Fiend" would give people less chance to say they are all standardized *Saturday Evening Post* stories, because, whatever can be said about them, they are not that. I know I am suppressing certain *Post* stories that in suspense and story interest are superior to these two—it is be the question of the book as a whole. If you decide to use "The Night Before Chancellorsville" the Table of Contents should be changed *so that it comes between "Two Wrongs"* and "*Jacob's Ladder.*"[3]

[1] The first two paragraphs and part of the postscript of this letter were included in *Scott/Max.*

[2] The phrase was deleted.

[3] "Jacob's Ladder" was not included in the volume.

TO: Maxwell Perkins — TLS, 1 p. Princeton University

1307 Park Avenue,
Baltimore, Maryland,
December 26, 1934.

Dear Max:

Growing increasingly ashamed about bothering you with details I want to suppress the forward to "Taps at Reveille."[1] Zelda didn't like it and her taste is usually good in such things and it doesn't read well to me. It has a kind of snappy-snooty sound which I intruded into the preface of Cerf's publication of "The Great Gatsby." If you can, without undue fermentation, arrange this, I think the fortunes of the book will be furthered.

Ever yours,
Scott

[1] The foreword was omitted and is now lost.

FROM: Arnold Gingrich[1] — ALS, 2 pp. Princeton University
Late 1934

Dear Scott, you are well nigh incredibly nice, about the nicest guy I ever met, I think, and I want you to know I think so, because probably I didn't convey that feeling at all coherently. If I didn't convey it at all, it is because I was drinking you up for the two hours I had and selfishly not giving a damn about maintaining the mutuality of the exchange.

For a long time after I left you I kept thinking about what guts it was to ask you for fiction and I'm sorry. I don't want to ask you to give it away when you know you can sell it.[2] If you do the short one for the book and something about it makes it unavailable for Scribners (which seems a hell of a remote possibility—) then of course I'll dance and make other appropriate gestures and noises if I can have it. But I would be an All-American heel to ask for it on any other basis.

As for the things you can write easily and in between the major efforts, that's different. Those I will ask for and hope to get often. This last one is a honey.[3]

Knopf likes my novel very swell, in fact better than I do myself. He says himself that he probably ought to be afraid of his own enthusiasm for it—that the chances are pretty slim that it's as good a book as he thinks it is. I asked him to send you a set of advance proofs, and if you would review it for the New Republic or somebody it would be of a piece with my idea of what a fine fella you are, but if you should decide not to that idea would still not be affected.[4]

Rupert Brooke was my first idol, in '17 and thereabouts, but you were the second and you wear better.

It would be awful to see you piss away your talent in Hollywood again, and I hope it won't come to that. Because, regarding the written word like a musical instrument, you are the supreme virtuoso—nobody can draw a purer finer tone from the string of an English sentence—and what the hell has the written word to do with Hollywood?

Have been busy as hell since I started this, and now the day's gone. Better sign off. I'll write you again when I get a chance. They moved my office while I was gone and all is pandemonium here.

I'll return the Necromancers.[5] Haven't had a chance to look at it yet.

If I can do you any good in any way let me know.

Cordialy
Arnold Gingrich

[1] Editor of *Esquire* magazine.

[2] Fitzgerald's first fiction appearances in *Esquire* were "The Fiend" (January 1935) and "The Night Before Chancellorsville" (February 1935). The top price *Esquire* paid was $250.

[3] "Sleeping and Waking," *Esquire* (December 1934).

[4] *Cast Down the Laurel* (1935). Fitzgerald did not review Gingrich's novel but provided a statement for the dust jacket: "Beautifully written, startling in form, and promising other equally good things to come. It pleases me beyond measure that Arnold Gingrich has brought off this book, which has the same scope and appeal of his editorial ventures."

[5] Possibly Robert Hugh Benson's *The Necromancers* (1909).

FROM: Sara Murphy
c. 1934

ALS, 4 pp. Princeton University

Sunday

Dear Scott,—

We were sorry not to see you again—but it seemed, under the circumstances better not to—

Please don't think that Zelda's condition is not very near to our hearts,—(+ we hope + *pray* it is + will not be as serious as you seemed to think)—and that all your misfortunes are not, in part, ours too—But at times it seems best, for the very sake of our affection for you,—not to let your manners (let us call it)—throw it off its equilibrium—even momentarily—We have no doubt of the loyalty of your affections (+ we *hope* you haven't of ours)—but consideration for other people's feelings, opinions or even time is *Completely* left out of your makeup—I have always told you you haven't the faintest idea what anybody else but yourself is like—+ have never (yet) seen the slightest reason for changing this opinion, "half-baked" as you consider it! You don't even know what Zelda or Scottie are like—in spite of your love for them. It seemed to us the other night (Gerald too)—that all you thought and felt about them was in terms of *yourself*—the same holds good of your feelings for your friends—in lesser degree,—Why,—for instance *should* you trample on other people's feelings continually with things you permit yourself to say + do—owing partly to the self-indulgence of drinking too much—+ becoming someone else (uninvited)—instead of the Scott we know, + love + admire,—unless from the greatest egotism, + sureness that you are *righter* than anyone else? I called it "Manners" but it is more serious—It is that you are only thinking of yourself.

Be as angry with me as you like, Scott—it may be true that "toute verité n'est pas bonne a dire" but I feel *obliged* in honesty of a friend to write you: that the ability to know what another person feels in a given situation will make—or ruin lives.

Please, please let us know Zelda's news. Dos[1] is here + says she seemed *so well* when you all went out together 10 days ago—I think of her all the time—

Forgive me if you can,—but you *must* try to learn, for your own good, + your adored family's good—Some distrust for your behaviour to *all* other human beings. Your infuriating but devoted + rather wise old friend—

Sara

[1] John Dos Passos.

FROM: G. B. Stern[1] ALS, 4 pp. Scrapbook. Princeton University

Jan 3rd [1935]

Dear Scott Fitzgerald

There's a genial old man in New York who collects celebrities; + about twice a week he rings me up + bellows: "Good morning. How are you?" ("Not at all well")—"That's *fine!* Now is there any one you'd like especially to meet + I'll get him for you!"

Then, regularly, I answer: "Yes: Scott Fitzgerald," + that seems to stump him. . . . So he rings off.

But it happens to be true. And as it looks as though we were not going to meet, I'll take Dorothy Parker's advice + write to you. Because we were talking, yesterday, about "Tender is the Night," + what a magnificent piece of work it was, + how it made these Massive Masterpieces look silly + heavy-jowled, + how it turned us inside-out when we read it + didn't put us back again, + what lovely sensitive ironic writing was in it; + we talked like that for quite a long time, till Dorothy said that you'd like to hear, perhaps, how I felt about it. As a matter of fact, if you read your reviews, you would know, to a certain extent, how I felt about it, because I did it for the Daily Telegraph. But one fan letter more or less in your mail can't do any harm. And I'm not altogether sure that "Tender is the Night" was appreciated enough or for the right reasons. People are such chumps.

You won't stop writing, will you, whatever happens. I'll give you a list of at least a Hundred Best Authors (Ancient + Modern) whose books I could easily spare. But not yours.

Yours
G B Stern

[1] Gladys Bronwyn Stern, English novelist who had reviewed *Tender Is the Night* in the *London Daily Telegraph*. She was best known for her *Matriarch* series, published 1919–35.

TO: Brooks Bowman[1] TLS, 2 pp. Princeton University

1307 Park Avenue,
Baltimore, Maryland,
January 16, 1935.

Dear Mr. Bowman:

As one of those who considers this year's performance the best in ten years and also as one of those who consider your achievement both as actor and composer the brightest spot in it I take the liberty of addressing this suggestion to you. For a long time there has been the lack of any new

Princeton songs, either suitable to stadium or to senior singing. Several people have spoken to me about it recently on the basis that I used to write the lyrics and a greater part of the shows back in '15, '16, '17 and was a former officer of the club.

My suggestion is this: that your song "East of the Sun" with a few changes in the lyric could be made a fine piece for senior singing. The general line would be:

"East of the sun, west of the moon
Lies Princeton,
South of the south, north of the north
Lies Princeton,
Here in my heart etc. etc.
Lies Princeton."

The idea being, of course, that Princeton to Princeton men lies outside of time and space. It's an over-sentimental conception but perhaps might mean something to the older alumni. If practical, you might try it out with the Glee Club quartet.[2]

Again congratulations to all of you for a really fine show which indicated that there's life in the old girl yet, as I had begun to doubt.

Yours
F. Scott Fitzgerald '17

[1] Princeton undergraduate who wrote "East of the Sun" for the 1934–35 Triangle Club show, *Stags at Bay*.
[2] Fitzgerald's suggestion was not acted on.

TO: Maxwell Perkins — Wire. Princeton University

1935 FEB 12 PM 9 46
TRYON NCAR[1]

TITLE SEEMS INCREASINGLY MEANINGLESS COULD YOU KILL JACKET AND PRINT PLAIN ONE SUGGESTIONS LAST NIGHTS MOON STOP IN THE LAST QUARTER OF THE MOON STOP GOLDEN SPOONS STOP MOONLIGHT IN MY EYES STOP OLD TITLE INVITES DISASTER WOMEN COULDNT PRONOUNCE AND WOULD FIND NO INTEREST I HAVE CONSIDERED THIS CAREFULLY[2]

SCOTT.

[1] Fitzgerald had gone to North Carolina for the benefit of his tuberculosis.
[2] Perkins wired back on 13 February that changing the title of *Taps at Reveille* would "increase already extravagant expenses and further delay publication." See Perkins' 18 February letter to Fitzgerald in *Scott/Max*.

TO: Chatto & Windus — TL(CC), 3 pp. Princeton University

1307 Park Avenue,
Baltimore, Maryland,
February 26, 1935.

Dear Sirs:

My books of short stories have had unusual success in this country. Three have been published, selling 15,000 to 20,000 copies each, and another is to be published this spring. Save for the short stories of O'Henry they are about the only collections that have had much sale in this country for a decade. I wonder if you would be interested in publishing a volume of them containing twenty-one of my stories selected from the four volumes.[1] They would be

(1) The Offshore Pirate
Bernice Bobs Her Hair
The Ice Palace
Benediction

These four from "Flappers and Philosophers" which Collins published in England twelve years ago without success

(2) May Day
The Diamond as Big as the Ritz
The Curious Case of Benjamin Button

From "Tales of the Jazz Age" which Collins published in England ten years ago, also without success.

(3) The Rich Boy
Absolution
The Baby Party
Rags Martin Jones and
the P— of W—

From "All the Sad Young Men" never published in England.

(4) The Scandal Detectives
The Freshest Boy
He Thinks He's Wonderful
First Blood
The Woman with a Past
The Last of the Belles
A Short Trip Home
Crazy Sunday
Babylon Revisited

From "Taps at Reveille" which appears here next month.

(5) The Intimate Strangers
(from McCalls Magazine 1935)

The actual bulk of such a collection might be appealing to the library patron in England. I know that there also only occasional Katherine

Mansfield catches the popular fancy. Nevertheless, I put this up to you in the hope that by publishing my books there and publishing them closer together I might build up some sort of English public, as both from the press and from the individual reports there is nothing in my work which is necessarily unintelligible or antipathetic to the British mind.

Very truly yours,

[1] This collection was not published.

FROM: Zelda Fitzgerald
After February 1935

ALS, 2 pp. (fragment). Princeton University
Sheppard and Enoch Pratt Hospital
Towson, Maryland

some forgotten nursery rhyme. There are human bodies without identities as I am myself. But I hope life is very important in your hotel; that the lobby is full of people making estimates of each one's worldly goods. Places where life transpires under a cloud of suspicion are more exciting. Your interest, inexhaustible tolerant and expansive, has always made anywhere a desirable spot.

D.O.—take care of yourself. I wish I could have done it better. You have never believed me when I said I was sorry—but I am.

Some day you will be well + happy again. Maybe you will be at Norfolk, salty and sun-burned. Your eyes will glow in the darkened room and the hum and drone of deepest summer will seep in under the blinds. Sand in the bath-tub, sticky lotion and a towel for your shoulders. I'll have to sprawl on my stomach till this sun-burn clears away and cut the sleeves from my softest shirt. Your hair is so gold against your golden skin. And your legs stick to-gether as you sit with them crossed. The room is so still because of the vibrance of the heat outside. Have a good time. Of cource it's cooler in the grill, and clandestine, and there are gusts of bottled breezes.

North Carolina should be pines and pebbles, geraniums and red tile roofs—and very concise. Breathe in the blue skies. It's a good place to get up early; there's a very polished sun to burnish the mountain laurel before breakfast. And the brooks gleam cold in the thin early shadows. Biscuits and grits all floating in butter; resin on your hands and frogs bouncing out of the twilight.

D.O—

D.O—

What is there to say? You know how much I have loved you.

Zelda

TO: Lois Moran TLS, 3 pp. Lois Moran Young

1307 Park Avenue,
Baltimore, Maryland,
March 8, 1935.

Note the date! Had no adress till
Lew Azrael gave me one a few minutes ago[1]

Dear Lois,

I was touched that you all called me up on your wedding day,[2] and it more than made up for the somewhat chilled receptions I had come to expect from your telephone. Could I have been there I'd have loved it—the marriage of Columbine, (and Lou Azrael told me it wasn't far from that, with all sorts of amusing circumstances,).

I believe you are going to be just as happy as it is possible for anybody to be with a dash of the Celt in them. For many reasons I want to see you again before many more years drift by and hear about the singing and hear about you and how all your funny old idealisms have worked out. (You will probably like me better because I don't drink any more.)

I have a book of short stories called "Taps at Reveille" coming out in a few weeks and I thought of including that old piece "Jacob's Ladder"[3] but I found that I had so thoroughly disemboweled it of its best descriptions for "Tender is the Night" that it would be offering an empty shell.

This seems an odd congratulatory letter to write to a lady who once played such an important rôle in my life, but it doesn't seem from this distance that your marriage has changed anything about you—I think one of the strongest impressions I ever got of the absolute seperateness of people, of old friends, of differing destinies and directions was that day in the Belvedere three years ago when you unwound a little of your life for me—gave me glimpses into all the years that I knew nothing of. Somehow we always expect old friends to be static until we see them again, and after thirty this is to some extent realized—but in case of one who started so early and so galvanically as you did, the changes are rung so quickly that no one could be anything but rather confused and dazzled.

I have never quite forgiven you, by the way, for the remark that you made in the dressing room at Ford's that you "had me on the spot" that day. My mind was never working faster than then; all that was true was that I was tired and abstracted. You probably don't even remember the episode, but keep it in mind, young lady, to quote old Sage Fitzgerald, you can stab a man anywhere but in his pride; never touch that unless you mean murder. Anyhow, I love you tremendously always and wish all happiness to you and yours.

Your Chattel
Scott Fitzg

[1] In holograph; the envelope is postmarked 6 May. Louis Azrael was a Baltimore journalist.

[2] Miss Moran had married airline executive Collier Young.

[3] *The Saturday Evening Post* (20 August 1927). Fitzgerald had written this story about a young actress after meeting Miss Moran.

TO: Mrs. Bayard Turnbull — TLS, 1 p. Princeton University

1307 Park Avenue,
Baltimore, Maryland,
March 15, 1935.

Dear Margaret,

I was delighted to have the Little *Review* as I never see it, however, I do not like Canby as I think he is a coward, a trimmer and a hedger. The book[1] is certainly getting all the publicity that could be demanded. I was personally disappointed in it coming after "Look Homeward Angel." But nothing that he did could be undistinguished in its way. What disappointed me was the gawky and profuse way in which he handled his material. I will have a copy by the end of next week. Would you like to read it, or have you it?

It was very sweet what you had to say about Zelda. Things are black there and I do not know how it is going to turn out. I want to see you soon.

Ever yours,
Scott

[1] Thomas Wolfe, *Of Time and the River* (1935).

TO: Roger Burlingame — TLS, 1 p. Syracuse University

1307 Park Avenue,
Baltimore, Maryland,
March 23, 1935.

Dear Roger:

I was surprised and delighted at the tremendous advances that your book makes.[1] I was interested in Dan Andrews from start to finish and thought his problem was handled with great imagination and sympathy.

The only story I can compare it to is the ancient and honorable high flight of Mr. Hugh Walpole (whom I don't otherwise admire) in "The Gods and Mr. Perrin" which you may have read. But I think yours is superior in every way. Many congratulations! I am especially delighted in your aptness in choosing the theme. I felt that in your first novel[2] about the young man in business that you were handicapped from the start.

With all congratulations,
Scott Fitzgerald

[1] *Cartwheels* (1935).
[2] *Susan Shane* (Scribners, 1926).

TO: James Boyd[1] TLS, 2 pp. University of North Carolina

1307 Park Avenue,
Baltimore, Maryland,
March 26, 1935.

Dear Jim:

It was great seeing you and your removal honestly leaves a gap. I made a short trip to New York which, while it reminded me that I have lost much of my old enthusiasm for talk and groups, also reminded me of the vacuum in which I have been living down here. If I have anything in common with a man intellectually here our pasts seem to have been very different, and if, on the contrary, our pasts have been the same, there is no intellectual meeting ground. I feel like the old maid you mentioned one day who "grew less desirable and more particular."

Max was tremendously enthusiastic about your new book[2] feeling that it was immensely in advance of the part published. I mean he was enthusiastic in his absolutely Grade A manner and left me full of curiosity.

I see a faint chance of a jaunt toward North Carolina in six weeks or so, but only a faint one, and I'd love to spend a day or two with you if things are breaking right.

I hope you and your wife are both much better and that we will all look back to this winter simply as a winter of discontent.

Ever yours,
Scott Fitzg—

[1] Princeton-educated novelist; author of *Drums* (1925), *Marching On* (1927), and *The Long Hunt* (1930).
[2] *Roll River* (Scribners, 1935).

TO: V. F. Calverton TLS, 1 p. New York Public Library

1307 Park Avenue,
Baltimore, Maryland,
March 26, 1935.

Dear George:

The best thing I can think of is a recent strain of poetry.[1] The trouble of sending fiction is that Gingrich of *Esquire* has stepped into the breach with an honorarium of $250 for such pieces as cannot possibly get into the popular magazines. So as long as this lasts, selling stories for less is giving money away—and I can't do that while I am still in debt. That, frankly, is the situation.

You are right that the house here is growing to be a habit and it takes a tidal wave to move me out of it. However, I am growing damn sick of it and would love to see you, but if I go to your house what the hell could I do with Scottie? Let's hope she is invited somewhere next week end or the one after that. She *is* invited Fri. I think[2]

Ever yrs
Scott

[1] Calverton had solicited a contribution from Fitzgerald for *The Modern Monthly*. Fitzgerald did not appear in this magazine.
[2] The last sentence was added in holograph.

TO: Maxwell Perkins TL, 2 pp. Princeton University
Baltimore, Maryland

Dear Max:
You might file this
F Scott Fitzgerald[1]

March 26, 1935.

To Maxwell Perkins

This collection will be published only in case of my sudden death. It contains many stories that have been chosen for anthologies but, though it is the winnowing from almost fifty stories, none that I have seen fit to reprint in book form. This is in some measure because the best of these stories have been stripped of their high spots which were woven into novels—but it is also because each story contains some special fault—sentimentality, faulty construction, confusing change of pace—or else was too obviously made for the trade.

But readers of my other books will find whole passages here and there which I have used elsewhere—so I should prefer that this collection should be allowed to run what course it may have, and die with its season.

If the Mediaeval stories are six or more they should be in a small book of their own. If less than six they should be in one section in this book. Note date above—there may be other good ones after this date.

CHOOSE FROM THESE
not more than 16

1921 Two for a Cent

1924 One of My Oldest Friends
The Pusher in the Face

1925 Presumption
Adolescent Marriage
1926 The Dance
1927 Jacob's Ladder
The Bowl
Outside the Cabinet Makers

1929 The Rough Crossing
At Your Age

1930 One Trip Abroad
The Hotel Child
1931 A New Leaf
Emotional Bankruptcy
Between Three and Four
A Change of Class
A Freeze Out

1933 More than Just a House
I Got Shoes
The Family Bus
1934 No Flowers
Her Last Case
1935 The Intimate Strangers

THESE ARE SCRAPPED

1919 Myra Meets His Family
The Smilers
1921 The Popular Girl
1923 Dice Brass Knuckles and Guitar
1924 John Jackson's Arcady
The Unspeakable Egg
The Third Casket
Love in the Night
1925 Not in the Guide Book
A Penny Spent
1926 Your Way and Mine
1927 The Love Boat
Magnetism

1928 A Night at the Fair
1929 Forging Ahead
Basil and Cleopatra
The Swimmers
1930 The Bridal Party
A Snobbish Story
1931 Indecision
Flight and Pursuit
Half a Dozen of the Others
Diagnosis

1932 What a Handsome Pair
The Rubber Check
On Schedule

1934 New Types

1935 Shaggy's Morning

And, to date four mediaval stories

[1] Added in holograph.

TO: Robert Penn Warren[1] TLS, 1 p. Yale University

1307 Park Avenue,
Baltimore, Maryland,
April 5, 1935.

Dear Mr. Warren:

Thanks for your letter. I wish to God I had something for you, especially as I undertand that Louisiana State University is to be the Athens of the nation. Seriously, I haven't a thing available but I'll certainly send something when I have.

You have the beginnings of a nice list there and I wish you the greatest success in your venture.

I, too, am sorry we did not meet again in Paris. My God, how I'd like to be there now!

Sincerely,
F Scott Fitzgerald

[1] Warren was at that time editing *The Southern Review*.

TO: Bert Barr TLS, 2 pp. Princeton University

1307 Park Avenue,
Baltimore, Maryland,
April 24, 1935.

Dearest Bert:

Your letter came at a moment when I was thinking of you. Twice in the last three years I've tried to get in touch with you when in New York but each time you were in Europe or Florida. Naturally, much has happened since that time. My wife recovered, and relapsed, and is still in uncertain health in a sanitarium; we have lived in Montgomery, Alabama, and Baltimore, Maryland, where were are now; I have published two books and wonder if you have read them; I no longer drink and have gotten very old; have never run into such easy pickings since that white purse, though the fence I went to still insists it was a phoney and the $23.70 he gave me was mostly for the letters he found inside it.

Often think of your wild wit and of our three curious pilgrimages ending with a somewhat unfortunate one in Paris with a hotel keeper's wife shrieking curses through the telephone.

I have your address and on every one of my infrequent visits to New York I will faithfully give you a call and see if I can round you up.

Always affectionately yours,
Scott

TO: C. A. Wright[1] TLS, 2 pp. Princeton University

1307 Park Avenue,
Baltimore, Maryland,
April 24, 1935.

Dear Mr. Wright:

I was on the "Tiger" staff at Princeton for three years and got out many issues of it, though I was not chairman. It was never as big a thing at Princeton as was the "Record" at Yale or the "Widow" at Cornell because most of the local wit was concentrated on producing the hullabaloo of the Triangle show, and lately the "Intime" reviews. My time was chiefly notable for the first acknowledgment in print that girls would be girls and the first use in the east of such words as "necking" and "petting" exemplified by a series which I started and Arthur Hope, the author of "She Loves Me Not," continued. It was called "International Petting Cues."[2]

With best wishes,
F Scott Fitzgerald

[1] An editor of the University of Pennsylvania *Punch Bowl* who had written Fitzgerald for a statement about college humor magazines.
[2] "Intercollegiate Petting Cues," *The Princeton Tiger* (10 November 1917).

TO: Mrs. Albert Kibble, Jr.[1] TL(CC), 2 pp. Princeton University
Baltimore, Maryland

The Penetentiary,
Louisville, Ky.,
April 24, 1935.

Dear Mrs. Kibble:

I got your letter here in the Penetentiary just as I was about to be hanged for murder. I think I am probably your half-brother and another half-brother is in the Maryland State Penetentiary charged with forgery. It is all a put up job as we Dukes are descended from the great Duke of Marlborough and have always been able to make a living by crime without being caught. There is a big petition here to spare my life and if I am spared the noose I would love to visit you in Pickford and stay as long as you like—like a year or so. I am not a harmful man except sometimes when I am irritated or when the food is bad, so you can feel perfectly safe. I am also handy around the house to crack safes, forge checks or deal with wicked neighbors as I am a good shot.

Please write me care of my attorney, F. Scott Fitzgerald, 1307 Park Avenue, Baltimore, Maryland, as they will not let me receive mail here.

Yours till the trap falls,
Basil Duke

[1] Mrs. Kibble had seen one of the Basil Duke Lee stories and had written to Basil Duke Lee c/o *The Saturday Evening Post* inquiring if he was her lost half-brother. Fitzgerald exchanged letters with Mrs. Kibble, pretending to be Basil Duke and Duke's lawyer. He mentioned these letters in "Author's House" (*Esquire*, July 1936), reproving himself for his cruelty: "You can pay a little money but what can you do for meddling with a human heart? A writer's temperament is continually making him do things he can never repair."

TO: H. L. Mencken — TLS, 2 pp. New York Public Library

1307 Park Avenue
Baltimore, Maryland,
April 29, 1935.

Dear Menck:

Here is the Gertrude Stein story "Melanctha." Remember that it came out around 1909. Anderson and Hemingway have acknowledged their enormous debt to it. And the curious power achieved by repetition wisely used is here at a peak that she never reached again. I am particularly fond of the passages where Melanctha is "so blue" and I think by God that it is the best conveying of an inconsolable gloom that I have ever read. Please read some of it.

The very loneliness in which its huge jump landed her is responsible for the crazy warping of her career and I hate to see you making generalities about her that made me definitely feel bad, just as when you jumped at conclusions about Hemingway's early work.

Got an odd reaction from seeing you the other night—of finding you, if I may be so bold as to say it, in a curious state of isolation neither sought for nor avoided. I suppose if one creates a world so wilfully, effectually and completely as you have for instance, there is nothing much to do except to live in it. I find myself increasingly in a similar position, a barber who trusts only his own razors. At present everybody is too young for me or too old, too malleable or too set, and for my purposes there is really not a great selection of food at the intellectual banquet. This is too complicated to elaborate here. I simply want to say that I can understand and respect your aloneness.

Always cordially and admiringly,
Scott Fitzg

P.S. I hope Sarah is improving with the season—Zelda is.

TO: James Boyd
Spring 1935

ALS, 2 pp. University of North Carolina
Baltimore, Maryland

Dear Jim:

I groan when I think what a bore I must have been the other night—reading you two of my own pieces + telling you a preposterous story of an Eton-Harrow cricket match (Jack Churchill *did* take us to one + we left early, but it wasn't like that at all. And then keeping you up with an entire scenario of a prospective novel. You must have envied yourself the evening with Pat O'Mara.

Almost always when I've been working hard what little color there is in my personality goes out of it. I should insert a proper interval of prayer before seeing anyone. It was, however, great to see you, and if I'd been content to let you + Bill[1] have a good time without intruding myself things wouldn't have been so irritating (this is on the assumption that you are fond of me as I am of you, else you wouldn't have stayed at all).

Anyhow apologies are always a little more wearying than what they apologize for. Warm regards to the progeny and to Kate and high hopes that she, and the rest of us, will climb out of this valley of illness

Ever Yours
F Scott Fitzgerald

[1] Probably William Leonard of Baltimore.

TO: Ernest Hemingway

Wire. Kennedy Library

BALTIMORE MD 1935 MAY 13 AM 7 07

WANT TO SEE YOU AS AM GOING TO CAROLINA FOR SUMMER COULD MAKE THREE DAY STAY KEYWEST ARRIVING THIS THURSDAY BUT WANT TO INTERFERE YOUR PLANS STOP NOT UP TO ANYTHING STRENUOUS PROBABLY RESULT OF TEATOTALING SINCE JANUARY WIRE THIRTEEN NAUGHT SEVEN PARK AVENUE BALTIMORE[1]

SCOTT.

[1] Pauline Hemingway wrote on the telegram: "Wired Scott Ernest in Bimini, forwarding your message so sorry Love P." Fitzgerald never visited Hemingway in Key West.

TO: H. L. Mencken
Late May 1935

ALS, 2 pp. Goucher College
Grove Park Inn letterhead
Asheville, North Carolina

Dear Menk: I'm sorry as hell about all this nuisance to Sara. That's the hell of getting older. It occurred to me the other day that I'm never in a group any more without their being one deaf person—

—My God! There is a convention of laundrymen here + a party next door has been telling for 10 minutes how a man named Bill vomited on his two long-haired dogs.

Anyhow you shouldn't have gone to that trouble of writing me about Gertrude Stien though your conclusions interest me.[1] I remember the contradiction in sense—somebody is dead + then alive again, in *Melanctha,* I think. But I believe you would have felt the book more remarkable had you read it in 1922 as Wilson + I did. She has been so imitated + thru Ernest her very rythm has gone into the styles of so many people. I agree that Carl[2] is too inclined to rapture on his Ronald Firbanks ect. but I still believe Gertrude Stien is some sort of a punctuation mark in literary history.

I am here resting, very bored + rather uninspired by my surroundings but here I stay another month by Doctor's orders. So I wont be able to have an evening with you, much as I'd like it. Saw George[3] a moment in New York—he looked handsome + young for his years. He was with the embryonic Tully.

With Warmest regards to you both

Scott Fitzg

There hasn't been a novel worth reading in one solid year, English or American.

[1] See Mencken's 23 May 1935 letter about *Three Lives* in *Letters of H. L. Mencken,* ed. Guy J. Forgue (New York: Knopf, 1961).

[2] Probably Carl Van Vechten.

[3] George Jean Nathan.

FROM: Gertrude Stein
Spring 1935

ALS, 2 pp. Scrapbook. Princeton University

My dear Scottie

Here we are at home and the birds and some of the birds nightingales and at first coming back was very strange but now it is very nice, very nice and quiet I thank you, I did like being with you all in Baltimore and here we have Zelda's picture and it is a very beautiful picture and it gives us a lot of pleasure, I wonder where you are and what you are doing, and I hope you are doing it very well whatever it is, you know that I am very fond of you and hope this finds you the same, do let us know about yourself we are here until October and love to you all over and over again

Always
Gtde Stein

TO: H. L. Mencken
1 June 1935

ALS, 1 p. Goucher College
Grove Park Inn letterhead
Asheville, North Carolina

Dear Menk:

It is so terribly sad. Sara's fine life was all too short. My thoughts are all with you tonight[1]

Scott Fitzg

[1] Sara Haardt Mencken died on 31 May 1935.

FROM: Zelda Fitzgerald
June 1935

ALS, 4 pp. Princeton University
Sheppard and Enoch Pratt Hospital
Towson, Maryland

Dearest and always
Dearest Scott:

I am sorry too that there should be nothing to greet you but an empty shell. The thought of the effort you have made over me, the suffering this *nothing* has cost would be unendurable to any save a completely vacuous mechanism. Had I any feelings they would all be bent in gratitude to you and in sorrow that of all my life there should not even be the smallest relic of the love and beauty that we started with to offer you at the end.

You have been so good to me—and all I can say is that there was always that deeper current running through my heart: my life—you.

You remember the roses in Kinneys yard—you were so gracious and I thought "he is the sweetest person in the world" and you said "darling." You still are. The wall was damp and mossy when we crossed the street and said we loved the south. I thought of the south and a happy past I'd never had and I thought I was part of the south. You said you loved this lovely land. The wistaria along the fence was green and the shade was cool and life was old.

—I wish I had thought something else—but it was a confederate, a romantic and nostalgic thought. My hair was damp when I took off my hat and I was safe and home and you were glad that I felt that way and you were reverent. We were gold and happy all the way home.

Now that there isn't any more happiness and home is gone and there isn't even any past and no emotions but those that were yours where there could be any comfort—it is a shame that we should have met in harshness and coldness where there was once so much tenderness and so many dreams. Your song.

I wish you had a little house with hollyhocks and a sycamore tree and the afternoon sun imbedding itself in a silver tea-pot. Scottie would be running about somewhere in white, in Renoir, and you will be writing books in dozens of volumes. And there will be honey still for tea, though the house should not be in Granchester—[1]

I want you to be happy—if there were justice you would be happy—maybe you will be anyway—

Oh, Do-Do
  Do-Do—

Zelda.

I love you anyway—even if there isn't any me or any love or even any life—

I love you.

[1] Rupert Brooke, "The Old Vicarage Grantchester" (1912).

Dearest and always
Dearest Scott:

I am sorry too that there should be nothing to greet you but an empty shell. The thought of the effort you have made over me, the suffering this nothing has cost would be unendurable to any save a completely vacuous mechanism. Had I any feelings they would all be bent in gratitude to you and in sorrow that of all my life there should not even be the smallest relic of the love and beauty that we started with to offer you at the end.

You have been so good to me — and all I can say is that there was always that deeper current running through my heart: my life — you.

You remember the roses in Kenney's yard — you were so gracious and I thought — he is the sweetest person in the world — and you said "darling". You still are. The wall was damp and mossy when we crossed the street and said we loved the south. I thought of the south and a happy past I'd never had and I thought I was part of the south. You said you loved this lovely land. The wistaria along the fence was green and the shade was cool and life was old.

— I wish I had thought something else — but it was a confederate, a romantic and nostalgic thought. My hair was damp when I took off my hat and I was safe and home and you were glad that I felt that way and you were reverent. We were glad and happy all the way home.

Now that there isn't any more happiness and home is gone and there isn't even any past and no emotions but those that were yours where there could be any comfort — it is a shame that we should have met in harshness and coldness where there was once so much tenderness and so many dreams. Your song.

I wish you had a little house with hollyhocks and a sycamore tree and the afternoon sun imbedding itself in a silver tea-pot. Scottie would be running about somewhere in white, in Renoir, and you would be writing books in dozens of volumes. And there would be honey still for tea, though the house should not be in Grantchester.

I want you to be happy — if there were justice you would be happy — maybe you will be anyway

Oh, Do-Do
Do Do —

Zelda I love you anyway — even if there isn't any me or any love or even any life — I love you.

TO: Don Swann
c. July 1935

ALS, 2 pp. Unlocated[1]
Grove Park Inn letterhead
Asheville, North Carolina

Dear Don:

If I seemed unappreceative of the etching of Tudor Hall it was because I was in a somewhat distraught mood—I'm delighted with it + very proud to own it. The reason I didn't want the one of Hampton was because the Pleausance Ridgely from whom I descended, antedated the present mansion by a generation + I thought it would be pretentious of me to hang it for that reason. But direct ancestors *did* live in Tudor Hall so you can imagine the pleasure it gives me.

(What do copies sell for by the way?)

I was a little disturbed by Don Junior—he is a fine man; and I'm sorry he has such sharp edges + hope that girl isn't putting him through any special hells.

Affection to All of You
Scott Fitzg—

[1] Published in facsimile by *Architectural Digest*, 33 (July-August 1976), 113.

TO: James and Katherine Boyd
Summer 1935

ALS, 4 pp. University of North Carolina
Hotel Stafford letterhead
Baltimore, Maryland

Dear Boyds:

Thank you. In better form I might have been a better guest[1] but you couldn't have been better hosts even at a moment when anything that wasn't absolutely—that wasn't near perfection made me want to throw a brick at it. One sometimes needs tolerance at a moment when he has least himself.

Jim—remember all the things *I did like about "Roll on Sweet Missoula"* (I forget the exact name)[2] and not my theoretical objections to certain ideas of yours as to what the novel should drive at. In spite of everything those are dangerous subjects as we grow older, no matter what we say, unless the discussion is remote from anything of ours, like discussing someone elses children in any terms except polite compliments. It comes so close to our only justification for living.

So if you ever get in doubt about anything about the theory of the novel, consult young Burt—he will set you straight. From now on I'm never going to embark on European travel without a few words with him. He must have been invaluable to Struthers[3] + Katherine.

I hope that the ills of the flesh plague you both less + less. I feel much better and have just sold the *Post* an idea that occurred to me on the train about Lincoln as our best writer, for $5000.[4] I make him something like Geo. Lorimer, though—with a touch of Hoover + J. P. Morgan.

Page just caught the train + we talked for an hour—gosh he's interesting, + I stupidly hadn't guessed it. The depression governor of N.C. then came along + I went to bed leaving them to their sins.

So farewell to the pines + gracious houses + happy children, + all good things to you both from

Your Friend
Scott F.

P.S. If you're ever wrapping things, send *The Long Hunt* to Ashville. I'll be there in a wk.

[1] Fitzgerald had visited the Boyds at Southern Pines, N.C.
[2] Fitzgerald was playing on the title of Boyd's *Roll River*.
[3] Writer Maxwell Struthers Burt.
[4] This was a joke.

TO: Laura Guthrie[1]
Postmarked 29 July 1935

ALS, 3 pp. Princeton University
New York City

Sweet Laura:

This is no longer funny. Just what has happened will not surprise you, but it fills me with a profound disgust. I have become involved again + am moving to another hotel, because it means no more work is possible here. Dont women have anything more to do than to sit around and make love + drink beer? This time my emotions arn't even faintly involved and I'm such a wreck physically that I expect the heart, liver and lungs to collapse again at a moments notice–six weeks of late hours, beer and talk, talk, talk.

So I'm moving to the Hotel Pennsylvania, not half so nice to write in but where I'll be completely anonymous + not possibly run into anyone I know, and I'll try to get this silly preoccupation off my mind.

A long telegram from "Terre Haute" reached me here. It was sent to the Algonquin (how she remembered I stayed here?) + to lake Lure in duplicate. Utterly indiscreet as they might have been returned to her as undelivered. They leave Terre Haute the first of August + the ladies "may remain at the Inn a few days after that. I dont mind another parting, if it is a real parting + is not in that atmosphere of scandal + desperate risk so I shall probably go to Lake Lure from here (that is by way of Baltimore to arrive August 2nd. When I know she's alone I'll get in touch with her—not before. I don't even think I want to return to the Inn while she's there. It would be the same story over again + everyone would be less amused + less patient. And if it *wasn't* the same story it would just spoil something that was very nice.

Oh hell, I don't know what to do—about anything. All this seems very trivial when compared to such major problems as Zelda's health or your projected divorce, and work, + the revolution. Anyhow—wires to the Pennsylvania till further notice—hold mail for awhile.

With Love Always
Scott Fitzg

A telegram from Terre Haute has just cleared up matters somewhat. Evidently Eleanor wants to go back to Ashville—in other words I am to be driven away, at least temporarily. So I think I'll go to Hendersonville or Saluda—Lake Lure is too hot.

So—my schedule will be

Hotel Pennsylvania till Tuesday—then Princeton (The Princeton Inn) for one night, then Baltimore for Wed night + Thursday. (Hotel Stafford). Arrive Ashville Friday morning— not going to hotel but as follows:

Before going to Hendersonville I want to see her—I want to see you too of course but I want to see her first because my plans depend on her stay at Grove Park. So I wish you would get word to the little devil when she returns to the Inn (not thru Eleanor, not in writing, + preferably after the consort leaves Wed.), that I will meet her at 11.30 Friday at that rathskeller place in the same position as Battita's bk. shop but one street further down the hill. She'll understand—tell her the place we had the bad caviarre. *Don't* tell her I'm arriving that morning. Tell her nothing.

Probably we'll talk for a couple of hours. If you are engaged that afternoon leave word where you are. You might tell the hotel I'll be back eventually—but as vaguely as possible—Ive been delayed by business + by sickness of my wife, any damn thing. But that if Im not back within another wk. I'll clear out my stuff.

All right—well, there's a plan at last. Nothing hurt but old man work—who is most important of all.

[1] A fortune-teller at the Grove Park Inn who had literary ambitions and became Fitzgerald's secretary-confidante. See Laura Guthrie Hearne, "A Summer with F. Scott Fitzgerald," *Esquire* (December 1964).

TO: Beatrice Dance[1] AL, 6 pp. Princeton University
August 1935 Asheville, North Carolina

I guess nobody won + everybody lost. This is your first tragedy—my second. I think I shall never let my heart go out of myself again. I somehow think you will, and if you do, that you will have learned something from all this so that your bill from the florist will be for laurel + gardenias —instead of white roses.

As this day wanes there is still no image of you emerging—only a memory of beauty and love and pain. The whole thing became a complete universal transcending the *You* that I first envisaged, so that what you did didn't matter because you could do no wrong. What you did became the standard of rightness.

Things are falling into shape a little—I managed to write several nessessary letters, send out laundry + get a little of what passes for sleep. However, if I don't feel better tomorrow I shall get me a doctor + join the procession of casualties which has followed in the wake of all this. Still no solid food, skin in a shambles, a hell of a cough + a vision so blurred that I'm beginning to hang on to things again. I know its all beer + cigarettes but I want to be reassured. If I could ever get it through my head that I'm thirty-eight not twenty-eight!

I broke off my letter to lie down a minute and opened a magazine to an article about Texas—you are everywhere around me, I cant see myself going into that dining room again or on to the verandah. Except that I have reached a zero hour as to work I would move on somewhere. I wonder if you went to New Orleans + saw your friend Cagen and what you think about + if you are all set up in your house and seeing old friends and with new plans stirring. Summer is full + rich tonight with heat lightening over the mountains. I wish I liked something except you.

There are so many memories and such varied ones that an endless series of images passes before my eyes Mostly unconnected, without hope and without solution. Something is over. I had been looking for you a long time I think here + there about the world and when I found you there occurs this tragedy or this mess depending on whether Im introverting or extraverting on the matter. All I know is I'd like to sit for a thousand years and look at you and hear your voice with the lovely pathetic little "*peep*" at the crecendo of the stutter. I think the word lovely comes into my mind oftenest when I think of you.

Everything harsh that passed between us that awful day I blame on that champagne which I practically forced on you + my own garrulousness with Eleanor so let's try to think of happier things that came before. There was some rouge, do you remember? And a moon at the castle and some soap and Mr Hirsch, and thousands of Sanos and some tears and an insurance mans parade + Mr. Fry's odd find, and some stairs and an elevator and taxis and beer at breakfast, and so much laughter. And a

rathskeller and a green lake and a bandage on my arm and a pink dress and a blue dress and rayon shirts and canned ale and a few golden hairs on my black sweater and you in my heart when I woke up + when I went to sleep and—
Goodbye darling Beatrice.

[1] A married woman with whom Fitzgerald had an affair in Asheville while she was staying at the Grove Park Inn with her invalid sister Eleanor.

TO: Beatrice Dance — ALS, 5 pp.[1] Princeton University
August 1935 — Asheville, North Carolina

The writ of *habeus corpus* that extradited you was not a surprise but it was a shock. Of *course* you were right to go—anything less than a complete separation would have been a perfectly futile temporizing.

But you have become the only being with whom I have any desire to communicate any more and when you were gone there was the awful stillness of a desert.

Love seems to be like that, unexpected, often tragic, always terribly mortal and fragile.

When this reaches you a little of the past, our past, will have already died, so I'm trying to write without the emotion I feel. For the moment we are both life-tired, utterly weary—and unreconciled. The old dizziness has come back (dont worry—it'll probably leave in a day or so) + I simply lie + think. Except that I hate to think of you in the heat of Tennesee I am glad I didn't have to go again. And to stay here with Hop + Doctor Cade[2] between us was impossible. I didn't even mind much when they ganged up on us + could have faced fifty more of them with you at my side—but that was not to be.

This is letter number 4, the others having been destroyed, each one antiquated by the changing conditions. Some day darling Beatrice I will write something about you "that the world will not willingly let die," but that time isn't yet and I cannot get much into the form of a letter. So let me simply clear up some loose ends:

The telegram fell into my hands by utter accident. (Do not blame Laura—she has been so kind and patient, and even wise within the limits of her curiously warped cosmos with its archaic demonology). I did not brood about it but I *did* think about it, and am still unaware what was in your dear distraught mind. It seemed to refer to some *specific harm I had done you*. And while there's been plenty of *general* harm done, any battle presupposes certain casualties. So I could only decide that you suspected some disloyalty to *us*. There has never been any, there have been some indiscretions but *darling,* in all good humor and even delight in your naïvette the palm must certainly be handed to you in that regard. But after you called from Chattanoga I am quite agreed to consider it as something hysterical and exhausted, and unless you choose to bring it up again it is forgotten. There could be an indefinate series of post mortems about these last four days—but let's dont.

Eleanor is out of my thots. Dr. Cade doesn't agree with me, + broadminded as he was about the triangular situation, he was very firm about "hands off" on the question of Eleanor. So, while I preserve my own opinions, I wont even restate them to you. And niether of us can be very smug about the neglect she came in for. Nevertheless there's a contradiction somewhere + I don't see why—oh hell, let's as Scotty says, skip it. I am too sick + miserable to think today. There doesn't seem to be anything in the world but you + me. You are the lovliest human being I have ever known.

Oh darlin I cant write any more. There is lots more to say + if you'll send me some safe adress I'll write you there. I love you—you are chrystal clear, blown glass with the sun cutting always very suddenly across it.

Thank you for the Sanos.[3] I am sending you some books

Your loving
Scott

Goodbye goodbye, you are part of me forever

[1] Although it contains no salutation, this letter appears to be complete.
[2] Mrs. Dance's husband and their family physician.
[3] Denicotinized cigarettes.

TO: H. L. Mencken — ALS, 3 pp. New York Public Library
c. 6 August 1935 — Asheville, North Carolina

Dear Menk:

Without any desire to begin a sleeveless correspondence I have found the urge to write you irresistable. In a world that in the last five years has become for me a world of children it was so damn nice to meet a man again, to know that one's shoulders wern't the only ones that were broken + bowed a bit trying to carry the awful burden of responsibility out of this dark cavern (Jesus, what a metaphor!)

We have both lived too deeply in our own generations to have much communication except with a mutual respect but that you accepted me as an equeal—even tho it was the exterior factor of a terriblee mutual grief that acted as the catylitic agent—settled something that had been haunting me about my relations with men since my tacit break with Ernest Hemmingway. I suppose like most people whose stuff is creative fiction there is a touch of the feminine in me (never in *any* sense *tactile*—I have always been woman crazy, God knows)—but there are times when it is nice to think that there are other wheel horses pulling the whole load of human grief + dispair, + trying to the best of their ability to mould it into form—the thing that made Lincoln sit down in Jeff Davis' chair in Richmond and ask the guards to leave him alone there for a minute

Dont answer this. It's really nothing but a bread + butter letter

Yrs
F. Scott Fitzg

Postsript

As to George.[1] It was so damn hot + it seemed awful to keep you standing there in the hall, so I didn't finish what Id intended. There was one point in 1920 when Geo. was older than me, + then there was suddenly a point where I was older than he was—about the time I was 26. Geo. was + wanted to remain a young man + I wanted to grow old + live + break, with my race. There was no further communication except my gratitude to him for first recognizing that I had a style. In the matter of discussing him no apologetics (your word!) are nessessary between you + me.

FSF

[1] George Jean Nathan.

FROM: Gerald Murphy — ALS, 2 pp. Princeton University

11 Aug. '35

Dear Scott:—

If at any time during this late summer or Fall you are to be free for a week-end (one during which I am going to Saranac Lake) I'd like so much to take you up with me. I go every 2 weeks. A train leaves at 1015 p.m. (daylight),—one reaches here at 730 Monday a.m.

It has occurred to me in all this that you alone have always—known shall I say?—or felt?—that Sara was—that there was about Sara—something infinitely touching,—something infinitely sad. Life begins to mark her for a kind of cumulous tragedy, I sometimes think.[1] Surely only those who have been as honest and trusting with life as she has really suffer. What irony! She needs nourishment—from adults—from those who are fond of her.

[Patrick's temperature and pulse remain where they descended. His appetite is failing. The poison causes this, the doctors say. He has lost 7 pounds since he went to Saranac Lake.][2] This drains Sara. I can tell from her voice.

I wonder so much how Zelda is.—It has been worrying us too,—your health. Be careful, Scott,—about everything!

your affectionate admonisher,
Gerald

I'd like to feel I know where you are from time to time.[3]

G.

[1] One of the Murphys' sons, Baoth, had died that year; the other son, Patrick, had tuberculosis.
[2] Murphy's brackets.
[3] See Fitzgerald's 15 August letter to Sara Murphy in *Letters*.

TO: Beatrice Dance — Wire. Princeton University

ASHEVILLE NCAR 506P 1935 AUG 20 PM 4 40

TAKE YOUR MEDICINE AND GO ON STOP THE WORLD WASNT BUILT FOR A PARLOR CAR BUT THE BRAVE INHERIT THE RAILROAD SYSTEM STOP COURAGE OUGHT TO MEAN SOMETHING TO US NOW[1]

UNSIGNED.

[1] Beatrice Dance had been hospitalized in San Antonio.

FROM: Sara Murphy — ALS, 4 pp. Princeton University

Aug 20 [1935]

P.O. Box 423 Saranac Lake

My dearest Scott,—I was (+ am) touched beyond words at your sweet letter—it did me a lot of good too—*thank* you for wanting to,—+ writing it—(I so often want to do things + then don't) It *is* a moment when I am raw to the feelings toward me of my friends (like the man who scraped his fingers to feel the combinations of safes.)—So that any demonstration of affection,—not to mention a regular "letter of recommendation" such as you sent me,—throws me into a comfortable state of basking—

I don't think the world is a very nice place—And all there seems to be left to do is to make the best of it while we are here, + be *very* VERY grateful for one's friends—because they are the best there *is*,—+ make up for many another thing that is lacking—And it seems not to matter *nearly* so much what one thinks of things—as what one feels about them.

I hope you *are* coming up to see us in Sept.? Gerald said he thought you would + we are all delighted. Would you like to bring Scotty?

There isn't the least danger, as the guest-house is separate—and all Patrick's dishes, silver, + laundry even are done apart. And we have had lots of guest-children + so take infinite precautions. We should love to see her again. I should love to see Zelda too—I think of her face so often, + so wish it had been *drawn* (not painted, drawn.) It is rather like a young Indian's face, except for the smouldering eyes. At night, I remember, if she was excited, they turned black—+ impenetrable—but always full of impatience—at *something*—, the world I think—she wasn't of it anyhow—not really

I loved her. + felt a sympathetic vibration to her violence. But she *wasn't throttled,*—you mustnt ever think she was except by herself—She had an inward life + feelings that I don't suppose anyone ever touched—not even you—She probably thought terribly dangerous secret thoughts—+ had pent-in rebellions. Some of it showed through her eyes,—but only to those who loved her. Why do I use the past tense?—Because she may *very well* be all right yet. I have been thinking about her a great deal lately—I read a Christian Science book the other day—(to please a C. Scientist friend)—And it said the easiest people (for them) to cure were those who were out of their minds. Why don't you try it? It might very well be true. *Anything* might be true, Scott, + will for you, if you like. Because God knows we have all of us tried every material aid we or anybody else could *think* of—It might be a good thing to turn to the spiritual + hope the bon Dieu won't notice that it is a last resort!

We all send love, + hope to see you Sometime Soon. And thank you for the Comforting letter—I needed it—

Your old halfbaked but affectionate friend—

Sara. ↑

How *are* you? for good, as You must know.

TO: Cyril Clemens[1] Typed statement signed, 1 p. Bruccoli
Before 30 November 1935 Asheville, North Carolina

Huckleberry Finn took the first journey *back*. He was the first to look *back* at the republic from the perspective of the west. His eyes were the first eyes that ever looked at us objectively that were not eyes from overseas. There were mountains at the frontier but he wanted more then mountains to look at with his restless eyes—he wanted to find out about men and how they lived together. And because he turned back we have him forever.

F Scott Fitzgerald

[1] President of the Mark Twain Society. Fitzgerald provided this statement for the banquet marking the centenary of Samuel Langhorn Clemens' birth, 30 November 1935.

TO: Gerald and Sara Murphy Wire. Honoria Murphy Donnelly

BALTIMORE MD

1935 DEC 26 AM 8 15

WE THREE WERE TOGETHER TODAY AND WE THOUGHT OF ALL FIVE OF YOU AS ALWAYS TOGETHER

SCOTT AND GELDA.

FROM: Gerald Murphy ALS, 3 pp. Princeton University

I suppose that we are two blatherskites living in stone huts in some distant Irish valley. You and I, I mean. I count so on my rare dish of talk with you. I guess we are Irish.

31 Dec. '35

Dear Scott:—

I have been here since the 24th. Honoria[1] was here also with us and went to the Myers at Bedford Village for New Year's day. To-morrow I return to New York.

We have thought of you very much these days and wondered if our wire would reach you. It was good to hear from you and that you were able to be together. Thank you for that message, Scott. Of all our friends, it seems to me that you alone knew how we felt these days,—still feel. You are the only person to whom I can ever tell the bleak truth of what I feel. Sara's courage and the amazing job which she is doing for Patrick make unbearably poignant the tragedy of what has happened—what life has tried to do to her. I know now that what you said in "Tender is the Night" is true. Only the invented part of our life,—the unreal part—has had any scheme any beauty. Life itself has stepped in now and blundered, scarred and destroyed. In my heart I dreaded the moment when our youth and invention would be attacked in our only vulnerable spot,—the children, their growth, their health, their future. How ugly and blasting it can be;—and how idly ruthless.

When you come North let me talk to you. I am probably going to England to the factories late this month. "Trade" has proven an efficient drug,—harmful but efficient.

Our love to you all,
Gerald

Hotel Russel, 45 Park Avenue N.Y.C.

[1] The Murphys' daughter.

TO: Laura Guthrie
1935

Inscription for *Tender Is the Night*.[1]
Bruccoli
Asheville, North Carolina

F Scott Fitzgerald
request the
pleasure of Laura
Guthrie's company
in Europe
1917 — 1930

[1] The inscription page has been removed from the book.

TO: Beatrice Dance TLS, 4 pp. Princeton University

Cambridge Arms Apartment,
Baltimore, Maryland,
March 6, 1936.

Six months have passed away and I think I can write you objectively. For myself don't take that little trilogy in *Esquire* too seriously.[1] For yourself I knew you would come back to life. The occasion for this letter is the disturbing note about Eleanor. Has she destroyed, or do you think she has the data that I got from New Haven?

There is one last article to appear next month in *Esquire*. I started to enclose it but haven't it.

My regards to Hop and to Dr. Cade, though the former will naturally not feel very warm about them, and for the latter I have a certain cynicism. I don't think a diagnostician can set himself up as a psychiatrist. The field is simply too large. We've been over that before in Asheville.

What on God's earth I could have told him that upset you has been on my mind all autumn, and I still can't imagine how in the short conversation between Cade and me anything disturbing could have transpired. Still, I remember how I upset Eleanor in ten minutes, so anything is possible. I remember our conversations as about like this:

a. His career as a medical man in Texas.

b. You and Hop and my instinctive liking for Hop and continued reiteration on my part that there was no question of any further continuance of our "affair." To resume: that the grief it inevitably caused Hop would be an essentially maturing element in his life—a viewpoint from which I privately was in doubt about, but didn't argue over.

c. Some stray talk on his part about Tula's[2] custody, as if you and I were headed for divorce and remarriage, and about the fact that you had once been rich—as if I was some sort of fortune hunter. An idea that he persistently couldn't erase from his mind.

d. That Eleanor was a blind—my concern about her and such matters being utterly bogus. I showed him something from the *American Psychiatric View* that had just come in, to convince him differently, but it didn't seem to take.

That's all I can remember of our conversations on those tragic mornings with all of us in a state of frayed nerves.

I know Hop and I talked only of college and the military profession, and vaguely of Eleanor—and of perhaps a few trifles. We were both so upset we might have murdered each other if we'd discussed you so we instinctively avoided the subject.

With all my heart I appreciate your remembering me at Christmas with the gift of *Fortune*, and with all my heart I am sorry to have brought so much sorrow into your life.

But the purpose of this letter is again Eleanor (and you can show this letter to Hop, but not to Dr. Cade, because their are strictures on him in it.) I think the place for her is Chicago. See if she has that data. If the situation becomes difficult write or wire me here and I can get information from the tops in Baltimore without any trouble.

With dearest affection always,
Scott Fitzg

P.S. I did also say to Dr. Cade: that *I went away to avoid the situation.* Not in any case to avoid *you*! Perhaps that confused what he told you.

P.S. 2. Remember this: houses grow larger and streets bigger after we have left them. At least I have always found it that way.

[1] "The Crack-Up" (February 1936), "Pasting It Together" (March 1936), and "Handle with Care" (April 1936).

[2] Tylah Dance.

TO: Mrs. Richard Taylor
c. Spring 1936

TLS, 1 p. (with holograph postscripts).
Princeton University
Asheville, North Carolina

Tuesday afternoon

Dearest Ceci,

Things have been in a wild mess here since Christmas with literally nothing but sickness. Zelda's been worse and your correspondent (for several months now a worthy citizen who touches no liquor in any form) is a very distracted man. Hence he is not the best company for a child on her spring vacation, especially as Scottie has been living high on a diet of parties and is beginning to believe all life is a dance. If you can keep her three or four days while I get a story in motion you'd be a life saver indeed.

I enclose check for fifteen dollars which would cover her expenses.

With much love to you all and wishes that I could see you too.

Scott

This seems silly—but Scotty is precocious—don't let any 15 yr. old rake kill her in a drunken auto—ah me—the sins of the fathers!

P.S. 2 She has a ghost of a cold. If she seems stuffy + cross it may mean a tempo. This is just an improbability from an old worrier.

FROM: Sara Murphy ALS, 8 pp. Princeton University

April 3 [1936]

Dearest Scott,—I was so glad to get your news—we have wondered So often, Gerald and I,—and Dos + Katy[1] and I—and Alice-Lee Myers and I, *Where* you were + how Zelda is doing + how big Scotty is,—+ how *you* were. Gerald is back—since the 16th March—he was gone 6 weeks—and though according to himself he had a dull + terribly busy time it must have been good for him, as change always is, as he came back looking 100% better or at least 100% more interested in the world--(which I suppose means the same thing + is the best we have.) Is that the Worthwhile school of thought? (If so, I take it back—) Anyhow he is back in harness in Mark Cross Co—+looks awfully nice, + *better*. A little too thin perhaps—but he says I always say that. We here on the Magic Mountain are really doing better too. I am *really encouraged* about Patrick—,you will be glad to hear, I know. He is still in bed (a year + a half!) + still has temperature—if that went down he could get up—And though he has his ups + downs which we expect, + scared us to death by having grippe about 5 or 6 weeks ago—he looks + acts—+ the symptoms are better,—+ from weighing 59 lbs last Sept. now weighs 80—So you see that is concrete evidence, even if one couldn't see + feel the change. I am sure, Scott, he is going to be allright + will yet have a good life, quiet perhaps, without violence, + yet maybe better than any of ours—in the end. I hope so indeed.

I did indeed read your trilogy in Esquire—+ think you must feel better for it—as it seemed to me to accomplish that,—get something off your chest,—if not much more not more for anybody else, I mean. *Do* you feel better? Do you know, I never realized, till I read those pieces (of course you won't care what your "half-baked" old friend thinks,—but you can tell me so in yr next letter.) I never realized, to what *extent* you thought you could run things + control your life by just wanting to—(Even *I* knew THAT much.) Do you *really* mean to say you honestly thought "life was something you dominated if you were any good"? Even if you meant your *own* life it is arrogant enough,—but life! Well if you thought *that*,—out of College, married, a father, travelled, seen life, etc etc—I give up. I can't fight you on paper, but there are several very loose stones in your basement, rocking the house. Let us have another argument—Sometime—(proving nothing, + neither side giving way an inch!!) Oh how wrong you are,—Scott, about so many things—but nevertheless go on,—I hope you *do*?—regarding Gerald + me—as your "inalienable friends"—But I *do* think Henley's man who said "my head is bloody but unbowed" is better than you on your old rifle range—They are both heroics if you like, —but the first is cheerfuller. If you just *won't* admit a thing it doesn't exist (as much.)—Even not admitting,—rebelling, dragging one's feet +

fighting every inch of the way, one must admit one can't *control* it—one has to *take* it,—+ as well as possible—That is all I know—I remember once your saying to me—in Montana at Harry's Bar,[2] you + Dotty[3] were talking about your disappointments, + you turned to me + said: I don't suppose you have ever known despair? I remember it so well as I was furious, + thought my God the man thinks no one knows despair who isn't a writer + can describe it. This is my feeling about your articles.—You mustn't think from this that I can't know + feel what you have been through—+ *do* think + feel about it oftener than you think—You have been cheated (as we all have been in one way or another) but to have Zelda's wisdom taken away,—which would have meant *everything* to you, —is crueller even than death. She would have felt all the right things through the bad times—and found the words to help,—for you, + for her real friends—I miss her too—You have had a *horrible* time—worse than any of us, I think—and it has gone on for so long—*that* is what gets us, + saps our vitality—your spirit, + courage are an example to us all—(Even though I do think your thinking procèsses are faulty!) And we will always have a warm spot in the heart, + a lighted candle for you—That is forever.—

With love—Your old + very devoted (though irritating) friend—

Sara

I didn't know I was going to write such a long letter! And no writer either. When are you coming up to see us? And you never said how you were *yourself*?[4]

[1] John and Katy Dos Passos.

[2] When Patrick was being treated for tuberculosis at Montana-Vermala in the Swiss Alps, the Murphys took over a local tavern and named it Harry's Bar.

[3] Dorothy Parker.

[4] See Fitzgerald's 30 March letter to the Murphys in *Letters*.

TO: Beatrice Dance — TLS, 2 pp. Princeton University

Grove Park Inn,
Asheville, N.C.
April 21, 1936.

Dear Beatrice,

Just got your wire about my story[1] and being at the Grove Park Inn I am irresistibly impelled to write you. The wire was forwarded from Baltimore.

My wife had reached a stalemate there and I had brought her here to Dr. Robert Carroll's[2] hospital. He seems to stand as one of the best psychiatrists in the East—and naturally in finding out that a man of such stature was in Asheville, I was reminded of our men at Appalachian Hall last summer. But apparently that is regarded in high psychiatric circles as mostly front.

Dr. Carroll's place is on the outskirts of town here, and Zelda seems comparatively happy there. She is no longer in a suicidal state but has an equally difficult halucination which I won't go into. It seems pretty certain she will never be able to function in the world again, at least not without a companion. But I am always full of hope, and a miracle may still happen.

In my quarter things are brighter than they were last year at this time when life was a matter of the sick trying to help the sick. The other day I took her to Chimney Rock where her family used to come when she was a child. And in trying (unsuccessfully) to locate the boarding house where they had stayed, the cloud of tragedy seemed sometimes to lift. As I told you, sometimes one would never know she was ill.

Thanks for your remembering about my story. Daughter also liked it and it seems to be having quite a circulation at her school.

The winter went with the usual difficulty specified for men these last few years, and I was glad to get back to Asheville with a few weeks of rest in view. My daughter is going to Miss Walker's school next fall and Vassar two years from this autumn—at least that is the plan. She wants to have some sort of debut, East or West, and I am taking her to Saint Paul this summer for the first time since she was an infant. Then I think we will go to Europe for a few weeks in June.

This letter seems largely taken up with my domestic affairs. I meant it to be otherwise. The hotel is startlingly familiar with Mr. Frye, Mrs. Reeves, and Mrs. Guthrie telling fortunes sometimes, and Mr. Barnett, and Mac and Ulysses and Charlie, and Mr. Rickey, who married his daughter the other day to a man about his own age, and Mrs. Dooley always looking like a diamond. And Asheville is the same with brightly painted working girls down town. I asked whether the set-up at the Castle had changed, but it seems Mrs. What's-her-name has sold out.

The movie magazine clipping arrived—seems there was some prize offered for the best letter. But Scottie sent her letter to three magazines and they all published it. It was a Pyrrhic victory because she didn't get the prize. She said she constructed it on the best models.

I think of you always and hope that things go well with you. I am glad that Eleanor's illness was no more serious.

Always, with deepest affection,
Scott

[1] Possibly "Fate in Her Hands," *The American Magazine* (April 1936), a story about a fortune-teller that was loosely based on Laura Guthrie.

[2] Psychiatrist at Highland Hospital.

TO: C. O. Kalman
May 1936

ALS, 2 pp. Princeton University
Asheville, North Carolina (?)

Dear Kaly:

Thanks for your most prompt response. In general the plans are vague, largely hovering betwen taking Scottina to Europe or to St. Paul + contingent, as always, on the condition of my invalid. I dont know what the gddam hell to do about that + I am trying to be hard-boiled about it, but as you know, it's a life-long consecration + all the friends I ever had couldn't argue me out of the idea that that's where my first duty lies.

I'm getting sentimental on you when this was to be a practical letter. What I didn't make clear in my telegram was that I wanted a parking place for Scottie (who is a little beauty by the way + the current belle of Baltimore) and then to leave her there + go back to Zelda in N.C. I don't want her to go to a dude ranch but I want her to have some sense of life in the middle-west + to have some friends there. I guess I've left my idea as vague as I started it. My own heart is here as always, yet a part of me will always live in St. Paul which I think of as a tough + usually impolite titty and am indeblet to for the ability to take it. I am not a snooty man, Kaly, + you'll have to interpret this arrogance in the light of what you know of me. Its perhaps a weakness in myself that makes me cling to the civilized + sophisticated. But I want daughter to know St. Paul

I will write or wire more specifly next week

Ever Your Devoted Old Friend Scott

TO: Bennett Cerf

Wire. Columbia University

BALTIMORE MD 402A 1936 MAY 16 AM 5 17

WOULD YOU CONSIDER PUBLISHING TENDER IS THE NIGHT IN THE MODERN LIBRARY[1] IF I MADE CERTAIN CHANGES TOWARD THE END WHICH I SEE NOW ARE ESSENTIAL COMMA IT WOULD MAKE ALL THE DIFFERENCE IN THE SPLIT UP OF THE TWO PRINCIPAL CHARACTERS STOP OR DO YOU THINK THAT ONCE PUBLISHED A BOOK IS FOREVER CRYSTALIZED PLEASE ANSWER CAMBRIDGE ARMS CHARLES STREET BALTIMORE MARYLAND

SCOTT FITZGERALD.

[1] The novel was not included in The Modern Library.

TO: Beatrice Dance
After 15 May 1936

ALS, 2 pp. Princeton University

Cambridge Arms
Charles St.
Baltimore

That was a very beautiful Easter present. It came one day when I was feeling rather sorry for myself having just written the second of a new series for *Esquire* on the autobiographical side (to be called "Author's House," "Afternoon of an Author" ect.)[1] and they were so nice and white and filmy.

Your long letter cleared up many things that had puzzled me. Our medical tycoon was single-minded, to put it mildly. I was amused at the "gorilla" *motif* as I hadn't credited him with such powers of invention. I'm glad Eleanor is off luminol. I lived on those coal-tar derivatives for months last year and its really a form of getting mildly drunk and leaves a very definate hang-over.

I shall be in Ashville again about the 15th of June (it will have been a year since we first went to the Castle that night with Mr. Jewishman). After that my plans are very vague—I feel more acted apon than acting as Scottie grows up and I sign applications for school and for Vassar. I suppose there will always be bursts of vitality or impatience, but for the time I am simply a medium for the care of two helpless people in a somewhat formidable universe. I *could* go to Europe and absorb some ideas, I *could* go to Hollywood and absorb gold, but I feel ham-strung by circumstances and will possibly end by sending Scottie to camp again and staying in Ashville. I have such a nice appartment here with my library around me that I hate like the devil to go into storage again without even the prospect of really living abroad, but there is no particular point of my living alone in Baltimore now that I've moved Zelda to Carolina. One thing I'm sure of—that I'll spend next winter on the Caribean Sea. I'm starting a long thing that will take at least two years and I want to start it outside the borders of our melancholy nation, which I find more attractive at a distance.

This is all egotistic and remote to you. I never picture you as you are now but as you were last summer, in my sight and out of it, for you were just as real when you were in Highlands. I hope you awfully happy—someday, a long time from now, I'm going to write about you really but in a way that wont hurt anyone + that only you + I will understand

Scott

[1] Fitzgerald included a 15 May telegram from Arnold Gingrich:

GOOD IS HARDLY THE WORD ITS PERFECT STOP NOT A WORD MISSING AND NOT A WORD AMISS STOP VARIATIONS ON THAT THEME WILL BE WELCOME UNTIL DOOMSDAY STOP MANY THANKS AND BEST WISHES.

TO: Beatrice Dance TLS, 2 pp. Princeton University

1 East 34th Street,
Baltimore, Maryland,
June 10, 1936.

Beatrice:

The books were wonderful. The doctor's book I am in the middle of now; the Santyana novel seems to be one of those things one must at least look over though I approach it with a vast skepticism—not skepticism for the man as he is top notch in his profession, but skepticism for anyone trying to play with a metier that is not his own. However, I have always held that every intelligent person has at least one good novel in him and one of my favorite novels, Samuel Butler's "Way of All Flesh," was written by a man who was essentially a scientist. At any rate I will report on "The Last Puritan" later. As for the third book I am so glad to get it.[1] Mencken usually sends me his small books but a big expensive thing like that no writer could live and give all his friends copies. I have an earlier edition of the work but this, of course, supercedes it. Looking at my library at this minute I don't think I now have the earlier edition after all. In any case he seems to have added an awful lot—

—At all events your taste is always impeccable.

You enclosed me a story by Roarke Bradford and I am ashamed to say that I haven't dipped into it yet; I admired Marc Connelly's dramatization of "Green Pastures" but I've been in the middle of a couple of stories and I always hate to read anybody else's fiction when I am working on something myself.

Next point (does this sound very official?) I think you'll like a series of sketches I'm starting in *Esquire* next month, very personal and similar to the Crack-up series. The first one is "Author's House" and the second "Afternoon of an Author" and the third I haven't done yet. They will be respectively in the July, August and September issues and they can tell you more about myself than I ever could in a letter because unfortunately, in my profession correspondence has to be sacrificed to the commercial side of being a literary man and I am probably the worst letter writer in the world.

And you are one of the best.

I hope you'll have a good time in California. My plans are still as vague as vague but I think I shall be able to make up my mind by another week or ten days.

With dearest affection always,
Scott

[1] *The American Language, Fourth Edition* (1936).

TO: Mrs. Richard Taylor

TLS, 2 pp. Princeton University

2400 Sixteenth Street, N.W.,
Washington, D.C.,
June 13, 1936.

Dear Cici: This is less a bread-and-butter letter than a necessary expletive; there is certainly no use in rubbing it in on an ignorant and selfish person, but the little display that we witnessed yesterday is an illumination indeed. Supposing I had gone up to your mother and said "Tom[1] is a bad priest," or supposing I had gone up to Clifton[2] and said "you are a bad naval officer and a poor aviator," can you imagine the repercussion. And yet a certain party felt quite entitled to let me know that she hadn't liked any of my stories lately, that her husband agreed with her, and one was supposed to take it with equanimity. The insolence was such that I could only be amused at the time, but looking at it in perspective I have succumbed to a certain irritation.

However, that was the only bitter spot to mar a perfect day with all of you. Please deliver the following messages for me.

To Aunt Elise, that I looked over the little book she gave me the other night and got much pleasure from it.

To Sally Pope, that when I get back to Baltimore, I will do the little sentence of description that I wrote about her on the beach and send her a carbon so that she will know that I have used it.

To. Teah, that I congratulate her (as I do all your children) on their power of producing lovely progeny.

To Hume with thanks for the use of his razor, and to Charlie with regrets that we didn't meet this time.

And to you most of all my dearest love.

Mother has had a bad morning. She wasn't able to hold on any nourishment, so I had the nurse keep taking the pulse, and the medical doctor arrived about an hour and a half ago and gave her some intervenous nourishment, which is done with a hypodermic. I will be able to be here the rest of the day with her, but have got to get back to Baltimore tonight and think I will send Scottie over tomorrow rather than try to make it two days in succession myself, because it is still necessary to steer the middle course between keeping her old heart nourished and at the same time feed her enough sedatives to keep her from ruining the operation. The situation is well in hand and I can only thank you with all my heart for your cooperation. Am counting on Annabelle arriving Tuesday morning.

With dearest love always,

Scott

[1] Thomas Delihant.
[2] Fitzgerald's sister was married to Clifton Sprague, a naval officer.

FROM: Gilbert Seldes TLS, 1 p. Princeton University

Mantoloking New Jersey June 26 [1936]

Dear Scott:

I haven't minded my own business for years, why should I start now. Please don't be annoyed—I know you won't be offended—by my discussing your professional affairs with you.

Max told me of the book you are proposing and of his opposition and when I told him what I thought, he thought it wouldn't be a bad idea if I wrote you.[1] First, you must know that I have in ingrained dislike of all books not written to be books, but collected from scattering magazine pieces. That prejudices me right away.

But more important, Scott, is that you seem more and more to me an essential figure in America and sooner or later you will have to say your complete say, not only in fiction, but in the facts about yourself and the part you played at the beginning and what you think of it now. And that sort of book, of supreme importance, will have all the edge taken off it, if you now publish the raw material, the mere fact without the thought. (I know that some of the pieces, especially lately, haven't been mere fact. But the general turnout of such a book as you could make from unassociated pieces would be the jumble of episode and fact—and you have meaning to give to them.)

Moreover, I am convinced that out of such a book, the reviewers first and a great part of the public later, would select a few spectacular episodes from the golden age and slide over the rest. They couldn't do that if the whole thing were integrated, the trivial and the tragic and everything all part of a single thing.

I know that you've had hard going lately, Scott, and it always enchants me when, in spite of your difficulties, you come through so steadily and so well with your stories and your Esquire pieces have shown me, perhaps I'm wrong, a direction you're taking, although I don't follow you into ruin and the rest, but I think you are being thoughtful and this is precisely the time when a book would be germinating or gestating or whatever that process is. I don't think it's the time for a synthetic, put-together work.

See paragraph one of this letter and forgive me if you disagree with me. Amanda sends all her love to you and Zelda and Scotty and so do I.

Yours always
Gilbert

[1] On 2 April 1936 Fitzgerald sent Perkins a plan for a collection of his articles. Perkins responded 16 June: "My great objection to it is that you could do such a very fine book of reminiscences at some time, and if you publish this, you greatly compromise the possibilities of ever doing such a book."

TO: Earl Donaldson[1] TL(CC), 1 p. Princeton University

July 5, 1936

Dear Earl:

With the help of a suggestion of John Biggs Jr. I went to the Scribner Company and arranged to borrow enough to cover the two deficient payments of March 15 and June 15. From his office I called up your office in Newark, New Jersey and found that you are equipped to handle such assignments in emergencies. The time is short now because my interests must be protected before the fifteenth of July, and this is already the sixth; so would you send me the following documents which I must fill out?

(a) An assignment to the Charles Scribner Company, 599 Fifth Avenue, New York City, of first rights, in case of my death, of $1500.00 to them, I am told that you must send me three papers to be signed and assigned. Mr. Charles Scribner will, in return, pay you $1500.00 to cover the payments overdue on March 15 and June 15. According to your letter, it is important that all of this should be done before July 15, up to which time I am protected, after that I think I shall be able to carry the $700.00 per quarter. I don't want any slip up to happen here, because this is the only protection that my wife and child have.

(b) My life insurance might lapse for non-payment; therefore, I would like to have my policy changed so that the beneficiaries, in the event of my death, will be, first: Charles Scribner, to the amount of $1500.00; and second: Harold Ober, of 40 E. 49th Street, New York City, to the extent of $8,000.00, balance to go to such heirs and assigns as may be made in my will.

Please send all necessary forms in triplicate to provide for the Charles Scribner's Sons, and for Harold Ober, to reach me by special delivery here.

Ever yours,
F. Scott Fitzgerald

P.S. I am sending this registered mail and hope for a registered letter from you.

Cambridge Arms Apts, Baltimore, Md.

[1] Of the Sun Life Insurance Co.

FROM: Charles Scribner   TL(CC), 2 pp. Princeton University

July 10, 1936.

Dear Scott:

Eben Cross called me up on the telephone the first of the week and I sent him the cheque for $1,500.00 to pay your back insurance premiums. I also thought that it was a good time to check up on the advances we had made in order that no misunderstanding might ever arise.

Most of the ancient indebtedness was written off against the serial publication of "Tender is the Night" and the royalty advance on this book. The advance still stands us out $1,671.50 but this is of course only an obligation against "Tender is the Night."

Since its publication we loaned you $2,000.00 which Ober thought would be met by the sale of motion-picture rights but unfortunately that never came off. On this it was agreed that you should pay 5% interest and it was not to be regarded as a charge against your account with us.

Your open account shows that we have advanced you from time to time $4,400.00 and that this has been reduced by the fact that you have earned since that time $1,188.99 in royalties. We have also paid $100.00 for customs duties which I do not know about personally, and for sundry charged $39.83 plus a bill in the retail of $390.03, and $77.22 interest on the $2,000.00.

Therefore, after deducting the unearned balance on "Tender is the Night," there is a deficit in your account of $5,818.09, not taking into account the $1,500.00 which you have just assigned on your life insurance policies.

I have thought of asking you to include the loan of $2,000.00 in the assignment as there does not seem to be any prospect in the next few years that you will be able to take care of it, and had I known that Ober was willing to do so I would have spoken to you, but I rather hated to see your daughter's heritage cut down any.

All this is rather painful and I hope it will not give you a headache. Max and I thought it only fair, however, by you as well as ourselves to get the figures on paper, to make sure that we agreed with you.

I certainly hope that you may be able to find time to write a novel in the next few years but I can very well appreciate the difficulties you are up against.

I overlooked giving you a book which I thought might interest you and when you have a permanent address I wish you would let me know and I will send it on.

With all best wishes

Sincerely yours

TO: Dr. Robert S. Carroll TL(CC), 2 pp. Princeton University

Grove Park Inn,
Asheville, N.C.,
July 21, 1936.

Dear Dr. Carroll:

Not take up your time unduely, let me sketch my last meeting with Zelda so that before I go away, which will be on next Sunday night, we can have some talk with a little of the underbrush cleared away.

. . . .[1]

Since I have been here I have gotten off of liquor and I am in the condition that I had meant to be on my arrival. I feel so much better that it seems almost on the cards for me to come back to Asheville for the rest of the summer after these few days that I must spend on my mother's business in Baltimore. I have no report yet from Dr. Ringer about whether or not there is any lingering t.b. but I know I am pretty damn well worn out and I know too that I would not want to make a change of base to another health place nor to to some trolley-end like Blowing Rock where I could not get typing down or find any of the props of civilization. So even if you do not think it advisable for me to see much of Zelda, would object to me remaining here through August—here at the Inn, I mean, or at the Manor if I can get more satisfactory rates there? (I am summer-conditioned and my best chance of recuperating vitality comes in summer, and something tells me that this one may just be my last chance.)

Giving you time to answer that question, let me say a word about Mrs. Sayre. Her relations with her daughter are as rudimentary now as they were at the nipple stage. I verily think in spite of the straight talk last April she fully expected to spend this summer in a rocking chair talking to her and going against all your attempts to activate Zelda's mind and body. The sick part of Zelda of course welcomes the chance to sit on her bottom and stay a few months in slow motion. So far as Mrs. Sayre is concerned my influence is null. She has only to tag me with "drinks too much" and for her simple mind that counts my judgment out. So I wish you would take as much of that on your broad shoulders as you conveniently can. You will see her today, Tuesday, and I will get in touch with you the day following.

Very truly yours,

[1] One hundred fifty-six words omitted by the editor.

TO: Rita Swann TLS, 1 p. Bruccoli

Grove Park Inn,
Asheville, N.C.,
July 21, 1936.

Dear Rita:

I am afraid that was somewhat confused over the phone but I was in such confusion when leaving that I scarcely understood the thing myself. It seems that for a son or daughter to declare a parent incompetent some *third* party, beyond the testifying child and testifying doctor, is required to give a disinterested opinion as to whether the heir or prospective trustee is acting in good faith or is trying to racket the aged out of their wherewithal.[1] Now, Rita, if I have to ask you to testify that I was not insane, you are the last person I would call upon because I know that you have always thought that I was. All the more reason for your knowing that I would not have the Caponi-craft to wizard my mother out of her money.

A letter from Ed Poe[2] says that I must appear in my stocking feet at the Rockville courthouse at 2 o'clock next Monday the 27th. Whether you, as the mysterious ghost assuring the law of my probity, will have to appear or not or merely make a deposition will best be answered if you call Ed Poe at Plaza 5610.

If necessary and if you can spare the time we could all ride over together.

I find in my papers among unanswered a carbon of the preface to Don's book of etchings. You remember in the first version I ghosted for Governor Ritchie, then revised it leaving him out, and I have a dim memory that you wanted something further done to this one; or am I wrong and did the draft get there by mistake?

Very best to you all,
Afftly, Scott

[1] The matter was dropped; Fitzgerald's mother was not declared incompetent.
[2] Edgar Allan Poe, Fitzgerald's Baltimore lawyer.

TO: Zelda Fitzgerald TL(CC), 1 p. Princeton University

Grove Park Inn,
Asheville, N.C.,
July 27, 1936.

Dearest,

It was too bad on your birthday that everything went so badly. I left the hotel for the hospital that morning fully intending to be back here in time to lunch with you as it looked at first like merely a severe strain that could be cured with hot applications and rest and a sling, but the x-ray showed that there was a fracture in the joint of the shoulder and a dislocation of the ball and socket arrangement of the shoulder so that it looked in the x-ray as though it were an inch and a half apart.

They sent for a bone specialist and he said it would have to be set immediately or else I would never be able to raise my arm as high as my shoulder again so they gave me gas about like when they pulled your tooth and I fell asleep thinking you were in the room and saying, "Yes, I *am* going to stay; after all it's my husband." I woke up with a plaster cast that begins below my navel, estends upward and goes west out an arm. I am practically a knight in armor and only this afternoon have been able to get out of or into a chair or bed without assistance. It has postponed all my plans a week so I will not leave here until next Sunday, the second, instead of tonight as I had planned and this will of course give me a chance to see you before I go. I am sorry your mother had indigestion the same day and served to make our birthday utterly incomplete.

The accident happened in a swan dive *before* I hit the water. It must have been the attempt to strain up in the first gymnastics I had tried for almost three years and the pull of the actual bone pressing against the feeble and untried muscles and ligaments. It was from a medium high board and I could feel the tear before I touched the water and had quite a struggle getting to the rail.

However, I am in good hands and they have saved me from any permanent crippling of the arm though I am afraid I will have to spend the week dictating to Jim Hurley rather than scribbling the rest of my story in pencil which comes much more natural.

With dearest, dearest love,
Scott

TO: Scottie Fitzgerald — Typed copy, 1 p. Princeton University
Asheville, North Carolina

July 1936

Darling:

I'm afraid the candy would reach you in a glucose mass if I sent it across the heat wave. So buy it yourself or get someone to buy it in Dartmouth.

A very tiresome day. In mid-story and along comes a wire from Hollywood from an agent, who wants to buy sound rights of *This Side of Paradise* (Paramount owns the old silent rights but never made it) for sale to some big company. Query: What will I ask? If I ask a few thousand and he sells for a big sum I'll feel stung—if I ask too much he'll lose interest. Dont want to bring in Ober because if *two* agents commissions.

We got 7500 for *sound rights alone* to *Gatsby,* but that, being a play too, had already brought 60,000 for silent rights while Paradise only brought 10,000. Think I'll ask 5,000. Rats! I'm too tired to think straight. I wish I wasnt such a rotten business man and I wish Ober wasnt such a perfect gentleman. It takes a heel to deal with those vermin out there.

Dont see why I'm inflicting you with this. Tell me about the French (or math or latin) Congratulations on the back-jack—it's a pretty dive. I think of you constantly and if I ever prayed it would be that the irritations, exasperations and blow ups of the past winter wouldnt spoil the old confidence we had in each other.

Good-night darlin' Scottina
Daddy

FROM: Gerald Murphy — ALS, 2 pp. Princeton University

30 July '36

Dear Scott:—

I find that I can go just so long without knowing how you all are;—where you all are. Just so long is at an end now. Send me a card or something. I leave the hospital to-morrow without my tonsils,—and go to camp for most of August. Sara has taken—or rather bought very advantageously—a well-built one of Edith Wharton's era which she has somehow transformed into something outside of New Orlean's—gay, light, colored rooms, white rugs, a small jungle of indoor exotic palms and plants,—mexican metalware partout, etc. The old guard of Upper St. Regis is fluttered in the dove-cote. We are on a quiet remote lake. Patrick likes it very much and is holding his own. It is Sara who needs attention now. I want to get her to Europe for a month. Her inconsolability,—and her present anxiety over Patrick begin to tell on her. She refuses to release her tense grip and is burning white. The same .pride in not sparing herself that her mother had,—has come to her now. There is little one can do for her. Even her loneliness I cannot reach. She is gay,—energetic,—but is not well.

One day riding down alone through Vermont I had a long conversation with you and asked you many questions,—abstract, they were. I wish I might know yr. answers one day.

We have seen Dos + Katy often. They are so fond of you as are we. Please send us some word. We *wonder* so and somehow must know,—soon. Just a telegram or card.

Aff'y.
Gerald.

Camp Adeline
Paul Smith's, New York.

TO: Scottie Fitzgerald

Typed copy, 1 p. Princeton University
Asheville, North Carolina

July 1936

Darling:

O.K. about the tutoring. Let it slide. But I hate to let one season slip by at your age without one difficult advance.

Do something for me! I'm proud of the swimming but summer's only summer. Give me a time maybe, and know always I'm thinking of you and for you, and my plans will come to you as soon as crystallized, sometime in August. Slim chance of my getting up to Pennsylvania. All Europe ideas definitely out. Spain was what I wanted to see and Spain is in what the newsmen call the "throes of revolution."

Your mother likes your letters so much. Hope you have nice tent mates. I dont agree with Mrs. Tappan on that subject, but that's a whole story and I know whatever the situation is you'll make the best of it in your own courageous way

Oh darling Scottie—I don't want to force you but it does please me when you can make a connection between the Louisiana Purchase and why Fred Astaire lifts up his left hind foot for the world's pleasure. I want you to be among the best of your race and not waste yourself on trivial aims. To be useful and proud—is that too much to ask?

I enclose you the jacket of my latest book. I have decided to write in Scandinavian! from now on!

Your devoted
Daddy

TO: Ethel Walker Smith[1]

TL(CC), 2 pp. Princeton University

Grove Park Inn,
Asheville, N.C.,
August 17, 1936.

Dear Mrs. Smith:

Your letter has encouraged me very much because both daughter and I had long looked forward to the time she could enter your school, which by every evidence seems "tops."

To go to bat financially the situation is as follows. Stretching my budget every which way I do not see how I can afford more than $100 a month plus the $400 dressing charge and there seems to be an awful gap between that and the $2200 which it ordinarily comes to. From that you can judge whether you think any adjustment of your rates in this case is possible.

Just for my satisfaction daughter took the French examinations at Bryn Mawr for the two classes below the final class (they have curious designations of their own which I have never quite been able to master) and got marks of 98 and 96 without having cracked a French book except for her private pleasure in eight months. She led her class in English and English composition with marks in the early 90s and was third in her class in history with 89, fell off a little in Latin to, I think, 79 and made a curious flop in mathematics. She is a year ahead in that and her year's standing was enough to pull her over but she carelessly did not turn over her paper and find four more questions on the other side until five minutes before the hour was up and came home to me in dispair saying she had answered only a little over half the questions. For the whole year I think her standing was either third or fourth in an exceptionally smart class of twenty-eight. There is no exact rating at Bryn Mawr as to that.

She is a conscientious, straight-forward person and I don't honestly want her to be brilliant in the scintillating sense and dread it when I see the signs of fatal facility in her. At Vassar I want her to follow some such line as a premedical course or one that will equip her for scientific research. If she is going to write (which God forbid!) I'd rather the necessity came from anything except a fundamentally literary training.

The world seems full of people seeking for self-expression with nothing to express. So often during the depression friends have sent me manuscripts accompanied by condescending little notes:

> "Not so much doing in the real estate line now so I thought I would take a little time off and write some short stories and I'd like you to look this one over."

It is much as if I should rush into Johns Hopkins Hospital demanding a scalpel to take out an appendix with on the basis that I had always thought it would be fun to be a surgeon.

In the event that you see your way clear to taking daughter it is of course understood that if the sky brightens for me next year I will try to pay the regular rate; my address will be here until further notice. A few weeks ago I managed to break my shoulder swimming and it is even now doubtful whether I can travel within the next fortnight after which I may have to go to Hollywood to recoup my battered finances.

I should try to fly back, however, for a day or so in order to make your acquaintance and bring daughter personally to the school.

Arthritis is a terrible thing. I have seen two good friends through awful sieges of it and can think of nothing that makes one more helpless and gives one the sense of the awful futility of illness. My deepest sympathy.

Sincerely

[1] Headmistress of the Ethel Walker School in Simsbury, Conn., which Scottie entered in fall 1936.

FROM: Gerald Murphy ALS, 3 pp. Princeton University
August 1936

Dear Scott:—

The mood of my letter must have been wrong. I feel a kind of disloyalty to Sara in giving you the impression that she admits to herself even remotely the fact of what she is withstanding. Her resilience is formibable,—when one considers that she faces squarely the truth about everything every minute of the day. I do not know what goes on in her mind. I doubt if two human creatures ultimately succeed in sharing grief. But I should never have made you think that she *shows* the slightest sign of what she's undergoing. Indeed everyone remarks her gayety and becomingness. She's never looked prettier. This camp is a bower.

Your article I have not read due to an oath I took with myself upon returning here from Europe last March that I would no longer read the newspapers and magazines. As a result I've lived with: "Le Rouge et le Noir," "The Return of the Native," "The Last Puritan," "Arctic Adventure," "Barchester Towers," "Le Crime de Sylvestre Bonnard,"—and now Dos' new book,—which I admire very much.[1] It has all recreated a kind of distant region in which I enjoy living,—and I find my mind freed.

As for life (as they call it) I find it turning out to be the very thing that I'd always suspected it to be: a very badly-schemed and wasteful process. Having felt it to be such, I find that I don't mind it as much: For those who believe in it (and believe in being in it and of it) [such as—Sara,—and you, I suppose][2] it must be a very painful experience. I find that my only fear is what *other* people may be suffering. Sometimes the thought is well-nigh intolerable. However, I find myself learning *again* not to take life at *its own* tragical value.

Your shoulder sounds painful. I hope it doesn't continue so long. Thank you for your letter. It brought much with it. Santayana describes his man at the end as an "ascetic without belief,"—I find that I have inadvertently been enjoying a kind of self-imposed incredulous self-denial for more than a year. It's insulation, at least against idle wear and tear. It's not what we do but what we do with our minds that counts. Our greatest affection to you,

Gerald.

Cummings says:—
"We live for that which dies, and die for that which lives." Is it true? G

[1] *The Big Money* (1936).
[2] Murphy's brackets.

TO: Scottie Fitzgerald
Summer 1936(?)

ALS, 4 pp. Princeton University
Grove Park Inn letterhead
Asheville, North Carolina

Scottina:

It was fine seeing you, + I liked you a lot (this is aside from loving you which I always do.). You are nicer, to adults—you are emerging from that rather difficult time in girls 12–15 usually, but you are emerging I think rather early—probably at 14 or so. You have one good crack coming but—well:

"Daddy the prophet!" I can hear you say in scorn. I wish to God I wasn't so right usually about you. When I wrote that "news-sheet" with events left out, you know: the letter that puzzled you, + headed it "Scotty loses Head," it was because I saw it coming. I knew that your popularity with two or three dazed adolescent boys would convince you that you were at least the Queen of Sheba, + that you would "lose your head." What shape this haywire excursion would take I didn't know—I couldn't have guessed it would be writing a series of indiscreet letters to a gossipy + indiscreet boy who would show them to the persons for whom they were *not* meant (understand: I don't blame —— too much—the fault was yours—he didn't, will you notice, put into writing an analysis of his best friends of his own sex!)

However, that's of no seriousness. But I think that the next kick will be a bad one—but you will survive, and after that you will manage your affairs better. To avoid such blows you almost *have* to have them yourself so you can begin to think of others as valuing themselves, possibly, quite as much as you do yourself. So I'm not afraid of it for you. I don't want it to be so bad that it will break your self-confidence, which is attractive + is fine is founded on positive virtues, work, courage, ect. but if you are selfish it had better be broken early. If you are unselfish you can keep it always—and it is a nice thing to have. I didn't know till 15 that there was anyone in the world except me, + it cost me *plenty*.

Signs + portents of your persistent conciet: Mrs Owens said to me (+ Mrs. Owens loves you)

"For the 1st time in a long while Scotty was *nice*, + not a burden as I expected. It was really nice to be with her."

Because, I guess, for the 1st time you entered into *their* lives, humble lives of struggling people, instead of insisting that they enter into yours—, a chance they never had, of belonging to "high society." Before, you had let them be aware of what *you* were doing, (not in any snobbish sense, because heaven knows I'd have checked you on that)—but because you never considered or pretended to consider their lives, their world at all—your own activities seemed of so much more overwhelming importance to you! *You did not use one bit of your mind, one little spot!* to think what *they* were thinking, or help *them!*

You went to Norfolk + gave out the information (*via* the Taylors, *via* Annabel, *via* mother that you were going to Dobbs. That doesn't matter save as indicative of a show-off frame of mind. You know it was highly tentative. It was a case, again, of boasting, of "promoting yourself," But those signs of one big catastrophe (it'll come—I want to minimize it for you, but it cant be prevented because only experience can teach) are less important than your failure to realize that you are *a young member of the human race,* who has not proved itself in any but the most superficial manner. (I have seen "popular girls" of 15 become utterly declassé in six months because they were essentially selfish. You (who isn't selfish, I think) had a superficial head-start with prettiness, but you will find more + more that less pretty girls will be attacting the solider, more substantial boys as the next two years will show. Both you + Peaches are intelligent but both of you will be warped by this early attention, + *something tells me she wont lose her head;* she hasn't the "gift of gab" as you have—her laughter + her silence takes the place of much. That's why I wish to God you would write something when you have time—if only a one act play about how girls act in the bath house, in a tent, on a train going to camp.

I grow weary, but I probably wont write again for a month. Don't answer this, justifying yourself—of *course* I know you're doing the best you "can."

The points of the letter are.

1st You did spill over, rashly!

2nd You are getting over the selfish period—thank God!

3d But it'll take one more big kick, + I want it to be mild, so your backside won't suffer too much.

4th I wish you'd get your mind off your precious self enough to write me a one act play about other people—what they say + how they behave.

With DEAREST love

Your Simply So-perfect Too too
Daddy

PLEASE, turn back + read this letter over! It is too packed with considered thought to digest the first time. Like Milton—oh yeah!

TO: Annabel Fitzgerald Sprague TL(CC), 2 pp. Princeton University

Grove Park Inn,
Asheville, N.C.,
September 10, 1936.

Dear Annabel:

Thank you for your fully detailed letter about Mother's effects, etc.[1] In answer to your questions, do what you think advisable. Scotty might like the radio but there are so many things on my mind that I can't say what to do about her personal property, though such things as a suitcase etc. are of some value you can estimate to each of us and the clothes I leave entirely up to you.

There are certain household articles that you may already have disposed of or that may not be worth putting in storage, such as the marble fisher boy. Can't we let all that wait, because the business of the money and the coincidence of my illness have become very pressing to me.

Since a year ago last February I have succeeded in getting myself into more debt than you can imagine and the two months of sickness here in Asheville have made the situation much worse. You can imagine such items as $450 for the operation and being so helpless so far as moving around was concerned that it was necessary to have day and night nurses and it comes down to a choice with me of either keeping up my insurance which for $60,000, though I have borrowed on it heavily or sacrificing the insurance and keeping what comparatively small amount may still be due me from mother's legacy. It is infinitely more logical for me to convert my share into cash and keep up the insurance because the possibilities (you must understand that I have been out of my room twice in the last six weeks and that all work has been terrifically crippled both in amount and in its general cheerfulness and salability under the influence of pain and of worry about mother, the usual concerns of Zelda and Scottie)—so much is this so that my insurance policy is in danger unless I could convert my inheritance into cash.

At first glance this would seem a pity but it is absolutely inevitable. I have got to take six weeks rest as the doctors have told me frankly the chances of my lasting out another winter are getting thinner and thinner and I would either be dead or be a jibbering nervous wreck in some sanatorium, in either case leaving very insufficient protection for two helpless dependents.

I have thought the matter over from every angle. There is nothing to borrow on the insurance. My debt to Scribner's has reached its limit and my agent, Harold Ober can afford to lend me no more until I can complete two or three stories necessary to cover it.

I am already writing again and will continue to write under any circumstances but it would be suicidal to keep on writing at this nervous tensity, often with no help but what can be gotten out of a bottle of gin. Save for one month last May and some enforced weeks' vacation after this accident I have taken no time off for over eight years except for three weeks in Bermuda where I lay in bed with plurisy. A few week ends at Virginia beach are no substitute as the tendency is to make whoopee and come back feeling worse than when you started.

I want six to eight weeks of not worrying about a single thing and of not writing under pressure and only for a couple of hours a day.

This story of becoming a nervous wreck at forty is not pretty but I want to make you understand that the only way such a rest can possibly be arranged is the aforesaid conversion of my share of mother's money into protection for my life insurance policy. There is no use reproaching me for past extravagances nor for my failure to get contol of the liquor situation under these conditions of strain.

During this time I have been in a night club exactly three times and have used the liquor for purposes of work or of accomplishing some duty for which I no longer have the physical or nervous energy. I am completely on the spot, have talked the matter over and thought it over from every angle and I think that mother and father would have agreed with me. In fact, most of the money that mother advanced me was for purposes of just such a rest but unfortunately it always had to be poured into taking care of Zelda, paying nurses and doctors' bills of my own during past two and three day breakdowns and the inevitable insurance.

My earning powers have been inevitably dimmed in the last two years by this and by the depression which has cut almost in half my actual income before 1932 up to this year when it was going along at a better clip until mother's collapse and this accident. There is no reason why in decent health I couldn't write myself out of this mess, being still under forty and having the necessary connections and reputation.

I want you to talk this over with Cliff. Meanwhile there will occur the inevitable business of dividing the estate. Mrs. Owens has in my files the exact amounts which mother lent me and the best thing would be for me to technically return them to the estate by means of vouchers and then when we started the fifty-fifty division it would be necessary for me to take out my vouchers while you chose the equivalent from paying bonds. Once I had back all my vouchers then I in turn would choose turn, and turn about with you till we had reached the wonderful South American stocks which Wharton-Smith managed to unload upon her and so on.

I want to do this as soon as possible and I would like to do it in Rockville, Maryland according to the advice in the enclosed letter of Mr. Bartlett's.

It looks now as if this ten day arthritis which has actually extended much longer than that is almost over. At least I am on my feet in the room today and have been able to finish a story by dictating it. I should like to come north by the 20th.

Cliff and Annabel would have to renounce their executorship to some banker or lawyer in Rockville which was her legal residence when she died. Outside of actual division the word "administering" in this letter seems meaningless. Once you have your share you are yourself administratrix of it, are you not?

Had mother known the whole situation I am sure whe would have agreed to the emergency because the difference between $60,000 and $7,000 or $8,000 is quite apparent in my case and you could do as you like about clipping your own coupons or having an administrator do it. Any extra expense incurred by this procedure I should expect to meet. To you it would seem to make so little difference and to me so much. Anxiously awaiting your answer in general to this arrangement I am

Your brother,

[1] Mrs. Fitzgerald had died in early September, leaving an estate of $42,000.

TO: Annabel Fitzgerald Sprague TLS, 1 p. Bruccoli

Asheville, N.C.,
September 16th, 1936

Dear Annabelle:

This letter is a sort of general O.K. I note the objections instead of marking them:

Zelda would like handkerchiefs and kimono, but I am sure not the dress.

The radio might as well be kept for Scottie as I gave away ours when I left in payment for some small debt. It was the same type.

Whatever became of that gorgeous opera cloak, sort of Venitien brocade?

Take what furniture you want, naturally. You might divy up on things like good pratical wardrobe trunks and suit-cases—I leave that to you.

We do not want the oil painting of the sheep but I somehow *would* like the marble Fisher boy.

I gather from Clif's telegram that there is nothing in my letter to you with which he disagrees. In that case, it is plain sailing.

I had an idea that Mother might have meant that the estate was to be administered and beneficiaries receive only the income. With this, as I told you in my letter, I disagree emphatically because of the reasons stated in the letter. I agree with Clif as to having Ed Poe be made

Administrator of the estate. I do not understand by what possible technicality it will take six months to settle the estate but knowing that the capital will be divided, I will be enabled, if necessary, to borrow on the expectation and with the proceeds fix up my insurance and thus get over this difficult autumn.

I still have a drawer full of stuff of Mother's, mostly old stubs, which have gone over to the best of my ability. Can you think of anything that I should do with them?

I shall always regret not having been able to be with you during this and appreciate all that you did and the way you did it.

Love,
Scott

TO: C. O. Kalman — TLS, 2 pp. Princeton University

Asheville, N.C.,
Sept. 19th, 1936

Dear Colly:

Thank you for your letter.

Mother did not know she was dying and did not suffer.

A most surprising thing in the death of a parent is not how little it affects you, but how much. When your Father or Mother has been morbidly perched on the edge of life, when they are gone, even though you have long ceased to have any dependnce on them, there is a sense of being deserted.

Mother's death was rather wretched from a purely selfish point of view because I could not be there. I split the clavicle of my shoulder and am just out of bed after seven weeks of it—caused by trying to show off for Zelda, on the first day that I could swim in a year and a half.

Mother's death made me sad in connection with so many deaths of people dear to me in the last two years, beginning with Ring's cashing in; after that Emily Vanderbilt shot herself on a lonely Montana ranch last summer which gave me the blues. (Do you remember the girl that looked like an ashe blond's scroll on a telephone board, whom you liked so much one night in Paris—well that is as melancholy a subject as the financial one). As you asked me to give you the whole history:

I am sort of floating at the moment and will probably go back to Hollywood as soon as my arm heals.

Talbert's[1] final collapse is the death of an enemy for me, though I liked the guy enormously. He had an idea that his wife and I were playing around, which was absolute nonsense, but I think even so that he killed the idea of either Hopkins or Frederick Marsh doing "Tender is the Night."[2]

All story prices are cut somewhat. Book sales are no where but established Writers are better off than the poor bastards who are just getting started.

The Esquire pieces[3] were written in a mood of depression. Don't put too much credence in them as being reflections as to how I feel now.

Have I answered your principal questions? Oh! one more, Scottie got a scholarship to a very expensive school, the Edith Walker School in Connecticut, on her fine record with remission of tuition of about one-half, and Zelda of whom you were most anxious to hear, and whom I seem to have left until the last moment, is infinitely better. There is a chance, which I go to sleep hoping for, that she may be out into the world again—on a somewhat short string to be sure, by April or May.

I hope you and Sandy did not go to much trouble preparing for us because I wrote you in a weird and at an undetermined time.

With all appreciation of your hospitality and affection to you both always, I am

Sincerely yours,
Scott

[1] Irving Thalberg.

[2] Neither Miriam Hopkins nor Fredric March was under contract to MGM at the time.

[3] The "Crack-Up" articles.

TO: John Dos Passos — TLS, 1 p. University of Virginia

Asheville, N.C.,
Grove Park Inn,
Sept. 21st, 1936

Dear Dos:

Just finished reading the Book.[1] Parts of it simply interferes with everything that I do, so that I quote back to them in my own mind as though they were things I experiended. I said to some one the other day, "A Cuban boy that I knew once"—and then I said, "Girl I knew that knew a Cuban boy once," and then I said, "A book I read about a Cuban boy once." It goes right into everything I have ever read, felt or experienced and I am writing this because I am living here and I haven't read "Mary French" which I hear is the best of all, but "Margle"[2] and "Charlie" and the "Incidentals" have been the most exciting things to me, that is, between the time I broke my shoulder last July and the blowing up of Gerald and Sallie[3] in the Alcazar.

With affectionate regards to you both always,

Scott

dictated—I have a cracked shoulder

[1] *The Big Money.*
[2] Fitzgerald drew an arrow from this word and noted: "God help us!"
[3] Fitzgerald drew an arrow from this word with a question mark; the reference is to Gerald and Sara Murphy.

FROM: Bob and Raye Sylvester[1] TLS, 1 p. Princeton University

Sept 26. [1936]
4 A.M. no less!

Dear Sport;

Have just finished reading a particularly atrocious story by some heeb working for the N.Y. Post[2] (and wouldn't old man Curtis[3] spin in his grave if he ever saw a copy of it?) about my favor*ite* author a-wasting and a-pining away down there in the fairly deep south.

Well, I'm sorry but you've just got to quit it. To quote that other melancholy soul, the late Dr. Lardner, I and Mother just won't have it. This is no time for you to be falling apart and if you haven't already thrown this somewhat impertinent message down the . . . . er . . . receptacle I intend to tell you why you've got to quit it.

In the first place, you're too old. Like the man with incipient tuberculosis, or whatever it is, you should have become more and more immune with the passing of each year. The time for you to have done a tailspin is long since past—so stop trying to catch up with something that's way behind you.

Secondly, you know too much. If the only writer in this whole goddamned, beJesus world who can understand kids and write about them as they should be written about is going to go off on some screwball tear and act like a child then the time has come for us all to run screaming up the steps of St. Patricks and give up.

Thirdly, and pardon my grammar, you can't let us down. When I think of the thousands—nay, millions—of words I have wasted in arguing your value in oh, how many, saloons with such kindred souls as Walker, Connelly, Sullivan, Lardner pere, Lardner fils, Hecht, O'Hara, March etc., I feel that I should warn you that in folding up on me you are robbing someone you don't even know of a very valuable saloon argument. And you know how hard it is to find an A No. 1 saloon argument. Mine is "Fitzgerald will live. Ceasar's Gallic Wars will be forgotten!"

Seriously, Mom and I are terribly sorry to hear that you're ill and unhappy. I suppose you get all sorts of letters from such screwballs as ourselves and perhaps this won't cheer you at all, much less amuse you. But we'd like to cheer you and we'd like to see you well in a hurry and have you turn out one such really *fine* book as was "Tender Is The Night." Anyone who has been through anything or thought of life at all knows what an exceptional piece of work that was, and how much of your life's blood must have gone into its making.

The Best
Bob and Raye Sylvester

[1] Sylvester was a *New York Daily News* columnist.

[2] Michel Mok had interviewed Fitzgerald in Asheville on his fortieth birthday and published an article in the *Post* depicting him as a broken drunk: "The Other Side of Paradise/Scott Fitzgerald, 40,/Engulfed in Despair/Broken in Health He Spends Birthday Re-/gretting that He Has Lost Faith in his Star." (25 September 1936)

[3] Cyrus Curtis, publisher of the *New York Evening Post*.

TO: Ernest Hemingway ALS (on Western Union form; in unknown hand).
Kennedy Library
Asheville, North Carolina

Sheville—N.C.
via N.Y.C. 9/28/36

Ernest Hemmingway
Ranch—Cooke City

If you ever wanted to help me your chance is now Stop A man named Michael Moch has taken advantage of an interview to spread me all over the N.Y. Evening Post in an absurd position Stop It cuts in on me directly and indirectly—[1]

Scott

[1] Fitzgerald's answer to Hemingway's offer of assistance implies that he had sent two telegrams: WIRED UNDER IMPRESSION THAT YOU WERE IN NEW YORK NOTHING CAN BE DONE AT LONG RANGE AND ON COOLER CONSIDERATION SEEMS NOTHING TO BE DONE ANYHOW THANKS BEST ALWAYS SCOTT. (Carlos Baker, *Ernest Hemingway: A Life Story*, p. 295) It is noteworthy that Fitzgerald turned to Hemingway after the "Poor Scott" reference in "The Snows of Kilimanjaro."

TO: C. O. Kalman — Wire, 2 pp. Princeton University

ASHEVILLE NCAR 442P 1936 OCT 5 PM 5 20

OSCAR KALMAN, BROKER WELL KNOWN

PHONE AND DLR OFFICE OR REISDENCE TONIGHT

MOTHER LEFT ME SECURITIES OF MARKET VALUE OF ABOUT TWENTY THOUSAND DOLLARS AND AN ADMINISTRATOR HAS ONLY JUST BEEN APPOINTED WHO TELLS ME THAT BY MARYLAND LAW I CANT HAVE THEM FOR SIX MONTHS AND NO BALTIMORE BANK WILL ADVISE[1] MONEY ON THEM UNDER THOSE CONDITIONS STOP I HAVE BEEN IN BED TEN WEEKS WITH BROKEN SHOULDER AND CONSEQUENT ARTHRITIES INCAPACITATING ME FOR WORK UNTIL THIS WEEK AND AM HEAD OVER HEELS IN DEBT TO PUBLISHER AND INSURANCE COMPANY ANDSOFORTH WITH PERSONAL OBLIGATIONS EMBARRASSING TO STATE IN TELEGRAM STOP CANNOT EVEN PAY TYPISTS OR BUY MEDICINE STOP I NEED ONE THOUSAND IMMEDIATELY AND FIVE THOUSAND WITHIN THE WEEK STOP[2] CAN YOU CONSULT WITH ANNABEL MCQUILLAN[3] HOW I CAN RAISE THIS AS PERSONAL LOAN SECURED BY NOTE OF HAND OR LIEN DUE ON LIQUIDATION OF LEGACY AT ANY INTEREST AND WIRE ME TONIGHT IF POSSIBLE AT GROVEPARK INN ASHEVILLE AS TO WHAT MIGHT BE DONE STOP THIS IS ABSOLUTELY LAST RECOURSE

SCOTT FITZGERALD.

[1] ADVISE was crossed out and ADVANCE written in.
[2] Kalman arranged the loan.
[3] Fitzgerald's aunt.

TO: Maxwell Perkins — Wire. Princeton University

ASHEVILLE NCAR 1936 OCT 6 AM 2 23

EVEN THOUGH ADMINISTRATOR HAS BEEN APPOINTED BALTIMORE BANK WILL NOT ADVANCE MONEY ON MY SECURITIES OF TWENTY THOUSAND I MARKET VALUE AT THEIR ESTIMATE UNTIL SIX WEEKS BY WHICH TIME I WILL BE IN JAIL STOP WHAT DO YOU DO WHEN YOU CANT PAY TYPIST OR BUY MEDICINES OR CIGARETTS STOP ANY LOANS FROM SCRIBNERS CAN BE SECURED BY LIEN PAYABLE ON LIQUIDATION CANT SOMETHING BE DONE I AM UP AND PRETTY STRONG BUT THESE ARE IMPOSSIBLE WRITING CONDITIONS I NEED THREE HUNDRED DOLLARS WIRED TO FIRST NATIONAL BALTIMORE AND TWO THOUSAND MORE THIS WEEK WIRE ANSWER[1]

F. SCOTT FITZGERALD.

[1] This loan was not made. See Perkins' 6 October letter to Fitzgerald in *Scott/Max*.

TO: Barrett H. Clark[1] TLS, 1 p. Yale University

Grove Park Inn
Asheville, N.C.
October 16, 1936

Dear Mr. Clark:

"Vegetable" reads well, but it simply won't play, and I would be doing you a disservice and you would be doing an equal disservice to the prospective producers to offer it to them as part of any repertory. It reads well, but there is some difference between the first and second acts that is so disparate that every time a Little Theatre has produced it (and many of them have tried it), it has been a failure in a big way. This is not to say that I do not realize that the thing reads well, or that I am not tremendously grateful for your interest, but simply to say that I can't give you the permission that you ask.

Sincerely yours,
F Scott Fitzgerald

[1] Drama critic who was at that time executive director of the Dramatists Play Service.

TO: Marjorie Kinnan Rawlings[1] TLS, 1 p. University of Florida

Grove Park Inn
Asheville, N.C.
October 16, 1936

Dear Miss Rawlings:

I will answer your questions individually. The best bootlegger in Asheville is the liquor store opposite the George Vanderbilt Hotel, behind the Battery Park. It is a liquor store selling, in a respectable way, wines, beers, port and sherry, but not above yielding up a pint of Bourbon or gin or what have you. Just mention me, and if that doesn't work try to put a tough look on your face.

I do want to meet you very much. I admire "South Wind Under"[2] and that so-often-reprinted story about the man who had been in prison and came back,[3] and also the other long short story (again I forget the name—maybe you are too complicated with your titles) that won the O. Henry Memorial prize the year before last.[4]

Somehow, I don't want to go to Pisgah Forest, and the idea of going shopping with a woman, even if she had pottery in mind, makes me a little jittery, much as was reported in a recent issue of Time magazine. In short, papa is an invalid, and if you want to see him enough you can always find him pacing up and down in his room at Grove Park Inn.

I didn't know that you had had a serious injury, and please accept my condolences. Mine has been a most absurd thing; I contracted it by trying to do a swan dive from a high board after a year of enforced quietude—probably the first man that ever broke his shoulder in the air.

Can't I be a stop on your way to Pisgah Forest? Give me warning and I shall be shaven and, if not dressed, at least properly attired.

Your admirer,
Scott

[1] Scribners author who wrote fiction set in Flotida; Perkins had asked her to look up Fitzgerald.
[2] *South Moon Under* (1933).
[3] "The Pardon."
[4] "Gal Young Un."

TO: Adelaide Neall[1] TLS, 1 p. Library of Congress

Grove Park Inn
Asheville, N.C.
October 23, 1936

Dear Miss Nealle:

I hope you are going to be able to schedule *Trouble*[2] soon. I have practically finished a story I think you will like, and naturally I don't want too much time to elapse between stories in the Post. I have thought that you underestimated *Trouble* as a story, and if you can make any possible constructive suggestion about it, please do so, but I like it as it stands now. In reading over the carbon copy, I am still sure I like it.

The new story has been delayed by an arthritis that set in on top of my breaking my shoulder.

In the Clipping Bureau I saw that the interview by Michael Mock had been repeated in a Philadelphia paper and I thought you or Mr. Lorimer might have seen it. The thing was so absurd that I am ashamed of myself for my credulity in being taken in. I had it investigated and found that the pictures showing the difference between Scott Fitzgerald at 21 and Scott Fitzgerald on his fortieth brithday, as well as the whole tone of the interview, before he arrived here in Asheville. It was so little true that the nurse who was on duty with me at the time was shocked at what he had written. He had composed the whole thing from two old articles in *Esquire* of about a year ago, and I can no more imagine myself saying the things that were attributed to me than you can. When I want to be dramatic I do it in my own way, certainly, and my own style. All my friends were shocked, and I was almost glad that my mother was dead so as not to have seen it, and I wired my daughter's school, Miss

Walker's, at Simsbury, Connecticut, so that she could not see it, when excerpts of it were reprinted in *Time* magazine.

With best wishes always,

F Scott Fitzgerald

1 Fiction editor at *The Saturday Evening Post.*

2 Fitzgerald's last *Saturday Evening Post* story (6 March 1937).

TO: Scottie Fitzgerald — TL(CC), 1 p. Princeton University

Grove Park Inn
Asheville, N.C.
October 28, 1936

Dearest Scottie:

When I go up Thanksgiving I am given the choice of taking you to dinner at either Pettibone Tavern, Old House, Farmington Country Club, Farmington Inn, Wampanoag Country Club or Avon Country Club. That part of Connecticut is a blank to me. Can you give me any steer as to where you prefer to go and whether there is some girl you are fond of that you would like to have go with us, whose parents will not be there. Possibly Aunt Rosalind will go up with me.

The regulations certainly seem to be strict. I am told that you are not to be allowed any chicken bones, and no morphine, under any conditions, and if I give you champagne and you roll in at midnight, you will be marked down 5% in each subject. Also, the regulations prescribe that you must go in your basketball uniform, balancing a copy of the Old Testament on your head, and if it slips just once—mind you, just once—you will be put back three grades and won't be able to enter Vassar until 1950.

Seriously, Pie, let me know about which one you prefer and whether you want any company with you—by which I mean that I don't feel like chaperoning any considerable group of girls, but if you have some special friend who would be lonely that day and you would like to bring along, it would be a pleasure.

Sorry about the birthday boquet being late. There don't seem to be any flower stores in Simsbury, and it had to go by way of Hartford.

Ever your loving daddy

FROM: Marjorie Kinnan Rawlings TLS, 2 pp. Princeton University
Fall 1936

Sunday Night

Dear Scott:

I've just finished "The Great Gatsby" again—

I have no business trying to write you about it now, because I'm all torn up again—much worse than when I read it ten years ago—You were wise so young—I'm only beginning to know some of the things you must have been born, knowing—

The book resolves itself into the strangest feeling of a crystal globe, or one of the immense soap bubbles we achieved as children, if it could hold its shape and color without breaking—It is so beautiful, it is so clairvoyant, it is so heart-breaking—

Please, how can you talk of security when the only security is the loveliness of the dream? And you are right to think that anything can be mended, and life can be cut to order, like a diamond—But turn about is fair play, and you must give life the same privilege—to mend and change you, and to cut new facets—I suppose you know that nothing is wasted—The hell you've been through isn't wasted—All you have to do, ever, is to forget everything and turn that terrible, clear white light you possess, on the minds and emotions of the people it stirs you to write about—That's your security—

I enjoyed myself unreasonably talking with you, and have no apologies for not letting you get the rest your nurse was having fits about—I think you probably needed that kind of talk as much as I did—only we kept darting up so many alleys—and a perfectly sane outsider would have thought we were a pair of articulate panthers, the way we took turns pacing up and down—You'll have to pace with me on my thirty-foot farmhouse porch this winter—we could pass each other comfortably—

I was high from the really very decent wines and I suppose the talk, as far as Spruce Pine—I got absent-minded once and found myself at the foot of Mt Mitchell—a man told me I *could* go over the mountain—having been up it in broad daylight, driving myself and paralyzed with terror that I wouldn't admit, I about-faced shamelessly and retraced the fourteen erroneous miles—

The reason I keep doing this—and this—is that the period broke off my typewriter a few days ago—When I try to end a sentence in all decisiveness, I just get a blur, like this There are always connotations in dashes, anyway—none in blurs[1]

So many thanks for your hospitality—

I'm writing Max, who sounded to me a bit worried about you, a favorable report—and an honest one—Good God, man, you're all right—Don't let anybody hurry you—not that you would—When you're sore through and through—I don't mean physically—it has to heal in its own way—Don't I know—If anyone knew how good my little 32 revolver has looked to me sometimes—

Don't ever write to me politely, answering a letter—but anytime you really want to call me "obvious" or what else was it, I'd enjoy having you do it—

Don't repeat to Max or anyone the small bit I told you about the book I have in mind after this one—But I'm longing to get to it, and dreading it, for if I can say one-tenth of what I want to, it will be perfectly beautiful—Then, when of course, it isn't, I'll consider the 32 again, or maybe do a Cross Creek Cleopatra with a rattlesnake—

Again, thank you—

Marjorie

[1] The blurs have not been transcribed.

TO: V. F. Calverton — TLS, 1 p. New York Public Library

Grove Park Inn
Asheville, N.C.
November 4, 1936

Dear George:

The Man Inside[1] *came and filled me with strange emotions.* I hardly know what to say until I have looked over parts of it again. You remember a conversation we had late one night in which you told me something about your relations with your wife—probably the best conversation we have ever had. It reminded me of that and I was alternately attracted and repelled by your use of documentation, which I suppose comes from your long journalistic and scientific training, and your attempt to weave Joli Coeur into a romance that hesitates between being realistic and picaresque.

To a great extent I have used the accepted technique of my time, feeling that what observations I have made need all the help that I can give the reader to carry on with them, and the more radical (I thought) my idea was, the more determinedly have I clothed it in sheep's wool and sugar-coated it, to change the metaphor.

If you do not mind criticism from a friend who admires you and who admires *The Man Inside,* I feel that the more nebulous your thought has been, the more inclined you are to throw a cloud around it, and again and again to try to resolve that cloud into a simple declarative fact expressed as an opinion or an apposition, with the naivete of a child pricking a balloon. I will have to see you to talk about it more fully. I hope to God it does well. You have done so much for other people that I would like to see you evolve some form in which your talent for fiction can appear to best advantage, and you are on the way to doing that here.

As ever yours,
F. Scott Fitzgerald

[1] Calverton's *The Man Inside: Being the Record of the Strange Adventures of Allen Steele Among the Xulus* (Scribners, 1936).

TO: Scottie Fitzgerald — Typed copy, 3 pp. Princeton University

November 10, 1936

GROVE PARK INN
Asheville, N.C.

Dearest pie:

I got a School letter about Thanksgiving saying that Thanksgiving Day is best, and it is much better for me that way. There is no particular advantage in going out two or three times rather than one, without any particular objectives; the idea is to go out once and have a good time. I will be delighted to meet Agnes, and our engagement is on Thanksgiving day.

Now, this is a parenthesis in my letter: I got the little charms that you sent me for my birthday: the bells dangling from the string and the mule, and I appreciated your thought of me—in a reverse way, you little donkey.

Park Avenue girls are hard, aren't they? My own taste ran to kinder people, but they are usually the daughters of "up-and-coming" men and, in a way, the inevitable offspring of that type. It is the Yankee push to its last degree, a sublimation of the sort of Jay Gould who began by peddling buttons to a county and ended with the same system of peddler's morals by peddling railroads to a nation.

Don't mistake me. I think of myself always as a Northerner and I think of you as a Northerner. Nevertheless, we are all one nation now and you will find all the lassitude and laziness that you despise among those girls, enough to fill Savannah and Charleston, just as down here you will find the same "go getter" principle in the Carolinas.

About the happy medium—which usually means to establish a state of happiness that has happened before and may possibly, under favorable circumstances, happen again: you have got to throw yourself one way or another, that is to say, you have got to say that I am dedicated to a scholastic life for the moment, or I am going to play around. Knowing your wise moderation in all things, I am not presuming to give your advice in this matter, except such advice as we can all take, whether we are Eleanor Turnbulls or Monseigneur Voltaires.

If you really were a happy medium you would probably be the most popular girl in school, which is the last thing I would want of you. I would like you to be a defiant little point of light at the end of a diamond, and if you have fools to be with, to make them a setting.

I don't know whether you will stay there another year—it all depends on your marks and your work, and I can't give you the particular view of life that I have, which as you know is a tragic one, without dulling your enthusiasm. A whole lot of people have found it a whole lot of fun. I have not found it so. But, my God, I had a hell of a lot of fun when I was in my twenties and thirties; and I feel that your duty to justify your inheritance is to accept the sadness, the tragedy of the world we live in with a certain *esprit*.

You have seen the shallowness of the Park Avenue girls, but if you had gone to school down here you would have seen the sort of half-ass attitude with which Southern women accept the decay of their race and cowardice of their men.

Now, insofar as your course is concerned, there is no question of your dropping mathematics and taking the easiest way to go into Vassar and being one of the girls fitted for nothing except to reflect other people without having any particular character of your own. I want you to take mathematics up to the limit of what the school offers. I want you to take physics and I want you to take chemistry. I don't care a damn about your English courses or your French courses. If you don't know two languages and the ways that great men chose to express their thoughts in those languages by this time, then you are not my daughter. You have got to do something hard and tough before you justify yourself with me entirely. You are an only child, but that doesn't give you any freedom of consonance with egotism.

I want you to know certain basic scientific principles, and I feel that that is impossible to learn unless you have the schooling of an East side newsboy or that of a scholar who has gone as far into mathematics and its inevitable results as coordinate geometry. I don't want you to give up mathematics next year. I learned about writing from doing something that I didn't have any taste for. If you don't carry your mathematics such as coordinate geometry (conic sections—or they may have some new name for it now) up to the point of calculus, you will have strayed far afield from what I had planned for you. If you don't care to carry beyond the calculus, it will show in the result of what struggles you may have with it; but you are not planning your course of study. I am doing that for the moment. Whether or not you make a success of it is my business and yours, but it is nothing to be decided by what is easiest. I have put too much thought into your education for that. You are going into Vassar with mathematical credits and a certain side of your life there is going to be scientific, and, as I used to say, it is not a subject of discussion: it is simply what I wish.

Honey, I wish I could see you. It would be so much easier to go over these important matters without friction, but at a distance it seems rather tough that you are inclined to take the easiest way and slide into the subjects that are easy for you, like languages.

No more until I see you Thanksgiving.

Daddy

TO: Bob and Raye Sylvester TL(CC), 1 p. Princeton University

November 12, 1936

GROVE PARK INN
Asheville, N.C.

Dear Bob and Raye Sylvester:

The thing is this: that you go along thinking, this is the way things are, and that is all right; you go along at the same time saying that this is the way things should be, but you are not sure; and you keep your tongue in your cheek about how things will be, but the safest prophecy is the most dismal.

Now, second: you go along thinking that *you* will get by no matter what; you think that the methods you have used are all right. Then you come up, because the first two don't fit together, and you never thought you had any character, anyhow.

Sincerely yours,

TO: Maxwell Perkins Wire. Princeton University

ASHEVILLE NCAR 1936 DEC 3 PM 7 44

CANT EVEN GET OUT OF HERE UNLESS YOU DEPOSIT THE REMAINING THOUSAND STOP IT IS ONLY FOR A COUPLE OF MONTHS STOP I HAVE COUNTED ON IT SO THAT I HAVE CHECKS OUT AGAINST IT ALREADY STOP PLEASE WIRE ME IF YOU HAVE WIRED IT TO THE BALTIMORE BANK STOP THE DOCTORS THINK THAT THIS SESSION OF COMPARATIVE PROSTRATION IS ABOUT OVER

SCOTT FITZGERALD.

TO: C. O. Kalman TLS, 1 p. Princeton University

GROVE PARK INN
Asheville, N.C.

December 12, 1936

Dear Kally:

The situation is essentially the same. For more than six months I have been too ill to do any decent work. But it is changed in this regard: that since you loaned me that $6,000 I have also borrowed $2,000 from the Scribner Company (to whom I already owe heavy advances on books yet to be written and marketed). I am up and around to the extent that I am finishing a story this week, and I am going to meet daughter, Scottie, in Baltimore, on the 22nd.

Will you lend me $1500, on assignment to be mailed you as soon as it can be prepared by Ed Poe, in Baltimore (already asked for, on the presumption that you will be able to lend me this money)?[1]

There is no reason in the world why you should not charge me interest on this. God knows, nobody else has hesitated during this time of the plague of the locusts; and while I know that it has been a gesture of friendship on your part, still it would aid my self respect if you would pretend that it has a business foundation. *Please wire me if such an* arrangement is practicable, or if your other commitments make it impossible.

Ever yours,
Scott

[1] Kalman made the loan.

For Annah Williamson
—other people were young once, just like you. They broke their hearts over things that now seem trivial. But they were their own hearts, and they had the right to

TAPS

AT REVEILLE

meddle with them in their own way

F Scott Fitzgerald
Ashville 1936

Courtesy of D.W.

[1] A relative of Dorothy Williamson ("D.W."), Fitzgerald's nurse in Asheville.

For Carroll Davis
from an old
editor of The Nassau
Litt. to a young
Editor of the Yale Litt

F Scott Fitzgerald
Baltimore
B 1936

[1] At that time a Yale undergraduate; later a biographer and essayist.

TO: Shirley Britt[1]

Inscription in *Tender Is the Night*.
Pennsylvania State University

For Shirley Britt
from the man
who winked at her
in the subway on
Easter Day 1914
F Scott Fitzgerald
Asheville, 1936

Tipped off
by
Martha Marie
Shank

[1] Proprietor of an Asheville secretarial service.

FROM: Zelda Fitzgerald
1936/1937

ALS, 4 pp. Princeton University
Highland Hospital, Asheville, North Carolina

Dearest, dearest Do-Do:

What a funny picture of you in the paper. I wish we had just been swimming together, the way it seems—I'll be so glad when you come home again. When will we be three of us again—Do you remember our first meal in the Biltmore when you said "And now there'll never be just two of us again—from now on we'll be three—"And it was sort of sad somehow and then it was the saddest thing in the world, but we were safer and closer than ever—Oh, I'll be so glad to see you on the tenth.

Scottie was as sweet as I had imagined. She's one inch shorter than I am and weighs four pounds more—and I am her most devoted secret admirer—

Maybe I can come home—

O my love
O my darling } Yes, I mean it

That's what we said on the softness of that expansive Alabama night a long long time ago when you envited me to dine and I had never dined before but had always just "had supper." The General was away. The night was soft and gray and the trees were feathery in the lamp light and the dim recesses of the pine forest were fragrant with the past, and you said you would come back from no matter where you are. So I said and I will be here waiting. I didn't quite believe it, but now I do.

And so, years later I painted you a picture of some faithful poppies and the picture said "No matter what happens I have always loved you so. This is the way we feel about *us*; other emotions may be super-imposed, even accident may contribute another quality to our emotions, but this is our love and nothing can change it. For that is true." And I love you still.

It was me who said:

I feel as if something had happened and I dont know know what it is

You said:

—Well and you smiled (And it was a compliment to me FOR you had never heard "well" used so before) if you don't know I can't possibly know

Then I said "I guess nobody knows—

And

you hoped and I guessed

Everything's going to be all right—

So we got married—

And maybe everything is going to be all right, after all.

There are so many houses I'd like to live in with you. Oh Wont you be mine—again and again—and yet again—

Dearest love, I love you
Zelda

Happily, happily foreverafterwards—the best we could.

Holograph document, 1 p.[1] Princeton University

c. 1936 Asheville, North Carolina (?)

Works of F. Scott Fitzgerald

Novels

This Side of Paradise
The Beautiful + Damned
The Great Gatsby
Tender is the Night
In the Darkest Hour (2 Vols.)
Through the Night (Contemp.)
Last Word

Stories

Flappers
Jazz
Sad
Taps
More
More
Savings

Plays + Poetry

1 Vol. Vegetable, New One: 39 , New One: 42

Essays

(Total 17 Vols)

Pub at

40 1st of Darkest
41 2nd of Darkest
42 Stories V
46 The Night
47 Stories VI
50 Last Word
51 Stories VI
53 Plays + Poetry
55 First + Last Words

Revised Edition
55–60
will Contain
19 Volumes

1 Fitzgerald's plan for a projected edition of his collected works.

TO: Marie Shank | Wire. Princeton University

BALTIMORE MD JAN 7 A [1937]

MISS MARIE SHANK

FAR FROM LEAVING ASHEVILLE FOR GOOD IT LOOKS LIKE MY HEADQUARTERS FOR A LONG TIME MY IDEA IS TO CONSTITUTE YOU AS SORT OF A ONE PERSON UNOFFICIAL TRUST FUND ARRANGEMENT IN MY EFFORT TO PAY OFF MY DEBTS THAT IS TO SAY I WOULD PAY YOU SOME SIZEABLE AMOUNT EACH WEEK AND YOU WOULD DISTRIBUTE IT AS YOU THOUGHT PROPER AND THAT ALL MAIL WOULD COME THROUGH YOU SO THAT I COULD GO TO A HIDEAWAY WITHOUT THE EVERPRESSING WORRY OF DEBT ON MY BACK STOP NATURALLY YOU WOULD TAKE WHAT COMMISSION YOU THOUGHT JUST FOR SUCH SERVICE BUT IN ANY CASE IT IS TOO MUCH FOR ME STOP THIS IS ENTIRELY CONFIDENTIAL NATURALLY STOP WILL BE IN ASHEVILLE TOWARD END THIS WEEK AND WILL GET IN TOUCH WITH YOU

S SCOTT FITZGERALD.

TO: Beatrice Dance | ALS, 5 pp. Princeton University
Early 1937 | Hotel Stafford letterhead
Baltimore, Maryland

Beatrice:

Your letter reached me an hour after I had left Hopkins where I had been laid up a week with grippe—so its odd you mentioned it.

The clinic there which goes in for diagnosis over a long or short period is the Phipps Clinic. The head is Dr. Adolph Meyer but you could communicate through Dr. Thomas Rennie, whom I will speak to, with the assurance that my name wont ever be mentioned to Eleanor.

I'm glad to say goodbye to the most calamitous year of my life and it was fitting end to spend Xmas to New Years in hospital instead with Scotty. I stayed up long enough to give her a tea dance (supposedly for 50 children, actually for 80) + then collapsed + handed her over to friends. She went down alone to Ashville to spend a few days with her mother + Nora Flinn.[1] She is with me now—when I've put her on the train I'll go south again probably either Tryon or the East Coast of Florida. I have got back almost the complete use of my arm and plan a year of intensive work to make up for this summer + fall.

So much for my somewhat uninspiring history. Did you or did you not send me another subscription to *Fortune*—I guess as much for a December issue arrived. It is a gorgeous magazine and this may amuse you—Scotty picked out her school from their article on the "ten best schools" last year + it was the one I wanted her to choose, even tho the article said frankly it was the strictest school in the country. She has done extremely well there, leading the school in two subjects + her class in two more. I think I told you she has a scholarship—else I couldn't have afforded it this year.

My God! This certainly is the proud parent. But you are too. I'd love to have seen Tulah in her long taffeta. I somehow don't think you will lose her as I have managed to lose Scottie. The latter is simply a carefully chaperoned waif and I hope it wont end by her flinging herself into some too early and disastrous marriage.

There is a phone call from below that my lawyer is here—his name is Edgar Allen Poe Jr. Concieve of that—Edgar Allen Poe and Francis Scott Key, the two Baltimore poets a hundred years after!

So goodbye and dearest affection always

Scott

[1] Nora Flynn was a friend of Fitzgerald's in Tryon, N.C., who tried to help him stay on the wagon.

TO: Beatrice Dance — ALS, 2 pp. Princeton University
Early 1937 — Tryon, North Carolina

Beatrice:

Your letter was disturbing. Its awful that you have been sick again. Finding that liquor was out of all controll with me I simply stopped it entirely the first of the year, even my beloved beer, and life seems niether better nor worse except better a little in the early morning and somewhat lonlier at night. Hated to stop as I enjoyed it so but it was responsible for that silly accident to some extent—I mean the dive was all right but I wouldn't have tried it without Dutch rashness. And that silly piece in *Time* was read by all friends, relatives ect, giving a general impression that papa was really thru this time.

After a quiet winter, seeing only a few old friends, I'm going north + then perhaps to Hollywood for a few months, first showing myself at daughter's school where she complains I'm the mystery man. My invalid, after vast improvement, so that I even planned to take her to the beach for awhile, has distressingly collapsed again. With each collapse she moves perceptibly backward—there is no good end in sight. She is very sweet and tragic   For the majority of creative people life is a pretty mean trick. There are only moments and its childish to hope for more. And hope was once so much fun, such a *graceful* virtue.

Im so glad about Eleanor. It really solves her problem doesn't it—I mean completely.

Letters are so egotistic nessessarily but about my recent stuff that you've liked I can't agree with you. It seems to lack any special brilliance or glow and in an attempt to get a new attitude I'm writing a play, or rather some plays.[1] Being such an experienced technician I've been inclined and tempted lately to cover lack of story + feeling about the story with mere description or else set off damp fireworks to give an artificial life. A play has such bare bones that it makes me aware always of the characters + whether or not they're travelling. My first (in 1923) was a failure, my only serious flop, + I have a detached interest to see what the drama, my first love, holds for me. (God that sounds stilted, but it's true)

Fortune + Life come + I think of you—as if I needed that. I wish I could see you but of course it's impossible. I'm going to write a play for you—I love your letters

Devotedly
Scott

[1] These plays were not completed and are unidentified.

TO: Adelaide Neall — ALS, 1 p. R. Sherrod
Early 1937 — Tryon, North Carolina

Dear Miss Neall:

Thanks for your note and for scheduling the *Trouble* story. 1937 *better* be good—'35 and '36 were one long doctor's bill.

"Gwen" (otherwise "Scottie")[1] is the healthy member of the family—she has a sort of half scholarship at Miss Walker's in Conneticut. My wife is better and for the first time in a long time I have no ailment to complain about.

I hope all goes well with you and I'd like to see you. I am thinking of taking up horses and dogs so I can write for the *Post* again—joking aside I want to discover some new vien which will interest both me and the public. I feel as if I were a contemporary of Richard Harding Davis and Eleanor Glynn[2] and yet my seniors by twenty years—Willa Cather, Ferber et al. seem to live zestfully in the present. Its a little too early for an autobiography of my era though I've even considered that.[3] In any case I'll be sending you something within a fortnight. I've sold you only 16 stories in 5 years, as compared to 36 straight in the five years before that. Of course there was a novel in there, two yrs. long. With Best Wishes

F Scott Fitzgerald

[1] Fitzgerald had sold two stories to the *Post* about a teenage girl named Gwen who was based on his daughter Scottie.

[2] Davis was an adventure writer and war correspondent at the turn of the century; Elinor Glyn was best known for her romantic novel *Three Weeks* (1907).

[3] Written in the margin in another hand: "No, it isn't too early."

TO: Fred B. Millet[1]
Postmarked 27 February 1937

ALS, 3 pp. Yale University
Tryon, North Carolina

Dr. Professor Millet:

This is pretty complete to date, more so than any bibliography I have ever written. Hope it answers your purpose

Sincerely
F Scott Fitzgerald

Scott Fitzgerald Sept 24th, 1896—St. Paul, Minn
Son of Edward + Mary Fitzgerald. Married—Zelda Sayre
(1920) Montgomery Ala
(Author of a novel
Save me the Waltze
and of short stories
alone + with her husband

One daughter
Frances Scott Fitzgerald (1921)

Educated Princeton Univ (1913–1917)
2nd Lt. 45th Inf.
1st Lt. Aide-de-Camp to Brig. Gen J. A. Ryan } War (not overseas)
Has lived near New York, in Europe (six years), in Wilmington, Baltimore and North Carolina.

Adress % Charles Scribners, 599 5th Ave
New York City

Works *Novels.* This side of Paradise 1920
The Beautiful and Damned 1922
The Great Gatsby 1925
Tender is the Night 1934

Stories Flappers and Philosophers
Tales of the Jazz Age
All the Sad Young Men
Taps at Revielle

(Contributed to thirty or forty magazines, principally the *Saturday Evening Post.* First story accepted by Mencken + Nathan for the old *Smart Set* in 1919. Previously had written for undergratuate publications and written the libretto several years for the Princeton Triangle Club—once with Edmund Wilson Jr.)

Play *The Vegetable* produced in Atlantic City 1923 with Ernest Truax

Movies The Chorus Girl's Romance. Metro 1920 Viola Dana
(*From my story* Head + Shoulders)

The Off Shore Pirate. Metro 1921 Viola Dana
(*From my story same title*)
The Husband Hunter Fox 1921, Elien Percy
(*From my Story,* Myra Meets His Family)
Conductor 1492
(*From my story* The Camel's Back. Warner 1922
The Beautiful and Damned Warner 1922
(Kenneth Harlan + Marie Prevost)
(*From my novel*)
The Great Gatsby Paramount 1926
(Warner Baxter + Lois Wilson
(*From my novel*)
Have also worked on several movies in New York and Hollywood.

Hobbies: Swimming, mild fishing, history, especially military, bucolic but civilzed travel, food and wine, imaginary problems of organization, if this makes sense.

Oil Picture Painted by David Silvette
5 N. 2nd St. Richmond Va.
He has reproductions of it.[2]

[1] Author of *Contemporary American Authors* (1940).
[2] Now at the National Portrait Gallery, Washington, D.C.

TO: Ernest Hemingway

Wire. Kennedy Library

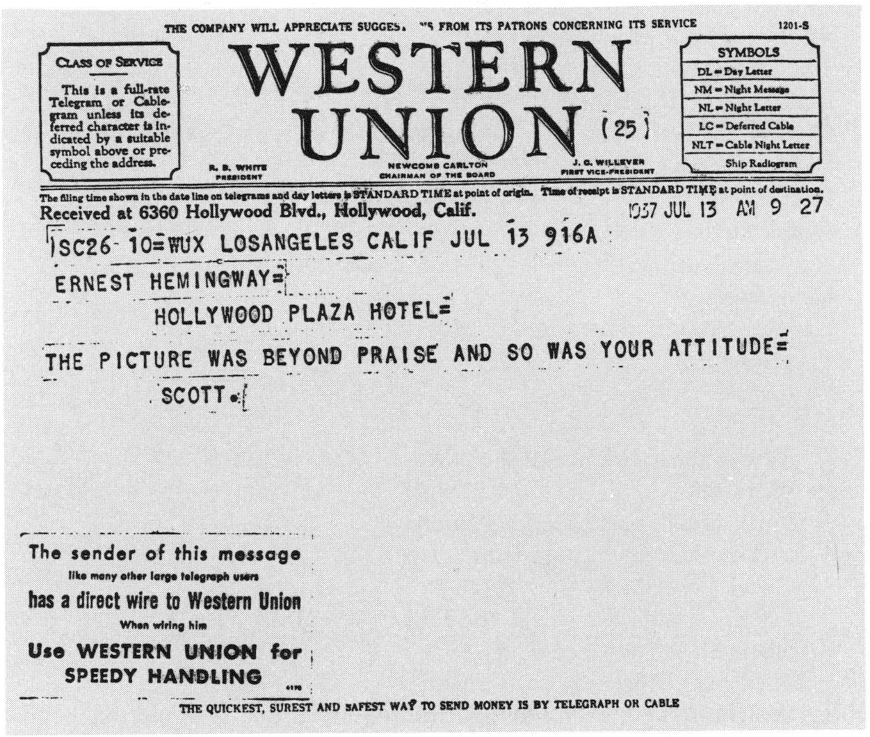
THE COMPANY WILL APPRECIATE SUGGESTIONS FROM ITS PATRONS CONCERNING ITS SERVICE 1201-S

WESTERN UNION (25)

CLASS OF SERVICE: This is a full-rate Telegram or Cablegram unless its deferred character is indicated by a suitable symbol above or preceding the address.

R. B. WHITE, PRESIDENT — NEWCOMB CARLTON, CHAIRMAN OF THE BOARD — J. C. WILLEVER, FIRST VICE-PRESIDENT

SYMBOLS: DL = Day Letter; NM = Night Message; NL = Night Letter; LC = Deferred Cable; NLT = Cable Night Letter; Ship Radiogram

The filing time shown in the date line on telegrams and day letters is STANDARD TIME at point of origin. Time of receipt is STANDARD TIME at point of destination.

Received at 6360 Hollywood Blvd., Hollywood, Calif. 1937 JUL 13 AM 9 27

SC26 10=WUX LOSANGELES CALIF JUL 13 916A

ERNEST HEMINGWAY=

HOLLYWOOD PLAZA HOTEL=

THE PICTURE WAS BEYOND PRAISE AND SO WAS YOUR ATTITUDE=

SCOTT.

The sender of this message like many other large telegraph users has a direct wire to Western Union. When wiring him Use WESTERN UNION for SPEEDY HANDLING

THE QUICKEST, SUREST AND SAFEST WAY TO SEND MONEY IS BY TELEGRAPH OR CABLE

Note: Shortly after Fitzgerald moved to Hollywood, Hemingway showed *The Spanish Earth* there to raise money for the Spanish loyalists. Fitzgerald had a six-month contract with MGM at $1000 a week, with an option for a year's renewal at $1,250.

TO: Edwin Knopf[1]

TL(CC), 2 pp. Princeton University
Hollywood, California

July 19, 1937

Dear Eddie:

A sight of me is Zelda's (my wife's) life line, as the doctor told me before I left. And I'm afraid the little flying trips would just be for emergencies.

I hate to ask for time off. I've always enjoyed being a hard worker, and you'll find that when I don't work through a Saturday afternoon, it's because there's not a thing to do. So just in case you blew off your head, (as David Belasco so tactfully put it), I'd like to put the six weeks a year, one week every two months, into the contract.

It will include everything such as the work left over from outside, as indicated below.

First here is a memo of things that might come up later.

Stories sold but not yet published

The Pearl and the Fur Make Yourself at Home	—*Pictorial Review*[2]
Gods of the Darkness	—*Red Book*
In the Holidays *Pub*[3] Room 32[4] Oubliette[5]	—*Esquire*
New York (article)[6]	—Cosmopolitan
Early Success	Cavalcade[7]

Unsold but in the Possession of my Agent in June, 1937

Financing Finnegan

Dentist's Appointment[8]

Offside Play[9]

(All the above belongs to the past)

In Possession

One play (small part of last act to do.)[10]

To write sometime during the next two years

2 Sat. Eve Post Stories

(I've never missed a year in the *Post* in seventeen years)[11]

1 Colliers Story (advance paid)[12]

3 Short Esquire pieces (advance paid)

So the total time I should ask for over two years would be twelve weeks to write these things while near my wife. It could be allotted as two weeks apiece for the stories, a week apiece for the articles, three weeks for finishing Act III of the play. Though if convenient, I shall in practice, use the weeks singly.[13]

Sincerely,

[1] MGM producer.

[2] "The Pearl and the Fur" was not published; "Make Yourself at Home" appears to have been published as "Strange Sanctuary," *Liberty* (9 December 1939).

[3] Added in holograph.

[4] Published as "The Guest in Room Nineteen."

[5] Published as "The Long Way Out."

[6] "My Lost City" was first published in *The Crack-Up*.

[7] Line added in holograph.

[8] Published as "The End of Hate," *Collier's* (22 June 1940).

[9] Unpublished.

[10] This play had the working title "Institutional Humanitarianism"; it was never published or produced.

[11] Fitzgerald did not appear in the *Post* after 1937.

[12] *Collier's* accepted "The End of Hate" for this advance.

[13] Fitzgerald's MGM contract stipulated that he had the right to work on his own writing during layoff periods.

TO: Anthony Powell[1] — TLS, 1 p. Powell
MGM letterhead. Culver City, California

July 22, 1937

Dear Powell:

Book came.[2] Thousand thanks. Will write when I have read it.[3]

When I cracked wise about Dukes, didn't know Mrs. Powell was a Duke. I love Dukes—Duke of Dorset, The Marquis Steyne, Freddie Bartholomew's grandfather the old Earl of Treacle.

When you come back, I will be in a position to have you made an assistant to some producer or Vice President, which is the equivalent to a Barony.

Regards,
F. Scott Fitzgerald.

[1] British novelist who had met Fitzgerald in Hollywood. See "Hollywood Canteen," *London Times* (3 October 1970), reprinted in *Fitzgerald/Hemingway Annual* 1971.

[2] Powell's novel *From a View to a Death* (1933).

[3] Powell did not receive a second letter from Fitzgerald.

FROM/TO: F. Scott Fitzgerald — Holograph postcard signed.[1]
Summer 1937(?) — Princeton University

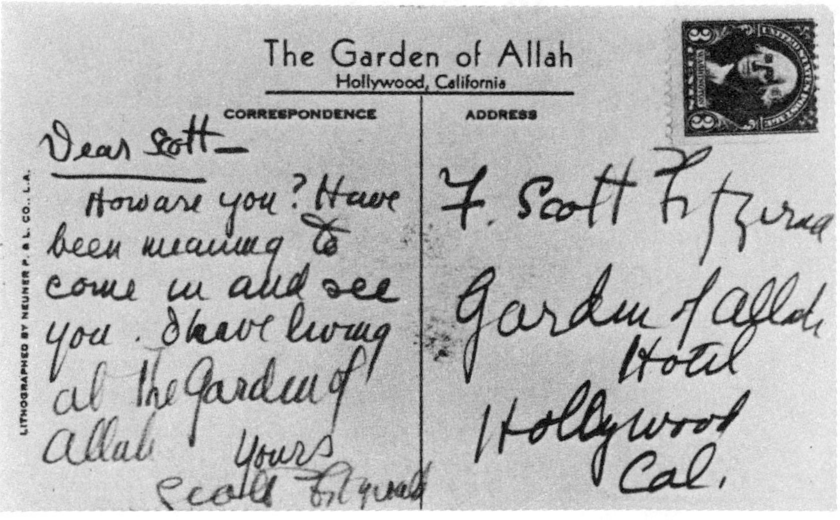

The Garden of Allah
Hollywood, California

CORRESPONDENCE

Dear Scott—
How are you? Have been meaning to come in and see you. I have living at the Garden of Allah
Yours
Scott Fitzgerald

ADDRESS

F. Scott Fitzgerald
Garden of Allah Hotel
Hollywood
Cal.

LITHOGRAPHED BY NEUNER P. & L. CO., L.A.

[1] Not mailed.

TO: Joseph L. Mankiewicz[1] TL(CC), 1 p. Princeton University
Hollywood, California

Sept. 4, 1937

Dear Joe:

This letter is only valid in case you like the script very much.[2] In that case, I feel I can ask you to let me try to make what cuts and rearrangements you think necessary, by myself. You know how when a new writer comes on a repair job he begins by cutting out an early scene, not realizing that he is taking the heart out of six later scenes which turn upon it. Two of these scenes can't be cut so new weak scenes are written to bolster them up, and the whole tragic business of collaboration has begun—like a child's drawing made "perfect" by a million erasures.

If a time comes when I'm no longer useful, I will understand, but I hope that this work will be good enough to earn me the right to a first revise to correct such faults as you may find. Then perhaps I can make it so strong that you won't want any more cooks.[3]

Yours,

P.S. My address will be, Highlands Hospital, Ashville, N.C., where my wife is a patient. I will bring back most of the last act with me.

[1] MGM producer.

[2] Fitzgerald had written the first draft of the screenplay for *Three Comrades* alone and was concerned that he would be assigned a collaborator. See *F. Scott Fitzgerald's Screenplay for Three Comrades* (Carbondale: Southern Illinois University Press, 1978).

[3] On 9 September Mankiewicz wired Fitzgerald in Charleston, S.C., complimenting him on the script and assuring him that he would not have to work with a collaborator. When Fitzgerald returned to Hollywood, E. E. Paramore was assigned to collaborate with him on *Three Comrades*.

TO: Sheilah Graham
Fall 1937(?)

Inscription in *This Side of Paradise*.
Princeton University
Hollywood, California

For my darling Sheilah
— after *such* a
bad time
from
Scott

THIS SIDE OF PARADISE

TO: Clayton Hutton[1]
Late October 1937

ALS, 1 p. Princeton University
Hollywood, California

Ex-1st Lt. INFANTRY
Headquarters Co. 1917

3d Football Team
St Paul Academy 1910

EX-EMPLOYEE
BARON G COLLIER
CAR CARDS, 1920

Worked Unsuccessfully
on
REDHEADED WOMAN
with JEAN HARLOW
1932

WON FIELDMEET
(JUNIOR)
NEWMAN school
1912

AFFAIR
(unconsumated)
with
ACTRESS (1927)

WROTE
22
Unsuccessful
Stories 1920.
OFFERED TO
SATURDAY
EVENING
POST
ect

PLAY VEGETABLE
RAN 2 WEEKS
ATLANTIC CITY
(with Ernest TRUAX)
1923

Dear Mr.

Unable to match the apt phrasology in your letter to Miss Graham of recent date, I can only repeat it: "You show both poor sportsmanship and bad manners"—the former because when a girl neglects two dozen phone calls it is fair to suppose you didn't make an impression—the latter because you wrote such a letter at all.

It is nice to know that it is all "a matter of complete indifference" to you, so there will be no hard feelings. But you worry us about the state of the English colony in Hollywood. Can it be that there are other telephones that —but no—and anyhow you can always take refuge behind that splendid, that truly magnificent indifference.

Very Truly Yours
F. Scott Fitzgerald

1 English movie producer whose attentions to Sheilah Graham annoyed Fitzgerald and prompted him to draft this letter, which was not sent. Hutton's stationery listed his productions.

TO: Drs. Robert S. Carroll and R. Burke Suitt

TL(CC), 2 pp. Princeton University
Hollywood, California

Oct. 22, 1937.

Dear Dr. Carroll or Dr. Suitt:

You will remember that we discussed the question of Zelda making a trip to Alabama by herself and that I thought it was out of the question—the reasons being that while she would have perhaps a seventy per cent chance of getting away with it for a week without serious damage, the risk, if she doesn't, would be tremendous and irrepairable. Having no judgment of any kind, a few drinks of sherry or a few highballs would be as liable as not to turn her into completely irresponsible channels, and there isn't a force in Montgomery strong enough to handle the situation which would then arise. Mrs. Sayer isn't such a force, nor anyone else in her family nor among her immediate friends, and it might lead to an awful mess before she could be rounded into shape again and brought back to you. After that there would be the consequent reaction of loss of confidence, melancholia etc. However, I am very keen that she should go there with a nurse—a nurse picked for being quiet and "a lady," not one who would try to obtrude herself and "make things go."

When I left Zelda on September 15th, we talked over the question of my making an intervening visit and decided then that it was better not to come until Christmas. There is, however, a faint possibility that I might fly down in November, stay for one night and fly back. However, that is problematical. So the question was when Zelda should spend her week in Montgomery. I suggested about midway between my visits, which would be about the fifth of November. Her counter-suggestion was that she should go Thanksgiving. I should suggest that if she now shows signs of restlessness, the former date would be better, though for sentimental reasons she would naturally prefer the holiday. I wish, after talking to Zelda, you would answer this by air mail, estimating the funds required for such a trip, which I will forward.

Her letters are few and far between, though the spirit seems approximately the same as before. The idea of coming to California doesn't appeal to her. She has expressed some desire to go off on her own and reconstitute herself, an intention which under the circumstance seems rather meaningless. When she lived with me in Baltimore, I left her alone on several occasions—sent her once to the World's Fair, two or three times to New York, and went off myself several times for periods of three or four days—but every time made sure there was a trustworthy friend, our secretary of whom she was very fond, her sister or mother close at hand, and also that there was something definite to distract and entertain her. On those occasions she acted more than usually well. On the other hand, all through that year and a half that we lived in the country (and we can't conclude that she is better now than she was then), there would be episodes of great gravity that seemed to have no "build up," outbursts of temper, violence, rashness etc. that could neither be foreseen or forestalled. Now I assume that in shushing any desire of hers to walk right out into the world, we are entirely in accord.

Do write me how things progress. I suppose she has been moved to the other room according to our conversation.

Always sincerely and gratefully,

TO: Beatrice Dance
Postmarked 27 November 1937

ALS, 7 pp. Princeton University
Garden of Allah letterhead
Hollywood, California

Beatrice:

The confusion of my life is typified by the fact that it is over a month since you so sweetly remembered my birthday with the fine hankerchiefs. They were lovely as a snowfall. Won't you stop wringing my heart that way? This is said lightly but I was more touched than you know. *Life + Fortune* have become part of my life + my fortune but I think of you when the Postman puts them on the door step.

So much has happened, most of it at last in process of digestion for a new novel though I think I'll stay here another year + fully recoup my finances. I like it—everything awful about it you hear is true but it has a strange mercurial sort of life. Ive been working on a script of *Three Comrades,* a book that falls just short of the 1st rate (by Remarque)—it leans a little on Hemmingway + others but tells a lovely tragic story. It will be done presumably by Tracy, Taylor, Tone + Margaret Sullivan.

There have been alarms + excursions beside and a new point of view since the drinking finally fell away (it's been over a year now). Daughter came out with Helen Hayes and spent August under her chaperonage, living a sort of Alice-in-Wonderland life in the pools of the stars—just what any 15 year old would dream of. The talent scouts were after her but I shipped her back East to Miss Walkers. She did well on her Vassar exams + goes there in Sept—age 16. It is a choice between 2 evils, Hollywood or Yale + Princeton proms + I guess the second is the least threatening.

Zelda is no better—I took her to Charleston on a trip from the sanitarium in Sept + she held up well enough but there is always a gradual slipping. I've become hard there and don't feel the grief I did once—except sometimes at night or when I catch myself in some spiritual betrayal of the past.

The emotional life is healthier than for several years—a somewhat hectic affair in which Winchell spared me by simply calling me a "love-story novelist" and an amusing meeting with Ginevra King (Mitchell) the love of my youth. Ive seen old friends again, friends again with Ernest + Gerald Murphy + so many people who'd drifted away in my cloistered (or perhaps wolf's den) years. Here introspection melts away in the thin yellow air and at Palm Springs last week I felt as you must have at the Casa de Manãna.[1]

Proust you'll love till the end + then you'll finish it from sheer intention—up to *Le Prisonniere* its fine + *Albertine disparu* picks up at the end but the last 3 volumes could have been revised with profit. *Mice + Men* has been praised all out of proportion to its merits. I hope you didn't read my recent *Esquire* stuff. It was all dictated when I had the broken shoulder + sounds like it.

San Antonio was hot when my train stopped there last July—of course I was tempted to call you up but of course didn't. Later with Scottie I spent a night in Juarez + El Paso + several times, waiting for planes I wandered about desolate breathless airports + thought of you + of how "Slinging Sammy Baugh" beat Southern Methodist—the only two events in Texas since the Alamo as far as I'm concerned.

I have two plays to be produced—one (a dramatization *The Diamond as Big as the Ritz*) in Pasadena this winter[2] + also a play from *Tender* in New York this Spring I hope.[3] My own play remains unfinished because of work here. Xmas I give Scottie her usual Baltimore party + spend Xmas with my invalid. And so it goes.

This is all egotistic news. From your letters I see a good deal but not as much as I would wish to. I do not feel as certain about anything as I did two years ago or I would be full of preachments—not that I doubt my judgements then but I feel something fermenting in me or the times that I can't express and I dont yet know what lights or how strong will be thrown on it. I don't know, even, whether I shall be the man to do it. Perhaps the talent, too long neglected, has passed its prime

Ever your Devoted Scott

[1] Nightclub at the Dallas Pan-American Exposition.
[2] By an amateur group.
[3] Not produced.

TO: Charles A. Post[1] — TL, 2 pp.[2] Western Reserve Historical Society
MGM letterhead. Culver City, California

Nov. 30, 1937.

Dear Mr. Post:

Hope this will be what you want: I was born in St. Paul, Minnesota, September 24th, 1896, the son of a broker, Edward Fitzgerald, who once wrote a novel with another young man, fortunately never published. My great-grandfather's brother, Francis Scott Key, wrote the "Star Spangled Banner," and those were the only signs of literary activity in the family until I came along.

I was educated at the St. Paul Academy in St. Paul; Newman School, New Jersey; and Princeton University, where I wrote for the literary and humorous monthlies and composed musical comedies which were given by the Triangle Club. I was Lieutenant of Infantry during the World War and Aide-de-Camp to Brigadier General John A. Ryan, and when I reached the port of embarkation and was loaded up with gas masks, steel helmet and iron ration, the Germans decided they'd better quit. That's the true story of the armistice. Have ever since suffered from non-combatant shell-shock in the form of ferocious nightmares.

I became an advertising man for nine months and then a writer for life. Published THIS SIDE OF PARADISE, a novel, in 1920 at the age of twenty-three. This seemed to catch on and was followed by THE BEAUTIFUL AND DAMNED, 1922, and THE GREAT GATSBY, 1925. Then after a long interval came TENDER IS THE NIGHT in 1934. Meanwhile I wrote about 150 short stories for the Saturday Evening Post, Scribners, American Mercury, Harpers, etc., about a third of which are collected into four books: FLAPPERS AND PHILOSOPHERS, 1920, TALES OF THE JAZZ AGE, 1922, ALL THE SAD YOUNG MEN, 1926, TAPS AT REVEILLE, 1935. At one point, 1923, I wrote a play, THE VEGETABLE, which was produced with Ernest Truax in Atlantic City, but it was such a dismal failure that it never reached New York. There have also been numerous articles and three trips to Hollywood, which is my present address. All in all very much the usual career of an American writer, even including the five years spent abroad as an expatriate.

I married, in 1920, Zelda Sayre, daughter of Judge A. D. Sayre of the Alabama Supreme Court, and have one daughter, Frances Scott Fitzgerald, born in 1921, preparing to enter Vassar next year. Most of what has happened to me is in my novels and short stories, that is, all the parts that could go into print.

My favorite American authors are Dreiser, Hemmingway and the early Gertrude Stein. I am an admirer of Mencken and Spencer Tracy, but not of Benny Goodman or Father Coughlin. I would like to be a G-Man but I'm afraid it is too late, like to swim, hate large parties and have insomnia. Like living in France, though New York is my favorite city.

Thanking you for your interest and apologizing for the unavoidable egotism of the above,

Sincerely,
F. Scott Fitzgerald

[1] Post was preparing a paper on Fitzgerald for the Novel Club in Cleveland.
[2] This letter was signed for Fitzgerald.

TO: Edwin Knopf — TL(CC), 1 p. Princeton University
Hollywood, California

Dec. 7, 1937

Dear Eddie:

Just received my notice about renewal and am delighted that you think I'm of use to you.[1]

I want to put in writing the one worry which you didn't think important yesterday. As I said, my play had for two acts a prison background which has since been overplayed by the release of ALCATRAZ, THE LAST GANGSTER and other pictures. When I get to it, which may be in three to six months, I want to rewrite it, preserving the plot and most of the characters but changing this element to another. So the element "institutional humanitarianism" which I supplied hastily for the contract in order to avoid divulging the plot, will be lacking from the new version.

My worry is only that my right to produce the play remain intact, especially if I should enlist a collaborator who would naturally want to know that my work in this regard is all free from strings or tails. I may add that I never had, nor have now, the faintest idea of finishing the piece on any but my own time, but the playwriting venture is of great importance to me in keeping my name known during this time when I will be behind the comparative anonymity of the screen. I know that in this regard my interests can in no way run contrary to yours.

Ever yours,

[1] MGM had renewed Fitzgerald's contract for one year at $1,250 per week.

TO: Sheilah Graham — ALS, 2 pp.[1] Princeton University
Early 1938(?) — Hollywood, California

So glad it went well, my blessed. Will be back when you wake up in the very late afternoon

Scott

Second Note

I am here (it is 5:30) + you are getting rapidly out of the ether + very sick.[2] You want to be anyhow. You asked me sweet questions and said you couldn't believe they did it while you were asleep. I love you + I am coming back in the morning quite early + sit with you. It has been a day for all of us + I must go eat + get a bit of sleep. Thank God it is over + youre well again

Scott

[1] Numbered 2 and 2A; the first page is missing.
[2] Miss Graham had undergone surgery.

TO: Hunt Stromberg[1]

TL(CC), 2 pp. MGM
Hollywood, California
Feb. 22, 1938

Dear Mr. Stromberg:

Working out this somewhat unusual structure was harder than I thought, but it's at last on a solid basis. I began the actual writing yesterday.[2]

The first problem was whether, with a story which is over half told before we get up to the point at which we began, we had a solid dramatic form—in other words whether it would divide naturally into three increasingly interesting "acts" etc. The answer is yes—even though the audience knows from the mysterious indifference that the characters are headed toward trouble. They know before we go into the retrospect that the two characters are not finished or "accomplished," they know that the husband's love still lives and all is not lost. Even without the prologue the audience would know that the wife is going to find the guilty pair and their interest is in the *way* and *how*.

The second problem was that during the secretary-husband affair, which will require about twenty-five pages to do justice to, Joan is almost completely "off scene" and the audience's interest is in the other girl. I've turned the handicap into an asset by the following change:

At the point when the husband is being involuntarily drawn toward the old secretary, we dissolve to the wife in Europe with her mother. Her old sweetheart comes into the picture for the first time—in this episode she is not even faintly tempted—only disturbed—but disturbed enough so that she books a quicker passage to America. At this point we dissolve back to the secretary and the husband.

This point, her decision to sail, also marks the end of the "first act." The "second act" will take us through the seduction, the discovery, the two year time lapse and the return of the old sweetheart—will take us, in fact, up to the moment when Joan having weathered all this, is unpredictably jolted off her balance by a stranger. This is our high point—when matters seem utterly insoluble.

Our third act is Joan's recoil from a situation that is menacing, both materially and morally, and her reaction toward reconciliation with her husband.

So much for the story. Now, will the following schedule be agreeable to you? The script will be aimed at 130 pages. I will hand you the first "act"—about fifty pages—on March 11th, or two weeks from Friday. I will complete my first draft of the script on or about April 11th, totalling almost seven weeks. That is less time than I took on THREE COMRADES, and the fact that I understand the medium a little better now is offset by the fact that this is really an original with no great scenes to get out of a book. Will you let me know if this seems reasonable? My plan is to work about half the time at the studio but the more tense and difficult stuff I do better at home away from interruptions. Naturally I'll always be within call and at your disposal.

With best wishes,

[1] Producer at MGM.

[2] Fitzgerald was writing the screenplay for a Joan Crawford movie, *Infidelity*, which encountered censorship problems and was never made. See R. L. Samsell, "Six Previously Unpublished Letters to Hunt Stromberg," *Fitzgerald/Hemingway Annual* 1972.

TO: Dr. Robert S. Carroll — TL(CC), 2 pp. Princeton University

Garden of Allah
8152 Sunset Boulevard
Hollywood, California
March 4th, 1938

Dear Dr. Carroll:

I have not heard from you as to when you think Zelda can make her tentative sortie into the world—though I gathered from our conversation in Greenville that you thought it would be about the end of March.

I am trying to arrange a week off here, so that I can see my daughter for the first time since September. (I got a glimpse of her at her school but, as you remember, they held me over here Christmas and New Year's.) The best time for me would be somewhere between March 23rd and 30th, and that would fit my daughter's vacation.

If you have found a companion, Zelda could meet us somewhere, perhaps in Virginia. Otherwise, my daughter and I could come to Tryon, though there seem to be no children there my daughter's age, and we seem to have rather exhausted the place's possibilities.

My slip off the wagon lasted only three days. It was the reaction from a whole lot of things that preceded it and is not likely to recur because I have taken steps practically and mentally to prevent the set-up that caused it: the physical exhaustion and the emotional strain.

I have, of course, my eternal hope that a miracle will happen to Zelda, that in this new incarnation events may tend to stabilize her even more than you hope. With my shadow removed, perhaps she will find something in life to care for more than just formerly. Certainly the outworn pretense that we can ever come together again is better for being shed. There is simply too much of the past between us. When that mist falls—at a dinner table, or between two pillows—no knight errant can transverse its immense distance. The mainsprings are gone.

And if the aforesaid miracle should take place, I might again try to find a life of my own, as opposed to this casual existence of many rooms and many doors that are not mine. So long as she is helpless, I'd never leave her or ever let her have a sense that she was deserted.

Next week, I will begin clearing up the balance of what I owe you. The $500 a month[1] that we settled on for Zelda had best be sent her in weekly payments, through my agent—that is, sent to her companion, because Zelda has no idea whatsoever of money. I expect in another year to be completely out of debt and will make a more liberal allowance, though, of course, at your discretion, as you said you wanted her to live rather in the class of poor scholars than to return to the haunts of the rich.

Since seeing you, I have run into two of the most beautiful belles of my time—utterly ridden and ruined by drugs. I know scarcely a beautiful woman of Zelda's generation who has come up to 1938 unscathed.

For myself, I work hard and take care of myself. I had a scare a few months ago when, for a long stretch, tuberculosis showed signs of coming back—just portents—weakness, loss of appetite, sweating. I took an X-ray, lay very low for a few weeks, and the feeling passed.

I don't think I could keep up this work for more than two years at a stretch. It has a way of being very exhausting, especially when they put on the pressure. So what income I achieve here is not to be considered as an average. Zelda understands this and that my true career is as a novelist and she knows that at that time the squirrel must live on what nuts he has accumulated.

I wish you would let me know as soon as possible your time plans for Zelda. As I wrote Dr. Suitt, I don't think she should go home to Montgomery until she has had a definite period of adjustment to the companion because they might "gang up" against the companion. Mrs. Sayre, when it comes to Zelda, is an entirely irrational and conscienceless woman with the best intentions in the world.

Likewise, all I have told you should be spoken of vaguely in front of any of Zelda's family. If it ever comes to a point when a divorce should be in the picture, I think I would rather have you watch over Zelda's interests. As I told you in Greenville, you've been more than a father to her—doing a much more difficult job than Dr. Forel had in bringing her to this level of stability. Everything that you recommended for her has proved correct, and don't think I don't understand your theory of the danger to her of any toxic condition. I gave her a few cigarettes and a few glasses of sherry in the spirit of a wickedly indulgent grandfather, merely to turn her gratitude toward me for a few hours—and realized it should never be the regular thing for her.

Yours always, with deepest gratitude,

[1] This figure covered hospital expenses and Zelda's allowance.

TO: Beatrice Dance

TLS, 2 pp. Princeton University

Metro-Goldwyn-Mayer
Culver City, California
March 4th, 1938

Dearest Beatrice:

Subscription to Life came and it's nice to see it lying on my office desk every Wednesday. I always lie right down on the couch and read it on Metro's time. However, now they have taken our secretaries away from us in a fit of economy, so I work at home out of spite—home being a parlor, bedroom and bath in the Garden of Allah Hotel.

I am writing a picture for Joan Crawford, called "Infidelity." I feel they should not have given me a subject that I know so little about. However, I am asking all my friends about their experiences, and will try to make it convincing. Of course, infidelity in the movies is somewhat different from infidelity in life, being always forestalled in time and having beautiful consequences.

"Three Comrades," the picture I have just finished, is in production and though it bears my name, my producer could not resist the fascination of a pencil and managed to obviate most signs of my personality. Nonetheless, I am now considered a success in Hollywood because something which I did not write is going on under my name, and something which I did write has been quietly buried without any fuss or row—not even a squeak from me. The change from regarding this as a potential art to looking at it as a cynical business has begun. But I still think that some time during my stay out here I will be able to get something of my own on the screen that I can ask my friends to see. But if you go to see "Three Comrades," only credit me with the parts you like.

I think of you often. Twice I have been to La Jolla. Each time I have asked about you, and tried to imagine you in the court, or at the bar, or riding through those lovely woods. It's a grand place and I made up the whole act of a play there in two days. (By the way, "Tender Is the Night" has been dramatized and may be in New York next year.)

The phone has just rung and I go to meet my fate in the person of Mr. Hunt Stromberg, who is going to hear the first third of my script.

Goodbye, dear Beatrice, and I hope this finds you happy.

Scott

TO: Louis Trinkaus[1] TLS, 1 p. Trinkaus

Metro-Goldwyn-Mayer Studio
Culver City, California
March 4th, 1938

Dear Mr. Trinkhaus:

Thank you for your letter. It was very nice of you to go to that trouble and it gave me a sense of "Gatsby" still existing. I am sorry you didn't like Daisy's "voice full of money." I don't know whether "a voice full of money" would charm me now, but I suppose I meant that it had a certain deep confidence that money gave in those days. And Daisy's speech about "the most advanced people" was very definitely ironic when I wrote it—imagine me in my right mind using the phrase "advanced people" which is consecrated to theosophists and such idiots.

I have been to Cagnes-sur-mer and found it full of artists waiting for remittances.

"Gatsby" was made into a movie with Warner Baxter in 1927. Clark Gable wants to do it, but Paramount is playing dog-in-the-manger about the rights.

Thank you again.

Sincerely,
F Scott Fitzgerald

[1] On 14 February Trinkaus had written Fitzgerald complimenting him on *The Great Gatsby* and rebuking Hemingway for his slighting remark about Fitzgerald in "The Snows of Kilimanjaro." (Princeton)

TO: Mrs. Mary Leonard Pritchett[1] TL(CC), 1 p. Princeton University

carbon copy to
Mrs. Cora Jarrett, c/o Harold Ober, 20 East 49th St. NYC

Metro-Goldwyn-Mayer Studios
Culver City, California
March 4th, 1938

Dear Mrs. Pritchett:

Sorry I could not get word to you before you sailed.

I am out of touch with the stage in New York, but have talked to Sidney Howard and several other playwrights here regarding your suggestions for the casting of "Tender Is the Night." Invariably, Margaret Rawlins has seemed a very good choice for Nicole to those who have read the book, and, equally unanimously, they have been against Beulah Bondi.

Nicole should have not merely glamour but a practically irresistible glamour. In fact, my ideal casting would be Katherine Hepburn or Margaret Sullavan, with the beauty of Loretta Young.

Oddly enough, the character of Tommy, or rather some of the mannerisms of Tommy, were taken from Mario Braggiotti,[2] the brother of Stanio. It would be a delightful coincidence if Stanio played the part.

Thank you for your interest in the casting. They have really done an awfully good job and, in the reading, all the parts seemed very fat and tempting. Bob Montgomery out here is one of several actors who keep recurring to the playing of Dick Diver.

With very best wishes,

Sincerely yours,
F. Scott Fitzgerald

[1] Agent representing Kate Oglesby and Cora Jarrett, who were dramatizing *Tender Is the Night.*

[2] Composer, pianist, and conductor.

TO: Dr. Robert S. Carroll and Dr. R. Burke Suitt

TL(CC), 3 pp. Princeton University
Hollywood, California

April 7, 1938.

Dear Dr. Carroll or Dr. Suitt:

The first thing that struck me in regard to Zelda was her illusion or rather her exaggeration of what she is to do during these experimental trips away from the sanitarium that we talked of. How much I am to blame for this I don't know, but I know it is hard for you to tell at any exact point what she can do or what she can't. However, it seems to me that her *thinking* about it was more in proportion a few months ago than it is now.

The idea first took shape, as I remember, in a vague promise that she could go to her mother in the Spring. Around Christmas I began to be assured by letters from her mother and sister that she was to be discharged by then—I did not believe this was possible but dared to hope that some scheme of traveling with a companion, at the end of a radius with the clinic as its center, would be feasible.

When Dr. Carroll and I talked in Greenville last February, he even mentioned such locales as the Coast of Maine. With this as a foundation, however, Zelda has, I find, erected a bizarre edifice. To change the metaphor, she imagines herself as a sort of Red Scourge in golden heels, flitting East and West, back and forth across the ocean, munificently bicycling with Scottie through Provence etc., with a companion chosen by herself, now reduced to the status of a sort of lady's maid, who will allow her to do anything she wants. She even has one picked out, a former patient; and she intends to control the purse strings herself—her theory being that the hospital (and she should know that she was carried by the hospital at cost over very hard times) intends to profit greatly by the excursion. My part is to stay here and pay for this grandiose expedition, with no control over it.

The thing changes then in its aspect from a humble attempt at some gradual adjustment to a glorious jail break. Also in her gloomier moments she is going to exact from us all the last farthing in spiritual and financial payment for this long persecution.

To say I am disappointed is putting it mildly. The hope was that if the idea of her coming back to me were removed, as she has wanted it to be, it would give her more responsibility, make her walk with even more guarded steps. The notion of her parading around irresponsibly, doing damage that might be irreparable, is as foreign to your ideas, I know, as to mine.

(After about two days of this rigmarole, I added to the general confusion by getting drunk, whereupon she adopted the course of telling all and sundry that I was a dangerous man and needed to be carefully watched. This made the whole trip one of the most annoying and aggravating experiences in my life.[1] I had been physically run down and under a doctor's supervision for two months, working with the help of injections of calsium, sodium, iron and liver, living on too much caffeine by day and sleeping on clorol at night and *touching no liquor;* and I was looking forward to this as a much needed rest. In fact, the doctor who is apprehensive that the trouble in my lungs is about to flare up again, begged me to go to the country or someplace near here and rest for a week. But because I had been held here Christmas and New Years, I was anxious to see my daughter at least once. I think she was the only one on our corridor of the hotel that Zelda did not convince that I was a madman. Luckily I sent Scottie off to Baltimore before matters attained their final pitch of the ridiculous—on the boat coming up from Norfolk where I had some words with the idiotic trained nurse whom, by the way, Zelda had invited to accompany her on her exit into the world. All this isn't pretty on my part, but if I had been left alone, would have amounted to a two day batt—in fact, I sobered myself up the second I had gotten Zelda off for Carolina and caught the plane from Washington that night, arriving here Monday and reporting for work.)

One thing is apparent: that my present usefulness is over in the case. Living a vegetable life in Tryon, I got along with her all right; even had some *fairly* good times together—now our relations are about as bad as at any time in our lives—even worse on my part, for I am unable to feel any of the pity which usually ameliorated whatever she did. In the old days, I could interpose someone between her and our daughter; now, the rasp of temperament between the two simply makes me want to shut her up violently; makes daughter and I feel like conspirators when we can have a minute alone together away from the sing-song patronage which she thinks is the proper method of addressing children. The daughter in turn treats her like an individual, and over it all the well-meant hypocrisy of trying to pretend we are just a happy family, is hard to keep up. The daughter is sorry for her mother, but they are very different in temperament and if more than a few hours together, Mrs. Fitzgerald runs to me with her face red, talking about Scottie as if she were a potential criminal for not having exactly the same interests. To Zelda's mind, I have separated them—the fact is that life has done it beyond my power to add or detract by the tiniest fraction.

Beyond all this, Zelda made a concrete effort during all the mornings and most of the afternoons toward a sort of sweetness which, to me, seemed thin and which apparently my cousins in Norfolk found winning and quite normal. This was even exerted toward me at times, but toward the end I was so irritated that I was unable to judge whether it was sincere or a complete mask, because the moment its objects were out of sight, she had no good words for anyone in particular.

I am enclosing check for the bill received April 1st. I do not know how far this runs.

Meanwhile I await hearing from you, even a note as to what condition you feel she is in and what your plans for her are, so I will be able to estimate what the financial obligations will be. She considers the sum Dr. Carroll wanted her to have as ridiculously inadequate, not realizing the proportion of my salary, my only income, which is going back to pay former debts run up over these years of sickness and trouble. As I told you, at the very best, it will take me two years to be out of debt; and during the second of these years, I want also to put aside some sum which will give me a year off to write a novel. In case of her making trips, I should infinitely prefer you to regulate what she should spend, and I am sorry if these two extravagant flights, which were an attempt to make up for the long time apart from her, gave her any ideas of my scale of living. I am still driving a 1934 Ford and shall probably continue to drive it, as far as I can see ahead.

Sincerely,

[1] In March Fitzgerald went east and took Zelda and Scottie on a trip to Virginia Beach and Norfolk.

TO: Dr. Robert S. Carroll TL(CC), 4 pp.[1] Princeton University

Garden of Allah Hotel
Hollywood, California
April 19th, 1938

Dear Dr. Carroll:

Your letter came last night and I have spent many hours trying to regard it from all angles. Since I have no more constructive plan for Zelda, it would seem a presumption to do anything but accept the program outright. Yet I am haunted by the sense that, considering Zelda in her saner moments and knowing her in those moments as possibly no one else ever can, the program lacks two things which are or can be of great importance to her—I feel that it lacks provision for hope and for sex.

As to the hope, I realize that in a sense there is no hope. I mean simply the illusion of hope, the sort of thing that runs away with her at times and makes her plan excursions and careers far beyond her capacity but that, within bounds, is pretty much what we live for, isn't it?

There was a period when she was at the Sheppard Pratt Hospital, when she had been hospitalized a year, gone through a katatonic state and come out of it and been moved to a free ward, when I was in a blue mood myself—when her attitude and morale changed suddenly and she went into a deep, suicidal melancholy. It happened very suddenly. She tried self-strangulation, etc., almost without warning. And this attitude developed out of a time when things were not so bad, but only that existence seemed to have settled into an appalling monotony. Hope meant a lot in the best part of our lives, the first eight years we lived together, as it does in the lives of most young couples—but I think in our case it was even exaggerated, because as a restless and ambitious man, I was never disposed to accept the present but always striving to change it, better it, or even sometimes destroy it. There were always far horizons that were more golden, bluer skies somewhere. It seems to me, therefore, that if she realized that her stay in the hospital was forever, the effect might be very dangerous. And in her saner and more morose moods, she is quite capable of realizing that. If she sinks down a couple of more notches, she might not, but at this point, I would be surprised if she didn't make that realization.

And I thought that a companion might be found who would realize her struggle toward some *private* life of her own. At 37, she is externally a most attractive woman, as you know; very pretty and well preserved and, when not dressed outrageously, an extremely personable individual. Judging by myself and the anchorite life that I perforce led during the years when I had T.B. and the broken bones, I know what a difference all that can make in morale.

For these two reasons, and perhaps with a sense of conscience that as the provider I would be in a sense making a final judgment on her, betraying all our old closeness, the old bond of justice that existed between us, if I formally gave up hope myself and simply waited by the psychological deathbed (this may seem strange from one who has no desire ever again to personally undertake her supervision. That period has gone, and each time that I see her something happens to me that makes me the worst person for her rather than the best, but a part of me will always pity her with a sort of deep ache that is never absent from my mind for more than a few hours: an ache for the beautiful child that I loved and with whom I was happy as I shall never be again.) For these reasons, I should ask you to consider a modification between the plan of your letter and the plan we discussed in Greenville. In your letter, the center of gravity is so markedly in the hospitalization, that very little time is given for any possible establishment of a place in life, even as a transient. I know that she is hospital-minded, but she was thirty when she first entered a hospital and there is a vision in her mind of a practical and pleasant world that is not a hospital. If I should seem to favor her staying on any longer than necessary, it puts me in an extremely difficult position with her and with her family, who have seen her in an extremely pleasant and hopeful light of late. It is the "two weeks every three months" that frightens me. Two weeks out of every two months,[2] or one month out of every three, would still leave the center of gravity in the hospital and yet give her some life outside. She loves Asheville, but inevitably, the fauna and flora have worn off their original novelty, and I somehow dread her going into another winter there without a few more hopes to live with. It must be her center, at present, for it has done wonders for her. But there have been lonely letters at times when she dreamed of tropical skies in December—

Your suggestion of the West Indies or Honolulu would appeal to me if only they were a little less remote in time. Who knows but that in another year a change for the worst might make such things impossible? Also, the coast of Maine suggestion of yours seemed to carry with it a certain promise. Right now is the time I fear, if she knows that the next step is a summer in Asheville, after all this hope, this so pitiful, so exaggerated hope, and again next November, when the gray days shut down. This part of Zelda I know well. She has a flowerlike quality of blooming or hibernating with the seasons. So this letter is to ask you to consent to a little more extended program, with me realizing its dangers, but also shunning the responsibility of what amounts to a drawing of the curtain upon her. If I were near there and things had gotten better between us, as they seemed to for a while when I was in Tryon, and if I had nothing to do save devote myself to her, taking her out for week-ends, etc., the prospect might seem different, but I am in the best working time of my life, my mind never quicker nor more desperately anxious to store a little security for old age and to write a couple more decent books before that light goes out, and I cannot live in the ghost town which Zelda has become. Do three weeks[3] of the year outside, scattered in weeks here and there, seem too much to allow her? If she is hopeless, there would be not so much to lose. Can't we compromise on something like this?

Now as to the money. My contract here expires next February, and there is not a possibility of my standing the strain of this work longer than that. I give myself about fifteen more working years and I think that I can average, with half of the years out here and half writing novels, about $20,000 clear a year, of which I would give Zelda one-third. But I should expect her to dress herself on that. It is rather awful to reach forty-one and realize that if I died at this moment, my wife and daughter would have only $30,000 of life insurance to live on, so weekly a check goes to the company from here to build up what I borrowed on my policy, and giving Zelda one-third of $20,000 will be something of a strain at first. Her illness has cost a small fortune, and double that if I count those who have had to take her place in my life and my daughter's in various ways.

So I imagine that I could meet the sum you mention, even this year, if it included some dress allowance and if, as I hope, you can see your way to giving her a little longer leash. Won't you write me as to this? I am afraid that my report on the trip may have contributed to your opinion and that is unfair to Zelda. As I said, other people who saw her, my cousins, were impressed with her normality. I think that she, and her family, too, would think that it was an act almost of malfeasance on my part to put her on such narrow bounds. Can't three months out of the year be arranged—two weeks in every eight?

Again, expressions of my faith in your wisdom and my gratitude for your kindness. Most anxiously I await some word from you. She is on my mind night and day, as she has been for eight years. Do please write.

Ever sincerely,

[1] Fitzgerald numbered this letter "II" and wrote at the head of his copy: "This was my answer."

[2] Fitzgerald bracketed this phrase and noted "(as above)."

[3] Fitzgerald emended "weeks" to "months" and noted in the margin: "This typist's error was caught in the copy sent to Carrol."

TO: Hunt Stromberg

TL(CC), 2 pp. MGM
Hollywood, California

4/21/38

Argument for Stromberg

Hunt—

Let us suppose that you were a rich boy brought up in the palaces of Fifth Avenue.

Let us suppose that—and I was a poor boy born on Ellis Island.

Let us suppose that's the way it was—you a rich boy—me a poor boy, get me?

Well, now, me the poor boy has done a bad thing and I am going to tell you, a rich boy, how it happened, and I am going to say to you:

"Picture yourself in my place."

And suddenly as I begin to tell my poor boy's story, you begin to listen very interestedly, with great concentration and in a minute you, the rich boy, begin to be able to *picture* yourself in my place—what I would have done, thought, said—and as I talk you would begin to really picture yourself having the experience that happened to me.

For instance, at the very start—as I begin to tell you what brought me to this bad spot when I describe myself as an immigrant baby, you would begin to imagine what that immigrant baby looked like—and suppose it had been you—and you look in your mind at that baby and it turns around and, so convinced are you of my sincerity and so deep is your interest that as the baby turns around, it *is* you. *You,* who are going through the experience of the narrator, you who are having the same experiences as he has, step by step, your face, your voice, following out the pattern of what happened to *me.*

Picture yourself in that situation is a phrase we all use but here I have tried to dramatize it. You will see how. This all is to prepare you for what I think may be a radical departure in pictures.[1]

[1] The project did not develop.

TO: Mrs. A. D. Sayre

TL(CC), 1 p. Princeton University
Hollywood, California

April 23rd, 1938

Dear Mrs. Sayre:

Thanks for your letter.

Zelda is off on the wrong foot about my plans for her. Far from wanting her to stay there, I have been pleading with Dr. Carroll to give her a longer leash. This is the first time she has ever abused me on that point, and I am considerably irritated.

I am sending you copies of the last correspondence between Dr. Carroll and myself, in which you will see that it is I who wants her to have a wider scope, and Dr. Carrol who does not think she is able to.

Very few lines of mine are left in "A Yank at Oxford." I only worked on it for eight days, but the sequence in which Taylor and Maureen O'Sullivan go out in the punt in the morning, while the choir boys are singing on Magdalene Tower, is mine, and one line very typically so—where Taylor says, "Don't rub the sleep out of your eyes. It's beautiful sleep." I thought that line had my trade mark on it.

However, "Three Comrades" should be released within ten days, and a good third of that is absolutely mine.

Zelda seems to have had an awfully good time in Montgomery, but I am sorry she doesn't like this companion.

Affection, always,

TO: Scottie Fitzgerald

TLS, 1 p. Princeton University

Hollywood
April 27, 1938

Dearest Pie:

Well—the cards are certainly on the table. It is apparent that, in borderline cases such as yours:

Entrance to Vassar depends on the Good Will of your school.

The Good Will of your School is likewise borderline in your case—good possibilities and somewhat smelly results; good extra curricular activities and disturbing conceit (which I hope won't go into your letter to Vassar.)

The Good Will of the School can be said to depend entirely on the next six weeks. *The fortnight of waiting is when they will be making up their final report.* If you are a leader as you consider yourself, perhaps you could exert yourself so that what happened to last year's Fifth Form won't happen to yours.

I have written Alice Lee Myers that the trip to Europe depends entirely on whether your school recommends you for college. If not, I don't think you'd get anything out of the trip and it can wait till next Summer when you're more mature. Something less expensive can be arranged here in America.

About New York shopping—can't Aunt Rosalind do it?

You ask about your mother—it goes to and fro. Dr. Carroll wants her to stay there with only six weeks out a year. I don't see that—so hopeless and dismal, so I'm asking for three to four months. Her family thinks I'm *behind* Carroll! So I've sent them the whole correspondence.

When I'm away from your mother I feel always an intense pity for her. She was one of the eternal children of this world, the nuisance makers, the charming excuse-artists—a thing people will stand until they realize the awful toll exacted from others.

I have waited to write the Finneys[1] till I heard from you. Perhaps if it can't be arranged in June it may be in Autumn.

It's pretty unlikely for me to come in June—would you like your mother to come with an attractive, well-dressed nurse?

Answer me this—and always

Dearest love
Daddy

[1] Fitzgerald was planning a trip to California for Scottie and her friend Peaches Finney.

TO: Zelda Fitzgerald
April 1938

ALS, 2 pp.[1] Bruccoli
Hollywood, California

I couldn't bring myself to write you last week—I was plenty sore with myself and also a good deal with you. But as things settle down I can regard it all with some detachment. As I told you I was a sick man when I left California—had a beautiful little hemorage the end of March, the first in two years and a half—and I was carrying on only on the false exaltation of having done some really excellent work. I thought I'd just lie around in Norfolk and rest but it was a fantastic idea because I should have rested before undertaking the trip. There has been no drink out here, *not a drop of it,* but I am in an unfortunate rut of caffiene by day and chloral by night which is about as bad on the nerves. As I told you if I can finish one *excellent* picture to top *Three Comrades* I think I can bargain for better terms—more rest *and* more money.

These are a lot of "I"s to tell you I worry about you—my condition must have been a strain and I thought you had developed somewhat grandiose ideas of how to spend this money I am to earn which I consider as *capital*—this extravagant trip to the contrary. Dr. Carrol's feeling about money is simply that he wants to regulate your affairs for the time being and he can do so if you live on a modest scale and within call. He doesn't care personally whether you spend a hundred a month or ten thousand—doubtless for the latter you could travel in state with a private physician instead of a nurse. Here is the first problem you run up against trying to come back into the world + I hope you'll try to see with us and adjust yourself. You are not married to a rich millionaire of thirty but to a pretty broken and prematurely old man who hasn't a penny except what he can bring out of a weary mind and a sick body.

Any relations you want are all right with me but I have heard nothing from you and a word would be reassuring because I am always concerned about you

Scott

Oh, Zelda, this was to have been such a cold letter, but I dont feel that way about you. Once we were one person and always it will be a little that way.

[1] This letter may not have been sent.

TO: Dr. Robert S. Carroll TL(CC), 4 pp.[1] Princeton University

Hollywood, California

May 19th, 1938

Dear Dr. Carroll:

In an odd way, I believe my attitude at the moment is the most detached of all. Yours is detached in the sense of a general who, measuring the capacity of his army against the other army, decides that this or that is the point to throw in his reserves. In the history of wars, battles have gone wrong because of such accidents as the failure of a supply train, the wet bowstrings of archers, the astonishing morale of a despised race, or the unexpected rising of a stream. Considered only as a topographer, my opinion must be taken into consideration—the whole terrain over which we must maneuver—my life and Zelda's. I can give myself arguments on both sides which have impersonality if only because they balance each other. For example:

If Zelda is hospitalized, there is a certain safety, a certain calculability about the next few years. If she is not entirely hospitalized, there is the chance that the renewal of contacts may lead her away from her dependence on me and, consequently, lessen my responsibility, which I selfishly want. On moral grounds, if she is hospitalized, I will have the reproach of not having given her every chance, as I would want it to have been given to me; but if she is not hospitalized, I will have put her in some danger by letting her go more into the world. Continuing the antitheses, on material grounds, if hospitalized, she would cost a certain sum, expensive when I include the fact that I would have to come East to see her three or four times a year. The cost of these trips, since they are in no sense vacations for me but periods of intense unhappiness and since, moreover, my salary stops when I leave Los Angeles, would add two or three thousand dollars, making a total, with the Honolulu trip, of eleven or twelve thousand for her, much more than half the money there is to spend on the three of us—condemning me pretty much to the galleys here, sick or well, and bringing my chances of ever writing another book practically to a minimum; on the other hand, if not hospitalized, she might cause damage, make bills, make material trouble that would be even worse than all this.

All in all, you see, I have as many pros and cons as a topographer or, to change the metaphor, as a historian, if such obscure tragedies ever rate recording.

So I would ask you to open your mind once more to the situation from my point of view. Isn't there possibly someone who, under your guidance and your authority, could devote four or five months a year to Zelda, if they had $600 or $650 a month to include *everything*, with Zelda to spend the rest of the time in the hospital at the same price, the whole to include clothes, all incidentals, etc.? Supposing Zelda at best would be a lifelong eccentric, supposing that in two or three years there is certain to be a sinking, I am still haunted by the fact that if it were me, and Zelda were passing judgment, I would want her to give me a chance, even though, as you say, "She suffered more in one short period of the agonies of impending self-destruction than even in the petulant period that inspired the letter you sent."

There is, at the moment, such a difficulty as this: I am sending my daughter abroad on a tourist-class, station wagon tour of Europe with a chaperon and some other girls; I have taken a small cottage or shack at the beach here. I am frightened to write Zelda of these two facts because I know the picture immediately forming in her mind—that her daughter can run over to the Europe that she so dearly loves, and that she can't; that I am near a beach for the summer, and the swimming that she loves so. As long as she sees her daughter in school and me in an office, she can accept the work and weariness of the world, but her own childish sense of justice would be wildly hurt at thinking that we should have such pleasures and she should not.

There is also one side of Zelda which is not even faintly provided for because it is most destroyed, and yet it is infinitely recurrent. At one time she had a very extraordinary mind, schizoid, but given its premises, rational. Under a complete hospitalization scheme, this would have no exercise at all except as a sort of rebuttal or, as they say here, "stoogie" to more definitely formed and powerful minds such as the physicians'. Her vocabulary must be allowed three times that of most people she is liable to come in contact with in a hospital. It would be like an artist only allowed to paint in certain tempera. This is one of many things that influence me when I say that your last letter does not make me happy. Could you not draw me up an alternative based on the chance of your finding such a person as we discussed in Greenville, perhaps finding such a person in the more cultured North (I hate that word "culture" and yet that is approximately what I mean)? If I felt that you had really considered that, I would be able to lie down knowing that the best possible had been done from all angles. At present, I am terribly perturbed and upset—after this hope and struggle, certainly we could give her *a month's trial.* The other plan makes my own set-up for the next ten years simply hopeless.

Please do answer this this week. It has gotten to a state where sleep is departing from me.

With deepest gratitude always,

[1] Fitzgerald numbered this letter "IV" and wrote at the head of his copy: "Next I sent Carrol this."

TO: Rosalind Sayre Smith

TL(CC), 4 pp. Princeton University

Hollywood, California

May 27th, 1938

Dear Rosalind:

These letters tell their own story. Any vote in the matter will be considered—that is any vote based on the entire situation and past history, not merely on the superficial fact that Zelda can put up a good front for a week. Dr. Carroll and your mother have taken up opposite stands and I am almost as much the football as Zelda. I am on your mother's side in that I want *more* trial of Zelda's capacities but *I will not override Carroll* and have it all thrown back on me again—I have proven my incapacity for the job. And the idea of your mother assuming the responsibility is, of course, fantastic—it would simply mean turning Zelda loose. To do that at present would be, to use Carroll's parallel, like entering a tubercular person for the Golden Gloves Tournament.

Scottie is somewhat snobbishly worried that her mother may not be dressed correctly for the commencement. I don't think Zelda needs anything at the moment but if any accessories are necessary, get them. She seems to be over the circus phase.

About a car. Perhaps the best thing would be to *hire one cheaply in New York for Friday to Sunday*. You would have trouble getting one in Hartford with all the schools around there graduating. I know this is expensive and I don't mean a Playa limousine but I think you could get a good rate somewhere if you made inquiries. *You will need it*—you won't be *at* the school but in a house chosen by:

The Pettibone Tavern
Weatogue, Connecticut

which is about a mile from Simsbury. The reservations are in my name—if Newman is going, better phone or wire them.

One thing I haven't told Zelda—that I've been shy about telling Zelda: I am sending Scottie abroad this summer on a tourist-class station-wagon tour of France with three girls from Spence under Alice Lee Myers (Mrs. Dick Myers), an old friend. Last year she took Honoria Murphy and some other girls with great success. She is a fine woman and knows Europe like her pocket. It will be wonderful for Scottie's French and keep her out of harm at the dangerous age of sixteen.

Zelda will resent this—of course she thinks she is quite capable of doing it herself despite the fact that they can't be together ten minutes without a quarrel and have about as many tastes in common at this phase of life as an Ethiopian and Eskimo. But there will undoubtedly be a lot of one-syllable logic when Zelda hears about it. And it will be a foretaste of the logic to expect if she should be released outright. Her idea seems to be that this final attempt of mine to earn some security should be used for her to raise hell, though she puts it in such mild terms as wine at dinner and bicycling through Greece. The facts that we have *no* capital—that over $100,000 has gone into her illness directly, that we will be another year or two in debt, simply don't exist for her.

But you will find her pleasant and sweet and, except on the subject of her illness and her capabilities, quite logical. If she'd like to see Alice Lee Myers, she can get her address through Gerald Murphy.

I think that's all. Your plan sounds fine—I wouldn't want her to go to the Algonquin.[1] She arrives Thursday, the 2nd, you should be in Simsbury by Friday evening and return to New York Sunday. Tuesday night she leaves for the South. So you have Thursday and Monday at least for the legitimate theatre—perhaps you'd better get tickets in advance. I hope the nurse will be able to amuse herself in what time you have to give to Zelda, as I know you don't want her (the nurse) always along. Better give the nurse a little spending money for movies and sight-seeing—of course she doesn't go to Simsbury unless you want to take her along one way for the ride and drop her at Hartford to go back immediately by train. She could rejoin you in the unlikely event of any trouble but of course her presence in Simsbury would embarrass Scottie.

I think that's everything. I insist Zelda treats *you* to theatres and all excursions as times are better for us and we are immensely in your debt. Advance Zelda what is necessary but she *shouldn't use charge accounts.*

"Three Comrades" is awful. It was *entirely* rewritten by the producer. I'd rather Zelda didn't see it.

Will you send me back the enclosures which I want for my files. Needless to say, Zelda shouldn't see them. As you can see, the correspondence with Carroll is so far inconclusive but of course the situation wasn't helped in Montgomery by encouraging Zelda's extreme plans. Unless she is steered gently away from anything bitter or controversial, you will notice a sharp reaction. She always seems quite happy and pleasantly distracted when with you.

With thanks for everything and best to you both,

Enclosed { Check $300
Letters

P.S. I've sent the hospital the ticket money. I don't know whether the enclosed will be enough for everything or what. Don't stint on the automobile anyhow. Scottie would react to a taxi like Billie Baxter to the hound dog in "Seventeen."[2]

[1] The Hotel Algonquin in Manhattan.
[2] A 1916 novel by Booth Tarkington.

FROM: Zelda Fitzgerald — Wire. Princeton University

NEWYORK NY 820A JUN 3 1938

QUOTE MISTERS FITZGERALD AND PARAMORE HAVE ADAPTED THE BOOK FAITHFULLY AND DISCRIMINATELY RETAINING ITS LIGHTER PASSAGES WITHOUT SACRIFICING ITS HEAVIER ONES THE SOUL OF AUTHOR BECOMES A LIVING FIRE IN A MEMORABLE MOTION PICTURE MARGARET SULLAVAN GIVES A TRULY GREAT PERFORMANCE THE ACTING IS UNIFORMLY EXCELLENT THERE IS A GREAT DEAL OF FUN WITH THE SHADOW OF THE WORLDS UNREST HANGING ABOVE FRANCHOT TONE GIVES ONE OF THE FINEST PERFORMANCES OF HIS CAREER THE REST ARE ONLY SLIGHTLY LESS PERSUASIVE NEWYORK TRIBUNE MANY CONGRATULATIONS

ZELDA.

FROM: Zelda Fitzgerald — ALS, 4 pp.[1] Princeton University
After 3 June 1938 — New York City

The love scene on the beach was superb, acting, dialogue, set and direction[2]

The street fighting was splendidly handled: a good suspense in the picking off of the lonely figure, and an adequately renderred sense of cavernous emptiness of cities deprived of their safety. The men are pretty good throughout, without much chance for moving acting.

The comedy is excellent all the way through; sophisticated, realistic, and of a bitter delight—The picture got lots of good sound laughs—

The girl was all that she could have been; and very convincing; and utterly charming and deeply moving when he carried her in in the blanket. She looked like a child—But somehow it seemed rather arbitrary that 3 men should so have avowed their lives to her well-being—

The dialogue is par excellence; the individual sceens excellent; the acting excellent (Margaret Sullavan) and first rate (the men). The music adds lots—

But there isn't any dramatic continuity—which robs the whole of suspense. I know its hard to get across a philosophic treatise on the screen, but it would have been better had there been the sense of some inevitable thesis making itself known in spite of the characters—or had there been the sense of characters dominated by some irresistibly dynamic purpose. It drifts; and the dynamics are scatterred + sporadic rather than cumulative or sustained.

The audience was most responsive, and applauded The music *montage* and technical side in general was beautifully handled.

—In casual vein, or what I would have said *had* it been the product of a stranger: beautifully adequate and intellectual dialogue (unusual)—*fine* acting from the heroine—of a convincing seriousness + portentuousness that was never realized because there wasn't any plot: spiritual or material—

Most of the scenes are gratifyingly strong + full—

Many congratulations.
Zelda

[1] The beginning of this letter may be lost.
[2] Zelda Fitzgerald had seen *Three Comrades* in New York City after attending Scottie's graduation from Miss Walker's school.

TO: D. Mildred Thompson[1] TL(CC), 2 pp. Princeton University

Metro Goldwyn Mayer Studio
Culver City, California
June 12th, 1938

My dear Dean Thompson:

Some two years ago I wrote you entering my daughter for Vassar. One week ago, after her graduation from the Ethel Walker School, there occurred something in the nature of a catastrophe which you will have to examine before determining her qualifications for entrance. By now the school has probably written you—after the graduation week-end was over and the honor system put aside, my daughter and another girl went to New Haven in violation of the regulations, had dinner with two Yale students and were caught coming back at nine o'clock that night. One of the undergraduates was the "fiance" of the other girl—my daughter knew neither of them. The other girl telephoned to the fraternity house of her friend and they met in a restaurant, after which the boys immediately drove them back to Simsbury. The Walker School were particularly annoyed that they had "picked up a ride" to New Haven,—this was by no means the first time it had been done at the school, but it was the first time for my daughter and she was the first one caught. It was broad daylight and they chose a car with a single man in it, so they didn't feel it was risky—an adult has an entirely different reaction. Mrs. Smith telephoned me that she could not let my daughter remain for the rest of the Board preparations. I agreed and have no resentment whatever toward the school which had treated her with every kindness.

The picture at first glance is in perfect focus—the kind of a girl on whom a college education is wasted, probably boy-crazy, irresponsible, almost delinquent. Now compare it with this—a judgement of contemporaries, those who lived with her in the school for two years. A month ago her class of thirty-odd voted their likes and dislikes. Among them I copy these from the school paper:

Most likely to succeed .... Fitzgerald (1st)
Most entertaining .... Fitzgerald (1st)
Most artistic .... Fitzgerald (2nd)
Most original .... Fitzgerald (1st)
Frankest .... Fitzgerald (2nd)

In the choice for the composite "Most Perfect Girl" I find:

Personality .... Fitzgerald (1st)

The two pictures simply do not go together, for the above represents, I think, the sort of girl who *does* deserve a college education. Editing the school magazine and writing the school musical play took away from her marks somewhat this year but such things do indicate an active mind and a useful surplus of energy.

If I were able to take the blame for an act which the child herself is now trying desperately to understand, I would, but she is sixteen and must stand on her own feet. That she has been motherless for ten years and homeless for five is no explanation, for such a deprivation should make a girl more, not *less* mature. It is more to the point that this is only the second trouble she ever got into in her life—the other being a piece of insolence which culminated a long friction with a housemother at Miss Walker's.

But I'd like the two pictures to stand on their merits. Just as you now take more into account than the mere numerical aspect of a grade, so I wanted to present to you the other face of this coin. Because I don't know what one does in a case like this. To the majority of Walker girls the answer would be a debut in New York, but every arrow in this child points toward a career, points away from an idle, shiftless life. And at the very moment when school seems behind and the gates seem opening, she yields to this uncalculated impulse—something that a week later would have deserved no more than a strong rebuke from me. If this closes the gates where does all that talent and personality go from here? Only a month ago, she was "most likely to succeed." What is she now?

Sincerely,
F. Scott Fitzgerald

P.S. I need not add that she is not now the same child who did this rash thing, and will never be again.

[1] Dean of Vassar College in Poughkeepsie, N.Y.

TO: Scottie Fitzgerald — Wire. Princeton University

CULVERCITY CALIF 223P 1938 JUN 20 PM 6 37
LETTER FROM VASSAR ENCOURAGING AS TO LATE UNPLEASANTNESS BUT WORRIES ME ABOUT WORK HOPE YOU ARE PUTTING EIGHT OR TEN HOURS A DAY ON HISTORY KNOWING EVERY CORNER OF IT LOVE

DADDY.

[1] Sent c/o Harold Ober in Scarsdale, N.Y., where Scottie was staying.

TO: Hunt Stromberg — TL(CC), 5 pp. MGM
Hollywood, California

June 27, 1938

Dear Hunt:

For a month I have been thinking about INFIDELITY, inventing and rejecting solutions.[1] I have arrived at some clear thinking about it and the chief difficulty has been how to present it to you. Perhaps the best way is to tell it to you exactly as it came to me, so while Sidney[2] is in the hospital, I'm stealing this day from THE WOMEN, to do just that.

In the first place, I have been stymied all through by my mental picture of the casting. It isn't my business, but such conceptions are not easy to get out of one's mind:

Instead of seeing our heroine Althea pursued by *two* attractive men, Gable and Cooper, as you suggested, I kept seeing Joan Crawford between Gable and Tone—between a star and a leading man. It was a dull thought. It was hard to tell the story, knowing that the audience was thinking ahead of you.

To clear my mind I have assumed a new cast of characters. For the sake of the picture, let me imagine that Althea is Myrna Loy, Nicolas is Clark Gable, and Alex, her old sweetheart, is Robert Taylor. Immediately the whole thing brightened for me. I could imagine Myrna Loy loving either one of them, I could imagine either one of them losing her without making the picture ridiculous. And I could imagine an exciting doubt up to the very end as to which one was going to win. For there is no question about it—this is a Three Star Picture.

With this set-up, let me recapitulate our story and see where it takes us. Until I get some time, I cannot do much more than suggest the backbone, but I am more interested than at any time since I reached the fatal page 90 of the first script.

We begin showing Clark and Myrna married but living with the door closed between them. This has been the situation in their lives for six months.

As before we go to a retrospect in which we show Clark and Myrna saying goodbye, as she starts for Europe to see her mother.

In Florence she comes across Robert Taylor, the man she loved and almost married five years ago. He will love her always but Myrna is deeply possessed by her love for Clark.

For the moment Taylor scarcely exists for her.

Back in America Clark has run across his former secretary and drifted into an affair with her.

Returning unexpectedly from Europe, Myrna finds them together. She cannot forgive—she is unable to forgive. That is the end of the retrospect—Clark and Myrna have drifted along for six months and are acutely miserable.

At this point, Bob Taylor comes back from Europe. His arrival, the fact that Myrna encourages his attentions, provoke a divorce. Perhaps Myrna had not intended it to go so far but her nerves and Clark's have been under a terrific strain and the marriage blows up with fireworks. Almost immediately Myrna marries Taylor.

Five years pass. Myrna and Bob Taylor live together happily. Perhaps their marriage has not the quality of ecstasy that her marriage with Clark Gable had but it is a good marriage. Gable has faded from her mind to be thought of, if at all, with bitterness and resentment.

Now Something Happens which Brings Gable Back Into Myrna's Life—Something That Throws them Suddenly Together, perhaps Isolate them in some Natural but Original way—Entirely against their Wills.

This Situation Endures from One to Two Weeks.

What would be her natural reaction, considering our premise—that she had honestly been happy with both men? At first she would be tremendously critical of Gable. She is now used to Taylor's way of doing things and everything that Gable does irritates her. She even wonders how she ever managed to live together with him.

But as she and Clark meet some Exterior Crisis together, this feeling changes. She sees that Clark's way of doing things, his attitude, his sense of humor is quite as good as Bob's—perhaps rather more exciting. In other words she gets used to him.

And the next step—sudden and surprising—is that one night when life has forced them into close proximity, she is physically attracted to him.

Myrna has always been so sure of herself, and is so set against him, that she is taken entirely off guard. It seems so natural, so familiar to be close to him, that now for a moment the years with Taylor seem vague, seem like a dream. This is life, this is what she is born for. She could now melt right into him once more and forget that Bob ever existed.

And at this precise moment, when she has half yielded to him, her heart going out to him utterly—the situation which threw them together is abruptly terminated. They are thrown back into the world again—

—and—in the world—she belongs to Bob.

Bob is her duty—Myrna is never one to shirk duty—and besides she loves Bob.

But things are now not the same. The happiness and tranquility that she had with Bob is now destroyed. She knows plainly that this is not the sort of ecstasy that she had with Clark.

What shall she do? Bob knows nothing, or she thinks he knows nothing.

She must keep it from him forever—she must forget if she can.

And then—in a most roundabout way—*Bob* finds how close she has been to Clark during that week or two.

Is it plain where we are, where the plot has brought us? It should be as plain to us as it is to Myrna: She has been guilty of the exact same crime for which she condemned Clark, five years before. An old love has reached up out of the past and called to her—an old love has trapped her, brought her to the point of Infidelity—so close that it was only an accident that she was not unfaithful to Bob, so close that Bob thinks that she *was* unfaithful.

Now, will she understand Clark's old sin, for which he has paid so dearly? *Now* will she forgive? It seems possible, extremely likely.

And if so, it seems likely that Bob, being of fine, sensitive stuff, might gracefully retire from such a situation.

Whichever Myrna does, stay with Bob or remarry Clark, we have fulfilled the original contract—and with a deep bow to the censors. We have shown how, when faced with a situation parallel to the one with which her husband was faced, Myrna might have yielded too.

Perhaps now you can have the story you wanted.

Yours,

[1] After he was assigned to *The Women,* Fitzgerald continued to volunteer help for *Infidelity.*

[2] Producer Sidney Franklin.

FROM: Zelda Fitzgerald — ALS, 3 pp. Princeton University
Summer 1938 — Highland Hospital, Asheville, North Carolina

Dear Scott:

It fill me with dread to witness the passage of so much time: another summer is half gone, and maybe there'll never be anymore sun-burns and high hot noons.

Do you suppose they still cook automobiles at Antibes, and still sip the twilight at Kaux, and I wonder if Paris is pink in the late sun and latent with happiness already had.

Anyway, I now know the address of summer, where it lives and breeds and makes its home, where daisy fields come from and bird-song is brewed, and where is the home of secret heavens It's not very far away, and Mamma and I may spend a couple of weeks there: if permission resolves

Meantime, Newman thinks *Three Comrades* one of the best picture's he's ever seen, and all sorts of scatterred opinions are very *pro*—so maybe we'll get some more money and more prestige and more liberties and all sorts of other desirable attributes˙

—and meanwhile Mamma is here; and lovely and eager as ever, but a year older than she was last year which makes me sad—

I hope she has a happy holiday—The mountains are very green and of as insistently splendid proportions as before—and Ashville is the highest point east of the Rockies. It says so on the radio—

Zelda

TO: D. Mildred Thompson — TL(CC), 2 pp. Princeton University
Hollywood, California

Aug. 16th
19 38

Dear Dean Thompson:

The wire was a godsend and your thought in sending it made me happier than the formal announcement possibly could have. I was jubilant for a week; then there set in a reaction in which I wondered how sincerely I can guarantee you a good scholar. My daughter's cards are so plainly on the table and so obviously marked that it seems as if even a "sucker" would know how to play the hand—but the "sucker" never does. By a new attack on her work, daughter assures herself a tenure in the East which she loves, a freedom such as neither school nor business college could give her, a far wider range of contacts—all of these the most immediate benefits, not to mention the more substantial ones. Yet, if she gets off on the wrong foot there, thinking of the college as a convenient parking place between glamorous dashes to Princeton and Baltimore, she will have washed up the whole effort in three months and duped us all—herself most of all.

I imagine there is a good deal of subtle supervision of Freshmen at Vassar and of course I am counting on that as well as on the moral homilies, the special privileges and the control of the pursestrings which are my contribution. But most of all I am counting on some girls or group of girls catching her imagination as certain men caught my imagination at Princeton. The first undergraduate Vassar girls I knew were the present Mrs. Hart Fessenden and Mrs. Lawrence Tighe, both somewhat before your time, I think. I remember hearing reports from them of a horrible girl called Edna St. Vincent Millay and defending this Miss Millay on the basis of a few things she had published. But that was doubtless a healthy attitude on their part and they were much broader than that sounds. (Katherine corrected the galley proofs on "This Side of Paradise"—and did an extremely quaint job of it.) They are the sort Of girls I wish Scottie would find there. She seems, however, to be teaming up with a certain —— —— whom I gather is rather a belle, which wasn't exactly my idea. At the same time to link her with an unsophisticated type full of moral earnestness might be too severe a vaccine. Anyhow I hope that when she finds her level it will be with girls whose attitude toward education is on a par with a boy's. If she should show any inclination to group up with those whose interest lie only in New York I trust my antennae to detect it before it has gone too far. I am really more concerned about that for her second year than for her first.

I have forbidden her all writing, acting or such extra curricular activities for the first term or until she shows me definite results as a scholar.

In relation to this I want to ask if you have any system of Freshman advisorship. When a girl wants to leave college how is the check made on where she is going, whether it is advisable, what is the chaperonage, etc. I know you have no time to answer these questions individually but is there any booklet or committee that is concerned with this matter who could give me some information? If remote control is impossible I will have to give power of attorney to someone in the East.

Again many thanks for the telegram and for your interest generally. I shall try to be on hand the opening day with my daughter and catch a glimpse of you then.

Sincerely—
F. Scott Fitzgerald

TO: Screen Writers Guild

TL(CC), 1 p. Princeton University
Hollywood, California

Aug. 29th
19 38

Gentlemen:

I think this question of Screen Credits is a matter on which the young writer's opinion is important. An established author can call it vanity to see ones name in lights but we boys of twenty-five have kindlier words for it.

If the balance of work is 70-30 in favor of one worker, precedence should be settled in the writer's office—and would be, I think, more times than not. If it's around 50-50 it should certainly turn on the toss of a coin. If there's a credit-hog concerned, big name or not, the matter could go to the Guild. The greedy boys would turn up in enough cases to identify themselves and be disciplined. But the alphabetical idea has a robot quality. In such well-known teams as Hecht-MacArthur, Campbell-Parker, the Hacketts, etc., it's of no importance but I am haunted by poor Zeno Zimmerman who always does a little more than his share of the work and who has to keep explaining to his wife and friends in Kansas City why his name always has third or fourth billing.

And what of the ridiculous situation of entrenched writers carefully choosing collaborators with initials that come after theirs? Zoe Akins could afford to be generous but poor Akins Zoe would have to be very choosy.

Very truly—
F. Scott Fitzgerald

TO: Scottie Fitzgerald

TLS, 3 pp. Princeton University
MGM letterhead. Culver City, California

Sept. 6th
1938

Dearest Pie:

Please read this whole letter carefully at the first opportunity. These instructions are absolute, and subject to no revision, because the next week is going to be somewhat difficult for me.

I decided to bring Peaches out because the matter had gone too far in their minds to be called off without rudeness and possibly injuring your whole relationship there. You are leaving for Hollywood Wednesday night to stay out here until Sunday afternoon—both ways by plane of course. I will try to give you the best available time though it won't be like last time at all. So don't expect too much. And the less you say to Peaches about whom you know here the better, because then less people will fail to remember you when they see you. This is very important, to save yourself any possible loss of prestige in front of Peaches. As an old snob, I know you will understand me.

Meanwhile you will go to Harold Obers when the boat docks Saturday (I'm not asking him to meet you because you know how much his Saturday afternoons mean to him) and I want you to be *very specially* nice to them all day Sunday—I mean really "give." They think it is asinine for me to bring you out here now but there is no use trying to explain to them—just tell them you think Daddy is crazy or that you left a toothbrush out here that you have to get, or anything you want. The point is I don't want you to spend all day Sunday in telephoning your New York clientele and making plans for the winter via the Ober's telephone. I know that at sixteen one wants to announce one's whereabouts to the world as an event of cosmic importance but please suppress this for one day and let them have a pleasant impression and *their Sunday peace*. You can leave for Baltimore any time you want to Monday—that is, any time when it is convenient for Peaches or her family to meet you. I don't want you to celebrate your homecoming by anything tricky. I mean having yourself met by a boy or arriving late at the Finneys, etc.

All arrangements about buying clothes, etc., etc., I will tell you about when you come out here. But I really have so many things to discuss with you that I will only say now that I don't want you to make any dates in Baltimore or New York for this winter without seeing me. I mean specifically no football games, school or college dances, etc. This applies to Baltimore, Princeton, New York and everywhere else.

As to the clothes, a proper budget is being figured out for you and you will have a suitable allowance. Concurrently with that, I have stopped all charge accounts in New York because with you charging odd things it would be impossible to figure just what you were costing. So you will be on a *cash* basis and perhaps—though it is a Utopian dream—you may learn more about handling money than I ever did.

Your Mother is coming to New York about the 20th and will ride up to Vassar. It gives her such great pleasure to think she is contributing to your education and it is the kind thing to carry on the illusion. Aunt Rosalind will be with her and it will interfere no more with you than did her coming to Commencement last June.

Mrs. Finney knows that you had some row with your headmistress and that you flew out here and took the Vassar exams in New York. She knows *no more* than that nor have I spoken of it to anyone including your Mother and your Aunt Rosalind.

On Monday before you leave for Baltimore be sure and call the Murphys, call *on* them if possible, to thank them for bringing you home. This will be a little courtesy which will be tremendously appreciated both by me and by them. Failing this—I mean if they're not there—write them a "thank you" letter from Baltimore. Also before you come out here I wish you will have written a letter to Alice Lee Myer to reach her on her arrival. You must get these things out of the way. There will be absolutely no time for me to "play mama."

Now about Hollywood: As to my personal life here, do me the courtesy not to discuss it with Peaches in any way either before you get here or while you are here. It will not touch you in any way. Any friend will be simply encountered as a friend and no more. You should not even say to Peaches that such-and-such a person is a "great friend" of mine. It is most decidedly not Peaches' business.

I hope you enjoy your two days in Baltimore—hope you will also be wise enough not to put your hands on the wheel of a car. It is unfortunate that it hasn't been convenient for you to learn to drive—I mean to be at ease with a car in traffic but that takes at least two months. Be wise and let it alone until next summer when I promise you it will be arranged. Handling another person's car clumsily isn't either pleasant or pictorial for them. The matter of smoking I will discuss with you here.

Again let me ask you to read this letter over *twice* or at least look it over twice—preferably after half an hour. Because every point here is of great importance and I would like you to spend the four days until I see you without displeasing me.

. . . .[1]

Hoping that your attention to this letter will preclude any unpleasant brushes on our brief contact, I am

With dearest love—
Daddy

Please Re-read[2]

1 Ninety-one words omitted by the editor.
2 Written in large letters at the bottom of the page.

TO: Mrs. A. D. Sayre

TL(CC), 1 p. Princeton University
Hollywood, California

Sept. 9th
19 38

Dear Mrs. Sayre:

Thank you for both your letters. Things have been tremendously busy here and I apologize for not answering sooner. Hope the New York trip goes off well and I am sure it will.

Have seen Irving Cobb[1] half a dozen times this last year and last time he told me quite a story about you when you were young. How your father was being groomed for Governorship of Kentucky with the possibility of running as candidate for President in 1872 and how that put a sharp end to your aspirations to go on the stage in Philadelphia. He remembers his "Cousin Minnie" so vividly and with much admiration and told me many stories of your youth.

With affection, always—

[1] Kentucky humorist Irvin S. Cobb.

TO: Dr. Robert S. Carroll TL(CC), 2 pp. Princeton University
Hollywood, California

Oct. 11th
1938

Dear Dr. Carroll:

I have your letter of October 3rd and I have tried to put myself in your place as well as I am able. Your letter, frankly, recommends more hospitalization rather than less—that is the gist of it, isn't it? It really puts it up to me again to decide whether extra money should be spent on supervised vacations, which are regulated for the good of a large number of persons or for specialized vacations which permit what she herself considers fun. I mean "fun" in its purest sense, from the sight of an ocean wave to an occasional breakfast in bed and choice of a dress and hat. Ironically enough, with your letter came one from her family, now pretty well consolidated in the vicinity through her sister's move to Atlanta, saying that you "have consented to letting her live in Asheville outside the hospital with a nurse." I don't know in what state of agitation they go to the hospital to get such twisted versions of what you recommend or whether the policy has been rather to stall them off. The fact is however that they still charge the main responsibility for all hospitalization to me and should I vote against Zelda's vacations at home there would be a terrific uproar.

As I told you before I am going along here pretty much from month to month and there is not a possibility of my being able to keep up this sort of work for more than another year and I've *got* to watch what we are spending. The money spent this year on Zelda's vacations has already been out of proportion to what it should be, but to send her to Florida instead of allowing her a little time at her Mother's would simply irritate her family beyond measure—while the cost would be the same or greater.

Certainly I don't want Zelda to face the world's problems, or to drink or smoke (she absolutely refrained from both during the last vacation), but I can't believe that such pleasures as she has found in her last two vacations, such as the one in New York and the one in Montgomery, can do much damage considering all the factors involved.

Perhaps the anticipation of them and the utterly delighted letters she has written me when enjoying them are signs that they have been benevolent.

I want to come and see you within the next six weeks and talk all this over.

With best wishes, always—

TO: Beatrice Dance

TLS, 2 pp. Princeton University
MGM letterhead. Culver City, California

Oct. 11th
1938

Beatrice:

I got word that *Fortune* was to smile on me again for a year. In the first issue I found something useful—the article on Elizabeth Arden. Am engaged and have been for several months on the screen play of "The Women"—a rather God-awful hodgepodge of bitter wit and half-digested information which titillated New York audiences for over a year. Most of the work has been "cleaning it up" for Norma Shearer—anyhow there is a beauty parlor scene which must be strictly according to Hoyle. So the article interested me. You seem far away—not the past you but the present you. You must have passed through many mutations since that August evening in 1935 when we sat downstairs in the Battery Park Hotel, and that funny doctor was going to solve us as briskly and easily as if we had been a minor operation. I am still amazed at his lack of perspicacity. Another year is finished here and I have a sense of very little accomplished. Only about one-third of "Three Comrades" was mine and a third ReMarque's. The rest was straight Hollywood, the work of an ignorant and vulgar gent who was "producing" the picture. For the rest, my invalid is still in Asheville (that odd town that in youth I thought was a fashionable resort, confusing it with Aiken) which has played such a large part in my life—where I broke my back and where Zelda is eking out her poor empty years. She is better; I have even taken her on trips—to Charleston, to Palm Beach, to Virginia Beach—all in the last year. She will always be an invalid. Daughter, after a summer abroad, is in Vassar. She is sixteen and much too much of a belle to make a good record there but I am hoping she will stay it out for two years. I have a sort of life here that is typical of Hollywood—in the strange atmosphere of a mining town in Lotus land—people have a tendency to find each other and cling together and retire out of the picture completely. Only when daughter is here have I gone into Hollywood society at all. I have a cottage on the Pacific which I gaze at morning and night with a not too wild surmise—my capacity for wonder has greatly diminished. And anyhow, it automatically stops whenever I cross the Mississippi River. I have a grand novel up my sleeve and I'd love to go to France and write it this summer. It would be short like "Gatsby" but the same in that it will have the transcendental approach, an attempt to show a man's life through some passionately regarded segment of it. This letter was to have been about you but there is only the old you that I knew—knew very well I think—yet I always enjoyed the thrill of surprise when you made some new romantic gesture. *Almost* you always made all your dreams plausible—so often they quivered on the edge of fulfillment, but there were ranges of mountains higher than the Rockies in the way.

Thank you again—

Scott

TO: Scottie Fitzgerald

TL(CC), 3 pp. Princeton University
MGM letterhead. Culver City, California

November 11, 1938.

Dearest Scottie:—

I *still* believe you are swimming, protozoa-like, in the submerged third of your class, and I still think your chance of flunking out is all too rosy—two 'B' tests in your easiest subjects are absolutely no proof to the contrary. You would have to be a complete numbskull to write a lower test than that in French or English. As a freshman at Princeton we had to struggle with Plautus, Terrence, Sallust and Integral Calculus.

However, the point of this letter is that I am compelled at last by this telegraph matter to dock your allowance. I pay you almost as much as some stenographers on this lot get for a hard week—and you treat me to this childish monkey business! You see I put a tracer on that call and the telegraph company reports that *you* told them the telegram was received by your roommate. Your letter tells quite another story. On the basis of it I am claiming damage from the Company for non-delivery, which unless your conscience is clear may lead to some trouble in Poughkeepsie. If your conscience *isn't* clear you'd better come clean right away.

I'm habituated to the string of little lies (such as you telling Dorothy that you went to the Navy-Princeton game, telling me that Gordon Meacham was Captain of the Freshman football team) but this sort of thing can lead into a hellish mess. I once saw a pathological liar in police court, her face blazing with pimples, her blue eyes straight as a die, as she told the sargeant the most amazing circumstantial story about where her boy friend had been the night of the holdup. I knew that the sargeant had the proof of the guilt on his blotter but there was something admirable, even awe-inspiring, about the way the girl invented even though she must have been squirming inwardly. If you should happen to be there next term I want you to take music and continue making up your songs and plays, because I kept thinking how, if life had been a little kinder, that girl might have been a great creator of fiction.

Instead she got two years.

Anyhow, the allowance is definitely docked to $3.85 until you come clean on the following questions:

1. The telegram matter. I think it would be wiser to settle it with me instead of the Dean.

2. I wrote you a letter, unacknowledged, of which the purport was that I didn't want you to go to debutant affairs in New York this year. I still don't want you to go to them. That includes Dorothy Burns' tea. My reasons are manifold and I will be glad to go into them with you further

3. I want you to go to Baltimore this Thanksgiving, leaving on the first day of vacation and remaining until Sunday. It shames me, and you too, to have to say that I must put a check on this, and that if you let me down I will consider that there is no use keeping you at Vassar another day.

4. I have asked you to stay at Vassar the week-end after the Yale game.

5. You can certainly find time to read eighteen Elizabethian lyrics. If I could spare the time and trouble to try to fix up the matter of the English course, what do you do with your hours?

On another slip I have listed these questions. Until I get a clear answer on every one, together with an affirmation that you intend to play square with me and stop this line of opposition, you will have to get along with pin money.

I know that you must have worries of your own and I hate to add to them. What I ask seems so very little. This year of many liberties is something I gave you with money and care (do you remember the schedules at Bryn Mawr?) Do you think it's fair to use these privileges against *me*? I've made every sort of appeal to your more civilized instincts and all I get is the most insincere "Can't we be friends?"—in other words, can't we be friends on *your* terms.

Friends!—we don't even speak the same language. I'll give you the same answer my father would have given to me—at seventeen, eighteen or nineteen or twenty. Either you can decide to make concessions to what I want in the East or you can come out here Thanksgiving and try something else.

Since you've finished the "Farewell To Arms" the second bit of reading includes only the following poems. The reference is to the index of first lines in either the Oxford book or the Golden Treasury.

Come Unto These	Shakespeare
Tell Me Where	"
Hark, Hark the Lark	"
Take Oh Take	"
Go Lovely Rose	Waller
Oh Western Wind	Anon
Art Thou Poor Yet	Dekker
Fear No More	Shakespeare
My True Love	Sidney
Who Is Sylvia	Shakespeare

The question will be along about *Wednesday*. If you read these ten poems you can answer it in a flash.

TO: Sidney Franklin

TL(CC), 1 p. Princeton University
MGM memo. Culver City, California

12/22/38

Dear Sidney:

Barring illness and (I have a sty as big as a Jefferson nickle—and less valuable) I will deliver you the stuff Tues. the 28th at midday. *So save Tuesday afternoon!* Singing! Dancing! Thorium! One of the Fitz Brothers in person! Soft-ball finals: Script vs. Sound!

I could give it to you Mon. the 26th at 11:45 P.M. but it would be an inferior script—hurried, careless and full of Christmas neckties. Wait till Tuesday for the genuine article.[1]

Ever yours,
F. Scott Fitzg.

P.S. Seriously I'm sorry it's taken five weeks—I didn't think it would be 75 pages.

[1] Fitzgerald's script for *Madame Curie* was rejected.

TO: Sheilah Graham
1938/1939

Inscription in Frank Norris' *The Octopus* (1901).
Princeton University
Hollywood, California

Sheilah from Scott.

Frank Norris after writing three great books died in 1902 at the age of just

1938
THE SUN DIAL PRESS, INC.

thirty. He was our most promising man and might have gone further than Dreiser or the others. He claimed to be a disciple of Zola the naturalist, but in many ways he was better than Zola.

PRINTED IN THE UNITED STATES AT
THE COUNTRY LIFE PRESS
GARDEN CITY, N. Y.

The time of the events is about 1880

FROM: Zelda Fitzgerald — ALS, 2 pp. Princeton University
Fall 1938 or 1939 — Highland Hospital, Asheville, North Carolina

Dearest Do-Do:

I'm sorry the passage of time is wearying you again: there's frost on the mountains and a chrystalline world too stimulating to permit the corporeal.

We ate supper yesterday in the pine-dust in the slant of a late mellow sun, in a world haunted to unrest by the unattained peace flooding the woods + sky.

Joseph Urban[1] had been there: and a house had dropped out of somebodys note book, and so much land-at-peace stretched over the brow of a "comprehended" world: just tentatively subjugated.

Will you be East for Christmas? Why dont you come through the Panama Canal? It's only a week I think, and would contribute sun + rest + the happy hum of newness. And would be the glamour of the Cosmopolitan Magazine, of Get-Rich-Quick Wallingford[2] + of the adventures of Anthony Somebody,[3] of James Montgomery Flagg[4]—a world of unnecessitated adventure that we've never known save in the tall + dark + beautiful card-shap or something of Capri—

—Anyhow I'll be glad about my dress—and whenever you just cant wait to know I'll tell you what I want for Christmas—

Devotedly
Zelda

[1] Interior decorator and architect.
[2] Character created by George Randolph Chester.
[3] Possibly a reference to *Anthony Adverse* (1933).
[4] Artist and illustrator.

FROM: Zelda Fitzgerald — ALS, 2 pp. Princeton University
1938–1940 — Highland Hospital, Asheville, North Carolina

Dearest Scott:

The weather does its eccentricities, and now its cold, and fair and a brittle and "unchosen" world confronts us again. I'll be so glad when the winter desists from its barbarianisms and one can breathe again.

Meantime I'm painting lampshades, instead of souls; just for a little while, and meantime I play the radio and moon about considerably and dream of Utopias where its always July the 24th 1935. Thats my chosen happiest equipment: to be 35, in the middle of summer forever.

Where is my book on architecture? Not that I would ever have time to master it, but it says in the funny-papers that a wife should follow her husbands interests so that she will be better material for the funny papers.

There's nothing to write: shall I just ask you for things instead? The bad old shoe-maker poured glue in my moccasins, which I love, and so now—what days does Mr. Goldwyn do the shopping?

I've been very expensive lately and ought to be able to produce a glamorous chronicle. I long for home; for all the so-poignant indispensibilities of a life that cant have so much longer. Things that people have cared about, and places that have housed their aspirations are ceaselessly moving

with Love, and gratitude
Zelda

TO: Scottie Fitzgerald
1938–1940

AL, 1 p. Princeton University
Hollywood, California

Instruction
Read carefully Keat's Ode to a Nightingale

In this poem is a phrase which will immediately remind you of my work.[1] First find this. In the *same* stanza is another phrase which I rather guiltily adapted to prose in the 2nd paragraph on p. 115 of *The Great Gatsby*.[2]

The question
When you have found what I refer to have you learned anything about the power of the verb in description?

1 "Already with thee! tender is the night,
And haply the Queen-Moon is on her throne,
Cluster'd around by all her starry Fays;
But here there is no light,
Save what from heaven is with the breezes blown
Through verdurous glooms and winding mossy ways."

2 "He lit Daisy's cigarette from a trembling match, and sat down with her on a couch far across the room, where there was no light save what the gleaming floor bounced in from the hall."

TO: Mrs. A. D. Sayre

TL(CC), 2 pp. Princeton University
Hollywood, California

Dear Rosalind: You have written me the same letter three times and I have probably been as repetitious in answering it. I sympathize with your concern over Zelda but there are limits about what I can do

Scott[1]

January 3, 1939.

Dear Mrs. Sayre:

Thank you for the lovely handkerchiefs. I'm wearing one in my breast pocket today.

I have a letter from Zelda in which she says she had a wonderful time Christmas. Have also one from Rosalind in which she complains that I am not doing anything about establishing Zelda in the world again. She seems to feel that establishing Zelda in the world is a simple matter—like the issuing of a pass—not at all the problem that the best people in the profession have been working at for ten years. These people, Carroll (and Myers who has more than once been called into a consultation) are of the opinion that the only thing which has given Zelda her present stability, her comparative health and her general sanity about things is the climate of a hospital. By "climate" I mean the regime, the sense of order and routine—all that goes with it. You're asking me to take this away, utterly against their advice. It is a very difficult business—a decision of tremendous moment. Because Carroll says that if I take her away he will not take her back—he feels that I will weakly destroy his entire work of bringing her from a state of horror, shame, suicide and despair to the level of a bored and often grouchy but by no means miserable invalid. He feels sure that another slip would occur within two or three months and that such a slip and the consequent years to recover from it would leave her at an imbecilic level if she recovered at all.

There is no favorable prognosis for dementia praecox. In certain diseases the body builds new cells, drawing on its own inner vitality. When there has been destruction in the patterns of the mind only the very thinest shell can be formed over them—so to speak—so that Zelda is always living in a house of thinly spun glass. Most of the time she functions perfectly within this house because the hospital protects her from any of life's accidental stones or from any damage that she might carelessly or absent-mindedly do herself. Carroll believes that that is the only way that she will ever be able to function.

Having always been a chance-taker and knowing that there have been remarkable cures (though seldom when the disease has ever been severe and protracted) I want *more* than that. I do not want what you want, because I believe that your desires proceed from a loving blindness. But I want three or four months outside the hospital this year with a nurse instead of the sparse seven weeks that she had outside during 1938. The constant objection that you and Rosalind make to the nurse has hampered me tremendously in arranging this and it seems to me that it has sprung from a family pride which has little place in a case as serious as this. It frightens us because it makes us think that you would soon have a provocation to dismiss the nurse and it has made the doctor think that none of you have any conception of the truth and you simply want to set up a false image of Zelda's cure for your own peace of mind. Rosalind has a suggestion that Zelda should live in an apartment in Ashville, which she claims that the doctor has approved of, but he says that he has never approved of such a thing nor seen any merit in it.

I am again taking up the question of finding a suitable woman to accompany Zelda on trips outside the hospital. There is never a day that I do not think of her comfort and cherish the hope, however faint, that she may be restored completely to life.

With love.

[1] Note in holograph to Rosalind Smith.

TO: Bernie Hyman[1]

Wire (copy). Princeton University
Hollywood, California

January 6, 1939.

RESPECTFULLY SUGGEST THE BEST WAY TO GET $5000.00 WORTH OF USE OUT OF MY CONTRACT IS TO ORDER A 12000 WORD ORIGINAL FOR SOME SPECIAL ACTORS STOP I HAVE AN IDEA FOR BEERY AND GARLAND AND COULD CERTAINLY PRODUCE A COMEDY OF MANNERS IDEA FOR SOME YOUNG ACTRESS STOP AM AT YOUR SERVICE OF COURSE BUT ORIGINAL IDEAS ARE PART OF MY STOCK IN TRADE THAT YOU HAVEN'T YET TAPPED STOP BEST WISHES

F. SCOTT FITZGERALD

[1] MGM producer. Fitzgerald's MGM contract was due to expire at the end of January.

TO: John Considine[1]

TL(CC), 2 pp. Princeton University
MGM memo. Culver City, California

1/6/39

Dear John:

Sorry you're layed up. Here are some ideas on the musical.

Hope you've had time to read *Infidelity*.

BABES IN WONDERLAND

Hunting for a comic opening to your idea, the following suggestion might appeal to you:

Frank Morgan the big movie producer (played by Frank Morgan) has a poor relation, a distant cousin whom he has placed as a clerk—the clerk who checks people in and out of the studio. (This part is also played by Frank Morgan—or Wallace Beery would do very well). The two men differ just as you would imagine: the Producer Morgan is hearty, hale and confident, although at the moment a little down-in-the-mouth and weary of his metier; the Clerk Morgan after a hard life of batting around is very glad of this little bone tossed him by his rich relative.

It is not generally realized but there are people working for years as clerks and stenographers on this lot who have never seen the movies being made. My last secretary had been here a year and during that time had never been on a set and, far from being the exception, many of the population arrive at eight, do a day's stint and leave at six without ever being in touch with any activities of the lot except what is before their eyes.

Anyhow, such is the case with Morgan the Clerk (or Beery the Clerk). We imagine the domain over which he presides as being a mixture of casting office and waiting-room. He has sent many people through the interior doors to their fate and he has once or twice been up the stairs to the majestic offices of his cousin Morgan the Producer, but though he is always hoping in some way to get on a set without annoying his wealthy relation, he has yet to view an actor in make-up except in the commissary, where he goes hastily once a day to down his thirty-five cent luncheon.

We get a glimpse of the two Morgans to begin with but we concentrate first on Morgan the Clerk. It is the end of a terrific day and the waiting-room is full of hopefuls who are whiling away the time by doing their stuff. Outside the rain is pouring down—a California flood—automobiles driving up to the door through pools a yard deep. Finally, no automobiles can get through. Word comes that many of the people are spending the night in the studio. Frank the Clerk is too kind-hearted to send the poor ill-dressed, ill-shod people out into the storm, so he stays past his usual time. They sleep. Frank sleeps. When he wakes, the rain has stopped and some circumstance, not yet invented, leads him to take them on a tour of the studio on one of those open gasoline trams which transport people between the dressing-rooms and the sets. With Frank at the wheel, the various people, some of whom we know by this time, start out through the night-bound streets of the little city.

Half a dozen of them, the most ingenious, form a plan. They will conceal themselves somewhere on the lot, adopting some kind of protective coloration, and stay there forever. They don't know yet how they will eat, what they will pretend to be but they are all romantics and they're determined that since it has been so hard to get into the studio they will now never leave it. They disappear. Aghast, Frank the Clerk drives the car back to the gateway, counts out the passengers and finds that six are missing. How is he ever going to find them?

We go now to Frank the Producer. Frank the Producer is stale. He is tired of the talent available and the new talent coming up leaves him unmoved. Nothing interests him. He is like a glutton surfeited with entertainment. His co-workers find him difficult, snappy . . .

Does this opening interest you? It seems to me to have more zip and naturalness than the other and the situations to which it leads can be guessed at. They could certainly include almost everything that we talked about yesterday.[2]

Ever yours.

[1] MGM producer.
[2] This project did not develop.

TO: Lloyd Sheldon[1]

TL(CC), 1 p. Princeton University
MGM memo. Culver City, California

Jan. 7, 1939

Dear Lloyd:

Went through the second batch and found two things that interested me. One "GET A HORSE" and the other "COURRIER de PARIS". I think the latter has a very solid structure and transposed to New York might have a very interesting and rather novel quality. Actually we have never had a shooting like the one that this is founded on—do you remember just before the war? But there is no reason why we shouldn't have and the value transposed to New York might be very glamorous and melodramatic.

"AND SO GOODBYE" might have the same sort of appeal as "A CHRISTMAS CAROL" did without the topical attraction. It seems a bit on the religious side and I think you'd have to get a true believer to write it. Also, it is reminiscent of several pieces of the type—yet not at all bad.

Also I felt that for another type of writer "GET A HORSE" might be very amusing.

I just heard this morning that Selznick wants me to do some polishing on "GONE WITH THE WIND"[2] and I'm being shipped over there immediately. I'm sorry we haven't been able to get together this time as I would very much like to work with you. Maybe the future will give us an opportunity.

Ever yours.

[1] MGM producer.
[2] Fitzgerald worked for only a few days on *Gone with the Wind*.

TO: Scottie Fitzgerald

Wire. Princeton University
Hollywood, California

Night Letter
Jan. 7, 1939.

FORGOT TO SAY I GOT THE PRESENT IT IS LOVELY AND I'M WEARING IT NOW STOP SUGGEST THAT TO MAKE SOUTHERN THEME INTERESTING YOU MUST GIVE EXAMPLES AND ANECDOTES FROM LIFE AND EVEN PUT IN DIALOGUE STOP BELIEVE IT OR NOT HAVE BEEN LOANED TO SELZNICK TO DO THE FINAL POLISH ON SCARLET DEAREST LOVE

DADDY

TO: Scottie Fitzgerald
After 11 February 1939

ALS, 2 pp.[1] Princeton University
Encino, California

Dearest: Please! Come clean with me. I do not want you to run charge accounts. Let's call that $40.00 extra—a present—and start over. Enclosed is your allowance for Mon 13th, Mon 20th + Mon 27th of March. *Please pay off your debts + live frugally till vacation.* (over)
I am quite likely to stop work here for several months (*next week*) and I want to be able to cut our standard of living in half at any time to do other work not so immediately profitable. Your "lady bountiful" complex is really not becoming; and wouldn't it be better to have my confidence for next autumn when you'll want a more mature wardrobe?

The poem *was* Cynara—and by Ernest Dowson. Some day you'll recognize great poetry when you see it, + when you send me doggerel such as your last *have some wit in your closing lines*. I knew you were in the doggerel stage + asked you to read W. S. Gilbert because his is at least the *best*—Cole Porter knows it by heart.

Send me your essay—I'd like to see it before recommending it, if you please!

Somehow I got the impression that while you had worked in Dec and tried to in Jan, in spite of sickness, you were now gliding along in that dangerous state that ends at a mountain-side. *Please* give me *one* good subject—I need encouragement.

Love Daddy

Who flunked out of Yale + Princeton—anyone I know?

[1] Written in the margin and on the verso of an 11 February letter from the Peck & Peck store in Poughkeepsie, requesting Fitzgerald's authorization of a charge account for Scottie. The account elicited Fitzgerald's 19 February 1940 comment: "Have paid Peck + Peck + Peck + Peck + Peck."

TO: Budd Schulberg
February 1939

ALS, 1 p. Schulberg

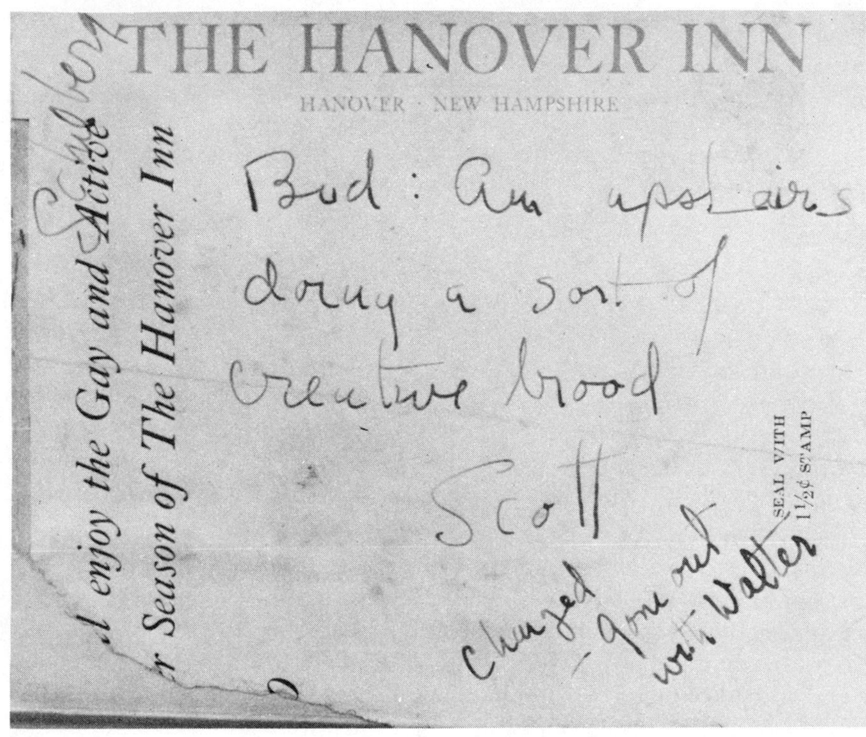
THE HANOVER INN
HANOVER · NEW HAMPSHIRE

Bud: Am upstairs doing a sort of creative brood

Scott

Changed—gone out with Walter

...l enjoy the Gay and Active
...r Season of The Hanover Inn

SEAL WITH 1½¢ STAMP

Note: After the expiration of his MGM contract Fitzgerald went on location at the Dartmouth College Winter Carnival with Budd Schulberg to collaborate on the *Winter Carnival* screenplay for producer Walter Wanger. Fitzgerald went off the wagon and was fired. Schulberg later wrote a novel, *The Disenchanted* (1950), based on these events.

FROM: Nathanael West

TLS, 1 p. Princeton University
Universal Pictures letterhead

April 5, 1939

Dear Scott Fitzgerald:

I'm taking the liberty again of sending you a set of proofs of a new novel.[1]

It took a long time to write while working on westerns and cops and robbers, but reading the proofs I wish it had taken longer.

I never thanked you for your kindness to me in the preface to the Modern Library edition of "The Great Gatsby." When I read it, I got a great lift just at a time when I needed one badly, if I was to go on writing.

Somehow or other I seem to have slipped in between all the "schools." My books meet no needs except my own, their circulation is practically private and I'm lucky to be published. And yet, I only have a desire to remedy all that *before* sitting down to write, once begun I do it my way. I forget the broad sweep, the big canvas, the shot-gun adjectives, the important people, the significant ideas, the lessons to be taught, the epic Thomas Wolfe, the realistic James Farrell,—and go on making what one critic called "private and unfunny jokes." Your preface made me feel that they weren't completely private and maybe not even entirely jokes.

Gratefully,
Nathanael West

6614 Cahuenga Terrace
Hollywood, Calif.

[1] *The Day of the Locust* (1939). Fitzgerald sent an appreciation through S. J. Perelman; see *Letters*.

FROM: Charles Scribner ALS, 3 pp.[1] Princeton University

May 16th 1939

Dear Scott—

I was sorry to have missed seeing you when you were in New York but it was great news to hear from Max that you had a novel in mind and the time to do it. Had been hoping for years that this time would come. I know what a tough time you had working on your last novel, but knowing you and realizing that you had your health and courage back again I feel certain that this novel may go as easily as any you have ever done and will put you out in front again.

Max and I have always thought that, apart from squaring you with the world, living where you have should give you a vast source of material that someday you should be able to use. There has been plenty about Hollywood but no one to my knowledge has told anything about it that made the people live, and while their surroundings and the form of life they lead may make them absurdly glamorous or dissolute they must have originally been born like other men and women and fundamentally have the same insides.

Well I don't know why I am writing you all this rot except that I know your book would be swell & that I have such a hell of a cold in my head that I can scarcely see out of one eye—and therefore with death at my shoulder I certainly hope to live long enough to read your novel and the sooner the better.

Ever sincerely
Charlie Scribner

[1] This letter has been corrected.

FROM: Zelda Fitzgerald
April 1939

ALS, 4 pp. Princeton University
New York City

Dearest Scott:

I'm so sorry about the turmoil:[1] I antagonized you apparently, so I did the best I could to see you well provided for, and will leave for Ashville to-morrow *Tuesday*.

Don't feel too badly about the children. They went to the club at Larchmont, and had dates and were provided with an adequate evening.

Mr. Case[2] is the truest of friends. He shielded you from any possible criticism, and at the expense of his whole day managed to help John Palmer see you to safety.

Your eye was most distressing; but the hospital will take care of it better than could otherwise have been provided and will be able to give you a good looking over as well. Your cough is awful; and you are exhausted. Please take care of yourself. There is a possibility of so much happiness if you will be of a more conservative intent.

I got money from Ober ($70): most of which I paid on account to the troublous times. To-day, I'll have to ask him for more. Mr. Case said he would send those bills straight to Ober; I didn't know what else to do with them.

D.O.: I pray that your eye will soon be well, that you will be better for your rest, and will be awaiting a more auspicious meeting—

We are indebted very heavily to

John Palmer, who solved the situation by at last finding a doctor who was willing to assume responsibility; and to Mr. Case who kept you off the street at considerable effort and who was as gracious as possible through out—

Good luck

Devotedly
Zelda

P.S. Needless to say I never heard of such a thing as regards the hospital—

[1] Fitzgerald had drunk heavily on their trip to Cuba; when they returned to New York and checked into the Hotel Algonquin, his condition was so bad that he had to be hospitalized. Zelda Fitzgerald returned to Highland Hospital by herself. This was to be their last meeting.

[2] Frank Case, owner of the Algonquin.

FROM: Zelda Fitzgerald | ALS, 4 pp. Princeton University
April 1939 | New York City

Dearest Do-Do:

It seems useless to wait any more; I know that you are better; and being taken care of; and I am of no assistance; so I'll go back to the hospital on the 2:30 train.

I am distressed about your lungs. Why dont you come to Tryon? It's the best place in the world for such and we could keep a little house on the lake and let you get better. We might have a very happy summer in such circumstance—you like it there, and I am very clever at serving bird-song and summer clouds for breakfast

Scottina could visit us; and we could find a better meaning to so many things.

Meantime: I have seen a fascinating exhibit of pictures at the Metropolitan during which I thought how you would have loved the "evolution of the American Scene" as portrayed from croquet lawns and corner stores, through the first rail-roads and steam-boats and minstrelsy and every known sort of adventure straight up to the present. I wonderred had you known the wharf at Buffalo as it was presented, and rememberred the summer at West Port.

I saw a news-reel movie of irrelevant if pictorial life in distant parts, and visited Ober to the extent of $150; and had the situation permitted of peace-of-mind would have had a very agreeable time.

Please believe that I stayed over solely to the purpose of helping you if I could I know from experience what a difference it makes in life when somebody cares about your troubles.

—We owe John Palmer a debt of gratitude of considerable proportions. He found the doctor; and "discussed" with Mr. Case; and handled the whole situation.

Mr. Case also was most gracious and was ultimately considerate of you. I know that I have written you all this before but, as you know my letters are censored from the Hospital and I wont have another chance to communicate until we meet again.

To the Hospital, this version: We had a most enviable trip; and everything was according to the rules This last refers to cigarettes and wine concerning which I will follow our agreement. As to any irregularity of arrival your lungs are bad, and required attention, and I am capable of travelling alone so there wasnt any use in your adding another tiring journey to what you had before you.

D.O. please take care of yourself—So you will be well again and happier than these last times. There are so few people of our era who have made original contributions to the life about us, and not many who can be so charming, and almost not any with a greater capacity for enjoyment.

There are still a great many things which could give us pleasure

And there are such a lot of people fond of you.

I havent bought *anything* save the dress + hat in which I appear, the flowers thereon, some stockings + 4 pr. of pants.

The money is simply *disparu*—

With the BEST of good wishes, and devotion, and aspirations to a mutual purpose sometime.

Zelda

TO: Scottie Fitzgerald

TLS, 2 pp. Princeton University
Hollywood, California

June 3, 1939

Dearest Pie:—

You asked for it about that "instructive" business when you spoke of taking a course at U.C.L.A. It seems what you really dread is a travel trip and I think you're awfully foolish because to my mind this really *will* be the last summer when it will be safe to travel in Europe. In any case, I want you to consult immediately with your Freshman director or whoever handles such things and find out what parties, if any, are making that Scandinavian trip touching in Russia—what is the shortest trip available; what is the latest you could go on such a trip—specifically *is there any trip of that kind leaving in August* and how much it would cost. Heaven knows I am not going to force anything like that on you against your will, but so far no suggestion of yours nor any idea of mine has carried the plot more than a month or so forward.

I *don't* want you to try to get a job through the Vassar Employment Bureau. It would mean (quite selfishly) a worry for me for I would have to come East and investigate the job. And though I appreciate the remorse and the intensity of purpose that inspired your five-and-dime suggestion, I assure you that Barbara Hutton is not going to let a rival in there. She kind of feels she owns it, you know.

So this letter is going to have, to some extent, an inconclusive ring. This much is certain. I gather that you want to spend from a week to ten days in Baltimore and will be at Finney's or Law's (please let me know) which brings us to about the 18th—when I want you at the *very latest* to appear in Asheville prepared to spend at least from a week to ten days with your mother. This seems to me to be an absolute obligation which has been too long put off and I know that you will not regard it as a trial since your relations with her are so much better.

During your visit in Baltimore (which I gather begins the 9th) you will receive a call from one of my old friends, Dr. Hammon or the handsome Dr. Ben Baker (just married, alas!) They will ask you to make an appointment with them in town for an examination of your appendix which will not take more than half an hour. I am doing this not because I doubt the infirmary physicians at Vassar but because I want a double opinion about the immediacy of the matter before we decide about the operation. In any case it will not occur in Baltimore. However, when they do call, I wish you would conform as much as possible to their convenience and not put it off till the last day of your visit. It's simply a check up. By the time you're in Asheville which is to be by the 18th, I will have decided the next steps—such as when you are coming out here, etc.

The idea of being counsellor in a summer camp doesn't appeal to me for reasons which I'll explain to you when I see you. If you do want to do some actual wage earning yourself this summer, we can arrange a little while of that too and speaking of that, I am sorry I cramped your style in that *Mademoiselle* affair.[1] I really don't care what they do in the line of captions and headings, but appreciate your refusing to let them change your text. I am sorry that it should be that way and I hope it works out all right and that you get the fifty bucks. I know what you wrote must have had some life and merit or they wouldn't have considered it. I hope you've kept a carbon.

All goes well here. I am just finishing a story—[2] to get my hand in after a lapse of almost four years—and then will probably do an original for Carole Lombard and Dave Selznick wants.[3] My illness while serious enough is not at all critical—merely a question of time and patience and rest, so please stay out of *too* much trouble.

I am sorry that that letter about the bills reached you when you were threatened with measles but those coincidences will happen, but I am delighted that the measles have turned out to be imaginary. Good luck in your exams.

With dearest love,

~~Scott~~ I mean
Daddy

P.S. Make the money go as long as possible.

[1] "A Short Retort," *Mademoiselle* (July 1939), an article by Scottie about her generation.

[2] Probably "Design in Plaster," *Esquire* (November 1939), or "Temperature" (unpublished).

[3] Fitzgerald did not get this assignment.

TO: Lawrence Lee

TL(CC), 1 p. Princeton University
Hollywood, California

June
21
1939

Dear Lawrence:—

There have been times in the past where I've had fiction that did not fit the commercial magazines that I sent to Mencken for his old *Mercury*. But this time doesn't happen to be one of them. The health hasn't been so good the past few years and I even owe *Esquire* a piece that I have never gotten around to doing.

I've thought of you often. I was near you last Fall for three hours and tried to telephone you, without success, from Monticello. Before our train left for the South Zelda too wanted to see you. The custodian at Monticello knew you by sight or reputation but all the centrals in Charlottesville could not locate you.

I shall always remember your grand hospitality to me on a rather desperate pilgrimage that I was making some half dozen years ago.

Ever your friend,

P.S. If you have time would you get some member of your Subscription Department to look up and send me the copy of the *Virginia Quarterly* in which appears an article by John Peale Bishop which refers to me.[1] It may be the article about Ernest Hemingway—anyway several people have spoken to me about it and out here among the Barbarians it is hard to find such a civilized periodical as yours. If he finds it, I hope the enclosed dollar will cover cost and postage.

P.S.2—With appreciation, I have chalked up on my blackboard the fact that you *would* like to publish some material of mine and shall not forget it if anything seems appropriate.

[1] "The Missing All," *Virginia Quarterly Review* (Winter 1937). Fitzgerald was bitterly hurt when he read Bishop's evaluation of his career.

TO: Maxwell Perkins

Wire. Princeton University

ENCINO CALIF JUL 3

HAVE BEEN WRITING IN BED WITH TUBERCULOSIS UNDER DOCTORS NURSES CARE SIS ARRIVING WEST. OBER HAS DECIDED NOT TO BACK ME THOUGH I PAID BACK EVERY PENNY AND EIGHT THOUSAND COMMISSION. AM GOING TO WORK THURSDAY IN STUDIO AT FIFTEEN HUNDRED CAN YOU LEND ME SIX HUNDRED FOR ONE WEEK BY WIRE TO BANK AMERICA CULVERCITY. SCOTTIE HOSPITAL

WITH APPENDIX AND AM ABSOLUTELY WITHOUT FUNDS. PLEASE DO NOT ASK OBERS COOPERATION

SCOTT

JUL 4 730A.

TO: Arnold Gingrich ALS, 1 p. Princeton University

July 1939

Hide-out adress! Now that I've paid off 99/100 of my debts people want me to contract more

5521 Amestoy Ave.
Encino, Cal.

Dear Arnold:

My account books are on their way out here and Ive forgotten what you used to pay me for stories. Anyhow will you credit these[1] against my balance and airmail me how much that leaves? (also whether you like the stories)?

One more thing—and here I'm intruding into your province. Both these stories depend on *surprise* as much as an old O. Henry did—and sometimes your editors give away what used to be called the "jist" in the top caption. I know for some pieces that's advisable—here it would be absolutely fatal. Could you note this on the stories?

With thanks and best wishes

Scott Fitzgerald

Excuse pencil but this is one of those days. The stories are shorter than I thought but I'd made a last cut.

[1] After two years of working on screenplays Fitzgerald resumed writing fiction and sent two stories to *Esquire*—probably "Design in Plaster" and "The Lost Decade."

TO: Maxwell Perkins TL(CC), 2 pp. Princeton University

July
19
1939

Dear Max:—

I expected to go to work last Wednesday and have been offered two jobs and had to turn them down—though there is no connection with the old fairy tale of the man who always started looking for a certain kind of game immediately after it passed out of his sight. I can do any kind of work except (a) the kind with producers who work all night which the doctor says is absolutely out, and (b) stories of the *Tarzan* and *Mark of Zorro* persuasion which require the practically stationary brain. I am even strong enough to work within the studio walls now and it is a question of days until a romantic comedy or a boy-and-girl story shows up.

The main point of this letter is confidential for the most important reasons. Harold Ober and I are parting company. Whether he is throwing me over or me him may be a subject of controversy—but not on my part. I think he is doing it even if Madame Ober uses me for the rest of her life as an example of gross ingratitude. She was very kind in taking Scottie during many of the intervals between vacations from camp and school in '35 and '36 when I was so ill—I have always wanted to do something for her boys in return. Also I shall be forever grateful to Harold for his part of the help in backing me through that long illness, but his attitude has changed and I tell you this without any anger, but after a month's long and regretful consideration. He is a single-tracked man and the feeling that he once had of definite interest combined with forgiveness of my sins, has changed to a sort of general disapproval and a vague sense that I am through—this in spite of the fact that I paid him over ten thousand dollars in commissions in the last year-and-a half and refunded the whole thirteen thousand that I owed him.

I think something to do with it is the fact that almost every time I have come to New York lately I have just taken Zelda somewhere and have gone on more or less of a binge, and he has formed the idea that I am back in the mess of three years ago.

Anyhow, it is impossible to continue a relation which has become so strained and difficult. Even though there has been no spoken impoliteness there is a new fashion of discussing my stories as if he was a rather dissatisfied and cranky editor and of answering telegrams with delayed airmails and, most of all, completely changing his old policy of backing me up to the limit of what the next story will probably be sold for which makes it impossible to go on. He fairly earned the fifty thousand dollars or so of commissions that I've paid him and nothing snows one under quicker than a send of disbelief and disillusion in anyone close. The final touch was when I had to sell two stories to *Esquire* at $250., when I wanted cash quick—one of them was worth at least $1000., from *Liberty* if he could have given me enough advance to survive the wait.

So while I feel regret I have no moral compunction. This is a matter of survival. A man lost in the Arctic for the second time cannot sit waiting while a former rescuer refuses to send out another relief expedition. I would rather deal personally with the editors, as I deal always with you, and get opinions at the source. Harold's greatest help was when I lived in Europe. As you know we have never been very close either intellectually or emotionally (save for his kindness to Scottie) . . . .[1] I stuck with him, of course, when he left Reynolds, but now he has many correct and conventional Agatha Christies, etc., on his list who never cause any inconvenience, so I doubt if I will be missed.

I thought you should know this—know also that he has always treated me fairly and generously and is above reproach as an agent. The blame which brought about this situation is entirely mine. But it is no such illogical step as the one which made Tom Wolfe leave Scribner's. A few weeks ago when three Fitzgeralds at once were in the hands of the medical profession he found it inconvenient to help and under the circumstances of the last year and a half the episode served to give me a great uncertainty as to his caring what becomes of me.

Above all things I wish you wouldn't discuss this with him. I have not, nor will ever say, nor *could* say anything against him either personally or professionally, but even the fact that I have discussed the matter with you might upset him and give him ideas that I had, and turn what should be a peaceful cleavage into an unpleasant affair.

I am better day by day and long only to make some picture money and get back to the novel.[1]

Ever your friend,

5521 Amestoy Avenue
Encino, California

[1] Twenty-three words omitted by the editor.
[2] See Perkins' 26 July letter to Fitzgerald in *Scott/Max*.

TO: H. N. Swanson[1] TL(CC), 2 pp. Princeton University

July
20
1939

Dear Swanie:—

From our phone conversation the other day I think that you've formed perhaps a false impression of my relation with Harold. It's been a case of two unlike people accepting each other for business reasons and while I think that he has honestly admired my short stories our closest jointure has been in his real affection for Scottie. This must have been the case or there wouldn't have been this change of attitude in such a short time. Only a few months ago he was telling me not to be in such a hurry about paying him back the debt, but on the contrary to put some money away.

I feel toward him a great gratitude and we've naturally had a pleasant friendship, but our communication was almost entirely by letter until about 1930 and I have never felt such confidence in his editorial opinions (save as that I would feel to an average literate layman) that I have felt in the constructive suggestions of, for example, Max Perkins of Scribners—who gave me very good advice in a rewrite of both "This Side of Paradise" and "Gatsby." And I don't think that Harold has ever felt qualified to advise me except in telling me frankly that in his opinion a story clicked or didn't click—he has never claimed to be the creative type and has left that problem to me.

So if he no longer thinks that I "click" the only thing for me to do is to establish relations with the editors directly because they know presumably what they want. (In the case of the *Post* it gradually grew to be the case that I talked over changes personally with Lorimer and dealt with him about as directly as I did with you in that *College Humor* series—Harold acted only as fiscal agent.)

In the East, conditions are not as in Hollywood where a man must be represented. Harold, being no longer prepared to back me up to the probable price of my next short story, becomes almost a barrier between the magazines and me. He and Paul Reynolds were most valuable in raising my prices during the rising magazine market of the '20's, especially while I was abroad. But now Harold seems to sense that I want to vary my work between pictures, novels and stories, rather than spend years at one type of stuff. His attitude seems to reflect the fact that I am not likely to be as good a client as I was in other days. I sent him a telegram and the enclosed answer is typical of his attitude. I was even grateful for the telegram because lately he has confined himself to airmail in answering wires. I am feeling rather hopeless about dealing much further with him under these conditions and am quite reconciled to Ann thinking for the rest of her life, that it is *me* who is deserting *him* and turning out to be a prize specimen of ingratitude.

I may or may not have told you the *Post* wants a complete revise of the story I wrote;[2] meanwhile I am doing a story for *Collier's*;[3] meanwhile I did two things for *Esquire* one of which (2800 words long) would have brought twice as much from *Liberty* if Harold had provided the means to wait.[4]

This is a long letter, but I want to clear it up with you that anything I may have to do in the East is done from necessity and not from irrational temper.

Ever yours,

5521 Amestoy Avenue
Encino, California

[1] Fitzgerald's Hollywood agent.

[2] "Temperature" was declined by *The Saturday Evening Post*.

[3] "Discard," which was declined by *Collier's* and published posthumously in *Harper's Bazaar* (January 1948).

[4] Probably "Design in Plaster" (November 1939) and "The Lost Decade" (December 1939).

TO: Maxwell Perkins

TLS (with holograph additions), 1 p.
Princeton University

July
24
1939

Dear Max:—

Supplementing Saturday's letter, I would like to have, in case of emergency, the names of the two or three best agents in New York—just in case this difficulty with Harold gets too hard to handle. I will not use your name in any way nor will I act on it immediately, but at this distance one feels rather powerless in obtaining information suddenly and I may need it.

Curtis Brown wouldn't do or any English Company. (Have considered Pinker, but they have that mail restriction at Sing Sing.)[1] Seriously who are the top men in that line? Would you airmail me this information?

Ever yours
Scott

5521 Amestoy Avenue
Encino, California

[1] Agent Eric S. Pinker had been sent to prison for misappropriating his clients' royalties.

TO: Kenneth Littauer[1]

TL(CC), 1 p. New York Public Library
Encino, California

July 25, 1939

Dear Kenneth:—

Here is your Hollywood story[2] and thanks for your letter. It is an ironic thought that the last picture job I took—against my better judgment—yielded me five thousand dollars five hundred and cost over four thousand in medical attention—plus an inestimable amount for two months time spent basking upon the dorsal region. Our Hollywood greed! The great idea is to do a picture, then something else, then another picture, but no one—especially producers and agents—want you to live without some trouble to match their own stomach ulcers.

About this story—here are two copies to help you to a quick decision. I don't know what the company rules cover but (in spite of the fact of returning to the studio for a polish job) the government, etc., are going to crack down so hard on me the end of this month that I have to know all, and, in case you like it, receive emolument Monday by wire. I don't know what my price is—only once did I get under $3000. from the *Post* and that was in a year (1937) when they got only one story.

No one has seen this—including Harold Ober. I don't know the exact trouble there—in fact a novel and highly dilatory evasiveness is responsible for my attitude toward our relationship. I am under past moral obligations to him—somewhat covered by having paid him about $50,000. in magazine commissions. But this is *now,* and one cannot subsist on the food of four years ago. I suspect various personal elements, for which I am perhaps greatly to blame—anyhow I am trying to postpone a rupture at least till I see him next month out here. But anything may happen—may have to happen—and, as *I am bound by no contract,* let this story be between Collier's and me. I shall send him a commission or not, depending on how much I can find out about his attitude. It would be a relief to have the break come from him—if come it must. It is sad that human relations have a way of wearing out. And after that remark I almost hesitate to subscribe myself.

Ever yours,

P.S. Please don't write—*telegraph.* The picture business has given me a phobia about waiting.

P.S. 2. If the story is a few hundred words overweight please wire that too and let me cut it here.

[1] Fiction editor of *Collier's.*
[2] "Discard."

TO: Helene Richards[1] TLS, 1 p. Princeton University

July
27
1939

Dear Miss Richards:—

Attached is some biographical data.[2] Sorry I have no picture but I may say that out here I am known as the old "oomph man." So any haberdasher's advertisement will do as a portrait.

Will you tell that so-called Mr. Gingrich that I am accustomed, in my haughty way, to some word of approbation if not ecstacy about my contributions. Bland and chaste as your check was it somehow lacked emotion. However, we are accepting it.

Sincerely
F Scott Fitzgerald

5521 Amestoy Avenue
Encino, California

[1] Arnold Gingrich's secretary at *Esquire.*
[2] Missing.

TO: Cam Kennedy TLS, 1 p. Princeton University

August
2
1939

Dear Cam:—

I *did* write you a letter—I wrote it in front of the art book. I think of you often, especially in relation to Daughter's visit, which is quite close now.

This business about horses and swimming is very easy and the only trouble is that the Rancho has the technique reversed: One should *dive* upon a horse from a safe height, while in the case of a swimming pool one should come *up from below* preferably through the drain, which is my method. Once up, I whip the waves like wind and away we go. If there is any other advice you would like I have a 1910 edition of the World's Almanac and though they tell me that things have changed a little since then I will be glad to look up anything for you.

Two things we're all agreed on in this country are that we should avoid all inter-planetary treaties and policies and that girls should not marry before the age of eleven. If there is any other unanimous opinion at large I failed to hear of it.

Always your friend,
Scott Fitzgerald

5521 Amestoy Avenue
Encino, California

TO: Dr. R. Burke Suitt TL(CC), 1 p. Princeton University

August
16
1939

Dear Dr. Suitt:—

Several matters: First, I am at last actively employed on a job to which my health is equal—I mean a movie job.[1] Trying to write in bed sick was not a great success. Movies are a salaried affair and along architectural rather than emotional lines and I hope I am going to be able to stick along with it and you and the government will be the first people to be paid. I will be able to send something for the cash account when I get my first check Monday, because of course I don't want Zelda to feel this any more than possible.

In regard to her, wasn't it settled a long time ago that she was capable of swimming and didn't she swim in Florida? Is it some old standing order that was left about this? I see absolutely nothing against her swimming there because swimming has been so very much to her always and I thought that there might be some confusion in the office about it. Daughter couldn't understand why she wasn't allowed to swim with the others. In my wife's letters she mentions a possible trip to the World's Fair. As you know, I like her to have every possible treat but as far as I can see ahead that will be beyond my means this Autumn. On the other hand, if things go well and my health holds up a trip to her mother's in Montgomery in September might be possible, if she did it cheaply.

This unexpected illness and sudden change of fortune has made me realize the difference between this present America and that of ten years ago. I am amazed at the fact that there seems to be no credit abroad—one can no longer follow on one's capabilities or one's past record as a money-maker. The whole scale of American life seems to be changing in its relation to the individual.

Ever yours, gratefully

P.S. Will you drop me a line about the swimming?

5521 Amestoy Ave.
Encino, Calif.

[1] Fitzgerald was working for Universal on *Open That Door*, which was not produced.

TO: Edgar Allan Poe — TL(CC), 1 p. Princeton University

September
18
1939

Dear Ed:—

You have an early Chaldean handwriting but an excellent heart. And our tastes must be similar because the dressing gown is a beautiful piece of lechery. Thank you. I have named it Celalume and shall think in its depths.

Best to Babe—sorry I didn't see her. I've been on the run between Universal and United Artists (where Niven is and isn't going to finish his picture) and on the point of suing R.K.O. for keeping me awake on their lot across the street. I am so tired of being old and sick—would much rather be a scared young man peering out over a hunk of concrete or mud toward something I hated than be doing this here stuff.

Ever yours

5521 Amestoy Avenue
Encino, California

TO: C. O. Kalman — Wire (copy). Minnesota Historical Society

ENCINO, CALIFORNIA SEPTEMBER 21, 1939

WAS TAKEN ILL OUT HERE LAST APRIL AND CONFINED TO BED FOR FIVE MONTHS AND NOW UP AND WORKING BUT COMPLETELY CLEANED OUT FINANCIALLY. WANT DESPERATELY TO CONTINUE DAUGHTER AT VASSAR. CAN YOU LEND THREE HUNDRED SIXTY DOLLARS FOR ONE MONTH?[1] IF THIS IS POSSIBLE PLEASE WIRE ME 5521 AMESTOY AVENUE, ENCINO, CALIFORNIA.

SCOTT FITZGERALD

[1] Kalman was in the hospital; Fitzgerald obtained the money from Gerald Murphy.

TO: Gerald Murphy — Wire. Honoria Murphy Donnelly

ENCINO CALIF 1135A 1939 SEP 21 PM 5 39

WAS TAKEN ILL OUT HERE LAST APRIL AND CONFINED TO BED FIVE MONTHS AND NOW UP AND WORKING BUT COMPLETELY CLEANED OUT FINANCIALLY WANT DESPERATELY TO CONTINUE DAUGHTER AT VASSAR CAN YOU LEND 360 DOLLARS FOR ONE MONTH IF THIS IS POSSIBLE PLEASE WIRE ME AT 5521 AMESTOY AVENUE ENCINO CALIF

SCOTT FITZGERALD

TO: Gerald and Sara Murphy — ALS, 4 pp. Honoria Murphy Donnelly
22 September 1939 — Encino, California

Gerald + Sara:

What a strange thing that after asking every other concievable favor of you at one time or another I should be driven to turn to you for money! The story is too foolish, too dreary to go in to—I was ill when I saw you in February and for a week had been going along on drink. Like a fool—for I had plenty of money then—I took two more jobs and worked myself up to a daily temperature of 102° + then just broke + lay in bed four months without much ability to do anything except lie to the world that I was "fine." I couldn't even reduce costs—there were the doctors and the government + the insurance, and the "face."

Well, I'm up now. I've even worked two weeks + tomorrow may find the financial crisis over—an idea at Metro—but the way all ones personal prides + vanities melt down in the face of a situation like not being able to continue a child's education is astonishing. Not having any credit, What a thing! When credit was exactly what one thought one had.

Last year for example I payed my Eastern agent $12,000 which he had advanced me over two years plus 10% of my gains (of about $68,000). Would he back me again—for $1000—$500? No—in spite of the $70,000 in commissions I've paid him in the past. All this may interest you, Gerald, as an indication of the fluctuation of talent value—I can see Sara yawn + I don't blame her. Anyhow it has been frightening and lost + strange. One's own reaction was:—I couldn't call on the impecunious, and eternally so, to whom I had "lent" or rather given many thousands—not only because they didn't have it—but because some relation established at the time of the lending forbade it. There were the bores I have tolerated because they have been nice to Zelda or some such reason, but once in a faintly similar situation years ago I sounded out one—+ buttoned up my overcoat quickly at the chill in the air.

Then there were relatives + friends. My relatives are all poor now, except my sister. . . .[1] And, as Gerald once remarked, your friends are the people you see. Forty-eight hours went into worry as to whether or not to ask you to help me. And then I wired, knowing somehow that if you were in America it would be all right, presuming on your grace. Next day came your wire—telephoned, but I went down and got a copy of it.

You had probably been going thru hell yourselves with Honoria on the high seas. And how easy too, in these times, to have been irritated by the intrusion of this preposterously personal problem—how can that Idiot, who has such abilities to be solvent, get himself in such a hole? Let it teach him a lesson!

You went a good deal further than that—you helped me perhaps because I would *never* learn—or "for help's sake itself," to paraphrase E. Browning. Anyhow it made me feel much too sentimental than is proper to one of our age + experience. And it is nice to know that when I send it back to you it will in time probably go to aid some other "unworthy case" (—do you remember Ernest's passage in "The Sun Also Rises" about being sorry for the wrong types, unsuccessful whores, ect.?)

You saved me—Scottie and me—in spite of our small deserts. I don't think I could have asked anyone else + kept what pride it is nessessary to keep.

Scott

[1] Three words omitted by the editor.

TO: Dr. R. Burke Suitt TLS(CC), 1 p.[1] Princeton University

Hollywood, California

September

27

1939

Dear Dr. Suitt:

I have a note from Miss Sheffler about my bill. You are no more at a loss than I am. For two months I have been up and around but the numerous movie offers that came in while I was at Temperature 100° just simply stopped. I've had exactly enough work, two weeks of it, to pay an income tax instalment. Somewhat in a panic I have shuttled between stories, "originals" for the movies and some very short pieces, with a total result of settling into a nice financial jam. I came out here to pay debts, worked as a faithful hack for twenty months and landed right back into tuberculosis. The man to whom I paid back the debts, my agent, decided not to back me any more.

So that's why I am unable to answer Miss Sheffler. My only idea is that (a) I have a high earning power which in the past has been affected only by overwork (T.B.) and that broken shoulder. (b) I hope you will find it possible to let things go on as they are for another month trusting me as you did before. I hope that this does not mean that Zelda will be deprived of the ordinary necessities. As you know I tried to give Zelda every luxury permissible when I could afford it (the trip to Florida, etc) but it is simply impossible to pay anything, even on instalments when one drives in a mortgaged Ford and tries to get over the habit of looking into a handkerchief for blood when talking to a producer.

If things go as bad as they have for another month, the hospital can reimburse itself out of life insurance. This is a promise.

Ever sincerely and gratefully,
Scott Fitzgerald

[1] Seventy-four-word postscript omitted by the editor.

TO: Kenneth Littauer TL(CC), 4 pp.[1] Princeton University

5521 Amestoy Avenue
Encino, California
September 29, 1939

Dear Kenneth:—

This will be difficult for two reasons. First that there is one fact about my novel, which, if it were known, would be immediately and unscrupulously plagiarized by the George Kaufmans, etc., of this world. Second, that

I live always in deadly fear that I will take the edge off an idea for myself by summarizing or talking about it in advance. But, with these limitations, here goes:

The novel will be fifty thousand words long. As I will have to write sixty thousand words to make room for cutting I have figured it as a four months job—three months for the writing—one month for revision. The thinking, according to my conscience and the evidence of sixty pages of outline and notes, *has already been done.* I would infinitely rather do it, now that I am well again, than take hack jobs out here.

* * *

The Story occurs during four or five months in the year 1935. It is told by Cecelia, the daughter of a producer named Bradogue[2] in Hollywood. Cecelia is a pretty, modern girl neither good nor bad, tremendously human. Her father is also an important character. A shrewd man, a gentile, and a scoundrel of the lowest variety. A self-made man, he has brought up Cecelia to be a princess, sent her East to college, made of her rather a snob, though, in the course of the story, her character evolves *away from this.* That is, she was twenty when the events that she tells occurred, but she is twenty-five when she tells about the events, and of course many of them appear to her in a different light.

Cecelia is the narrator because I think I know exactly how such a person would react to my story. She is *of* the movies but not *in* them. She probably was born the day "The Birth of a Nation" was previewed and Rudolf Valentino came to her fifth birthday party. So she is, all at once, intelligent, cynical but understanding and kindly toward the people, great or small, who are of Hollywood.

She focuses our attention upon two principal characters—Milton Stahr[3] (who is Irving Thalberg—and *this is my great secret*) and Thalia,[4] the girl he loves. Thalberg has always fascinated me. His peculiar charm, his extraordinary good looks, his bountiful success, the tragic end of his great adventure. The events I have built around him are fiction, but all of them are things which might very well have happened, and I am pretty sure that I saw deep enough into the character of the man so that his reactions are authentically what they would have been in life. So much so that he may be recognized—but it will also be recognized that *no single fact is actually true.* For example, in my story he is unmarried or a widower, leaving out completely any complication with Norma.[5]

In the beginning of the book I want to pour out my whole impression of this man Stahr as he is seen during an airplane trip from New York to the coast—of course, through Cecelia's eyes. She has been hopelessly in love with him for a long time. She is never going to win anything more from him than an affectionate regard, even that tainted by his dislike of her father (parallel the deadly dislike of each other between Thalberg and Louis B. Mayer). Stahr is over-worked and deathly tired, ruling with a radiance that is almost moribund in its phosphorescence. He has been warned that his health is undermined, but being afraid of nothing the warning is unheeded. He has had everything in life except the privilege of giving himself unselfishly to another human being. This he finds on the night of a semi-serious earthquake (like in 1935) a few days after the opening of the story.

It has been a very full day even for Stahr—the bursted water mains, which cover the whole ground space of the lot to the depth of several feet, seems to release something in him. Called over to the outer lot to supervise the salvation of the electrical plant (for like Thalberg, he has a finger in every pie of the vast bakery) he finds two women stranded on the roof of a property farmhouse and goes to their rescue.

Thalia Taylor is a twenty-six year old widow, and my present conception of her should make her the most glamorous and sympathetic of my heroines. Glamorous in a new way because I am in secret agreement with the public in detesting the type of feminine arrogance that has been pushed into prominence in the case of Brenda Frazier,[6] etc. People simply do not sympathize deeply with those who have had *all* the breaks, and I am going to dower this girl, like Rosalba in Thackeray's "Rose in the Ring" with "a little misfortune." She and the woman with her (to whom she is serving as companion) have come secretly on the lot through the other woman's curiousity. They have been caught there when the catastrophe occurred.

Now we have a love affair between Stahr and Thalia, an immediate, dynamic, unusual, physical love affair—and I will write it so that you can publish it. At the same time I will send you a copy of how it will appear in book form somewhat stronger in tone.

This love affair is the meat of the book—though I am going to treat it, remember, as it comes through to Cecelia. That is to say by making Cecelia at the moment of her telling the story, an intelligent and observant woman, I shall grant myself the privilege, as Conrad did, of letting her imagine the actions of the characters. Thus, I hope to get the verisimilitude of a first person narrative, combined with a Godlike knowledge of all events that happen to my characters.

Two events beside the love affair bulk large in the intermediary chapters. There is a definite plot on the part of Bradogue, Cecelia's father, to get Stahr out of the company. He has even actually and factually considered having him murdered. Bradogue is the monopolist at its worst—Stahr, in spite of the inevitable conservatism of the self-made man, is a paternalistic employer. Success came to him young, at twenty-three, and left certain idealisms of his youth unscarred. Moreover, he is a worker.

Figuratively he takes off his coat and pitches in, while Bradogue is not interested in the making of pictures save as it will benefit his bank account.

The second incident is how young Cecelia herself, in her desperate love for Stahr, throws herself at his head. In her reaction at his indifference she gives herself to a man whom she does not love. This episode is *not* absolutely necessary to the serial. It could be tempered but it might be best to eliminate it altogether.

Back to the main theme, Stahr cannot bring himself to marry Thalia. It simply doesn't seem part of his life. He doesn't realize that she has become necessary to him. Previously his name has been associated with this or that well-known actress or society personality and Thalia is poor, unfortunate, and tagged with a middle class exterior which doesn't fit in with the grandeur Stahr demands of life. When she realizes this she leaves him temporarily, leaves him not because he has no legal intentions toward her but because of the hurt of it, the remainder of a vanity from which she had considered herself free.

Stahr is now plunged directly into the fight to keep control of the company. His health breaks down very suddenly while he is on a trip to New York to see the stockholders. He almost dies in New York and comes back to find that Bradogue has seized upon his absence to take steps which Stahr considers unthinkable. He plunges back into work again to straighten things out.

Now, realizing how much he needs Thalia, things are patched up between them. For a day or two they are ideally happy. They are going to marry, but he must make one more trip East to clinch the victory which he has conciliated in the affairs of the company.

Now occurs the final episode which should give the novel its quality—and its unusualness. Do you remember about 1933 when a transport plane was wrecked on a mountain-side in the Southwest, and a Senator was killed? The thing that struck me about it was that the country people rifled the bodies of the dead. That is just what happens to this plane which is bearing Stahr from Hollywood. The angle is that of three children who, on a Sunday picnic, are the first to discover the wreckage. Among those killed in the accident besides Stahr are two other characters we have met. (I have not been able to go into the minor characters in this short summary.) Of the three children, two boys and a girl, who find the bodies, one boy rifles Stahr's possessions; another, the body of a ruined ex-producer; and the girl, those of a moving picture actress. The possessions which the children find, symbolically determine their attitude toward their act of theft. The possessions of the moving picture actress tend the young girl to a selfish possessiveness; those of the unsuccessful producer sway one of the boys toward an irresolute attitude; while the boy who finds Stahr's briefcase is the one who, after a week, saves and redeems all three by going to a local judge and making full confession.

The story swings once more back to Hollywood for its finale. During the story *Thalia has never once been inside a studio*. After Stahr's death as she stands in front of the great plant which he created, she realizes now that she never will. She knows only that he loved her and that he was a great man and that he died for what he believed in.

This is a novel—not even faintly of the propoganda type. Indeed, Thalberg's opinions were entirely different from mine in many respects that I will not go into. I've long chosen him for a hero (this has been in my mind for three years) because he is one of the half-dozen men I have known who were built on the grand scale. That it happens to coincide with a period in which the American Jews are somewhat uncertain in their morale, is for me merely a fortuitous coincidence. The racial angle shall scarcely be touched on at all. Certainly if Ziegfield could be made into an epic figure then what about Thalberg who was literally everything that Ziegfield wasn't?

There's nothing that worries me in the novel, nothing that seems uncertain. Unlike *Tender is the Night* it is not the story of deterioration—it is not depressing and not morbid in spite of the tragic ending. If one book could ever be "like" another I should say it is more "like" *The Great Gatsby* than any other of my books. But I hope it will be entirely different—I hope it will be something new, arouse new emotions perhaps even a new way of looking at certain phenomena. I have set it safely in a period of five years ago to obtain detachment, but now that Europe is tumbling about our ears this also seems to be for the best. It is an escape into a lavish, romantic past that perhaps will not come again into our time. It is certainly a novel I would like to read. Shall I write it?[7]

* * *

As I said, I would rather do this for a minimum price than continue this in-and-out business with the moving pictures where the rewards are great, but the satisfaction unsatisfactory and the income tax always mopping one up after the battle.

The minimum I would need to do this with peace of mind would be $15,000., payable $3000. in advance and $3000. on the first of November, the first of December, the first of January and the first of February, on delivery of the last installment. For this I would guarantee to do no other work, specifically pictures, to make any changes in the manuscript (but not to having them made for me) and to begin to deliver the copy the first of November, that is to give you fifteen thousand words by that date.

Unless these advances are compatible with your economy, Kenneth, the deal would be financially impossible for me under the present line up.

Four months of sickness completely stripped me and until your telegram came I had counted on a buildup of many months work here before I could *consider* beginning the novel. Once again a telegram would help tremendously, as I am naturally on my toes and

[1] Edmund Wilson included in his edition of *The Last Tycoon* (1941) the text of this letter from the section beginning "The story occurs during four or five months. . . ." through "It is an escape into a lavish, romantic past. . . ." Littauer's copy of the letter has not been found.

[2] Brady.

[3] Monroe Stahr.

[4] Kathleen Moore.

[5] Norma Shearer Thalberg.

[6] New York debutante.

[7] Fitzgerald's carbon copy of this letter has his note "Orig Sent thru here" after "Shall I write it?" The fragmentary continuation of the letter beginning "As I said" survives with the *Last Tycoon* notes.

FROM: Kenneth Littauer — TLS, 2 pp. Princeton University

10 October 1939

Dear Scott:

This is to confirm our telephone talk of yesterday. We are all greatly interested in the outline for a novel which you sent us under date of September 29. Its success is dependent of course upon how you do it. Therefore we don't want to say yes to your proposal until we have seen a substantial sample of the finished product. We realize the necessity of giving you some sort of subsidy if you are to follow the work through to the end. And so we are willing to say that if you will send us fifteen thousand words of the proposed novel in more or less finished form we will undertake to say yes or no upon the basis of that much manuscript. If we say yes we will forthwith advance to you five thousand dollars to apply against the total price of the novel. And upon delivery of an additional twenty thousand words we will advance to you an additional five thousand dollars. Thus we would undertake to advance ten thousand dollars in all against a total purchase price which remains to be negotiated but which we are hopeful will not be unreasonable.

We have nothing on which to base an offer except the price we paid you for your last story which was $2500. Ordinarily we offer an author as much per serial installment as we would pay per short story. How would it be, then, if we based our offer upon the number of seven-to-eight-thousand-word installments into which the story falls, undertaking to pay at the rate of $2500 per installment; and provided we agree to give you, in addition to the sum of these payments, a bonus of $5,000 to cover the extra value inherent in the cumulative appeal of any good serial story?[1]

Let me hear more from you soon so that I may know whether to put your name at the head of our 1940 progrom or not. All the best,

Sincerely yours
Kenneth Littauer
Fiction Editor

P.S. Your wire of October 9 with corrections for the new story has just reached me. The story isn't here yet.

[1] A reply to Littauer has not been found; Fitzgerald probably responded by phone. He regarded Littauer's proposed terms—which would have meant more than $20,000 for the serial rights—as inadequate and asked Perkins to negotiate with Littauer for a larger advance. At the bottom of the first page he calculated: "Ten thousand for 35,000 words—5–6000 installments." Across the top of the first page he wrote "*Attention Frances,*" referring the letter to his secretary Frances Kroll.

TO: Maxwell Perkins — Wire. Princeton University

ENCINO CALIF OCT 11 AM 5 41

PLEASE LUNCH IF YOU CAN WITH KENNETH LITTAUR OF COLLIERS IN RELATION TO SERIAL OF WHICH HE HAS THE OUTLINE. OBER TO BE ABSOLUTELY EXCLUDED FROM PRESENT STATE OF NEGOTIATIONS I HAD MY LAST DRINK LAST JUNE IF THAT MATTERS TELL LITTAUR THAT I FOOLISHLY TURNED DOWN LITERARY GUILD OFFER FOR TENDER. NIGHTLETTER ME IF YOU CAN. NOVEL OUTLINED ABSOLUTELY CONFIDENTIAL AS EVEN A HINT OF IT WOULD BE PLAGIARIZED OUT HERE EVER YOURS

SCOTT FITZGERALD.

TO: Maxwell Perkins — Wire. Princeton University
14 October 1939

VANNUYS CALIF OCT 14

PLEASE DO GET IN TOUCH WITH LITTAUER HAVE OUTLINED EVERY SCENE AND SITUATION AND I THINK I CAN WRITE THIS BOOK AS IF IT WAS A BIOGRAPHY BECAUSE I KNOW THE CHARACTER OF THIS MAN EVER YOURS[1]

SCOTT FITZGERALD.
906A.

[1] On 16 October Perkins reported to Fitzgerald on his meeting with Littauer: "I think he is now very optimistic, but they must see some substantial part to do what is necessary. Couldn't you write that part very quickly, even if not in absolute final form. . . ?" (Princeton)

TO: Arnold Gingrich Wire. Princeton University

ENCINO CALIF 505P 1939 OCT 16 PM 7 30

THIS REQUEST SHOULD HAVE BEEN INCLOSED WITH PAT HOBBY'S CHRISTMAS WISH[1] WHICH IS THREE THOUSAND WORDS LONG IF YOU CANT GO UP BY $150 I WILL HAVE TO SEND IT EAST I HATE TO SWITCH THIS SERIES BUT CANT AFFORD TO LOSE SO MUCH PLEASE WIRE ME

SCOTT.

[1] *Esquire* (January 1940).

FROM: Arnold Gingrich Wire. Princeton University

CHICAGO ILL 955A

F SCOTT FITZGERALD

5521 AMESTOY AVE ENCINO CALIF 1939 OCT 17 AM 8 19

DEAR SCOTT: SENDING $150 TODAY WHICH WILL CREDIT AGAINST PURCHASE OF PAT HOBBYS CHRISTMAS WISH IF YOU INSIST SINCE THAT ONE HAS BEEN RUSHED THROUGH FOR JANUARY ISSUE AND I CANT DO OTHERWISE. HOWEVER IF YOU INSIST UPON THIS ARRANGEMENT FOR THIS STORY WILL HAVE TO DECLINE WITH REGRET ANY MORE IN THIS SERIES. WOULD HAVE BEEN PLEASED TO GO ON STOCKING THEM UP AGAINST FUTURE REQUIREMENTS AS FAST AS YOU COULD TURN THEM OUT BUT CANNOT DO SO ANY MORE UNLESS AND UNTIL YOU LET ME BE THE JUDGE OF HOW MUCH WE CAN HONESTLY AFFORD TO PAY FOR THEM. REALIZE YOU HAVENT ASKED FOR MY ADVICE BUT WOULD NEVERTHELESS ADVISE YOU FRANKLY NOT TO JEOPARDIZE OLD RELIABLE INSTANT PAYMENT MARKET LIKE THIS BY USE OF STRONG ARM METHODS WHICH I AM BOUND TO RESENT AS REFLECTION ON MY SIX YEAR RECORD OF COMPLETE FRANKNESS IN DEALING WITH YOU. IN ANY CASE YOU HAVE THE EXTRA $150 AND NEXT MOVE IS UP TO YOU BUT ON BIRD IN HAND THEORY BELIEVE YOU WOULD BE BETTER BUSINESSMAN TO REGARD IT AS ADVANCE AGAINST ANOTHER STORY.[1] REGARDS,

ARNOLD.

[1] Fitzgerald was paid $250 for each *Esquire* story and had tried several times to negotiate an increase. The great advantage of the *Esquire* arrangement was that Gingrich would accept anything Fitzgerald submitted.

FROM: Arnold Gingrich Wire. Princeton University

CHICAGO ILL 144P 1939 OCT 17 PM 12 34

F SCOTT FITZGERALD

5521 AMESTORY AVE ENCINO CALIF

DEAR SCOTT WE MENNONITES COOL DOWN QUICKER THAN YOU FIGHTING IRISH SO SUGGEST YOU DONT ANSWER THIS UNTIL TOMORROW BUT AFTER YOU HUNG UP I REALIZED THAT IF MY UNFORTUNATE CHOICE OF WORDS IN MY WIRE HURT YOU HALF AS MUCH AS YOUR LAST SPOKEN WORDS HURT ME THEN IT IS INEFFFABLY SILLY FOR TWO ADULTS TO FIGHT A MUTUALLY UNWANTED WAR OVER A RELATIVELY SMALL AMOUNT OF MONEY AFTER SIX YEARS OF FRIENDLY AND PEACEFUL GIVE AND TAKE IN WHICH MUTUAL UNDERSTANDING AND FORBEARANCE HAS SMOOTHLY OILED THE EXCHANGE OF SOME SEVENTY FIVE THOUSAND WORDS AND SEVENTY FIVE HUNDRED DOLLARS WITHOUT DAMAGE TO FRIENDSHIP WHICH LATTER COMMODITY IS TO ME AT LEAST A MORE PRECIOUS CURRENCY THAN CASH. UPON REREADING OUR TWO WIRES I NOW FRANKLY CONFESS THAT YOURS DID NOT WARRANT MY USE OF THE PHRASE "STRONG ARM METHODS" FOR WHICH I APOLOGIZE AND CAN ONLY ASK YOU TO FORGIVE AND FORGET. MEANWHILE I ASSURE YOU THAT OUR CORPORATE TROOPS MAY ALWAYS BE COUNTED UPON AS ALLIED TO BE SUMMONED AT WILL TO YOUR BREAD AND BUTTER MAGINOT LINE.[1] AND I DEEPLY REGRET THAT MY CUMULATIVE ILL TEMPER THE PRODUCT OF ABOUT TWENTY STRAIGHT MONTHS OF REVERSES ON ALL FRONTS, SHOULD HAVE BURST SO UTTERLY WITHOUT PROVOCATION AND SPATTERED SUCH A SENSITIVE SOUL AS YOUR GOOD SWEET SELF. EXCUSE IT PLEASE

ARNOLD.

MAGINOT.

1 Fitzgerald referred to the Culver City branch of the Bank of America as his "Maginot Line."

TO: Dr. Robert S. Carroll TL (draft with holograph revisions), 2 pp. Princeton University

October
20
1939

Dear Dr. Carroll: (or Dr. Suitt)

I have been in bed for ten days with a slight flare-up of T.B. Regularly three mornings a week, come letters such as these from Zelda. I blew up the other day and wired her sister in Montgomery that Zelda could leave the hospital only on condition that I can not be responsible for setting loose a woman who, at any time may relapse into total insanity. A divorce would have to be obtained first.

It is the old story down there—that the only thing that counts is the peace of mind of an old lady of eighty. Unless you could assure me (and I know from your letters that you can't) that Zelda is 80% certain of holding her ground outside and not becoming a general menace or a private charge, I don't see how I can ask you to release her—except on the aforesaid basis of an agreed-upon divorce.

My daughter is of age now and can probably manage to keep out of her mother's way, so if the Sayres want to take over they are welcome. But I do not want a maniac at large with any legal claims upon me. She has cost me everything a woman can cost a man—his health, his work, his money. Mrs. Brinson and Mrs. Sayre have made fragmentary attempts to act impartially, but on the whole, have behaved badly, from the moment their first horrible accusation in 1932 that I put Zelda away for ulterior purposes. Mrs. Smith is simply a fool. I wish none of them any harm and I think Mrs Brinson has tried intermittently to execercise some of her Father's sense of justice but in these ten years I feel that every fragment of obligation on my part has been gradually washed out.

For me, life goes on without very much cheer, except my novel, but I think if there is any way to stop this continual nagging through Zelda it will be a help. I had every intention of sending her to Montgomery with a nurse this October, but there was no money. Of course, at present I am not in any mood to give her anything—even if I could afford it. After a few weeks in Montgomery, her first attempt would be to beg or borrow enough to get out here and hang herself around my neck—in which case a California State Asylum would be her last stop on this tragic journey.

All pretty black, isn't it? *Please try to persuade her not to send me any more of those letters.*

Ever yours, gratefully,

P.S. Of course I approve of what you've done about the room, ect. Scottie and I are living hard. A friend lent me enough to pay her first term in college. For better or worse Scottie + I form a structure—if that worm-like convolusion in Montgomery is a family then lets go back to the age of snakes.

5521 Amestoy Avenue
Encino, California

TO: Harry Joe Brown[1] TL(CC), 1 p. Princeton University

October
31
1939

Dear Harry Joe:

Here is your book. I don't want to work in pictures this next month because I am finishing a novel, but if anything magnificent comes up after that, keep me in mind as I would like to try your foundry.

Sorry you couldn't use the snowblind idea or the one about Sonja[2] skating badly, but maybe we will click another time.

Ever yours,

5521 Amestoy Avenue
Encino, California
Van Nuys 8591

[1] Producer at Twentieth Century–Fox.

[2] Sonja Henie; Fitzgerald had suggested plot ideas for her movie *Everything Happens at Night* (1939).

FROM: Zelda Fitzgerald ALS, 4 pp. Princeton University
Fall 1939 Highland Hospital, Asheville, North Carolina

Dear Scott:

I'm sorry about our present estate. So many years ago when we were just married and making Holiday about the Biltmore corridors, money was one of the things one simply stated the necessity for, went through the requisite ritual and waited. Now that 50¢ this way or that way, any day, begin to count it is become of vastly more relevance. In view of the fact that the war will probably make jobs a lot harder to get in California, wont you consider curtailing our expences as seems exigent? There is so little necessity for keeping me here: I would be of service in Montgomery besides being happy to be there, and keeping up two ménages is that much easier than keeping up three. Meantime, you promised me two years ago that you would pursue the matter of my going home Time goes on, as you have perhaps remarked, and still I have no social status beyond that of a liability.

I play tennis, and paint pictures and go to the movies. There is occasionally a party. Last week the Hospital gave a most entertaining folk-dancing festival; and, as you know, we climb mountains and brood It's an awfully nice place; do not think that I am ungrateful that I ask you most urgently to remember how long I have been devoting myself to the observance of the strictest of regimes: medical observation: and to remember that life is not an inexhaustible store of Efforts to no deeper purpose than that of ameliorating the immediate circumstance

I too am most grateful to the Finneys for their courtesies to Scottie. Has her party been cancelled? She seemed very controlled and reconciled to whatever curtailment had to be made when she was here. She is really of a very judicious temperament and makes adverse adjustment with a most commendable philosophy.

I suggested to you before that short of an actual job in Hollywood, this part of the world is far more conducive to good health: also it is cheaper—Why dont you consider it again?

Outside of offering suggestions, I am not in a position to be of any assistance—

Colleeen Moore's[1] dolls-house is now on exhibit in Ashville. I remember a most depressing evening of sitting around her house while people withheld their approbrium until they had placed what was wrong with each other—It would no doubt have made interesting reminiscence had I not fogot all save the aura of House-detective that pervaded the gathering

DEVOTEDLY
Zelda

[1] Movie actress.

TO: Dr. Robert S. Carroll — TL(CC), 1 p. Princeton University
Fall 1939 — Encino, California

Dear Dr. Carroll:—

I want to give you some idea of the financial situation. As far as the movies are concerned I am temporarily through. It was never to any extent a matter of drink. My agent here would testify at having seen me in the daytime and evening a hundred times and had *never* smelt liquor on me. After I quit the movies I *did* do some heavy drinking for some weeks. But during the twenty-two months that I worked in pictures the problem was one of health and more particularly of nerves. My tendency was to get myself into a constant struggle with the producers about how I wanted a picture to be. Naturally, I made some enemies. The health matter, of course, made it increasingly difficult to deal with the business which resolves itself largely into a matter of endless cigarettes and benzedrine tablets and twelve and sixteen hour conferences. You can't do that with T.B. and though I don't consider myself licked in that regard, it is out for the present.

The enclosed will indicate what I am doing to rehabilitate my fortunes. It is all highly confidential but the idea is that I have sent the synopsis of a novel to Collier's and they have agreed to back me if they like the first section. I mean back me to a very substantial amount. (it is something to have a reputation—even if it is the only thing you have left) These letters are from my publisher who is going to try to cooperate in the matter. It looks like the best way out. I seem to have completely lost the gift for the commercial short story, which depends on the "boy-meets-girl" motif. I can't write them convincingly any more which takes me completely out of the big money in that regard. This isn't anything new. After doing one hundred and fifty short stories of that type my enthusiasm began to fall off as far back as 1934. It requires a certain ebullience about inessential and specious matters which I no longer possess.

I am sending you these letters of Max Perkins because I hope you will be able to be as lenient as possible with Zelda the next two weeks, for now that things have bucked up I shall begin shortly to pay you a proportion of what money comes in. Particularly I refer to her oil painting. She doesn't complain about it—in fact her last letter is awfully sweet, and not restless and demanding, which I know indicates that you have talked with her and which I *hope* indicates that the Sayres have found some other mischief with which to occupy their idle hands. My God, how I detest "good people." I mean people that are good and think it is quite sufficient as a career. The one hundred dollars which I think I mentioned in that frantic telegram is hypothetical and has been spent a long time ago. But I am enclosing $50. which I hope can supply Zelda with a few oil paints.

Thank you for having grasped this situation so completely with so little evidence. Would be you so kind as to ask your secretary to return the Perkins letters?

Ever yours,

TO: Zelda Fitzgerald — AL (draft), 9 pp.[1] Bruccoli
Fall 1939 — Encino, California

Dearest Zelda:

It is two in the morning. I have been sleeping since ten. All day I've been working on a novel for which the magazine publishers have agreed to back me if they like the first twelve thousand words. It looks like a way out and Im putting everything I have into it. At twelve the mail came but certain letters I put aside unopened as I've done for a week—letters of quiet abuse from your family.

I am not very well—one lung is all gone now and I broke two fingers in the hand writing this when I tried to lift off my bed-desk by myself last Saturday. But of course that is all a secret because if the magazine knew I was not quite well it wouldn't help me write the novel. I care about the novel but not especially about anything else anymore. That a fifty dollar ticket to Montgomery would in some way purchase your eternal mental health is a proposition I will not debate. I wont even debate it with Dr Carrol—if he says it will, then Godspeed you. I should think that before Christmas–if I can get some peace—you could go south (to Montgomery) for a long trip *with* supervision. But the other story is too dreary—what would you do—because if you did go on your own I would fold up completely—for paints or amusements or clothes? Scottie would have to work + not be able to send you much for some time. Id lie very quietly in my grave out here but I think the spectre of you walking the streets of Montgomery in rags as the last of the Sayres, followed by curious urchins, would haunt me.

There'd be no one to help—even Newman hid behind his wife's skirts in an emergency. Just a horrible death in life.

For, Zelda, if you were capable of organizing anything you would do it there. What would I not give for the right to liesure—have you ever known me to have it? To be well, to be kept well, to have my pencil + paper bought for me, to not think of taxes and insurance and other peoples health and bringing up a child. I'd love to wake up some morning once and say: No cares today, no debts, no money-lenders, no mental prostitution, nothing between me and my canvas except my hand—and that well, not broken—the little finger trails across this page. I am not sorry for you this time—I envy you. And I am infinitely more sorry for my expiring talent which you tell me will be helped "by releasing you." That is equivalent to the great peace I should find if Scottie begged to contribute to the family fortunes by entering a steel mill or a whore-house.

You are a darling sometimes—I cant claim this distinction—but unfortunately you have given no signs that you can be anything more. And being a darling isn't enough. You've got to have the energy to sell your pictures—I can't forever find you Cary Rosses—and to live a literary life outside of mine. And where is that energy to proceed from? Are you to find it in Montgomery conversing with the shades of Mrs Mckinney? It is all right to concieve of life in terms of a vast nostalgia if it has an artistic purpose, or if it is a personal idiosyncracy like collecting old coins—but the world wont permit it unless it is self supporting. It's a luxury that even the rich, now, can scarcely afford. *We*—we consumptives, mistaken people, workers, die-ers, we must live—not at your expence, God knows, but in spite of you. We have our tombstones to chisel—and can't blunt our tools stabbing you back, you ghosts, who can't either clearly remember or cleanly forget.

I would rather do what I did in August—club the whole archaic Brenda Fraser idea out of Scottie's mind, by separating her from her roommate—and have her indignation forever, than present the picture of a brood of unmatured pigs sucking at my nipples forever. If this be treason make the most of it. As a fighter, if she were contemporary, I admire your mother. In her present rôle of sinister old witch, I think she adds no dignity to anyone's stature. Why doesn't she get Tilde home? Or Rosalind?

Do you think she cares or ever has cared about you or your impersonal interest? Do you think she would ever quarrel with you for your impersonal good? She constructed herself on a heroic romantic model as a girl and you were to be the stuffed dummy—true or false, screwed or chaste, honest or bogus,—on which she was to satisfy her egotism. She chose me—and she did—and you submitted at the moment of our marriage when your passion for me was at as low ebb as mine for you—because she thought romanticly that her projection of herself in you could best be shown thru me. I never wanted the Zelda I married. I didn't love you again till after you became pregnant. You—thinking I slept with that Bankhead—making all your drunks innocent + mine calculated till even *Town Topics*[2] protested. I'd been drunk, sure—but find any record of me as a drunk at Princeton—or in the army, except one night when I retired to the locker room. You were the drunk—at *seventeen,* before I knew you—already notorious.

This is the very questionable element I bought and your mother asks to be given back—for some vague reason known fully in the depths of your family psycholoay. The assumption is that you were a great prize package—by your own admission many years after (and for which I have [never] reproached you) you had been seduced and provincially outcast. I sensed this the night we slept together first for you're a poor bluffer and I loved you—romantically—like your mother, for your beauty + defiant intelligence; but unlike her I wanted to make it useful. I failed, as she did, but my intentions were a hell of lot purer and since you could have left me at any time I'd like to discover the faintest basis for your family's accusation that I drove you crazy. In so far as it was the conscious work of man, that old witch drove you crazy. You were "crazy" in the ordinary sense before I met you. I rationalized your eccentricities and made a sort of creation of you. But dont fret—if it hadn't been you perhaps I would have worked with more stable material. My talent and my decline is the norm. Your degeneracy is the deviation

(end of thought)

[1] This letter, which was not sent, survives in a nine-page holograph draft and a secretarial typescript.

[2] Gossip magazine.

TO: Sheilah Graham Wire. Princeton University

ENCINO CALIF 1939 NOV 9 AM 3 47

THE COUNTRY IS BEHIND YOU NOW STOP JUST RELAX AND DO YOUR HOUR[1] STOP NEWS JUST REACHED HERE ENGLAND IS AT WAR STOP IS DENIED AND AFFIRMED BY LOCAL PRESS SEEMS INCREDIBLE SIGNED CONSTANCE CAROL HEDDA STOP I STILL MISS YOU TERRIBLY

SCOTT.

[1] Sheilah Graham was on a speaking tour.

TO: Chairman of Cottage Club Elections Committee TL(CC), 1 p. Princeton University

Encino, California

November

13

1939

Dear Sir:—

To many Cottage men of my generation it has been a source of regret that Baltimore (once almost as much a Cottage Town as St. Louis) now contributes so many of their boys to Ivy and Cap and Gown. This was frankly for several reasons—in the post war years a few prominent Baltimoreans, who were graduates of Princeton and of Cottage, succeeded in drinking themselves out of life and sight and Cottage was quite unjustly blamed for the business. The truth of the matter was that in those days the Baltimore boys were pretty sturdy drinkers before they headed northward. I'm told this has changed—but anyhow the origins of the charge are forgotten in Baltimore—but the prejudice remains.

Maryland will always be a great feeder for Princeton so I think such a prejudice is to be deplored. I lived in Maryland many years and made somewhat of a protegee of young Andrew Turnbull—used to take him and my daughter as moppets to the games from 1932 to 1935. I always took the children to the Cottage for lunch. Now of course if young Turnbull, a sophomore, is already tied up with some other group (I've never been really posted on the new system) then this letter is futile. But if he *isn't*, he might be an opening wedge to the Baltimore trade worthy of consideration. He was a brilliant kid and fearless, despite his small stature. He had strong convictions, not always popular ones, which kept him from being a leader at Gilman, but I believe he was very well liked at St. Andrews. He will make his mark somewhere, sometime, I believe, and carry on the tradition of a prominent Baltimore family. His father graduated from Johns Hopkins; his grandfather graduated from Princeton in the early seventies.

This kid should be a good organizer and a credit to any club. Will you kindly call on him? If he's sewed up for Cap, as might be the case, it's no use, because Pepper Constable was long his hero. Otherwise, I think it might turn out as valuable an interview for the club as for him.[1]

Humbly—and with Softly-Falling Grey Hairs,

[1] Turnbull—who became Fitzgerald's biographer—did not receive a bid from the Cottage Club.

TO: Gene Buck TL(CC), 1 p. Princeton University

November
14
1939

Dear Gene:—

Daughter is co-author of Vassar musical show. Has one piece which is spreading like wildfire through eastern colleges.[1] Like Brooks Bowman's Triangle piece "Love on a Dime" in 1933. (do you remember?)

Query: I am oddly unaware how she would get professional attention. Pictures are adamant against unknowns and probably think Vassar is an ointment anyhow. Have you any printed form telling her what to do with it? Or better still, could you recommend her to someone. If you can, I am enclosing an envelope addressed to her.

My God, how they grow up—I'd like to see yours now.

Your old friend,

5521 Amestoy Avenue
Encino, California

[1] Scottie's song was "The Right Person Won't Write" in *Guess Who's Here.*

FROM: Kenneth Littauer Wire. Princeton University

NEWYORK NY 232P 1939 NOV 28 PM 12 04

F SCOTT FITZGERALD

5521 AMESTOY AVE ENCINO CALIF

FRIST SIX THOUSAND PRETTY CRYPTIC THEREFORE DISAPPOINTING. BUT YOU WARNED US THIS MIGHT BE SO. CAN WE DEFER VERDICT UNTIL FURTHER DEVELOPMENT OF STORY? IF IT HAS TO BE NOW IT HAS TO BE NOW[1] REGARDS

KENNETH LITTAUER.

[1] Fitzgerald had sent the opening chapter of *The Last Tycoon,* but Littauer was unwilling to make an advance on the basis of this sample.

TO: Kenneth Littauer — Wire. New York Public Library

ENCINO CALIF NOV 28 1939 107P

NO HARD FEELINGS THERE HAS NEVER BEEN AN EDITOR WITH PANTS ON SINCE GEORGE LORIMER

SCOTT FITZGERALD.

422P

TO: Maxwell Perkins — Wire. Princeton University

VANNUYS CALIF 100P 1939 NOV 28 PM 4 56

PLEASE RUSH THE COPY AIR MAIL TO SATURDAY EVENING POST ATTENTION JOE BRUAN[1] STOP I GUESS THERE ARE NO GREAT MAGAZINES EDITORS LEFT ALWAYS YOURS

SCOTT FITZGERALD.

[1] Joseph Bryan. *The Saturday Evening Post* was unable to negotiate with Fitzgerald because the material in *The Last Tycoon* was considered too strong for the magazine.

FROM: Maxwell Perkins — Wire (typed draft). Princeton University

Nov. 29, 1939

A beautiful start. Stirring and new. Can wire you two hundred fifty and a thousand by January.[1]

Max.

[1] Perkins was making a personal loan to Fitzgerald—not an advance from Scribners on *The Last Tycoon.*

TO: Maxwell Perkins — Wire. Princeton University

VANNUYS CALIF 316P 1939 NOV 29 PM 6 44

THANK YOU WILL YOU GET THE PROSPECTUS I SENT COLLIERS HAVE IT RE-TYPED IN YOUR OFFICE AS IF IT HAD BEEN ORIGINALLY SENT TO YOU AND SEND IT TO THE POST. YOUR TELEGRAM WAS VERY ENCOURAGING ON A DAY THAT LOOKED RATHER BLACK. THE COLLIERS BUSINESS WAS WISH FULFILLMENT ANYHOW AS I HAVEN'T SEEN A PIECE OF FICTION IN THERE FOR SEVERAL YEARS THAT WOULD SERVE THE PURPOSE OF A SEARS ROEBUCK CATALOG. EVER YOURS

SCOTT.

TO: Maxwell Perkins Wire. Princeton University

VANNUYS CALIF 1939 NOV 29 PM 11 29

LELAND HAYWARD WILL CALL YOU TOMORROW PLEASE TRY TO SHOW HIM THE OUTLINE I SENT TO COLLIERS IN YOUR PRESENCE NOT BECAUSE I DISTRUST HAYWARD WHO IS AN OLD FRIEND BUT BECAUSE DISCRETION IS RARE AND NECESSARY IN THIS CASE POSSIBLY HE MIGHT MAKE A DEAL WITH THE STUDIO TO FINANCE THE WRITING OF SUCH A PICTURE BUT OF COURSE NOT WITH THE STUDIO IDENTIFIED WITH THE LEADING CHARACTER ASK HAYWARD TO COME AND SEE ME WHEN HE GETS BACK AND DONT TELL HIM HOW POOR I AM THIS WOULD SERIOUSLY INTERFERE WITH NEGOTIATIONS[1]

SCOTT.

1 Agent Hayward was unwilling to negotiate for Fitzgerald until the novel was completed.

TO: H. N. Swanson TL(CC), 1 p. Princeton University

November
29
1939

Dear Swanie:—

I didn't hear from you further about the radio work. Thanks anyhow for your interest. My destiny is probably not worth watching over, though, such as it is, I don't feel that you're sufficiently interested to continue as the watch-dog in the case.

So please consider this as officially terminating our business relations. I thank you for small favors in the past. Once you reviewed a book of mine in "College Humor." You said, "What would I give to write like that!" It was probably rather a thin dime, but you got what you wanted. And that's certainly your business. But so is my business my own, and I feel that I cannot do it with you any longer.

Sincerely
F. Scott Fitzgerald

5521 Amestoy Avenue
Encino, California

TO: Sheilah Graham

TLS, 1 p. Princeton University
Encino, California

December
2
1939

Dear Sheilah:

I went berserk in your presence and hurt you and Jean Steffan.[1] That's done.

But I said things too—awful things and they can to some extent be unsaid. They come from the merest fraction of my mind, as you must know—they represent nothing in my consciousness and very little in my subconscious. About as important and significant as the quarrels we used to have about England and America.

I don't think we're getting anywhere. I'm glad you no longer can think of me with either respect or affection. People are either good for each other or not, and obviously I am *horrible* for you. I loved with everything I had, but something was terribly wrong. You don't have to look far for the reason—I was it. Not fit for any human relation. I just *loved* you—you brought me everything. And it was very fine and chivalrous—and you.

I want to die, Sheilah, and in my own way. I used to have my daughter and my poor lost Zelda. Now for over two years your image is everywhere. Let me remember you up to the end which is very close. You are the finest. You are something all by yourself. You are too much something for a tubercular neurotic who can only be jealous and mean and perverse. I will have my last time with you, though you won't be here. It's not long now. I wish I could have left you more of myself. You can have the first chapter of the novel and the plan. I have no money but it might be worth something. Ask Hayward. I love you utterly and completely

I meant to send this longhand but I don't think it would be intelligible.

Scott

[1] Fitzgerald went on a bender after *Collier's* declined to make him an advance on the basis of the first chapter of *The Last Tycoon,* and Sheilah Graham broke off with him. Jean Steffan was a friend of Miss Graham's.

TO: Sheilah Graham
Early December 1939

ALS, 2 pp.[1] Princeton University
Encino, California

When I finally came to myself last Tuesday I found this,[2] which seems to be yours.

It is very quiet out here now. I went in your room this after noon and lay on your bed awhile, trying to see if you had left anything of yourself. There were some pencils and the electric pad that didn't work and the autumn out the window that won't ever be the same. Then I wrote down a lot of expressions of your face but one I cant bare to read, of the little girl who trusted me so and whom I loved more than anything in the world—and to whom I gave grief when I wanted to give joy. Some things should have told you I was extemporizing wildly—that anyone, including Scottie, should ever dare critisize you to me. It was all fever and liquor and sedatives—what nurses hear in any bad drunk case.

I'm glad you're rid of me. I hope you're happy and the last awful impression is fading a little till someday you'll say "he can't have been *that* black."

Goodbye, Shielo, I wont bother you any more.

Scott

[1] Possibly part of a longer letter.
[2] Unidentified.

TO: Leland Hayward TL(CC), 2 pp. Princeton University

December
6
1939

Dear Leland:—

Here's the information you wanted:[1]

1. Metro—I worked there longest, a little over a year and a half. I was very fond of Edwin Knopf who I think likes my work very much. Joe Mankiewicz asked me to come back and work with him, but our relations were so definitely unpleasant after he decided to rewrite "Three Comrades" himself that I don't think I could do it. I worked with Sidney Franklin on "The Women" and on "Madame Curie." Whether he would be interested in having me work for him again I don't know. Anyhow his boss, Bernie Hyman, quite definitely doesn't like me. I don't know why because I've scarcely exchanged two words with him. Nor do I know Mayer, Mannix or Katz except that at some time I've shaken hands with all three of them. Hunt and I reached a dead end on "The Women." We wore each other out. He liked the first part of a picture called "Infidelity" that I wrote so intensely that when the whole thing flopped I think he held it against me that I had aroused his hope so much and then had not been able to finish it. It may have been my fault—it may have been the fault of the story but the damage is done. John Considine is an old friend and I believe asked for me in midsummer during the time I was so ill, but I believe he has kind of slowed down lately and I don't think I'd like to work for him. There's another producer I hardly know whose name I can't remember now, but he was a young man and was

once Stromberg's assistant. I believe he was the producer of "These Glamor Girls." Merian Cooper and I once talked over a story. We get along very well personally, but his reputation among authors is that he is never able to make up his mind and I imagine that he wouldn't be quite the man though I'd just as soon work for him if he knows pretty much what he wants when we start off. The other producers there, Cohn, etc., I don't even know by sight. King Vidor who is a personal friend several times asked me what I was doing and talked about a picture we were going to do together sometime.

2. Paramount—I worked for Jeff Lazarus. I've been told that he has been fired and I know that he is at present in Europe but I liked him very much and we got along in fine style always. On the same picture I worked with Griffith who has always wanted to do "The Great Gatsby" over again as a talkie. I do not know Mr. Le Baron or Mr. Hornblow. I know Tony Veiller slightly and he was interested in having me work on Safari but at the time I wasn't interested in pictures. This again goes back to last June and July. I don't think I know anybody else at Paramount.

3. Twentieth Century Fox—I met Harry Joe Brown. Don't think I know anyone else.

4. R.K.O. Radio—Don't think I know a soul.

5. Universal—Some producer asked for me one day when I was finishing a story but I've forgotten his name and the next day when I was ready to report to him and talk it over he had gone on vacation. My relations with Stahl were just a little too difficult so there's no use trying anything there.

6. United Artists—Wanger is out absolutely. Goldwyn I know nothing about. Sam Wood and I had always gotten along before, but during this week that I worked there on "Raffles" everything got a little strained and I don't think that he would welcome me as a collaborator. That seems to cover everyone I know at United Artists. Eddie Knopf and I have always been friends but I have no idea how much power he has there and my impression is that it is comparatively little. However, if such is not the case I think I'd rather work with him than any man I've met here.

7. Columbia—I don't know a soul except that I think that Sam Marx is there and I always thought of Sam as a rather dull fellow though very nice.

8. Selznick International—I find this studio the pleasantest studio that I have worked in (I was on Gone With the Wind about eight or nine days) but what Dave thinks of me I haven't any idea. I know that I was on the list of first choice writers on "Rebecca" but that may have been Hitchcock's doing. I think that Dave is probably under the impression that I am a novelist first and can't get the idea as to what pictures are about. This impression is still from back in 1921 when he wanted me to submit an original idea for Elaine Hammerstein.

9. Warner Bros.—The Warner Bros. I don't know personally though they once bought a picture right from me in the "Beautiful and Damned." I have talked to Bryan Foy on the telephone, but of course a quickie is exactly what I rather don't want to write.

Whatever company made "In Name Only" also asked for my services last July, but that was when I was sick and had to turn down offers.

I think that pretty well covers everything and, Leland, I would rather have $1000. or $750., without being rushed along and pushed around than go into a nervous breakdown at $1500.

Ever yours,

5521 Amestoy Avenue
Encino, California

[1] Fitzgerald was seeking free-lance screenwriting assignments while working on *The Last Tycoon.*

TO: Editors of *The Saturday Evening Post* TL(CC), 1 p. Princeton University

December
6
1939

Dear Sirs:—

Another job prevented me from getting as far on with this revise as I had intended. However, this additional thirteen hundred words introduces my heroine and should give you an idea of the "climate" of the story. The only thing I can think of is to push along with it little by little on Sundays until I have enough to enable you to make a tentative decision, but I felt I wanted you to get a glimpse at my leading girl.

Cecelia is a sort of juvenile in the old fashioned use of the term. She is my device for telling the story and though she has adventures of her own she is not one of the characters I am primarily interested in.

Please be discreet about the idea because I think it's one of those naturals that almost anybody could do only I'd like to be the one.

Sincerely
F. Scott Fitzgerald

5521 Amestoy Avenue
Encino, California

TO: Arnold Gingrich TL(CC), 1 p. Princeton University

December
19
1939

Dear Arnold:—

You have already paid $150. for this.[1] Frankly, I don't know how good it is. If you think it's worth $300., I could certainly use the balance and please remember by telegraph to the Bank of America, Culver City. At the same time wire me if you still want more Pat Hobby's. I can go on with them.

On the other hand I have a couple of other short pieces in mind. I'd like to do two or three for you within the next week to cover me over Christmas as I've been sick in bed again and gotten way behind.

Best wishes always,

P.S. I felt in spite of the title being appropriate to the season it was rather too bad to begin the Pat Hobby series with that story[2] because it characterizes him in a rather less sympathetic way than most of the others. Of course, he's a complete rat but it seems to make him a little sinister which he essentially is not. Do you intend to use the other stories in approximately the order in which they were written?

5521 Amestoy Avenue
Encino, California

[1] Probably "Two Old-Timers," *Esquire* (March 1941), which was posthumously published.

[2] "Pat Hobby's Christmas Wish."

TO: Marguerite Ridgeley[1] TL(CC), 1 p. Princeton University

December
19
1939

Dear Marguerite:—

It was damn sweet of you to write me that letter. I guess it was inevitable that Scottie would be somewhat Baltimorean because those adolescent years were so important. I had always assured her she was a big rugged middle-westerner like me and someday I would take her back to the Falls of Minneaha and let her dance with Hiawatha by the light of the Minnesota moon—but it worked out differently. It was nice of you to write me. It gave me a vivid little picture of her that night.

As for the dress, I made every stitch of it with my own hands. The ruching around the neck and collar-bone came from a fichu worn by Mrs.

Francis Scott Key the night of repeal. The sequins and the *petite polonaisse* at the back (rear) had been kicking around the family for years and I wasn't going to stand it anymore so I tacked it on with a bit of basting at the last moment as she went out the door thinking—"There, there—the child is launched at last! Oh, if young Lord Molyneux will only look at her he can have her for twelve thousand bucks a year and a mere pittance to me so I can have my drop of port of an evening. Out she went, my little one, propelled by the foot that had once sent kick after kick over the goal post for dear old Princeton and if she ever pulls that stuff of coming back with a baby in her arms—well, Marguerite, I wouldn't do it again for all the whiskey in the magazine advertisements.

Seriously, Marguerite, I wish you would tell me more of Marjorie,[2] of the music. It's all very confusing this career business. Just when I thought that I wouldn't go in for the current nonsense that every child who could turn a white paper into a gray one was a young Whistler, and had written Scottie that her chances of being a successful professional writer were one in a thousand, she turns about and sells a story to the New Yorker![3]

I hope Marjorie will turn out to have what Cole Porter called "listening in advance." He had an instinct about his music. In writing what he himself wants to hear he anticipates other peoples wants. Of course I know Marjorie's aims are more ambitious as to the sort of thing she wants to write. I wish you would write me sometime at more length about her.

Ever your friend,

5521 Amestoy Avenue
Encino, California

[1] A Baltimore friend of Fitzgerald's.
[2] Scottie's friend Marjorie Ridgeley.
[3] "A Wonderful Time," *The New Yorker* (19 October 1940), by-lined Frances Scott.

TO: Arnold Gingrich — Wire. Princeton University

ENCINO CALIF 221P DEC 22 1939

THAT YOU WIRE A HUNDRED ADVANCE ON REALLY EXCELLENT STORY TO REACH YOU TUESDAY SO I CAN BUY TURKEY IS PRESENT CHRISTMAS WISH OF

PAT HOBBY FITZGERALD.

TO: Arnold Gingrich TLS, 1 p. Princeton University

December
25
1939

Dear Arnold:—

Please wire money. Thanks. Did you know that last story[1] was the way 'The Big Parade' was really made King Vidor pushed John Gilbert in a hole—believe it or not.

Your chattel
Scott

5521 Amestoy Avenue
Encino, California

[1] "Two Old-Timers."

TO: Marjorie Sayre Brinson TLS(CC), 2 pp. Princeton University

December
27
1939

Dear Margery:

Enough time has passed so that I can write you calmly in relation to that telegram. After Zelda had written me fourteen straight letters, some from the hospital and some from places downtown telling me about the $50. which was miraculously to make her well I simply blew up. The telegram was ill-advised and ill-worded, but I thought that from my angle you were taking advantage of my illness to force us into something which both the medical authorities and I thought would be disastrous.

If you will calmly reconstruct Zelda's recent visits to Montgomery, you will remember that in the winter of 1931 she got a severe asthma, that after I left her in the best and most comfortable circumstances to go to California, she had such a severe setback that when I returned at Christmas time she was scarcely the same girl and shortly after had to go to Hopkins for three months.

Twice she has returned since and each time the asthma has attacked her violently, something that has never happened in either North Carolina or Florida. Of course she has enjoyed Montgomery and always I sent her all the money she wired for even though it was by no means in the budget. But any evidence that Montgomery by itself did operate as a curative factor or that the sudden change from a life of order and discipline to one of complete laissez-faire would allow her even to hold her ground—any evidence of that is absolutely lacking. Therefore I could not help considering those continual prods about the ticket in relation to the whole situation and especially to your mother's conviction that if Zelda was ever ill she is well now. Zelda is not a person who has gotten over an acute pneumonia but one who, so to speak, has permanently less than one lung. If either your mother or Rosalind had ever been able to think of it this way there would have been much trouble and bitterness averted. That Zelda is able to conduct herself charmingly for several weeks even under quite trying conditions has been demonstrated. That such a fact entitles us to the rashest of all experiments, her complete release, is not predicated upon that fact in the mind of any alienist in the world.

I want to send her home as soon as I can for a visit, a short one, not only because this is the asthma season in Alabama, but because I have been having the damndest physical and financial struggle of my life since about mid-August. If I work, I cough and if I don't work I lie awake all night worrying. I finally made up my mind to Hell with it and I am trying to get along on a sort of skeptic's Christian Science. It looked for a while as if Scottie wasn't going to be able to get to Vassar which would have been a pity as she may end by making rather a record there. She has already sold one story to the New Yorker which is pretty smart for 18. At the very least I am going to send her to Asheville to spend a few nights with her mother next week. The next thing will be to arrange Zelda's visit South. This must be handled delicately because of course I am in arrears with Carroll and from his point of view it would seem a luxury. However, I know how much such a visit will mean to your mother and you can have at least the consolation that if it had been Christmas it would be over now and this way it is still to be enjoyed.

This letter is not an atonement for that telegram. Though it was inexcusably rude, there is a point of torture beyond which a sick and struggling man cannot be driven and Zelda's letters had begun to amount to that. But we have so many kind memories in the past it is sad to think of it all ending that way in a burst of temper and cross purposes.

With sincerest love to you all,

Scott

5521 Amestoy Avenue
Encino, California

FROM: Zelda Fitzgerald ALS, 2 pp. Princeton University
1939 Highland Hospital, Asheville, North Carolina

Dear D.O:

It rains, and sleets; and is indeed as malevolent a time as ever attacked. The hills are steeped in Cosmic regrets and the valleys are flooded with morose and aimless puddles.

However, the stores bloom and blossom and ingratiates themselves with the brighter of spring-times and the newest of aspirations. The drugstores are still fragrant of chocolate and aromatic of all sorts of soaps and bottled miracles. This town is so redolent of hushed rendez-vous: I always think of you when I wait in Faters for the bus or hang around Eckerts before a movie—or even after a movies, thus making orgy.

"The Hunchback of Notre Dame" is the most magnificent fusion of music and action and the signifigance of lines that I have seen. The acting is far more than usually compelling: and the orchestration does not confine itself to the music but includes the whole performance.

There does not seem to be any news: which some people think of in terms of an advantage, but which, to me, presents itself vaguely in terms of disaster. Well anyway we're better off than the Finns + the Russians.

I cant understand about your stories. The school that you started and the vogue which you began are still dictating the spiritual emulation of too many people for your work to be irrelevant: and certainly the tempo of the times ought to bring you some success.

Would it be a good idea if you tried Harold Ober again? That seems to me a most sensible way of handling the situation: Ober knows so much better than anybody else how to handle your work.

Devotedly
Zelda

Peter Liddle might be a lucky nom-de-plume.

TO: Dr. Harry Nardini
c. 1940

TL(CC), 1 p.[1] Princeton University
Hollywood, California

Dear Dr. N——:

I will be on my feet in a day or so and I would very much like to have you here to put you across my knee and spank this dope phobia out of your system. Some day you're going to make that accusation against a patient who really *uses* it and he's going to stick you with a syringe which will not be imaginary—probably in the back, out of respect to your Sicilian customs.

I have to thank you for keeping me sick for a year with your digitalin and think you should send in a small contribution to your competitor Capone in Alcatraz, who also unfortunately escaped the earthquake at Messina in 1902.

I would be "glad to see you in my office any time."

Sincerely

[1] Fitzgerald wrote at the head of this copy: "Answered [corres]."

FROM: Maxwell Perkins

TLS, 2 pp. Princeton University

Jan. 2, 1940

Dear Scott:

I hope you got safely through the so-called holidays. I feel pretty exhausted though I didn't do much but read manuscripts.—Only one party.

Now these drafts are raising Cain. I think we have at last got them straightened out, but they wouldn't take a Connecticut bank check, and I had to do a lot of shifting things around. But Scott, do remember that I have done all I can for the present. There was one draft more than I expected at that. I am still in debt in that matter I told you of, though not much; and the bequest I told you of begins to seem somewhat improbable. It appears that the sum was badly invested some twenty-five years ago, and at least has seriously diminished. I just have to tell you about it because of the way things are.

Always yours,
Max

improbable. It appears that the sum was badly invested some twenty-five years ago, and at least has seriously diminished. I just have to tell you about it because of the way things are.

Always yours,

Mac

To Mr. F. Scott Fitzgerald

TO: Maxwell Perkins
3 January 1940

TLS, 1 p. Princeton University

January
3
1939

Dear Max:—

I'm sorry that your kind impulse should have brought trouble down upon you. If it is any consolation the effect on my morale of getting your letter offering to lend me $1000. was tremendous and has already born the most tangible results—enabled me to get off a piece that should bring in something substantial and to approach the matter of working here with much more confidence.

Now that I learn that you may not get the bequest I have put you on the first list to be paid with one other friend and the groceryman. What a mess the drafts must have caused, my God! But it still adds up in my calculation to $1000.—unless you meant that the $250. you first sent me before the $1000. was intended to have been part of it. Here is the account.

On or about November 29 you sent me $250. and spoke of $1000. more which you could lend me before the first of the year. To my debit there stands:

1 draft—	$205.
1 draft—	150.
1 draft—	122.44
12/14 you sent—	150.00
12/28 your check—	372.56
total	$1000.00

I have checked with the bank and find that this is right. But I'm sorry you were disappointed in the inheritance and that the drafts should have caused you trouble on perhaps a busy day and in the middle of the holidays. I know you must feel a little like Scottie makes me feel, sometimes.

Ever yours, gratefully, apologetically and a good deal more,

Scott

5521 Amestoy Avenue
Encino, California

TO: Maxwell Perkins — ALS, 1 p. Princeton University
Before 9 January 1940 — Encino, California

Dear Max:

Beneath the surface of your letter and in the cartoon of the man with coco cola I detect a certain perturbation. What happened the first part of December or thereabouts was that I quarrelled with S.G.,[1] and then encountered a New Orleans prick named —— from *Colliers* who told me my novel was no good. Christ, how did I think the editorial staff that goes for the servant girl romances of Kathleen Norris could ever like any serious effort of mine!

That was all—after about five heavy days in which I stayed close to home, S. G. and I were reconciled. Even while I was tight I wrote a short Esquire piece.

And that's all. I havn't had a drop for four weeks tomorrow—no question of virtue. It has come to make me deathly sick—even a single drink.

Scott

[1] Sheilah Graham.

FROM: Maxwell Perkins — TL(CC), 1 p. Princeton University

Jan. 9, 1940

Dear Scott:

I am not a subtle fellow. I am a simple fellow. There was nothing implied by that drawing. I thought you would admire the art.—And the man was not meant to be you. It was meant to be me, and to indicate my own good resolutions. Don't read any hidden meanings into what I write or draw. I only wanted to reveal to you *another* talent.

Always yours,

TO: Maxwell Perkins — TLS, 1 p. Princeton University

January
13
1940

Dear Max:—

I thought drafts were something that everybody knew about except me. I had to ask somebody how they were drawn. The fact that you did not know about them completes my disillusion as to New York and New Yorkers. It represents the utmost in unsophistication.

But I shall never draw a draw a draft again, nor even sit in one, nor get in the one they're going to have for the next war.

Ever your friend,
Scott

P.S. I *insist* on reading meanings into things. Do you remember when I accused you of sending me the memoirs of General Grant because you thought I was a failure?

5521 Amestoy Avenue
Encino, California

TO: Arnold Gingrich — TL(CC), 1 p. Princeton University

January
15
1940

Dear Arnold:—

I don't get a word from you except in telegrams. Please do take time to answer this if you possibly can. You have one story of mine "Between Planes"[1] which doesn't belong to the Pat Hobby series. It is a story that I should hate to see held up for a long time. If your plans are to publish it only at the end of the Pat Hobby series would you consider trading it back to me for the next Pat Hobby story? I might be able to dispose of it elsewhere. Otherwise I very strongly wish that you could schedule it at least as early as to follow the first half dozen Pat Hobbys.

The weakest of the Hobby stories seem to me to have been "Two Old-Timers" and "Mightier Than The Sword."[2] If you could hold those out of type for a while I might be able either to improve them later or else send others in their place. You remember I did this in the case of a story sent you a few years ago.

Ever your friend,

5521 Amestoy Avenue
Encino, California

[1] "Three Hours Between Planes," *Esquire* (July 1941).
[2] *Esquire* (March and April 1941).

TO: Leland Hayward TL(CC), 2 pp. Princeton University

January
16
1940

Dear Leland:—

Another week having gone I make the assumption that the Kitty Foyle deal is cold.[1] I am rather disappointed as I know there are three or four dull jobs for every attractive one but thanks for trying. I am sufficiently acclimated to Hollywood to realize how uncertain anything is until a contract is signed.

Looking at it from a long view the essential mystery still remains, and you would be giving me the greatest help of all if you can find out why I am in the doghouse. Having dinner the other day at the Brown Derby I ran into Swanson and he began talking about jobs, mentioning that Kenneth McKenna had wanted me at Metro and why hadn't I answered his wire about it. I told him again that you were my agent now. That was all—nothing unpleasant. But it reminded me that both Knopf and McKenna who were my scenario heads for nine-tenths of the time that I have been employed in pictures seem to want me, yet when it comes to the question of a job there's always some barrier.

Once Bud Shulberg told me that, while the story of an official blacklist is a legend, there is a kind of cabal that goes on between producers around a backgammon table, and I have an idea that some such sinister finger is upon me. I know also that if a man stays away from pictures deliberately like I did from March to July he is forgotten, or else people think there's something the matter with him. And I know when that ball starts rolling badly, as it did in the case of Ted Paramore and a few other pinks, it can roll for a long time. But I have the feeling that there is some unfavorable word going around about me. I don't know whether a man like Edington would refer to Dave Selznick who thinks I should "write originals," or perhaps to Mannix who would say that I didn't come through for Hunt Stromberg, or to Bernie Hyman. I only know that I have a strong intuition that all is not well with my reputation and I'd like to know what is being said or not said. . . .[2]

And if you do, wouldn't it be well when another offer comes up for you to tell the producer *directly* that certain people don't like me? That I didn't get along with some of the big boys at Metro? And refer them to people who *do* like me like Knopf, Sidney Franklin and I think, Jeff Lazarus. Isn't that better than having them start out with enthusiasm like Hempstead[3] and then find out that in certain quarters I am considered a lame duck or hard to get along with. Or even that I drink, though there were only three days while I was on salary in pictures when I ever touched a drop. One of those was in New York and two were on Sundays.

In any case, it seems to me to be a necessity to find out what the underground says of me. I don't think we'll get anywhere till we *do* find out, and until you can steer any interested producers away from whoever doesn't believe in me and toward the few friends that I've made. This vague sense of competence unused and abilities unwanted is rather destructive to the morale. It would be much much better for me to give up pictures forever and leave Hollywood. When you've read this letter will you give me a ring and tell me what you think?

Ever your friend,

5521 Amestoy Avenue
Encino, California
STate 4-0578

[1] Fitzgerald did not work on this movie.
[2] Twelve words omitted by the editor.
[3] David Hempstead, RKO producer.

FROM: Arnold Gingrich — TLS, 1 p. Princeton University

January 18, 1940

Dear Scott:

While I liked the "Between Planes" story very much I didn't figure on using it before the Pat Hobby series had run its course. I don't like to break the continuity of a series. So maybe it might be better, at that, to let it go elsewhere, just switching it against the next Pat Hobby story. But if there is any hitch in getting it placed satisfactorily elsewhere then I would like to buy it back again. But there'd be no hurry about it as we probably can keep Pat Hobby going through 1940.

I must confess a rather special weakness for the "Two Old Timers." That one seems to me to be anything but weak. I particularly recall the moment when the guard, speaking of how soon they may be out, differentiates between how soon the ex-star may be let out as opposed to how long poor old Pat may be held.

I have been figuring on running these in the order in which they were received, as that was the way you wanted them after the Christmas story which was stuck into the January issue for reasons of topicality. But if you would much prefer a reshuffled sequence, let me know and I'll be glad to follow it.

Cordially yours,
Arnold

P.S. My own particular favorite of all the Pat Hobby stories is "Boil Some Water, Lots of It."[1] In fact, in or out of the Pat Hobby series, that's one of my all-time favorite stories, both for structure and for content.

[1] *Esquire* (March 1940).

FROM: Zelda Fitzgerald
Postmarked 13 February 1940

Signed card (with holograph postscript).
Princeton University
Highland Hospital, Asheville, North Carolina

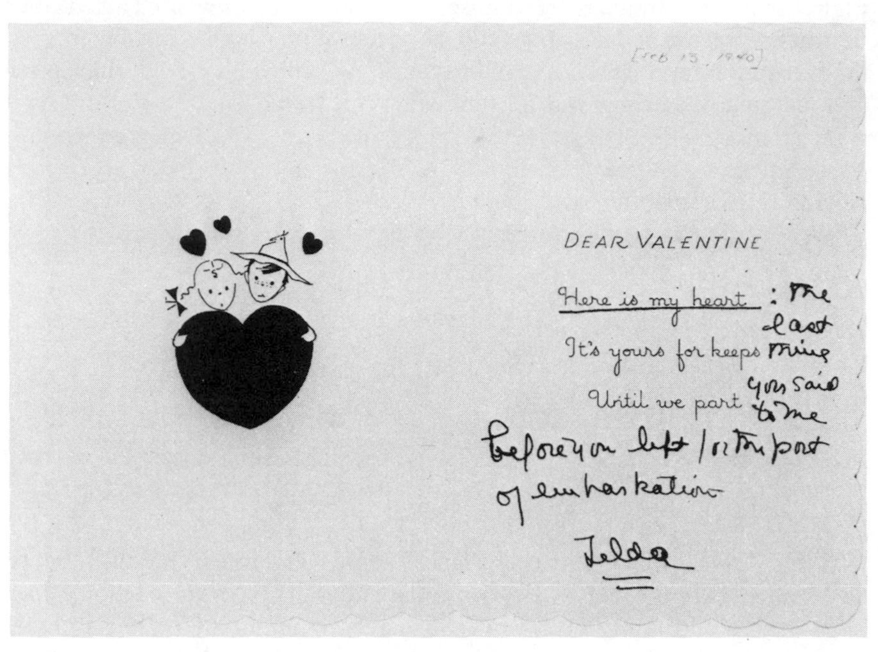

[Feb 13, 1940]

DEAR VALENTINE

Here is my heart : the last
It's yours for keeps thing
Until we part you said to me
before you left for the port
of embarkation

Zelda

TO: Robert Bennett[1]

TL, 1 p.[1] Bruccoli
February
21
1940

Dear Mr. Bennett:—

The Plato and Shaw were excellent. On the other hand, the type is too fine in this copy of "Crime and Punishment." I will just have to wait till a good clear type turns up. Also as I told you on the phone this is not Kipling's Collected Verse to 1918, but simply some casual collection made about 1911.

Again thanks for the other two books.

Yours
F. Scott Fitzgerald

5521 Amestoy Avenue
Encino, California

P.S. Am sending books under separate cover.

[1] Associated with Holmes Book Co., a Los Angeles bookstore.

TO: Arnold Gingrich TL(CC), 1 p. Princeton University

February
23
1940

Dear Arnold:—

As you know Edward J. O'Brien wants "Design in Plaster" for his anthology.[1] Also Edward Everett Horton[2] has approached me with the idea of making the Pat Hobbys into a theatrical vehicle for him. So my stuff is getting a little attention.

I intended to write you before about my nom de plume, John Darcy.[3] My suggestion is that the first story be "Between Planes"; the next, the enclosed "Dearly Beloved";[4] third "The Woman from 21"[5] and if you happen to like this poem, "Beloved Infidel,"[6] and will seriously guard Mr. Darcy's identity, it might interest your readers. It has a touch of Ella Wheeler Wilcox about it and some shadows of Laurence Hope and the early Kipling.

With best wishes always,

P.S. There will be another Pat Hobby on soon. I have written half of one but didn't like it. The enclosed story, "Dearly Beloved" is so short you can have it for $200., but I wish you would wire the money.

5521 Amestoy Avenue
Encino, California

1 *The Best Short Stories 1940.*

2 Character actor who was Fitzgerald's landlord at "Belly Acres" in Encino.

3 Since the Pat Hobby stories were appearing monthly in *Esquire*, Fitzgerald wanted to publish other stories under the pseudonym John Darcy, which was never used. See Fitzgerald's 7 February letter to Gingrich in *Letters*. One Fitzgerald story, "On an Ocean Wave," appeared posthumously under the pseudonym Paul Elgin in *Esquire* (February 1941).

4 Gingrich declined "Dearly Beloved"; it was first published in the *Fitzgerald/Hemingway Annual 1969.*

5 *Esquire* (June 1941).

6 The poem, addressed to Sheilah Graham, was declined by *Esquire*; it was first published in *Beloved Infidel* by Sheilah Graham and Gerold Frank.

TO: Phil Berg–Bert Allenberg Agency[1] TL(CC), 1 p. Princeton University

February
23
1940

Messers Berg, Dozier and Allen

Following is the data I promised—from August 1937 when I arrived here on a six months Metro contract.

1. Two weeks on *Yank at Oxford* with Jack Conway and Michael Balcan. They used two scenes of mine.

2. Six months with Joe Mankiewicz on *Three Comrades*. Received the first credit. My contract was renewed with rise from $1000. to $1250.

3. Three months with Hunt Stromberg on "Infidelity" when we struck censorship problem and project was abandoned. Up to this point Hunt seemed highly pleased with my work and about then Joe Mankiewicz asked for me on another picture but I chose to stick with Hunt.

4. Five months with Stromberg on *The Women*, first working with Sidney Franklin and then with Don Stuart. Hunt was difficult to please on this and toward the end Don and I lost interest.

5. Three months with Sidney Franklin on *Madame Curie*. We were bucking Bernie Hyman's preconception of the thing as a love story. Hyman glanced at what we had done and shelved the whole project. Franklin had been very interested up to that time.

6. There had been many offers to borrow me by other studios. When Knopf told me that my contract was not to be renewed I went directly to Dave Selznick for *G.W.T.W.* Things were in a mess there and I went out after two or three weeks.

7. At this point I wanted to quit for a while—health bad and I was depressed about the Metro business. But Swanson argued me into a job with Wanger on *Winter Carnival* with a rise to $1500. This was a mistake. I blew up after a trip to Dartmouth and got flu and got drunk and walked out.

8. After a month's rest I took a job with Jeff Lazarus on *Air Raid*. We progressed for a month and then the picture was put aside for *Honeymoon in Bali* and I went to Cuba.

9. I found in the East, that I was sicker than I had thought and I came back here in May to lie around in bed till my health picked up. I had the refusal during these months of *In Name Only*, *Rebecca* and half a dozen others, but by July, when I wanted to work again, the offers seemed to stop. The first thing that came along was a week's job with Stahl on some vaguely projected original (at $1500.).

10. In September Eddie Knopf wanted me for *Raffles*. They were already shooting and I came in on a violent quarrel between Goldwyn and Wood.[2] I refer you to Eddie Knopf on the matter. Somewhere around

this time Harry Joe Brown called me over to Twentieth Century Fox on a Sonja Heine picture but it was apparently only for a day's pumping. Anyhow save for a nibble on the part of Hempstead for Kitty Foyle, no one has shown interest since then.

Such is the story of two and one half years.

5521 Amestoy Avenue
Encino, California

[1] The Berg-Allenberg Agency represented Fitzgerald in Hollywood after he left the Swanson and Hayward agencies. William Dozier was head of the story department.

[2] Director Sam Wood.

TO: Scottie Fitzgerald TL(CC), 2 pp. Princeton University

February
26
1940

Dearest Scottie:—

I am sorry you've got the February blues. Schoolmasters have told me that in small schools they look forward to February as a time of horror. I understand about the prom. Isn't it a question of your popularity turning on you—most people assume that a popular girl has surely been asked and are afraid to try. By this time you will either have gone or not gone and are no longer staying awake at night over it.

The Alumni Weekly has repercussions of the Princeton editorials. I have been very interested.[1]

With my own career at low ebb I have been hesitant to write you—because what at least carried financial pressure before hasn't that, much less any trace of authority. There are a couple of things though that have preyed in my mind come Maundy Thursday to wit: that the reason you missed the Messelaeni is because you were a little Walker School about it. "I didn't know enough about politics" etc—what it really means is you are in the midst of a communist dominated student movement at Vassar which you do nothing about. The movement will go both up and down in the next few years. You can join it or let it simmer but you have never even considered it outside of classroom work—except to say, perhaps, that your father is rather far to the left. It would be foolish ever to make enemies of those girls. Silly and fanatical as they seem now some of them are going to be forces in the future of that section. You must have some politeness toward ideas. You can neither cut through, nor challenge nor beat the fact that there is an organized movement over the world before which you and I as individuals are less than the dust. Some time when you feel very brave and defiant and haven't been invited to one particular college function read the terrible chapter in Das Kapital on *The Working Day*, and see if you are ever quite the same.

I do not want you to lose your gayety ever—or ever your seriousness.

Do you know any lawyers? Ask somebody at the next Y.H.P. function who's gone on to law at Harvard. Then ask a law student who are the top prospects for the Editorship of the *Harvard Law Review*. Why not meet the lawyers. But for Christ's sake meet the people, meet the communists at Vassar and at least be politician enough to be absolutely *dumb* about politics and if you [ ] make them on their side.[2]

P.S. I can't accentuate this too much as you move in such varying worlds so at the risk of being a bore I beg you once more to consider politics as being a religion, something that you can only discuss freely among those of the same general attitude as your own. With other people you will find yourself in intolerable arguments—friendships are being made and broken over questions of policy, a state of things which is liable to increase month by month. It is all white hot and the long pinchers of tact can be very useful.

1403 N. Laurel Avenue
Hollywood, California

[1] Articles on changing the Princeton club system in the *Princeton Alumni Weekly* (16 and 23 February).

[2] The bottom of this page is torn off, removing words on the last line.

TO: Edward Everett Horton TL(CC), 1 p. Princeton University

March
1
1940

Dear Messers. Horton:—

Reading over the Pat Hobby material I think someone could put together a play out of it. For the first act there is a situation in the question as to whether or how he will get a job and he might very well get it through his sick wife as in the story, "No Harm Trying." Act II would probably be concerned as to whether he will make good and his hilarious failure. In Act III, I see him as a desperate man. The question might now be whether he is to go to jail for blackmail, perhaps following the story, "Pat Hobby's Christmas Wish."

As I said before I do not feel capable of undertaking the job, but I'd be delighted if your eastern managers can hit on a playwrite who would be interested. There are doubtless young men out here who would be both competent and eager but how to uncover them is beyond me.

With best wishes for the continued success of the tour.

Believe me, most sincerely yours

5521 Amestoy Avenue
Encino, California

TO: Dr. Robert S. Carroll TL(CC), 1 p. Princeton University

March
7
1940

Dear Dr. Carroll:

Zelda wrote me, without any criticism or complaint that she is confined to barracks. I am terribly grieved about this. I have been able to do so very little for her for ten months that it made me happy to think that she had earned a little freedom.

I do not know what her offense was. I do know though, that she was utterly determined not to abuse her liberty; that it made her letters much more alive; and that in the last fortnight a note of deep despondency has crept in.

I do hope that the period of discipline will be shortened as much as is consistent with your policy. These months have meant for her a curtailment of most other privileges and treats—the sight of her mother, etc. It makes me sad that I can't help.

Sincerely, and gratefully
F. Scott Fitzgerald

5521 Amestoy Avenue
Encino, California

TO: Dr. Robert S. Carroll TL(CC), 1 p. Princeton University

March
8
1940

Dear Dr. Carroll:

Your letter was a complete surprise, but of course I am delighted that you feel the way you do.[1] The news that she had been home alone in December was a complete surprise to me though as you know I would have been in agreement if you had ever thought before that a journey without a nurse was desirable. I have written Mrs. Sayre telling her of your letter and my agreement with it.

You have been magnificent about the whole thing and I am completely sensible of my financial and moral obligation to you. I may say privately that while I have always advocated her partial freedom my pleasure in this is qualified by an inevitable worry. Still one would rather have the worry than the continual sadness added to by her family's attitude. The attitude will continue but it will be on a different basis and easier to disregard.

I certainly hope that you will be able to write Mrs. Sayre at length about her responsibilities in the matter and about Zelda *doing* something. I still wish there was someone there a little keener and younger, but since I am utterly unprepared to take on the job again I suppose it is lucky that there is any sort of home where she will at least be loved and cherished. The possibility of dissipation frightens me more than anything else—which I suppose is poetic justice.

Again gratefully and sincerely yours,

5521 Amestoy Avenue
Encino, California

[1] Zelda Fitzgerald was allowed a furlough from Highland Hospital and was planning to stay with her mother in Montgomery. This arrangement held until her death in 1948; she returned to the hospital voluntarily when she anticipated relapses.

TO: Zelda Fitzgerald — TL(CC), 1 p. Princeton University

March
8
1940

Dearest Zelda:—

It is wonderful to be able to write you this. Dr. Carroll has for the first time and at long last agreed that perhaps you shall try to make a place for yourself in the world. In other words, that you can go to Montgomery the first of April and remain there indefinitely or as long as you seem able to carry on under your own esteem.

So after four years of Dr. Carroll's regime interrupted by less than twenty scattered weeks away from the hospital, you will have the sense of being your own boss. Already I can share your joy and I know how Scottie will feel.

I am sorry your entrance will not be into a brighter world. I have no real finances yet and won't until I get a job. We have to live on those little pieces in Esquire and you know how little they pay. Scottie speaks of getting a job in Lord and Taylor's this summer but I do not want her to do that for all sorts of reasons. Maybe by the time you get home things will be brighter. So there we are.

With dearest love,

5521 Amestoy Avenue
Encino, California

TO: Mrs. A. D. Sayre TL(CC), 1 p. Princeton University

March
8
1940

Dear Mrs. Sayre:—

This morning I have a letter from Dr. Carroll in which he suggests for the first time that Zelda try life in Montgomery. This is a complete about-face for him, but I do not think that his suggestion comes from any but the most sincere grounds. If it was being influenced by any financial consideration he would have suggested a state hospital in Alabama. So he must believe she now has a good chance of standing on her own.

I feel as if an enormous moral burden had lifted from my shoulders. To be able to think that Zelda will have a life in the world for the first time since 1933 will be a joy indeed and if my streak of financial difficulties has brought this about it may turn out to have been a lucky thing. I think Scottie, too, will feel a terrific relief and I know how much it means to you there.

I am in pretty good health and there is a very good chance I may get a job next week, working on my own story, "Babylon Revisited." I will, of course, send Zelda everything that I can afford for a modest life. Scottie and I have been living on the Esquire stories which bring in very little indeed. But things must get better.

Dr. Carroll says in part, "What do you think of letting her go home, say about the first of April giving the mother an outline of certain danger signs which, should they appear, indicate a tendency to relapse. Thus we let the family share the responsibilities as long as all is well. *She can return to the hospital from Montgomery at any time need should develop,* and I am quite sure the mother will make every effort to cooperate intelligently."

The news about the trip home in December was a complete surprise to me. For two years Dr. Carroll had insisted entirely upon the nurse accompanying her. I would not have made any objection had the suggestion of a solo trip come from him. My one fear was that in case I went against his wishes he would not take her back in an emergency—a fear which is removed by the sentence underlined above.

Well, all good luck to the experiment. It may be some time before I can get East myself, and of course I do not want her to come out here under these harassed circumstances. I am getting in touch with Dr. Carroll and with Zelda about the details.

5521 Amestoy Avenue
Encino, Calif.

TO: Scottie Fitzgerald — TLS, 1 p. Princeton University

March
8
1940

Dearest Scottie:

Delighted to be able to tell you that your mother is going home in April for an indefinite stay. A letter came from Dr. Carroll to that effect this morning. It is the first time he has ever considered such a thing and I hope to Heaven that he is deciding with all the acuteness of his judgment. I think he is. He has always been right so far so today I have written your mother that she can go and you can imagine what her joy will be.

I was so pleased with your letter. It seems like a fulfillment of something that you should go up to the library of Cottage and see that old poem hanging there.[1] I am glad of course that you did go to Princeton and glad for every happiness you had this year.

Please let me know the news about what clubs the boys go, or did I ask you that before. Too bad you didn't go to St. Andrews this year and crash *Life*. The one thing I didn't like in your letter was the suggestion of working in the college shop at Lord and Taylor's this summer. It seems to me utterly uninteresting and unconstructive. I would even prefer the dramatic school idea or the summer stock. The hours are long and hard and New York in summer can be pretty tough. The experience you got would be pretty damned routine and dull after the first week unless you were planning to work up to be a lady buyer, which God forbid. Commercial genius like scientific genius is something that I'm afraid was denied to you and me.

They have remade that old Hepburn picture "The Bill of Divorcement" with Maureen O'Hara. It is based on a falsity and I hear this remake is very poor, but I should not advise your seeing it or if you go to see it, go alone, though as I say it is not worth seeing.

I am still in consultation on doing the screenplay for "Babylon Revisited" but not on salary, yet. Enclosed is $10.00.

With dearest love, always,
Daddy

5521 Amestoy Avenue
Encino, Calif.

[1] A manuscript poem by Fitzgerald in the Princeton Cottage Club.

TO: Arnold Gingrich — TL(CC), 1 p. Princeton University

March
15
1940

Dear Arnold:

Thanks for your telegram about Pat Hobby's Secret.[1] You have no idea of the moral effect of such appreciation.

I have as usual come across a few changes. Will you kindly have them made?

Page 6—6th line from bottom for "with his breath" substitute "with their small plunder"

Page 9—Last paragraph should begin "For many years Mr. Banizon would be, etc.

" 9—Last paragraph, second sentence. Substitute commas for dashes.

" 9—Last sentence—"If only ideas could be—

Your last two issues have misnumbered the numbers of the stories in order of publication. Orson Welles[2] will be the fifth not the fourth of the series. Are you going to publish "Between Planes" as a John Darcy story as I suggested?[3] If you agree that this is a very good story I suggest that you slate it ahead of Two Old Timers, Pat Hobby's Preview, On the

Trail of Pat Hobby, Pat Hobby's College Days, A Patriotic Short or Mightier Than the Sword which seem to me the less interesting.

And can the money for this be wired?

Ever your friend,

5521 Amestoy Avenue
Encino, California

P.S. Arnold, this is 2750 words long and is a real story not a sketch. I can't believe it isn't worth $400.00.[4]

[1] *Esquire* (June 1940).
[2] "Pat Hobby and Orson Welles," *Esquire* (May 1940).
[3] "Three Hours Between Planes," *Esquire* (July 1941), was published posthumously under Fitzgerald's name.
[4] Fitzgerald did not succeed in raising the price.

TO: Neal Begley — TL(CC), 1 p. Princeton University

Encino, California
March
26
1940

Dear Mr. Begley:—

Thank you very much for your letter. It was a great disappointment for me not being able to go on with that series. It was intended for the Saturday Evening Post, refused in favor of some stories by Austin Chamberlain about medieval times, stories which seemed to me well enough written but without any interpretative point of view. I wrote four of them, three of which were published by *The Red Book* (at a very inadequate price) and one of which they bought but still hold for reasons of their own.[1] Together they have come to 30,000 words and I have often considered writing a few more and launching them as a book.

That, however, would be only half my intention as I intended to carry Philippe through a long life covering the latter part of the ninth and early part of the tenth century, a time that must simply be vibrant with change and would be intensely interesting in view of new discoveries (such as the new data on the witch cult) and the new Marxian interpretation. But if I did publish a shorter book to begin with do you think it would have any buyers? There are waves of interest in historical fiction and I wonder if this is one of those times.

Thanking you very much for your interest.

Sincerely,
F. Scott Fitzgerald

[1] Three of Fitzgerald's Count of Darkness, or Philippe, stories were published in 1934–35; the fourth was published posthumously in 1941.

TO: Dr. Robert S. Carroll — TL(CC), 1 p. Princeton University

March
26
1940

Dear Dr. Carroll:

Zelda writes me that she is to be released the 15th of April. Now in the past I have always taken over a more or less protective custody but this time it will be different, for she is going to live for awhile with her family in Alabama by mutual agreement, though theoretically released to me.

Up to a month ago your letters have conveyed, have they not, that you did not believe it probable that she was susceptible to entire recovery and stabilization. Circumstances however make it advisable that she take this chance. If you are agreed on this could you make me further your debtor by writing a letter stating this general situation. Then, in case of a relapse (which, you have indicated is possible) the long and difficult business of diagnosis and legal position is simplified. The letter I should think should be such as to make plain to the ordinary doctor the circumstances of her release. I think that the Sayres also should be armed with such a document, if only in the most informal form in their case. They have no recourses or mental preparation for dealing with any sudden homicidal or suicidal tendency.[1]

I am almost sure of signing a picture contract this week after a full year of sickness and will send you a substantial check.

Ever yours gratefully,

5521 Amestoy Avenue
Encino, California

[1] No such problems occurred.

TO: Scottie Fitzgerald

TLS, 1 p. Princeton University
Encino, California

April
1
1940

Dearest Scottie:

Enclosed find fifteen dollars. I expect to go back to picture work next Monday.

Hope you enjoyed your vacation. I gathered from your impassioned reluctance to visit the old folk that there was a boy in the background. I hope it went well.

Love,
Daddy

P.S. Thinking of Venice today reminded me of when I was there with you. You don't remember going to Venice though you rode in a gondola and ate Venetian ices. But then there's no reason why you should remember—it was five months before you were born. "Oh daddy—don't be vulgar."[1]

[1] The last sentence was added in holograph.

TO: Arnold Gingrich

TL(CC), 1 p. Princeton University

April
3
1940

Dear Arnold:—

I have found some bad errors in "The Homes of the Stars."[1] Could you possibly have these corrections made:

Page 2, line 8—for *dirty* should read *soiled.*
" 2, line 12—for *presently* should read *After awhile*
" 2, 8th line from bottom—cut word *smugly*
" 2, last line should read *thrusting itself at him.*
" 3, line 15—should read *or passed away.* (paragraph) *And he did not know. . . . . .*
" 4, line 16—cut the word *Well*
" 4, line 18—? after *first*
" 6, line 8—should read *jumped into his car and the sound*
" 6, 4th line from bottom should read *leze-majesty*
" 8, line 7—quotation mark a misprint.
" 9, line 14—for *a sister* read *brothers*

" 9, line 15—cut the word *out*
" 9, 4th line from bottom—for *thoroughly* read *almost entirely*
" 10, last two lines should read: *another recognizing clue and hoped that Ronald Coleman did not know his last name.*

You did not tell me whether you liked the story. Don't you think it's one of the best?

Ever your friend,

5521 Amestoy Avenue
Encino, California

[1] The eighth Pat Hobby story, published in *Esquire* (August 1940).

TO: Mrs. A. D. Sayre — TL(CC), 1 p. Princeton University
April 1940

c/o Phil Berg
9484 Wilshire Boulevard
Beverly Hills, California

Dear Mrs. Sayre:—

Enclosed are money orders for $15. and $20. Zelda may have written you that I am going back to picture work but in a very small way. The work I am going to do is suitable to my present state of health and it should be pleasant for it consists of picturizing one of my own stories, but unfortunately is badly paid. I am doing it, in fact, "on spec"—that is the producer is allowing me a small sum of money and if he manages to resell the picture to his company I will presumably share in his profits. I never wanted money as much as I do now but this is the best arrangement that I can make.

For the present I want Zelda to be able to get along on $30. a week of which she will pay you $15. for her contribution to the household. I will send the money in alternate weekly amounts of $25., $35., $25., $35., etc., so that on alternate weeks she will have cash enough for any larger purpose such as a dress etc. The enclosed is for the first week beginning Monday, April 15. $20. for her, $15. for the household. Next week it will be $10. for her, $15. for the household, etc. If and when my work goes better and my debts begin to be paid—I owe the government and about everybody else—I will increase this. For the present I sincerely hope that she can keep within it. Above all she should avoid running up bills as there is literally no cash to respond to telegraphic requests for funds. I am afraid this is going to be hard for her because the hospital supplied more in the way of diversion than one would think and for the present she will be poorer in material things, as I am, than at any other time in her life, since I was a second lieutenant drawing almost exactly the same pay that I am sending her.

I know how delighted you will be to have her home and I hope things will go well. I suppose the doctor is sending you an advisory letter. My only advice is that if things seem to be going badly get confidential medical advice at once. A week saved in this regard may forestall a serious slip-back. I found this to my bitter experience.

Best to all.

Always affectionately,

P.S. I am moving into town to be nearer my work, but have not yet an address. For the present will you or Zelda write me either care of my new agent at the above address, or else "General Delivery, Encino, California," as they will forward it.

TO: Maxwell Perkins

TLS, 1 p. Princeton University
Encino, California

April
19
1940

Dear Max:—

"You remember a couple of weeks ago I asked you to mail a letter for me in New York. To explain: it was the answer to a dunn for some money which I do not owe. The claimant is, of all things an undertaker. Not that I owe him for a corpse, but for an ambulance which he claims that I ordered. In any case he now writes me threatening to serve me with a summons and complaint.

"Now you will notice that this letter is headed by date only. Actually I am leaving my old address and I have no new one as yet. This is an actual fact. Also I have a new agent here whose name you do not know, so if this man tries to serve a summons and complaint on me through Scribner's you can conscientiously and truly tell him that you don't know whether I'm in New Orleans or the North Pole."

I hope they don't bother you with this. The sum is just $50., but it is an absolute gyp and I don't intend to do anything about it. I hope I'll have some good news of myself pretty soon. I worked on the novel for two weeks last month.

Ever your friend,
Scott

TO: Nathan Kroll[1]

TL(CC), 1 p. Princeton University
Encino, California

May
6
1940

Dear Nathan:—

This is in lieu of a meeting which doesn't seem practical this week not from lack of physical time, but simply from lack of any intellectual energy at the end of a day's work. My only, and I accentuate *only*, idea about the realistic treatment of the play[2] is that Act I might concern the question as to whether Pat will get a job at all. In other words, will he get a last chance. That Act II would concern not so much whether he would make good at this last chance but his stretching it out through some female complication into something that approaches the criminal and is too big for him because he is only a small time rat. The suspense of Act III in this sort of line-up would be as to whether worse than starvation would be his lot leaving complete latitude as to what should happen to him—all the way from a brief respite up to a lucky break as would seem appropriate.

Horton's man who has gone on some other job and abandoned the notion was struck by the idea of Pat's having a son—though not an East Indian son as in the story of "Pat Hobby's Young Visitor." As a playwright it seemed to appeal to him as a starting point.

This is really all I have to suggest except what I told Frances, that the series is characterized by a really bitter humor and only the explosive situations and the fact that Pat is a figure almost incapable of real tragedy or damage saves it from downright unpleasantness. The play should attempt to preserve some of this flavor. It is the only thing actually new about the original conception.

I hope next week the worst of this scenario work will have cleared away as per a schedule that Francoise and I made out this morning.

Ever yours,

1 Frances Kroll's brother.
2 Kroll was attempting to dramatize the Hobby stories.

TO: Bill Dozier TL(CC), 1 p. Princeton University

May
15
1940

Dear Bill:—

The enclosed letter will explain itself.[1] I'm sorry not to be a well-heeled client.

Lester Cowan[2] is coming back *Friday* and I should suggest—if you think it practical—that you simply *show* him or *read* him the enclosed letter. I think he will understand that this is a matter of the job having run over the money allotted to it, and *in no sense* an attempt to chisel anything out of him.

He is likely to call me up first thing Friday so if you could find it convenient to take the matter up with him as soon as possible after his arrival it would probably go off more smoothly. I think I have a pretty fine continuity here if I can have another week's peace of mind about it. Though I've sweated over it, it's been pleasant sweat, so to speak, and rather more fun than I've ever had in pictures.

Ever yours,

5521 Amestoy Avenue
Encino, California

[1] Unlocated.

[2] Producer who had purchased the movie rights to "Babylon Revisited." Fitzgerald wrote the screenplay, but the movie was not made.

TO: Isabel Owens TL(CC), 1 p. Princeton University
Encino, California

May
29
1940

Dear Mrs. Owens:

Thanks ever so much for your very thorough letter. I don't know whether you kept a carbon so I am enclosing it with this. All your suggestions seem O.K. to me with the following suggestions:

I want to keep the lampshades that Zelda made irrespective of how damaged they are. And I want to keep at least that one good lamp with the heavy China base. About the clothes better go on the conservative side. There can't be many of them but throw out only what is useless. Keep three pairs of ballet slippers and throw out the rest.

Do as you like about the Victrolas. The Finneys have the best one and didn't Scottie take the Swiss one? But the records I want to keep. The Xmas box can go.

As to bric-a-brac it is hard to say. For some reason I do want to keep the lead soldiers and also the war slides, etc. If a piece of bric-a-brac is utterly useless and has no special artistic value let it go, but I know there are small China ornaments Zelda was fond of, etc. and I can't believe that what remains would take up a great deal of space. I want to hang on to all pictures, certainly—for instance that Braque which looks like nothing but is probably the best thing we have. Canvasses do come under the pictures to keep. I wouldn't dare give away anything of Zelda's.

I will quite possibly be East in the early fall but I certainly want to cut down these storage charges as soon as possible. It was a rather funny situation. My library which I can't use yet couldn't bear to get rid of, etc. for so many things.

Let me again ask you to use your infallible judgment.

Ever your friend

TO: Victoria Schulberg[1]
After 26 May 1940

Inscription in *Tender Is the Night*.
Schulberg

75E

For Victoria Schulberg
in memory of a
three day mountain-climbing
trip with her illustrious
father — who pulled me
out of crevices into which
I sank and away from
avalanches —
with affection to you
both

F Scott Fitzgerald
Beverly Hills
1940

[1] Newly born daughter of Budd Schulberg. Fitzgerald phoned Schulberg at Cedars of Lebanon Hospital after her birth and lectured him on the father-daughter relationship.

TO: Lester Cowan TL(CC), 1 p. Princeton University

May
28
1940

Dear Lester:

My idea is to lie up in Santa Barbara or Carmel for a week or ten days. Bill Dozier will give you the addresses and when I have a permanent one I will wire it to you myself. I don't know how anybody can get away from anything these days and I'm even taking a radio. But just the idea of having the house off my back is a relief.

The picture was fun to write. The only snag was in the final Swiss Sequence. I found out that there is no trace of winter sport in Switzerland *before the middle of December* and the stockmarket crash occurred very definitely the *last part of October* so, instead of a routine based on bob-sleds such as we talked about, I had to resort to an older device. I think this sequence carries the emotion of the others but it is the one with least originality of treatment, and audiences are more and more responding to originality after five years of double-feature warm-overs.

Sheilah has several times mentioned to me a little actress named Mary Todd (aged eight). She was the child who played the piano in "Intermezzo" and also did a touching scene in George Cukor's "Zaza"—when the child had to receive her father's mistress not understanding the situation at all. She is certainly somebody to keep in mind, though I can't seem to visualize her face at this moment.

Also the actor[1] who played the chief commissar in "Ninotchka" and the bookkeeper in "Shop Around the Corner," might be worthy of consideration for Pierre, though the types he has played so far are largely South European. And for this he would have to be a sprucer and more attractive man externally to match up with Marion.

Lester, I'm terribly sorry that I didn't get around to reading the Hilton script. I did actually go through it quickly and enjoyed it—but not enough to give any constructive suggestions. I wish it the greatest success.

There are so many new things in our script that I thought it best to deliver it to Bob under seal. So many of the scenes are easily repeated in the most innocent way, and the ear of Hollywood is notoriously hungry. I think you will like the title.[2] It is an unusual name with a peculiarly sonorous quality and so many of the more popular pieces—Babbitt, Rebecca, David Copperfield—have been only names. I think if you sleep on it, it will grow on you.

Looking forward to seeing your face or hearing your voice. Best to Ann.

With warm personal regards

P.S. This of course, is the best and final version of the 1st draft.
Encino, California

[1] Felix Bressart.
[2] The working title for the screenplay of "Babylon Revisited" was "Honoria"; Fitzgerald also considered calling it "Cosmopolitan."

TO: Scottie Fitzgerald — TLS, 1 p. Princeton University

June
14
1940

Dearest Scottie:—

By my mistake the money was *not* sent to Mary Law. I wired you $15. care of Ober and here's another $15. The allowance for the week of June 17 will be sent you tomorrow and you can use it to get to Montgomery.

Things not so bright here.

Dearest love,
Daddy

P.S. Gloria[1] was a much more trivial and vulgar person than your mother. I can't really say there was any resemblance except in the beauty and certain terms of expression she used, and also I naturally used many circumstantial events of our early married life. However the emphases were entirely different. We had a much better time than Anthony and Gloria had.

1403 N. Laurel Avenue
Hollywood, California

[1] Gloria Patch of *The Beautiful and Damned.*

TO: Arnold Gingrich — TLS, 1 p. Princeton University

June
25
1940

Dear Arnold:—

Believe it or not this is the fourth story about Pat in the last two weeks.[1] One of the others was good but I wanted a story that would be up to the late ones. It is rather more risqué than those in the past—a concession to war times. I hope you can put it ahead of those I have designated in other letters as being mediocre.

You haven't answered my question about "Between Planes." I do wish you would publish it but I wish if it is not already set up that the nom-de-plume could be changed to John Blue instead of John Darcy.

Ever your friend
Scott

P.S. I do hope you can *keep this title* rather than change it to something with the word Pat in it. In the case of "Putative Father" changing the title anticipated the first climax.[2] If you want to use the word Pat in a subtitle, O.K., but the title is really an intrinsic part of a story, isn't it?

P.S.S. If you like this will you wire the money?

1403 N. Laurel Avenue
Hollywood, California

[1] Probably "Fun in an Artist's Studio," *Esquire* (February 1941).
[2] "Pat Hobby, Putative Father," *Esquire* (July 1940).

TO: Mrs. Richard Taylor — TL(CC), 1 p. Princeton University

June
26
1940

Dearest Ceci:

Haven't heard about you or yours for years it seems. I was sick in bed for almost a year but am up and back at work now.

Did you see a very poor story of mine that was in Collier's a few weeks ago?[1] It was interesting only in that it was founded on a family story—how William George Robertson was hung up by the thumbs at Glen Mary or was it Locust Grove? Aunt Elise would know. The following[2] from last month's New York Post will tell you of Scottie's progress along the fatal line of literature.

When you tell me about the daughters, tell me also whether Clifton Sprague has become a great power in the Navy.

With dearest love,

1403 N. Laurel Avenue
Hollywood, California

[1] "The End of Hate."
[2] Unlocated.

TO: Arnold Gingrich TL(CC), 1 p. Princeton University

July
15
1940

Dear Arnold:

My name is Paul Elgin and Paul will presently send you some contributions.

I see that your next scheduled story is "Pat Hobby Does His Bit" and I hope that the one after that is "No Harm Trying." It certainly seems to me next in order of merit. You didn't comment on "Fun in an Artist's Studio." Perhaps if your secretary told me in which order the remaining stories are scheduled I might be able to make some changes in one or two of them before they go into type. There are a couple there that don't please me at all.

Thanks for your note. Best wishes.

Ever your friend,

1403 N. Laurel Avenue
Hollywood, California

TO: Zelda Fitzgerald TL(CC), 1 p. Princeton University

July
29
1940

Dearest Zelda:—

The Temple[1] thing is this: she's too old to have a child's appeal and though they've put everything in her last pictures—song, dance, sleight of hand, etc.,—they fail to hold the crowd. In fact the very last is rather nauseous in its sentimentality.[2]

So this "independent" producer Cowan, now of Columbia, shortly to be at Paramount, had the idea of a romantic drama for her and bought my *Babylon Revisited* last year for $900. for that purpose. I should have held out for more but the story had been nearly ten years published without a nibble. So then, in a beautifully avaricious way, knowing I'd been sick and was probably hard up, Mr. Cowan hired me to do the script on a percentage basis. He gives me—or *gave* me—what worked out to a few hundred a week to do a quick script.[3] Which I did and then took to bed to recuperate. Now he says he wants me to do another. . . .[4]

Anyhow I *think* it's been a good thing except for the health angle and if and when he sells Mrs. Temple and Paramount the script there'll be a little more money—if he doesn't think of a way to beat me out of it.

So that's the story. Tell me—did the watch come? You never mentioned it.

With Dearest Love,

1403 N. Laurel Avenue
Hollywood, California

[1] Lester Cowan wanted Shirley Temple to play the role of Honoria in *Babylon Revisited.*

[2] Two Shirley Temple movies were released in 1940: *The Blue Bird* and *Young People.*

[3] Fitzgerald received $5,000 for the screenplay.

[4] Fifty-five words omitted by the editor.

TO: Bill Dozier TL(CC), 1 p. Princeton University

August
19
1940

Dear Bill (—or Phil?)

Whatever comes of this, I mean if I'm engaged by Zanuck,[1] please don't give it to the *Reporter.* As I told you I'm still behind on income tax and they jump you at the *moment* your name appears, long before you collect any money. That's why I got so upset at Lester paying at his own convenience.

Also I'd rather wait till I get into production—I was announced on two or three big pictures on which I didn't get credit in the end. Let me slip up on them and surprise them. I should like Messers. Swanson and Stromberg to writhe at their short-sightedness, but I've made a few real enemies here and I don't want any casual crack to interfere with this possible relation with Twentieth Century. I don't know why *I* should be advising *you,* but for all these reasons I don't think advertisement is advisable at the moment.

Ever yours,

1403 N. Laurel Avenue
Hollywood, California

[1] Twentieth Century–Fox was considering hiring Fitzgerald to work on the screenplay for *Brooklyn Bridge.* He was hired September–October to work on Emlyn Williams' play *The Light of Heart.*

TO: Garson Kanin[1] TL(CC), 1 p. Princeton University

August 23 1940

Dear Mr. Kanin:—

Having seen "A Man to Remember," "The Great Man Votes," "Bachelor Mother" and "My Favorite Wife" several times each, and with ever increasing interest, my spirits went up when Lester Cowan read me your letter in which you said pleasant things about my script "Cosmopolitan."

I understand all too well that confused feeling when one has finished a difficult job. Any project, no matter how promising, presents itself in dark and foreboding aspects. I could wish though, that you were twins. The idea of an old-line director dipping this one in the traditional fishgue would make me sad indeed. Most pictures are still being written and directed for the credulous audiences of ten years ago—now actually reduced to the children and the old—while people between eighteen and forty stay away in droves. Your work is so fresh and new that I hope you will uncover material worthy of it.

With thanks and admiration,

1403 N. Laurel Avenue
Hollywood, California

[1] Writer-director at RKO.

TO: Zelda Fitzgerald TL(CC), 1 p. Princeton University

August 30 1940

Dearest Zelda:—

It seems odd to be back in the studio again. Monday morning they called up to tell me they wanted me for a four weeks' job.[1] I only get about half of what I used to but all of it is owed to everybody imaginable, the government, insurance, hospital, Vassar, etc. But four weeks pay does insure a certain amount of security for the next three months if I spread it over the time wisely.

I'm going to get a suit in two or three weeks and will send you the money for a dress as you must be short on clothes. I'm still running the fever and there's a couch in my office and while they insist on your physical presence in the studio there are no peepholes they can look into and see whether I am lying down or not. It gives me a very strange feeling to be back.

I suppose Scottie will be with you this week. She tells me that she has grown two years this summer. Do write me at length about her. I'm sorry to miss a glimpse of her at this stage of her life, but of course it seems much more important to stay here and keep her going. It is strange too that she is repeating the phase of your life—all her friends about to go off to war and the world again on fire.

With dearest love,

1403 N. Laurel Avenue
Hollywood, California

[1] Probably *The Light of Heart*.

TO: Lester Cowan
c. August 1940

TL(CC), 1 p. Princeton University
Hollywood, California

Monday night.

Dear Lester:

I phoned but you were gone. I saw the *Great McGinty* and heard the crowd respond and I think your answer is there and not in this wretched star system. When you said you were not going to begin with the prologue and seemed to give credence to some director's wild statement that Petrie was the best character—I felt that you were discouraged about the venture and it was warping your judgment. If it is such a poor script that it can be so casually mutilated then how will it be improved with two slipping stars?

The virtue of the Great McGinty was one and singular—mark this—it had only the virtue of being told to an audience as it was conceived. It was inferior in pace, it was an old story—the audience loved it because they are desperately tired of s—— put up every week in new cans. It had not suffered from compromises, polish jobs, formulas and that familiarity which is so falsely consoling to producers—but read the last *Variety* (N.Y. edition) and what the average man gives as his reason for staying away. That scene of familiarity which seems to promise out here that old stuff has made money before, has become poison gas to those who have to take it as entertainment every night—boy meets girl, gang formula, silk-hat western. The writing on the wall is that *anybody* this year who brings in a good new story *intact* will make more reputation and even money, than those who struggle for a few stars. I would rather see new people in this picture than Gable and Temple. I think it would be a bigger and better thing for you.

Ever your friend,

TO: H. N. Swanson TL(CC), 1 p. Princeton University

September
11
1940

Dear Swanie:—

Your office told me that the offer of $200., for the radio rights of "The Dance" came through Harold Ober. I agreed to it with that understanding.

The implication of this announcement in the *Reporter* is that you are still my representative out here. This is emphatically not true. Your preposterous suggestion outside the theatre the other night that I advertise some commercial product is as near as you have come to representing me for almost a year. I must ask you to make no further announcements of this kind.

Sincerely,
F. Scott Fitzgerald

1403 N. Laurel Avenue
Hollywood, California

TO: Scottie Fitzgerald TLS, 1 p.[1] Princeton University

September
14
1940

Dearest Scottie:—

Two letters from your mother have discussed your not going back to Vassar and you have mentioned it yourself. You were quite right that I tended in my letters to give your mother a one-sided view of things. *Technically* everything I have told her is true. I *do* run a small fever and in place of doing an *Esquire* story I *did* rest up for a week by hocking the car so I would be ready for this job. But I would be working anyhow as I can't imagine simply lying on my back; and believe me things were much worse a year ago when the car was hocked in need and I had to borrow money to send you to college.

So forget it. All goes well here. I'm having some etchings framed for you. Do you want a picture of me in my palmy days or have you got one?

With dearest love,
Daddy

1403 N. Laurel Avenue
Hollywood, California

[1] A holograph postscript has been torn off the letter.

TO: Scottie Fitzgerald

TLS, 1 p. Princeton University

September 21 1940

Dearest Scottina:

Thanks for your letter. I can imagine your surprise about Bob and Bobby, and don't think me callous when I say that the main thing is to get the right letters *in the right envelopes.* I shall never forget getting a picture of your mother (which I had paid for) autographed tenderly to Bobby Jones, the Atlanta golfer. And with Bob and Bobby—well, a girl can't be too careful.

Tell me if you like Spanish.

With dearest love,
Daddy

P.S. Have sent $10. to Raymond's Art Shop, 354 Main St., Poughkeepsie, together with three etchings, one Princeton, one Bryn Mawr School, and one of a family home. (Francis Scott Key, Jr., wasn't particularly closely related—I have some etchings of the old Key places in St. Mary's County but they're buried somewhere.) The fourth picture you can pretend is "Old Bobs Roberts"—your boy on the West Coast. (if you don't want this one send it back as thousands are clamoring for it—really, *I* want it if you don't.) Anyhow you'd better drop into the shop and see how they're framing them.

1403 N. Laurel Avenue
Hollywood, California

TO: Robert Bennett

TLS, 1 p. Bruccoli

September 25 1940

Dear Robert Bennett:

I am sending you the Chapman[1] to your house with postage—just in case they should go back. I am tremendously in your debt for getting them for me.

I had read Lang, Leaf and Myers' Iliad and Butler's Odyssey and most of Pope's dribble but for years have wanted to read Chapman—

probably on account of Keat's sonnet. Now I have, thanks to you and feel greatly improved and highly Elizabethean.

I'll be in soon to see you.

Sincerely
F Scott Fitzgerald

1403 N. Laurel Avenue
Hollywood, California

[1] The George Chapman translation of Homer.

TO: Lester Cowan TL(CC), 1 p. Princeton University

September
28
1940

Dear Lester:

Don't know whether you're here or not. The more I think about Shirley Temple, the less I think she is appropriate to the part—the very thought of her doing it at thirteen reduces my interest in the picture. On the other hand, I think Franchot Tone and some beautiful unknown little girl might be magnificent and I do hope he is still interested.

This feeling was probably inspired by some interview I read with Mrs. Temple in which she said that she felt Shirley wouldn't do anything till after the first of the year—not realizing that she is growing right out of the part. I wouldn't give a nickel for a plot based on a man and his adolescent daughter like those gloomy sequences of Fred March in "Susan and God."

Ever your friend,

1403 N. Laurel Avenue
Hollywood, California

TO: Walter L. Bruington[1] TL(CC), 1 p. Princeton University

October
9
1940

Dear Walter Bruington:

This letter was to have gone with the books. Certain books I wanted were out of print and I substituted others for them, and because of this I was rather alarmed to notice that as a whole the list seemed to present a somewhat pinkish aspect. I fear that, on this account, perhaps the choice will seem to have been somewhat impertinent—but certainly I didn't mean to intrude my opinions upon yours—I was anxious to send you books that have given me stimulation or pleasure.

Let me say again how tremendously obliged I am for your kindness and courtesy in this entire matter. After a year "on the wagon," my visit to Mr. Dracula seems rather nightmarish but I know it could have developed into a hell of a mess if you hadn't acted so swiftly.

Looking forward to our meeting, I am

Sincerely and gratefully yours,

1403 N. Laurel Avenue
Hollywood, California

[1] Lawyer who represented Fitzgerald in an unknown matter.

TO: Arnold Gingrich — Wire. Princeton University

LOS ANGELES CALIF 1146A 1940 OCT 15 PM 2 26

PATRIOTIC SHORT[1] SO CONFUSED IT WILL STOP INTEREST IN SERIES STOP SEVERAL PEOPLE CONCUR IN THIS STOP CANT YOU SET IT UP AGAIN STOP YOUR LETTER PROMISED TO HOLD IT OUT

SCOTT.

[1] *Esquire* (December 1940).

TO: Scottie Fitzgerald — TLS, 1 p. Princeton University

October
19
1940

Dearest Scottina:

This is going to be a mercenary letter. First place, I suggest that the enclosed birthday gift be combined with any other you receive to buy something as substantial as a *coat*—I mean a good payment on one.

Second—what do you think of this suggestion. Writing Peaches and Mary letters which say frankly that you have no way of repaying them at the moment for many courtesies and much hospitality and would *they* like you to pick them out a little dress, or the money you had to spend for them to use themselves. I feel conscious about your going to Baltimore now without *some* gift and can give you $30 for each (total $60.) if you approve and write me immediately. It isn't much—I know your friendships really pay for it but it's a sort of token of appreciation that I think they'd appreciate. I would so much like to do something for both those families.

Gerald and Sarah Murphy both write how they missed you. Could you go there some time and not *overwhelm* them. Excuse me—I know you have tact. But their tragedy won't die while they live.[1]

This time maybe I'll finish my novel. You can help by acknowledging the weekly check when received. And you would oblige me by acknowledging the *other* birthday gift from the coast at once.[2]

With dearest love,
Daddy

P.S. About not showing the Birth of a Nation: By the Vassar Trustees' ruling (II[7] July 1896, still in force) Not more than ten or less than five negro or mullato girls can be admitted to Vassar in any given year. This was modified (in 1903 minutes of the Trustees 3[VI]) to admit 8 quadroons or 16 octaroons. Can you wonder they're sensitive? The new ruling admits 64 macaroons.[3]

P.S. (2) O God that I could ever again feel as old as you do now!

1403 N. Laurel Ave.
Hollywood, Calif.

[1] Both the Murphys' sons had died.

[2] From Sheilah Graham.

[3] The brackets in this paragraph are Fitzgerald's. The last sentence was added in holograph.

FROM: Ernest Hemingway
After 21 October 1940

Inscription in Hemingway's
For Whom the Bell Tolls (1940). Bruccoli

To Scott with
affection and esteem

Ernest/

TO: Bill Dozier TL(CC), 1 p. Princeton University

November
5
1940

Dear Bill:

I had forgotten tomorrow was election eve and I promised to sit up with some sick Republicans. Let me come in and see you toward the end of the week—unless this is something crucial. My general plan is to go on with my novel as long as my ill gotten gains hold out. If anything more comes in from Lester I think I can finish it.

Phil probably showed you my letter about the 20th Century job.[1] The fault seems to be mine—at least I can find no one to blame it on—but I still don't know what was the matter or exactly in what way it was unsatisfactory. It never felt quite alive from beginning to end yet there were excellent things in it.

When I see you we can discuss what future, if any, I seem to have in this business.

With best wishes always,
F. Scott Fitzgerald

1403 N. Laurel Avenue
Hollywood, California

[1] Fitzgerald's screenplay for *The Light of Heart* had been rejected.

TO: Edmund Wilson TL(CC), 1 p. Princeton University

Hollywood, California

November
25
1940

Dear Bunny:

I've been reading your new essays with interest and if you expect (as Max Perkins hinted) to republish them sometime, I'd like to put you on to something about Steinbeck. He is a rather cagey cribber. Most of us begin as imitators but it is something else for a man of his years and reputation to steal a whole scene as he did in "Mice and Men." I'm sending you a marked copy of Norris' "McTeague" to show you what I mean. His debt to "The Octupus" is also enormous and his balls, when he uses them, are usually clipped from Lawrence's "Kangaroo." I've always encouraged young writers—I put Max Perkins on to Caldwell, Callaghan and God knows how many others but Steinbeck bothers me. I suppose he cribs for the glory of the party.[1]

[1] This paragraph was omitted in the text published in *Letters*.

TO: Arnold Gingrich TL(CC), 1 p. Princeton University

November
27
1940

Dear Arnold:—

Thank you for your letter of October 16. I'm going to try to get to "Two Old Timers." Miss Richards tells me the deadline for this is December 10. There is not an awful lot I can do to it but the last two[1] I'm certainly going to revise or send something else in their place.

Am far past the middle of a novel and I want to finish it by February. I expect it to sell at least a thousand copies.

With best wishes always,

1403 N. Laurel Avenue
Hollywood, California

[1] Possibly "Mightier than the Sword" and "Pat Hobby's College Days," *Esquire* (April and May 1941).

TO: Robert Bennett TLS, 1 p. Bruccoli

November
28
1940

Dear Bennett:—

I just got back from the East today[1] and read the Elizabethean poems with my batch of mail. This didn't give me time to do them justice and I'm going to read them again. But I enjoyed them immensely, especially "Phoenix in April."

I will be coming down soon.

With best wishes
Scott Fitzgerald

Hollywood, California

[1] Fitzgerald had not been east.

TO: Tax Commissioner,
State of California

TL(CC), 1 p. Princeton University

December
15
1940

Dear Sir:

I am sending you the last instalment of my 1939 Income Tax. You asked me to tell you about any change of address. I had to leave my apartment at 1403 N. Laurel Avenue because it is on the third floor and three weeks ago I had a severe heart attack. I'm living at the moment with a friend and meanwhile looking for an apartment on the first floor.[1] My mail will reach me at the other apartment (1403 N. Laurel) and I can be reached by telephone here at Hollywood 7730.

I'm managing to work but must stay in bed for two or three months and life is one cardiogram after another which is a pleasant change from X-rays. I have a few hundred dollars to carry me along but I'm afraid to send you any instalment on the 1938 tax at this writing as I may not be able to go back to picture work until February even if they should want me.

Sincerely
F. Scott Fitzgerald

1403 N. Laurel Ave.
Hollywood, Calif.
Encl. chk. $66.74

[1] Fitzgerald was staying in Sheilah Graham's apartment at 1443 N. Hayworth Ave., where he died on 21 December.

TO: Norma Shearer Thalberg
c. 1940

Inscription (holograph draft) for *The Last Tycoon* (1941). Princeton University
Hollywood, California

To Write in Copy to Shearer

Dear Norma:

You told me you read little because of your eyes but I think this book will interest you—perhaps you could see it as an attempt to preserve something of Irving ~~and~~ though the story is purely imaginary ~~and~~ ~~He inspired~~ My own impression of him ~~short but~~ shortly recorded but very dazzling in its effect on me, inspired the best part of the character of Stahr—though I have put in ~~much~~ something drawn from other men and, inevitably, much of myself.

~~It is a tragic story~~ I invented a tragic story ~~because~~ and ~~Stahr's~~ Irving's life was, of course, not tragic except his struggle against ill health because no one has ever written a tragedy about Hollywood (a Star is Born was a pathetic story and often beautiful story but not a tragedy) and doomed and heroic things do happen here.

With Old Affection and Gratitude

~~Scotty~~

Appendix: Undatable Material

TO: Harold Ober

Inscription in George Barton's *The Bell Haven Eight* (1914), with annotated frontispiece. Bruccoli

For Harold
Ober, the best
back-stop the
Crimson crew ever
had. From
The Yale Athletic
Association
(see frontispiece)

THE UNEXPECTED MOVE LOOKED LIKE A DELIBERATE ATTEMPT TO THROW THE RACE AWAY

TO: Margaret Orr Green

Inscription in *This Side of Paradise*.
University of Tulsa

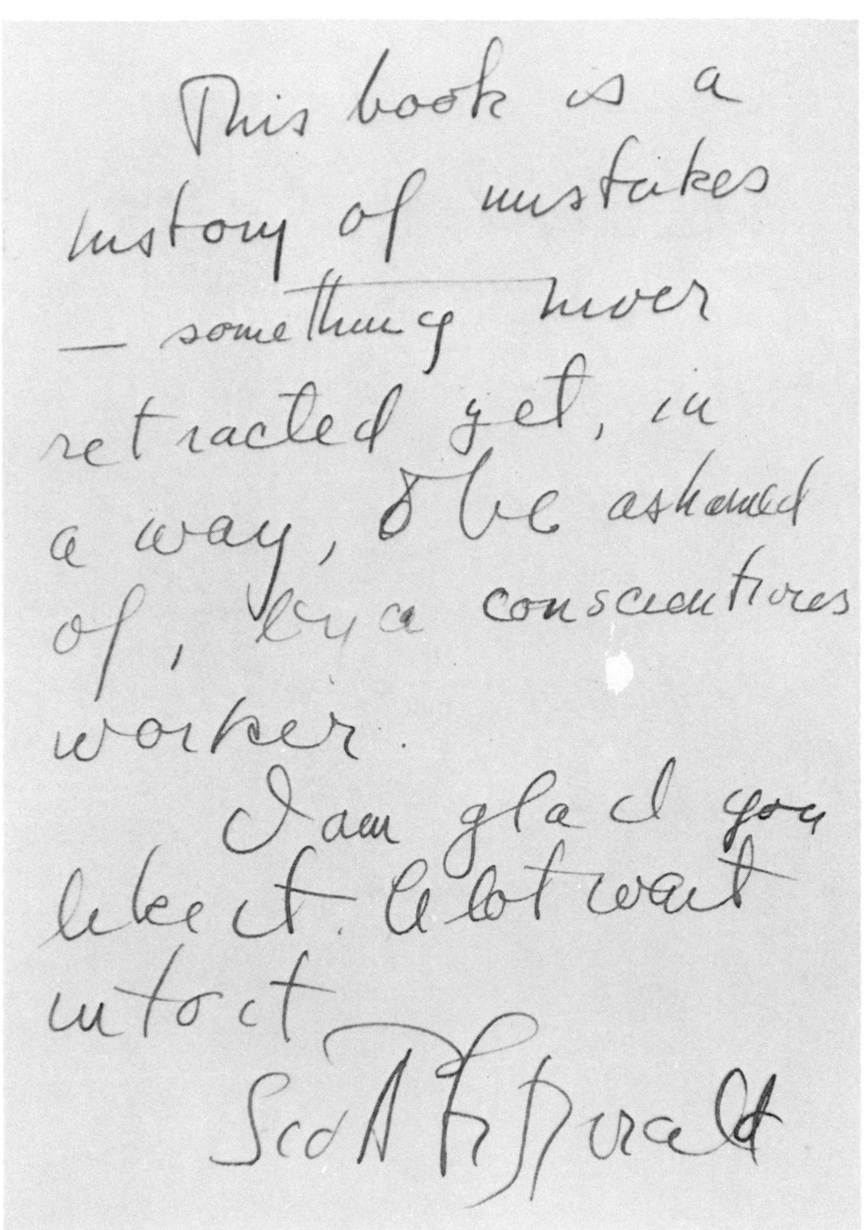
This book is a history of mistakes — something never retracted yet, in a way, to be ashamed of, by a conscientious worker.

I am glad you like it. A lot went into it

Scott Fitzgerald

Note: On the bookplate, which shows bookshelves and a fireplace, Fitzgerald wrote: "F Scott Fitzgerald crowds to the nice fire-place."

TO: Unknown

Inscription in *The Beautiful and Damned.*
University of Virginia

The phrase:
"Beautiful but ~~B~~ Dumb"
was this book's contribution
to its time.

F Scott Fitzgerald

It has awful spots
but some good ones.
I was trying to
learn.

FORM LETTERS AL, 1 p. Princeton University

FORM I

My Dear ——

Thank you for your very kind letter. One of the satisfactions of writing is to find that someone who has read your work thinks enough about it to write the author

Sincerely

FORM II

Thank you for your letter. My excuse for the long delay in answering is that a pile of letters were sidetracked into an answered file just before I moved from one house into another

Message

Again thank you for the interest that inspired your letter.

Sincerely

Index

ABOUT THE EDITORS

MATTHEW J. BRUCCOLI, Jefferies Professor of English at the University of South Carolina, is a leading authority on F. Scott Fitzgerald. He has written or edited some thirty volumes in the field of American literature. Among his recent books are *Scott and Ernest* and *The Notebooks of F. Scott Fitzgerald.*

Dr. Bruccoli, a graduate of Yale University and the University of Virginia, lives in Columbia, S.C., with his wife and four children. He is a partner in Bruccoli Clark Publishers.

Margaret M. Duggan and Susan Walker are graduate students at the University of South Carolina.